American Educational History

WILLIAM H. JEYNES
California State University, Long Beach

American Educational History

SCHOOL, SOCIETY, AND THE COMMON GOOD

SAGE Publications
Thousand Oaks ▪ London ▪ New Delhi

For information:

Sage Publications, Inc.
2455 Teller Road
Thousand Oaks, California 91320
E-mail: order@sagepub.com

Sage Publications Ltd.
1 Oliver's Yard
55 City Road
London EC1Y 1SP
United Kingdom

Sage Publications India Pvt. Ltd.
B-42, Panchsheel Enclave
Post Box 4109
New Delhi 110 017 India

Printed in the United States of America

Library of Congress Cataloging-in-Publication Data

Jeynes, William.
American educational history : school, society, and the common good /
William H. Jeynes.
    p. cm.
Includes bibliographical references and index.
ISBN-13: 978-1-4129-1420-8 (cloth)
ISBN-13: 978-1-4129-1421-5 (pbk.)
    1. Education—United States—History. I. Title.
LA205.J49 2007
370.973—dc22

2006025766

This book is printed on acid-free paper.

07   08   09   10   11   10 9 8 7 6 5 4 3 2 1

Acquisitions Editor:	Diane McDaniel
Editorial Assistant:	Ashley Plummer
Copy Editor:	Carla Freeman
Typesetter:	C&M Digitals (P) Ltd.
Proofreader:	Doris Hus
Indexer:	Diggs Indexing Services
Cover Designer:	Michelle Kenny
Marketing Manager:	Nichole Angress

Brief Table of Contents

Contents

10 The Civil Rights Movement and Federal Involvement in Educational Policy

11 The Turbulence of the 1960s

Foreword

In the conclusion to her book *Who Are We?* Jean Bethke Elshtain (2000) reminds us that there is "such a thing as a historical record and we are not permitted to 'rearrange the facts' in order that they might better comport with our own perspective" (p. 134). Years of studying and teaching in the discipline of education have made me aware that many of our texts are so driven by the ideological perspective of the author that facts are included or omitted in such a way as to confirm that perspective (e.g., liberal, conservative, critical, feminist, or constructivist). For example, a popular history of philosophy text omits as much as entire millennia without a word about why, and almost every chapter refers to the contributions of a single 20th-century philosopher. If these "rearrangements" or limitations are not understood and their alternatives not made explicit, texts for educators will limit as much as they elucidate. It is not the fact that our own perspectives influence what we write and how we read a text that is regrettable; it is that there are so few contemporary attempts in the social sciences these days to strive to move beyond personal perspectives to offer readers a more accurate and straightforward description of history. Not so with this thorough and balanced history of education by Professor William Jeynes.

Seven characteristics make this history of education unique, timely, and inspiring. First, Jeynes is careful in every chapter to embed the history of education into the larger history of what was going on in the United States and the world at the time. He reveals how the early educators worked hand in hand with those forming the nation to coordinate the special purposes and needs of the new republic. For example, here we will find answers to questions such as the following: How did the Revolutionary War result in the most rapid educational transformation ever documented in history? What role did churches play in abolition and the establishment of schools for people who had been enslaved? What did the early textbooks teach, and how was the content related to the goals of the founders in establishing a democratic republic? How did the *Sputnik* crisis encourage federal funds to flow into state education agencies, and how did the early civil rights movement encourage even more federal involvement?

Second, the reader will encounter a presentation of the history that goes back to primary sources and early histories, including letters and other documents from as early as the 17th century all the way up to today's essential documents. The exploration of these reveals a far more complex and thoughtful history than our revisionists claim; for example, Jeynes unveils the thoughts and intents of early settlers such as the Puritans who developed a rich network of educational opportunities, from founding church schools for young children to Harvard, both of which initially included Native Americans. The use of these sources yields a history that is both authentic and alive.

Third, readers will find special chapters and special attention in all the chapters on the education of groups of special interest in the history of education, for example Native Americans, Latinos, women, and Asians, as well as a chapter devoted entirely to the education of African Americans and issues of slavery, including differences between education in the North and South. It is sobering to realize that from the early Puritans who developed schooling opportunities for Native Americans to the establishment of the early charity and later common schools all the way to the No Child Left Behind, there have been consistent efforts to develop educational opportunities that would "level the playing field." Jeynes's history helps us understand that issues of equity did not somehow emerge for the first time in the 1950s and 1960s and to see historically the variations in solutions proposed over the centuries.

Fourth, and perhaps most refreshingly, Jeynes is not afraid to step right into controversial issues from the 1600s to today and lay out both the facts and the controversies, rather than lapsing into an analysis from the left or the right. For example, one chapter is devoted to distinguishing the liberal and conservative educational philosophies going back to the influence of early European thinkers. Another chapter directly addresses more contemporary divisions between left and right by chronicling reform efforts under Democratic versus Republican administrations. A special chapter on the rise of multiculturalism includes both its major proponents and critics. Here, the reader will take the multicultural journey learning from the left and the right, from Kunjufu to Sowell, Sleeter to Schlesinger; and the same is true of issues surrounding the education of speakers of primary languages other than English. Woven throughout the text, Jeynes also documents the nation's struggle to use education to strengthen the moral fiber of its citizens, from the early founders' and educators' conviction that there was too much freedom in the Constitution of this new democratic republic for an unrighteous people all the way to today's more meager efforts to address character, ethics, and virtues in public education contexts.

Fifth, alongside this emphasis on presenting our history from left to right and everything in between, at various points in each chapter, under headings such as "Educational Debate" and "Contemporary Focus," the reader is presented with questions, encouraging their own reflection and analysis of the history and/or controversies just presented. Jeynes seems to actually trust readers to develop their own perspectives and supplies us with the voluminous data, as well as the range of competing interpretations across history in order to develop our own perspectives. We are not told by Jeynes what to think about any issue; we are told what has happened and what others believe and believed so that we may have the necessary historical fodder to see how these issues impact our current work and to encourage our own development of responsive alternatives. In addition to these points of reflection in the text, we are given extensive timelines and vignettes of events as well as short biographies of major figures.

Sixth, in presenting this 15-chapter history of our nation's struggles to develop a world-class education for all of its citizens, Jeynes uses a two-pronged approach: epochal and topical. Some chapters detail particular eras such as the periods surrounding the colonial age,

Revolutionary War, Civil War, World Wars I and II, Great Depression, Cold War, civil rights movements, and the turbulent 1960s. Other chapters focus on issues such as the education of Native, Latino, Asian, and African American students and women; liberal versus conservative philosophies; Democratic versus Republican reform; and the rise of public criticism. The last chapter brings us up-to-date on contemporary issues such as school violence, special education, international comparisons, technology, and the struggle for equity and equalization in school funding. Should any reader want to go deeper into any subject or era, the book's references alone are a wealth of information for anyone serious about education in America.

Last, this is not just a history of education from kindergarten to high school; Jeynes also provides us with the history of the American university. In this is revealed the parallels and common intents and transformations of both schools and universities. Once again, all these are embedded in the larger historical context of the United States and the world.

Jeynes's thoughtful and provocative history provides us with a most inclusive context from which to measure our current experiences, policies, and opportunities and from which to imagine and develop new possibilities. This text emerges in a time when there is a dire need for a more complete and honest account of our great experiment in educating the most diverse peoples ever in any democracy. It tells the whole story, from the triumphs and tragedies of the past to the paradoxes, challenges, and opportunities of the present. As an educator, I am deeply grateful for such a brilliant and balanced history of American education. I look forward to reading it again and again and to sharing the wealth with my students, whom I sincerely want to be able to engage with the whole story so that they may develop more successful educational environments for the future of America and the world.

—Mary Simpson Poplin
Former Dean of the Graduate School of Education and Professor of Education
Claremont Graduate University
July 2006

REFERENCE

Elshtain, J. B. (2000). *Who are we?* (p. 134). Grand Rapids, MI: Eerdmans.

Preface

PURPOSE OF THE TEXT

Reading *American Educational History: School, Society, and the Common Good* will be a unique experience for a variety of reasons. First, it is designed to stimulate dialogue. In recent years, the majority of educational history authors have attempted to lead the reader into making certain specific conclusions. In this sense, objectivity and fairness are not the foremost goals of these books. In contrast, this book is not designed at every junction to lead the reader to certain conclusions. Rather, I believe that for American society to be strong, it is vital that adults reach their own conclusions about educational debates. Consequently, for many educational issues, if there are two sides of a debate, this book will present both sides as fairly as possible.

Moreover, as much as possible, I will present some perspectives that are rarely highlighted in educational history textbooks because these views do not agree with the viewpoints maintained by their authors. One would make a mistake to assume that simply because I present some perspectives that are rarely highlighted in other books that therefore I agree with their viewpoints. In fact, at least half the time I disagree with these perspectives. However, these perspectives are included because they are opinions that are important to know in order to have an intelligent dialogue about education. In addition, different perspectives are presented so that the reader can appreciate the fact that often advocates on both sides of a debate have a point and that neither side is totally right or totally wrong. In a society that is often deadlocked in political and educational debates, whether it is in the form of filibusters, name-calling, or the erection of straw men in philosophical debates, it is essential to instead enter into dialogue with an open mind, understanding that those with different perspectives often possess valid points.

Second, this book will seek to place education events in a proper historical context. It is undeniable that concurrent historical events had a tremendous impact on educational practice. It is also true that many people have a difficult time understanding certain historical developments in education because they are unaware of the surrounding historical contexts. Most books on American educational history examine the topic almost in isolation from some of the most tumultuous and transforming changes in history. To really comprehend the dynamics of schooling and how it both reacts to surrounding events and influences them, it is imperative that the reader understand the general historical context in which events took place. On many occasions, education was a cog in a greater conglomeration of historical events that caused the United States to move in a given direction. At other times, schooling was the engine of change or renewal. Appreciating the educational experience in each of these scenarios is key if one is to learn from the multifaceted nature of the history of schooling.

Third, this book focuses more attention on post–World War II events than most books of its kind. I believe that the time has come for educational historical books to reflect the degree to which education has taken center stage more frequently in the modern era. This emphasis is also consistent with this book's emphasis on the magnitude of the interaction between broader historical events and America's school system. This dynamic has become even more patent during the post–World War II era, because political leaders have realized the relationship between educational health and geopolitical realities. For example, many Americans blamed the American education system for the fact that the Russians (via the *Sputnik*) beat the Americans into space. Presidents George H. W. Bush, Bill Clinton, and George W. Bush all claimed that they were "educational presidents." To the extent that post–World War II America became more cognizant of the inextricable connection between education and the broader forces of history, a particular emphasis on this period appears warranted.

Fourth, a primary goal of this book is to serve as a means for making American education better than it is today. Just what seem to be the best ways to reach this goal will vary from one reader to the next. However, whatever one's worldview, he or she will doubtlessly conclude that there are some ways in which the nation's system and practice of schooling surpass previous achievements. However, it is equally true that readers will identify areas in which American school leaders need to learn from past educational practices. Ultimately, then, the most influential and potent educational history book is one that not only reviews the past but also illuminates the present and spawns ideas for the future. It is my desire, therefore, that the journey through time that the reader takes by reading this book will be one that stimulates dialogue, places educational events in a broader historical perspective, and stimulates a train of thought that will yield a more effective education system for the generations to come.

ORGANIZATION OF THE TEXT

The book is written in a way that is sensitive to the chronology of educational events and also the most notable events in educational history. These chapters reflect not only the influence that schooling has had on broader American society but also the impact of major historical events on education:

1. The Colonial Experience, 1607–1776

2. The Effects of the Revolutionary War Era on American Education

3. The Early Political Debates and Their Effect on the American Education System

4. Education, African Americans, and Slavery

5. The Education of Women and Native Americans, Latinos, and Asian Americans

6. The Widespread Growth of the Common School and Higher Education

7. The Effects of the Events During and Between the Civil War and World War I

8. The Liberal Philosophy of Education as Distinguished from Conservatism

9. The Great Depression and the Long-Term Effects of World War II and the Cold War on American Education

10. The Civil Rights Movement and Federal Involvement in Educational Policy

11. The Turbulence of the 1960s

12. The Rise of Public Criticism of Education

13. The Rise of Multiculturalism and Other Issues

14. Educational Reform Under Republicans and Democrats

15. Other Recent Educational Issues and Reforms

The layout of these chapters will help the reader understand just how various educational practices came into existence and how many of the school debates of today emerged to become a part of the American fabric of life.

PEDAGOGICAL FEATURES AND BENEFITS TO EDUCATIONAL HISTORIANS, STUDENTS, AND INSTRUCTORS

When compared with other American educational history books currently on the market, this book not only provides more content but also includes pedagogical features that will add greater depth to the knowledge that one procures about educational history:

- *Timelines.* The timelines will help the reader place the most important events in educational history in proper historical context not only in relation to other educational events but also with respect to other major historical events as well. This is extremely important because the significance of educational events can best be accurately comprehended when understood in proper historical context.
- *A Closer Look.* Some scholars, teachers, and educational events were sufficiently prominent and pervasive in their influence that they deserve a more intricate examination to fully appreciate their contributions. This pedagogical feature gives a special place to such people and events.
- *Added Insight.* This pedagogical feature provides added information that will give the reader added knowledge in order to better comprehend the educational forces at work at the time covered in the chapter.

- *Contemporary Focus.* Through the issues addressed in this feature, the reader will understand how many of the events in the history of schooling strongly relate to salient educational issues today.

- *Educational Debate.* This pedagogical feature encourages historians, students, and others to engage in debates that have deep historical roots and are some of the most vital controversies facing education today.

- *Key People and Terms.* This section is near the end of each chapter and lists some of the most important people and terms occurring in the chapter.

- *Discussion Questions.* Near the conclusion of each chapter, a set of questions will appear that are designed to stimulate thought and discussion about educational events relevant to the American educational experience, past and present.

A FINAL NOTE

American Educational History: School, Society, and the Common Good will be not only an extremely informative book but also an enjoyable one. Ideally, the learning experience should be one that stimulates thinking and fosters intellectual hunger. There are an interminable number of lessons one can learn from educational history, and it is my hope that once these lessons are learned, they will yield a greater system of schools than this nation has ever seen before.

Acknowledgments

I am very thankful to many individuals who played a large role in making this work possible. I want to thank numerous people in the academic world at Harvard University and the University of Chicago for helping me give birth to this project and in guiding me through the early stages of writing many of these chapters. I especially want to thank the late Bob Jewell for his encouragement in writing on many of these topics. I want to thank a number of academics whose initial reviews helped shape my writing, even before my submission of the drafts to Sage Press. These individuals include Wendy Naylor, Chris Ullman, Huong Nyugen, Ken Calvert, and Dick Carpenter. I want to thank the reviewers who examined the drafts submitted to Sage, including H. Rich Milner of Vanderbilt, Vincent Anfara of the University of Tennessee, J. Randolph Cromwell of Averett University, and J. Gina Giuliano of SUNY at Albany. I want to thank the people at Sage for their wonderful support. I also want to thank several dear friends whose encouragement with respect to this project touched me deeply. Among these dear friends are Wayne Ruhland, Jean Donohue, Rick Smith, and Larry and Vada DeWerd. Thank you so much for your support!

I am incredibly blessed to have been married for 20 years to my wife, Hyelee, whose support has been exemplary. Without her prayers and support, this work never could have been completed. I am blessed and honored to have three wonderful boys, whom I thank for their love and inspiration. The support of my wife and children gave me the encouragement I needed to rely on God's strength and providence to complete this project. I am very grateful for that encouragement and strength.

CHAPTER 1

The Colonial Experience, 1607–1776

The educational undertaking of the early European settlers who came to the United States was especially important because it established a foundation from which all other Americans built (Bailyn, 1960; Cubberley, 1920, 1934). The contributions that each group made varied, depending largely on the degree of their educational orientation and whether they were able to operate in an atmosphere of peace with the Native American population (Bailyn, 1960; Cubberley, 1920, 1934; Willison, 1945, 1966).

Some of the most salient accomplishments in American educational history were made, in particular, in the first few decades after the arrival of the Pilgrims, in 1620, and the Puritans, in 1630 (Bailyn, 1960; Cubberley, 1920, 1934; Willison, 1945, 1966). Their educational success in establishing Harvard College, the nation's first secondary school (Boston Latin School), and compulsory education helped launch the nation's schooling system that would one day become the envy of the world (Jeynes, 2004). Despite these successes, the early settlers also faced challenges in dealing with other cultures, which would spawn a litany of debates that would endure for centuries (Tyack, 1974). Clearly, these debates and successes still live on in American education today.

Although many groups of settlers came to the United States during the 1600s, the Puritans and Pilgrims undoubtedly had the greatest impact on American education (Bailyn, 1960; Cubberley, 1920, 1934). There are two primary reasons for this: First, the Puritans and Pilgrims emphasized education to a considerable degree (Bailyn, 1960; Cubberley, 1920, 1934). Second, for many years, they had a positive relationship with Native Americans that served as a model for other settlers for over half a century (Bailyn, 1960; Cubberley, 1920, 1934; Willison, 1945, 1966). In contrast, many of the other European settlers varied in their academic orientations and the state of their relationships with Native Americans. The importance of an academic emphasis in a community is patent in its impact on the establishment of schools. The state of relations with Native Americans was essential because the presence of peace with one's neighbors greatly facilitates the starting and operating of schools, especially for the young. In the absence of peace, schools could become easy targets for attack.

In terms of chronology, it is somewhat surprising that the Puritans and Pilgrims had a greater impact on the future of American education than other European groups that preceded them, as well as their contemporaries. However, when one takes a closer look at the Jamestown colonists, who arrived in Virginia in 1607, and the Spanish, who arrived even earlier, in comparison with the Puritans and Pilgrims, one can understand why the latter groups had far greater impact.

THE COLONISTS AT JAMESTOWN

Jamestown was settled by 144 males in April of 1607 (Urban & Wagoner, 2000). The early days at Jamestown were very arduous for the settlers. Within a short time of their arrival, they encountered raids by the Powhatan Native Americans and deleterious diseases, such as malaria and typhoid (Urban & Wagoner, 2000). By the end of 1608, half of the original settlers had died (Johnson, 1997, pp. 24–25). One reason the colony survived despite these calamities was the strong leadership of John Smith. Smith was born in Lincolnshire, England, in 1579. He spent his young adulthood as first a merchant and then a soldier in the Austrian army. Eventually, he was taken prisoner by the Turks and sold as a slave (Stephens, 1872). As a slave, Smith was treated cruelly and later escaped and joined up with the first settlement sent to Jamestown. His difficult experiences taught him how to survive. Consequently, under Smith's leadership, the emphasis of the Jamestown colony was on survival rather than on education.

The settlers who arrived at Jamestown were sponsored by investors who desired that the settlement be profitable. As a result, the settlers were sometimes greedy, and that was reflected in their treatment of the Native Americans living around them. In the worst episode, Thomas Hunt sailed up the East Coast and captured and enslaved a group of Native Americans. It is also true that the Native American inhabitants in the area around Jamestown were not especially friendly; they were divided regarding whether they should be aggressive or peaceable toward the people of the Jamestown. A Native American whom the settlers called "Jack of the Feather" was one who wanted war with the settlers. He killed a resident, but when a settler's servant attempted to bring Jack of the Feather to the governor, a struggle resulted and the servant shot him (Eggleston, 1998).

As a result of Jack of the Feather's death, the local Native American population determined that they would wipe out the population of Jamestown, which had by then grown to 900 or so inhabitants (Eggleston, 1998). They might have succeeded were it not for a Native American boy who lived in a White man's house and heard of the plot and warned the settlers. As a result, the settlers were able to either flee or defend themselves. Nevertheless, the Native Americans were successful in slaying a large percentage of the Jamestown colonists, killing nearly 350 individuals (Eggleston, 1998). Amongst this kind of hostility, a system of education could not flourish in Jamestown (Marshall & Manuel, 1977).

THE SPANISH COLONISTS IN FLORIDA

The Spanish arrived in what is now Florida in August of 1565, well before the arrival of the English in Jamestown and New England (Milanich & Milbrath, 1989). Initially, 600 Spanish settlers arrived in what became St. Augustine, in the eastern part of the region, on the Atlantic coast. The Spanish colonists arriving there, and later in areas of the Southwest, were looking to profit from the wealth of the area (Blackmar, 1890; Zavala, 1968). The Native

Americans throughout Florida, and later other areas that the Spanish settled, did not especially appreciate this emphasis and viewed the Spanish as materialistic and focused on gold (Blackmar, 1890; Zavala, 1968). Primarily because of their focus on profit, the Spanish often mistreated the Native Americans in Florida (Zavala, 1968).

One of the primary reasons that the Spanish did not emphasize education that much is that their goals in colonization were different than those of the English. First, there was generally a much closer connection between the motherland and the "New World" colony in the case of the Spanish than with the English (Landers, 2005; Super, 1988). In the case of the Pilgrims and the Puritans, in particular, these groups fled the religious persecution that they had faced in England (Bailyn, 1960; Cubberley, 1920, 1934). As a result, Spain possessed a more meticulous strategy for their colonies than did the English (Cubberley, 1920; Landers, 2005; Super, 1988). For example, Spain had a detailed plan of how to provide food for their settlements, both via shipping and the self-support of a given colony (Super, 1988). Second, partially because of the close relationship between Spanish colonies and the motherland, the Spanish in Florida and other areas desired to govern the Native Americans under the auspices of the Spanish government (Blackmar, 1890; Landers, 2005; Zavala, 1968). In contrast, the English desired to establish settlements that were distinct and separate from the Native American tribes (Cubberley, 1920, 1934; Landers, 2005). As Landers (2005, p. 28) notes, this attempt at governance caused a series of Native American revolts against Spanish law, and Florida was strung together "by small forts" in order to help enforce Spanish governance. Sporadic attacks by Native Americans continued throughout the 1600s, especially as the Spanish continued to expand their influence throughout much of Florida. This fact caused the Spanish to focus on a military strategy more than an educational one (Blackmar, 1890; Landers, 2005; Zavala, 1968).

Although the Spanish did make incipient attempts to educate both their people and Native Americans by what Landers (2005) calls "rudimentary missions" (p. 28), education was not a primary Spanish focus. However, the Spanish thought that the most exigent problem facing the settlers was to govern successfully and fabricate an affluent economy (Landers, 2005). Therefore, the Spanish settlers concentrated their efforts on the colonists and their Native American subjects, using their skills to produce a healthy economy rather than educate the community (Landers, 2005).

In addition, the Spanish colonists in Florida and the Caribbean lived in a very hostile environment (Marshall & Manuel, 1977). Some Native American tribes practiced cannibalism, and those that did not made the sacrifice of the flesh of the colonists an integral part of their religious rituals (Marshall & Manuel, 1977). Even before the Spanish arrived, numerous Native American groups practiced human sacrifices of their own (Marshall & Manuel, 1977). Surely, a system of education could not exist in the presence of such a threat.

THE PILGRIMS AND PURITANS

The Pilgrims and Puritans arrived in the New World in 1620 and 1630, respectively. Although they were technically two distinct groups, the fact that they both arrived in Massachusetts caused them to eventually function with much the same goals and priorities (Bailyn, 1960). The religious beliefs of the two groups were somewhat different, but they both believed in the need to establish a more pure church. As time passed, the Puritans

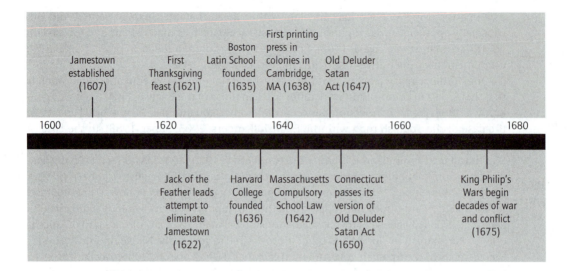

would far outnumber the Pilgrims, and the two groups tended to increasingly merge in their political and religious beliefs. Given that the similarities of these two groups far outnumbered their differences, many historians treat them accordingly as one societal entity, and that will often be the approach of this author as well.

Puritan Educational Emphasis and Educational Philosophy

Most of the Puritan ministers who first came over to America graduated from Oxford and Cambridge universities (Marshall & Manuel, 1977). At this time, Oxford and Cambridge were considered the finest colleges in England and perhaps in the world (Brooke, Highfield, & Swaan, 1988). Therefore, Puritan leaders were accustomed to the highest educational standards and maintained that the Puritans needed to establish similar standards in New England. They quickly realized the necessity of training ministers born in America to be as educated as possible (Pulliam & Van Patten, 1991). To the Puritans, serving God was of utmost importance, and education was a means to that end.

The Puritans were conservative in their philosophy of education. Cotton Mather and John Cotten were among those Puritan leaders who gave a written detailed description of this philosophy. They believed that both parents and children had certain responsibilities when it came to education (Pulliam & Van Patten, 1991) and promoted what might be called a "holy triad" in education, consisting of the home, the church, and the school.

The Home

The Puritans, as a whole, believed that the home was the central place of education (McClellan & Reese, 1988). They surmised that if the home environment were not right, even if the child attended the best church and the best school, the child would not grow up to be properly educated. The colonists asserted that the home was where the spiritual training given at church and the academic training given at school were applied to everyday living (McClellan & Reese, 1988). The child's experience at home was therefore to be a type of spiritual, academic, and job-related apprenticeship. To the extent that this was true, the educational training that a child received at home was very child centered.

In colonial days, particularly among the Puritans, the father was much more involved in the raising of the children than we commonly see today (McClellan & Reese, 1988). Part of this paternal involvement resulted from the Christian concept of the Trinity: the Heavenly Father, the Son, and the Holy Spirit. Many colonists believed that children form an image of the Heavenly Father based on their relationships with their own fathers. Therefore, they concluded that the father had a very special role in raising the children. The Puritans inferred a child could gain a sense of the love and holiness of the Heavenly Father only by examining the life of his or her earthly father. This noteworthy role was especially prominent in raising boys. The colonists understood that boys obtain a true concept of what it meant to be a godly man from their fathers. In the eyes of the colonists, therefore, the more time a boy spent with his father, the better off he would be (Eavey, 1964; McClellan & Reese, 1988; Willison, 1966).

When a Puritan boy reached school age, when he was not in school, he often followed his father like a shadow. If the father worked in the fields, the boy worked there with him. If the father owned a shop, the boy often worked with him there as well. Similarly, the girls generally followed their mothers in much the same way. The girls, thereby, learned cooking skills, sewing skills, and the fine points of what it means to be a godly woman (McClellan & Reese, 1988). If the mother ran the village market, her daughter learned how to do this job by her mother's example.

Most colonial families had what they called "family devotionals," in which they studied the Bible and prayed together as a family. This family time served the purposes of fostering spiritual growth and family unity, increasing the children's reading skills, and implanting seeds of spiritual wisdom within the children (Hiner, 1988). During the family time, the Puritans also read the classics of literature and the newspaper together (Hiner, 1988). To the colonists, increasing one's knowledge was important. Nevertheless, they surmised that unless an individual was grounded in spiritual wisdom, the increased knowledge could be used indiscreetly and could create much harm.

Some people have inaccurate stereotypes of the way Puritans viewed children, believing that Puritans viewed children as "little adults," though this was actually not the case (Smith, 1973). The Puritans did maintain higher expectations of children than is present in contemporary American society, but this was largely due to necessity (Smith, 1973). The life spans of people were shorter than they are today, and the agriculturally based society meant that work participation depended on one's physical size more than on one's age. The larger families of the day also meant that parents needed the help of their older children to care adequately for the young. The Puritans practiced a balance between discipline and encouragement when they raised their children. Cotton Mather (1708) said, "We are not wise for our children, if we do not greatly encourage them."

The Church

Regarding life as whole, the Puritans regarded the church as the most important member of the triad. However, they believed that the family had more of a salient role than the church in educating children. The church's purpose in education was to educate the colonists regarding the teachings of the Bible and how to be loving and godly people. People came to church to obtain wisdom. The church was also the educational administration center for the vast majority of educational undertakings and generally operated the elementary and secondary schools, worked together with other churches to develop colleges, and instructed members of their congregations regarding how they should edify their families at home (Hiner, 1988).

Given that the church emphasized knowing the Bible, teaching children to read was considered essential. The Puritans and Pilgrims placed an emphasis on reading the Bible in both American and European schools, where they resided at this time as well.

The School

In Puritan/Pilgrim culture, the school was responsible for fostering the academic development of the child. The Puritans maintained that the most important function of the school was to help produce virtuous individuals. John Clarke, a leading educator, expressed views that were quite representative of New England educators at the time. He believed that a schoolmaster must, "in the first place be a man of virtue. For . . . it be the main end of education to make virtuous men" (Clarke, 1730).

Academically, the greatest emphasis was placed on reading, so that children could read the Bible as soon as possible. The colonial school itself was not child centered. The colonists believed that the children were to listen closely to instruction at school and then apply the lessons at home. The Puritans viewed schools as having a stabilizing influence on society via drawing children closer to God (Pulliam & Van Patten, 1991). In one respect, however, the Puritan/Pilgrim education was more child centered than the schools of the 1800s. With the onset of increased division of labor, industrialization, and urbanization, the role of the home in education decreased considerably over time. As a result, most American homes were less child centered in the 1800s than they were in colonial times (Hiner, 1988; McClellan & Reese, 1988). Men became involved in jobs away from home, and their children only on rare occasions worked by their sides.

Educational Debate: Parent-Teacher-Community Partnerships

The Puritans and Pilgrims were strong advocates of a strong partnership between the family, the school, and the church. Given the religious nature of the "holy triad," this triangular relationship could not be duplicated today. However, many claim that educators can at least attempt to build a greater unity between parents and schools. Moreover, some assert that schools should also welcome the participation of various facets of the community, including churches and other places of worship, community centers, and nonprofit organizations, that are desirous of helping children do well in school. However, some contend that such a close relationship is no longer possible in modern society because there is no longer the sense of community that there was in the past. In many cases, parents are busy working away from the home and have little contact with their schools and neighborhoods. In addition, communities are not as well-defined as they were in previous generations. Especially in large cities, the identity of certain communities has been lost in the complex mosaic of the metropolis. In fact, one is often unaware of where one suburb ends and another begins unless one sees a sign indicating a boundary. In addition, people do not trust one another to the extent to which they did in past generations.

Some social scientists acknowledge that while it is probably more difficult to build these parent-teacher-community bounds, it is nevertheless imperative that Americans try and that with patience and individual sacrifice, victory can be achieved.

- Do you think it is possible to build strong teacher-parent-community ties, or is this bound to be a rarity in modern society?
- If so, what do you think teachers, parents, and community entities can do to make such partnerships a reality?

Puritans' and Pilgrims' Relationships With Native Americans

A second important reason that education developed in New England first is that the Puritans and Pilgrims had a much better, more positive relationship with the Native Americans than any of the other early colonist groups. This meant that they could freely establish schools and colleges without fear of those schools being attacked. This was an important concern, because schools were filled with women and children, who were defenseless in case of attack. It was indeed foolish to run schools unless a sense of peace existed.

One situation that helped facilitate peace with the Native Americans was a series of events preceding and including the arrival of the Pilgrims at Plymouth Rock in 1620. Prior to their arrival, a Native American tribe by the name of the Patuxets inhabited the area. One of the more aggressive Native American tribes, the Patuxets were detested by many other Native American groups for their abundance of attacks (Goodman, 1971). The Patuxets favored the elimination of Caucasians from the shores of America and were quite successful in implementing their plans along these lines. An interesting thing happened, however. Four years before the Pilgrims arrived, the entire Patuxet tribe was hit by a mysterious plague and was wiped out. The Native American tribes surrounding the area believed the plagues were a divine judgment against the Patuxets because of their violent tendencies. None of these tribes took the vacant land, because they believed the land was cursed (Goodman, 1971).

As a result of all of this, when the Pilgrims arrived, they were surprised not to find Native Americans in the area (Willison, 1945). Captain Myles Standish led a few men around, only to find vacated Native American huts (Willison, 1945). Eventually, they met a Native American named Samoset, who surprised them with the greeting, "Welcome" (Willison, 1966)! Samoset felt relaxed with the Pilgrims and asked them for some beer. The Pilgrims did not have any beer, but instead gave him some "strong water" (possibly brandy) (Willison, 1966, p. 90). The next time the Pilgrims met Samoset, he brought another Native American named Squanto who "had been in England and could speak English better than himself" (Willison, 1966, p. 92).

The Pilgrims, amazingly, just happened to set foot on the land previously inhabited by the Patuxets. When the Pilgrims first met the neighboring Native Americans, the inhabitants communicated to them what had happened to the tribe that had previously inhabited the land. The Pilgrims also believed that the plague had been an act of divine judgment (Goodman, 1971; Marshall & Manuel, 1977). The Pilgrims were told that because the neighboring tribes had no interest in the land, the settlers were welcome to inhabit the 50-mile stretch of land. The Native Americans believed that divine intervention had enabled the Pilgrims to land on the vacant land.

Samoset and Squanto then introduced the Pilgrims to Massasoit, who, generally speaking, was regarded as the leader of a large number of the Native American tribes in the southeast section of New England (Willison, 1945). In their first meeting with Massasoit, the Pilgrims gave Massasoit many gifts in order to set the foundation for a peaceful relationship (Willison, 1945). The Native Americans were equally kind to the Pilgrims, afraid that if they were unkind to them, the same fate that met the Patuxets would also fall upon them (Willison, 1945). The Native Americans showed the settlers the kinds of crops that grew best in the area. In addition, they shared their food with the Pilgrims during that first cold winter and saved a number of them from starvation. Squanto was especially helpful along these lines. He showed the Pilgrims how to grow corn, without which they probably would have perished during the first winter. Squanto's willingness to help is quite amazing, given that years before, he had been captured by a British captain and temporarily sold as a slave in England (Willison, 1966). The Pilgrims shared with Squanto that this particular captain, Captain Hunt, was infamous for his treachery and that he was not representative of British people as a whole. To the contrary, Hunt was well known for being untrustworthy and deceitful (Young, 1974).

For their part, the Pilgrims, and later the Puritans, shared their medicine with the Native Americans, which also saved a number of lives. In one event that helped solidify the relationship between these groups, the Pilgrims saved Massasoit's life (Willison, 1945). Massasoit was seemingly on his deathbed and sent word to the Pilgrims and Puritans that he was about to die. The settlers quickly dispatched people who were knowledgeable in medicine to help Massasoit (Willison, 1945). When the settlers arrived, they found that he had been blinded by the disease and was truly about to die. Numerous other individuals in his tribe were infected with the same or similar diseases (Willison, 1945).

Edward Winslow and two other settlers administered various kinds of medicine to bring Massasoit and the other tribespeople back to health. Within a few days, the leader and his tribespeople responded to the medical treatment and recovered (Willison, 1945). Massasoit rejoiced in his dramatic recovery and announced, "Now I see the English are my friends and love me and whilst I live, I will never forget this kindness they have showed me" (Willison, 1945, p. 222). On another occasion, Squanto, despite his early helpfulness, betrayed the Pilgrims by trying to initiate a plot to attack them (Willison, 1966). Squanto succeeded in convincing many Pilgrims and Native Americans that Massasoit was behind the plot (Willison, 1966). Fortunately, the Pilgrims trusted Massasoit enough to investigate the matter and discovered that the leader knew nothing of the plot (Willison, 1966). Massasoit was infuriated at Squanto and wanted to kill him, but the settlers remembered Squanto's earlier kindness and asked that his life be spared. Massasoit showed himself faithful not only by being proven innocent, but by agreeing not to kill Squanto.

The Pilgrims and Puritans also shared with the Native Americans their rather sophisticated methods of water purification (Willison, 1945). The Pilgrims survived their earliest winters of New England because of the generosity of the Native Americans and the strength of their faith in a sustaining God (Marshall & Manuel, 1977). They believed that the trials of life made them stronger and more compassionate human beings. The Puritans managed to overcome a hurricane in 1635 and an earthquake in 1638 (Bartlett, 1978).

The early treaties that the Pilgrims and the Puritans made with the neighboring tribes served as a model for settlers and Native Americans desiring good relations with one another. The peace treaty of mutual aid and assistance that the Pilgrims made with Massasoit, and rulers over several smaller tribes as well, lasted for 40 years (Bartlett, 1978).

Contemporary Focus

Creating a Racially Harmonious Classroom Atmosphere

From the early years of elementary school, Americans are probably familiar with the fact that the Pilgrims invited the Native Americans to a huge "Thanksgiving" feast in October of 1621. This was the Pilgrims' way of expressing thanks to God for His providence toward them. They invited the Native Americans in order to reach out to them and thank them for their help in their first year in the New World. Massasoit came with 90 Native Americans and surprised their hosts by bringing plenty of food to add to what the Pilgrims offered.

The gathering was a tremendous example of an attempt to create racial harmony. How often do we hear of such gatherings that promote racial harmony today? People would do well to follow this example today. The Thanksgiving feast included feasting, games, and sports contests, including wrestling, running, and shooting. The feast was such a success that it was extended to 3 days (Marshall & Manuel, 1977). It was the first of many such Thanksgiving celebrations (Bartlett, 1978; Robinson, 1851).

Today, there is clearly a lack of racial interaction among school students (Brown & Gaertner, 2001; Cahill, 2004). Students of the same race often gather together at tables and often sit at totally different locations than students of other racial backgrounds. Many families have never invited people of different races to dine with them in their homes.

- What can we, as teachers, do to increase the interaction of students from different racial backgrounds in our classrooms?

The early successes between the Pilgrims and the Native Americans were largely due to a high degree of tolerance by both sides. The tolerance of the Pilgrims grew largely out of their experiences of persecution in England and their experiences after fleeing to the Netherlands (Bartlett, 1978; Robinson, 1851). In the Netherlands for 12 years, they were exposed to a broad range of religious views, as well as the education and the government of the Dutch). While in the Netherlands, many Pilgrims interacted with people from all the major Christian denominations, and they learned to speak Dutch and French (Bartlett, 1978). Bartlett notes, "They embarked on a new course toward universal thinking, led by John Robinson, who was a pioneer in religious fellowship" (p. 20). Robinson, who had been a professor at Cambridge University, built relationships with many of the Dutch intellectuals of the day (Bartlett, 1978).

The tolerance of the Pilgrims/Puritans and the Native Americans were extended to other groups as well, contrary to stereotypes held by certain people. It is true that the Pilgrims/Puritans did not permit all groups of people to live with them, but they regularly helped others and were very hospitable to all kinds of people, including the homeless, strangers, shipwreck victims, and even enemies who had committed deleterious acts against them (Bartlett, 1978). Pilgrim/Puritan court-proceeding records indicate that the administration of justice was often done with leniency and flexibility. They acted this way largely because they believed that courts in England were often too severe in the ordering of punishment (Bartlett, 1978).

Nevertheless, the peace between the Puritans and the Native Americans would not last forever, and this will be dealt with later in the chapter.

EDUCATION CONTRIBUTIONS OF OTHER GROUPS

Dutch and Other Settlers in the Mid-Atlantic Colonies

The Dutch exerted a fair degree of educational emphasis, although not as much as the Puritans. The Middle Colonies probably had the next most developed elementary education system after those in the New England area. The Dutch in New York tried to establish a school at every church that was founded (Eavey, 1964). In these schools, "schooling on a tuition or charitable basis came to prevail" (Cubberley, 1920, p. 369). This educational orientation enabled all children, no matter what socioeconomic level, to go to school (Cubberley, 1920). In Pennsylvania, a large number of Protestant denominations sponsored schools. Like their New England counterparts, Pennsylvanians and those in the mid-Atlantic states believed that school children needed to read the Bible (Cubberley, 1920). A similar diverse sponsorship of schools existed in New Jersey. Churches in the mid-Atlantic States did their best to enable poor children to go to school for free (Cubberley, 1920).

The fact that many churches wanted all children to be educated even if they could not pay is not surprising. The greatest contribution of the early Christians of biblical times and the centuries that followed is that they considered all people worthy of receiving an education (Dupuis, 1966; Marrou, 1956). This belief was principally built on the verse from the Bible that asserts, "There is neither Jew nor Greek, slave nor free, male nor female, for you are all one in Christ Jesus" (Galatians 3:28, *Holy Bible,* 1973). Early Christians believed that all people were worthy to be educated, first in biblical truths and then in other ways as well.

The Quakers, in particular, were quite vigorous in starting religious schools in both Pennsylvania and New Jersey. The Quakers founded 60 to 70 schools in Pennsylvania and about 35 in New Jersey (Curran, 1954). Pennsylvania, with even more religious groups than in the area including New Netherlands (also known as New Amsterdam and New York), put an even greater emphasis on literacy and education than the Dutch had (Eavey, 1964). In 1683, Pennsylvania passed a law that required parents to teach their children to read at a level sufficient to be able to read the Bible (Eavey, 1964). Religious groups like the Morovians, Lutherans, Friends, and Mennonite groups attempted to establish schools in virtually every one of their churches in Pennsylvania (Eavey, 1964). Despite the educational orientation of these groups, it did not reach the level attained by the Puritans. Nevertheless, the educational emphasis of the Middle Colonies was certainly greater than that of Jamestown, where survival was emphasized, and was more formal and developed than education in Maryland and in the remainder of the South.

Other groups contributed as well. The first Jewish settlers to arrive in the United States came from Brazil in 1654 and settled in New Amsterdam. In 1760, the Spanish and Portuguese Congregation of Shearith Israel started the first Jewish American school within their synagogue (Gartner, 1969). Although each group of settlers asserted some degree of educational emphasis, none approached the degree that was enjoyed by the Puritans and Pilgrims (McClellan & Reese, 1988; Smith, 1973).

Settlers in Maryland and Other Areas in the South

In Maryland and the South, education was viewed as more of a family matter than even in New England. Settlers in Maryland and other southern locations, outside of Jamestown, maintained that as long as the family ensured that education was taking place, schools really were not requisite. As a consequence of possessing this perspective, most families in these areas either taught their children themselves or hired tutors to do the teaching (Urban & Wagoner, 2000). Education in the South also tended to be more home based, because the distances between farms and plantations made community schools impossible (Wright, 1957). Nevertheless, the hired tutors taught a copious number of subjects, including reading classical works of literature, math, one to three foreign languages, science, geography, history, and proper moral conduct (Wright, 1957). Some educators did establish some free private schools in Virginia, including Syms, in 1647, and Eaton, in 1659, but these types of schools were far more numerous in New England (Welling, 2005).

In the late colonial period, some tutors developed a considerable reputation in the art of teaching. Probably the most acclaimed tutor was Philip Fithian (Urban & Wagoner, 2000). He was a theological graduate from Princeton and taught a vast array of subjects, including foreign languages. Tutors who taught foreign languages were especially in high demand. Nevertheless, most families could not afford private tutors, and therefore they themselves undertook the task of educating their children. In addition to this form of homeschooling, missionary societies were also engaged in educating children. They were cognizant of the fact that most people could not afford to hire a professional tutor and that others did not feel adequately equipped to train their children in all academic disciplines. As a result, some missionary societies volunteered to teach children either for free or for a free-will donation (Cremin, 1970). The most prominent of these missionary groups was the Society for the Propagation of the Gospel, which secured 170 missionary stations for education between 1701 and 1776. This network of missionary stations was so vast that it covered nearly the entire gamut of the East Coast (Cremin, 1970).

THE EXTENT OF THE PURITAN CONTRIBUTION

The Puritans placed a great degree of emphasis on education largely because they believed that the Bible commanded people to be educated. The belief was based on the biblical declaration, "You shall know the truth and the truth will set you free" (John 8:32, *Holy Bible,* 1973). Of course, this statement referred primarily to spiritual truth. And, indeed, when the Puritans founded Harvard and Yale and other groups founded Princeton and most other early schools, it was with the teaching of spiritual truth that these people were most concerned. Nevertheless, the attitude of the Puritans toward education was very forward looking. They believed that since all of God's creation represented His truth, that education in a more general sense was worth pursuing. Today, America's system of higher education is generally regarded to be the best in the world. The United States owes much of this fact to the Puritans. One hundred and forty years before the founding of the United States of America, Harvard was founded. Many Puritans had taught and/or studied at Cambridge University in England. It was for this reason that they established the town of Cambridge in Massachusetts and that Harvard was located in Cambridge. Virtually all leaders of the Pilgrims and Puritans were academically oriented.

When they arrived in Massachusetts, the Pilgrims elected Deacon John Carver to be governor. Carver died only a few months after being chosen. His successor, William Bradford, was a strong believer in supporting an intelligent gospel (Bartlett, 1978). Bradford, like many of the Puritan leaders of the time, owned a prodigious number of books (400) in his library (Bartlett, 1978). The fact that the Puritans kept records of the number of volumes owned by the leaders demonstrates the emphasis that they placed on literacy. Even though the Pilgrims were economically poorer than the Puritans, Bartlett (1978) notes, "Like the Puritans, the Pilgrims honored education" (p. 48). The Bible was considered the most important book that one could own, and virtually every Puritan home possessed at least one copy (Bartlett, 1978).

The years from 1635 to 1637 were some of the most crucial years in the history of America. In those 3 years, advances by the Puritans and Pilgrims set the stage for the base of the United States to be developed. In 1635, these settlers founded America's first secondary school; in 1636, they founded the continent's first college; and in 1637, they held America's first election with more than one candidate, with John Winthrop being elected governor. The educational and democratic foundation of the future United States of America was established (Johnson, 1997).

The Puritans and Pilgrims emphasized education at every age level. Elementary and secondary schools were founded shortly after the Puritans and Pilgrims arrived in the New World. In 1635, just 5 years after Boston was founded, the public voted in the formation of the Boston Latin School (Fraser, 2001). The Boston Latin School was the first secondary school established in the United States (Rippa, 1997). It was based on the European Latin School Model, which emphasized the learning of religion, Latin, and the classics of literature. The ability to speak more than one language was a central educational theme, much more so than one presently sees in contemporary American society. The Boston Latin School became distinguished, such that some of its best teachers became famous. One of these famous teachers was Ezekiel Cheevers, who taught over 50 years at the grammar school level, much of that time at Boston Latin (Pulliam & Van Patten, 1991).

The Puritans and Pilgrims also started primary schools that were often less formalized than the secondary schools. Primary school education often took the form either of parents teaching their children or of "Dame Schools," based on the European model, in which either young or widowed women instructed young children for a small fee. Reading and writing schools were also available for both the primary and secondary school level, for those who either could not or chose not to pay a fee (Rippa, 1997). The Dame School originally emerged in England following the Reformation, and its development in the United States and Europe served two purposes: First, it helped more elementary school age children to learn how to read, and, second, it enabled some women to make a little money. In the United States, the Dame School was the forerunner of the elementary school (Cubberley, 1920).

The early curriculum of the New England settlers focused on reading, writing, arithmetic, and religious instruction (Pulliam & Van Patten, 1991). Both boys and girls usually started attending school at the age of 6 or 7. School was in session 6 days each week, except during the summer (Pulliam & Van Patten, 1991). School days were generally longer than in

America today. There was a considerable degree of variation in how many years boys and girls remained in school. This was largely dependent on how badly they were needed at home to tend to more mature duties, like planting and harvesting the crops. Prayer, Bible reading, and moral instruction were essential parts of the school day, especially at the beginning and the end of each school day (Pulliam & Van Patten, 1991). Ray Hiner (1988) notes,

> Beyond the creation of a regenerate man, the Puritans had other educational goals, equally explicit. Most of these were encompassed by the characteristics of the civil man. . . . He respected authority, obeyed the laws of the community, and accepted his responsibilities as parent, provider, husband. (p. 6)

Over time, the education system of these settlers became more defined. In 1642, the Massachusetts legislature passed a law requiring that the head of every household teach all the children in one's home, both male and female (Hiner, 1988). This law is often referred to as the "Massachusetts Compulsory Education Law." There was a special emphasis on helping children to read and understand the principles of religion and the capital laws of the country (Cubberley, 1934). Cubberley (1920) noted the significance of the 1642 law when he stated that "for the first time in the English-speaking world, a legislative body representing the State ordered that all children should be taught to read" (p. 354).

The importance of religious and moral training was even more apparent in legislation passed in 1647 that is commonly referred to as the "Old Deluder Satan Act." The essence of the legislation was an assertion that Satan wanted people to be ignorant, especially of the Bible. Therefore, it was the responsibility of each community to ensure that ignorance did not prevail among the youth. The legislation required that each community of 50 or more householders assign at least one person to teach all the children in that community (Fraser, 2001). This teacher was to instruct the children to read and write and would receive pay from the townspeople (Fraser, 2001).

The contents of the legislation further instructed towns of 100 households or greater to begin grammar schools. These schools were designed to prepare children so that they would one day be equipped to study at a university (Fraser, 2001). The emphasis of these laws was not on compulsory education as much as it was on learning. These early laws reasserted the Puritan belief that the primary responsibility for educating children belonged to the parents. They believed that even if the schools failed to perform their function, it was ultimately the responsibility of the parents to ensure that their children were properly educated (Cubberley, 1920).

George Martin (1894), in his book, *The Evolution of the Public School System,* stated that there were six major principles that supported this legislation: (1) "the universal education of youth is essential to the well-being of the state" (n.p.); (2) the primary obligation for education rests with the parents; (3) the state can justifiably enforce this edict; (4) educational opportunity must be provided, even if it is at public expense; (5) the state has the right to establish a minimum educational standard; and (6) tax money may be used to fund education (Martin, 1894).

The Puritans and Pilgrims claimed that it was ultimately the responsibility of the parents to make sure that their children were educated. Often Puritan parents trained their children in the home during the early elementary school years and then sent their children to a Latin grammar school to prepare them for higher education (Pulliam & Van Patten, 1991). Benjamin Franklin's (1961) autobiography offers some insight into the educational experience of many Northerners during the colonial period:

I was put to the grammar school at eight years of age, my father intending to devote me as the tithe of his sons to the service of the church. My early readiness in learning to read (which must have been very early, as I do not remember when I could not read) and the opinion of his friends that I should certainly make a good scholar, encouraged him in this purpose of his. . . . But my father, burdened with a numerous family, was unable without inconvenience to support the expense of a college education. . . . He gave up his first intentions, took me from the grammar school, and sent me to a school of writing and arithmetic. (p. 5)

The fact that Puritans passed the 1642 and 1647 education laws affected the educational policies of other states as well. As the Puritan movement matured, the Puritan religious tradition became known as the "Congregationalist" denomination. The Congregationalists, educationally speaking, were also the dominant group in the states of Connecticut and New Hampshire, which border Massachusetts. Given this background, it is not surprising that Connecticut in 1650 and New Hampshire in 1689 passed their own versions of the "Old Deluder Satan" laws (Smith, 1973; Stewart, 1969). Through these educational laws, the settlers once again declared that Satan was the author of spiritual and intellectual incognizance. This was in contrast to the biblical declaration mentioned earlier, "The truth will set you free" (John 8:32, *Holy Bible,* 1973). To the Puritans, God's truth was revealed not only in His inspired Word, the Bible, but also in His creation at large (Romans 3:20, *Holy Bible,* 1973).

A Closer Look: Compulsory Education

In 1642 and 1647, Massachusetts activated the process toward compulsory schooling that would eventually include every state in the country. In 1642, Massachusetts passed a compulsory education law that, as Cubberley (1920) notes, particularly emphasized reading. Communities could choose to school children either in the home or in an actual school building (Cubberley, 1920; Hiner, 1988; Urban & Wagoner, 2000). However, if a community failed in its obligation to educate children, it could be fined (Cubberley, 1920; Urban & Wagoner, 2000). The Old Deluder Satan Act was inaugurated to focus on more specific enforcement of compulsory education and the importance of reading the Bible.

Today, although the present compulsory schooling laws differ to some degree, state by state, most states require that children attend school between the ages of 6 and 16. Taiwan recently passed a law mandating schooling until the end of high school. Some people believe that the United States should take the same action because it would provide a better life and standard of living for many Americans. Others argue that there are at least three reasons why this would not be a good supposition. First, no one benefits by insisting that students remain in school who do not wish to be there. Second, it is insensitive to some students who must succor their families instead of going to school. Third, some educators, such as John Holt (1976, 1981) and Daniel Pink (2005), assert that the current organization of schools is outdated and that many children will benefit the most if they are educated in the more natural and loving environment of the home. These educators assert that extending compulsory education laws will only make more inveterate a system of schooling that usurps power from parents and grants more ownership to the state and the status quo.

- What do you think about requiring schooling until the end of high school?

Charles Chauncy (1655), an early leader in Massachusetts, argued that education was necessary in order to prevent children from becoming intellectually "naked." The Puritans placed a great deal of emphasis on literacy, especially with the long-term goal of reading and understanding the Bible. To the Puritans, literacy was not essential to experiencing salvation, but it surely facilitated salvation. To this end, the Puritans in Massachusetts became the nucleus of the printing industry in the New World (Cremin, 1976). The first printing press in the colonies was set up in Cambridge, in 1638 (Smith, 1973). The Puritans' emphasis on using the printing press was consistent with their emphasis on literacy. The establishment of printing presses outside of Massachusetts really did not take place until they appeared in St. Mary's City and Philadelphia, in 1685 (Cremin, 1976).

The Puritans/Congregationalists in Connecticut were closely connected with their brethren in Massachusetts but were nevertheless distinct (Stewart, 1969). These New Englanders gave less responsibility for schools to the states and more responsibility to the churches. In 1712, an important law was passed in Connecticut whereby the people took control of the schools away from the towns and put it into the hands of the churches (Stewart, 1969). The churches continued to enjoy control over the schools until 1795 and 1798, when control was given to the school societies (Stewart, 1969). Throughout much of the 18th century, the Congregationalists had the power to determine most educational decisions.

Nevertheless, the power of the Congregationalists decreased substantially following the "Great Awakening" of 1740 to 1741, in which a tremendous revival spread across many of the colonies. As a result of the Great Awakening, many religious denominations increased in number and obtained greater power in determining educational policy (Stewart, 1969). Even though the Congregationalists were still the most powerful religious group in New England after the Great Awakening, their numerical dominance was diminished. As a result of the church system of education, the financial support of education came from church collections. Church collections were often taken to support the act of teaching, the educational facilities, and book purchasing for settlers and Native Americans (Stewart, 1969). The importance of teaching Native Americans especially became an issue when a number of them, to the surprise of the settlers, "put out their children to the English, to be brought up by them" (*Connecticut Record,* 1736, pp. 102–103). In such cases, it was especially important to the settlers to educate the Native American children.

Max Weber (1864–1920), one of the founders of modern sociology, in his book *The Protestant Ethic and the Spirit of Capitalism* traces the American Protestant work ethic all the way back to the Pilgrims and the Puritans (Weber, 1930). Weber argued that Calvinism, as exemplified in the Puritans and Pilgrims, had a profound effect on the American work ethic. In this perspective, spirituality, education, and hard work were inextricably connected. All of these disciplines were involved in the pursuit of God (Weber, 1930). According to Weber, Protestants were highly influenced by the Apostle Paul, who emphasized hard work and was a highly educated individual (Weber, 1930). Of course, Weber's work was of limited scope in some respects, because certainly all Christian groups, including Catholics and Eastern Orthodox Christians, were also influenced by the Apostle Paul. In fact, recent research suggests that there is a broader Christian ethic, rather than merely a Protestant work ethic, that encompasses the other Christian groups as well (Mentzer, 1988).

GROWTH OF HIGHER EDUCATION BEFORE THE REVOLUTIONARY WAR

In 1636, Harvard College became the first institution of higher education founded in the United States, primarily as a college for training ministers (Pulliam & Van Patten, 1991). The goal was to train "learned and godly ministers" (Beard & Beard, 1944, p. 65), so that ministers would be both spiritual and educated. This was not only the belief of the Puritans, but of most settlers at that time. The ministers of that time, in both Europe and America, were more educated than the people of any other occupation. In the colonial period, people believed that ministers were already sagacious individuals. They knew the most about how to live life. Therefore, since they were so wise, the colonists believed they were the people that could be best entrusted with knowledge. As much as the colonists valued knowledge, they valued wisdom more. They believed that knowledge was best entrusted with the sapient. As a result, colonial times ministers were frequently the intellectual leaders of their communities. Later, Harvard became a nucleus for inculcating people from other professions as well, including lawyers and doctors (Beard & Beard, 1944).

Harvard initially started as a nameless university in 1636. But in 1638, when Rev. John Harvard decided to dedicate nearly all his possessions to the full establishing of the college, the institution took his name. The university started as a very religious institution and remained that way for most of its history. Crimson was chosen as the official color of the college, representing the blood of Christ. The official Harvard crest showed three books. Two of them were open, representing those aspects of knowledge that could be obtained by man's inquiry. One of the books remained closed, pointing to those aspects of knowledge that only God could know. Interestingly enough, about 100 years ago, the third book was "opened" on the Harvard crest. But in Harvard's early days, the school served as more of a seminary than anything else (Spring, 1997).

The second American college, William and Mary, was founded in Williamsburg, Virginia, in 1693. In other words, even though colonists settled in Virginia well before they settled in what we now call Massachusetts, a formal center for higher education did not develop in Virginia until 57 years after the founding of Harvard. Furthermore, the enrollment at William and Mary was almost always considerably smaller than at Harvard, even though (a) Virginia's population was higher throughout most of the colonial period and (b) Harvard had the nearby competition of Yale, beginning just 8 years after William and Mary was founded.

Again, this had much to do with the nature of the respective colonists themselves in New England and Virginia. The New England colonists were there because they had fled religious persecution. The Virginia colonists were there, for the most part, to improve their lives and make a lot of money. During the latter half of the 1600s, a lot of religious people, particularly of the Episcopal faith, began to move into Virginia. They possessed priorities that resembled those of the Puritans. They believed people should live upright lives, and they also espoused education (Urban & Wagoner, 2000).

Over time, as an increasing number of religious people moved into Virginia, friction developed between these newcomers, who were concerned about education and the more monetary-minded people, who were enthused about the new cash crop, tobacco. The friction accrued when the religious faction founded the College of William and Mary. The less religious, monetary-minded faction thought that the founding of the college was a waste of time and that Virginia's resources were best directed into tobacco. The friction came to a

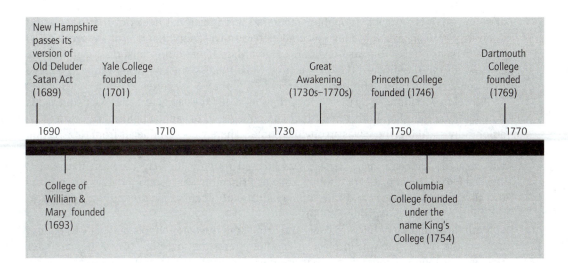

New Hampshire passes its version of Old Deluder Satan Act (1689)

Yale College founded (1701)

Great Awakening (1730s–1770s)

Princeton College founded (1746)

Dartmouth College founded (1769)

1690 — 1710 — 1730 — 1750 — 1770

College of William & Mary founded (1693)

Columbia College founded under the name King's College (1754)

head when the president-elect of the soon-to-be-founded College of William and Mary applied for a charter through England's Attorney General Edward Seymour. Seymour saw no use for the school, but James Blair, a missionary representative of the Bishop of London, pointed out that souls needed to be saved. "Souls," replied Seymour, "damn your souls! Make tobacco!" (Urban & Wagoner, 2000). That was also a common response from many monetary-minded people in Virginia. And so the religious people went their way, led by Blair in the movement to start William and Mary and eventually succeeding, convinced that smoking tobacco was a vice. And the people involved in tobacco went their way, convinced that beginning a college in Virginia was a waste of time. Before William and Mary was founded, some elite, primarily religious people had been able to send their college-age children to study in England, but this was an option only for the very few (Schlesinger & White, 1963). The purpose of the school, much like Harvard, was "to provide a seminary for the training of ministers and to make possible the right training of the young that the cause of the Gospel might be advanced" (Eavey, 1964, p. 202).

How could anyone think higher education was a waste of time? This may be hard for people to conceive today. But in reality, that is how many less religious people in the world at that time viewed higher education. Devout Christians, on the other hand, saw higher education as a means to spread the gospel. As a result, Christian groups started virtually all of America's universities of the first 160 years after the Pilgrims. Although there were a couple of state universities founded immediately following this period, the state university movement really did not begin in earnest until the 1820s (Tewksbury, 1932).

In fact, Christendom was so convinced that higher education was one of the keys for the development of moral behavior and the spreading of the gospel that missionaries started most of the highest-quality universities in many nations in the world. Even in nations in far-off places, such as Japan, Korea, China, and Africa, many top schools were started by missionaries (Big List of Korean Universities, 2002; Cui, 2001; *Index of Ewhaeng,* 2002; Pepper, 1990; Reynolds, 2001).

Shortly after William and Mary was founded, Yale was founded by the Congregationalists (the Puritan line). As the colonial population ascended in the New York and Connecticut area, the colonists urgently sought to address the educational needs of that population (Stewart, 1969). In addition, they saw a need to found a school that was of a more conservative persuasion than Harvard. Of course, Harvard itself was quite conservative at the time as viewed from the modern-day perspective. Nevertheless, the colonists wanted a college that would satisfy their definition of *conservative* (Urban & Wagoner, 2000).

Princeton was founded by the Presbyterians in 1746 for essentially the same two reasons that Yale was founded. With three American colleges in existence before Princeton, geographically speaking, there was an obvious "hole." There were no colleges from New Haven, Connecticut, where Yale was located, all the way down to Virginia, where William and Mary was located. Princeton, New Jersey, was located roughly halfway between the two. It seemed like a logical place for another college. Princeton was also founded as a conservative alternative to Harvard and Yale, which had already become the preeminent colleges in the country (Urban & Wagoner, 2000).

With the founding of Harvard, Yale, and Princeton, the core schools of what was later to become the Ivy League was in place. It is quite interesting that now, over 370 years after Harvard was founded, more than 300 years after Yale was founded, and over 260 years since Princeton was founded, these schools are still referred to as the "Big Three," generally considered overall to be the three best universities in the United States. Schools like the University of Chicago, Stanford, and MIT are also now regarded as prestigious, but the "Big Three" have pretty much retained their positions as the nation's top-three academic institutions. Perhaps even more interesting, they are still ranked in prestige in the order of their founding.

Added Insight: The Importance of High Expectations

Puritans, Pilgrims, and certain other European settling groups set very high expectations for their youth. They often not only emphasized English literacy but also insisted that their leaders possess literacy in several languages. High expectations and setting the appropriate expectations of students are two reasons that may help explain the educational proficiency of the Puritan people.

The place of high expectations and classroom atmosphere is not limited to the Puritans, but research suggests that parental and teacher expectations, as well as classroom atmosphere, have a prominent place in modern-day instruction as well (Jeynes, 2005; Rosenthal & Jacobson, 1968).

Rosenthal and Jacobson (1968) performed an intriguing study in the San Francisco area. They wanted to point out that teacher expectations played a remarkable role in presaging student outcomes, sometimes acting as a self-fulfilling prophecy. They called this role of teacher expectations the "Pygmalion effect." They visited schools and administered a test. They then communicated to various teachers that the results of their examination demonstrated that about 20% of the students were special. In reality, the researchers chose the 20% of the students randomly, and they were really no more "special" than any of the other students. The researchers shared that the teachers were not allowed to convey this information to the students, and they hypothesized that the teachers would treat these designated students accordingly. At the end of the school year, Rosenthal and Jacobson returned to the schools and again administered tests. They found that the 20% of the students that they had randomly labeled as "special" had their scores increase considerably more than the remainder of the students. The Rosenthal and Jacobson hypothesis was supported that asserted that teacher expectations does influence student outcomes.

One of the interesting findings of the Rosenthal and Jacobson (1968) study is that they found that teacher expectations played a more decisive role at the elementary school level than for secondary school students. Why do you think this might be so?

Elementary school teachers encounter students closer to the "ground floor" than do secondary school teachers. However, one should note that elementary school teachers do not meet children at the absolute ground floor. Therefore, preservice teachers should be cognizant of the fact that even kindergarten children vary considerably in their abilities. Some kindergarten children can do simple algebra problems, while others do not comprehend even a single letter in the English alphabet. For any given elementary school class, children often vary in their abilities by plus or minus 2 years from the average grade level. In other words, a teacher instructing at the third-grade level can expect that the students in the class will vary in their abilities from the first-grade level (minus 2 years) to the fifth-grade level (plus 2 years). Teaching students with this wide range in their abilities is one of the most difficult challenges in teaching.

The period between the 1740s and 1750s, immediately following the Great Awakening and before the time of the Revolutionary War, was a "golden age" for starting colleges. During the Great Awakening, many preachers rallied the people into an awareness of the importance of educating the religious leadership. As a result, some of America's greatest colleges were founded, including Princeton, Columbia, and Penn. The founding of Brown University, some years later, was also said to be a result of the effects of the Great Awakening (Michaelsen, 1970). After the establishment of these schools, the percentage of Americans who attended college slowly edged upward, although it was some time before any significant percentage was reached (Michaelsen, 1970).

Columbia was the fifth American college founded and the fourth among the Ivy League schools. The Episcopals founded it in 1754 as King's College. The name was changed to Columbia in 1787. The idea that the rank of the Ivy League schools follows chronological order may or may not continue with Columbia. Most would agree that Columbia is in the middle tier among the Ivy League schools, but Dartmouth is often considered the fourth best among the Ivy League schools, and that was not founded until 1769 (Urban & Wagoner, 2000).

Devout religious people founded all the Ivy League schools, with religious purposes in mind. It was understood that these schools would serve as a conduit for spreading the gospel. Columbia, of course, served the growing population of New York. Because Harvard and Yale had been established longer, however, New York's elite generally preferred to attend one of those two. Even today, Columbia aggressively recruits those who have been rejected from Harvard or Yale. The reason the date of their founding played less of a role for the later Ivy League schools is that beginning in 1754, the founding of colleges became much more frequent. Meanwhile, Harvard, Yale, and Princeton had a clear jump on the rest of the pack in terms of establishing themselves, and other Ivy League schools had somewhat less of an advantage. After Columbia and Penn, Brown and Dartmouth were founded in the 1760s. The Dutch Reformed church also founded Rutgers during the same period. After that, as will be addressed later, immediately following the Revolutionary War, the number of colleges increased significantly (Tewksbury, 1932).

In many respects, the colonists faced greater challenges in establishing elementary and secondary schools than they did in establishing colleges, largely due to the threat of Native

American attacks upon the schools: College-age individuals could defend themselves, but primary and secondary school children were far more helpless. Thus, although the extent of the development of a college in an area often reflected the extent of the development of education for the young, the education of the young became even more dependent on good relations with the Native Americans than was the case with colleges.

DETERIORATION OF PURITAN AND NATIVE AMERICAN RELATIONS

The relationship between the Puritans and the Native Americans was largely a good one as long as Massasoit lived. During this time, the Native Americans and the settlers offered each other their practical and cultural strengths (Marshall & Manuel, 1977). The Native Americans offered their knowledge of agriculture and survival. The settlers offered their medicine and education. For decades, the Native Americans and the Puritans peacefully enjoyed the benefits of each other's strengths. They helped each other live and thrive agriculturally and medically. From early in Harvard's history, in the 1640s or before, the Puritans made it a priority to educate Native Americans (Lin, 2005). As a result, some Native Americans began to attend Harvard along with the other students (Adams, 2005; Marshall & Manuel, 1977).

Over time, Puritans became more committed to educating Native Americans at Harvard. Harvard's charter of 1650 specifically states that the college was committed to "the education of the English and Indian youth of the country" (Wilson, 2004, p. 3). The Puritans eventually concluded that to make this invitation to Harvard more attractive, there needed to be a distinct building within Harvard College to educate Native Americans (Adams, 2005). The issue of whether instructors should teach Native Americans alongside Euro-Americans was one that Puritans pondered at both the elementary school and college level (Marshall & Manuel, 1977; Szasz, 1988). Early on, the Puritans believed that Native Americans and Euro-Americans should be taught concurrently (Cremin, 1970; Marshall & Manuel, 1977). Cremin (1970) notes, "There is evidence that early as 1650, Indian children were attending the common schools of Massachusetts side by side with whites" (p. 194). However, as time passed, the Puritans concluded that for practical reasons and due to Native American preference, at the college level, separate facilities were best (Cremin, 1970; Marshall & Manuel, 1977). The building of the Native American facet of Harvard College was initiated in 1653 and completed in 1655 (Adams, 2005; Cremin, 1970; Lin, 2005). The Puritans offered Native Americans the occasion to attend Harvard, often free of charge (Marshall & Manuel, 1977). Therefore, opportunities given to make it easier for some people of color to gain access to higher education has deeper roots than both opponents and proponents of this idea might lead one to believe.

As the next generation of Native Americans gained dominion in their tribes, their relations with the colonists began to deteriorate. Two of Massasoit's sons, Wamsutta (Alexander) and Metacomet (Philip) viewed the Puritans quite differently than their father did (Fager, 1980; Markham, 1883; Strange, 1675). Wamsutta and Metacomet had three primary concerns. First, they believed that many actions that their father viewed as acts of cooperation, such as inviting Native Americans to study at Harvard, were really acts of compromise (Fager, 1980; Markham, 1883; Strange, 1675). And truly, one can see both sides. From the standpoint of the Puritans and the first generation of Native Americans with whom they had relations, this was an act of kindness. But Metacomet, in particular, noted that the Native Americans who returned from college were thinking too much like the White people (Fager, 1980; Strange, 1675). Second, Alexander and Metacomet also believed their father had sold too much land to the settlers at too low a price (Marshall & Manuel, 1977). Third, as Puglisi states (1991) "Metacomet and his people were troubled by the growth of the English population in New England" (p. 2). Alexander's and Metacomet's perspective changed relations between the Puritans and the Native Americans considerably (Puglisi, 1991).

Temporarily, after his father's death, Alexander, the son of Massasoit, became chief of the Wampanoags (Abbot, 1899; Morris, 1876). Alexander was cool toward the Puritans, and evidence suggests that he might have been plotting with the Narragansett tribe against them (Abbot, 1899; Markham, 1883). The Puritans first heard of the scheme from members of the tribe, who claimed that Alexander was conspiring with the tribe's leaders (Abbot, 1899). However, because the Narragansetts and Wampanoags were enemies, at first the Puritans doubted the veracity of these claims. They thought the Narragansetts were simply trying to make trouble for Alexander (Abbot, 1899; Markham, 1883). When the Puritans asked Alexander about the claims, he replied that the rumors were false and that he had no dealings with the Narragansett tribe, because they were enemies. The Puritans then asked Alexander to speak to them before the Plymouth Court and reassure them that they had nothing to fear and that the Narragansetts' claim of a plot was false. Alexander seemingly gladly agreed, but on the day he was scheduled to speak, he did not show up (Abbot, 1899; Markham, 1883). Worried about this turn of events, the Puritans sent out a group to locate Alexander and became very distressed when they discovered him meeting with the Narragansetts. The Puritans then dispatched Major Winslow to force Alexander to explain his actions, and Alexander was insulted (Abbot, 1899; Markham, 1883).

When Alexander died the following year after becoming chief, Metacomet became chief of the Wampanoags (Fager, 1980; Markham, 1883; Strange, 1675). As the years passed, it became more evident to the Puritans that relations with the Native Americans were deteriorating. Puritan crops were often growing better than those of the Native Americans. Although the Puritans shared their produce, the Native Americans felt embarrassed by their need and sometimes stole from the colonists (Marshall & Manuel, 1977). Metacomet maintained a belief that Native Americans were increasingly becoming Westernized, in part through Puritan schools and Harvard College, and that the increasing number of English would only exacerbate this trend (Abbot, 1899; Puglisi, 1991; Strange, 1675). Although only a minority of Native Americans were schooled by the English and only a small number attended Harvard, it was generally the most gifted Native Americans who were educated in this manner, and this was of great concern to Metacomet (Abbot, 1899; Puglisi, 1991; Strange, 1675).

The real turning point occurred when the Puritans found a Native American they called "John Sassamon" dead in a pond (Ranlet, 1999). Sassamon had studied at Harvard and previously had been regarded as instrumental in keeping peace between the Native Americans and the colonists (Adams, 2005; Ranlet, 1999; Strange, 1675). However, two actions by Sassamon apparently enraged Metacomet. First, Sassamon had learned of a plot led by Metacomet to gather together a confederation of Native American tribes to attack the Puritans, and he had communicated this scheme to them (Morris, 1876). Second, Sassamon apparently communicated to Metacomet that the latter needed to change his ways; he exhorted Metacomet to have a more peaceable approach toward the Puritans, like Massasoit, and adopt Western ways (Strange, 1675). Consequently, Metacomet considered Sassamon a traitor (Strange, 1675). After the death of Sassamon, a Native American named Patuckson came forward and "could not resist talking about it" (Ranlet, 1999, p. 146). Patuckson revealed that he had seen three Native American men, including one of Metacomet's right-hand men, kill Sassamon (Adams, 2005; Marshall & Manuel, 1977; Ranlet, 1999). One of the three accused of the murder confessed to his participation and testified against the other two (Marshall & Manuel, 1977).

Large numbers of armed Native Americans roamed the countryside. The Puritans became intimidated, and many retreated to more densely populated areas. Shortly thereafter, in June 1675, the Native American attacks began. They first attacked the Plymouth colony, but the fighting eventually spread throughout a large part of New England, including a substantial portion of the settlements in Massachusetts, Connecticut, and Rhode Island (Abbot, 1899; Calloway, 1997; Church, 1716; Drake, 1999; Freeman, 1878; Leach, 1963; Markham, 1883). The attacks were a brilliant work of a highly organized military strategy (Abbot, 1899; Freeman, 1878; Markham, 1883). The essence of the strategy was for the Native Americans to assault nearby towns simultaneously so that none of them could send reinforcements to help the others (Abbot, 1899; Freeman, 1878). Leach (1963), of the Rhode Island Historical Society, notes that according to a Rhode Island resident of the period, William Harris, Metacomet had intended to launch the attacks as early as 1671, but heavy rains thwarted his plans. If it is true, as Harris and a number of historians suggest, that Metacomet had been planning for war for some years, this might help explain the adroit strategy and execution of these plans in the early stages of the conflict (Abbot, 1899; Ranlet, 1999).

In addition to the brilliant military strategy of concurrent attacks on nearby cities, Metacomet maintained a second military strategy. He knew that his armies would be unable to kill all the settlers in many towns, so his primary aim was to burn down their sources of food and shelter (Calloway, 1997; Freeman, 1878; Morris, 1876). The Native Americans' mode of attack was generally to shoot at the settlers and burn down their houses, barns, and farms (Calloway, 1997; Morris, 1876). In another example of Metacomet's military acumen, the Native Americans saved some of their largest attacks for September through November, when burning the barns and crops would mean that the Puritans, Quakers, and other set-tlers would not have enough food for the winter (Calloway, 1997; Drake, 1999). Indeed, Metacomet's strategy was so meticulously planned that nearly every major historian agrees that the leader came very close to success, and most settlers in New England barely made it through the winter (Calloway, 1997; Drake, 1999; Freeman, 1878).

Although Native Americans did not target schools to the extent that they attacked homes, barns and crops, on many occasions, they destroyed or nearly destroyed entire towns (Calloway, 1997; Freeman, 1878; Haefeli & Sweeney, 1997; Puglisi, 1991). Therefore, schools, in addition to Dame Schools, were naturally among the buildings destroyed (Slotkin & Folsom, 1978; Weddle, 2001). As Slotkin and Folsom (1978) note, even in just the initial con-flicts of the first year, called "King Philip's War," "It pushed the colonies perilously close to ruin. Half the towns in New England were severely damaged—twelve completely destroyed" (p. 3). Weddle (2001, p. 94) estimates those numbers to be somewhat higher, with 12 settle-ments "razed to the ground" just among the Puritan settlements alone. Large settlements, such as Providence, Rhode Island, and Springfield, Massachusetts, were especially hard-hit (Weddle, 2001; Slotkin & Folsom, 1978). Providence lost 84% of its houses due to fire and all but two of its homes overall, partially because the Quakers, in accordance with their non-violent beliefs, refused to defend their city, and fled (Schultz & Tougias, 1999; Weddle, 2001). Quakers in other Rhode Island cities were also attacked (Schultz & Tougias, 1999). If the Puritans were relatively pacifistic in their practical lives, the Quakers were totally pacifistic. Despite the pleading of Roger Williams to at least defend their homes, the Quakers simply left the areas under assault as the Native Americans approached and ransacked their towns (Ammerman, 1995). Springfield lost two thirds of its homes, and other large towns, such as Brookfield, Northfield, and Deerfield, "were abandoned" (Drake, 1999, p. 86).

Clearly, within the early months of King Philip's War, the English settlers experienced many defeats (Weddle, 2001; Schultz & Tougias, 1999; Slotkin & Folsom, 1978). Many women and children were either killed or taken captive, and even babies were "scalped" (Abbot, 1899; Church, 1716; Pugilisi, 1991; Slotkin & Folsom, 1978). The beating that the young were taking in homes and schools caused a substantial disruption in New England schooling (Weddle, 2001). Weddle notes the extent to which the English feared being attacked: "But the colonists came to mistrust all Indians in the months following the outbreak of the attacks. They regarded the individual battles as an all-encompassing race war" (p. 79).

King Philip's War was the first in a succession of many wars that continued until approximately 1713 (Pugilisi, 1991). King Williams War was among the largest, beginning in 1689 (Pugilisi, 1991). The relationship between Native Americans and New Englanders was never the same.

The Native American attacks of this era had two profound effects. First, the schooling of the Puritan children came to a standstill. Rather than fight to keep the schools open, the Puritans chose to close the schools down. Although some Puritan towns initially attempted to keep the schools open, there were simply too many children being killed to justify this. Naturally, as a result of the wars, Native Americans no longer attended Harvard (Adams, 2005). As the wars became prolonged, by 1700, discouraged by the continued deterioration in their once tranquil relations with Native Americans, the Puritans tore down the Native American college within Harvard (Adams, 2005).

The second profound effect is that the attacks radically changed the attitudes of the settlers toward the Native Americans. As news of the attacks spread to faraway colonies, the settlers became bitter and angry. It was well-known among the settlers that the Puritans and the Quakers were pacifistic. It was also well-known, among settlers and Native Americans alike, that the Puritans and the Quakers generally treated the Native Americans with the greatest kindness of all the settling groups. Thus, other colonists were astonished at the attacks on these two groups, in much the same way people might be if the Amish, whose lifestyle is similar, were attacked today (Marshall & Manuel, 1977; Williston, 1945).

Historians generally take one of two perspectives regarding the Native American attacks. The first group of historians believes that the settlers should never have landed in the New World in the first place. The Native Americans inhabited the land before them. Therefore, the Europeans should never have set foot there. According to these historians, the desire by the Native Americans either to wipe out the new arrivals or to send them back to Europe was a natural consequence of the settlers growing in number; and they targeted the schools in particular to ensure that the next generation of settlers would not be greater than the early generation of European newcomers. In the eyes of these historians, the Native American attacks were both justifiable and understandable (Marshall & Manuel, 1977).

The second group of historians believes that human migration was worldwide and inevitable, especially considering that groups like the Puritans were facing persecution. They claim that for each race to have a continent all to themselves without permitting other races to enter is unrealistic. This was not the case in any other part of the globe, so why should it be the case in North America? According to these historians, the issue was whether the Native Americans and colonists could peacefully coexist in North America, and they are less sympathetic regarding the Native American attacks, for violence was not consistent with the notion of peaceful coexistence (Marshall & Manuel, 1977).

The purpose of the Native American attacks on the schools had been to (a) to discourage further colonization of the New World (it was hoped that the attacks would communicate to the Puritans and the Quakers that New England was not a hospitable place for colonization) and (b) to lower the overall population, especially the population of the next generation of settlers (Marshall & Manuel, 1977).

The Native American plan backfired, however, because American colonists were shocked by the mass slaughter of Puritan and Quaker children in particular. The attitude of most of them of that time was "If you can't get along with the Puritans and Quakers, you can't get along with anyone" (Marshall & Manuel, 1977). The colonists concluded that the Native Americans were barbarians. As Puglisi (1991) observes, "King Philip's War also transformed most New Englanders' attitudes toward the Indians" (p. 31). Drake (1999) adds, "King Philip's War changed the political environment with which such Indians operated. The war precipitated a tremendous shift in the attitudes of the English toward the Indians" (p. 172) The colonists in many sections of the country cried out for vengeance (Pugilisi, 1991; Weddle, 2001). Immigrants coming to America were told to bring their guns, because in the minds of the existing colonists, the Native Americans were cruel and aggressive (Marshall & Manuel, 1977). This turn of events, together with President Andrew Jackson's mistreatment of Native Americans years later, did more to influence Euro-American and Native American relations than any others.

The Native American attacks of 1675 to 1713 were a pivotal point in relations between the Native Americans and the colonists. By the early- to mid-1800s, there was another turning point as well. Previous to 1800, many people had come to America for reasons of religious and intellectual freedom. Therefore, their hunger for land and wealth was minimal. But by the early to mid-1800s, most people came to America for that very reason and had very little interest in religious and intellectual freedom (Johnson, 1997). Their motives revolved around selfishness and avarice. These new settlers had heard of the Native American attacks on the Puritans and Quakers. They regarded the Native Americans as the enemy, and they showed little forbearance for the idea of peaceful coexistence. They were convinced of the cruelty of the Native Americans not merely because they attacked, but because of whom they attacked: Puritans, Quakers, and children.

The nature of the settlers moving West was also of concern to the clergy, who were concentrated in the East. The clergy was concerned about the lawlessness and the "anything goes" attitude of many settlers pushing their way out West. Throughout the late 1600s, 1700s, and 1800s, eastern clergy became so concerned about the failure of western frontier people to abide by the law and by treaties that they raised an urgent plea for pastors to go to the region and start churches to tame the land (Beecher, 1835; Eavey, 1964). Because vengeance and greed were on their minds, those who settled the western frontier committed many wrongs against the Native Americans. From the perspective of the settlers, they were justified in doing this because of the way the Native Americans had treated the early settlers. The emphasis of the western settlers was much more on vengeance than it was on peaceful coexistence (Johnson, 1997).

Once the wars ended, the New England settlers were able to reestablish their schools (Cubberley, 1934). Between 1713 and 1776, elementary, secondary, and postsecondary institutions grew considerably in number. Despite various obstacles, the foundation of a strong educational system had been developed. It was a foundation that would serve people as well as a new nation prepared to be born. The solid foundation would also help make it possible for a new nation to flourish and for the United States to quickly possess one of the most respected education systems in the world (Cubberley, 1934).

CONCLUSION

There is no question that the commitment to education among the settlers varied widely. The Europeans who came to North America arrived with often significantly different goals from one another. The Puritans and Pilgrims undoubtedly valued schooling the most of the first European settlers. However, what the new Americans probably did not anticipate is the extent to which relations with their neighbors, the Native Americans, would influence the extent to which schooling would be possible. Nevertheless, the fact that peace did facilitate education should remind one that the ravages of war almost never provide fertile ground for education.

Perhaps the most amazing accomplishment of the Puritans is the speed and the efficacy with which they established what became some of the nation's most exemplary educational expressions, including Harvard, Yale, Boston Latin School, compulsory education laws, and so forth. They even saw the need to include an emphasis on educating people of color (Wilson, 2004). In other words, a great deal of educational practice today finds its roots in Puritan traditions established between 1635 and 1647. The Puritans clearly made some mistakes educationally, especially in their inability to grasp why certain Native Americans would embrace Puritan schooling while others would grow to resent the Westernization that accompanied instruction. The Puritan example should inspire one to esteem the great academic goals that humans are capable of reaching and yet foster a greater comprehension of the fact that many people of color still regard American education as a Westernizing influence.

Contemporary Americans have many educational institutions and practices for which to thank the Puritans. And yet as ironic as it may seem, some of the challenges faced by the Puritans were in a real sense very similar to those faced today. With these thoughts in mind, one can unquestionably see a great need to learn from the people of that era.

DISCUSSION QUESTIONS

1. Before the Pilgrims and the Puritans arrived in North America, the Wampanoags and other Native American tribes had to endure the aggression of the Patuxet tribe. Similarly, the Pilgrims and the Puritans were victimized by widespread religious persecution in England. Do you think that the fact these groups suffered made them more desirous of

getting along with one another? How can familiarity with the experiences of various cultures and nations help teachers understand why certain people behave the way they do?

2. One trend that is apparent in higher education is that usually the first 50 years in a college's history determines how successful the institution will be in the long run. Why do you think that this is often the case?

3. How important do you think the work ethic is as a determinant of children's achievement? How important do you think this factor is in the rise of a nation to economic prominence?

4. Two chief emphases of the Puritans in education were teaching by example and maintaining good relationships with their neighbors, the Native Americans. These two emphases remain important in teaching today. Students see whether we are living according to what we claim to value, and they will be more influenced by our deeds of love, acceptance, and understanding of people from different races and backgrounds than they will by just our words. If we teach using words of acceptance and understanding regarding people of other races but we never spend much time with those of other races, what conclusions do you think children will draw from our lives?

REFERENCES

Abbot, J. S. C. (1899). *History of King Philip*. New York: Harper.

Adams, J. (2005, December 7). Harvard excavates past in Indian college anniversary. *Indian Country Today*, p. 3.

Ammerman M. (1995). *Roger Williams*. Uhrichsville, OH: Barbour.

Bailyn, B. (1960). *Education in the forming of American society*. Chapel Hill: University of North Carolina.

Bartlett, R. (1978). *The faith of the Pilgrims*. New York: United Church Press.

Beard, C. A., & Beard, M. R. (1944). *A basic history of the United States*. New York: Doubleday, Doran.

Beecher, L. (1835). *A plea for the West*. Cincinnati, OH: Truman & Smith.

Big list of Korean universities. (2002). Duke University. Retrieved May 1, 2003, from http://www.duke.edu/~myhan/c_blku.html

Blackmar, F. W. (1890). *Spanish colonization in the West*. Baltimore: John Hopkins University.

Brooke, C. N., Highfield, J. R., & Swaan, W. (1988). *Oxford and Cambridge*. New York: Cambridge University Press.

Brown, R., & Gaertner, S. L. (2001). *Intergroup processes*. Malden, MA: Blackwell.

Cahill, S. (2004). *Inside social life: Readings in sociological psychology and microsociology*. Los Angeles: Roxbury.

Calloway, C. G. (1997). Introduction: Surviving the Dark Ages. In C. G. Calloway (Ed.), *After King Philip's War: Presence and persistence in Indian New England* (pp. 1–28). Hanover, NH: Dartmouth College.

Chauncy, C. (1655). Charles Chauncy on liberal learning. In W. Smith (Ed.), *Theories of education in Early America* (pp. 15–23). Indianapolis, IN: Bobbs-Merrill.

Church, B. (1716). *The entertaining history of King Philip's War*. Boston: Thomas Church.

Clarke, J. (1730). John Clarke's classical program of studies. In W. Smith (Ed.), *Theories of education in Early America* (pp. 38–45). Indianapolis, IN: Bobbs-Merrill.

Connecticut Record, Vol. VII, 1726-1735 (1736).

Cremin, L. (1970). *American education: The colonial experience, 1607–1783.* New York: Harper & Row.

Cremin, L. A. (1976). *Traditions of American education.* New York: Basic Books.

Cubberley, E. (1920). *The history of education.* Boston: Houghton Mifflin.

Cubberley, E. (Ed.). (1934). *Readings in public education in the United States: A collection of sources and readings to illustrate the history of educational practice and progress in the United States.* Cambridge, MA: Riverside Press.

Cui, D. (2001). British Protestant educational activities and nationalism of Chinese education in the 1920s. In G. Peterson, R. Hayhoe, & L. Yongling (Eds.), *Education, culture, and identity in the twentieth century China* (pp. 137–160). Ann Arbor: University of Michigan Press.

Curran, F. X. (1954). *The churches and the schools.* Chicago: Loyola University Press.

Drake, J. D. (1999). *King Philip's War.* Amherst: University of Massachusetts.

Dupuis, A. M. (1966). *Philosophy of education in historical perspective.* Chicago: Rand McNally.

Eavey, C. B. (1964). *History of Christian education.* Chicago: Moody Press.

Eggleston, E. (1998). *A history of the United States and its people.* Lake Wales, FL: Lost Classics Book Company.

Fager, C. (1980). *Quakers and King Philip's War, 1675–1676.* Falls Church, VA: Kimo Press.

Franklin, B. (1961). *The autobiography of Benjamin Franklin.* New York: New American Library.

Fraser, J. W. (2001). *The school in the United States.* Boston: McGraw Hill.

Freeman, F. (1878). *Civilization and barbarism.* Cambridge, MA: Riverside Press.

Gartner, L. P. (1969). *Jewish education in the United States.* New York: Teachers College.

Goodman, S. E. (1971). Squanto. In L. D. Geller's (Ed.), *They knew they were Pilgrims: Essays in Plymouth history.* New York: Poseidon Books.

Haefeli, E., & Sweeney, K. (1997). Revisiting the redeemed captive: New perspectives on the 1704 attack on Deerfield. In C. G. Calloway (Ed.), *After King Philip's War: Presence and persistence in Indian New England* (pp. 29–71). Hanover, NH: Dartmouth College.

Hiner, N. R. (1988). The cry of Sodom enquired into: Educational analysis in seventeenth century New England. *The social history of American education* (pp. 3–22). Urbana: University of Illinois Press.

Holt, J. C. (1976). *Instead of education: Ways to help people do things better.* New York: Dutton.

Holt, J. C. (1981). *Teaching your own A hopeful path for education.* New York: Delacorte Press.

Holy Bible. (1973). Grand Rapids, MI: Zondervan.

Index of Ewhaeng. (2002). Seoul: Ewha University. Retrieved on May 1, 2003, from http://www.ewha.ac .kr/ewhaeng.

Jeynes, W. (2004). Immigration in the United States and the golden years of education: Was Ravitch right? *Educational Studies, 35,* 248–270.

Jeynes, W. (2005). A meta-analysis of the relation of parental involvement to urban elementary school student academic achievement. *Urban Education, 40,* 237–269.

Johnson, P. (1997). *A history of the American people.* New York: HarperCollins.

Landers, J. (2005). Social control in Spain's contested Florida frontier. In J. F. d. Teja & R. Frank (Eds.), *Choice, persuasion, and coercion: Social control on Spain's North American frontiers* (pp. 27–48). Albuquerque: University of New Mexico.

Leach, D. E. (1963). *A Rhode Islander reports on King Philip's War.* Providence, RI: Rhode Island Historical Society.

Lin, J. C. (2005, April 11). Indian tribe back in yard. *Harvard Crimson,* p. 6.

Markham, R. (1883). *A narrative history of King Philip's War and the Indian troubles in New England.* New York: Dodd, Mead.

Marrou, H. I. (1956). *A history of education in antiquity.* New York: Sheed & Ward.

Marshall, P., & Manuel, D. (1977). *The light and the glory.* Grand Rapids, MI: Fleming Revell.

Martin, G. (1894). *The evolution of the Massachusetts public school system.* New York: Appleton.

Mather, C. (1708). A master in our Israel. In W. Smith (Ed.), *Theories of education in early America* (pp. 9–24). Indianapolis, IN: Bobbs-Merrill.

McClellan, E. B., & Reese, W. J. (1988). *The social history of American education.* Urbana: University of Illinois Press.

Mentzer, M. S. (1988). Religion and achievement motivation in the United States: A structural analysis. *Sociological Focus, 21,* 307–316.

Michaelsen, R. (1970). *Piety in the public school.* London: Macmillan.

Milanich, J. T., & Milbrath, S. (1989). *First encounters: Spanish exploration in the Caribbean and the United States.* Gainesville: University of Florida Press.

Morris, H. (1876). *Early history of Springfield.* Springfield, MA: F. W. Morris.

Pepper, S. (1990). *China's education reform in the 1908s.* Berkeley: Regents of the University of California.

Pink, D. (2005). *A whole new mind: Moving from the information age to the conceptual age.* New York: Riverhead Books.

Puglisi, M. J. (1991). *Puritans besieged: The legacies of King Philip's War in the Massachusetts Bay Colony.* Landham, MD: University Press of America.

Pulliam, J. D., & Van Patten, J. J. (1991). *History of education in America.* Upper Saddle River, NJ: Merrill/Prentice Hall.

Ranlet, P. (1999). Another look at the causes of King Philip's War. In A. T. Vaughan (Ed.), *New England encounters* (pp. 136–155). Boston: Northeastern University.

Reynolds, D. R. (2001). Christian mission schools and Japan's to-a-dobun shoin: Comparisons and legacies. In G. Peterson, R. Hayhoe, & Y. Lu (Eds.), *Education, culture, and identity in twentieth century China* (pp. 82–108). Ann Arbor: University of Michigan.

Rippa, S. A. (1997). *Education in a free society.* White Plains, NY: Longman.

Robinson, J. (1851). *Works.* London: John Snow.

Rosenthal, R., & Jacobson, L. (1968). *Pygmalion in the classroom: Teacher expectations and pupil's intellectual development.* New York: Holt, Rinehart & Winston.

Schlesinger, A. M., & White, M. G. (1963). *Paths of American thought.* Boston: Houghton Mifflin.

Schultz, E. B., & Tougias, M. J. (1999). *King Philip's War.* Woodstock, VT: Countryman Press.

Slotkin, R., & Folsom, J. K. (Eds.). (1978). *So dreadful a judgment: Puritan responses to King Philip's War, 1676–1677.* Middletown, CT: Wesleyan University Press.

Smith, W. (1973). *Theories of education in early America.* Indianapolis, IN: Bobbs-Merrill.

Spring, J. (1997). *The American school 1642–1996.* White Plains, NY: Longman.

Stephens, A. H. (1872). *History of the United States.* New York: Hale & Son.

Stewart, G. Jr. (1969). *A history of religious education in Connecticut.* New York: Arno Press & New York Times.

Strange, R. L. (1675). *The present state of New England with respect to the Indian war.* London: Dorman Neumah.

Super, J. C. (1988). *Food, conquest, and colonization in sixteenth-century Spanish America.* Albuquerque: University of New Mexico.

Szasz, M. (1988). *Indian education in the American colonies, 1607–1783.* Albuquerque: University of New Mexico Press.

Tewksbury, S. (1932). *Founding of American colleges and universities before the Civil War.* New York: Teachers College.

Tyack, D. (1974). *The one best system: The history of American urban education.* Cambridge, MA: Harvard University Press.

Urban, W., & Wagoner, J. (2000). *American education: A history.* Boston: McGraw-Hill.

Weber, M. (1930). *The Protestant ethic and the spirit of Capitalism* (T. Parsons, Trans.). New York: Charles Scribner's Sons.

Weddle, M. B. (2001). *Walking in the way of peace: Quaker pacifism in the seventeenth century.* Oxford, UK: Oxford University Press.

Welling, G. (2005). *From revolution to reconstruction.* Groningen, Netherlands: University of Groningen.

Willison, G. F. (1945). *Saints and strangers.* New York: Reynal & Hitchcock.

Willison, G. F. (1966). *Saints and strangers.* London: Longmans.

Wilson, R. (2004, April 13). 350th anniversary of Indian College commemorated. *Harvard University Gazette,* p. 3. Retrieved on May 15, 2005, from httpwww.news.harvard.edu/gazette/2005/04.14/03-indian.html.

Wright, L. B. (1957). *The cultural life of the American colonies, 1607–1763.* New York: Harper.

Young, A. (1974). *Chronicles of the Pilgrim fathers.* Baltimore: Genealogical Publishing.

Zavala, S. (1968). New viewpoints on the Spanish colonization of America. New York: Russell & Russell.

The Effects of the Revolutionary War Era on American Education

The Revolutionary War was one of the major historical events that had a profound impact on the American system of education. Before 1776, the United States had developed a system of education fashioned after the European, and particularly the English, system of education. Although Harvard, Yale, and Princeton were flourishing by 1776, many of America's elite still chose to study in Europe. In 1776, however, the United States severed its relationship with England as a colony. Oxford and Cambridge were certainly not the desirable places to study that they had been before the Revolutionary War (Tewksbury, 1932). Surely, if one attended there, one would receive the English, and not the American perspective, on history and life. Before the Revolutionary War, an American elementary and secondary school system was inveterately established in the English model and often operated by those loyal to the crown (Cremin, 1970). The new American nation recognized the need to develop its leaders with an American perspective (Brown, 1890; Tewksbury, 1932; Spring, 1990).

The post–Revolutionary War period distinguished the American from the European education system and enabled the fledgling nation to develop its own national educational identity. This transformation occurred both at the curricular and school levels. In addition, the charity school initiative, initially founded by the Puritans, matured into the defining school movement of the post–Revolutionary War era. As the American nation changed, so did the sophistication and broad appeal of the charity school movement. Post–Revolutionary War educational realities also catapulted the nation into an awareness that it was imperative that it develop a strong system of higher education. To be sure, the Revolutionary War created one of the most rapid and impressive educational transformations that the world has ever known.

DISTINGUISHING A TRULY AMERICAN SYSTEM OF EDUCATION

Key American leaders such as George Washington, Benjamin Rush (the country's most prominent physician), Thomas Jefferson, and Noah Webster argued that it was important

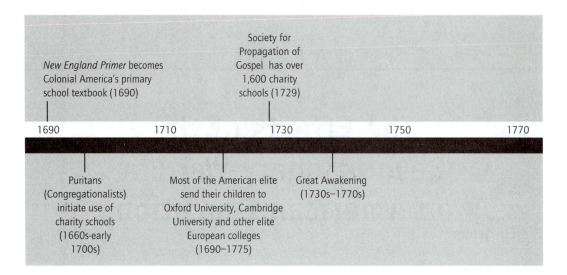

New England Primer becomes Colonial America's primary school textbook (1690)

Society for Propagation of Gospel has over 1,600 charity schools (1729)

1690   1710   1730   1750   1770

Puritans (Congregationalists) initiate use of charity schools (1660s-early 1700s)

Most of the American elite send their children to Oxford University, Cambridge University and other elite European colleges (1690–1775)

Great Awakening (1730s–1770s)

to build a puissant domestic system of education so that Americans could receive the highest-quality education at home rather than going overseas (Johnson, 1997; Tewksbury, 1932; Urban & Wagoner, 2000). Rush (1786/1951) asserted that the base of patriotism was formed in the first 20 years of one's life. He also believed that religious moral training was necessary in the schools in order for people to learn a self-disciplined and self-restrained lifestyle (Lewy, 1996; Urban & Wagoner, 2000). Rush claimed that this self-disciplined and self-restrained lifestyle was vital in order for freedom to survive (Urban & Wagoner, 2000). Without this moral restraint, America's freedoms could become abused and hurt people, causing these freedoms to eventually be reduced in response (Brown, 1890; Hunt & Maxson, 1981). Thomas Jefferson also claimed that he was very concerned about the idea of Americans getting their educational training overseas (Tewksbury, 1932; Urban & Wagoner, 2000).

The Revolutionary War influenced American education for other reasons as well. First, Americans and the peoples of various territories, soon to become states, recognized that the nation as a whole and the regions of the United States had distinct needs that could be best satisfied by schools and colleges that were in that area and could be sensitive to those needs (Tewksbury, 1932). Second, Americans realized that the United States as a fledgling nation had to develop its own resources (Tewksbury, 1932). The manpower and the brainpower of the British Empire could no longer be looked to as a protector. In other words, with America's new independence also came new responsibilities. Now, the United States had to develop its own brainpower and manpower. As a result, the number of colleges being founded increased dramatically during the post–Revolutionary War period. In fact, the founding of these early schools went a long way toward establishing an American perspective among its leadership and people that was quite distinct from the English or European perspective (Tewksbury, 1932; Urban & Wagoner, 2000).

Before the American Revolution, the vast majority of those concerned about education, especially higher education, were religious people. As a result of the Revolutionary War, a growing number of Americans realized the importance of education, and American schooling was influenced at three levels: the curricular level, the elementary/secondary level, and the college level. Although the leaders of this new emphasis on education were usually religious, they were happy to see that a greater number of people, even if they were less religiously inclined, realized the value of schools (Cubberley, 1909, 1920; Gangel & Benson, 1983). George Washington was a passionate advocate for a strong system of education. During his first annual address to Congress, Washington (1790) declared,

> Nor am I less persuaded that you will agree with me in opinion that there is nothing which can better deserve your patronage than the promotion of science and literature. . . . To the security of a free constitution it contributes in various ways.

The Curricular Level

The Revolutionary War had a tremendous impact on the U.S. education system. Before the Revolutionary War, the settlements in America operated largely as separate entities. They were brought together, to some extent, by attempts to organize colonial governments and a collective dislike for British rule. But the Revolutionary War would set into motion the move toward a national consciousness, national goals, and the building of a national consensus on various issues. It started slowly, of course. Some historians believe that a national consciousness in the fullest sense of the term really did not begin until after the Civil War.

Of course, this consensus following the American Revolution occurred first at the local level and then at the state level, developing gradually. The growing consensus among distinct American communities enabled different communities, in a unified fashion, to address their distinct educational challenges. Various books were written to help meet some of these educational needs. Noah Webster contributed to this "unification through books" more than any other individual. Webster fought in the American Revolution; was a lexicographer, lawyer, journalist, and teacher; and cofounded Amherst University, in Massachusetts, in 1821 (Moss, 1984; Rollins, 1980; Unger, 1998). Although today, he is best known for developing *Webster's Dictionary,* in the early decades of the American republic, he was best known for helping to shape the nation's school curriculum (Moss, 1984; Rollins, 1980; Unger, 1998).

In 1783, Webster completed the first of three books that together were entitled *A Grammatical Institute of the English Language.* By 1801, the speller had sold 1.5 million copies. By 1829, the number sold totaled 20 million, and by 1875, it stood at 75 million (Spring, 1990). Webster's writings were geared to moral education, which most educators of the day believed formed the basis of all constructive education (Hunt & Maxson, 1981; Yulish, 1980). To most early Americans, it was more important that one be a kind, loving, and holy individual than whether one had a high degree of intellectual sophistication. In other words, early Americans esteemed not only the development of knowledge but also the development of wisdom. It was their belief that knowledge could be used in the most constructive way when it was based on wisdom (Gangel & Benson, 1983; Hiner, 1988). Early Americans frequently quoted Proverbs 1:7, which states, "The fear of the Lord is the beginning of knowledge; fools despise wisdom and instruction" (*Holy Bible,* 1973).

The New England Primer (1690) was the primary textbook used to reach the goal of basic literacy for New England children. It was often referred to as "New England's Bible" (Spring, 1990). Webster wrote an updated version of this book that was suitable for the post–Revolutionary War period (Webster, 1789). In this book, children were guided through the memorization of the alphabet by referring to a biblical event or individual with each letter of the alphabet. For example, for letters A through C, Webster's *New England Primer* (1789) read as follows:

> In ADAM'S fall, we sinned all.
>
> Heaven to find, the BIBLE mind.
>
> CHRIST crucify'd, for Sinners dy'd. (Ford, 1962, p. 23)

Added Insight: Noah Webster, America's Schoolmaster

Noah Webster (1758–1843) was one of the most prominent and visionary educators of his era. He wrote scores of educational books and was nicknamed "America's schoolmaster." Born in West Hartford, Connecticut, Webster served in the Revolutionary War and then taught in a number of capacities and dramatically impacted America's early intellectual and educational development. He studied law at Yale University, founded a newspaper, and wrote religious, political, economics, and scientific works.

An ardent Federalist, Webster affirmed that Americans needed to unite and that in terms of strength, they were going to develop into a new Europe. However, Webster averred that in order for this to take place, the United States also needed to realize a distinctly American identity (Webster, 1807). For the nation to reach these goals, Webster insisted that the United States needed to establish a uniquely American, high-quality education system (Webster, 1834, 1965).

Noah Webster propounded a concept of a school system that was broad and practical. He believed that schools and colleges should encourage their students to travel throughout the United States, as part of their academic training (Webster, 1965). He contended that the school curriculum should be practical and train students in ethics, citizenship, law, and budgeting money (Webster, 1793, 1834, 1965). He thought it was equally important for both boys and girls to experience a teacher's tutelage in these disciplines (Webster, 1965). Noah Webster claimed that in the long run, such emphases would yield more benefits than studying "dead languages," such as Latin, Hebrew, and Classical Greek (Webster, 1965). He also believed that it was far more practical to determine the initiating point of a child's education based on his or her maturity rather than on age (Webster, 1965). Webster (1783) was very sensitive to children in the writing of his books. For example, he said, "Some of our hardest words to pronounce are monosyllables" (p. 6).

Webster contributed a great deal to the United States establishing its own academic and national identity. He wrote some of the nation's most popular first schoolbooks and gave the nation its first dictionary and Bible written in American English. He helped establish a foundation from which many generations of Americans would benefit.

On a broader scale, the curriculum of the colonial era included reading the classics in English literature and studying mathematics and foreign languages, such as French (Beard &

Beard, 1944). The mid-Atlantic colonies made a special attempt to consider the specific needs that the children would have as adults, in order to function well in society. Charles and Mary Beard (1944) state,

> At all events secondary schools gave thousands of Americans a more than elementary training for reading newspapers, pamphlets, and books; for taking part in the discussion of public affairs; and for sharing in the growth of social and intellectual autonomy. (p. 65)

The founders of America's post–Revolutionary War education system were extremely well educated and consequently established rigorous standards in the nation's schools and colleges (Barton, 1992; Holmes, 2001; Howard, 1943; Robson, 1985; Waller, 1950). American adolescents who continued in their education were expected to become fluent in two or three languages and have well-developed interdisciplinary expertise in government, economics, the classics, mathematics, and science (Moss, 1984; Rollins, 1980; Unger, 1998). Children frequently learned to read by the age of 4.

Although post–Revolutionary War expectations for those who pursued education were rigorous by contemporary standards, there are a number of reasons that will facilitate an understanding as to why this was so. First, people's life spans were shorter than they are today. In the 1700s and early 1800s, some people, like John Adams, lived into their 90s, but diseases frequently consumed people's lives, so that many died in their 40s, 50s, and early 60s (Fogel, 2004; Riley, 2001). This fact necessitated that schooling become more concentrated in time (Holmes, 2001; Howard, 1943; Robson, 1985; Waller, 1950). Second, boys and girls often helped their parents with harvesting the crops and domestic responsibilities, especially beginning in their adolescent and preadolescent years (Fogel, 2004; Riley, 2001). In other words, adolescents were expected to assume adult responsibilities at a younger age than is currently in vogue. To whatever extent that this trend translated into less years of adolescent schooling, it meant that teachers needed to teach more information in a shorter period of time than is the case today (Holmes, 2001; Howard, 1943; Robson, 1985; Waller, 1950). This trend intensified over time, so that by the 1840s, many schools required algebra in the fourth grade (Somerville, 2002). Third, because the United States was a fledgling nation, the nation's educational founders believed that it was imperative for the United States to produce a strong education system as a means of survival. In the post–Revolutionary War era, the United States was surrounded by a host of great powers, which could pose a threat to national security (Johnson, 1997; Kamen, 2003; McKay & Scott, 1983). Principally, Britain remained an adversary, and historians often refer to the War of 1812 as the "second war of independence" (Gerson, 1966; McKay & Scott, 1983). Spain was an expansionist power that longed to dominate North America (Kamen, 2003; McKay & Scott, 1983). Numerous Native American tribes were hostile to the new country; and the French, although they were allies during the Revolutionary War, soon had their own revolution and were eventually led by Napoleon, who had high aspirations consistent with his autocratic rule (McKay & Scott, 1983). The perilous nature of the times convinced school leaders that the United States needed to insist on high academic standards.

Moral education was an important component of the elementary and secondary school education of the post–Revolutionary War era (Hunt & Maxson, 1981). This fact is evident in the Northwest Ordinance, written in 1787. This government document asserted that "religion, morality, and knowledge, being necessary to good government and the happiness of mankind, schools and the means of education shall forever be encouraged" (Beard & Beard, 1944). In this sense, the post–Revolutionary War approach to moral education agrees with Elliot Eisner's (1994) assertion that "curriculum is a device not only for conveying the past but also for shaping consciousness" (p. 44). However, Eisner also valued "ambiguity" in cognitive and moral training (p. 71). In contrast, post–Revolutionary War educators valued a quest for truth, in reference to both academic subjects, such as math as science, and moral issues (Beard & Beard, 1944; Hunt & Maxson, 1981). James Sullivan, who was a Massachusetts Supreme Court justice, argued that a national system of education was needed to help shape the morals of American society (Beard & Beard, 1944; Hunt & Maxson, 1981). Although many American leaders agreed with Sullivan, Democratic-Republicans, who were strong in the South, valued states' rights, and many of the party's leaders in the South were afraid that this "moral teaching" could involve teaching against slavery. Horace Mann initially faced some of the same kind of resistance when he first introduced the idea of "common schools" (Spring, 1997).

The Elementary/Secondary School Level

The Revolutionary War set in motion a truly American system of education. This happened not only in higher education, but in preparing children as well. The sudden freedom that accompanied the end of the Revolutionary War opened the eyes of Americans regarding the need for educating America's future leadership and citizenry. In particular, many Americans did not care much whether the education of young children was done by private elementary schools or public elementary schools. Americans simply wanted their children properly educated, and this allowed both private and public schools to flourish at the same time.

Americans, on the whole, were very idealistic about the potential for schools creating better people and therefore a better society. Americans believed strongly that schools could make an impact on a child not only intellectually, but morally as well (Hunt & Maxson, 1981; Kliebard, 1969; Lewy, 1996; Spring, 1997). A lot of this optimism stemmed from the fruits of the Revolutionary War. Americans realized that their newly achieved freedom meant that they were free to engage in the grand experiment called "democracy." George Washington had often warned of the consequences of "unbridled democracy" without a commitment to morality (Barton, 1990, 1995; Hunt & Maxson, 1981). Most Americans believed, however, that if their children were properly trained in religion and morality, they could avoid this pitfall.

The Revolutionary War set in motion the vast expansion of private schools of a wider scope than ever would have been possible during the colonial period. The war also had a tremendous impact on the development of elementary and secondary schools. In 1789, the same year Washington became president, the Massachusetts Education Act was passed. Under this law, boys and girls would go to school at public expense in all communities with at least 200 people. A given community was required to supply children with an education through elementary school. Boys and girls were required to study the same

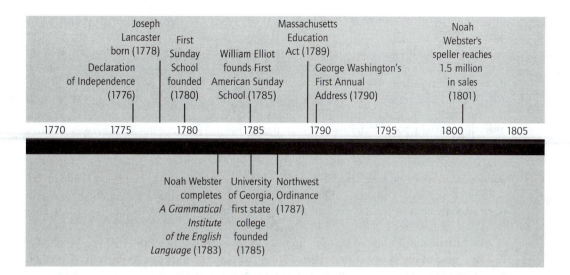

subjects. Previous to this time, boys were sent to school more frequently than girls. In addition, boys and girls often studied different subjects to prepare them for their distinct roles in society.

Even though there were advances in elementary and secondary schooling in the years immediately following the Revolutionary War, the United States was still a very poor country. The United States had incurred $75 million in debt from the war, and American people had other priorities, including gaining political and economic footing (Johnson, 1997; Kaestle, 1983). It really was not until after the War of 1812 that the nation became more secure politically and economically. As a result, the United States had more money to dedicate to building its elementary and secondary education system (Kaestle, 1983).

One of the great educational events following the Revolutionary War was Americans' alacrity to embrace the charity school concept on a broader scale. Although charity schools had been around since the days of the Puritans, these schools enjoyed unprecedented support after the Revolutionary War. At this juncture, it is wise to trace the history of the charity school movement.

THE RISE OF CHARITY SCHOOLS

The optimism that most Americans possessed led to the development of a vast network of private schools called "charity schools." One of the primary goals of the charity school was to reduce poverty and crime. Juvenile reformatories were also started with this goal in mind (*Report of the Prison Discipline Society,* 1855). These educational institutions were initiated with the idea of developing stronger character among America's young. The schools operated with the assumption that a weak family structure contributed significantly to potential problems and criminal tendencies among America's youth. If these schools could help develop strong moral character and enable children to stay away from a criminal element, they could perform an indispensable service for the community (Hunt & Maxson, 1981; Spring, 1997).

The idea for charity schools has deep roots, dating back to the early 1600s in Europe (Cremin, 1980; Jones, 1964). The Puritans in Europe believed it was absolutely essential to make schooling accessible to all, decoupled from one's ability to pay (Eavey, 1964; Jones, 1964). The Puritans were not the first to advocate this position. Many European church leaders, including Martin Luther, had propounded this perspective for centuries (Eavey, 1964; Jones, 1964; Raitt & McGinn, 1987; Randell, 1988). However, the Puritans were clearly the first group to successfully inaugurate a system that would make charity or free schools a widespread practice (Eavey, 1964; Jones, 1964). The movement was specifically a church-sponsored movement, with several goals in mind: (a) to reduce some of the social and moral ills often associated with those of lower socioeconomic status, (b) to spread the gospel, and (c) to educate children in the reading, writing, and mathematical skills they needed to succeed in society (Hunt & Maxson, 1981; Jones, 1964).

The British charity school system did not educate every single British child, which was the ideal goal of the system (Jones, 1964). Nevertheless, the charity school system reached hundreds of thousands of students, a number that was unfathomable even decades earlier (Jones, 1964). The British charity school movement was so successful that literacy among poor youth soared during the 1700s. The movement was a stunning success not only along educational fronts, but religiously as well (Eavey, 1964; Jones, 1964). In fact, Jones (1964) notes, "The schools were of greater consequence to religion than any other design which had been on foot since the Reformation" (p. 59).

Generally speaking, the populace was more enthusiastic about charity schools in the city than they were in the country (Jones, 1964). There were two primary reasons for this. First, in rural areas, students needed to travel long distances to school, which, given the transportation limitations of the day, was a major obstacle. Second, and partially related to the first point, families in rural areas favored home-based schooling (Jones, 1964). Nevertheless, over time, due to the dedication of itinerant educators and generous philanthropists, charity schools spread widely through the countryside. The expansion was so substantial that although the movement grew the most in London, over time, some of its greatest triumphs came in the Welsh countryside (Jones, 1964). The charity school movement help transform Wales from a simple, nonreligious, and ignorant society into a literate and religious one.

Given that the immigrants who came to America at the time were largely from England, it is no surprise that they brought the charity school with them to the New World. America's first charity schools were actually founded early in America's colonial history. Probably the largest organization sponsoring charity schools was the Society for the Propagation of the Gospel (Bailyn, 1960; Cubberley, 1920), which originated in England and soon expanded to the United States. By 1729, in England and the United States combined, the society had 1,658 schools, with a total of about 34,000 pupils (Cubberley, 1920).

Soon after the establishment of Harvard University and Boston Latin School, New England educators made it a priority to establish charity schools (Carter, 1824). The Puritans in England were the people most dedicated to the free-school concept (Eavey, 1964; Jones, 1964). It is therefore only logical that the Puritans were the most committed to the free school concept in the United States (Carter, 1824; Cremin, 1970; Cubberley, 1909, 1934; Fraser, 2001; Jones, 1964). The Puritans developed charity schools in the mid-1600s because they believed in the Christian-originated concept that all people were equal and therefore all people should be educated (Dupuis, 1966; Jones, 1964; Marrou, 1956; Rothstein, 1994). This principle was based on various Bible verses, including, "For there is neither Jew nor Greek, there is neither slave nor free, there is neither male nor female" (Galatians 3:23, *Holy Bible,* 1973). The Puritans realized that this could be achieved only by offering schooling on a sliding scale. For most people, this meant they paid no tuition (Rothstein, 1994). Within early American society, it was understood that the small number of wealthy people had a responsibility to support other members of society. Therefore, wealthy settlers would pay for 20, 50, or 100 students (Jones, 1964; Rothstein, 1994).

The Puritans passed laws in 1642 and 1647 to ensure that all the area's children would be educated (Cremin, 1970; Cubberley, 1934; Fraser, 2001; Gutek, 1997; Spring, 1997). George Martin (1894), in his book, *The Evolution of the Public School System,* stated that one of the key assertions of this legislation declared that the "universal education" of youth is essential to the well-being "of the commonwealth" (p. 9). In many towns and municipalities, public support helped ensure the survival of the schools (Carter, 1824; Cremin, 1976; Gutek, 1997). However, whatever the means of educational support, some families could not afford to send their children to school, nor could they educate them at home. The dedication of the early settlers, and especially the Puritans, to universal education dictated that free education be made available to all American children no matter what their financial conditions or the color of their skin (Carter, 1824; Cremin, 1976).

The Puritans strongly believed in a solid education system at every level and dimension and that training leaders was essential to a civilized society (Cremin, 1976). Therefore, shortly after their arrival in 1630, the Puritans founded Harvard University. At Harvard, ministers and, later on, lawyers, government leaders, and doctors, could be trained. The Puritans saw Harvard as serving another function as well, that is, as a source of spiritual training for those preparing to be leaders. Consistent with this emphasis, for many years Harvard's nickname was "the school of the prophets" (Carter 1969, p. 6).

Although the Puritans certainly advocated education at the university level, they also promoted the growth of elementary and secondary schools (Cremin, 1976). The problem was that many people could not afford to send their children to school and the settlers were generally much poorer economically than when they lived more established lives in Europe. The charity schools that the Puritans founded in Europe were made possible because of church philanthropists. These individuals believed that it was their Christian responsibility to support children who otherwise would not be able to go to school (Jones, 1964). However, in the New World, these generous philanthropists were usually less wealthy than those in Europe. This made supporting poor school children more difficult (Cubberley, 1920, 1934; Jones, 1964).

Despite the monetary obstacles to operating charity schools, many in the Puritan community donated to them so that free education could be made available to as many children as possible (Cubberley, 1920, 1934; Jones, 1964). Given that the financial resources of the wealthy were not as copious as their counterparts in Europe, it was crucial that the middle class also contribute to enable poor children to go to school. Fortunately, because providing universal education was such a deeply held conviction among the Puritans, many middle-class people responded to the need (Jones, 1964). The New England community was willing to support charity schools because the Puritans maintained deeply held convictions about the importance of citizens doing what they could to relieve social ills, eliminate slavery, spread the gospel, and promote the work ethic (Carter, 1824; Jones, 1964; Stewart, 1969).

The charity school movement started as a church-sponsored practice (Carter, 1824; Jones, 1964), which had certain advantages and disadvantages. Among these is that, first, it produced a passion to support the charity schools that otherwise probably would not have existed (Carter, 1824). Second, school leaders placed considerable emphasis on both spiritual and intellectual development (Carter, 1824; Hunt & Maxson, 1981; Jones, 1964). Among many of the lower-class children, this was particularly salient, because they often lived in a poor moral climate, in which drunkenness and adultery were prevalent, and generally received less parental instruction in right and wrong than in the case of middle-class children (Carter, 1824; Hunt & Maxson, 1981; Jones, 1964). Third, the Puritans were well-known for their work ethic, and they could pass down these values to their children (Hunt & Maxson, 1981; Kliebard, 1969; Stewart, 1969).

Two disadvantages accompanied the religious nature of the charity school movement. First, children who attended church were more likely to receive an education than those that did not attend. Even if many charity schools did not limit attendance to membership of their own church, church adherents were nevertheless much more likely to attend church-sponsored schools. As a consequence of this fact, over time, the church community tended to be considerably more educated than less religious individuals (Stewart, 1969). A second disadvantage is that because the clergy generally earned poverty-level salaries, it was nearly impossible for churches to start charity schools unless the congregation was reasonably wealthy (Jones, 1964). Most pastors were simply too poor to initiate the needed funding on their own. Many ministers averred that charity schools would benefit their communities, but they simply did not have the finances to follow through with their dreams. This limited the number of charity schools that were started.

Unique Aspects of the Charity School

Many facets of the charity school experience were quite unique and would be hard to relate to for most people living today. Other aspects of charity schools formed the foundation of the public school system and other educational developments that were to follow.

One of the most remarkable aspects of the charity school was the extent to which each teacher was "adopted" by the children's families, and vice versa. In today's society, most families know teachers only from a distance. However, in colonial New England, teachers went to church with their students, and they often sat side by side. Educators considered the practice of teachers sitting next to their children in church especially salutary, because it constituted a form of moral example (Hunt & Maxson, 1981; Jones, 1964). To New Englanders of the time, as crucial as intellectual education was to the proper development of youth, moral education was even more important (Hiner, 1988; Hunt & Maxson, 1981; Jeynes, 2003; Kliebard, 1969). In the minds of the educators of the day, church attendance was an integral part of education (Jones, 1964).

A second unique component of the charity school was that the pastors and teachers who ran the schools often provided after-school jobs for older children (Hiner, 1988; Jones, 1964). Through performing these tasks, the older children developed habits of responsibility, diligence, and community, which contributed to their growth.

Third, educators often went to great lengths at their own inconvenience to establish charity schools in rural and poor communities (Carter, 1824; Jones, 1964). It was difficult to establish charity schools in rural areas because many towns were very isolated and had little or no easy road access. Nevertheless, consistent with the settlers' belief in universal education, ministers and other educators often traveled from one town to another, during the course of a week, to establish and maintain these free schools (Carter, 1824; Jones, 1964).

One should not imagine that founding and continuing to support these schools was easy for the ministers and other educators who attended to them (Carter, 1824). Moreover, those who were willing to brave the elements to establish these schools were not always the most qualified teachers (Carter, 1824; Jones, 1964). Nevertheless, most parents who sent their children to charity schools had high expectations of the teachers. As a consequence, even rural schools had to ultimately prove that they were quality institutions, in order to avoid failure (Jones, 1964). This was especially true because in this day, many people opined that parents could do a better job of educating than teachers.

It is difficult to estimate just how many rural charity schools there were. Compared with most city charity schools, which regularly filed reports to their denominations, the rural free schools were not as well organized (Jones, 1964). Nevertheless, we do know that there were many hundreds, and perhaps thousands, of them (Cubberley, 1920). As a result, the unique contribution of these schools was considerable and encompassed a vast geographical area.

Forming the Foundation of Future Education

Charity schools helped form the foundation on which many future educational advances developed. First, charity schools introduced a higher level of organization and professionalism to the teaching profession than had ever been witnessed before. Contrary to the stereotypes people often have of early education, charity school teachers were often innovative and pioneered new methods of instruction in the schools. Some of these innovations included increasing the use of teacher aides to maximize the amount of one-on-one instruction, the integration of more memory games, and the use of students to help others understand the material (Carter, 1824; Jones, 1964).

The instructional and organizational sophistication of charity schools helped raise the stature of teachers of the poor to a new level of professionalism (Jones, 1964). Before the expansion of the charity school movement, teachers of the ruling elite enjoyed a high degree of respect not so much accorded to those who instructed those of low socio-economic status. However, an increasing percentage of the general populace soon came to acknowledge the fact that the charity school movement was the most successful effort of the 18th century to educate the poor (Jones, 1964). Americans in the 18th century generally held those who labored in humanitarian service to the poor in high esteem. As Americans acknowledged that the charity school movement was immensely effective, widespread, and well organized, charity school teachers became heralded as humanitarians (Carter, 1824; Jones, 1964).

Second, charity schools helped establish the way in which education would take place in the public schools that would develop many years later. The charity school, though private, was the forerunner of the public school. Both arose out of the quest for universal education. Charity schools were gradually converted into public schools in the mid-19th century; people realized that because of the considerable increase in the number of immigrant poor, taxation was necessary in order to make universal education a reality.

Given that public schools were essentially converted charity schools, it comes as no surprise, then, that public schools adopted charity school practices, including use of the same textbooks, teacher aides, recitation and memorization, and use of students to help other students in the learning process. The public schools also adopted the moral education curriculum practiced in the charity schools. This meant that there was little difference between the moral instruction taught in early public schools versus that which had been taught in church-based charity schools (Carter, 1824; Jones, 1964; Hunt & Maxson, 1981). Both were highly religious in nature. The only difference was that moral education in state-sponsored public and charity schools was less sectarian than that found in religious charity schools (Carter, 1824; Jones, 1964; Ulich, 1968; Yulish, 1980).

The religious emphasis of American charity and public schools of the period may seem foreign to people living now. However, to individuals living in the 18th and 19th centuries, education without religion was inconceivable (Jones, 1964). Moreover, most educators of this era viewed moral education as the most important aspect of education (Michaelsen, 1970; Yulish, 1980). To the extent that religion was foundational to morality, this meant that religious instruction was required in the schools.

Third, charity schools also contributed to the general thinking that would prevail in public schools, that the nation should practice a decentralized approach to education (Jones, 1964). Charity school leaders adhered to a fundamental belief that bureaucracy and "red tape" had negative effects on education and were therefore to be avoided. Charity school leaders believed that the best way to avoid these pitfalls was to hire wise teachers (Jones, 1964; Michaelsen, 1970). In other words, these leaders believed that great teachers were the best defense against potential effects of bureaucracy (Jones, 1964).

The Spread of the Massachusetts Charity School Model

The free-school model practiced by the Puritans in Massachusetts soon spread through the remainder of New England and the Northeast, became the model for pre–Revolutionary War America, and was also emulated during the years following the war (Stewart, 1969).

One facilitating factor that enabled the Massachusetts free-school model to proliferate was that many Puritans migrated and settled in Connecticut and, to a lesser extent, in other areas of New England (Stewart, 1969). Massachusetts had passed two laws requiring the support of schools (Spring, 2001). Since Connecticut people had come mostly from Massachusetts, they were accustomed to following the same kinds of laws as those in Massachusetts and therefore imitated the free-school model as early as the 1600s (Carter, 1824; Stewart, 1969). Connecticut followed the Massachusetts model for another reason as well. That is, leadership tried to develop a school system that would prepare students to go to Harvard, because until 1701, Connecticut could not afford to build a college (Carter, 1824; Stewart, 1969). The state's dependence on Massachusetts is documented by references made by Connecticut educational and government leaders to documents from Massachusetts (Carter, 1824; *Connecticut Record,* 1736, Stewart, 1969).

Like Massachusetts citizens, the residents of Connecticut maintained an educational emphasis (Stewart, 1969). Therefore, as time passed, they became determined that

Connecticut needed to establish its own university and upgrade its education system. However, leaders soon realized that certain circumstances needed to change in order to make this a reality. The colonies of New Haven and Connecticut were individually lacking sufficient resources to build an elaborate school system and college. Partially in order to make a vibrant school system a reality, the colonies of New Haven and Connecticut decided to combine (Carter, 1824). Furthermore, these combined colonies, together called "Connecticut," sold some land to Ohio in order to raise money for schools. With a more solvent state intact, Connecticut clergy acted collectively to establish Yale College (Carter, 1824).

Once the Massachusetts model had spread to other parts of New England, it spread to the mid-Atlantic states, including New York and Pennsylvania (Curran, 1954), and then to other eastern states as well. The Massachusetts model soon became the exemplary charity school model in the country.

SUPPLEMENTS TO CHARITY SCHOOLS

Charity schools were not the only means of educating the masses free of charge. The Sunday school movement also educated tens of thousands of mostly poor children. One should note that charity schools and Sunday schools were often not totally distinct from one another. Thousands of churches supported both a charity school and a Sunday school program. Sunday schools often made education an all-day affair. Naturally, since the instruction took place on the Sabbath, teachers placed special emphasis on religious and moral education (Hunt & Maxson, 1981; Kliebard, 1969). Nevertheless, this was not the only kind of curriculum that was taught. Churches desired to train children to serve as informed and skilled American citizens.

Some children attended both charity schools and Sunday schools. However, each type of school was often designed to reach a particular clientele. Charity schools were established with the purpose of reaching children who did relatively little work at home or in the factory and were therefore free to attend school regularly (Eavey, 1964; Jones, 1964). Sunday schools were designed to appeal to children who did work in the fields and factories during the week and were not at liberty to attend school every day. The nation needed both kinds of schools, and they each played a role in raising the literacy rate of the general population.

The curriculum that most American children were exposed to was also affected by the Sunday school movement, which started in England under the direction of Robert Raikes (1735–1811). Raikes founded the first Sunday school in Gloucester, England, in 1780 (Eavey, 1964). He had a real desire to help poor children, who otherwise had little or no opportunity to go to school, and encouraged all children in the area to attend Sunday school. Children attended school from 10:00 to 12:00 in the morning each Sunday. Then, they ate lunch, returned to school at 1:00, and went to church. After church, they received religious training and then returned home around 5:00 (Eavey, 1964). Raikes enjoyed the support and the friendship of many of the great English ministers of the day, both in general and for his specific Sunday school plan. Ministers like John and Charles Wesley, George Whitefield, and William Wilberforce were very supportive of his educational efforts. By 1811, over 400,000 students attended Sunday school in England (Eavey, 1964).

The Sunday school movement quickly came to the United States, where it also flourished, reaching its goal of drawing in thousands of poor children. The first Sunday school in the United States was started by William Elliot, in Virginia, in 1785 (Eavey, 1964). Elliot set aside this time to teach his children, his slaves, and his neighbors. In 1786, the second Sunday school was established in Virginia by Francis Asbury, who desired to teach his slaves (Eavey, 1964). Sunday schools probably developed in Virginia before they emerged in other states largely because there were fewer educational opportunities in Virginia versus other states, especially those in the North. Over the next 5 years, Sunday schools were created in other southern cities, as well as most major cities in the North (Eavey, 1964). For 40 years, the Sunday school movement grew as a way to educate the poor, the neglected, slaves, and immigrants. Many Sunday schools grew so large they could no longer be held in churches, and rented facilities were required. The Sunday school movement continued to be a major force in educating the poor throughout the 19th century and into World War I (Eavey, 1964). After World War I, as the common school grew, more and more poor people were able to procure an education by attending common schools.

FREE SCHOOLS AND AFRICAN AMERICANS

African Americans in the North quickly emerged as one of the primary beneficiaries of free schools (Andrews, 1969; Woodson & Wesley, 1962). Most African Americans in the North were freed slaves and did not have much money to pay for education (Klinker & Smith, 1999; Wilson, 1977; Woodson & Wesley, 1962). Consequently, free schools emerged as the ideal means through which many African Americans could capitalize on their first taste of freedom (Wilson, 1977; Woodson & Wesley, 1962).

In some cases, educators founded free schools that specifically focused on educating African Americans. In other cases, African Americans attended the same schools as Whites (Andrews, 1969; Spring, 1997). The question arises as to whether the African-American-only schools were founded at least in part in the spirit of racism. Carter Woodson, the foremost African American historian, believes that these schools were not founded with negative racial motives and that educators established Black-only free schools with the motive of sensitivity to the unique experiences that freed slaves had experienced (Woodson & Wesley, 1962). There is also evidence to suggest that African Americans often preferred going to these schools rather than the integrated ones (Andrews, 1969; Spring, 1997). Nevertheless, it would be hard to imagine a situation in which racism did not at least at times enter in to the desire to build African-American-only schools.

Educating African American children, whether in integrated schools or not, involved certain unique challenges. First, African Americans occupied a wide range of educational levels. Contrary to what some commonly think, the knowledge levels of some slaves were quite vast (Woodson & Wesley, 1962). Although the overall African American literacy rate was lower for African Americans than for Whites, especially in the South, it is also true that many African Americans were well versed in some of the most valued kinds of knowledge (Ashmore, 1994; Wilson, 1977; Woodson & Wesley, 1962). For example, many African Americans, both free and slaves, spoke a foreign language. Woodson and Wesley (1962) point out that many slaves lived among the same conditions as the wealthy and therefore were often exposed to a level of culture that most White people were not. Although some freed slaves came from this kind of background, the vast majority of slaves were not literate (Woodson & Wesley, 1962). Many freed slaves, therefore, came from a background of little educational opportunity (Hill & Jones, 1993; Klinker & Smith, 1999; Wilson, 1977; Woodson & Wesley, 1962). Teachers in charity schools faced the challenge of collectively teaching African Americans who were pretty sophisticated in their levels of knowledge and those who were not. It was not an easy task to concurrently teach children that were at such different levels.

A second challenge that educators of African Americans faced is that African American children often attended schools inconsistently (Andrews, 1969). There are probably a number of reasons for this fact. Most notably, given that many African Americans were from poor families, they were probably more likely to be called on to periodically help financially support the family than were White children (Ashmore, 1994). It may also be that after years of suffering under slavery, African Americans were less inclined to believe that schools could really ameliorate their way of life (Ashmore, 1994). They may have also had less access to transportation.

Despite certain challenges in educating African Americans, there were also certain dynamics working in favor of charity schools that helped the lives of many African American children. The most patent factor favoring African American education was the determination by many northern states to make the education of African Americans a reality. In addition to integrated charity schools that were available to African Americans in the mid- to late 1700s, most major cities and states opened up charity schools specifically geared toward the needs of freed slaves. Some religious groups, like the Quakers, were especially diligent in their efforts to open up schools for freed slaves. In just 1 year, 1797, the Quakers opened up seven schools for African Americans (Woodson & Wesley, 1962). The efforts of the Quakers resulted in Pennsylvania becoming the state with the most schools for African Americans (Curran, 1954; McClellan & Reese, 1988). Rhode Island started a school specifically for freed slaves. Other schools were started in Baltimore and what is now known as Washington, D.C. (Woodson & Wesley, 1962). In 1788, New Jersey passed a law making it mandatory to teach African Americans, or one would face a substantial fine (Woodson & Wesley, 1962).

Naturally, the alacrity of some in establishing African American schools was much more common in the North than it was in the South (Jeynes, 2003; Spring, 1997). There were some charity schools founded by southerners in the South, but northerners founded the vast majority of them (Woodson & Wesley, 1962).

Not only were educators willing to build charity schools for African Americans, but they were also desirous of reaching African Americans that could have easily been overlooked. For example, Andrews (1969) notes that educators made a special effort to target children who came from troubled backgrounds, particularly those who had committed crimes. School leaders also made certain that both African American girls and boys had an opportunity to go to charity schools.

A second strength that helped ensure the growth of charity school education for African Americans was the willingness of people to donate money to this cause. In fact, a number of the founding fathers gave generously to ensure that African Americans could go to charity schools for free. Alexander Hamilton, John Jay, and Benjamin Franklin donated particularly large amounts of money to further this cause (Andrews, 1969). Other famous philanthropists, including Abiel Smith and Anthony Benezet, also dedicated nearly all of their money to building schools for African Americans and other minorities (Spring, 1997; Woodson, 1968). Although clearly the education system tended to spend more money on White children than on Black children, the generosity of many people who put great value on African American education considerably reduced the extent of that expenditure gap (Woodson, 1968).

Where African Americans Attended Charity Schools

Where African Americans chose to attend school is an interesting area of study. Many different kinds of churches and state governments welcomed African American students. However, African Americans clearly felt more comfortable with some groups than with others (Woodson & Wesley, 1962). Two factors were especially important in determining where African Americans chose to send their children to school: first, the extent to which a school desired African Americans to reach a high status in life. Second, the style of worship of the church sponsoring the school (if indeed it was church sponsored) also played a factor.

Regarding the first factor, African Americans realized that for their children to have a better chance of living a fulfilled life, the school needed to guide the children in the direction of high-status jobs. African Americans considered this especially vital, because many prejudiced people lived in the nation who often believed that African Americans were incapable of holding such jobs (Hill & Jones, 1993). African Americans discovered that Baptist and Methodist schools were especially open to Blacks and, to some degree, their desire to obtain high-status positions (Woodson & Wesley, 1962). Both denominations were even open to African Americans becoming ministers, which, in the 18th and 19th century was regarded as the highest-status position of all. Some African American ministers, like Richard Allen, gained considerable respect, and White ministers traveled with them (Woodson & Wesley, 1962). Other denominations, like the Episcopals, also desired African Americans to advance in life. However, a second factor caused African Americans to favor the schools of other groups.

The style of worship of the denomination sponsoring the school was a second factor that determined where African American children attended charity schools. To comprehend why worship style was important, one must understand that most charity schools were closely connected with churches. Consequently, where people sent their children to school tended to be the same places where their families worshipped. Hence, the two were usually inextricably connected. Ironically, the religious groups that were the first to offer charity schools to African Americans in the North were not the ones that ultimately experienced the highest levels of African American participation in these schools. The Puritans were the first of the settlers to educate African Americans (Urban & Wagoner, 2000). The Quakers, Episcopals, and Presbyterians also welcomed Blacks and were among the earliest groups to offer charity school instruction. However, African Americans preferred the more demonstrative Baptist and Methodist worship styles (Woodson & Wesley, 1962). Therefore, they tended to enroll their children in Baptist and Methodist charity schools.

As one would expect, the educational opportunities for African Americans were much greater in the North than they were in the South. In Chapter 4, we will examine this issue more thoroughly. The states in the Deep South were the most restrictive, whereas states like North Carolina were somewhat more tolerant (Woodson, 1968). Although a number of northern groups established schools for African Americans in the South in the late 1700s and early 1800s, these groups also encouraged freedom for the slaves. Once plantation owners discovered this, they lobbied hard to shut these schools down (Wilson, 1977). As a result, by the 1830s, African Americans in the South found it difficult to obtain any kind of schooling (Wilson, 1977; Woodson, 1968). This situation persisted in the South until the end of the Civil War.

THE CHARITY SCHOOL MOVEMENT NATIONWIDE

The Massachusetts model for charity schools was highly regarded and emulated in many areas across the land. However, the charity schools that the Puritans had developed were intimate in nature and geared toward small communities and areas where there was not a disproportionate number of poor people. The Puritan model was educationally effective in small and moderate-sized communities, but it was not economically efficient. It could not accommodate student bodies in which there were large numbers of poor immigrants and relatively small numbers of wealthy people. By now, the settlements had become a new nation, the United States of America. A new economically efficient system of charity schools was needed.

Joseph Lancaster and the New Charity School Model

In this context, there emerged an innovative Englishman named Joseph Lancaster, who had a considerable impact on American schools. Lancaster was born in England, in 1778. He was an educational systematizer, as opposed to an originator. Lancaster greatly respected the Puritan charity schools as he saw them operate in England. As a Quaker, he had a great deal of appreciation for the dual emphasis that the Puritans placed on moral and academic education. Nevertheless, he believed that if charity schools were to reach the poor masses, they needed to be large and efficient (Kaestle, 1973). Lancaster's model called for one teacher in a room of perhaps 100 school children (Spring, 1997). Monitors, who were usually older students, served as teacher's aides and helped the individual students with their work (Spring, 1997). A typical class of 100 students might have six monitors (Kaestle, 1973; Spring, 1997). The Lancaster model was economically efficient because one teacher taught so many students. However, because of the presence of monitors, Lancaster argued that students would still get the individual attention that they needed (Kaestle, 1973; Spring, 1997).

A key factor in Lancaster's success, from a financial standpoint, was the willingness of many Quaker philanthropists to sustain the establishment and operation of his charity schools. Quakers were enthusiastic about Lancaster's schools because one of his emphases was that children be given a "Scriptural education" (Kaestle, 1973, p. 36). Consistent with this support, Quakers were some of the first to apply the Lancaster model in their charity schools (Kaestle, 1973). Urban churches also found the Lancaster system very practical. Other nonecclesiastical organizations believed that the Lancaster system provided a practical way of educating children who were not currently attending religious charity schools. The Lancaster method gained a new level of notoriety when the New York Free School Society, under the leadership of DeWitt Clinton, adopted the Lancaster system (Cornog, 1998; Spring, 1997).

Joseph Lancaster was probably the most admired educator of his time. Many Americans respected him because he was able to combine educational effectiveness with economic efficiency. Lancaster was revered because of his efforts to help the poor, his emphasis on moral education, his effective means of classroom management, and his effective use of teacher aides. Many educators believed that the use of teacher aides improved the education that children received (Bourne, 1870). Some educators argued that monitors, who could give children more individual attention than they would otherwise receive, would relate to children better than adult teachers and that the individual attention that monitors offered would especially benefit children who were either struggling or surging ahead in their studies. The use of monitors, some educators argued, would ensure that these children received the supplementary work that they needed.

Lancaster schools gained the reputation of being fun for students and yet having a disciplined atmosphere. Part of this resulted from Lancaster's use of merit tickets, which teachers used to reward students for good behavior (Kaestle, 1973).

Although most people perceived many strengths in the Lancaster system, these schools also had their critics (Cubberley, 1920). The primary objection to the Lancaster schools was a by-product of their emphasis on economic efficiency. That is, people sometimes thought his schools were too "mechanical" (Cubberley, 1920; Kaestle, 1973). There is likely some truth to this criticism. However, any time educators attempt to be sensitive to educational efficiency, they run the risk of being called mechanical. Whatever strengths and weaknesses existed in the Lancaster system, the truth remains that it had an undeniable effect on America's education system and set the stage for the development of the common or public school system.

The Place of DeWitt Clinton

As great an influence as Joseph Lancaster was on the American education system, he would not have had such influence had not DeWitt Clinton embraced his methods (Cubberley, 1920). DeWitt Clinton was both mayor of New York and the president of the New York Free School Society (Bobbe, 1933; Cornog, 1998; Cubberley, 1920). His position as head of the privately run New York Free School Society and mayor helped the Free School Society to eventually become the forerunner of publicly funded schools (Cubberley, 1920).

Clinton was one of the foremost political and educational leaders of his time. He was born in a political family as the nephew of George Clinton, who had been the governor of New York. Clinton was a bright individual and greatly valued education. He graduated first in his class from Columbia. In 1803, Clinton became mayor of New York (Bobbe, 1933; Cornog, 1998; Cubberley, 1920; Stephens, 1872). At the time, New York was the second-largest city in the United States. It is symbolic of Clinton's overall contribution to both the city and the state of New York that by the time he left his position as mayor in 1815, New York City had surged ahead of Philadelphia to become the largest city in the United States (Cornog, 1998).

Clinton perhaps contributed more than any New Yorker to laying the foundation for New York's future national and international leadership. He maintained a heartfelt conviction that New York should place great emphasis on the development of education, the military, and building a strong system of transportation. Clinton argued forcefully in Albany for a strong system of charity schools and the building of the Erie Canal (Bobbe, 1933; Cornog, 1998; Cubberley, 1920). Historians generally regard the building of the Erie Canal as the most important public works project in the nineteenth century.

Clinton realized that New York City was growing rapidly. He realized that the surge in New York's population was creating many poor people, who needed to be educated. Clinton was appreciative of the fact that many churches were actively engaged in teaching. He respected the presence of church charity schools and their emphasis on love and compassion (Cubberley, 1920; Fitzpatrick, 1969; McMillan, 1984). He believed, however, that the vast number of immigrants coming to New York made it impossible for church charity schools to teach all of the poor people who needed to be educated. Therefore, he argued that the city should establish charity schools in order to educate the poor who were not attending church charity schools (Bobbe, 1933; Cubberley, 1920; Pulliam & Van Patten, 1991; Spring, 1997).

After the Revolutionary War, many Americans became convinced that the nation needed to be active in educating as many people as possible. People began to realize that to accomplish this, the cities needed to supplement the educational activities of the church (Cremin, 1980; Pulliam & Van Patten, 1991; Spring, 1997; Ulich, 1968; Urban & Wagoner, 2000). In the 1790s, even before the Lancasterian system emerged as a major player in New York City education, private schools did all they could to accommodate those families who normally could not afford to send their children to school. Carl Kaestle (1983), in his book *Pillars of the Republic: Common Schools and American Society, 1780–1860,* notes that private schools often engaged in a practice "of adjusting tuition according to the income of the parents" (p. 15). But the hearts of those who operated the charity schools were larger than their pocketbooks. As school enrollment grew in the early 1800s, the private charity schools could not accommodate all of the new immigrants.

The New York Free School Society was founded in 1805. Clinton was the primary advocate for the growth and support of the society. Nearly all of the support came from private sources, so that these schools were indeed private schools. However, Clinton took the initiative to convince New York government leaders that it was also in the best interests of the city and the state to make sure that these schools prospered. Therefore, he argued successfully, the city and state government should give some support to these schools (Bobbe, 1933; Fitzpatrick; 1969; Urban & Wagoner, 2000). The interconnected nature of the private and public sector might be difficult for contemporary Americans to comprehend. However, in the early 1800s, there was not such a rigid distinction between the two sectors (McMillan, 1984; Ulich, 1968; Urban & Wagoner, 2000). Rather, people thought of the overall good of the country. For example, churches often intervened to support struggling state universities, and state and city funds were frequently used to help private schools. Americans believed that the presence of education was so important that it was imperative that the private and public sectors support one another for the greater good of the country (Blanshard, 1963; Cremin, 1980; Cubberley, 1920; Michaelsen, 1970; Pulliam & Van Patten, 1991; Ulich, 1968).

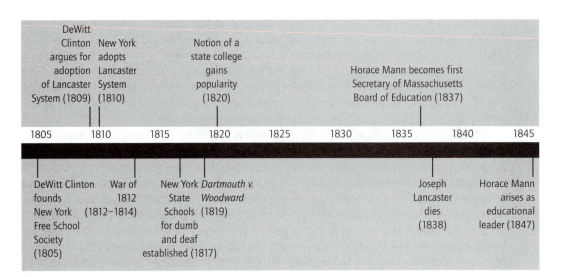

Clinton believed that the New York Free School Society should successfully emulate many of the aspects of church charity schools that made them thrive. He was particularly interested in the success that churches enjoyed in educating African Americans (Fitzpatrick, 1969). Clinton asserted that city charity schools, just like church charity schools, needed to educate children of all races and of both genders. Fitzpatrick notes that "just as Clinton drew no sex line in education, so he drew no color line" (p. 49).

The New York Free School Society was not the only organization of charity schools in New York. Nevertheless, it soon became the most dominant (Spring, 1997). Those who organized the society believed that criminal association was perhaps the greatest challenge facing parents attempting to raise their children in New York City. As a result of this perspective, it was a major aim of these schools to make children more loving, more civil, and more cooperative (Spring, 1997).

Overall, Clinton favored a broad reach for the education system. He believed that instructors should teach many disciplines in school and that the educational program should include a program of moral education, very similar to church schools (Fitzpatrick, 1969). Clinton (1829) called for teaching a wide range of disciplines and stated, "The outlines of geography, algebra, mineralogy, agriculture, chemistry, mechanical philosophy, surveying, geometry, astronomy, political economy, and ethics must be communicated" (p. 116). Clinton also propounded plans for the development of state schools for the deaf and dumb, established in 1817 (Fitzpatrick, 1969).

Given that churches undertook most of the country's education, the New York Free School Society emulated religious schools in many respects (Ulich, 1968; Yulish, 1980). The religious inspiration was especially prominent in the society's moral education program (Fitzpatrick, 1969; Ulich, 1968). Both Clinton and Lancaster believed in the teaching of the Bible in the classroom in a nonsectarian fashion (Fitzpatrick, 1969; Kaestle, 1973; Yulish, 1980). They averred that this teaching should serve as the foundation for a school's moral education program. Over time, Clinton became very proud of the effectiveness of the moral education program. He stated, "Of the many thousands who have been instructed in our free schools in the City of New York, there is not a single instance known of anyone being convicted of a crime" (Fitzpatrick, 1969, p. 54).

It would be hard to imagine a mayor of a major American city making this statement today. Indeed, it was a credit to the effectiveness of moral education that Clinton could make that statement during his era. Instruction in morality and literacy was considered the most important aspect of teaching at the time (Fitzpatrick, 1969; Ulich, 1968; Yulish, 1980).

A Closer Look: DeWitt Clinton, Building the Foundation of a Stronger Nation

DeWitt Clinton (1769–1828) was not only a powerful educator, but one of the most noteworthy American politicians in the early 1800s. Clinton was the nephew of George Clinton, who had been governor of New York (Bobbe, 1933; Cornog, 1998).

Clinton had always wanted to make a difference in society, ever since he was young. When he became a political leader, he earned a reputation for maintaining a presence in myriad spheres of influence. Before becoming head of the New York Free School Society, Clinton served simultaneously as both mayor and lieutenant governor of New York City and State, respectively (Bobbe, 1933). This was during a period of time when Americans did not consider it a conflict of interests to serve in two political posts simultaneously (Bobbe, 1933). The fact that Clinton functioned in two posts simultaneously was indicative of his yearning to act as a catalyst for change in a copious number of disciplines.

Clinton's quest to promote the good in various disciplines was no more evident than in education. Despite his political inclination since young adulthood, he also reveled in the approbation of the scholarly community (Cornog, 1998). Cornog observes, "He craved the approval of the learned for his intellectual efforts as much as, or even more than he desired the electoral approval of his fellow citizens. But he also had a sincere wish to make New York and the nation a better place" (pp. 35–36). In 1805, John Murray and Thomas Eddy approached Clinton regarding starting a free school society in New York, using the Lancaster system. The first school in the society opened in 1806, and the New York Free School Society began to fully use the Lancaster rubric a few years later (Bobbe, 1833).

Consistent with most of Clinton's undertakings, the New York Free School Society was an efficacious triumph and epitomized the potential of the Lancaster approach. Clinton's broad involvement was also ostensible in other undertakings. As Cornog (1998) notes, "The major was the functional as well as the nominal head of the city police. On occasion, Clinton had to lead forces into the streets to suppress riots of one sort or another" (p. 57). As grand as these accomplishments were, Clinton's crowning achievement was initiating the plan for the construction of the Erie Canal (Bobbe, 1933), which facilitated the development of the United States into a world power. Clinton's acumen undoubtedly also helped catapult the United States into being an educational power.

The state of New York realized the utility of charity schools well before the founding of the New York Free School Society. One indication of this is that as early as 1795, the state helped finance church charity schools (Fitzpatrick, 1969). This presaged the founding of the New York Free School Society 10 years later (Fitzpatrick, 1969; Pulliam & Van Patten, 1991). Although the founding of this state charity school system actually trailed the establishment of these schools in other states and cities, the determination of Clinton combined with the size of the city soon catapulted New York City to the forefront of the charity school movement.

In 1809, Clinton launched a major push to apply the Lancaster system in New York City's charity schools. He said, "It comprehends reading, writing, arithmetic, and the knowledge of the Holy Scriptures. It arrives at its object with the least possible trouble and expense" (Fitzpatrick, 1969, p. 150). In 1810, New York City adopted the Lancaster model for its school system. It was designed to be an efficient and inexpensive way of educating the poor and training them in moral character (Hunt & Maxson, 1981). The effective organization of the Lancasterian schools set in motion the future organization of the public schools. In 1818, the New York Free School Society invited Lancaster to New York to see whether the schools were operating according to his standards (Fitzpatrick, 1969). The more the society used the Lancaster method, the more Clinton and other New Yorkers fell in love with the system. Clinton, president of the New York Free School Society, literally adored Lancaster's system: "I consider his system as creating a new era in education, as a blessing sent down from heaven to redeem the poor" (as cited in Bourne, 1870, p. 128).

The Lancaster system was not new. Most of the major church denominations used the model (Fitzpatrick, 1969). However, the fact that the nation's second-largest city was inaugurating the system lifted the approach to a new level of renown and respectability. The New York Free School Society became the most famous state charity school system in the country. This contributed greatly to the expansion of the Lancaster rubric in America. In the early 1800s, New York was already well-known for having the nation's best high schools. The adoption of the Lancaster system to the high school level only added to this perception (Fitzpatrick, 1969).

The New York Free School Society experienced considerable growth. By 1830, over 7,000 students were enrolled in its schools, and by 1838, this number swelled to 20,000 (Fitzpatrick, 1969). African Americans made up 7% to 8% of the student body (Fitzpatrick, 1969). Although far more students, including African Americans, were educated in church charity schools than in the city system, under Clinton, the contributions of the New York Free School Society were considerable.

Clinton propounded many educational ideas that set the stage for academic developments for many years to come. He was able to secure state support for city charity schools in 1822, at a level of $150 per student (Fitzpatrick, 1969). Given that the New York Free School Society was a private organization, naturally, even after the breakthrough in state funding, most of the support came from private sources. Once Clinton was elected governor of New York in 1825, he showed the same devotion to expanding educational opportunities across the state that he had demonstrated as mayor. He advocated the establishment of technical schools and teacher-training institutes (Carter, 1826; Fitzpatrick, 1969). Clinton had the pleasure of signing into law the formation of a technical school in 1831. However, the first teacher-training institute was not established until 1844. Clinton even established the Infant School Society to train children age 2 through 5 (Fitzpatrick, 1969). He played a major role in the wide application of the charity school system and also laid the foundation for the modern education system.

Contemporary Focus

Pendulum Swings in Educational Policy

DeWitt Clinton was one of many politicians who became involved in education. Since the early 1980s, education has become a prominent topic in political circles. Presidents Reagan, George H. W. Bush, Bill Clinton, and George W. Bush have all made major attempts to wield power over educational policy. State political leaders are frequently even more involved in shaping school policy. There are some who believe that government should be more actively involved in shaping educational policy, because scholarly goals should become national concerns. However, there are others who claim that government involvement in education politicizes the process. For example, they claim that policy swings like a pendulum depending on who is in power. Some believe that these pendulum swings are healthy because they promote balance in the long run. Others claim that such swings are detrimental because they lead to inconsistency. Pendulum swings often take place regarding such issues as whole language versus phonics instruction as the best means to teach reading. Depending on the administration in power, the government will support one policy against the other. In this sense, some contend that pendulum swings are a consequence of the inherent effects of a democracy. The pendulum effect could encourage balance in the long haul. Nevertheless, other educators believe that a moderate approach incorporating both policies might be more effective and that a democracy need not function in such a polarizing fashion. However, they contend that as long as education is politicized, this moderate approach is unlikely to take place.

- To what extent do you think politicians should be involved in education?
- Do you view the pendulum effect as creating balance or inconsistency?

THE DECLINE OF THE CHARITY SCHOOL SYSTEM

As time passed, the increasing level of immigration made it unrealistic to rely so much on the private funding of charity schools. The ratio of poor-to-wealthy citizens was increasing considerably. Although the Lancaster system was only one of many methods of operating charity schools, it was the most widely applied. When in 1838, Lancaster was killed by a runaway horse, it symbolized the end of an era in schooling.

New York did continue to use the Lancaster system until the 1840s. Those educators who especially loved the plan tried to hold on to the system as long as possible and often implemented a "mixed plan" in the mid-1800s (Kaestle, 1973; Monroe, 1940). However, by the 1840s, a new prominent figure had arrived on the educational scene named Horace Mann (Mann, 1938; Monroe, 1940; Rippa, 1997; Troen, 1988; Ulich, 1968; Yulish, 1980). Although it would be some years before Americans would full fully embrace Mann's ideal of the common school, the transition had already begun (Mann, 1938; Monroe, 1940; Troen, 1988). The privately run charity school would now be supplanted by the publicly supported common school (Brandt & Shafter, 1960; Monroe, 1940). Yet it was also clear that the common or public schools were established on a foundation supplied by the charity schools.

Educational Debate: The Lancaster System

Most teachers probably would not like the idea of instructing a class of 100 students. However, in most major American cities, charity schools applied the Joseph Lancaster model, which encouraged 100 students per class. Lancaster's argument was that such a structure was necessary if people wanted all children to be able to go to school, including those who could not afford to pay. Although teachers each had six student-teaching assistants, the arrangement was doubtlessly difficult for teachers.

- How do you feel about this structure?
- Do you think congregating 100 students in a class subverts the educational process, or do you think that the people at the time were just doing the best they could in what was then a poor country?

THE COLLEGE LEVEL

The Revolutionary War had a profound impact on the system of American higher education. Americans realized that a strong set of colleges was absolutely necessary in order to train the new nation's leaders in a way that was distinctly non-European. Before the Revolutionary War, Ivy League colleges such as Harvard, Yale, and Princeton did not have the reputations that they enjoy now. Many of America's foremost leaders and scholars often sent their children to European colleges (Spring, 1997; Tewksbury, 1932). After the Revolutionary War, most Americans realized that the United States needed to train leaders to have an American perspective and that in addition to having a government independent from England, its education system needed to be independent as well.

Most early schools continued to be founded by religious groups. As Charles and Mary Beard (1944) assert, "It was mainly to religious motives that colleges, like elementary schools, owed their foundations" (p. 65). The members of these religious groups believed that salvation and moral character were essential to keeping the nation together (Hunt & Maxson, 1981; Kliebard, 1969). Now that freedom of religion was one of the cornerstones of the Constitution, various religious groups felt free to begin colleges in various places up and down the East Coast, including Washington College in Maryland (1782), Washington and Lee in Virginia (1783), Hampden-Sidney College in Virginia (1783), Transylvania Seminary in Kentucky (1783), Dickinson in Pennsylvania (1783), St. John's in Maryland (1784), Franklin and Marshall in Pennsylvania (1787), and Williams College in Massachusetts (1793) (Tewksbury, 1932). The Episcopals, Presbyterians, and Congregationalists were the most active denominations in founding colleges at this time. Later, the Methodists and Baptists would also participate more in the founding of colleges (Tewksbury, 1932).

In addition to the flowering of religious colleges in many places east of the Mississippi from 1776 to 1800 came the birth of the state school. The concept of the state college really did not gain notable popularity until the 1820s (Tewksbury, 1932). But in 1785, the University of Georgia was founded, and in 1789, the University of North Carolina was founded (Tewksbury, 1932). At first glance, it might seem surprising that the first state schools emerged in the South. But if one chooses to examine the situation more carefully, it should really come as no surprise. During the post–Revolutionary War period, most New England and mid-Atlantic states already enjoyed an excellent college reasonably close by. New England boasted the best two colleges in the nation, Harvard and Yale. The mid-Atlantic states had Princeton, Columbia, and the University of Pennsylvania. Even Virginia enjoyed the presence of the College of William and Mary. But the states south of Virginia did not possess a college of similar quality. In addition, southerners accurately argued that the needs of the future leaders of their states were different from those in either the New England or mid-Atlantic states. Therefore, southern schools were needed (Tewksbury, 1932).

The distinction between religious and state institutions was not that clear in the immediate postwar period. Certain schools that we now identify as state schools actually started as religious schools. The University of Tennessee, founded in 1794, started under the name Blount College and was founded by the Presbyterians (Tewksbury, 1932). This was also true of Rutgers University, the eighth American college, which was founded in 1766 by the Dutch Reformed Church and did not become a state college until 1917 (Tewksbury, 1932). New York University was founded by Presbyterians in 1831, and the Congregationalists and Presbyterians founded UC-Berkeley in 1855 (Tewksbury, 1932).

The "other side of the coin," however, elicited the greatest concern among America's leaders. The Revolutionary War had raised the awareness of secular leaders to a level that had previously been reserved only for religious leaders: The education of the American populace was a necessity. The problem with this late revelation for certain secular leaders was that the college landscape was already dominated by religious schools. And the quality of schools like Dartmouth, Harvard, and Princeton was so high that inaugurating state schools at this point to compete with these schools seemed futile. Yet the need of each state to educate leaders for their states was self-evident.

As a result of the combination of the educational landscape and the need for state colleges, state colleges did continue to arise in certain areas. The University of Vermont was founded in 1791 (Tewksbury, 1932). Unlike its New England neighbors of New Hampshire, Massachusetts, Rhode Island, and Connecticut, Vermont did not possess an outstanding privately run university. Therefore, Vermont emerged as about the only place in New England that was ripe for a state-run institution of higher education (Tewksbury, 1932).

Ohio also served as an excellent ground for a state university because of the lack of any outstanding private institution. In fact, the closest Ivy League institution was the University of Pennsylvania, hundreds of miles away. Ohio seemed to be a perfect place to found a state institution. Consequently, Ohio University (1802) and Miami University (1809) were started even before the founding of a private institution. In fact, Ohio was the only state in the Union to witness the founding of two state universities before a private institution of higher education had been founded (Tewksbury, 1932).

During the period after the Revolutionary War, two other state colleges were also founded: the University of South Carolina and the University of Maryland. Once again, these two schools were in areas in which there was no outstanding private institution with which to compete. At the same time, there was a real desire on the part of these states to educate their people.

The Revolutionary War acted to propel the U.S. system of higher education into a rapid period of growth that set the stage for its future glory. Specifically, the Revolutionary War had a tremendous impact on the U.S. system of higher education for the following reasons:

First, freedom from England made virtually all Americans aware of the need for American-based quality centers of higher education. The vision for building institutions of higher education was no longer limited almost solely to religious people. Second, the new emphasis on education enabled both religious and state institutions to grow. This fact set the stage for the unique coexistence of strong private and state institutions we enjoy today.

Nevertheless, the Revolutionary War in itself was not sufficient to produce the strength in the state university system we know today. Two other events needed to take place in order for state universities to blossom. The first was the Supreme Court case of *Dartmouth College vs. Woodward,* in 1819. This case affirmed the right of private institutions of higher education to exist without undue government interference (Bailyn, 1960). We shall return to this case later. Suffice it to say that although this case supported the rights of private institutions, by doing so, it also paved the way for the state university movement. Second, the Civil War also aided in the development of state universities, helping Americans to realize the need for commonalities to exist among Americans that would help bind the nation together. Some believed that the state could supply these commonalities better than religious universities.

Overall, the Revolutionary War era made its mark on higher education. Educators had established religious colleges faster than ever before, and the state university movement had begun.

CONCLUSION

The Revolutionary War period had a considerable impact on education that forever altered school practices in the United States. It helped unite the country via a common curriculum that was presented through particular books, especially those written by Noah Webster. The war and the independence that followed also caused educators to energetically found a long list of colleges that greatly strengthened the American education system. Finally, the Revolutionary War era established the charity school system as the broadest educational model for American elementary and secondary schools. The charity schools laid the foundation for the establishing of the public schools that were to follow. Whether one likes it or not, wars and their aftermath often change a society, including its education system. The Revolutionary War, as the nation's first war, clearly had a foundational impact on American education. The intensity of the political "moment" ultimately affected the intensity of the educational "moment." There is little question that the flurry of educational events that followed the war was largely a product of the weighty nature of America's assertion of independence. That intensity played a large role in producing an education system that developed to great heights very quickly. Even today, Americans are beneficiaries of that enthusiasm and intensity.

DISCUSSION QUESTIONS

1. In the days leading up to the Revolutionary War, a number of Americans went to Europe to obtain the best university education available. Now, according to surveys from

Germany, China, and Britain, academics believe that nearly all of the top universities are in the United States. Consequently, many foreign students from all over the world come to the United States to attend prestigious institutions such as Harvard, Yale, Princeton, Stanford, and the University of Chicago. Would you be willing to go overseas if you felt that meant getting the best education possible? What are some of the advantages and challenges experienced by the students who do this?

2. Do you think American higher education would have progressed as rapidly as it did if it had remained an English colony? Why or why not?

3. The charity school movement was able to succeed largely because there was an understanding that the wealthy people in society should pay to make it possible for the poor to go to school. Do you think this understanding still exists in American society today? Why or why not?

4. The *Dartmouth College v. Woodward* (1819) Supreme Court decision affirmed the right of private colleges and universities to exist. Greater competition in higher education resulted. In what ways do you believe both private and public universities are better as a result of this competition? How do you think this competition likely affects class sizes, the number of course offerings, the number of majors available, the level of individual attention received, and so forth?

REFERENCES

Andrews, C. C. (1969). *The history of the New York African free schools.* New York: Negro Universities Press.

Ashmore, H. S. (1994). *Civil rights and wrongs: A memoir of race and politics.* New York: Pantheon.

Bailyn, B. (1960). *Education in the forming of American society.* Chapel Hill: University of North Carolina.

Barton, D. (1990). *Our godly heritage* [Video]. Aledo, TX: Wallbuilders.

Barton, D. (1992). *Education and the founding fathers* [Video]. Aledo, TX: Wallbuilders.

Barton, D. (1995). *The myth of separation.* Aledo, TX: Wallbuilders.

Beard, C. A., & Beard, M. R. (1944). *A basic history of the United States.* New York: Doubleday, Doran.

Blanshard, P. (1963). *Religion and the schools.* Boston: Beacon Press.

Bobbe, D. (1933). *DeWitt Clinton.* New York: Minton, Balch.

Bourne, W. O. (1870). *History of the Public School Society.* New York: Wood.

Brandt, C. G., & Shafter, E. M. (Eds.). (1960). *Selected American speeches on basic issues, 1850–1950.* Boston: Houghton Mifflin.

Brown, A. (1890). *The genesis of the United States.* Boston: Houghton, Mifflin.

Carter, J. G. (1824). *Letters on the free schools of New England.* New York: Arno Press.

Carter, J. G. (1826). *Essays upon popular education, containing a particular examination of the schools of Massachusetts, and an outline of an institution for the education of teachers.* Boston: Bowles & Dearborn.

Clinton, D. (1829). In C. Z. Lincoln (Ed.), *Messages from the governors* (Vol. 5, p. 116). New York: State University of New York Press.

Connecticut Record, Volume VII 1726–1735 (1736).

Cornog, E. (1998). *The birth of empire: DeWitt Clinton and the American experience, 1769–1828.* New York: Oxford University Press.

Cremin, L. (1970). *American education: The colonial experience, 1607–1783.* New York: Harper & Row.

Cremin, L. (1980). *American education: The national experience, 1783–1876.* New York: Harper & Row.

Cremin, L. A. (1976). *Traditions of American education.* New York: Basic Books.

Cubberley, E. P. (1909). *Changing conceptions of education.* New York: Houghton Mifflin.

Cubberley, E. (1920). *The history of education.* Boston: Houghton Mifflin.

Cubberley, E. (Ed.). (1934). *Readings in public education in the United States: A collection of sources and readings to illustrate the history of educational practice and progress in the United States.* Cambridge, MA: Riverside Press.

Curran, F. X. (1954). *The churches and the schools.* Chicago: Loyola University Press.

Dartmouth College v. Woodward, 17 U.S. 518 (1819).

Dupuis, A. M. (1966). *Philosophy of education in historical perspective.* Chicago: Rand McNally.

Eavey, C. B. (1964). *History of Christian education.* Chicago: Moody Press.

Eisner, E. W. (1994). *Cognition and curriculum reconsidered.* New York: Teachers College Press.

Fitzpatrick, E. A. (1969). *The educational views and influence of DeWitt Clinton.* New York: Arno Press.

Fogel, R. W. (2004). *The escape from hunger and premature death, 1700–2100.* New York: Cambridge University Press.

Ford, P. L. (Ed.). (1962). *The New England primer.* New York: Teachers College Press.

Fraser, J. W. (2001). *The school in the United States.* Boston: McGraw-Hill.

Gangel, K. O., & Benson, W. S. (1983). *Christian education: Its history and philosophy.* Chicago: Moody.

Gerson, N. B. (1966). *Mr. Madison's war, 1812: The second war for independence.* New York: Messmer.

Gutek, G. L. (1997). *Historical and philosophical foundations of education.* Upper Saddle River, NJ: Prentice Hall.

Hill, H., & Jones, J. E. (1993). *Race in America: The struggle for equality.* Madison: University of Wisconsin Press.

Hiner, N. R. (1988). The cry of Sodom enquired into: Educational analysis in seventeenth century New England. In B. E. McClellan & W. J. Reese (Eds.), *The social history of American education* (pp. 3–22). Urbana: University of Illinois Press.

Holmes, S. (2001). *God of grace and God of glory: An account of the theology of Jonathan Edwards.* Grand Rapids, MI: Eerdmanns.

Holy Bible. (1973). Grand Rapids, MI: Zondervan.

Howard, L. (1943). *The Connecticut wits.* Chicago: University of Chicago Press.

Hunt, T. C., & Maxson, M. M. (1981). *Religion and morality in American schooling.* Washington, DC: University Press of America.

Jeynes, W. (2003). *Religion, education, and academic success.* Greenwich, CT: Information Age Publishing.

Johnson, P. (1997). *A history of the American people.* New York: HarperCollins.

Jones, M. G. (1964). *The charity school movement: A study of eighteenth century Puritanism in action.* Cambridge, UK: Cambridge Books.

Kaestle, C. (1973). *Joseph Lancaster and the monitorial school movement.* New York: Teachers College Press.

Kaestle, C. (1983). *Pillars of the republic: Common schools and American society, 1780–1860.* New York: Hill & Wang.

Kamen, H. (2003). *How Spain became a world power, 1492–1763.* New York: HarperCollins.

Kliebard, H. M. (1969). *Religion and education in America.* Scranton, PA: International Textbook Company.

Klinker, P. A., & Smith, R. M. (1999). *The unsteady march: The rise and decline of racial equality in America.* Chicago: University of Chicago Press.

Lewy, G. (1996). *Why America needs religion.* Grand Rapids, MI: Eerdmanns.

Mann, H. (1938). *Letter to F. A. Packard.* Boston: Massachusetts Historical Society.

Marrou, H. I. (1956). *A history of education in antiquity.* New York: Sheed & Ward.

Martin, G. H. (1894). *The evolution of the public school system.* New York: Appleton.

McKay, D., & Scott, H. M. (1983). *The rise of the great powers, 1648–1815.* London: Longman.

McClellan, E. B., & Reese, W. J. (1988). *The social history of American education.* Urbana: University of Illinois Press.

McMillan, R. (1984). *Religion in the public schools.* Macon, GA: Mercer University.

Michaelsen, R. (1970). *Piety in the public school.* London: Macmillan.

Monroe, P. (1940). *Founding of the American public school system.* New York: Macmillan.

Moss, R. J. (1984). *Noah Webster.* Boston: Twayne.

Pulliam, J. D., & Van Patten, J. J. (1991). *History of education in America.* Upper Saddle River, NJ: Merrill/Prentice Hall.

Raitt, J., & McGinn, B. (1987). *Christian spirituality: High Middle Ages and Reformation.* New York: Crossroad.

Randell, K. (1988). *Luther and the German reformation, 1517–1555.* London: Edward Arnold.

Report of the Prison Discipline Society, 1832. (1855). Boston: Boston Press of T. R. Marvin.

Riley, J. C. (2001). *Rising life expectancy: A global history.* New York: Cambridge University Press.

Rippa, S. A. (1997). *Education in a free society.* White Plains, NY: Longman.

Robson, D. W. (1985). *Educating republicans: The college in the era of the American Revolution, 1750–1800.* Westport, CT: Greenwood Press.

Rollins, R. M. (1980). *The long journey of Noah Webster.* Philadelphia: University of Pennsylvania Press.

Rothstein, S. W. (1994). *Schooling the poor: A social inquiry into the American educational experience.* Westport, CT: Bergin & Garvey.

Rush, B. (1951). Benjamin Rush letter to Richard Price, May 25, 1786. In L. H. Butterfield (Ed.), *Letters of Benjamin Rush* (Vol. 1, pp. 388–389). Princeton, NJ: Princeton University Press.

Somerville, M. (2002). *Tapestry of grace.* Purcellville, VA. Retrieved May 19, 2005, from www.tapestryofgrace.com/usingTOG.htm.

Spring, J. (1990). *The American school 1642–1990.* White Plains, NY: Longman.

Spring, J. (1997). *The American school 1642–1996.* White Plains, NY: Longman.

Spring, J. (2001). *The American school 1642–2000.* Boston: McGraw-Hill.

Stephens, A. H. (1872). *History of the United States.* New York: Hale & Son.

Stewart, G. Jr. (1969). *A history of religious education in Connecticut.* New York: Arno Press and New York Times.

Tewksbury, S. (1932). *Founding of American colleges and universities before the Civil War.* New York: Teachers College Press.

Troen, S. K. (1988). Popular education in nineteenth-century St. Louis. In E. McClellan & W. J. Reese (Eds.), *The social history of American education* (pp. 119–136). Urbana: University of Illinois Press.

Ulich, R. (1968). *A history of religious education.* New York: New York University Press.

Unger, H. G. (1998). *Noah Webster: The life and times of an American patriot.* New York: Wiley.

Urban, W., & Wagoner, J. (2000). *American education: A history.* Boston: McGraw-Hill.

Waller, G. M. (1950). *Puritanism in early America.* Boston: Heath.

Washington, G. (1790). *First annual address to Congress.* Retrieved July 11, 2004, from odur.let.rug.nl/~usa/P/gw1/speeches/gwson1.htm.

Webster, N. (1789). *New England primer.* New York: Patterson.

Webster, N. (1793). *Effects of slavery on morals and industry.* Hartford, CT: Hudson & Goodwin.

Webster, N. (1807). *Education of youth in the United States.* New Haven: CT.

Webster, N. (1834). *Value of the Bible, and the excellence of the Christian religion: For use of families and schools.* New Haven, CT: Durrie & Peck.

Webster, N. (1965). On the education of youth in America. In F. Rudolph (Ed.), *Essays on education in the early republic* (pp. 54–68). Cambridge, MA: Harvard University Press.

Wilson, P. (1977). Discrimination against Blacks in education: An historical perspective. In W. T. Blackstone & R. D. Heslep (Eds.), *Social justice and preferential treatment* (pp. 161–175). Athens: University of Georgia Press.

Woodson, C. G. (1968). *The education of the Negro prior to 1861.* Washington, DC: Associated Publishers.

Woodson, C. G., & Wesley, C. H. (1962). *The Negro in our history.* Washington, DC: Associate Publishers.

Yulish, S. M. (1980). *The search for a civic religion.* Washington, DC: University Press of America.

CHAPTER 3

Early Political Debates and Their Effect on the American Education System

One of the outstanding features of the American education system is that many of the early political decisions regarding education have had a profound impact on education for centuries afterward (Bailyn, 1960; Cremin, 1976, 1980; Cubberley, 1920, 1934; Marshall & Manuel, 1977; Spring, 1997). Many of the most distinguishing qualities of American education today have their roots in political debates that took place in the first decades following the founding of the country (Cremin, 1976, 1980; Pulliam & Van Patten, 1999; Urban & Wagoner, 2000). This fact is not coincidental. Many of America's early statesmen wanted to be involved in every aspect of the birth of the country to make certain that the United States developed into a strong and vibrant nation (McClellan & Reese, 1988; Washington, 1790). Education had long played an important role in the development of the colonies. Now, however, as the country developed, education was regarded as helping to secure not only the welfare and future of individual settlers but also the welfare and future of a nation. Therefore, many of America's founders were desirous of expressing their views on schooling and entering into the debate on the development of America's education system.

VIEWS OF THE DEMOCRATIC-REPUBLICANS AND THE FEDERALISTS

Shortly after the formation of the new American nation in 1776, two primary political parties arose on the political scene, the Federalists and the Democratic-Republicans. Both political parties had distinct political and educational perspectives. Although these schools of thought were designed to be more political than educational, they each had inherent in them diverging educational philosophies. Even when these distinct philosophies were not immediately apparent, they manifested themselves as being inextricably connected with the overriding political perspective. Therefore, whatever differences existed in each of these political parties ultimately affected their educational policies as well. Some of the

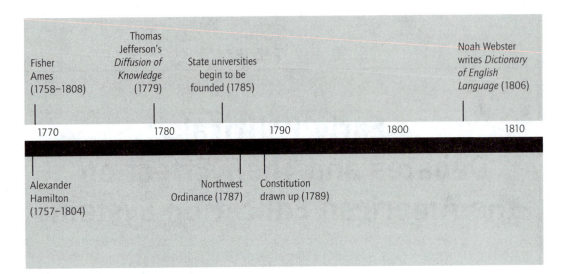

Fisher Ames (1758–1808)

Thomas Jefferson's *Diffusion of Knowledge* (1779)

State universities begin to be founded (1785)

Noah Webster writes *Dictionary of English Language* (1806)

1770   1780   1790   1800   1810

Alexander Hamilton (1757–1804)

Northwest Ordinance (1787)

Constitution drawn up (1789)

major political differences between the Federalists and Democratic-Republicans were as follows.

First, the Federalists, led by people such as Alexander Hamilton and George Washington, believed that the federal government should be the central source of power. The Democratic-Republicans claimed that the state governments should have the greatest power, to prevent concentration of power. The Federalists declared that the nation's political and economic systems would best flourish if there were an efficacious center of power. They believed that to decentralize power was inefficient and not in the best interests of a young nation trying to become established. The Democratic-Republicans contended that if there was too much power invested in the federal government, this enhanced the chances of retrogressing toward monarchy. The Declaration of Independence, according to these individuals, was a statement not only of independence as a political entity but also of independence from previous monarchical thought.

Second, the Federalists asserted that the United States should believe and act as a unified nation. They believed that there was moral strength and security in unity. The Democratic-Republicans, led by individuals such as Thomas Jefferson and James Madison, stood behind the salience of states' rights (Cremin, 1976, 1980; Johnson, 1997; Stephens, 1872). They claimed that the federal government should not be allowed to direct the affairs of states in a way contrary to what the states wanted. Each side had deep-rooted and logical reasons to believe this way. The Federalists believed that unification of the settlements was necessary for national survival and to develop strength. The Democratic-Republicans, on the other hand, given that the United States had just been freed from monarchical rule, were suspicious of centralized power and, in fact, sometimes referred to George Washington as "King George."

Third, the two parties differed on how the nation should resolve some of its most important conflicts. The Democratic-Republicans were led by Thomas Jefferson, the primary author of the Declaration of Independence, and James Madison, the primary author of the Constitution. The Democratic-Republicans were more likely than the Federalists to contend

Table 3.1 The First Six U.S. Presidents, Numbered by Order of Presidential Service and Listed by Party

Federalists	Democratic-Republicans
1. George Washington (1789–1797)	3. Thomas Jefferson (1801–1809)
2. John Adams (1797–1801)	4. James Madison (1809–1817)
6. John Quincy Adams[a] (1825–1829)	5. James Monroe (1817–1825)

a. Later changed political parties.

that the nation's most contentious debates should be resolved by consulting the Constitution (Jefferson, 1812). The Federalists respected the Constitution, but they were more likely than the Democratic-Republicans to admit that the Constitution was flawed. The Federalists, whose strongest base of support was in religious New England, were more likely to assert that one should consult a higher law, which was for them the Bible (Webster, 1834). Although Democratic-Republicans were often religious and Federalists respected the Constitution, they differed on this point.

In the early years of the country, both the Federalists and Democratic-Republicans were reasonably strong politically. However, by the early 1800s, the Democratic-Republicans had clearly gained an advantage. Eventually, they gained such an advantage that the Federalist Party ceased to exist (J. Adams, 1854; J. Q. Adams, 1850). As one might expect, the Democratic-Republican ideals of states' rights eventually predominated over the Federalist ideals. That is not to say that Americans no longer valued various Federalist ideals, but the Democratic-Republican perspective tended to be the dominant one (Brown, 1890; Johnson, 1997). This development had profound implications for the future of American education (Fraser, 2001; Gutek, 1997; Rippa, 1997).

PRESIDENTS AND EDUCATIONAL LEADERS

Both the distinctions between the Federalists and the Democratic-Republicans, as well as the ultimate Democratic-Republican triumph, can be more easily comprehended by look-ing at Table 3.1. The Democratic-Republicans did not have their first presidential victory until Thomas Jefferson (1801–1809) was elected as the third president of the United States. Before then, the Federalists had had the numerical political edge. However, John Adams's (the second president) unpopularity coupled with Democratic-Republican gains helped the party dominate the presidential elections for over two decades (Brown, 1890; Eggleston, 1998; Johnson, 1997). Democratic-Republicans Thomas Jefferson, James Madison, and James Monroe all served two terms each. John Quincy Adams started his political life as a Federalist and maintained Federalist beliefs. Years later, by the time he ran for president, the Federalists were nearly extinct, and it was almost impossible to win a presidential election as a Federalist. As a result, John Quincy Adams, with deep Federalist roots, chose to run as a Democratic-Republican. He was a Federalist in Democratic-Republican clothes, and his views on slavery were also of the Federalist persuasion (Marshall & Manuel, 1997). Therefore, in Table 3.1, John Quincy Adams is listed in the Federalist column.

One of the main ways the Democratic-Republicans and the Federalists differed was in their beliefs about how the United States Constitution should be applied to American daily life. Both parties had a high regard for the Constitution. Nevertheless, most Federalists strongly believed that the Constitution, as a document made by humans, should be regarded as quite fallible. In their view, it was subordinate to some absolute sense of right and wrong. The absolute authority to which most Federalists looked was the Bible (J. Adams, 1854; J. Q. Adams, 1850; Marshall & Manuel, 1997; Webster, 1853). The diaries of George Washington and John Quincy Adams indicate that both of these men were devoutly religious (Marshall & Manuel, 1997). The Federalists asserted that the Democratic-Republicans focused too much on states' rights. They averred that concentrating on individual and states' rights opened up the door for moral wrongs to be committed. They believed that if the federal government pointed the American people toward certain moral absolutes, this would reduce immoral behavior. John Adams (1854), for example, believed that a national morality was essential in order for the Constitution to be upheld:

> We have no government armed with power capable of contending with human passions unbridled by morality and religion. Avarice, ambition, revenge or gallantry would break the strongest cords of our Constitution, which was made only for a moral and religious people. It is wholly inadequate to govern any other. (p. 229)

John Quincy Adams (1850) was also very specific about what he believed was the highest law:

> The law given from Sinai was a civil and municipal as well as a moral and religious code; it contained many statutes . . . of universal application—laws essential to the existence of men in society, and most of which have been enacted by every nation, which ever professed any code of laws. (p. 61)

The Northwest Ordinance of 1787 reflected the importance of teaching moral education. The phrase of the ordinance most related to education (Article 3), states, "Religion, morality, and knowledge, being necessary to good government and the happiness of mankind, schools and the means of education shall forever be encouraged."

Thomas Jefferson and James Madison were the chief authors of the Declaration of Independence and the Constitution, respectively. It therefore comes as no surprise that both men viewed the Constitution as the final authority in deciding virtually all matters concerning the lives of American citizens. Democratic-Republicans often referred to the 10th Amendment of the Constitution, because it is unequivocal about states' rights: Whatever authority was not specifically assigned to the federal government was to be assigned to the appropriate state government. Education falls under this category. Therefore, Democratic-Republicans contended that education should be a function of the state government, one that is decentralized and relatively free from federal interference. The Democratic-Republicans were strong defenders of states' rights based on this constitutional argument (Johnson, 1997).

A Closer Look: What Is the Ultimate Authority?

The Democratic-Republicans and Federalists had disagreements largely because they differed on what the final authority was. The Democratic-Republicans had Thomas Jefferson, the primary writer of the Declaration of Independence, and James Madison, the primary author of the Constitution. Consequently, the party believed that the Constitution was the final authority to consult in order to resolve conflicts. This orientation helps one understand why the Democratic-Republicans maintained many of the perspectives they did on issues such as states' rights and slavery. The Federalists, naturally, also maintained a high degree of respect for the Constitution and its authority in controversy. However, the Democratic-Republicans generally regarded the Constitution as the final authority on controversial matters to a greater extent.

The Federalists' political stronghold rested primarily in New England, which was the nation's "Bible belt" for many years. George Washington and John Quincy Adams, in particular, were very religious leaders. George Washington attributed the strength of his Christian faith to an experience that he had had during the French and Indian War. In the midst of that conflict, Washington had two horses shot from under him, and four bullets pierced his jacket, though none of these even scratched the future president. Washington attributed this amazing incident to the intervention of God (Connell, 2004; Marshall & Manuel, 1977). John Quincy Adams wrote a diary in which he makes constant reference to the importance of his Christian faith. With all of this in mind, the Federalists were much more likely to see the Constitution as a valuable but flawed document. They believed that a higher law, the Bible, was the ultimate authority on controversial matters.

Even today, if one examines the chief controversies, the debate largely revolves around what the ultimate authority is for resolving conflicts. On issues of civil rights, abortion, war, and other controversies, the differences of opinion that people have are often founded on what they regard as the ultimate authority.

The greatest educational spokesmen for the Democratic-Republicans and the Federalists were Thomas Jefferson and Noah Webster, respectively (Gutek, 1997; Kirk, 1953). The debate between Jefferson and Webster delineated many of the differences between the Democratic-Republican and Federalist points of view (Brown, 1890; Johnson, 1997; Webster, 1853).

The crux of the Democratic-Republican scholastic proposals were contained in the Jeffersonian proposal titled "Bill for the More General Diffusion of Knowledge" (Fraser, 2001; Gutek, 1997; Rippa, 1997). Jefferson had first introduced this piece of legislation in 1779, when he was a member of the Virginia legislature. One of the central purposes of the bill was to establish a state system of elementary and secondary schools in Virginia. He called for 100 elementary schools to be built and maintained at public expense (Fraser, 2001; Gutek, 1997; Rippa, 1997). Boys and girls would attend for free for 3 years. The curriculum was roughly the same as was commonly taught in the private religious elementary schools of the time. Jefferson also called for the development of 20 secondary schools for children in order to prepare them for college. Students would have to continue to excel academically in school, or they would be dropped. This rubric sought to provide pragmatic direction for the future of Virginia schools. The gist of Jefferson's proposal called for schooling to be under local control and jurisdiction. The bill also introduced a state-based organization of free elementary school education. Although the Virginia State Legislature did not pass the bill, Jefferson's ideas served as a prototype for future public school educators (Fraser, 2001; Gutek, 1997; Rippa, 1997).

Added Insight: Geographically Based Political Power and How the Democratic-Republicans Eventually Prevailed

In the late 1700s, political party affiliation was strongly geographically based. The Federalists were dominant in the North, with New England as their center of power, while the Democratic-Republicans were dominant in the South, with South Carolina as their center of power. One might be tempted to say that political party affiliations are strongly geographically based today, but that trend is mild compared with the late 1700s. For example, in contemporary America, Maryland and Massachusetts may well be the two most Democratic states. However, Democrats represent only about 65% of the registered electorate in these states, indicating that there are nevertheless many Republicans. Similarly, Indiana and Utah may well be the two most Republican States. However, once again, only about 65% of the registered electorates in those states are Republicans, so there are also many Democrats. The situation in the late 1700s was very different. When George Washington was in office, it was extremely difficult to find a Democratic-Republican in Massachusetts. Similarly, it was also difficult to find a Federalist living in South Carolina. In fact, one reason George Washington was such a popular president is that even though he supported the Federalist perspective, he was from the South. Therefore, many Americans believed that he represented their interests. Given that the political affiliations of the North and South were antipodal, one can see that the seeds of the Civil War were being sown well before 1861.

Given that the country was geographically politically divided, one might wonder what changes and political strategies transpired to enable the Democratic-Republicans to become the dominant political party. First of all, John Adams, the second president and a Federalist, was not a popular president. His taxation and foreign policy, especially with regard to the French, upset many Americans. Under his administration, the Federalists began a precipitous decline from which they would never recover. Second, the Democratic-Republicans inaugurated a political strategy that focused on winning some of the mid-Atlantic States, such as New York. In the presidential election of 1800, the Democratic-Republicans managed to win New York City by a few hundred votes. This victory emerged as the difference in the race and enabled the Democratic-Republic Party to make further inroads into previously dominant Federalist territory. The Federalist Party died out in the mid-1820s.

Noah Webster was often called the "schoolmaster to America" because of his influence on American scholarship and instruction (Spring, 1997). *Webster's Dictionary* was the first comprehensive dictionary in American English. His textbooks for school children were so popular that they quickly sold more copies than there were people in the United States. Webster believed that it was important for schooling to be available to all Americans.

Therefore, he, like Jefferson, supported the idea of free schools (McClellan & Reese, 1988; Webster, 1853). He emphasized that moral education was the most important aspect of education and that national unity on important issues and patriotism were also desirable traits. Webster placed a great deal of emphasis on literacy, believing that an educated citizenry was essential for a strong democracy. Webster's ideas were especially popular in Massachusetts, where nearly all Americans were literate. Webster believed that literacy opened the door of opportunity to the knowledge of almost any academic discipline of one's choosing.

The Federalist Party enjoyed popularity from 1789 to 1801. During this time, the Federalist presidents George Washington and John Adams led the nation. During George Washington's presidential terms, the Federalist perspective enjoyed an advantage (Brown, 1890; Stephens, 1872). The country loved George Washington so much that his call for unity, conviction, and a sense of national consciousness prevailed. Under John Adams, the Federalist influence waned. Although the Federalists were still dominant in New England, the Democratic-Republicans made inroads into the mid-Atlantic States. Many Americans called for an expansion of states' rights. As a result, from 1801 to 1825, the Democratic-Republicans won most of the early deliberations regarding states' rights.

HOW VICTORIES BY DEMOCRATIC-REPUBLICANS INFLUENCED AMERICAN EDUCATION

A Decentralized Education System

The fact that the Democratic-Republicans won most of the early debates had a dramatic impact on the education system in the United States, including helping establish a decentralized system of education. In the eyes of many Americans, a decentralized school system was consistent with democracy. Some politicians, like Jefferson and others, argued that a democratic political system should have a democratic educational structure (Gutek, 1997; Urban & Wagoner, 2000). They asserted, in essence, that America's school system should naturally be of the people, by the people, and for the people. Democratic-Republicans averred that this could most easily be made a reality if decision making occurred as close to the classroom as possible rather than at the level of the federal government. This declaration convinced a plethora of Americans that a decentralized educational rubric was in the best interests of the country.

As a newly born country, myriad Americans had a natural distrust of centralization (Johnson, 1997). Numerous citizens believed that there was a close association between centralization and dictatorship. This is not to say that they maintained that centralization and monarchy were the same thing. Nevertheless, some Americans were fearful that a centralized government was more monarchical in nature. Therefore, a centralized government, in their view, was a few steps away from a dictatorship (Johnson, 1997). This being the case, in the minds of many, a democratic government was by definition a decentralized institution.

Many educators of the time opined that both teachers and families could maximize their influence on education if the system were decentralized. This was a particularly crucial issue to early Americans, because at this time most civilians believed that the parental role in academic training was even more important than the educator's role. As a result, Americans felt more amenable to the idea of parents having a major voice in schooling than to district superintendents and other school officials dictating most of the decisions.

In the early days of the American school system, parents were highly involved in their children's education both at home and at school. Teachers frequently visited the homes of their students to hone their knowledge of the school children and generate an enduring bond with the parents (Dupuis, 1966; Chamberlin, 1961; Gangel & Benson, 1983; Hiner, 1988). By doing this, a teacher could become aware of a child's strengths and weaknesses. In colonial and post–Revolutionary War America, people believed in mutual respect between the parent and the teacher. Individuals from this period had a great deal of admiration for the teachers because of their cognizance of the educational process (Chamberlin, 1961; Gangel & Benson, 1983; Hiner, 1988). However, teachers also had respect for parents because they knew more about their children than anyone else.

In the pre–Revolutionary War period, settlers were thankful that the English government did not attempt to run each colony's school system. Instead, the English government allowed each settlement to delineate its educational policy and establish schools. This was a very different practice than the one in England. In Britain, the government dictated the scholastic policies of most communities. Naturally, one can argue that Britain would have done this with North American schools had the continent been closer and more accessible. This assertion is likely correct to a large degree. Nevertheless, whatever the reason for the lack of British incursion into pre–Revolutionary War school practices, settlers came to enjoy a decentralized educational environment. This decentralization existed in both the private and government sectors.

Although most Americans probably take the decentralized school system for granted, it is undoubtedly unique and a by-product of the traditionally democratic form of government in the United States (Gutek, 1997).

If one examines the education systems of the nations of the world, he or she will notice an intriguing trend. Almost without exception, the structure of each nation's school system reflects the type of government that the nation possessed at the time of the education system's founding (Stevenson & Stigler, 1992). That is, if the nation's government was very centralized at the time an elaborate educational model was developed, the educational structure was also likely to be centralized. Similarly, if the nation's government was decentralized at the time a sophisticated education system was introduced, the system was also likely to be decentralized.

As a result of this historical trend, the educational rubric of nearly all European, Asian, and African nations is centralized in nature. This is due in large part to the fact that most European, Asian, and African nations developed their academic governance models when their governments were highly centralized. In the European perspective of a few centuries ago, for example, centralization was required to ensure efficiency and the establishing and fulfillment of common goals (Marrou, 1956).

Historically, most nations of the world have tended to centralize governments when founding their organized instructional systems (Marrou, 1956). The mind-set of numerous nations includes the association of decentralization with disorganization and factionalism. In these countries, centralization is viewed as a type of organizational salvation. This helps explain why in the 1870s, Japan imitated America's educational rubric in terms of curriculum and content but chose the French model of centralized administrative structure. The Japanese government was very centralized at the time. It was hard for them to conceive of constructing an organized education structure that was so decentralized (Amano, 1990; Keenleyside & Thomas, 1937; Khan, 1997).

Webster and other Federalists believed that local control would reduce the quality of schooling, particularly in the area of moral education (Webster, 1853). The Federalists believed that state and local control generally resulted in lower quality, whether one meant morally or academically. They asserted that establishing moral and academic standards at the federal level was the most efficacious way to ensure the nation's development. John Adams, the second U.S. president and an outstanding Federalist, distrusted popular and local impulses. In the view of Adams (1854), liberty should not be equated with the freedom to do whatever one pleased: "I would define liberty as a power to do as would be done by Christ" (p. 377). Therefore, in Adams's eyes, liberty could survive in the long run only when it was founded on love and morality.

Federalists claimed that localized and state-based morality was largely to blame for the problem of slavery (J. Adams, 1854; J. Q. Adams, 1850; Kirk, 1953). John Adams and other Federalists claimed that what was needed was more of a nationally based morality that would help eradicate evils like slavery. Adams and others believed that a decline in morality would ultimately pose a threat to liberty and would eventually lead to licentiousness. This, in turn, would cause people to desire to curb liberty because it would be seen as the origin of the trouble.

Fisher Ames, who is most famous for giving us the First Amendment to the Constitution, was also concerned about some of the excesses of state or local control. Ames contended that Democratic-Republicans maintained too optimistic a view of what local people would do if left to their own desires. Ames stated,

> Politicians have supposed that man really is what he should be; that his reason will do all it can, and his passions and his prejudices no more than they ought. . . . Popular reason does not always know how to act right, nor does it act right when it knows. (as quoted in Kirk, 1953, p. 72)

The Democratic-Republicans, however, believed that given that education in the New World had flourished at the local level, it was only natural for education to continue to operate at the local level (Spring, 1997). The fact that education in the United States was not centralized at this time and that this is what people were accustomed to greatly strengthened the eventual implementation of the Democratic-Republican perspective.

However, it took some time for the Democratic-Republican decentralization emphasis to take hold (Monroe, 1940). This was due not only to the prominence of Federalist ideas in New England and the mid-Atlantic states but also to the conviction of most Americans at that time that education was the responsibility of the church and not the government. As a consequence of this perspective, numerous Americans claimed that church leaders rather than government officials should resolve the centralization versus decentralization issue. This attitude initially influenced the success of certain Democratic-Republican educational proposals. For example, ironically, the Virginia Assembly did not, for the most part, pass Jefferson's Bill for the More General Diffusion of Knowledge. It took some time for Jefferson's ideas to gain adherents. Nevertheless, eventually other states, particularly in the Midwest, implemented plans similar to Jefferson's (Monroe, 1940; Pulliam & Van Patten, 1999).

The decentralized system of education had one special benefit for schools emerging in different states. It allowed the schools to acclimate to their own particular situations. It allowed Catholics in Maryland (where Catholics were initially congregated in large numbers) to operate schools in the way that they saw fit. It allowed people in New England to run their schools differently than in Maryland, and vice versa. As mentioned, it was particularly important to New Englanders at that time that the Bible be central to the curriculum.

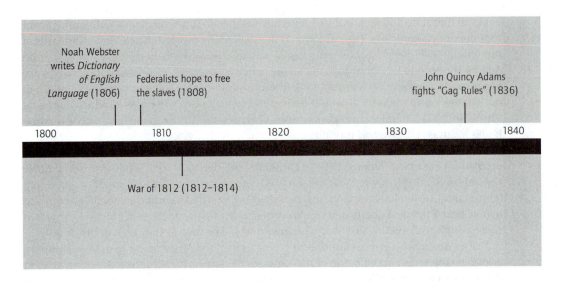

Noah Webster
writes *Dictionary
of English
Language* (1806)

Federalists hope to free
the slaves (1808)

John Quincy Adams
fights "Gag Rules" (1836)

1800   1810   1820   1830   1840

War of 1812 (1812–1814)

Because of the decentralized nature of the American education system, New Englanders and other Americans were free to structure their school curricula in any way they pleased.

Overall, most people believe that the decentralized nature of the American school system is a positive attribute (Urban & Wagoner, 2000). Nevertheless, there are certainly some positive and negative aspects of a decentralized system. Noting these positive and negative aspects is particularly interesting because the decentralized nature of our education system has been under attack in recent years.

Some of the positive aspects of having a decentralized education system in America are as follows: (a) It enables schools to be sensitive to the diverse array of people to be educated; (b) it allows teachers to have a stronger role in developing the curricula they use for their children; (c) it allows schools to offer a wider range of courses than could otherwise be the case; (d) it allows for a much higher level of parental and student input that can potentially be used to change the schools; and (e) it allows for a higher level of competition among the textbook manufacturers, so that, ideally, better textbooks will be used. However, one should note that states with large populations, such as California, Texas, New York, and Florida, have much more influence on the content of textbooks than states with small populations. Therefore, determination of textbook content is not a totally decentralized process.

For most of American history, this fact was considered a positive aspect of the American education system. Within the last 35 years, however, some have questioned whether having a decentralized system of elementary education and secondary school helps our education system or not. A lot of this skepticism arose during the 1960s and 1970s because of a perceived decline in the U.S. education system. This perception arose out of (a) a decline in the performance of American students on standardized tests, including the SAT (formerly known as the Scholastic Aptitude Test or Scholastic Achievement Test); (b) a decline in the relative performance of Americans on international comparison tests; and (c) a sense that perhaps one of the reasons that minority students did not perform as well on standardized tests is that they did not receive courses that were at the same academic levels as their White counterparts. Therefore, some politicians and educators believe that a decentralized education system is more likely to produce inequality (Gurule & Ortega, 1973).

Contemporary Focus

Are We Beginning to Lose Our Decentralized System of Education?

The American system of education is presently one of the most decentralized systems in the world. This fact is reflected in the fact that in most cases, less than 10% of a public school's educational dollar comes from the federal government (Swanson, King, & Sweetland, 1997; U.S. Department of Education, 2005). However, although state and local governments together generally contribute about 90% of the public school's expenditures, increasingly the federal government demands that certain standards be met, theoretically, to maximize the public good (Swanson et al., 1997; U.S. Department of Education, 2005). Moreover, if schools fail to meet these standards, the federal government can sometimes threaten to reduce its financial support of the public schools or intervene in school affairs when it deems that such intervention is for the welfare of the school children and in the best interests of the country (Swanson et al., 1997).

Presidents Bill Clinton and George W. Bush have expressed concern about the likelihood that America's decentralized system of education is part of the reason there exists an achievement gap between rich and poor students, as well as White and some minority students (Marcus, 1997; Neill, 1998). Increasingly, these leaders and others have claimed that children living in the suburbs are more likely to receive a demanding curriculum than their counterparts living in rural areas and in the inner city (Marcus, 1997; Neill, 1998). There are a variety of reasons to suspect that there probably is some gap in the rigor of the curriculum. First, students in areas in which low achievement is the norm may put pressure on teachers to require less homework. Second, in low-achieving areas, parents and teachers may have lower academic expectations of the young. Third, sometimes if schools do not possess enough students interested in higher-level courses, the classes are not offered.

President Clinton attempted to address some of these issues by creating a more centralized curriculum of what American students are expected to learn. Clinton argued that American fourth graders across the country should take a reading test and eighth graders should take a math test to determine whether individual schools were teaching sufficiently challenging curricula. Clinton advocated the use of these tests not to compare students, but to compare schools (Marcus, 1997; Neill, 1998).

Educators are very mixed regarding whether Clinton's moves will have a positive or negative overall effect. Nevertheless, Clinton was responding to the concerns of many regarding the possible negative effects of a decentralized school system. It may be that Clinton's actions, designed to make the American education system somewhat more centralized, will address some of the excesses that decentralization can have. However, some believe it signals the move toward a more centralized American school system.

President George W. Bush's "No Child Left Behind" program has taken the nation even further on the road toward centralization. Bush believes that the nation should rely even more on standardized tests to assess how well schools are educating the nation's children (U.S. Department of Education, 2002). He has also required states to establish guidelines and requirements regarding teacher credentials and standards to ensure that new and existing teachers are well trained. Although the states have a large role in establishing these guidelines, many argue that given that this is based on a federal initiative, it is accelerating the trend toward centralization.

- Given the above trends, some people argue that the U.S. schooling system has taken a major turn toward centralization. Others assert that Presidents Clinton and Bush have merely addressed some of the excesses of the decentralized system and that, in reality, America's education system is really not becoming more centralized at all. What do you think?

Strong Private and State Systems of Higher Education

A second product of the early political debates was that the United States developed strong private and state systems of higher education (Pulliam & Van Patten, 1999). The private system of higher education matured well in advance of the state system. As a result, initially the religious colleges had a substantial qualitative advantage over the state institutions. However, the fact that Democratic-Republicans favored state institutions tended to help state colleges close the quality gap.

Many social scientists believe that one of the reasons the U.S. system of higher education is so strong is that both the private and state institutions are vibrant (Pulliam & Van Patten, 1999). Given that the Federalists advocated the expansion of private religious education and the Democratic-Republicans backed state colleges, one can argue that the fact that the political parties backed different groups actually benefited the country. For many years, private religious colleges (e.g., Harvard, Yale, and Princeton) tended to be of higher quality than the state institutions. The fact that Democratic-Republicans were very supportive of state institutions enabled many state colleges to become prestigious as well.

One can argue that this educational disagreement between the political parties of the era actually ameliorated the quality of American education. This is one of the ironies of political debates. An abundance of individuals insist that one political party is completely right and the other is totally wrong. To the extent that some Americans have this perspective, they assume that the country is better off if one party always prevails over the other. Although there are certainly times in which this is accurate, there are many other situations in which the opposite is true. In the case of higher education, it actually worked to the nation's benefit for one political party to support state institutions and the other to favor private religious ones. In this way, both types of establishments became strong.

The fact that Democratic-Republicans, who were dominant in the South, wanted strong state colleges also helps explain why many of the early state colleges emerged in the South. The universities of Georgia, North Carolina, and Virginia were among the first state centers of higher education (Tewksbury, 1932). Similarly, the Federalist stronghold of the Northeast continued to host most of the nation's prestigious private colleges. Without the early political victories of the Democratic-Republicans over the Federalists, the state universities probably would not have developed as well as they did (Tewksbury, 1932).

A Likely Delay in Freeing the Slaves

The third effect that the Democratic-Republican victory had was probably to delay the freeing of the slaves. While educators often regard the decentralized school system as a positive result of the Democratic-Republican school system, their impact on the slavery issue was clearly a negative one. This is not to say that the Democratic-Republicans were pro-slavery (Eggleston, 1998; Stephens, 1872). Rather, (a) they may not have realized the ramifications of their push for the individual rights of states on the slavery issue, and (b) they were more reluctant to risk dividing the nation on the issue of slavery than the Federalists were (Eggleston, 1998). John Quincy Adams in particular probably did more in attempting to fight slavery than any other president before Lincoln (Marshall & Manuel, 1997).

To understand why the Democratic-Republican victory so dramatically impacted the slavery issue, one needs to understand the political landscape of the time. The balance of political power was much more geographically based than it is now (Eggleston, 1998; Stephens, 1872). Today, in the United States, many states have a long-standing tradition of voting for candidates of one party more than the other. For example, Maryland has a long tradition of voting primarily for Democrats, and Indiana has a similar Republican tendency. Nevertheless, despite these trends, there are many Republicans in Maryland and numerous Democrats in Indiana. Even in the most one-sided states in this regard, one party generally enjoys only about a 65%-versus-35% voter registration advantage.

Political parties were much more geographically based in the late 1700s and early 1800s. In the late 1700s, before the decline of the Federalist Party, the Federalists were dominant in the North, and the Democratic-Republicans enjoyed preeminence in the South (Eggleston, 1998; Stephens, 1872). Massachusetts was the strongest Federalist state. If you were from Massachusetts in the late 1700s, you were almost certainly a Federalist. South Carolina was the major Democratic-Republican stronghold. If you lived in South Carolina during this period, you were almost certainly a Democratic-Republican (Eggleston, 1998; Stephens, 1872). Eventually, the Democratic-Republicans did make inroads into some of the northern states, especially the mid-Atlantic states, where the Federalists had previously enjoyed a solid advantage. Nevertheless, from the beginning of the nation's history, one party dominated in the North and the other in the South.

Due to the fact that the tensions between the Federalists and Democratic-Republicans were largely along geographical lines, many politicians and other Americans feared that a civil war would eventually take place, years before it actually occurred (Brown, 1890; Eggleston, 1998; Johnson, 1997; Stephens, 1872). Although there were exceptions, the Democratic-Republicans were generally much more sympathetic to slavery than were the Federalists. Again, they were not necessarily pro-slavery, but what one would probably call "pro-choice." That is, they believed that each state and individual should have the right to choose whether slavery should be lawful or not. This perspective was quite consistent with their emphasis on states' rights. The Federalists were generally antislavery or pro-freedom. Again, this approach was in agreement with their belief in a common set of national laws, guidelines, and morals to help formulate American behavior (Brown, 1890; Eggleston, 1998; Johnson, 1997; Stephens, 1872).

The debate concerning slavery therefore focused on whether the Southern states had a right to maintain the institution of slavery. According to the Constitution, it certainly did have that right. When discussing the education of African Americans, it is important to note the nature of the slavery debate. The essence of the slavery debate was not so much an issue of whether people were for slavery or against it. Most people in the South did not own slaves. In addition, for those who did not own slaves in the South, the vested interest they had in continuing slavery was not sufficient to go to war over. Indeed, many people in the South thought slavery was an unacceptable practice. Even many Northerners, while they abhorred the institution of slavery, believed that it was the business of the individual states as to whether they would have slavery or not. Therefore, the debate over slavery was not so much a matter of whether a person was for or against slavery, but whether he or she believed that states and individuals had the right to choose whether to enslave others or not. So, it was a debate between pro-freedom and pro-choice forces (Brown, 1890; Eggleston, 1998; Johnson, 1997; Stephens, 1872).

Whether people of the North or the South were just in their views is easy to determine looking back in hindsight. However, to many living at that time, especially in the South, the matter was not clear at all. To Southerners, the Northerners were being dictatorial in much the way that the British had been during the colonial period, and the Northern politicians in Washington, D.C., were trying to inflict their will on the rest of the American people. Southerners argued that America was a democracy in which individual rights ruled the land. Therefore, many Southerners opposed the notion of forcing plantation owners to free the slaves with the same fervor with which they opposed British oppression during the Revolutionary War. Furthermore, Southerners believed that Northern politicians, living hundreds of miles from the South, could not possibly understand the extent to which the region relied on the slaves for its economic welfare (Brown, 1890; Eggleston, 1998; Johnson, 1997; Stephens, 1872). Many Southerners believed that to free the slaves would lead to economic peril and that the North would therefore be able to always predominate economically over the South. Some Southerners even believed that the primary reason many Northerners opposed slavery had more to do with their desire to dominate the South and less to do with any true convictions they held regarding slavery (Brown, 1890; Eggleston, 1998; Johnson, 1997).

Southerners also believed that the Northern politicians were very insensitive regarding the ramifications of freeing the slaves. Numerous leaders in the South tended to believe that if the Northerners had been the ones to have to live with the ramifications of setting the slaves free, they would not advocate such a position (Brown, 1890; Eggleston, 1998; Johnson, 1997; Stephens, 1872). The Southerners feared that freed slaves would quickly organize a mass rebellion and that mayhem would spread throughout the South. This fear shows the degree to which they were plagued by guilt regarding their treatment of the slaves.

Abolitionist forces in the North believed that the South's pro-choice perspective on slavery was totally insensitive to the experiences of the slaves and dismissed the issue of moral responsibility and a sense of right and wrong (McCarthy & McMillan, 2003; McKivigan, 1999; Miller & Cimbala, 1996). Abolitionists knew that if the slaves were given the liberty to articulate their views at the voting booth, they would declare that slavery should be abolished. In the view of many Northerners, the institution of slavery was deleterious enough but allowing these victims no voice in their own fate and instead declaring that slavery was a matter of individual choice maximized exploitation of the slaves (McCarthy & McMillan, 2003; McKivigan, 1999; Miller & Cimbala, 1996).

From the standpoint of the Northerners, they were fighting for human liberty and righteousness. From the standpoint of the Southerners, they were fighting the tyranny and dictatorial nature of the Washington politicians. It comes as no surprise, therefore, that both sides fought with such fervor. Northerners, in fact, often do not realize that the states of the Deep South and the Southern border states entered the Civil War for different reasons (Brown, 1890; Eggleston, 1998; Johnson, 1997; Stephens, 1872). Upon Lincoln entering office, the states of the Deep South were defiant and seceded, convinced that it was their right by the Constitution to preserve slavery. The Southern border states entered the war less over the slavery issue than on the basis of a state's right for self-determination.

Although the North fought to eradicate slavery and the South fought to preserve slavery, it is wrong to assume that racism existed in the South but did not exist in the North. Freed African Americans experienced challenges in the Northern states as well. Nevertheless, the challenges African Americans faced in the North were far less than anything they faced in the South.

Some Democratic-Republicans did occasionally speak out against slavery. Thomas Jefferson made one or two rather lengthy statements describing his distaste for slavery. Nevertheless, Jefferson himself was a slaveholder (Brown, 1890; Eggleston, 1998; Johnson, 1997; Stephens, 1872). In addition, the Democratic-Republicans clearly had much stronger views on states' rights than they ever entertained regarding slavery. Nevertheless, part of the division between the Federalists and the Democratic-Republicans was a North/South issue. Of the six presidents mentioned earlier, all three Democratic-Republicans were slave owners. Of the three Federalists, John Adams and John Quincy Adams did not own slaves. George Washington released his slaves upon his death. Apparently, he was well-known for being very kind to his slaves, although one might view that as a contradiction in terms. His slaves never wanted to leave his family, even upon his death.

To the Democratic-Republicans, if the United States were to remain together as a nation, states' rights had to be respected. The union of so many different colonies dictated that the individual preferences of each colony be respected. The Democratic-Republicans believed so strongly in this concept that they pushed to insert it as a major part of the Constitution. Many Federalist statesmen were particularly upset about this. They believed that the slavery issue should be solved sooner rather than later.

The tension between the Federalist-dominated North and the Democratic-Republican-dominated South even affected the way the Constitution was written. You might recall that in the Constitution, a slave is given the value of three fifths of a person, and this understandably offends a lot of African Americans. They assume that this was an expression of Southern racism at the time and a compromise between the Northern and the Southern politicians. But in reality, this was not the case at all. The slaves were not counted as less than full persons because of Southern racism, but because the North wanted to discourage slavery (Brown, 1890; Eggleston, 1998; Johnson, 1997; Stephens, 1872). At that time, federal aid was based on the population of a given state or city. The Northerners feared that if slaves were counted as full persons, this would encourage Southerners to import more slaves. Therefore, in order to discourage the importation of slaves, the North actually did not want the slaves to be counted at all. It was the Southerners who wanted the slaves to be counted as full persons, so that they could receive more federal money.

The Democratic-Republicans who were not especially fond of slavery probably did not realize the extent to which their insistence on states' rights would set the stage for the Civil War. The argument made by the Southern states for the existence of slavery was a Constitutional argument based on the rights of states to decide such matters. In fact, some of the Southern border states claim that they entered the Civil War only out of their anger over what they considered to be the flagrant violation of states' rights. The Federalists thought that the slavery issue should be resolved at the federal and not the state level. Most Federalists believed that no matter what the Constitution permitted, a higher moral law declared that slavery was wrong.

John Quincy Adams was the most outspoken politician of his time against slavery (Marshall & Manuel, 1997). As a Congressman, his strategy was to make slavery illegal in Washington, D.C. He believed that if this could successfully be accomplished, it would set the stage for slavery being abolished in the land (Marshall & Manuel, 1997). Each year in Congress, John Quincy Adams raised this issue of extirpating slavery from Washington, D.C. Each year, the issue was defeated. Adams's insistence raised the ire of many of his congressional peers, especially among the Democratic-Republicans. A large number of Congressmen wanted to act to remove him from office (Marshall & Manuel, 1997). In his diary, Adams expressed a great deal of frustration regarding the struggle to free the slaves. But, ultimately, he won an important victory. Repeatedly, Congress received petitions from the abolitionists calling for the end of slavery. In 1836, the House of Representatives adopted a group of resolutions, called the "Gag Rules," to keep such petitions from being read on the floor of the House (Marshall & Manuel, 1997). Adams believed that these Gag Rules were unconstitutional and eventually succeeded in having them abolished. In his diary, Adams was elated, overjoyed over a victory in what he called a "spiritual battle" (Marshall & Manuel, 1997, pp. 97–103).

The Federalists tended to argue their case from a higher authority, which for them was the Bible. Democratic-Republicans, even if they were religious, tended to argue their case from the Constitution. This fact illuminates not only the essence of the slavery debate following the Revolutionary War but also many other controversial debates that have taken place throughout American history. Two sides of a debate arise over a morally controversial issue because one side views the issue as a purely Constitutional issue and the other side views the issue as one that involves a higher moral law that overrules the contents of the Constitution (Eggleston, 1998; Marshall & Manuel, 1997).

In 1808, a major opportunity faced the United States. The Federalists and President Thomas Jefferson, a Democratic-Republican, worked together to pass legislation that would make the importation of slaves illegal. A number of Federalists saw the debate as the best opportunity since 1776 to free the nation of slavery. In the days leading up to the writing of the Declaration of Independence, America's founders were engaged in a debate about whether slavery should be addressed and the extent to which the signers of the document wanted to censure King George III for promoting slavery and causing the colonies to become embroiled in such an evil institution (Berlin & Hoffman, 1983; Bernstein, 2003; Johnson, 1997). Ultimately, this idea was not supported, because many believed it would alienate the South perhaps to the point that many people would not support a war for independence (Berlin & Hoffman, 1983; Bernstein, 2003; Johnson, 1997). Had the Federalists had their way, slavery would have ended in 1808. However, most Federalists also realized that their party was in decline and that they simply did not have the votes to ban slavery. The Democratic-Republicans, with strong roots in the South, were too powerful to defeat on this issue. Many Federalists were simply happy to have a Democratic-Republican president who would at least take a step in what they felt was the right direction. Under Jefferson's leadership, some Democratic-Republicans voted to declare importing slaves illegal who might not have voted that way had a president been in power who was more sympathetic to the slave owners (Brown, 1890; Eggleston, 1998; Johnson, 1997; Stephens, 1872).

Had the Federalists, their support base being in the North, been the majority party in 1808, it is likely that slavery would have ended at this time. One can only wonder how American history would have progressed if an "emancipation proclamation" had taken place in 1808 rather than five and a half decades later. Would the civil rights movement have occurred five and a half decades earlier? Would segregation have ended earlier? Would there have been a Civil War? If so, would it have occurred in 1808?

The fact that slavery remained an American reality impacted education to a large degree: (a) Education remained largely segregated, certainly in the South and to a lesser degree in the North; (b) a disproportionate amount of financial and physical resources went to White students rather than African American students for an even longer period of time; (c) the education that African Americans received would be largely dependent on White churches in the Northern states; and (d) one can argue that every advance that African Americans have made in education was delayed because the nation preferred to emphasize states' rights rather than national unity.

In fact, the effects of the Democratic-Republican victory can be discussed on an even more substantial level. If the nation had decided at an early time that the slavery/racial issue should be decided at the federal level, perhaps the whole movement toward civil rights for African American people could have been greatly expedited. Even after the Supreme Court ruled in 1954 that racially based segregation was unconstitutional, the push toward desegregation had to be won state by state.

One can argue about what African American history might have looked like if the Federalist philosophy had prevailed over that of the Democratic-Republicans. In all fairness, however, one should also ask how centralized the American education system would have been had the Federalists prevailed. John Quincy Adams proposed a federal university, but a Democratic-Republican Congress balked at his ideas. There is little question that the U.S. system of education would not be as decentralized as it is now had the Federalists prevailed in their debate against the Democratic-Republicans.

Educational Debate: How Would an Earlier Release of the Slaves Have Affected American Education and Society?

At the time of the founding of the United States, it was decided that although the slavery issue could not be resolved, it would be revisited in 1808. The Federalists hoped that by 1808, they would have enough political clout to put an end to slavery. Unfortunately, just the reverse happened, and by 1808, the Democratic-Republicans were the dominant political party. The Federalists realized that they would not be able to realize their dream and successfully pass legislation that would end slavery. Instead, President Thomas Jefferson initiated a compromise that banned the importation of slaves. Although this legislation was passed, plantation owners still imported 250,000 slaves between 1808 and the end of the Civil War.

An interesting question arises: What if the Federalists had enjoyed the political power to abolish slavery in 1808? In reality, slavery did not end until the Emancipation Proclamation of 1863, coupled with the end of the Civil War in 1865. Would American education today and the status of minorities be that much further along if the slaves had been freed in 1808? Would race relations be that much better today if the slaves had been released in 1808? There are two schools of thought on how one might answer this question. The first is that we as Americans would be considerably further along. After all, there was a 57-year gap between 1808 and the end of the Civil War. One could argue that certainly education and race relations would be better if the slaves had been freed earlier. In fact, it is likely that the Civil War would have taken place earlier. However, one could also argue that Martin Luther King Jr. needed television to successfully communicate his points to the American public. Many Northerners were not cognizant of the situation faced by African Americans in the South until they witnessed various scenes coming into their living rooms on television. Therefore, one can also argue that only through television were subsequent advances in civil rights possible.

- What do you think? Would the nation be farther along in education and in race relations had the slaves been set free in 1808?

CONCLUSION

The early political victories by the Democratic-Republicans not only influenced education at that time, but the entire course of American educational history. Often the foundational years of development directs the course of an undertaking for centuries to come. Therefore, one could argue that the decisions that are made in an institution's incipiency are especially important. Due to the Democratic-Republican political victories of the early 1800s, the United States possesses a decentralized elementary and secondary school system. Probably the main reason the United States enjoys such a strong university and college system is that the Democratic-Republicans and the Federalists particularly advocated the development of state colleges and private religious universities, respectively. Had the Democratic-Republicans not supported the founding of state colleges, state colleges likely would have developed more slowly and would not have the position of prominence that they have today.

Most Americans, although not all, would probably argue that the first two Democratic-Republican contributions are positive ones. First, most Americans value a decentralized system of education. Second, a majority of people also value the nation's strong system of state universities. However, the third contribution, a delay in freedom for the slaves is clearly not a positive one. It is quite possible, if not likely, that the Democratic-Republican political victories, and hence the Federalist defeats, delayed the end of slavery. As the major political party of the South, the Democratic-Republicans were far more tolerant of slavery than they should have been. In the year 1808, there was a grand opportunity to end slavery in America. However, the weak Federalist Party did not have the votes to do what many of them wanted to do, to put an end to slavery. The Democratic-Republicans, with the exception of a select group of men such as Jefferson, believed that states' rights should prevail and that compromising on slavery was the best political strategy. The failure of the nation to end slavery in 1808 may have delayed many of the educational advancements that African Americans did eventually make after the Civil War and after World War II.

To whatever extent the political victories by the Democratic-Republicans had both positive and negative consequences for education, it is clear that America's system of education was influenced for decades by their triumph and, in many cases, for two centuries. The salience of this early period was significant enough that one should expect that Americans, in several respects, will experience the Democratic-Republican influence for many years to come.

DISCUSSION QUESTIONS

1. Is it conceivable that a centralized system of education works best in some nations or settings and a decentralized system in others? What national qualities would make a centralized system or a decentralized system preferable?

2. Why is it that decisions made hundreds of years ago can have such an impact on education today?

3. Historically, people from different political parties tend to have distinct perspectives on education. Why is this the case? What are the advantages and disadvantages of certain educational philosophies being associated with particular political parties?

4. Which key educational debates taking place today do you think will have the most puissant effect on the schools of the future? Why?

REFERENCES

Adams, J. (1854). In C. Adams (Ed.), *The works of John Adams, second president of the United States* (Vol. IX). Boston: Little, Brown. Original statement, October 11, 1798

Adams, J. Q. (1850). *Letters of John Quincy Adams to his son on the Bible and its teachings.* Auburn, NY: James M. Alden.

Amano, I. (1990). *Education and examination in Modern Japan.* Tokyo, Japan: University of Tokyo Press.

Bailyn, B. (1960). *Education in the forming of American society.* Chapel Hill: University of North Carolina.

Berlin, I., & Hoffman, R. (1983). *Slavery and freedom in the age of the American Revolution.* Charlottesville: University Press of Virginia.

Bernstein, R. B. (2003). *Thomas Jefferson.* New York: Oxford University Press.

Brown, A. (1890). *The genesis of the United States.* Boston: Houghton, Mifflin.

Chamberlin, G. J. (1961). *Parents and religion: A preface to Christian education.* Philadelphia: Westminster Press.

Connell, J. T. (2004). *The faith of our founding father: The spiritual journey of George Washington.* New York: Hatherleigh Press.

Cremin, L. (1980). *American education: The national experience, 1783–1876.* New York: Harper & Row.

Cremin, L. A. (1976). *Traditions of American education.* New York: Basic Books.

Cubberley, E. (1920). *The history of education.* Boston: Houghton Mifflin.

Cubberley, E. (Ed.). (1934). *Readings in public education in the United States: A collection of sources and readings to illustrate the history of educational practice and progress in the United States.* Cambridge, MA: Riverside Press.

Cubberley, E. P. (1909). *Changing conceptions of education.* New York: Houghton Mifflin.

Dupuis, A. M. (1966). *Philosophy of education in historical perspective.* Chicago: Rand McNally.

Eggleston, E. (1998). *A history of the United States and its people.* Lake Wales, FL: Lost Classics Book Company.

Fraser, J. W. (2001). *The school in the United States.* Boston: McGraw-Hill.

Gangel, K. O., & Benson, W. S. (1983). *Christian education: Its history and philosophy.* Chicago: Moody.

Gurule, K., & Ortega, J. (1973). L. A. decentralization with problems. *Inequality in Education, 15,* 43–44.

Gutek, G. L. (1997). *Historical and philosophical foundations of education.* Upper Saddle River, NJ: Prentice Hall.

Hiner, N. R. (1988). The cry of Sodom enquired into: educational analysis in seventeenth century New England. *The social history of American education* (pp. 3–22). Urbana: University of Illinois Press.

Jefferson, T. (1812). *A manual of parliamentary practice.* Georgetown: Cooper & Milligan.

Johnson, P. (1997). *A history of the American people.* New York: HarperCollins.

Kaestle, C. (1983). *Pillars of the republic: common schools and American society, 1780–1860.* New York: Hill & Wang.

Keenleyside, H. L., & Thomas, A. F. (1937). *History of Japanese education and present educational system.* Tokyo, Japan: Hokuseido Press.

Khan, Y. (1997). *Japanese moral education: Past and present.* Madison, NJ: Fairleigh Dickinson University Press.

Kirk, R. (1953). *The conservative mind.* Chicago: Henry Regnery.

Marcus, J. (1997, September 19). Clinton faces testing war. *Times Educational Supplement,* p. 22.

Marrou, H. I. (1956). *A history of education in antiquity.* New York: Sheed & Ward.

Marshall, P., & Manuel, D. (1977). *The light and the glory.* Grand Rapids, MI: Fleming Revell.

Marshall, P., & Manuel, D. (1997). *Sounding forth the trumpet.* Grand Rapids, MI: Fleming Revell.

McCarthy, T. P., & McMillan, J. C. (2003). *The radical reader: A documentary history of the American radical tradition.* New York: New Press.

McClellan, E. B., & Reese, W. J. (1988). *The social history of American education.* Urbana: University of Illinois Press.

McKivigan, J. R. (1999). *Abolitionism and American religion.* New York: Garland.

Miller, R. M., & Cimbala, P. A. (1996). *American reform and reformers.* Westport, CT: Greenwood Press.

Monroe, P. (1940). *Founding of the American public school system.* New York: Macmillan.

Neill, M. (1998). National tests are unnecessary and harmful. *Educational Leadership, 55*(6), 45–46.

Pulliam, J. D., & Van Patten, J. J. (1999). *History of education in America.* Upper Saddle River, NJ: Merrill/Prentice Hall.

Rippa, S. A. (1997). *Education in a free society.* White Plains, NY: Longman.

Spring, J. (1997). *The American school 1642–1996.* White Plains, NY: Longman.

Stephens, A. H. (1872). *History of the United States.* New York: Hale & Son.

Stevenson, H. W., & Stigler, J. W. (1992). *The learning gap.* New York: Summit Books.

Swanson, A. D., King, R. A., & Sweetland, S. R. (1997). *School finance: Its economics and politics.* White Plains, NY: Longman.

Tewksbury, S. (1932). *Founding of American colleges and universities before the Civil War.* New York: Teachers College Press.

Urban, W., & Wagoner, J. (2000). *American education: A history.* Boston: McGraw-Hill.

U.S. Department of Education. (2002). *No child left behind.* Washington, DC: Author.

U.S. Department of Education. (2005). *Digest of education statistics.* Washington, DC: Author.

Washington, G. (1790). *First annual address to Congress.* Retrieved July 11, 2004, from odur.let.rug.nl/~usa/P/gw1/speeches/gwson1.htm.

Webster, D. (1853). *The works of Daniel Webster* (Vol. I, pp. 41–42). Boston: Little, Brown. Original statement, December 22, 1820.

Webster, N. (1834). *Value of the Bible, and the excellence of the Christian religion: For use of families and schools.* New Haven, CT: Durrie & Peck.

Education, African Americans, and Slavery

The schooling situation for African Americans was vastly different in the North than it was in the South, even before the Revolutionary War. From these early days, there was a potent connection between emancipation and education. Those who favored freedom for all American Blacks viewed education and emancipation as inextricably connected. "The truth shall set you free" was a Bible verse often quoted by educators of the time (Barry, 1870), who declared that education of African Americans was a necessary step toward emancipation and the fruits of full citizenship. In contrast, many slave owners in the South feared that if slaves learned to write, they would inspire rebellion (Van Horne, 1985; Woodson, 1915).

AFRICAN AMERICAN EDUCATION IN THE NORTH

Few statistics more patently delineate the contrast between African American education in the North and in the South than the comparison of literacy rates in the two areas. Estimates differ to some degree, but historians estimate that by the end of the Civil War, African American literacy in the South was no higher than 10% and was probably as low as 2% (Wilson, 1977). In contrast, in 1850, most major U.S. Northern cities had African American literacy rates of 64% to 97% (Bergman & Bergman, 1969). Generally, cities further north (see Table 4.1), such as Providence (97%), New York (88%), and Boston (90%), had higher rates of literacy than cities that bordered the South, such as Washington, D.C. (65%), and Baltimore (64%) (Bergman & Bergman, 1969).

A large part of the disparity in the North-vs.-South percentages finds its roots in differences in educational access. In New York, the same percentage of White and African American children attended school (Bergman & Bergman, 1969). In the South, states passed laws in the 1830s and 1840s to forbid the schooling of slaves (Bullock, 1970; Wilson, 1977). Although the gulf in educational opportunities for Blacks was especially vast in 1850, the disparity developed well before the Revolutionary War, because these two regions went in very different directions regarding the education of African Americans (Bullock, 1970; Copeland, 2000).

Table 4.1   Rates of Literacy for African American Adults in Major Northern Cities in 1850

Far-Northern Cities	African American Literacy Rate (%)	Northern Cities Closer to the Southern Border	African American Literacy Rate (%)
Providence, RI	97	Cincinnati, OH	81
Boston, MA	90	Philadelphia, PA	67
New York, NY	88	Washington, DC	65
New Haven, CT	83	Baltimore, MD	64
		Louisville, KY	63

The Puritans and the Quakers

Well before the Revolutionary War period, a number of British and American groups attempted to educate African Americans (Bullock, 1970; Harrison, 1893). The Society for the Propagation of the Gospel, the British missionary group, was founded in 1661 under the name the Propagation of the Gospel and assumed its permanent name in 1701 (Harrison, 1893; Urban & Wagoner, 2000). The Society for the Propagation for the Gospel was a Puritan-sponsored group that launched hundreds of schools designed to teach the gospel and to promote literacy (Harrison, 1893). The leaders of these schools encouraged many African Americans to attend, so they could learn to read the Bible, poems, and other eminent books (Bullock, 1970; Harrison, 1893). Given that the Puritans were located in the North, these efforts were far more rife in the North than in the South (Cornelius, 1991; Harrison, 1893). Nevertheless, Puritan leaders called on slave owners, concentrated particularly in the South, to furnish their slaves with Bibles and other books to help ensure that they could learn to read (Cornelius, 1991). John Eliot (cited in Cornelius, 1991, p. 14) excoriated slaveholders for perpetrating "a destroying ignorance" upon the slaves by not encouraging them to read and write.

The majority of the groups (including the Puritans, Quakers, and other groups) involved in educating African Americans viewed literacy as a major step to achieving liberation and equality for African Americans (Cornelius, 1991; Schwartz, 2000). In retrospect, one can see that the two were, in fact, closely related. African Americans who learned to read at these early Puritan-sponsored schools used their writing skills to compose pleas to the courts asking for freedom (Cornelius, 1991; Schwartz, 2000).

The Quakers also regarded African American literacy as a vital development if emancipation were to occur (Copeland, 2000; Schwartz, 2000; Sterling, 1991). The Quakers were the first in the colonies to formally organize an effort to ban slavery from America's shores, and in 1724, they went so far as to say that the seizure of slaves in Africa was an act of war (Copeland, 2000; Vahey, 1998). The Quakers were very tolerant of minority populations. For example, they had no objections to interracial marriage (Wilson, 1977). These attitudes carried over to their work in educating African Americans (Sterling, 1991; Vahey, 1998).

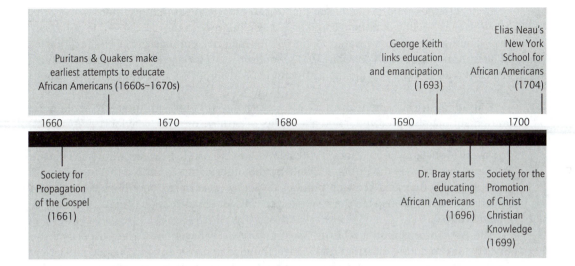

Puritans & Quakers make
earliest attempts to educate
African Americans (1660s–1670s)

George Keith
links education
and emancipation
(1693)

Elias Neau's
New York
School for
African Americans
(1704)

1660   1670   1680   1690   1700

Society for
Propagation
of the Gospel
(1661)

Dr. Bray starts
educating
African Americans
(1696)

Society for the
Promotion
of Christ
Christian
Knowledge
(1699)

The Quakers had a very proactive approach to purging slavery from the land, of which education constituted one prong. They formulated a plan for educating slaves and then returning them to their homeland in Africa. The Quaker plan was inspired by the words of George Keith, who in 1693 declared that religious and literacy training for slaves was needed in order to prepare them for emancipation (Woodson, 1915). The Quakers not only taught slaves to read the Bible and the classics but also put great emphasis on teaching them the "duties of citizenship" (Woodson, 1915, pp. 43–44).

The Quakers, however, thought that other aspects were also necessary to ensure emancipation and full educational opportunity. Quaker ministers such as Elias Hicks and John Wollman sponsored widespread boycotts of goods produced by slave labor (Vahey, 1998). Wollman went so far as to say that to buy products made by slaves was as bad as owning slaves (Vahey, 1998). In later years, other evangelical groups would apply the same techniques to pressure slave owners (Roth, 1999). James Milligan was another Quaker prominent in calling for putting political pressure on slave owners (Roth, 1999). Quakers believed that African Americans could experience a full and appropriate education only if they were free.

Added Insight

The Quakers were also the most active organized group involved in the Underground Railroad (Copeland, 2000; Sterling, 1991; Vahey, 1998). Several Quaker families, including the Coffins, Wittsets, Motts, and Hicks families, were especially renowned for their involvement in the organization. Levi Coffin was the so-called president of the Underground Railroad and was a major advocate for educating African Americans (Vahey, 1998). Across many cities in the United States, Quakers were highly organized in their efforts to free the slaves. In 1776 alone, Long Island Quakers successfully freed 154 slaves (Vahey, 1998). Once slaves were freed, the Quakers once again emphasized educating African Americans so that they could experience the joys of true citizenship (Sterling, 1991).

Even with these efforts to educate the African American community, there was not the progress in schooling that there could have been. In America overall, a low rate of literacy even among Whites contributed to the White majority emphasizing the education of Whites more than Blacks (Wilson, 1977; Woodson, 1915). Naturally, had a greater abundance of teachers emphasized the instruction of African Americans, more progress would have been seen.

Educating African Americans not only went hand in hand with the early abolitionist movement but also predated it and abetted its rise (Harrison, 1893; Taylor, 1999; Wilson, 1977). Shortly after 1700, there appeared in the colonies the first organized calls for an end to slavery (Copeland, 2000; Vahey, 1998; Zdrok-Ptaszek, 2002). However, efforts to educate African Americans by the Puritans, Quakers, and other groups predated this time. In fact, one can argue that as a growing number of people discovered how intelligent African Americans were, this inspired the systematized calls for emancipation (Vahey, 1998; Zdrok-Ptaszek, 2002).

The Puritan organizations of the Society for the Propagation of the Gospel and the Society for Promoting Christian Knowledge, founded in 1699, not only helped make New England develop the most minority-friendly education system in the New World but also enabled the area to become the center of the antislavery movement (Wilson, 1977). The Quaker efforts to educate African Americans ultimately yielded political clout via William Penn and Benjamin Franklin (Washington, 1969; Spring, 1997). Booker T. Washington (1969) notes that "the pious philanthropist, William Penn, tried in vain to embody his anti-slavery sentiments in the law of the province" (p. 114). Technically, his Pennsylvania bill of 1712 "was passed emancipating slaves by law, but was repealed by Queen Anne" (p. 114).

Benjamin Franklin was also influenced by an early Quaker, Anthony Benezet (Bergman & Bergman, 1969). Franklin became a mainstay of the emancipation movement by printing a book by an antislavery Quaker, Benjamin Lay (Bergman & Bergman, 1969), supporting Benezet's first free school for African Americans in Philadelphia (Bergman & Bergman, 1969; Woodson, 1915) and becoming president of the Philadelphia Abolitionist Society (Spring, 1997). In 1790, Franklin also appealed to the United States to remove slavery from the Constitution (Bergman & Bergman, 1969). Moreover, Franklin founded a school for African Americans that would last nearly a century (Copeland, 2000; Wilson, 1977).

Other Efforts Dedicated to the Education of African Americans

As time went by, a growing number of organizations and individuals focused on educating African Americans (Wimberly, 1977). Reverend Doctor Bray began educating African Americans in Maryland in 1696 (Woodson, 1915). After he died, his associates continued his work (Bergman & Bergman, 1969; Van Horne, 1985; Woodson, 1915). A group called "Associates of Reverend Doctor Bray" was one of the most remarkable groups dedicated to schooling African Americans. In 1723, the group sent money to establish schools and libraries to educate African Americans (Van Horne, 1985). In 1740, Associates of Dr. Bray inaugurated a school for African Americans in South Carolina, and, in 1759 and 1760, they started two in Philadelphia (Bergman & Bergman, 1969, Van Horne, 1985). The Associates gained enough repute that Benjamin Franklin joined the group (Bergman & Bergman, 1969).

Many influential individuals in the pre–Revolutionary War era also played a major role in educating African Americans. Ezra Stiles, later president of Yale, attempted to train African

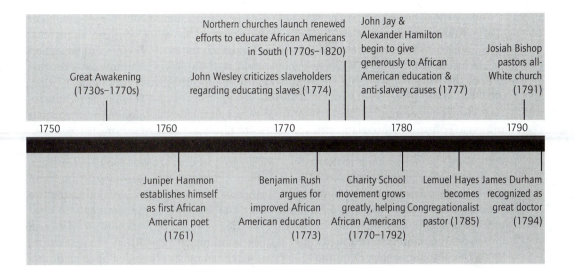

Great Awakening
(1730s–1770s)

Northern churches launch renewed
efforts to educate African Americans
in South (1770s–1820)

John Wesley criticizes slaveholders
regarding educating slaves (1774)

John Jay &
Alexander Hamilton
begin to give
generously to African
American education &
anti-slavery causes (1777)

Josiah Bishop
pastors all-
White church
(1791)

1750   1760   1770   1780   1790

Juniper Hammon
establishes himself
as first African
American poet
(1761)

Benjamin Rush
argues for
improved African
American education
(1773)

Charity School
movement grows
greatly, helping
African Americans
(1770–1792)

Lemuel Hayes
becomes
Congregationalist
pastor (1785)

James Durham
recognized as
great doctor
(1794)

Americans for the ministry (Harrison, 1893). Many northeastern churches opened up schools for freed slaves (Harrison, 1893). In 1704, Elias Neau launched a school for African Americans in New York City. By 1708, Neau had 200 students in his school (Woodson, 1915).

The growth of printed magazines and books, the antislavery views of most of the founding fathers, and the proliferation of antislavery societies all contributed to the expansion of schooling opportunities for African Americans (Copeland, 2000). Speeches like those of William Pinkney (1788) and Benjamin Rush (1773) helped many Americans to apprehend the intellectual abilities of African Americans. Pinkney (1788), in a speech before the Maryland House of Delegates, stated his belief that "Negroes are not worse than white people under similar conditions" (p. 6). Benjamin Rush (1773), a founding father and regarded as the nations foremost physician, argued that African Americans had a right to be educated. Two of the leading founders and Federalist Party members, John Jay and Alexander Hamilton, probably invested more money than anyone else into New York African American schooling (Jay, 1801). Jay dedicated much of his life, energy, and money to building free schools for African Americans. Hamilton helped toward this end as well and was secretary of the New York Abolitionist Society (Washington, 1969). The fact that both Jay, the nation's first Supreme Court chief justice, and Alexander Hamilton, the first secretary of the treasury, were both strong supporters of schooling for African Americans in New York helped catapult New York into the position of having the finest education for African Americans in the country, even eventually surpassing New England (Jay, 1801; Woodson, 1915). Jay believed that it was essential that African American schools ensure high attendance and have high standards in maintenance and supervision.

The growth of abolitionist societies in the 1700s and early- to mid-1800s also aided the growth of African American education (Taylor, 1999). By 1838, there were 1,300 societies in the United States, with hundreds of thousands of members (Filler, 2002; Zdrok-Ptaszek, 2002). On a number of occasions, abolitionist organizations specifically called for the increased education of slaves (Woodson, 1915). For example, in 1794, the American Convention of Abolition Societies called for the education of slaves in quality literature (Woodson, 1915).

The growing chorus of politicians, religious leaders, and abolitionist societies calling for African American education yielded another type of boon as well. Over time, an increasing number of White Americans were donating land and money for the cause of education for Blacks (Benezet, 1871; Wimberly, 1977; Woodson, 1915). When Anthony Benezet died in 1784, he left a considerable amount of wealth to educate African Americans (Spring, 1997; Woodson, 1915). Abiel Smith, the Massachusetts investor, and Thaddeus Kosciuszko, the Polish engineer and freedom fighter for America in the Revolutionary War, also left a fortune to construct schools for African Americans (Spring, 1997; Woodson, 1915).

Three other groups quite committed to educating African Americans were the Baptists, Methodists, and Presbyterians (Harrison, 1893; Wimberly, 1977; Woodson, 1915). Each group not only opened schools to educate African Americans but also was eager to train African American ministers (Harrison, 1893; Woodson, 1915). This was especially attractive to many African Americans because being a minister was one of the two or three most honored occupations of the time (Cornelius, 1991; Harrison, 1893; Woodson, 1915). Not all church denominations were as dedicated as these in training African Americans (Harrison, 1893). Generally speaking, denominations that had been most influenced by the spiritual revival called the "Great Awakening of the Mid-1700s" and its call for spiritual renewal and education were more involved in educating African Americans than were denominations that were not as influenced (Cornelius, 1991; Harrison, 1893; Marty, 1968). The Great Awakening was a religious revival that called for a renewed emphasis on one's relationship with God and influenced many of the nation's founders and leading educators.

The Debate Over the Need for African American Education

Even with these efforts to educate African Americans, many people, particularly in the South, strongly opposed the education of African Americans. First, some people believed that it was not very practical to educate Blacks and that it was valuable only insofar as it contributed to them working more efficaciously. This meant that according to these people, African Americans did not need much education at all.

Second, some Southerners, especially, believed that education would enable African Americans to organize and revolt (Copeland, 2000). This point is particularly interesting, because it reveals some guilt on the part of slaveholders and other opponents of African American education. If slavery was not that bad an institution, why would slaves revolt if they were educated? Clearly, many slaveholders knew deep down in their hearts that the slavery institution was oppressive. Third, some people viewed African Americans as inferior in the sense of either being stubborn or less intelligent. Therefore, some people argued that African Americans would not benefit from education in a way commensurate with that of Whites.

A number of leaders at the time of the American Revolution abetted the cause of African American education considerably (Copeland, 2000). A number of the founding fathers took positions that the federal government needed to take action to educate African Americans and even to extricate them. Benjamin Franklin supported the education of Blacks for three reasons: (a) It would make them Christians; (b) they were human beings also; and (c) it would make them more economically efficient (Copeland, 2000). His arguments were a clear rebuttal to most of the points raised by opponents of the education of African Americans. There is little question that Benjamin Franklin intended his views to totally undermine the assertions of these opponents. Franklin thought that those who argued that African Americans were intellectually inferior were simply giving a "silly excuse" (Woodson, 1915). He asserted that schooling Blacks would surely yield in them, as in anyone, great moral and intellectual benefits (Cornelius, 1991; Woodson, 1915). He further asserted that an educated worker was better than an ignorant one, because the former is more likely to suggest successful ways to improve productivity.

Anthony Benezet (1871) was straightforward in his assertion of the equality of African Americans: "I can with truth and sincerity declare I have found in the Negroes as great a variety of talents as amongst whites and I am bold to assert that" (p. 1).

John Wesley, the founder of the Methodist Church, and George Buchanan, an early abolitionist, were two of the most courageous individuals in challenging the slaveholders, who so many people feared. In addressing the slave owners, John Wesley (1774) declared, "Allowing them [the slaves] to be as stupid as you say, to whom is that stupidity owing" (p. 1). Wesley went on to say that not only were Africans Americans not inferior to Europeans, they were actually superior to some of them. Buchanan (1793) averred "that the Africans whom you despise, whom you inhumanely treat as brutes, and whom you unlawfully subject to slavery with tyrannizing hands of despots are equally capable of improvement with yourselves" (n.p.).

Despite these encouraging statements, advocates of African American education had to contend not only with people who thought that educating African Americans was a waste of time because they were intellectually inferior but also with those who claimed that schooling African Americans was a worthy endeavor despite their intellectual inferiority. Thomas Jefferson (1903) held this perspective, and it was of little help to those who emphasized the essential nature of educating African Americans. Jefferson and others like him contended that African Americans were capable of benefiting from education but were not apt to reach intellectual parity with White people.

Acceleration of the Charity School Movement

The formation of charity schools by northeastern settlers and their striking growth following the Revolutionary War yielded many benefits for African Americans. Charity schools focused on meeting the educational needs of the impecunious (Bobbe, 1933; Cornog, 1998). African Americans constituted one of the poorest ethnic groups. Therefore, efficiently run charity schools were one of the North's best answers to the socioeconomic enigmas faced by these individuals (Andrews. 1969). The African American population also faced another problem, in that a large portion of their population in the North were freed slaves.

The belief by the White majority at the time was that freed slaves had unique needs (Andrews, 1969; Woodson, 1915). The White majority knew that these former slaves had been treated as chattel and also that most of them had received little in the way of traditional educational training (Spring, 1997). It was therefore believed that special schools designed for these freed slaves would be most salutary in terms of mainstreaming them into society (Spring, 1997). How much of the establishment of these special schools came out of good will and how much was due to racism is hard to say. Woodson (1915), perhaps the greatest African American historian, believes that these schools were established with good intentions and were not a product of racism. The motivation, however, could well be some combination of these two motives.

African Americans in the North were lawfully permitted to attend any school that White children attended. No law in the North at that time forced segregation (Woodson, 1915).

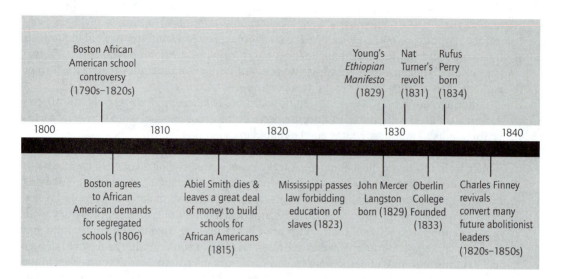

Boston African American school controversy (1790s–1820s)

Young's *Ethiopian Manifesto* (1829)

Nat Turner's revolt (1831)

Rufus Perry born (1834)

1800   1810   1820   1830   1840

Boston agrees to African American demands for segregated schools (1806)

Abiel Smith dies & leaves a great deal of money to build schools for African Americans (1815)

Mississippi passes law forbidding education of slaves (1823)

John Mercer Langston born (1829)

Oberlin College Founded (1833)

Charles Finney revivals convert many future abolitionist leaders (1820s–1850s)

Nevertheless, due to (a) poor economic conditions and (b) the awkwardness of attending school with Whites, numerous African Americans did not attend public and private schools that were operated by the White majority (Spring, 1997; Woodson, 1915). As a result, in the North, many African Americans felt more comfortable sending their children to schools solely designed to help freed slaves. Such schools were opened in Philadelphia in 1770, in New York in 1787, and in Baltimore in 1792 (Bergman & Bergman, 1969; Spring, 1997). The Lancasterian schools in New York were especially successful in reaching out to African Americans (Andrews, 1969; Bergman & Bergman, 1969). This was important, because there were few African Americans who could afford to pay tuition. Therefore, the more efficiently a school was run, the more poor people could be helped (Jones, 1964; Kaestle, 1973).

In most Northern cities, African Americans were in one of several school situations. Generally speaking, over 70% of African Americans went to some type of charity school (Woodson, 1915). For example, in Philadelphia, in 1859, about 77% of African American students attended charity schools (Woodson, 1915). Many African Americans attended schools with White children. However, over 40% of African American students attended schools designed for freed slaves (Woodson, 1915).

African Americans, particularly freed slaves, often struggled with the kind of schooling situation that was suitable for them (Jay, 1801). African Americans had Sunday schools and both Black and integrated charity schools (Woodson, 1915). However, some African Americans believed that education would best serve their youth if schools were self-run (Spring, 1997). During the late 1700s and 1800s, African Americans increasingly started their own schools, several by 1830 (Woodson, 1915). The struggle that African Americans faced regarding how best to educate their children is best exemplified in a situation that they faced in Boston, beginning in the 1790s. At this time in Boston, there were a total of 766 Blacks out of a total population of 18,038 (Schultz, 1973). In other words, about 4% of the student population was African American. The poverty of the African Americans and the unwelcome reception they sometimes received in Boston's public schools made some African Americans yearn for something better (Schultz, 1973).

Many African Americans in the 1790s concluded that their children could learn more productively in a segregated setting (Schultz, 1973). As a result, the African American community petitioned the Boston School Committee, asking for separate schools. However, the committee refused the request, concerned that if they did agree to it, they might have to give separate schools for all of Boston's ethnic groups (Schultz, 1973).

Given that the public schools frustrated the African American desire for separate schools, they obtained support from private White sources to begin all-Black private schools (Schultz, 1973). The public schools feared that they would lose all the Black students to the private schools. Consequently, the Boston School Committee finally agreed to the demands of African Americans in 1806 and secured the necessary funding for the schools in 1812. However, the Boston School committee could not obtain all the money they needed from public sources. They also had to rely on private donations. A substantial portion of the funding came from a White man named Abiel Smith (Schultz, 1973), who died in 1815 and "left the entire income from his shares in New England turnpikes and bridges and from United States bonds to be used for the support of black schools" (Spring, 1997, p. 87).

But by the 1820s, some people in the African American community began to question the wisdom of segregated schools (Schultz, 1973). In 1833, the Boston School Committee concluded that the quality of education that Blacks were receiving was inferior to that of White students. After complaints continued, the government of Massachusetts signed into law a bill calling for racial integration (Schultz, 1973). Technically, the law was not necessary, because Massachusetts law already allowed for school integration. Nevertheless, the state's political leaders believed it was wise to make a definite legal declaration calling for integration. The Boston School Committee's conclusion was a precursor to the 1954 *Brown v. Board of Education* Supreme Court decision, which declared that in those areas of the country with de jure (forced) segregation, schools that African Americans attended in large numbers tended to be inferior to schools with a majority of White students. No violence resulted from the integration (Schultz, 1973).

Contemporary Focus

Afrocentric Schools

The issue of self-run schools is particularly relevant because of the move among some African Americans, particularly supported by Molefi Kete Asante, toward Afrocentric schools (Asante 1987). Asante is a multiculturalist who believes that African American children should be able to attend Afrocentric schools. He believes that given the vast number of cultures now represented in American schools, it is impossible for African American students to adequately learn about their culture unless they attend Afrocentric schools. Many American educators have expressed concern that this amounts to segregation and is a move backward. Educational leaders, such as Gary Orfield (1996), have warned that the United States is becoming resegregated. However, Asante argues that this segregation is justified because, as in the 1790s-to-1820s Boston case described in this chapter, African Americans are asking to be segregated.

- What do you think? Are Afrocentric schools a positive development?

African American Leaders

Many African Americans educated in the North emerged as major American figures who made a difference in the history of the United States (Ross, 2003). They entered a variety of occupations and made an impact on American society in a number of ways. The fact that Northern schools provided a means for educating these African Americans served as a turning point in American educational history. In many respects, the hope for African American progress, self-determination, and the realization of potential depended on education. The fact that many of these leaders used their academic training to make great contributions to society served to raise the aspirations of other African Americans and to gain the respect of many White Americans as well. The accomplishments by these individuals across a gamut of disciplines established a foundation and example that many African Americans could follow.

Richard Allen was surely an African American hero and can best be described as the "Martin Luther King Jr. of his day" (Wilson, 1977; Woodson, 1915). Allen founded the African Methodist Episcopal (AME) church denomination and inaugurated the denomination's first church in Philadelphia. He enjoyed great renown within both the African American and White communities. On many occasions, Allen traveled with White pastors to minister jointly in sundry situations (Woodson, 1915).

Josiah Bishop was called on in 1791 to pastor an all-White church in Portsmouth, Virginia (Bergman & Bergman, 1969; Woodson, 1915). The fact that he was privileged to take such a post points to a number of encouraging realities. First, it indicates that Bishop was not a racist. Second, it shows that this all-White church in Virginia was not racist. Third, it suggests the high educational abilities of Bishop (Woodson, 1915).

James Durham was also an African American hero. Educated in Philadelphia, he moved to the South and became one of the foremost physicians in New Orleans (Brissot de Warville, 1794). Durham spoke three languages fluently (Spanish, English, and French) and was such a distinguished doctor that he gained the attention and praise of Benjamin Rush, the nation's foremost physician. Rush met with Durham and said of him, "I learned more from him than he could expect from me" (Rush, cited in Baldwin, 1834). Rush, a signer of the Declaration of Independence, no doubt helped establish himself as a humble man by making such a statement. Nevertheless, he also helped elevate the stature of Dr. Durham to one of the most intelligent physicians in the country.

The intellectual accomplishments of African Americans educated north of Washington, D.C., were broad. Benjamin Baneker, of Baltimore County, manufactured the first clock made in pre–Revolutionary War America (Woodson, 1915). Before this time, the British government discouraged the colonies from engaging in technological innovation. The British concern was that colonial technological innovation could subvert the balance of trade between England and the New World (Woodson & Wesley, 1968). They wanted the colonies to supply raw materials to England and be dependent on Britain for human-made goods (Woodson & Wesley, 1968). Baneker had little concern about this requisite. With no concern for how the British might respond, Baneker contributed to a growing sense of self-sufficiency among the settlers (Woodson, 1915).

Educated African Americans not only made advances in fields that were demonstratively practical but also penetrated the artistic realm (Bergman & Bergman, 1969; Woodson & Wesley, 1968). In 1761, Jupiter Hammon established himself as a writer and probably the first African American poet with *Salvation by Christ, With Penitential Cries,* the first piece of literature published in the United States by a person of African descent. In 1770, Joshua Johnston became the first African American painter, and in the 1800s, Robert Duncanson became an established Black artist (Bergman & Bergman, 1969). Ira Aldridge became a well-known African American actress, who performed Shakespeare (Woodson & Wesley, 1968).

Increasingly, during the early to mid-1800s, via education, African Americans were making substantial contributions, first in ministry and later in education (Woodson & Wesley, 1968). They gained a new level of recognition in the North as many became ministers (Ross, 2003). Although the vast majority of African American ministers pastored Black congregations, the availability of innumerable pulpits in the North gave them an opportunity to influence society and present their ideas to a degree that they had not enjoyed previously (Ross, 2003). This influence expanded as some African Americans pastored all-White churches. Congregationalist and Baptist churches were probably the most open denominations to this arrangement, and Lemuel Haynes was probably the most esteemed of these ministers. Haynes became a Congregationalist pastor in 1785 and became the first African American Pastor of an all-White Congregational Church in 1818 (Bergman & Bergman, 1969). An eloquent orator and thinker, Haynes' sermons appealed to both Blacks and Whites.

In the 1780s, the Baptist church declared slavery as a "violation of the right of nature" (Bergman & Bergman, 1969, p. 6). This attitude attracted many African Americans to the Baptist denomination who aspired to be ministers (Bergman & Bergman, 1969; Woodson, 1915). Other than Josiah Bishop's church in Virginia, perhaps the most well-known Southern all-White church pastored by an African American was Hard Shell Baptist Church, in Tennessee. The church was not only all White but also included many of the most prominent and wealthy people in the state (Woodson, 1915). Sojourner Truth, a woman who escaped slavery in 1826, preached many abolitionist messages that inspired both African Americans and Whites (Ross, 2003). In 1849, Rev. Charles Avery founded Avery College, an African American college in Pennsylvania (Woodson, 1915).

As the mid-1800s progressed, African Americans were making a mark in education and journalism (Bergman & Bergman, 1969). Edward Mitchell and Richard Theodore Greener became the first African Americans to graduate from Dartmouth and Harvard, respectively (Bergman & Bergman, 1969). Rufus Lewis Perry (1834–1895) became a highly regarded African American educator and journalist (Bergman & Bergman, 1969).

African Americans educated in the North also played an important role in government in the immediate post–Civil War period. Right after the Civil War, many African Americans were elected to Congress and state legislatures (Bergman & Bergman, 1969). African Americans were also appointed to various government positions, including five that were named superintendents of education for their respective states (Wilson, 1977).

John Mercer Langston (1829–1897) was an African American who graduated from Oberlin College and was elected to Congress. Nearly all African Americans elected to Congress were either educated in the North or instructed by people from the North (Bergman & Bergman, 1969; Woodson, 1915). A fair number of African Americans were elected to Congress shortly after the Civil War, including Alonzo Ranzier (1834–1882) and Jeremiah Haralson (1846–1916). In later years, Thomas Ezekiel Miller (1849–1937) would also be elected. African Americans excelled in other occupations as well. Robert Morris and George Vashon became lawyers. John Rock became not only a lawyer but also a dentist, physician, and teacher (Woodson & Wesley, 1968).

Early in the 19th century, it appeared that at least in the North, many aspects of the education of African Americans were headed in the right direction (Bergman & Bergman, 1969). But while many African Americans became productive citizens and did not stir up any trouble for society, others did encourage revolt (Woodson & Wesley, 1968). The fact that a number of educated African Americans were leading revolts in certain cities appeared to confirm the worst apprehensions of many Whites. Toussaint L'Ouverture led a successful Black revolt in Haiti over the seeming indomitable forces of France (Woodson & Wesley, 1968). This encouraged many Blacks to think that they could obtain freedom as well. African American revolts occurred, especially in the South (Child, 1794/2002). Nat Turners's revolt of 1831 may be the most famous, but there were other revolts as well, in places like Virginia and South Carolina (Wilson, 1977; Woodson, 1915). And, indeed, educated African Americans were leading these revolts. This fact confirmed the worst fears of many Southerners (Child, 1794/2002; Wilson, 1977).

Many of the African Americans who organized Black revolts were either educated in the North or were educated in the South by Northerners (Wilson, 1977). This brings us to tracing the history of the education of African Americans in the South.

EDUCATION OF AFRICAN AMERICANS IN THE SOUTH

Even during the colonial period, African Americans generally received a lesser degree of education than they did in the North. This does not mean that there was a dearth of attempts by certain groups to educate African Americans. Rather, the Southern governments acted to block many of these attempts (Woodson, 1915). Even in colonial days, many Southern governments resisted the education of African Americans. During the 1660s and 1670s, the Quakers were actively involved in educating African Americans (Woodson, 1915). But in the 1670s, the governor of North Carolina blocked the Quakers from educating African Americans unless they obtained a license from the Bishop of London. The Quakers were enraged and replied, "Who made you ministers of the Gospel to white people only?" (Woodson, 1915, p. 68). Even the Southern Methodist church, which supported slavery, nevertheless encouraged the education of Blacks. This may be one reason so many Blacks in the South joined the Methodist Church (Woodson, 1915).

The Southern governments turned their backs on educating African Americans. In addition, the Northerners were taking too little action to end slavery. Southern churches, philanthropists, and other individuals who could have taken more action to educate African Americans than they did often failed to take appropriate action because they feared the puissance of the slave owners (Woodson, 1915). Some ministers and educators established schools for African Americans. Samuel Thomas, a minister, founded a well-known school for Blacks in South Carolina in 1744 (Bergman & Bergman, 1969).

Alternative Means of Educating African Americans in the South

The fact that the United States failed to address the slavery issue head-on meant that alternative means of educating African Americans in the South had to be found. Those in the South generally made little or no attempt to educate African Americans. And when Southerners did educate their slaves, it was largely with the intent of making them more effective workers (Bullock, 1967).

Most Southerners, however, had no objection to African Americans learning the Bible, which opened a door for Northern Christians. Many Northern Christians and abolitionists were frustrated with the lack of action by the U.S. government to end slavery (Alley, 2002; Loveland, 1999; Miller, 1996). Many of these individuals had hoped for decades that a president would rise up with enough conviction and resolve to eliminate the cancer of slavery. They were frustrated that the government nearly always decided to go in the direction of compromise when addressing the slavery quagmire. This frustration lasted so many years that Northern churches and abolitionists, in essence, gave up on the possibility that the government could resolve the slavery issue (Loveland, 1999; Miller, 1996). Consequently, many Northern Christians and abolitionists decided to take matters into their own hands. The fact that the United States failed to address the slavery issue head-on meant that alternative means of educating African Americans in the South had to be found (Daniels, 1903; Jones, 1832; Sims, 1926; Stowell, 2000; Sutton, 1912).

Northern religious people and abolitionists saw education and liberation for the slaves as inextricably connected (DuBois, 1913). They maintained this perspective for two reasons. First, they viewed education as a liberation of the mind that could expediently accompany emancipation. Second, teaching would give instructors an opportunity to build relationships with the slaves, so that they could help them escape and/or instruct them that slavery was wrong (Copeland, 2000; Schwartz, 2000; Sterling, 1991). Numerous Northern religious organizations sent down teachers to the South hoping to bring freedom to the slaves and to raise the their literacy levels (Daniels, 1903; Jones, 1832; Sims, 1926; Stowell, 2000; Sutton, 1912; Woodson, 1915).

The Northern Christians believed they could both educate African Americans and see them become Christians by teaching them using the Bible, and vast numbers of individuals from different denominations participated in this attempt (Bullock, 1967; Daniels, 1903; Jones, 1832; Sims, 1926; Stowell, 2000; Sutton, 1912). Considering the obstacles involved, this educational outreach was quite effective. Bullock (1967) notes that in some Southern states, most slaves received an education as a result of these efforts. However, Bullock also notes that in other states, well under half of the slaves received this benefit.

Bullock (1967, p. 11) attributes a large amount of the success of these efforts to what he terms the "informal permissiveness" of many Southerners when it came to education. Bullock notes that this informal permissiveness allowed the Quakers, in particular, to make dramatic gains in literacy among slaves toward the end of the 18th century. Furthermore, Bullock (1967) adds,

> By the opening of the nineteenth century, permissiveness had eroded the plantation society's rational policy, and new educational opportunities had opened up for . . . slaves. . . . The institution of slavery had become infected with a form of indulgence that was eventually to create an educated group of slaves and would supply leadership on behalf on their own freedom. (p. 7)

Bullock goes on to say,

> Signs that informal permissiveness would result in formal education for the South's Negroes were already abundant . . . missions that arose around slavery were never killed; they were allowed to form the nucleus of a movement for formal schooling among free Negroes and slaves. (p. 11)

Bullock (1967) and other historians note that as time passed, various religious groups, including Presbyterians and Quakers, became more "bold" in establishing schools for African Americans in the South. Over time, tens of thousands of African Americans attended the literacy schools (Daniels, 1903; Sims, 1926; Stowell, 2000; Sutton, 1912). The long-term influence of these schools is best summarized by Bullock (1967), when he stated, "Probably the heaviest blow that Negroes struck against slavery came from those slaves who had gained their education under bondage and escaped North to join the antislavery movement" (p. 14). The literacy rates of African Americans skyrocketed from 2% around 1760 to 25% by 1820 (Bullock, 1967; Daniels, 1903; Sims, 1926; Stowell, 2000; Sutton, 1912; Wilson, 1977; Woodson, 1915). The literacy rates for African American males rose almost as high as that for Southern White males (Wilson, 1977; Woodson, 1915). But the Northern churches had an additional motive that they did not so readily reveal to Southern Whites: They taught African Americans that the Bible taught that slavery was wrong (Daniels, 1903; Sims, 1926; Stowell, 2000; Sutton, 1912). Unfortunately, in one of the saddest chapters in American educational history, these advances in literacy were not allowed to last.

Beginning in the 1790s, slaveholders and others opposing education for slaves were quick to blame White Northern Christians for slave revolts (Bergman & Bergman, 1969; Woodson, 1915). The tension grew to a climax when, in 1796, a North Carolina Grand Jury formally blamed the Quakers for slave revolts in a number of cities (Bergman & Bergman, 1969). Eventually, the attempt by religious and other abolitionist groups to educate slaves in the South would only reinforce that perspective. The efforts of these Northern educators along with three incidents particularly invoked the wrath of slaveholders against Northern educators. The first took place in February, 1829, when an African American educated in New York, Robert Alexander Young, wrote a widely circulated pamphlet titled *Ethiopian Manifesto, Issued in Defense of the Black Man's Rights in the Scale of Universal Freedom*. In this pamphlet, Young warned of God's judgment because of slavery (Cornelius, 1991; Young, 1829).

Nat Turner's revolt of August 1831 played an even more prominent role in arousing the hostility of slaveholders toward Northern educators of slaves (Cornelius, 1991; DuBois, 1913; King, 1995). Educated by White Baptists, Turner was a literate African American from Virginia who believed he was God's messenger to bring liberation to the slaves (King, 1995; Woodson, 1915). Nat Turner's revolt served to reveal the extent to which the efforts by Northern church groups to educate slaves had as much to do with encouraging liberation of the slaves as it did with educating them (Cornelius, 1991; Woodson, 1915). As a result, Turner's rebellion was called "the Baptist War." The revolt left 61 White men, women, and children dead (Cornelius, 1991; King, 1995, Woodson, 1915; Woodson & Wesley, 1968). The final event occurred when Boston-educated African American David Walker also warned of God's judgment for slavery (Cornelius, 1991). Walker's claim that God would send a series of physical and economic calamities upon the nation stirred many people in the country, especially with the onset of the 1857 recession.

Many slave owners had discovered dual motives of liberating and educating well before the preceding three events (Wilson, 1977), and they petitioned the Southern governors to pass laws to forbid the teaching of slaves (Van Horne, 1985).

As a result of the petitions of the slave owners, one by one, Southern governments either forced or intimidated the church schools into closing (Cornelius, 1991; Knight & Hall, 1951; Woodson, 1915). Each state had a slightly different legal technique to bring this goal to pass, but each law possessed the same intended consequence. For instance, in 1823, Mississippi made it illegal for five or more Blacks to meet together for educational purposes (Cornelius, 1991; Woodson, 1915). The procession of similar laws passed by other states gained real momentum after the publication of Young's pamphlet of 1829 and the Nat Turner revolt of 1831 (Cornelius, 1991). In 1829 and 1831, Georgia provided fines, whipping, or imprisonment for anyone teaching slaves to read and write (Cornelius, 1991; Knight & Hall, 1951; Woodson, 1915). North Carolina continued the trend in 1830 and 1835 by forbidding "teaching or giving books to slaves" (Cornelius, 1991). Also in 1830, Louisiana specified that there would be a 1- to 12-month prison term for anyone who taught slaves. Virginia and Alabama also passed laws punishing people who taught African Americans to read and write (Cornelius, 1991; Woodson, 1915).

South Carolina passed the most stringent law against teaching slaves (Cornelius, 1991; Woodson, 1915). One man in particular, State Senator Whitemarsh Seabrook, argued successfully for an austere law preventing the spread of literacy among slaves (Cornelius, 1991). The law was not only one of the most specific of the anti-literacy laws but also contained the fewest loopholes and threatened violators with some of the most severe punishments. The strong nature of the South Carolina bill caused many people from out of state to take action to attempt to force South Carolina to repeal the bill. However, these efforts were not successful (Cornelius, 1991).

Southern states that punished those who taught slaves generally sought to make a public example of the violators, so that other educators would be discouraged from teaching. This approach achieved the desired result, while minimizing the unsavory publicity that would result from enforcement (Cornelius, 1991). In 1854, Miss Douglass, in Norfolk, Virginia, was caught illegally teaching Blacks, the result of the Enactment of the Laws Restricting the Teaching of Slaves. This legal action caused others who engaged in educating African Americans to become intimidated by Southern law officials (Woodson, 1915).

As a result of the passage of these state laws, the education of Blacks by religious groups came to a sudden halt (Washington, 1969; Wilson, 1977). Some religious groups did educate African Americans in the South, but they limited their efforts to the Southern border states with less severe laws regarding educating African Americans. Even those efforts were done in a clandestine way (Washington, 1969; Wilson, 1977). There were some cases of both Whites and Blacks doing what they could to educate the slaves. The famous Black abolitionist Frederick Douglass got his first instruction from his White mistress (Washington, 1969). Douglass also initiated attempts to educate African Americans (Huggins & Handlin, 1980; McFeely, 1991). Douglass's self-sacrifice along these lines helped gain him the confidence, respect, and admiration of many African Americans and facilitated his rise to leadership (Huggins & Handlin, 1980; McFeely, 1991). Some other slaves also received instruction from either their slave owners or their family members (Cornelius, 1991; Woodson, 1915). Sojourner Truth not only preached a message of salvation, truth, and emancipation but also embarked on numerous efforts to educate African American slaves (Ross, 2003). And a Black woman in Savannah, Georgia, ran a school to educate Blacks for three decades without the knowledge of government authorities (Cornelius, 1991; Woodson, 1915). John Chavis, born in 1763, was one of the more fortunate Southern African Americans. A White neighbor paid his way to attend Princeton, and he became a well-respected educator (Woodson & Wesley, 1968). After the passage of all the laws forbidding the education of slaves, White children often taught slaves how to read and write (Woodson, 1915).

The fact that a number of Southern governments deliberately acted to suppress attempts to educate African Americans has tremendous significance. Today, part of the argument for insisting that state governments initiate programs of affirmative action is based on the fact that Southern state governments did so much to block the education of African Americans during the 1800s (Woodson, 1915).

Many people today oppose government intervention to help ensure that racial minorities have certain opportunities made available to them. Some people assert that government involvement in formulating racial policy only heightens the tension that exists between the races (Sowell, 1993). There may be a certain degree of truth to this. It is conceivable, however, that people who argue this way would be more tolerant of government intervention along these lines if they were more fully informed regarding the historical reasons behind contemporary government involvement. Those who insist that government should be involved in a policy of affirmative action are not always inherently fond of big government. Rather, there is a sense among those who support affirmative action that to the extent to which the government either forcefully excluded African Americans from living the American dream or neglected to help African Americans so they could move toward that dream, the government should be the first to help African Americans. It is on this basis that many civil rights activists argue that the government should be at the forefront of formulating any affirmative action plans. Once this historical background regarding blocking education and opportunity for African Americans is understood, the involvement of government in affirmative action plans becomes less threatening. The involvement of government in promoting educational opportunity for African Americans today appears to be a commonsense development in order to right the wrongs of the past that have been committed by various governments of the past.

Educational Debate: Historical Justification for Affirmative Action

One of the strongest arguments in favor of affirmative action is a historical one. That is, given that Southern state governments were often the first to shut down the doors of educational opportunity, should they not be the first to open them?

- Do you agree with this historical justification for affirmative action? Why or why not?

CHANGING AMERICAN EDUCATION FOREVER: EVENTS LEADING UP TO THE ELECTION OF LINCOLN AND LIBERATION FOR THE SLAVES

Perhaps no other event influenced American education more than the freedom of the slaves that resulted from the Civil War (Jenkins, 2002; Neufeldt & McGee, 1990; Richardson, 1986). Freedom for the slaves meant that all African Americans could now be educated, without the interference of slaveholders. Many Northerners and some Southerners had long opposed slavery, but some of them lacked the will to eradicate this practice. Consequently,

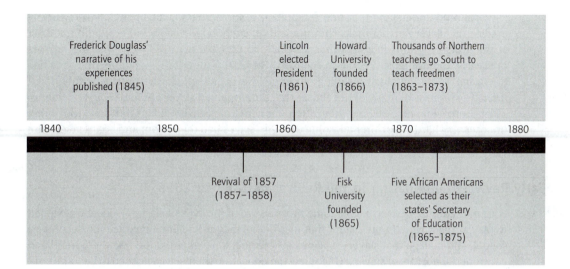

citizens often voted for presidential candidates who lacked the moral fortitude to attempt to eliminate slavery from the land (Hammond, 1974; Holt, 1978; Johnson, 1997; Ransom, 1989). Some of these candidates personally opposed slavery but sought means of compromise in public policy on this issue (Hammond, 1974; Holt, 1978; Johnson, 1997; Ransom, 1989). What caused Northerners to suddenly change their voting patterns to select a candidate, Abraham Lincoln, who vowed that he would not tolerate slavery? Whatever caused this voting pattern change was crucial in determining the future of American education. The election of Lincoln and the freedom for the slaves that followed was one of the most important events in American educational history.

Attitudes of Northerners Toward Slavery Before the Late 1850s

Before the late 1850s, although many Northerners opposed slavery, they did not oppose it with a great deal of zeal (Alley, 2002; Hammond, 1974; Zdrok-Ptaszek, 2002). Many Northerners had the attitude that although they personally disapproved of slavery, the Southerners had the right to own slaves under the Constitution. There were essentially two schools of thought regarding slavery: pro-freedom and pro-choice. People in the pro-freedom school favored the release of the slaves no matter what the Constitution said. People in the pro-choice school of thought were not always necessarily in favor of slavery (Alley, 2002; Hammond, 1974; Zdrok-Ptaszek, 2002). They simply believed that Southerners were within their constitutional rights to own slaves. While a grand majority of Northerners personally abhorred slavery, a fair number of Northerners were pro-choice. Even among these Northerners who were pro-freedom, many did not have a real sense of urgency about rooting slavery out of the land. Wherever Northerners stood on the issue, they tended to view slavery as a political issue rather than a moral or spiritual one (Alley, 2002; Hammond, 1974; Zdrok-Ptaszek, 2002). This fact kept the majority of Northerners from feeling strongly enough about slavery to desire to eradicate slavery from the land.

We should understand that one reason some Northerners lacked conviction regarding eradicating slavery is that mass communication such as television and radio did not exist at the time. Programs like *60 Minutes,* which could have divulged to people the horrors of slavery, did not exist. People in the North generally thought it was a horrible practice to engage in the buying and selling of people. Nevertheless, Northerners generally had a limited awareness of many of the abuses that accompanied slavery (Alley, 2002; Hammond, 1974; Zdrok-Ptaszek, 2002). They often thought that slaves did not endure too many unnecessary hardships. After all, some thought, slaves had their room and board taken care of by their owners (Alley, 2002; Hammond, 1974; Zdrok-Ptaszek, 2002).

Early Revivals Culminating in the Revival of 1857 to 1858

For Americans in the North to become more aware of the evils of slavery, education needed to play a major role. To the extent that instructors taught in elementary school, secondary school, and college that slavery was morally wrong, a new generation had the potential to confront the horrors of slavery. Of course, the educators themselves needed to become convinced. For this reformation to occur, a dramatic change had to take place. As Zdrok-Ptaszek (2002) notes, "Religious revivals swept the North during the late 1820s and early 1830s, and charismatic preachers such as Charley Finney won over a number of converts" (p. 16). In fact, Finney alone led 500,000 to conversion experiences (Hambrick-Stowe, 1996; Hardman, 1987). For one man, this was quite remarkable, given that the U.S. population was only about 10 million in 1820 and slightly over 20 million by 1850 (Bergman & Bergman, 1969). The revivals of the 1820s and 1830s culminated in the "Revival of 1857 to 1858" (Hambrick-Stowe, 1996; Hardman, 1987; Orr, 1989). So great was the influence of this revival that many historians termed it "the event of the century" (Long, 1998, pp. 13–15).

Ministers and religious educators had a dramatic impact on changing the North's perspective on slavery. In 1857, a great religious revival sprung up in America. The revival started in New York City via the efforts of a minister named Jeremiah Lanphier (Orr, 1989; Smith, 1980). He sponsored a lunchtime prayer meeting for New Yorkers. The prayer meeting became so popular that his church could not contain the thousands of people who attended each day. Therefore, other churches opened their doors so that the excess number of people could be accommodated in their facilities. Other churches, marveling at the enthusiastic response, opened their doors for lunch hour prayer as well. The churches enjoyed phenomenal success in these meetings. Soon, there were tens of thousands of New Yorkers attending churches all over the city (Orr, 1989; Smith, 1980. As Dieter (1996) notes, "Such meetings were common to a majority of the major cities of the east and Midwest" (p. 40). The revivals began in the 1820s, climaxed in 1857, and had a tremendous impact on American education and the election of Lincoln. The latter event in itself would ultimately change American education forever, because many African Americans from all over the South would have real educational opportunity for the first time.

The Revival's First Influence: On Educators

The revivals influenced education across a number of fronts. First, among the groups most influenced by the revival were educators (Burns & Furbish, 1901; Orr, 1989). Educators, particularly those teaching in private schools (the public school movement was gaining momentum from 1820–1857, but most American children still attended private schools) and colleges, were strongly influenced by the Revival of 1857 to 1858 and Finney's preaching even before this point (Burns & Furbish, 1901; Orr, 1989). Those who taught adolescents saw a new opportunity to raise up a new generation inculcated in the belief that slavery was a moral ill and had to be eliminated (Burns & Furbish, 1901; Orr, 1989; Zdrok-Ptaszek, 2002). Of Finney's 500,000 converts, many were educators (Hambrick-Stowe, 1996; Hardman, 1987).

Educators in the nation's colleges were even more influenced by the revival than were instructors in the private schools. This is largely because the Revival of 1857 to 1858 was a religious movement mainly among the educated leaders of the country and is often referred to as the "businessmen's revival" (Long, 1998, pp. 13–15). It also had a pronounced impact on colleges, because Charles Finney was himself an educator, as were many of his closest colleagues (Carnes, 2002; Hambrick-Stowe, 1996; Hardman, 1987; McKivigan, 1999). Finney, along with Timothy Weld, was the cofounder of Oberlin College, in 1833. Oberlin was the first college in the United States to admit African Americans. Finney also purposely spoke at or near many of the nation's colleges (Carnes, 2002; Hambrick-Stowe, 1996; Hardman, 1987; McKivigan, 1999). In fact, Finney's success at the University of Rochester helped catapult him to national prominence.

Some of the nation's most prominent colleges were deeply affected by the revivals of the 1820s and 1830s and the Revival of 1857 to 1858 (Davis, 1967). Finney and his converts Timothy Weld and the Tappan family became very involved in establishing antislavery colleges and in changing the spiritual and political environment of countless colleges across the United States (Davis, 1967; McKivigan, 1999; McKivigan & Snay, 2002; Wimberly, 1977). Oberlin College, the institution founded by Weld and Finney, was an overtly abolitionist college (Essig, 1999; Wimberly; 1977). A number of colleges, including Yale, Columbia, the University of Rochester, and Oberlin College, have given especially detailed descriptions of the attitudinal changes that took place (Burns & Furbish, 1901; Orr, 1989).

Particularly important to education is that the revival spread to many college campuses. Charles Finney was instrumental in seeing revival come to the University of Rochester through his meetings in Rochester, New York (Hambrick-Stowe, 1996; Hardman, 1987; Long, 1998; McKivigan, 1999). These revival meetings actually predated the vast Revival of 1857 to 1858, but the effects perdured for some time. Two of the most pronounced revivals were at the University of Michigan and the University of Virginia. Powerful revivals also took place at Harvard, Yale, Dartmouth, Columbia, Brown, Oberlin College, Williams, Amherst, Rutgers, Middlebury College (Vermont), Jefferson College, and numerous others (Hambrick-Stowe, 1996; Hardman, 1987; Orr, 1989).

The revival at Yale is summarized by Yale historians:

In 1858 occurred the last great religious awakening of the era under consideration. It had its rise in what is popularly known as the "prayer meeting revival." According to the testimony of H. E. Burns and E. B. Furbish (both members of the Yale class of 1860) it was characterized by multiplied and crowded prayer meetings, that sometimes embraced every member of a given college class. There were no special preachers. The members of the faculty most prominent were President Woolsely, Dr. Fisher, Professors Goodrich and Thatcher, and the Tutor Hutchinson. There were early morning "entry" prayer groups, and large numbers of students took part in the meetings held in the Central Church by the townspeople. On Sundays, many students went by twos to surrounding towns and held evangelistic services. One livery stable, Phil Hoadley, who never let horses on Sunday, gave free use of his teams for this purpose during the revival. The college church was greatly augmented by the conversions at this time. (Burns & Furbish, 1901, pp. 93–94)

The effects of the Revival of 1857 to 1858 spread even further into the Midwest and West, reaching the University of Wisconsin, UC-Berkeley (then called the College of California, which started as a private religious institution), Illinois College, Beloit College, Miami of Ohio, Denison, Ohio Wesleyan, and others (Hambrick-Stowe, 1996; Hardman, 1987; Orr, 1989). The revival was so extensive that it not only affected colleges, but secondary school students as well (Smith, 1980).

The Northern universities at the time contributed to unmasking some of the ugly truths about slavery (Hammond, 1974; Orr, 1989). Ministers and politicians were some of the primary beneficiaries of higher education at the time. When these leaders returned home to their congregations and constituents, respectively, they would often communicate to people the horror and injustice that surrounded slavery (Orr, 1989). In this way, education during this period had a dramatic impact on the history of the United States.

A Closer Look: Charles Finney, Religious Leader and Educator

Although Finney's contributions to the education of African Americans and the mainstreaming of the abolitionist movement were once a matter of great attention in American textbooks, historians today often do not elaborate as much on his accomplishments. Nevertheless, as the cofounder of Oberlin College, the first American college to accept African Americans, and the mentor of many of the leaders of the abolitionist movement, Finney's influence on the course of African American education is profound.

Historian Timothy L. Smith (1980) observes,

> As is now well known, religious radicals of both Unitarian and evangelical persuasions co-operated to kindle the first blaze of antislavery feeling which swept over the nation. Charles G. Finney probably won as many converts to the cause as William Lloyd Garrison. . . . Among these were Weld, Tappan, first president of the American Antislavery Society, and Joshua Leavitt, editor first of the *Evangelist* and then of the *Emancipator*. Revivalists like Edward Norris Kirk, Nathaniel S. S. Berman, and Jacob Knapp, together with hundreds of Methodist and New School pastors lent spiritual support to the movement. (p. 180)

The Revival's Second Influence: On Abolitionists

One cannot deny the phenomenal impact that abolitionists had on education (Carnes, 2002; Davis, 1967; McKivigan, 1999). Without freedom for the slaves, the tremendous educational advances for African Americans in the post–Civil War Period would not have materialized,

Brown v. Board of Education (1954) would not have happened, and American educational opportunity would not be as widespread as it is today. Zdrok-Ptaszek (2002) notes, "Future abolitionists such as Arthur and Lewis Tappan and Theodore D. Weld were among those to fall under Finney's sway and engage in social reform as a result" (p. 16). Zdrok-Ptaszek adds, "Although this spirit of reform is usually attributed to a renewal in religious and evangelical fervor, some reformers were motivated by secular, societal ideas rooted in the Enlightenment" (p. 17).

Increasingly, religious educators in particular called on Northerners to support only politicians who were against slavery (Roth, 1999). Theodore Dwight Weld, the Tappans, and James Binney called on the United States to end slavery immediately (Friedman, 1999; Loveland, 1999; Roth, 1999). Although they initially earned the label "radical abolitionists" for taking this stand, the fact that these individuals believed that abolitionist teaching could be accomplished as part of religious education caused many individuals to change their minds and voting patterns on the slavery issue (Perry, 1999). Quantitative research by Hammond (1974) indicates that religious education and teaching explain changes to antislavery voting patterns more than any single factor during the years and decades prior to the Civil War.

Although religious abolitionists, such as William Lloyd Garrison, had been around for many years, the Revival of 1857 to 1858 made the antislavery movement more of a mainstream movement, laudable among the majority of Northerners (Alley, 2002; Garrison, 2002). Timothy Smith (1980) notes, "Out of the heart of revival Christianity came by mid-century a platform more widely acceptable and realistically concerned with alleviating social evil" (p. 146). The Baptist publication, *The Watchman's Reflector,* frequently became a vehicle for expressing the effect that revival was having on antislavery sentiment. In 1857, the publication stated that men must "learn to regard slavery as not merely the denial of rights conferred in original creation, but as an outrage on the nature which the Son of God was pleased to make the temple of His divinity" (cited in Smith, 1980, p. 153). The writer went on to say, "The growth of slavery could only be halted . . . when Christians comprehended the infinite value which Christ had attached to every human creature through his incarnation, his sufferings, and atoning death" (cited in Smith, 1980, p. 153).

Religious educators were often quick to rebuke materialistic America for overlooking the needs of the oppressed. Historian Timothy Smith (1980) quotes one religious leader, Olin, who declared that Americans who were paying

> "decent attention to the externals of religion on the Sabbath" . . . while ignoring the sufferings of the poor and enslaved and laying an "embargo of almost famine prices upon bread," were guilty of "deep-seated, practical infidelity." God was "rising out of his place to hear the cry of the 'poor and needy' and visit rebuke on their oppressors." (p. 156)

The revival spread to Philadelphia, Boston, Chicago, Detroit, Cleveland, Washington, Cincinnati, Louisville, and virtually every major city in the North (Orr, 1989). It especially affected many businesspeople. The revival not only spread to the business centers of the United States but also reached almost every town in the North. New York, Pennsylvania, and

New Jersey were the first states influenced. Shortly thereafter, the revival spread to Connecticut, Rhode Island, and Massachusetts. Ohio, Michigan, and Indiana experienced the revival beginning in the latter part of 1857. Through these beginnings, the revival stretched to Illinois, Iowa, and Missouri, and into the northern New England states of Vermont, New Hampshire, and Maine. The revival even spread to the western territories and was especially prominent in California (Orr, 1989).

The effects of the revival were so pervasive that it soon became known by the names "The Great Revival" and "the event of the century" (Long, 1998, pp. 13–15). Dieter (1996) notes the incredible sense of unity that resulted from the Revival of 1857 to 1858:

> One of the most extensive descriptions of . . . hope for Christian unity and the role of holiness promotion in achieving it, is given in an 1857 report on the characteristics of the Tuesday Meetings. . . . The common experience of holiness united Presbyterians, Baptist, Methodist, Episcopalians, Quakers, United Brethren for Christ, Jews, and proselytes. (Dieter, 1996, p. 34)

The Revival's Third Influence: On Authors of Books Used in Schools

The third way the revivals influenced education is that they influenced authors who wrote books used in schools and colleges. Many of those involved in or influenced by the religious revivals or by other abolitionist efforts either became involved in education or wrote books read in colleges and schools (Barnes, 1964; Hammond, 1974; Kraiditor, 1969; Perry, 1999, Sorin, 1971). Harriet Beecher Stowe, daughter of the renowned preacher Lyman Beecher, wrote the book *Uncle Tom's Cabin,* which had a dramatic influence on the educated class in their views of slavery (Barnes, 1964, Hammond, 1974, Kraiditor, 1969; Sorin, 1971).

Concluding Thoughts on the Revival

The timing of the revival was right and enabled many Americans in the North to realize that God's aid could be counted on to overcome slavery. Smith (1980) adds,

> It is no wonder that when the intermittent and local awakenings characteristic of the years after 1842 gave way in 1858 to a Pentecost of seemingly miraculous proportions, revivalists were convinced that the conquest of social and political evil was nearly at hand. (p. 153)

In the years that followed, individuals gave due credit to the role of faith in ending slavery. In the 1880s, a Freewill Baptist minister said that the faith that had "swept slavery from the earth, elevated women from a state of bondage and had weakened the grasp of despots would ultimately triumph over every ill" (Freewill Baptists, 1880, p. 1). While faith had not yet overcome every ill, it went a long way in producing a moral determination to end slavery in the North. This, in turn, ushered in the election of Abraham Lincoln (Smith, 1980).

AMERICAN NORTHERN HEROES

Following the very sad chapter in American educational history in which Southern governments closed down schools for African Americans arose what is ironically perhaps the most inspiring period in the American educational record. Beginning with the last years of the Civil War and continuing into the Reconstruction Period, 9,503 freedman teachers, primarily from the North, instructed former slaves in the South (Knight & Hall, 1951; Swint, 1967). These teachers made profound sacrifices to complete their mission, including enduring the wrath of the Ku Klux Klan (KKK) (Anderson, 1988; Knight & Hall, 1951; Nieman, 1994; Swint, 1967). These individuals often sacrificed their families, jobs, and way of life in order to instruct former slaves. Swint (1967) notes,

> Many of the teachers had been abolitionists; practically all were profoundly religious. In fact, the outstanding characteristic of the Yankee teachers seems to have been piety. Many of the teachers were also ministers. A smaller number of teachers came for financial reasons, because although the pay was not great, it was fairly decent. (p. 35)

The largest number of these teachers came from the state of Massachusetts, followed by New York and Ohio (Swint, 1967).

Many prominent ministers and abolitionists were strong supporters of these organizations, including Henry Ward Beecher, Phillips Brooks, and William Lloyd Garrison (Garrison, 2002; Swint, 1967; Wimberly, 1977). The government encouraged as many Americans as possible to get involved in these efforts, viewing education as "the first essential of the new regime" (Swint, 1967, p. 57).

Although many people in the South received these instructors well, the KKK was filled with great animosity toward them. The KKK believed that the most efficacious way of stopping the education of African Americans was to attack and intimidate the instructors (Anderson, 1988; Nieman, 1994; Swint, 1967; Washington, 1969, 1901/1999). "The Ku Klux Klan (KKK) would threaten teachers, often beat them, or tar them and cover them with cotton" (Swint, 1967, p. 107). In Louisiana, Texas, Tennessee, and Arkansas, the KKK was especially dangerous. As Swint (1967) notes, "schools were burned, teachers threatened and beaten," and "teachers flogged" (p. 131).

The KKK frequently sent threatening letters to teachers in which they asserted that they would kill the teacher(s) unless that person ceased teaching African Americans (Anderson, 1988; Nieman, 1994; Knight & Hall, 1951; Swint, 1967). Some of these threatening notes were actually published in the magazines of the organizations that were sending them. These published accounts give us insight into the nature of the threats:

> Unholy teacher of the blacks, begone, ere it is too late! Punishment awaits you, and such horrors as no man ever underwent and lived. The cusped moon is full of wrath, and as its horns fill the deadly mixture will fall on your unhallowed head! Beware! When the Black Cat Sleeps we that are dead and yet live a-waiting you.

Fool! Adulterer and cursed hypocrite! The far-piercing eye of the grand Cyclops is upon you! Fly the wrath to come.

Ku Klux Klan (*American Missionary,* 1868, p. 183)

Another KKK warning read:

The KKK's are on your track and you will be in hell in four days if You don't mind yourself, mind that you don't go the same way that G. W. A. went some night.

Yours in hell,

KKK (*Freedman's Record,* 1868, pp. 80–81)

In the quotation, "G. W. A." refers to a prominent politician from Georgia who was murdered (Swint, 1967).

Given that the KKK was so aggressive, many teachers who taught in the rural areas had to live in the cities. It was far too dangerous for teachers to live in isolated areas. Although some instructors became intimidated and returned home, nearly all of them continued to teach the liberated African Americans (Anderson, 1988; Nieman, 1994; Knight & Hall, 1951; Swint, 1967).

No finer hour did the American teaching profession ever have than the period of 1863 to 1873, when many teachers risked their lives and safety in order to instruct African Americans (Anderson, 1988; Nieman, 1994; Knight & Hall, 1951; Swint, 1967). In the final years of the Civil War, teachers literally moved into cities right behind the Union army lines and started schooling immediately following a Union victory (Knight & Hall, 1951; Swint, 1967). Furthermore, the willingness of the teachers to voluntarily subject themselves to the wrath of the KKK demonstrates a level of heroism equal to that of any cohort of teachers in American history.

Those instructing the slaves not only established schools for African Americans but also helped them organize politically and were instrumental in establishing African American colleges (Anderson, 1988; Nieman, 1994; Knight & Hall, 1951; Swint, 1967). The American Missionary Association, the largest of the sponsoring organizations, was especially active in establishing these colleges, including Hampton, Fisk, and Atlanta (Roebuck & Murty, 1993).

During the Civil War and post–Civil War period, there was a considerable change in direction toward educating former slaves in the South. For the first time in the South's history, tax money was used to create a system of public education to instruct the citizenry (Wilson, 1977). The Northern troops worked to establish the first free public schools for African Americans, using property taxes in the South to fund the effort. Shortly after the Civil War, as mentioned briefly earlier, five states chose African Americans to be their superintendents of education (Wilson, 1977). A majority of the most prestigious Black colleges were founded during the period immediately following the Civil War, for example, Howard University, Atlanta University, Fisk University, and Morehouse College (Roebuck & Murty, 1993; Woodson & Wesley, 1968). Despite the strong beginnings, it would nevertheless take many decades before African Americans could really enjoy an education commensurate to what White-majority children were receiving.

The long-lasting, genuine educational advances of African Americans would naturally come following the Civil War. Every gain that African Americans had obtained before this point was short-lived and perfunctory in nature (Riggs, 2001). The events leading up to the election of Lincoln and the Civil War that resulted are essential to understanding the maturation of education in the United States. In fact, the developments leading up to the election of Lincoln are that much more interesting because America's education system played a large role in ushering in the Lincoln administration.

CONCLUSION

The education of African Americans has a place of central importance in the history of education. Included are some of the highest and lowest points of the development of schooling. Through it all, there are both many lessons to be learned and inspiring lives to be emulated. First, it is important for people to understand that historically, there has always been a strong relationship between education in truth and personal freedom. There is a sense that the biblical adage "You will know the truth and the truth will set you free" definitely applies to the struggle of the slaves but also to every generation. The Puritans and the Quakers were among the first to realize the strong connection between the education of the slaves and their eventual emancipation. However, it is also true that wherever oppression exists today, education in truth is vital for true emancipation.

Second, the educational history of this period is a vivid reminder of the heights and the depths to which human behavior can go, depending on one's motivation. The acts of Southern governments, pressured by slaveholders, to close down schools for African Americans beginning in the mid-1820s is one of the saddest chapters in American educational history. However, the sacrifices made by thousands of Northern teachers to educate former slaves in the South, despite being victimized by the wrath of the KKK, are perhaps the most heartwarming actions in this nation's educational history. It is a vivid reminder that present and future American educators can make a tremendous difference in the lives of others and in the course of history, if their hearts are filled with love and a passion to teach.

Third, this period also reminds the reader of the importance that this nation attaches to equality. Many Americans have made tremendous sacrifices to achieve greater equality of opportunity for all the nation's people. Education is an important component of the quest for equality.

The education of African Americans during this period gives Americans much to ponder, much to be thankful for, and much to strive toward.

DISCUSSION QUESTIONS

1. Why did the Quakers, and to a lesser extent the Puritans, see such a close connection between education and emancipation for the slaves? Why would education help hasten the liberation of the slaves and facilitate their adjustment once emancipation took place?

2. Why was it important for African Americans in the North to be educated to the degree that they could procure prominent positions in society? What positions do you think were particularly important in that era? Why?

3. The spiritual revivals culminating in the Revival of 1857 to 1858 had a dramatic impact on American schools and colleges and future opportunities for African Americans via the election of Lincoln. Why did the spiritual revival have such an impact? Have there been any events in recent history that have caused such a major change in our education system?

4. Racism is a worldwide problem. In most nations, racial equality does not have as high a priority as it does in the United States. In many nations, minorities receive no education, are not permitted to have White-collar jobs, and cannot hold political office. In some nations, slavery still exists. What events in American educational history made racial equality the priority that it is today? What can American teachers do to educate children about the racial problems around the world?

REFERENCES

Alley, J. B. (2002). Anti-slavery and the Republican party. In J. Zdrok-Ptaszek (Ed.), *The anti-slavery movement* (pp. 128–131). San Diego, CA: Greenhaven Press.

American Missionary (1868, August), *12*(8), p. 183.

Anderson, J. D. (1988). *The education of Blacks in the South, 1860–1935*. Chapel Hill: University of North Carolina Press.

Andrews, C. C. (1969). *The history of the New York African free schools*. New York: Negro Universities Press.

Asante, M. K. (1987). *The Afrocentric idea*. Philadelphia: Temple University Press.

Baldwin, E. (Ed.). (1834). *Observations on the physical and moral qualities of our colored populations with remarks* (p. 4). New Haven, CT.

Barnes, G. S. (1964). *The antislavery impulse, 1830–1844*. New York: Harcourt, Brace & World.

Barry, A. (1870). *True education: The truth shall make you free*. London: Lohmann & Cockhead.

Benezet, A. (1871). History of schools for the colored population in the District of Columbia. In M. B. Goodwins (Ed)., *Special report of the commissioner of education of the improvement of public schools in the District of Columbia*. Washington, DC.

Bergman, P. M., & Bergman, M. N. (1969). *The chronological history of the Negro in America*. New York: Harper & Row.

Bobbe, D. (1933). *DeWitt Clinton*. New York: Minton, Balch.

Brissot de Warville, J. P. (1794). New *Travels in the United States of America*. London.

Brown v. Board of Education 347 U.S. 483 (1954).

Buchanan, G. (1793). *An oration on the moral and political evil of slavery*. Delivered at a public meeting of the Maryland Society for the promoting of the abolition of slavery, and relief of free Negroes and others unlawfully held in bondage, July 4, 1791. Baltimore.

Bullock, H. A. (1967). *A history of Negro education in the South: From 1619 to the present*. Cambridge, MA: Harvard University Press.

Bullock, H. A. (1970). *A history of Negro education in the South: From 1619 to the present*. New York: Praeger.

Burns, H. E., & Furbish, E. B. (1901). In J. B. Reynolds, S. H. Fisher, & H. B. Wright (Eds.), *Two centuries of Christian activity at Yale, 1701–1901* (pp. 93–94). New York: G. P. Putnam.

Carnes, M. C. (2002). *Invisible giants: Fifty Americans who shaped the nation but missed the history book*. Oxford, UK: Oxford University Press.

Child, L. M. (2002). Slave labor versus free labor. In J. Zdrok-Ptaszek (Ed.), *The anti-slavery movement* (pp. 96–103). San Diego, CA: Greenhaven Press. (Original work published 1794)

Copeland, D. A. (2000). *Debating the issues in colonial newspapers.* Westport, CT: Greenwood Press.

Cornelius, J. D. (1991). *"When I can read my title clear": Illiteracy, slavery, and religion in the antebellum South.* Columbia, SC: University South Carolina Press.

Cornog, E. (1998). *The birth of empire: DeWitt Clinton & the American experience, 1769–1828.* New York: Oxford University Press.

Daniels, J. (1903). *The progress of Southern education.* Philadelphia: American Academy of Political and Social Science.

Davis, B. (1967). *Antebellum reform.* New York: Harper & Row.

Dieter, M. E. (1996). *The holiness revival of the nineteenth century.* London: Scarecrow Press.

DuBois, W. E. B. (1913). *John Brown was right.* New York: Knaus-Thompson.

Essig, J. D. (1999). The Lord's free man. In J. R. McKivigan (Ed.), *History of the American abolitionist movement* (pp. 319–339). New York: Garland.

Filler, L. (2002). Abolitionism and the age of reform. In J. Zdrok-Ptaszek (Ed.), *The anti-slavery movement* (pp. 57–65). San Diego, CA: Greenhaven Press.

Freedman's Record (1868), *4*(5), pp. 80–81.

Freewill Baptists. (1880). *Doctrine and life.* Dover, NH: Freewill Baptist Publishers.

Friedman, L. J. (1999). Confidence and pertinacity in evangelical abolitionism. In J. R McKivigan (Ed.), *History of the American abolitionist movement* (pp. 75–100). New York: Garland.

Garrison, W. L. (2002). Declaration of the sentiments of the American anti-slavery society. In J. Zdrok-Ptaszek (Ed.), *The anti-slavery movement* (pp. 66–80). San Diego, CA: Greenhaven Press.

Hambrick-Stowe, C. E. (1996). *Charles G. Finney and the spirit of American evangelism.* Grand Rapids, MI: Eerdmans.

Hammon, J. (1761). *An evening thought: Salvation by Christ with penitential cries.* Retrieved on August 30, 2001, from http://www.accd.edu/SAC/ENGLIsh/bailey/jhammon.htm.

Hammond, J. L. (1974). Revival religion and antislavery politics. *American Sociological Review, 39,* 175–186.

Hardman, K. (1987). *Charles Grandison Finney, 1792–1875: Revivalist and reformer.* Syracuse, NY: Syracuse University.

Harrison, W. P. (1893). *The gospel among the slaves.* Nashville, TN: M. E. Church.

Holt, M. F. (1978). *The political crisis of the 1850s.* New York: Wiley.

Huggins, N. I., & Handlin, O. (1980). *Slave and citizen: The life of Frederick Douglass.* Boston: Little, Brown.

Jay, J. (1801). *The correspondence and private papers of John Jay, 1782–1793* (H. P. Johnson, Ed.). New York & London.

Jefferson, T. (1903). *The writings of Thomas Jefferson, memorial edition. Autobiography, notes on Virginia, parliamentary manual, official papers, messages, and addresses* (A. A. Lipscomb & A. E. Bergh, Eds.). Washington, DC: Thomas Jefferson Memorial Association.

Jenkins, W. L. (2002). *Climbing up to glory: A short history of African Americans during the Civil War and Reconstruction.* Wilmington, DE: SR Books.

Johnson, P. (1997). *A history of the American people.* New York: HarperCollins.

Jones, C. C. (1832). *The religious instruction of the Negroes.* A sermon delivered before associations of planters in Liberty and MacIntosh counties, Georgia. Princeton, NJ: D'Hart & Connolly.

Jones, M. G. (1964). *The charity school movement: A study of eighteenth century Puritanism in action.* Cambridge, UK: Cambridge Books.

Kaestle, C. (1973). *Joseph Lancaster and the monitorial school movement.* New York: Teachers College Press.

King, W. (1995). *Stolen childhood.* Bloomington: Indiana University.

Knight, E. W., & Hall, C. L. (1951). *Readings in American in American educational history.* New York: Appleton-Century-Crofts.

Kraiditor, A. S. (1969). *Means and ends in American abolitionism: Garrison and his critics on strategy and tactics, 1834–1850.* New York: Pantheon.

Long, K. T. (1998). *The Revival of 1857–1858: Interpreting an American religious awakening*. New York: Oxford University Press.

Loveland, A. (1999). Evangelicalism and "immediate emancipation" in American antislavery thought. In J. R. McKivigan (Ed.), *History of the American abolitionist movement* (pp. 2–18). New York: Garland.

Marty, M. E. (1968). *Religious issues in American history*. New York: Harper & Row.

McFeely, W. S. (1991). *Frederick Douglass*. New York: Norton.

McKivigan, J. R. (1999). *Abolitionism and American religion*. New York: Garland.

McKivigan, J. R., & Snay, M. (2002). Religion & reform. In J. Zdrok-Ptaszek (Ed.), *The anti-slavery movement* (pp. 57–65). San Diego, CA: Greenhaven Press.

Miller, W. L. (1996). *Arguing about slavery*. New York: Knopf.

Neufeldt, H. G., & McGee, L. (1990). *Education of the African American adult*. New York: Greenwood Press.

Nieman, D. G. (1994). *African Americans and education in the South, 1865–1900*. New York: Garland.

Orfield, G. (1996). *Dismantling desegregation: The quiet reversal of Brown v. Board of Education*. New York: New Press.

Orr, J. E. (1989). *The event of the century*. Wheaton, IL: International Awakening Press.

Perry, L. (1999). Adin Ballou's Hopedale Community and the theology of antislavery. In J. R. McKivigan (Ed.), *History of the American abolitionist movement* (pp. 278–295). New York: Garland.

Pinkney, W. (1788). *Speech before the Maryland House of Delegates*. Baltimore.

Ransom, R. L. (1989). *Conflict and compromise: The political economy of slavery, emancipation and the American Civil War*. Cambridge, UK: Cambridge University Press.

Richardson, J. M. (1986). *Christian reconstruction: The American Missionary Association and Southern Blacks, 1861–1890*. Athens: University of Georgia.

Riggs, M. Y. (2001). African American children, "The hope of the mace": Mary Church Terrell, the social gospel, and the work of the Black women's club movement. In M. J. Bunge (Ed.), *The child in Christian thought* (pp. 365–385). Grand Rapids, MI: Eerdmans.

Roebuck, J. B., & Murty, K. S. (1993). *Historically Black colleges and universities*. Westport, CT: Praeger.

Ross, R. E. (2003). *Witnessing and testifying*. Minneapolis, MN: Fortress Press.

Roth, R. (1999). The first radical abolitionists: The Reverend James Milligan and the Reformed Presbyterians of Vermont. In J. R McKivigan (Ed.), *History of the American abolitionist movement* (pp. 34–57). New York: Garland.

Rush, B. (1773). *An address to the inhabitants of the British settlements in America on slave-keeping*. Philadelphia: J. Dunlap.

Schultz, S. (1973). *The culture factory: Boston public schools, 1789–1860*. New York: Oxford University Press.

Schwartz, M. J. (2000). *Born in bondage: Growing up enslaved in the antebellum*. South Cambridge, MA: Harvard University Press.

Sims, C. F. (1926). *The religious education of the Southern Negroes*. Unpublished doctoral dissertation.

Smith, T. L. (1980). *Revivalism and social reform: American Protestantism on the eve of the Civil War*. Baltimore: Johns Hopkins University Press.

Sorin, G. (1971). *The New York abolitionist: A case study of political radicalism*. Westport: Greenwood Press.

Sowell, T. (1993). *Inside American education*. New York: Free Press.

Spring, J. (1997). *The American school 1642–1996*. White Plains, NY: Longman.

Sterling, D. (1991). *Ahead of her time: Abby Kelly and the politics of antislavery*. New York: Norton.

Stowell, J. S. (2000). *Methodist adventures in Negro education*. Chapel Hill: University of North Carolina.

Sutton, W. S. (1912). *The education of the Southern Negro*. Austin: University of Texas.

Swint, H. L. (1967). *The Northern teacher in the South*. New York: Octagon.

Taylor, R. S. (1999). Beyond immediate emancipation: Jonathan Blanchard, abolitionism, and the emergence of American fundamentalism. In J. R. McKivigan (Ed.), *History of the American abolitionist movement* (pp. 392–406). New York: Garland.

Urban, W., & Wagoner, J. (2000). *American education: A history*. Boston: McGraw-Hill.

Vahey, M. F. (1998). *A hidden history: Slavery, abolition, and the underground railroad in Cow Neck on Long Island*. Port Washington, NY: Cow Neck Peninsula Historical Society.

Van Horne, J. C. (Ed.). (1985). *Religious philanthropy and colonial slavery*. Urbana: University of Illinois.

Washington, B. T. (1969). *A new Negro for a new century*. Miami, FL: Mnemosyne.

Washington, B. T. (1999). *Up from slavery*. New York: Norton. (Original work published 1901)

Wesley, J. (1774). *Thoughts upon slavery*. Philadelphia: Joseph Cruikshank.

Wilson, P. E. (1977). Discrimination against Blacks: A historical perspective. In W. T. Blackstone & R. D. Heslep (Eds.), *Social justice and preferential treatment* (pp. 161–175). University of Georgia: Athens.

Wimberly, W. W. Jr. (1977). *Missionary reforms in Indiana, 1826–1860: Education, temperance and anti-slavery*. Bloomington: University of Indiana.

Woodson, C. G. (1915). *The education of the Negro prior to 1861*. New York: Putnam's.

Woodson, C. G., & Wesley, C. H. (1968). *The Negro in our history*. Washington, DC: Associate.

Young, R. A. (1829). *Ethiopian manifesto, issued in defense of the Black man's rights, in the scale of universal freedom*. New York. Retrieved August 30, 2006, from http://chnm.gmu.edu/egyptomania/sources.php?function=detail&articleid=11.

Zdrok-Ptaszek, J. (2002). Introduction. In J. Zdrok-Ptaszek (Ed.), *The anti-slavery movement* (pp. 10–24). San Diego, CA: Greenhaven Press.

CHAPTER 5

The Education of Women, Native Americans, Latinos, and Asian Americans

One of the most interesting dimensions of the development of American schooling is the history of education for women and people of color, including Native Americans, Latinos, and Asian Americans. To be sure, the experiences of these groups were quite distinct from each of the others. For females, the first concern was providing elementary and secondary school education, since a college education was very unusual for either men or women. However, when a college education became somewhat more common, the gender gap at this level became an important concern and educators attempted to address this issue.

The education of Native Americans, Latinos, and Asian Americans was also influenced by combat in particular sectors of the globe (Barker, 1970; Eggleston, 1998; Gonzales, 1990; Houston, 1938; Lord, 1961; Slotkin & Folsom, 1978; Wallace & Foner, 1993; Weddle, 2001). Combat aroused distrust between Native Americans and Whites, and Latinos and Whites. Combat in Asia caused some Chinese men to disregard China's ban on emigration and come to America; and military conflict also generated friction between Chinese Americans and Japanese Americans (Gonzales, 1990; Yoo, 2000). Nevertheless, each situation faced in schooling these groups was unique and presented distinct challenges that educators needed to address.

EDUCATION OF WOMEN

When one conceives of the progress that has been made in educating women in the last 400 years, one must first cast aside the notion that advances have been made at a uniform pace. To be sure, the overall trend has been upward. Nevertheless, in the midst of what were mostly advances, setbacks frequently took place. Some of these setbacks were unpremeditated, but they nevertheless occurred. For example, when Congress passed the G.I. Bill in 1944, to extend educational benefits to those who fought in World War II, it clearly benefited primarily men and diminished the percentage of college students who were women (Polakow, 2004; U.S. Department of Education, 2002). Nevertheless, the overall inclination has been one of progress.

During the pre–Revolutionary War period, the settling groups that accentuated education the most overall tended to also attend most to the education of girls. However, generally, boys and girls were educated with different goals in mind. Boys were educated in order to be effective in community leadership and in their work (Hiner, 1988). Girls were educated in order to effectively instruct their children (Rush, 1786b). The fact that women were viewed as the paramount instructors of children, including boys, ultimately meant that there was a good deal of curricular overlap between boys and girls (Blinderman, 1976; Hiner, 1988; Rush, 1785, 1786b). Nevertheless, there was also a good deal of gender differentiation in the curriculum (Hiner, 1988; Rush, 1786a, 1786b). Boys received instruction that was consistent with their eventual functions as providers; girls received more domestically oriented instruction (Rush, 1785, 1786a, 1786b). Lest one think that this instructional dichotomy was merely practiced hundreds of years ago, it really was not until the 1960s and 1970s that girls were encouraged to take shop classes and boys seriously considered taking home economics classes (Gomersall, 1994; Spencer, 2004).

The earliest colleges were limited to males. In fact, they were limited to males who were both extremely bright and very rich (Geiger, 2000). Fewer than 1% of Americans went to colleges even through much of the 1800s (Geiger, 2000; U.S. Department of Education, 2002). College attendance was reserved for the bright elite. To be intelligent alone would not open the doors to college. Similarly, if one were wealthy alone, this also would not make college attendance plausible. One needed to be bright, wealthy, and male to attend college in pre–Revolutionary War America (Miller-Bernal & Poulson, 2004).

Influence of the Revolutionary War on Female Education

The Revolutionary War enhanced educational opportunities for women. Jan Lewis (2002) observes, "Women's education made stunning advances in the dates after the revolution" (p. 86). Women's literacy generally trailed that of men by a few percentage points. Nevertheless, as Lewis notes, "Almost all white women learned to read and write and many became learned" (p. 87).

During the Revolutionary War period, there were a number of notable advocates for women's education (Rush, 1947; Lewis, 2002). One of these individuals was Benjamin Rush (1786b), one of the original signers of the Declaration of Independence. During the first years of the United States, Rush (1947) emerged as one of the preeminent advocates of women's education. Rush was considered the most meritorious physicians in the United States (Good, 1918; Gorton, 1998; Rush, 1820). He was a professor of medicine and chemistry at the University of Pennsylvania (Crosscup, 1968; Good, 1918; Rudolph, 1965; Urban & Wagoner, 2000). Rush (1786a, 1786b) espoused equipping girls with a knowledge of the English language, including reading, writing, and spelling. He also insisted that women needed to know an ample level of math to be able to do bookkeeping. In addition, Rush (1820, 1947) believed women should be taught geography, the Bible, music, history, poetry, literature, and dance (Good, 1918; Rudolph, 1965). Noah Webster (1807, 1843) also argued that America should have a consequential program of women's education. Webster averred that women should be educated in the philosophy of republicanism so that they could train children in the principles of responsible citizenship and living in a democratic society (Beard & Beard, 1944; Blinderman, 1976; Gorton, 1998; Shoemaker, 1966; Webster, 1807, 1843). Thomas Jefferson (1818) argued that the position of housewife was as venerable as the man's place as farmer. Therefore, women should be educated.

In the immediate post–Revolutionary War period, various state governments, like Massachusetts, insisted that boys and girls be taught the same subjects at the elementary school level. Nevertheless, girls clearly received education of a somewhat different nature than boys in most areas of the country (Lewis, 2002).

Emergence of Women's Colleges

In the early 1800s, an increasing number of female institutions offered a more ambitious academic curriculum for women (Edwards, 2002; Lyon, 1835). Nevertheless, a large number of women wanted a college that was as demanding as the male institutions. At this time, women did not wish to attend a coed college. There was a general belief among both men and women that males and females both learned most effectively if they were separate (Albisetti, 2000; Riordan, 1990).

Women finally got the quality institution they were looking for when Troy Female Seminary was founded in Troy, New York, in 1822 (Fairbanks & Sage, 1898; Gordon, 2002). Troy supplied an ambitious curriculum and attracted the affection of many women. Between 1822 and 1872, 12,000 women received their education at Troy (Fairbanks & Sage, 1898). This was a large number of students for the day. Troy was the first institution of higher education designed to exclusively train women based on a curriculum that was essentially the same curriculum as the men received (Fairbanks & Sage, 1898).

The next half century after the founding of Troy, women's education made many advances. New spokespeople arose for the women's education movement. Mary Lyon, the founder of Mount Holyoke College, in 1837, became a major force in women's education. Lyon originally founded Mount Holyoke College as a seminary focused on the religious training of women (Boas, 1971; Lyon, 1835). However, she also wanted to elevate the quality of training that her students received in science and literature.

Women's education became a major priority in the minds of some of America's most prominent educators. A. W. Richardson (1847), in a letter written to Henry Bernard, on March 23, 1847, stated the following:

> Strange it is, but true, that, with us there is much more lively interest felt in the cause of female education than in the education of young men. Is this not an effort in the right direction? Educate the girls—thoroughly educate them—and the boys in order to render themselves respectable in their eyes, will find the means to educate themselves. (p. 1)

Charles Burroughs (1827), of St. John's Church in Portsmouth, New Hampshire, gave an address on female education in which he asserted that men and women were equal. Therefore, the education of each gender was equally important.

The declarations of many prominent individuals in support of women's education helped provide the atmosphere for rapid expansion. Although Troy Female Seminary was the first institution of higher education to offer the same level of curriculum as that for men, many other women's institutions had an influence as well (Boas, 1971). These institutions offered courses that can be best described as both high school and collegiate in level (Boas, 1971).

Added Insight: Catharine Beecher, Harriet Beecher Stowe, and the Beecher Family

The Beecher family was one of the most influential families in American educational history. The father, Lyman Beecher, was a minister and an educator. He was a pastor on the East Coast and then became president of Lane Seminary, in Cincinnati, Ohio (Snyder, 1991). Beecher was one of the most famous people of his era. He was a strong advocate of the expansion of the common schools, under the direction of his close friend Horace Mann. Beecher was also the founder of the temperance movement, which enjoyed considerable popularity during the 19th and 20th centuries. Beecher was most well-known for his preaching, educational leadership, and strong stand against alcohol and slavery (Schreiner, 2003; Snyder, 1991).

Beecher was a strong believer that if parents were strongly involved in their children's lives, they could train their children to change the world. Therefore, he spent a great deal of quality time with his children. Catharine Beecher, one of his daughters and an influential educator, wrote regarding her father, "And was there ever a parent who, in the first period of family training, more perfectly exhibited a happy combination of strong and steady government with the tenderest love and sympathy" (Beecher, cited in Snyder, 1991, p. 3). Catharine also wrote of her father, Lyman, "My father had that passionate love of children which makes it a pleasure to nurse and tend them, and which is generally deemed a distinctive element of a woman" (Beecher, 1874, pp. 15-16).

Lyman Beecher had 11 children, and they, in fact, changed the world. This is all the more remarkable because Reverend Beecher's first wife died, leaving the family devastated for a period of time. Jerald C. Brauer (1991, p. xv) notes, "Each Beecher was a major figure of the development of . . . American culture." Some of his most notable children included Catharine, Mary, and Harriet, who were prominent figures in starting and running religious schools and the precursors of women's colleges (Schreiner, 2003). Catharine became one of the leading educators in the country and wrote a number of books on Christianity and education. Mary helped promote the schools and publications of both Catharine and Harriet (Schreiner, 2003). Harriet, who after her marriage to Calvin Stowe, became Harriet Beecher Stowe, was the most renowned of the Beecher offspring and wrote the classic book, *Uncle Tom's Cabin,* published in 1852. The writing of this book did a great deal to turn the tide of Northern public opinion against slavery. Harriet Beecher Stowe became an instant hero in the North but was despised even more than William Lloyd Garrison in the South (Schreiner, 2003; Snyder, 1991). Given that Harriet Beecher Stowe was an educator, her connections enabled schools and colleges throughout the country to use her book.

Many of Beecher's other children also engaged in some combination of ministry and education, often in the form of pastoring a church and being a principal for a school (Schreiner, 2003; Snyder, 1991). Those of his children who combined ministry and education or at least focused on one or the other discipline included Thomas, Edward, William, George, and James.

Henry Ward Beecher, another of Lyman's sons, also helped *Uncle Tom's Cabin* become a well-known book, as he pastored a church that had 6,000 attendees weekly and was well-known for his strong oratory against slavery.

This one family accomplished many lionhearted feats that changed American education and the nation forever.

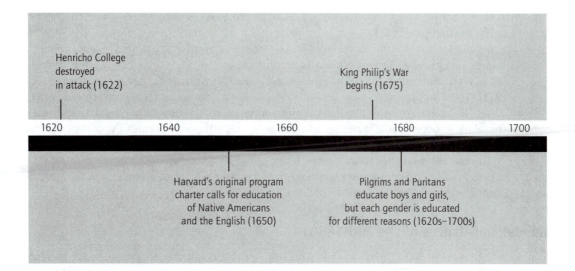

Henricho College
destroyed
in attack (1622)

King Philip's War
begins (1675)

| 1620 | 1640 | 1660 | 1680 | 1700 |

Harvard's original program
charter calls for education
of Native Americans
and the English (1650)

Pilgrims and Puritans
educate boys and girls,
but each gender is educated
for different reasons (1620s–1700s)

In 1814, Emma Willard opened up Middlebury Female Seminary (Boas, 1971; Miller-Bernall, 2000). Willard was one of the most heralded educators of her time and did a memorable job fund-raising in order to establish her institution (Fairbanks & Sage, 1898). Her efforts helped inspire the generosity of the people of Troy, New York, when she founded the Troy Female Seminary 8 years later (Boas, 1971; Miller-Bernall, 2000).

The Lyman Beecher household also had a major impact on women's education (Boas, 1971). Pastor Beecher had always encouraged all his children to try to make a major impact on society, and he strongly believed in the value of women's education (Boas, 1971; Snyder, 1991). One of his daughters, Catharine Beecher, founded Wheaton Female Seminary, in Massachusetts, and later established Hartford Female Seminary, in Connecticut, which many considered an equal to the institution at Troy (Boas, 1971; Edwards, 2002; Miller-Bernall, 2000). Like Willard, Beecher regarded teaching as far more than a profession, but as a type of ministry (Boas, 1971). Therefore, Beecher recruited only instructors to her seminaries who viewed education in the same way (Boas, 1971; Edwards, 2002). Beecher's Hartford Female Seminary was so extraordinary that it earned the reputation of being one of the three best female institutions of higher education in the country, along with Willard's Troy Female Seminary and Zilpa Grant's Female Seminary, in Ipswich, Massachusetts (Boas, 1971; Edwards, 2002).

Although the institutions at Troy and Hartford became more celebrated than those in Middlebury and Wheaton, it is interesting to note that both Willard and Beecher each started a school that served as a precursor to their greater successes at Troy and Hartford (Edwards, 2002; Miller-Bernall, 2000). Furthermore, although one would not consider the schools in Middlebury and Wheaton to be colleges, they helped these women establish the model for the institutions of higher education at Troy and Hartford (Boas, 1971; Miller-Bernall, 2000; Sicherman, 1988).

Although the highlights in the development of women's education occurred primarily in the North, for many years there were actually more female institutions of higher education in the South than in the North (Boas, 1971). However, most Northerners were not interested in going there because these colleges were regarded as lower quality. Southern women's colleges also played less of a role in the progression of women's education for the same reason (Boas, 1971).

A definite momentum was evident in women's education at the time. The education of women was gaining a growing level of attention (Boas, 1971; Edwards, 2002). For example, in 1827, the American Journal of Education lauded the work of Catharine Beecher (Boas, 1971). There appeared to be a nationwide movement to eradicate ignorance (Edwards, 2002). To Americans who lived at the time, ignorance was closely connected with vice. Therefore, it was essential to impart knowledge to strengthen the moral fabric of the country (Boas, 1971).

The gap between education for males and females was declining. In fact, European visitors to the United States often commented on the degree of gender equality in the United States compared with other nations (Boas, 1971).

Gender Imbalances of the Mid-1800s

By the mid-1800s, Americans were becoming more cognizant of two ostensible gender gaps in education (Edwards, 2002). The first has already been referred to in this chapter. That is, males were far more likely than females to attend college (Edwards, 2002; Troen, 1988). In fact, the gender gap was so substantial that by the middle of the 1800s, males were about 9 times as likely as women to attend college (DuBois, 1912; Troen, 1988; U.S. Department of Education, 2002).

There were a number of reasons for the presence of this gender gap. First, the few occupations that most necessitated a college education were male dominated at the time (Edwards, 2002). During the mid-1800s, people went to college most frequently to become a minister, doctor, or lawyer. All three occupations had a far greater number of males than females (Boas, 1971; Tewksbury, 1932; Troen, 1988). Clearly, the distribution in these occupations has changed dramatically since the mid-1800s (Edwards, 2002). Nevertheless, this was the state of affairs back then.

Second, most colleges at this time were male colleges. People at this time believed that males and females learned best if they were separated from one another and that if men and women learned in the same schoolroom, they could easily be distracted by one another (Albisetti, 2000; Riordan, 1990). Therefore, educators favored the strategy of having men's and women's colleges in close proximity but separated from each other. In this way, men and women could intermingle on the weekends but would not distract each other during school days.

Many people today might chuckle over this supposition. Nevertheless, lest one laugh too loudly, contemporary research suggests that both boys and girls generally perform better in single-sex rather than coed educational environments (Lee & Bryk, 1986; Lee & Marks, 1990). Consequently, there are movements in some circles to increase the number of single-sex schools. Issues of segregation and socialization restrict the extent to which this movement possesses momentum (Fliegel & MacGuire, 1993). Nevertheless, from a purely academic perspective, a growing number of educators favor single-sex schools. The fact that the number of male colleges far outnumbered the number of female colleges contributed to the gender gap of the mid-1800s (DuBois, 1912).

Third, people during this period encouraged males more than they did females to procure an education. Mid-19th-century Americans placed a high value on the role of a mother in raising children and believed that the more parents were present in the home, the more children would benefit. In addition, they declared that if a father could obtain a college education, this could help him be a better provider for the family. Nevertheless, less than 2% of males went to college (Miller-Bernal, 2000; Sicherman, 1988).

The second gender gap is less well-known among Americans. By about a 2-to-1 margin, girls were considerably more likely to procure a high school diploma than boys, and despite what modern-day stereotypes suggest, the girls of the 19th century often received more formal education than did boys (Troen, 1988; U.S. Department of Education, 2002; U.S. Department of Health, Education, and Welfare, 1951, 1970). At most city elementary schools that we have record of in the mid-1800s, by the seventh grade, girls began to far outnumber boys. By the teenage years, girls frequently made up more than 60% of the school population (Troen, 1988). This imbalance was not due to any preference for educating girls. Rather, it was due to practical reasons. By the time boys reached the age of 11, parents often believed that it was more important to have the boys at home helping in the fields rather than being educated in the schools (Troen, 1988). Although many Americans strongly believe in the vital nature of education, the exigency of survival often forced parents to take their boys out of the sixth grade. Although girls often helped out at home, too, their help was not considered as vital to the survival of the family. Therefore, it was more unusual to remove girls than boys from school after the sixth grade.

For the early part of the 19th century, the average amount of the formal education received by males and females probably did not differ that much. The gender gap in the percentages of males and females attending school was greater for higher education than it was for secondary education, which would seem to favor boys (U.S. Department of Health, Education, and Welfare, 1951, 1970). Nevertheless, because the total number of Americans pursuing higher education was so small, this number would not affect the average overall level of education as much as the absolute numbers of those attending secondary school (Miller-Bernal, 2000; Sicherman, 1988). The gender gap in higher education affected the overall level of education much more after the Civil War and into the 20th century, when the number of people attending institutions of higher education increased dramatically (U.S. Department of Health, Education, and Welfare, 1951, 1970).

Although the average education levels of males and females were probably about the same in the first half of the 18th century, the nature of the education that males and females received was often considerably different (Edwards, 2002). As a result, male rates of literacy were almost always higher than female rates of literacy during this time.

Although many females were taught to read in order to make them potentially good teachers, the education of girls was generally more domestically oriented than was the case for boys (Wollstonecraft, 1891). Girls were taught home economics in addition to the standard subjects one normally associates with school. Males were trained to be the providers of the home (Wollstonecraft, 1891). Therefore, teaching boys to read often received a higher priority than teaching girls to read.

Economic Development Reduces Gender Gaps

As the United States grew economically in the second half of the 1800s, both gender gaps were reduced. Economic development reduced the female advantage at the secondary school level, for two reasons in particular.

First, boys were somewhat less likely to be called on to work in an industrial setting than in an agrarian one (Troen, 1988). Second, economic development meant that boys needed to be more educated in certain respects, and this made families more likely to keep boys in school than had previously been the case (Troen, 1988). Nevertheless, families continued to be more likely to pull boys out of school than girls in order to provide economic support (Troen, 1988). Hence, although the secondary school gender gap was reduced, it was not eliminated. In fact, there remains a gender gap even to this day (U.S. Department of Education, 2002).

Economic development had a substantial impact on reducing the college gender gap, which helped females (Matthaei, 1982). It produced a number of household conveniences that unconstrained the time of mothers and wives for additional pursuits (Gordon, 2002). This fact contributed to a substantial increase in the number of occupations with a large number of females. The stage was set for a surge in women's education.

The Post–Civil War Surge

As great as the progress in women's education was beginning in the 1820s, the post–Civil War period produced advances in women's education that are unequaled in American history (U.S. Department of Education, 2002; U.S. Department of Health, Education, and Welfare, 1951, 1970). By 1890, women made up 36% of the college population (U.S. Department of Education, 2002). A great deal of this impressive increase was due to the founding of many women's colleges (Boas, 1971; Edwards, 2002; Tidball, Smith, Tidball, & Wolf-Wendel, 1999). By 1900, there were 150 women's colleges in the United States (Tidball et al., 1999). However, even though there was a great accretion in the number of women's colleges, most of the rise in female college attendance during the post–Civil War period was due to the proliferation of coeducational colleges (Miller-Bernal, 2000).

In fact, by 1870, more women attended coeducational colleges than women's colleges (Miller-Bernal, 2000; U.S. Department of Health, Education, and Welfare, 1951, 1970).

This trend was especially true in African American colleges, which were generally more likely to be coeducational than were White institutions (Gordon, 2002). Generally speaking, the gender gap among African Americans going to college was about the same as for Whites going to college (DuBois, 1912; Gordon, 2002).

Most of the prominent women's colleges were founded after the Civil War, including Smith, Barnard, Wesleyan, Bryn Mar, Stephens, the College of Notre Dame, and so forth (Tidball et al., 1999). Perhaps the two most prestigious women's universities, Vassar and Radcliff, were founded in 1865 and 1894, respectively (Gordon, 2002; Miller-Bernal, 2000).

Cornell, the final Ivy League college to open its doors in 1868, became a coeducational college. It quickly established itself as the most illustrious coeducational college in the country (Miller-Bernal, 2000). Ezra Cornell, the institution's founder, actually desired to unite Cornell with a women's college, Wells, but the leadership of Wells desired to remain separate (Miller-Bernal, 2000).

Women's education advocates became more numerous and unquestionably contributed to the exponential growth that was taking place in female education and in the discipline as a whole. Prudence Crandall opened up a girl's school in Connecticut for African Americans and mulattoes (Boas, 1971). One remarkable woman was Jane Addams

(1860–1935). Addams initially started as a medical student but ended up disliking the field (Gordon, 2002). A wealthy woman, she decided to spurn the lifestyle normally associated with wealth, and she became a social reformer. She established a settlement house for new immigrants, called Hull House, in the slums of South Chicago. Addams became an advocate for the education and well-being of the poor and advocated compulsory education, child labor laws, and improved health and sanitation for those living in the slums. Hull House became a major educational concourse that not only provided basic schooling but also helped immigrants to become socialized and to adapt to American culture (Edwards, 2002; Gordon, 2002). Addams attempted to highlight the artistic contributions and other dexterity of immigrants.

The late 1800s was a time of unparalleled growth in women's education (Edwards, 2002; Gordon, 2002; U.S. Department of Health, Education, and Welfare, 1951, 1970). Statistics on the number and percentages of women high school graduates and college attendees indicate that a surge occurred following the Civil War (U.S. Department of Education, 2002). Although this timing is incontrovertible, it seems that events that happened concurrently with the Civil War, rather than the Civil War itself, contributed most to the upsurge (Boas, 1971; Edwards, 2002; Gordon, 2002; Newcomer, 1959; Tidball et al., 1991; U.S. Department of Health, Education, and Welfare, 1951, 1970).

One significant event was the Morrill Land Grant of 1862, which mandated the sale of public lands at an extremely low price in order to support state universities (Gordon, 2002). The Morrill Land Grant Act contributed to the exponential growth of female collegiate education in two ways: First, the cheap land sales enabled state universities to charge low tuition rates, which made college education at state universities more affordable than at most private universities (Gordon, 2002; Newcomer, 1959). Second, state universities were almost always coeducational (Gordon, 2002; Newcomer, 1959; U.S. Department of Health, Education, and Welfare, 1970). This naturally increased the number of slots available to women.

Industrialization was the second major development that reached fuller fruition after the Civil War. It relieved many women of time constraints, permitting them to pursue academic interests, as was addressed earlier in this chapter (Gordon, 2002).

This progress that women's education made from 1865 to 1900 was broad in terms of who attended high school and college as well as in the development of the curriculum (Tidball et al., 1999; U.S. Department of Health, Education, and Welfare, 1951, 1970). African American females were among the primary beneficiaries of the growth in women's education, although discrimination continued to be real (Tidball et al., 1999). Between 1865 and 1900, African American illiteracy in the South was cut in half (Gordon, 2002). In 1881, the American Baptist Home Missionary Society founded Spelman College, the first African American women's college. The Atlanta-based institution educated some of the leading African American ladies of the era (Tidball et al., 1999).

The curricula that women were exposed to also broadened during this period. Naturally, at coeducational schools, women could take pretty much the same courses as men (Newcomer, 1959). In addition, many of the women's colleges actually emphasized physical education more than the men's colleges did. In a number of female colleges, physical education was required, whereas in the male colleges, it was only optional (Tidball et al., 1999).

The fact that nursing and teaching were becoming major occupations of women also helped augment the curricula to which women were exposed. By 1900, there were 400

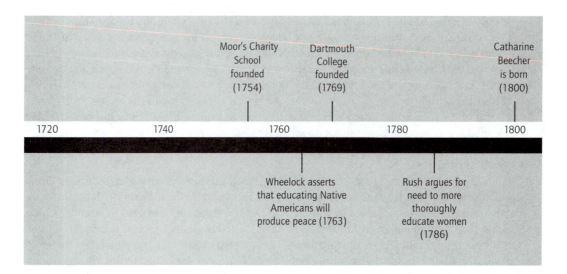

nursing schools in the United States (Tidball et al., 1999). Teachers became more organized, and as a result, groups like the Chicago Federation of Teachers were founded, the precursor of the American Federation of Teachers (Gordon, 2002). As teachers became more organized, this made the preparation of teachers, many of whom were women, more systematic.

The advances made by women from 1865 to 1900 were considerable. By 1898, 53% of the University of Michigan's undergraduates were women (Tidball et al., 1999). Truly the advances women had made were profound. The momentum that women's education enjoyed in the late 1800s continued into the early 1900s. By 1910, nearly as high a percentage of colleges admitted women as men (Tidball et al., 1999). The momentum continued until 1930, when a higher percentage of colleges admitted women than admitted men (Tidball et al., 1999). From 1900 to 1930, American college enrollment surged, especially among women (Miller-Bernal, 2000). The progress that women's education had made since the Civil War was quite amazing.

Prominent Female Educators

As women's education advanced, an increasing number of women moved to the forefront of instructional leadership. Some of the women, mentioned earlier in this chapter, such as Catharine Beecher and Jane Addams, represented some of the most outstanding leaders in education. Catharine Beecher (1800–1878) may well have been the most widely known woman of her day (Edwards, 2002). Her emphasis on teaching training enabled her to help elevate teaching to a "respectable" profession. The work of Jane Addams reminded Americans of the importance of reaching the immigrants for the work of education to be considered successful (Edwards, 2002).

Elizabeth Peabody (1804–1887) was another of the most influential educators of the time. Peabody became a leading proponent of the kindergarten and of the need for moral education to be an integral and foundational aspect of kindergarten (Edwards, 2002).

Elizabeth Blackwell (1820–1910) was the first woman to graduate from a regular medical school. Once she became a doctor, Blackwell delivered many lectures on health and hygiene to women and girls throughout the country. She started a women's hospital in New York and medical schools for women in both New York and London (Edwards, 2002).

Ellen Swallow Richards (1842–1911) was the first trained female chemist. She was also the first female graduate and faculty member at MIT. She generally receives credit for starting the ecology movement in the United States (Edwards, 2002).

Mary McLeod Bethune (1875–1955) was the daughter of freed slaves. She founded a boarding school for African Americans in Florida. The school was later combined with a male institution and became Bethune-Cookman College (Edwards, 2002). Bethune established the National Colored Women's Association, which helped ex-slaves become educated and established in society. In 1938, Franklin Roosevelt appointed her as director of Negro Affairs in the National Youth Administration (Edwards, 2002).

Post–World War II Advances

The percentage of the female college population dropped back to 35% in 1950, below 1890 levels (U.S. Department of Education, 2002). This was due largely to the G.I. Bill (1944) (Tidball et al., 1999). One should note that this legislation decreased the proportion of women college attendees because of the prodigious increase in the number of male college students. Even after the passage of the G.I. Bill, however, the actual number of women attending college continued to increase. Women continued to make advances in college admissions after the full effects of the legislation were realized (Tidball et al., 1999). The launching of *Sputnik,* the Russian satellite, and the onset of the Cold War gave renewed impetus to the advances made by women at the college level (Tidball et al., 1999). The influence of the Cold War on women's education will be examined in greater detail in Chapter 9. However, suffice it to say that largely due to the higher involvement of Soviet women in the sciences and in other disciplines compared with American women, Americans became more determined to see a larger percentage of women go to college and major in many of the disciplines traditionally dominated by men (Tidball et al., 1999).

The progress in women's education continued until 1979, when women college attendees outnumbered their male counterparts (U.S. Department of Education, 2002). By the turn of the 21st century, American college attendance was 57% female and 43% male (U.S. Department of Education, 2002). The percentage of females is expected to reach about 60% in the coming years (*Chronicle of Higher Education,* 2003).

African American Concerns About Women's Education Trends

The breakdown of the percentage of the college population that is male and female differs by race. Table 5.1 lists the percentages, according to race, based on the figures from 2002 to 2003, the latest year for which data are available.

One notices that while the gender gap is not particularly large for Whites and Asians, it is more substantial for Latinos and African Americans. The fact that among African Americans, females outnumber males in college by nearly 2 to 1 has produced concern in a number of African American leaders (Jeynes, 2005; Ogbu, 1992, 1993). Ogbu argues that

Table 5.1   Percentage of Female and Male College
                   Population, Broken Down by Race

Ethnicity	Female (%)	Male (%)
White	56	44
Asian	52	48
Latino	60	40
African American	63	37

SOURCE: *Chronicle of Higher Education* (2003) and U.S. Department of
Education (2002).

the gender gap among African Americans that favors females is no more desirable that the one that existed in past generations that favored males. He believes that action needs to be taken to rectify this gender gap, but asserts that it is important to understand why the gender gap exists in the first place.

Ogbu (1992, 1993) claims that the reason a gender gap exists among African Americans is that American society communicates to its youth that academic achievement is a "White thing" and a "female thing." Consequently, society discourages African American boys from doing well in school. First, Ogbu believes that American society communicates that education is a "White thing." White children are encouraged to go into "brainy" occupations, while African Americans are encouraged to excel athletically. Ogbu notes that if an African American boy chooses to emphasize academic pursuits, he is called an "Oreo cookie." Ogbu believes that most facets of society share in this orientation, so that teachers, the media, parents, and others must share some of responsibility.

Second, Ogbu (1992, 1993) believes that American society communicates that academic achievement is a "female thing." He notes that the overwhelming majority of elementary school teachers are female and that this communicates that education is more of a female than a male practice. He argues that although there are a fair percentage of male secondary school teachers, by the time students reach this age, it matters little, because modeling takes place and childhood impressions form primarily in the elementary school years. Ogbu further notes that there are very few African American male kindergarten and elementary school teachers through which Black boys can see that African American males can be educationally oriented as well.

There is assuredly research to support at least some of Ogbu's asseverations (Jeynes, 2005). There are few male elementary school teachers and even fewer Black male elementary school teachers (Ogbu, 1992, 1993). Furthermore, there is a culture among many male students that boys who are academics are either sissies or nerds. Society probably bears part of the blame for this emphasis (Ogbu, 1992, 1993). Nevertheless, one might also argue that the African American gender gap might be more complex than Ogbu acknowledges.

Educational Debate

John Ogbu (1992, 1993) represents a growing number of African Americans who are concerned that African American women in college outnumber their male counterparts by an almost 2-to-1 margin. He contends that the main reason is that American society communicates that schooling is a "female thing" and a "White thing." There is little question that boys who excel academically often run the risk of being called a sissy or nerd (Warrington, Younger, & Williams, 2000; Wilson, 2005). Similarly, terms like "Oreo cookie" (for African Americans) and "Twinkie" (for Asian Americans) are often applied by minority people to discourage people of these races from acting "too White" (Lee, 2004). Nevertheless, other people believe the gender gap among African Americans and Latinos is more complex and can be best explained by fatherless homes and other cultural factors. What do you think?

- Do you agree with Ogbu, or do you think the reasons are more complex?
- If you disagree, what do you think are the primary reasons for the college attendance gender gap among African Americans and Latinos?

Concluding Thoughts on the Education of Women

The fact that people are even discussing a college gender gap that now favors females shows just how far women's education has advanced in the past few centuries. The progress of women's education has been broad in its impact and deep in its influence. The unique schooling experiences that ethnic minorities have had also assists one in gaining insight into some of the unique encumbrances that different groups face today. These are all important sagas in the journey through time that is American educational history.

EDUCATION OF NATIVE AMERICANS

Different colonies faced distinct problems in educating Native Americans. Jamestown colonists were the first to attempt to educate them (Szasz, 1985). Long before the College of William and Mary was founded for the education of the White majority, there were plans for the colonists to build a college, called Henricho College, for educating Native Americans (Szasz, 1985). Henricho College was supposed to be the venue through which many Native Americans could come to Christ. But, as was mentioned in Chapter 1, the Virginia Bay Company advertised only that they were engaging in missionary activity (Marshall & Manuel, 1977). In reality, they showed little interest in pursuing missionary endeavors at all. They had raised a substantial amount of money from Christians in England under the pretense that missionaries were being sent to save the Native Americans. But the Virginia Bay Company deceived the Christians by not sending the missionaries they had promised (Marshall & Manuel, 1977). In similar fashion, as much as the Virginia Bay Company talked about Henricho College, it was never established. The company kept on diverting money that was originally designated for the college to other purposes (Marshall & Manuel, 1977).

Henricho College

In all fairness to the Jamestown colonists, part of the reason for diverting money from Henricho College stemmed from the fact that the Native Americans showed little interest in being educated and taught to read, because they were convinced that their culture was superior (Szasz, 1988). Margaret Szasz (1988) writes, "The powerful Powhatan Algonquin saw their culture as superior to the colonial culture. As a result, Virginians encountered overwhelming difficulty in attempting to educate their children" (p. 259). Had Henricho College been successfully founded, it would have stood out as a major educational event, indeed. This would have meant that the first college founded in America was not founded for the purpose of educating Whites, but educating Native Americans. But alas, it was never to be (Urban & Wagoner, 2000).

By the 1640s, settlers throughout the colonies concluded that establishing a college for the Native Americans was not the best way to proceed with educating them. John Eliot became known as "the Apostle to the Native Americans," because he attempted to minister to and educate Native Americans by learning their languages and cultures (Spring, 1997). Eleazar Wheelock and Samson Occom, a converted Native American, encouraged both Native American men and women to attend Dartmouth (Wheelock, 1763). In fact, one of the major reasons for founding Dartmouth was to educate Native Americans. Wheelock also founded Moor's Charity School, in 1754, to educate Native American boys and girls (Dickey, 1954; Spring, 1997; Wheelock, 1763). Wheelock (1763) believed that if the Native American children were educated, it would make them less aggressive and there would be less war between the Native Americans and the colonists (Dickey, 1954; McCallum, 1939; Wheelock, 1763).

Educating Native Americans in New England

The education of Native Americans was also a problem in New England. As early as the days of the Puritans, Europeans wanted to teach the Native Americans how to read and write (Marshall & Manuel, 1977). Many of the early religious colonists believed that reading was essential to understanding the Bible and that understanding the Bible was the key to entering into salvation. With this background in mind, many religious people of this period attempted to teach the Native Americans with almost as great a fervor as with their own people (Marshall & Manuel, 1977).

Religious colonists volunteered to teach many Native American adults and children how to read and write. The Puritans in particular volunteered to have some Native American leaders attend Harvard and Yale. The Puritans had founded these institutions only a short period of time before extending these invitations. The interpretation of these events was very different depending on whether one was an Native American or a colonist (Marshall & Manuel, 1977). The colonists thought they were doing a good deed. They were helping the Native Americans to develop to their highest potential. They were opening up Native Americans to a new world and to a means through which they could enrich their civilization.

To the Native Americans, however, what appeared to be a good deed on the part of the colonists was not always viewed that way. Initially, the Native Americans enjoyed having their people taught and enjoyed being treated as equals, in that they were being invited to read the books of the colonists and attend their universities (Marshall & Manuel, 1977; Szasz, 1988). But over time, some of the Native Americans changed their perceptions. This was particularly the case among the younger generation when they reached adulthood. These younger Native

Americans in particular believed that those among them who were receiving education from the colonists were changing and becoming "Westernized" (Szasz, 1985). Some of those being educated by Westerners were advocating maintaining a more conciliatory attitude toward the colonists. Some were even becoming Christians (Marshall & Manuel, 1977). After all, many colonists believed that the chief reason for learning to read was to facilitate salvation.

The younger generation of Native Americans, in particular, questioned the motives of the colonists and believed that the colonists were using education to destroy their culture (Spring, 1997). The idea that educating the Native Americans would lead to less war gained favor after the Revolutionary War as well. Many American leaders, including George Washington, believed that as the Native Americans understood the colonists more, they would fear the Americans less (Henderson, 1998; McKenney, 1846, 1933; Viola, 1974). American leaders believed that educating the Native Americans would induce less war and that instead of fighting over land, reasonable prices could be discussed when the Americans wanted to buy additional land.

A considerable number of the Native Americans, such as the Cherokees and the Mohegans, wanted to learn to read (Sylvester, 1910; Szasz, 1988). Many of the tribes began to realize that literacy was indispensable for the enrichment of their people and if they were to truly apprehend the ways, customs, and the thinking of the colonists (Szasz, 1988). They realized that the colonists could offer literacy to them, but literacy brought the risk of becoming "Westernized" (Szasz, 1985). In 1798, the Cherokees sought to address this problem by asking the Moravian missionaries to share their books, but not their culture (Szasz, 1988). Naturally, this was almost impossible. In addition, many religious colonists believed that they had the ability to help the Native Americans in many ways. Some of these ways involved the passing on of certain cultural values. For example, many colonists believed that they needed to train the Native Americans to work more assiduously (Spring, 1997). They believed that some of the debacles that came upon the Native Americans were because of the lack of a work ethic (Spring, 1997).

A Closer Look: Textbooks and Culture

Native Americans in both the pre–Revolutionary War period and after American independence faced a quandary. American educators of the time offered two advantages that were appealing to Native Americans. First, they offered instruction in English. Native Americans realized that learning English was important and practical in order to communicate with their Western counterparts. Second, American educators offered to convert Native American oral languages into written languages with alphabets. Most Native American tribes did not have written languages. Therefore, this, too, was very appealing to Native Americans.

Nevertheless, it is also true that Native Americans were concerned that receiving Western education would cause them to lose their culture. Spring (1997) notes that the Cherokees communicated to various White settlers that they were interested in learning to read the Western books but they did not want to be exposed to Western culture. This question emerges: To what extent is it possible to publish educational books that do not also reflect one's culture?

- What do you think? Are there some subjects in which this would be easier or harder to do than others?
- When you think of the content of American textbooks today, to what extent do you think they reflect American culture?

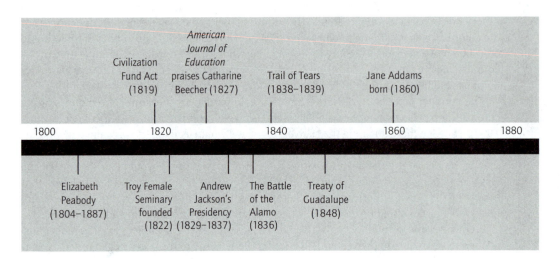

The differing interpretation of the colonial instruction of the Native Americans by each side reminds one of the thin line between helping people of other cultures and taking away their cultures—indeed, there may be many cases in which it is impossible. Given the extent to which one can influence a culture, the question then becomes whether one attempts to help members of another culture knowing that one might forever change their way of life.

The Role of Thomas McKenney

As time passed, Americans increasingly viewed education as a means to civilize the Native Americans (Szasz, 1985). Thomas McKenney, a Quaker, played an important role in educating the Native Americans early in the 19th century. As a Quaker, McKenney (1933) was very concerned about maintaining a peace between the Whites and the Native Americans. He was convinced that if the Native Americans could be successfully educated, war would be avoided and the highest potential for Native American civilization could be realized. McKenney asserted,

> I have no doubt then, nor do I now, the capacity of the Indian for the highest attainments in civilization, in the arts and religion, but I was satisfied that no adequate plan had ever been adopted for this great reformation. (p. 34)

McKenney's views played a large role in convincing the U.S. Congress to pass the Civilization Fund Act, in 1819, to provide monetary support for schools among the Native Americans (Spring, 1997). The act authorized the president to "employ capable persona of good moral character, to instruct them [Native Americans] in the mode of agriculture suited to their situation; and for teaching their children in reading, writing, and arithmetic" (McKenney, 1846, p. 334).

Although the Civilization Fund Act was designed to reach all Native Americans, more traditional Native Americans resisted any plans of instruction (Viola, 1974). The act contributed to creating a class structure in their society: The "progressive" Native Americans were open to American education and became literate and educated, and the more traditional Native Americans did not. (Viola, 1974). Without anyone realizing it, this differentiation by class within the Native American community set the stage for the peace treaties that they would sign with the government of the United States. What happened as a result of being educated is that the more Westernized Native Americans became the leaders of most of the Native American tribes (Viola, 1974). Native Americans naturally chose leaders that were literate and educated. They were not only perceived as the most intelligent but were also chosen because it was believed that those who could communicate in English could best handle the White majority (Spring, 1997).

Given this background, it is not surprising that the more Westernized Native Americans took control of directing policy among the Native American tribes (Hoxie, Mancall, & Merrell, 2001). Many of these leaders, especially among the Cherokee and Choctaw tribes, signed treaties with the United States government in which they agreed to sell much of their land (Hoxie et al., 2001). From the viewpoint of the traditionalist Native Americans, the education of these leaders who would ultimately become Westernized greatly hurt the Native American tribes (Hoxie et al., 2001).

The Election of Andrew Jackson: An Unfortunate Turning Point

Unfortunately for the Native Americans, Andrew Jackson defeated John Quincy Adams to become the seventh president of the United States. Adams probably fought for the rights of racial minorities more than any other president before Abraham Lincoln (Adams, 1969; Gottheimer, 2003; Miller, 1972; Miller, 1996; Ware, 1998). But Adams (1969) was at heart a Federalist. He had left the Federalist Party because it was going extinct as a political party, and when he was elected president, he was a member of the Democratic-Republican Party. Nevertheless, Quincy's Federalist leanings split the Democratic-Republicans. Andrew Jackson rebelled against the Federalist tradition and founded the Democratic Party (Gottheimer, 2003; Miller, 1972; Miller, 1996; Ware, 1998). Jackson totally reversed the tradition of every president since George Washington of treating Native American claims to land with respect (Schlesinger & Israel, 2003). The official policy of all previous American presidents had been to pay Native Americans for their land. But Jackson (1829, 1830; Wallace & Foner, 1993) dramatically reversed that policy. He proposed setting aside lands west of the Mississippi River that the Native Americans could govern, in exchange for the Native American lands east of the Mississippi (Jackson, 1829, 1830; Wallace & Foner, 1993). The president was then authorized to help the Native Americans make the transition to the western lands more easily. Nevertheless, many Native Americans died during the journey, in what is called the "Trail of Tears" (Wallace & Foner, 1993).

When the Native Americans settled down in the western territory, they developed schools for their people. A considerable number of Native Americans owned African American slaves. The Cherokees alone possessed thousands of African American slaves, but there was no attempt to provide schooling for them (Spring, 1997). After the Civil War, some Native American tribes did found segregated schools for African American children. The Cherokee and Choctaw tribes established respectable schools in the 1840s and established a highly organized system of schools (Spring, 1997).

Native American Boarding Schools and the Meriam Report

In addition to Native Americans establishing their own schools, in the late 1800s and early 1900s, the U.S. government supported a policy of establishing boarding schools for Native Americans (Morgan, 1889). This reflected the government's belief that a greater effort should be made to assimilate Native Americans into the culture of the United States (Morgan, 1889). The U.S. government also made a culturally insensitive mistake when it passed the General Allotment (or Dawes) Act in 1887 (Szasz, 1974). This piece of legislation called for Native American individuals, rather than the tribes, to own their land. This undermined the sense of community that had existed under tribal ownership (Szasz, 1974). In 1928, however, these policies were rejected via the government-sponsored Meriam Report (Szasz, 1974). The Meriam Report, written at the request of Hubert Work, Secretary of the Interior, stated that these U.S. policies had actually contributed to impoverishment of Native American peoples (Szasz, 1974).

The Meriam Report called for a complete overhaul of the Bureau of Indian Affairs and of national Indian policy. Furthermore, the report suggested that education should be the primary function of the Indian Bureau. It urged that Native American education be operated at the Native American community level and that assimilation not be the goal of this education. John Collier, the commissioner of Indian Affairs from 1933 to 1945, did much to follow the recommendations of the Meriam Report (Szasz, 1974). In some ways, a great deal of progress was made following the report in terms of self-determination in education among Native American people (Spring, 1997). However, there is actually a lower percentage of Native American children in school now than in 1930 (Szasz, 1974; U.S. Department of Education, 2002).

The Meriam Report established the foundation for U.S. government educational and economic policy with regard to Native Americans for the post–World War II era until present times (d'Errico, 2001; Senese, 1991). For example, in 1955, the Eisenhower administration initiated a program focused on "reservation rehabilitation and development" (Senese, 1991, p. 19). This initiative involved accelerating the movement of Native Americans out of boarding schools into public education facilities on the reservations (Senese, 1991). Consequently, temporarily during the 1950s and 1960s, Native American enrollment in public schools surged, especially among larger Native American tribes, such as the Navajo (Senese, 1991).

President Eisenhower was convinced, however, that better schooling was inadequate to produce the kind of advancements he envisioned. He believed that reservation industry needed to develop to provide jobs for Native Americans (Burt, 1982; Senese, 1991). At first, Eisenhower sensed that there was only minute progress in this regard. However, in 1955, the Eisenhower administration convinced the National Association of Manufacturers to participate in this goal. Eisenhower used tax and labor incentives, modeled after a similar program to increase industry in Puerto Rico, to attract businesses to Native American reservations (Burt, 1982; Senese, 1991). As Eisenhower's two-pronged approach of improving schooling and job opportunities for Native Americans gained momentum, Native American unemployment rates fell dramatically (Burt, 1982; Senese, 1991). Eventually, Congress assimilated the salience of Eisenhower's initiative and in 1960 passed a series of bills called Operation Bootstrap (U.S. Congress, 1960) in order to provide improved schooling and industrial jobs for Native Americans (Burt, 1982; Senese, 1991).

Under President John F. Kennedy's New Frontier program, Stuart Udall, the secretary of the interior, and Philleo Nash, the commissioner of Indian Affairs, guided the government's Native American policy in a new direction (Szasz, 1977). Nash believed that for Native

Americans to succeed, ultimately, one had to "supplant reservation culture with metropolitan culture" (as cited in Senese, 1991, p. 70). Initially, Native Americans and Nash enjoyed a good relationship. However, over time, Udall became frustrated with the lack of educational and industrial progress on the reservations and pressured Nash to produce more results. Nash blamed the slow progress on Native Americans, for, in his view, their dependence on the welfare system diluted their sense of motivation. The resulting friction between Udall, Nash, and Native Americans caused Nash to resign (Senese, 1991; Szasz, 1977). Nevertheless, the Nash government approach continued throughout the first half of the 1960s (Senese, 1991). During the 1960s, 100 industries established residence on Native American reservations, stimulating the demand for schooling on the reservations and slicing the Native American unemployment rate by one quarter (Senese, 1991). Nevertheless, the initiatives created deep divisions in Native American communities regarding whether industrialization was robbing them of their cultural traditions (d'Errico, 2001). Some Native Americans argued that educational and industrial progress were necessary to lift many Native Americans out of poverty, but others asserted that self-determination and not the Western concept of progress should be the ultimate goal of Native Americans (d'Errico, 2001).

Beginning in about 1965, under the Lyndon B. Johnson administration, self-determination and multiculturalism became of the focus of federal Native American policy (d'Errico, 2001). Instead of focusing on increased achievement and preparation for employment, the U.S. government concluded that Native Americans wanted to run their own schools (d'Errico, 2001; Senese, 1991). Although Native Americans appreciated the self-determination aspect of this approach, they could not relate to a multicultural perspective. As Peter d' Errico (2001) points out, "Native American self-determination does not fit neatly within a multicultural perspective of American society" (p. 483). To many Native Americans, multiculturalism means that they must exist within American society rather than exert self-determination and that they must study many cultures rather than study their own (d'Errico, 2001).

There is no question that the American "educational answer" to the challenges faced by Americans has changed over the years. In the 1600s and 1700s, Americans viewed literacy as the solution (Dickey, 1954; Viola, 1974; Wheelock, 1763). In the mid- to late 1800s and early 1900s, the United States emphasized Americanization (Morgan, 1889). Later in the 1900s, Americans thought that schooling Native Americans to prepare for prosperity and economic development was what they needed (Szasz, 1977). Since 1965, the United States has emphasized the salience of multiculturalism for Native Americans (d'Errico, 2001). In every one of these cases, these initiatives split Native American opinion (d'Errico, 2001; Szasz, 1977). In each instance, a large portion of Native Americans appreciated the need for these ideas. However, many Native Americans also resisted these ideas, believing that it was "cooperation" with the West as much or more than "warfare" that has worked to incapacitate many Native American cultural traditions (d'Errico, 2001; Dickey, 1954; Viola, 1974; Wheelock, 1763).

There is little question that the debate about what education options are best for Native Americans will continue for many decades to come. Part of the problem is that the Native American case is unique in terms of sovereignty, community, and the debate over integration versus tribal segregation. Americans value sovereignty, integration, independence, individual advancement, equality, and achievement all at the same time. In the case of the Native Americans, sometimes these values appear at odds with one another. For example, Americans are generally taught, based on *Brown v. Board of Education* (1954), that real equality cannot exist without integration. It is not always clear to the U.S. government or to the Native Americans which of these values are most important. Furthermore, even within these groups, there is much disagreement about what priority each of these values should have. Until there is greater consensus, the schooling of Native Americans is likely to remain one of the most challenging dilemmas facing educators.

Contemporary Focus

Education, Culture, and Right and Wrong

During the 1600s and 1700s, American educators believed instructing Native Americans should include teaching about respecting women and an emphasis on hard work. Regarding women, Americans particularly objected to the practice of polygamy among many Native American tribes. They believed that in the majority of tribes, women were treated as chattel. In this view, one manifestation of this attitude was that many tribes allowed males to engage in polygamous relationships. Americans at the time claimed that educators should discourage this practice.

Similar issues are very relevant in today's world. During the Afghanistan War following the September 11, 2001, attack on the United States, Americans became very concerned that the Afghan people forbade the education of females.

Americans had to make a decision to either focus on cultural sensitivity and allow the Afghan people to continue their previous practice or strongly urge the education of females based on principles of right and wrong. The American government decided to do the latter. The decision angered many Middle Eastern people, who believed that the previous Afghan practice was acceptable and that the United States had no right to act to ensure the education of females. Years from now, the Afghan people may well resent the United States for its actions in the education of Afghan females.

Balancing cultural sensitivity and acting according to one's convictions of right and wrong can be a sensitive issue.

- Many professors note that college students today enjoy using the phrase "Everything is relative," when there are many issues that people should address with a conviction that certain actions are right and other actions are wrong. What do you think about the observations of these professors and the comment of the students?

- Generally speaking, which do feel is more important, acting out of cultural sensitivity or based on a sense of right and wrong?

- What factors can help us determine when it is best to take actions based on cultural sensitivity and when we should act out of a sense of right and wrong?

EDUCATION OF ASIAN AMERICANS

Asian American migration to the United States was quite small in number until the 1960s. Until that time, all Asian groups combined made up less, and usually considerably so, than 5% of the total immigration population in a given year (Weinberg, 1997) Nevertheless, Chinese and Japanese people began to arrive in consistent flows beginning in the 1850s and

1880s, respectively. Other Asian groups, most notably Filipinos, did not arrive in significant numbers until 1900. The Chinese tended to settle in Northern California, and the Japanese established themselves in California and Hawaii (Weinberg, 1997).

Demographically, both the Chinese and Japanese who arrived in the United States were quite different from both other immigrant groups and those that still lived in their native lands (Weinberg, 1997). First, these Asian Americans were more likely to be middle-to-upper class than other immigrants or their remaining countrymen (Ng, 1998; Weinberg, 1997). Second, given that they were of higher socioeconomic status than most in their native lands, they also exhibited a greater level of educational orientation (Ng, 1998; Weinberg, 1997). Third, the Japanese immigrants in particular were more likely to be Christian than those in their homeland (Weinberg, 1997). The number of Japanese American Christians in the early 1900s was not far behind the number of Japanese Buddhists (Yoo, 2000).

The western region of the United States was substantially less developed than the eastern region. Consequently, the education that children received was often far more informal. Among all groups, especially outside of California, those with some educational experience often taught children in very informal settings (Kalman, 1982; Kaufman, 1984). Nevertheless, by the late 1800s, schooling became more formalized. Asian Americans viewed education as a key component of experiencing the American dream, as did many immigrants in the eastern United States (Weinberg, 1997; Yoo, 2000).

Although Asian Americans realized the importance of education, as did the immigrants in the eastern states, there were a number of key distinctions in the Asian educational experience. First, Asian Americans were more aggressive than European immigrants of the time in establishing schools to preserve their culture. Wealthy Chinese in San Francisco established academies and schools in the 1880s and 1890s designed for this purpose. In the early 1900s, Japanese Americans started language schools to preserve their language and culture (Weinberg, 1997).

Education of Chinese and Chinese Americans

The immigration of Chinese to the United Stats represents one of the most unique aspects of American educational history. Before the California Gold Rush of 1848, almost no Chinese came to the United States, because the Chinese government forbade emigration. Not only was emigration forbidden, but under Imperial Chinese law, it was also punished by decapitation (Gonzales, 1990).

As time progressed, however, the ruling Qing Dynasty (1644–1912) weakened due to internal warfare, political strife, and deleterious economic conditions (Gonzales, 1990). A year after it started, the Chinese began to hear about the California Gold Rush. Some, mostly single, males decided to take the chance of ignoring the prohibition on emigration, and they came to America (Gonzales, 1990). With the onset of the Taiping Rebellion (1850–1864), conditions in China became even more baleful, and eventually 25 million died in the warfare (Gonzales, 1990). Moreover, China was overpopulated with a population of 430 million and was unable to feed all its people, and starvation ensued (Gonzales, 1990). Although most families were too afraid of the consequences, especially for women and children, of emigration from their country to risk coming to the United States, many single males decided to take a chance.

Due to California's labor shortage in the early 1850s, Californians initially received the Chinese as a "godsend" (Gonzales, 1990). Initially, Chinese found jobs in the cigar industry, the restaurant business, and sometimes in prospecting for gold.

The fact that most individuals emigrating from China were single men caused a gender gap in the Chinese population in the United States. Chinese men outnumbered their female counterparts by about 27 to 1 (Gonzales, 1990). Most Chinese men remained single in the United States. In the short term, there was one respect in which this worked to the advantage of Chinese and Chinese Americans: Single men did not have to support a wife and children, and therefore they could work for lower wages than most people (Gonzales, 1990; Wollenberg, 1976, 1995). As it was, most Chinese in general were so grateful to be away from the abysmal economic and political conditions in China that they were willing to work for much less money (Gonzales, 1990). Many White and other non-Chinese Californians, most of whom supported families, felt that they could not compete with Chinese laborers for jobs and that the influx of Chinese was causing wages to spiral downward (Gonzales, 1990; Wollenberg, 1976, 1995).

However, as a consequence of the perceived threat from Chinese workers, a real disadvantage arose. White and other non-Chinese individuals formed labor unions, and discrimination against Chinese and Chinese Americans increased considerably (Gonzales, 1990; Wollenberg, 1976, 1995). California and San Francisco legislators, in particular, passed "anticoolie" laws designed to discourage immigration and citizenship for the Chinese (Gonzales, 1990). Concerns about Chinese cheap labor also culminated in the federal Chinese Exclusion Act of 1882, which prohibited the immigration of Chinese laborers (Gonzales, 1990; Wollenberg, 1976, 1995).

The fact that Chinese settlers were almost all male had a second disadvantage: There were not enough Chinese families to produce a second generation of Chinese that would emerge in the 1870s (Gonzales, 1990). Chen (1980) points out that even among the small number of Chinese women in California, most focused on short-term relations with the men, rather than starting a family.

The Chinese who arrived in the United States often formed "Chinatowns" (Chen, 1980). Although some might be tempted to be critical of this as a type of self-segregation, one should remember that the Chinese have long valued family and community ties. In addition, the Chinese government usually distrusted foreigners, as exhibited by the building of the Great Wall (Chen, 1980; Waldron, Hannan, & Twitchett, 1990). Chinese encounters with the Mongols and many other "outside" groups helps one understand this protective orientation. "Chinatowns" are found all over the world.

The existence of separate Chinese communities made it easy for public school educators, especially in San Francisco, to overlook the obvious need to school the Chinese. This tendency became even greater when churches started a number of schools in Chinatown in San Francisco, where so many immigrants lived (Wollenberg, 1995). From the 1850s to the 1870s, Presbyterians, Baptists, Methodists, Episcopals, and Congregationalists all started schools there (Wollenberg, 1976, 1995).

The most famous of the private religious school leaders was probably William Speer. Speer was a former missionary to China and became a major advocate for the Chinese, lobbying California leaders in order to stop discrimination (Wollenberg, 1976, 1995).

Despite the availability of private schools, the residents of Chinatown also wanted public schools (Wollenberg, 1995). Two church leaders, Reverend Otto Gibson and Reverend H. H. Rice, worked together with the Chinese to petition the state legislature demanding public schools. Pastor Rice said that the Chinese "must be educated or excluded and I do not think it is possible to exclude them" (California State Senate, 1876). Congregationalists argued that discrimination against Chinese and Chinese Americans in public school education was causing them to become bitter. Eventually, the municipal court ruled that the Chinese could not be denied public education (Wollenberg, 1995).

Education of Japanese and Japanese Americans

The immigration and educational trends of the Japanese had some similarities with the Chinese experience but also showed some real differences. One of the primary similarities is that, as in China, until Emperor Meiji came to power in 1868 (Beasley, 1972), it was illegal for Japanese to emigrate from their country. Even after this point, Japan did not allow laborers to go to other countries until 1885 (Gonzales, 1990). The United States, both at the corporate and governmental levels, applied some pressure on the Japanese to open up their country and allow laborers to emigrate. The Japanese who came to America settled primarily in Hawaii and California (Gonzales, 1990).

When one examines Asian American education, one must be careful to distinguish between the Japanese American and Chinese American experience. Japanese Americans, consistent with Emperor Meiji's emphasis on applying Western ways, were much more open to integrating with other groups than were Chinese Americans (Weinberg, 1997). One should also note that growing military conflicts in East Asia produced tension between Japanese Americans and Chinese Americans (Weinberg, 1997; Yoo, 2000). Between 1894 and 1945, Eastern Asia was the site of tremendous military conflict. The Sino-Japanese War of 1894 to 1895, the Russo-Japanese War of 1905, the Japanese invasion and annexation of Korea in 1910, and the subsequent conflicts between China and Japan leading up to and including World War II influenced the schooling situation in the western United States (Weinberg, 1997; Yoo, 2000). Great tensions developed between Chinese Americans and Japanese Americans, and they refused to go to school with one another. As the war continued into the late 1930s, Japanese Americans and Chinese Americans sent large amounts of money to support their native countries in the war effort (Yoo, 2000).

The tensions between Japanese Americans and Chinese Americans only added to the de facto segregation conditions that existed in many parts of California (Weinberg, 1976, 1997). Chinese Americans tended to be more segregated than Japanese Americans, largely because Chinatown in San Francisco was a far more segregated area than Little Tokyo in Los Angeles. Furthermore, Chinese Americans, originating in a racially homogeneous environment, balked at the idea of going to school with other racial minorities (Weinberg, 1997).

Until World War II, Japanese Americans often attended school with White children and performed quite well (Ng, 1998). Unfortunately, the strong financial support that many Japanese Americans gave the Japanese Imperial Army caused the Roosevelt administration to question the loyalty of the Japanese American community, and internment followed (Weinberg, 1997). Even during the internment, Japanese Americans maintained an emphasis on educating their young people. This is not surprising, given the fact that a high percentage of Japanese Americans had been attending California schools (Yoo, 2000). After World War II, Japanese Americans were more likely to be integrated with other children than were other minority groups (Weinberg, 1997).

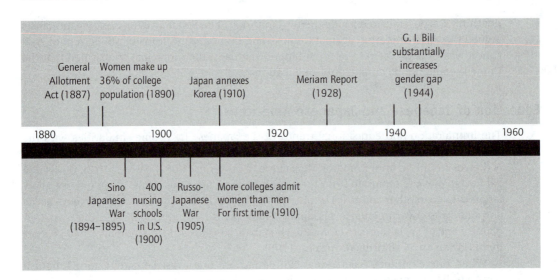

Asian Americans today are very successful financially and maintain a median income about 15% above the American average (U.S. Census Bureau, 2001). Part of this success is due to the educational emphasis found in many Asian American families.

EDUCATION OF LATINOS

Mexicans and Mexican Americans and Education

The Mexican educational experience was more complex than one might expect. Although Mexicans had the shortest distance to travel to the United States and in some cases were already settled in certain areas of the Southwest, most Mexicans from the mid-1800s until the mid-1900s crossed back and forth across the border. Often, Mexicans worked in the United States but would still return to Mexico (Clark, 1908; Vargas, 1999). This is particularly understandable because in the mid-1800s especially, Mexican people regarded much of Texas and other portions of the Southwest to be considerably less fertile than "the bountiful Valley of Mexico, the west-central region around Guadalajara, and the Pacific slope" (Vigness, 1965, p. 23). They did not view it as a pleasant place to live. To the Mexicans, and in previous years, the Spanish, "Texas did not seem to possess the natural wealth and mineral resources that other areas of Mexico possessed" (Vigness, 1965, p. 23). Texas was also regarded as too far inland, away from the primary population centers of Mexico. It was because Mexicans did not regard Texas as a favorable place to live that the Mexican government was so open to Moses and Stephen Austin developing the land (Barker, 1970; Lord, 1961; Lundy, 1970; Vigness, 1965).

The fact that most Mexicans crossed back and forth across the border made the educational experience arduous for Mexican children and those that inculcated them (Reynolds, 1933). Schools of formal education were initially sparse among the White population in Texas, and there were few Mexicans permanently settled in the desert Southwest, east of California, who could help school Mexican immigrants (DeLeon, 1982). By the time of the Alamo, in 1836, the Spanish-Mexican population in Texas, excluding soldiers, was only 4,000 (DeLeon, 1982; Vargas, 1999). Although Mexicans lived in the United States with the advent of the Treaty of Guadalupe, in 1848, the numbers of Mexican Americans living in the United States was still small—until the Mexican Revolution and World War I, which both took place during the period from 1910 to 1920 (Johnson & Hernandez, 1970). After this point, the Mexican American population surged, doubling every 10 years (Jencks, Lauck, & Smith, 1922).

In many respects, because of the extensive border crossing, the Mexican educational experience may have been the most unique of all. Neither the Mexicans nor the American educators really knew what schooling expectations were appropriate for such a transient population (Reynolds, 1933).

Some sections of the United States in which Mexicans settled were distant from the border, and the mobile way of life that was often a hindrance to education was not an issue. However, for many years, it was rare for Mexicans to settle beyond the states bordering Mexico (Clark, 1908; Vargas, 1999). For example, contemporary Americans know that Colorado has a high Latino population partially because it is just north of New Mexico. However, as late as 1900, there were only 274 Mexicans and Mexican Americans living in Colorado (Clark, 1908; Vargas, 1999). Therefore, although working and living on both sides of the American/Mexican border had its utilitarian advantages, the fact that so many Mexicans persisted in this way of life made their children's education a perplexing matter.

For most of the post–Mexican American War period until the early 1900s, Mexicans engaged in itinerant occupations. Initially, Mexicans worked primarily in agriculture, which often prescribed working in various farms in different towns, depending on what crop was in season. As the 1800s progressed, an increasing number of Mexicans and Mexican Americans took jobs with the railroad (Bryan, 1912; Vargas, 1999). However, working for the railroad also involved a high degree of mobility and was therefore also not conducive to educating one's children.

A second factor contributing to the challenge of educating Mexicans is that the vast majority of Mexicans in the United States were male, and the vast majority of males were single (Clark, 1908; Vargas, 1999). The abundance of single males enabled these individuals to work for lower wages than would be feasible for married men, and it made Mexican males very competitive in the labor market. However, those males whose wives and children were still in Mexico generally received little or no education in their homeland (Clark, 1908; Vargas, 1999).

A third factor is that unlike other minority groups, Mexicans had just completed a war with the United States. There were two reasons this influenced the attitudes of many Americans toward Mexicans. First, many Texans in particular were still bitter about the events surrounding the Alamo (DeLeon, 1999; Houston, 1938). Desperate to find people willing to endure the elements and develop Texas, the Mexican government had promised White settlers, led by Moses and Stephen Austin, an increasing degree of autonomy to do so. The Mexicans initially honored these agreements, although there was tension created with the Law of April 6, 1830 (Barker, 1928; Houston, 1938). However, when Santa Anna became dictator of Mexico in 1835, he declared the previous agreements null and void (Barker, 1970; Houston, 1938; Lord, 1961). This turn of events ultimately climaxed with the battle of the Alamo, in 1836 (Barker, 1970; Houston, 1938; Lord, 1961; Myers, 1948). Unfortunately, Texans, especially, remained bitter about the Alamo, and rather than implicate Santa Anna alone, they became resentful toward Mexicans generally (DeLeon, 1999; Houston, 1938). The bitterness caused discrimination. Consequently, if Mexicans had a choice (and due to finances, they often did not), they usually preferred to settle in California rather than in Texas (Ruiz, 1993; Vargas, 1999).

Another reason the war influenced the Mexican educational experience in the United States is that Americans questioned where the allegiance of Mexicans in the United States rested (DeLeon, 1999; Vargas, 1999). Overall, the recent Mexican-American War caused Americans to be less concerned with the presence of educational opportunities available to Mexicans than they otherwise would be (DeLeon, 1999; Vargas, 1999).

Like many Americans of the time, a dearth of financial reserves had an impact on the schooling of Mexicans. Most Mexicans came from impecunious circumstances, where even the most fundamental levels of education were rare, and nearly all male Mexicans engaged in unskilled labor, which eventuated in low wages (Gamio, 1930). There is also some indication that employers probably discriminated against Mexicans in the wages they furnished, but the indicators are mixed (Bryan, 1912; Vargas, 1999). In a 1908-to-1909 study addressing this issue, the findings indicated that when wages were paid on the basis of piecework, Mexicans received the same pay as Whites and Asians (Bryan, 1912; Vargas, 1999). However, a study of railroad workers indicated that the average Mexican received under $1.25 per day in wages, whereas the average White and Asian worker received an average of over $1.25 a day in wages (Bryan, 1912; Vargas, 1999). It is true that this difference does not in itself indicate discrimination. Historically, among late 19th and early 20th century, railroad and other workers with seniority received more compensation than new workers (Chiswick, 1992; Howlett, 2000). In addition, for most of the nation's history, employers believed that workers who supported families should receive more compensation than those who were single (Chiswick, 1992). Given that Mexican workers were much more likely to be single than were Japanese and White workers, this likely explains some of the wage differential. However, it is also true that many people maintained a stereotype of Mexicans at the time that they were not sedulous workers (Bryan, 1912; Vargas, 1999). It is likely that this stereotype also explicates some of the wage differential and therefore indicates discrimination.

Changes Over the Decades

The Mexican American educational situation was very different than that faced by Asian Americans. The Mexican Americans who came to the United States were generally poor and relied on farming for family survival (Sanchez, 1997; Torres, 1997). Given that different agricultural crops matured at different times, Mexican Americans often lived as migrant farmers, which made getting an education problematic (Torres, 1997; Sanchez, 1997). Although Mexicans were required by U.S. law to go to school, 40% of Mexican American children did not attend (Cooke, 1949; Miranda, 1990; Schermerhorn, 1949). One California study in 1928 showed that an even higher percentage, 90%, did not attend school (Tashakkori & Ochoa, 1999). Mexican American families did not place a high priority on education because they needed their children to work in the fields in order to help the family financially (Reynolds, 1933; Tashkkori & Ochoa, 1999).

Given that Mexican American children received little education either in Mexico or in the United States, few were literate in Spanish or able to speak English (Getz, 1997; Sedillo, 1995). Getz (1997) notes that many Mexican Americans were frustrated with the Mexican government's failure to provide good schools and living conditions. A 1921 California study found that out of 1,081 Mexican American families, 55% of the men and 74% of the women could not speak English (Sedillo, 1995). The fact that so few Mexican American children attended school contributed to the lack of English knowledge, as did a desire to preserve the Spanish language and Latino culture (Garcia, 1997; Sanchez, 1997). In addition, many Mexican Americans lived in "colonies," isolating them from most urban and rural population concentrations (Reynolds, 1933; Tashakkori & Ochoa, 1999).

The lifestyle patterns mentioned above created many misconceptions in the minds of numerous Americans regarding the nature of Mexican Americans (Reynolds, 1933; Tashakkori & Ochoa, 1999). Many Americans interpreted the presence of the colonies and a disinclination to learn English as an expression of voluntary segregation. This misinterpretation contributed to the de facto segregation of Mexican Americans in Texas and California (Reynolds, 1933; Tashakkori & Ochoa, 1999).

In addition to the reasons just listed, many Texans and Californians were reluctant to have their children attend schools with Mexican Americans because they were concerned about the lack of English proficiency in many Mexican American students. They believed that working with many students weak in English language skills would curtail the academic pace of the school (Cooke, 1949; Getz, 1997). Although there were no laws in California, Texas, or New Mexico requiring the segregation of Mexican American students, schools with a large number of Mexican Americans quickly developed a reputation for being "slow" academically (Cooke, 1949; Getz, 1997; Schermerhorn, 1949). Misunderstandings, racism, and the unique situations all worked together to produce de facto segregation.

From about 1910 to the early 1920s, the Mexican American population was concentrated only in certain areas and was small in number (Jencks et al., 1922). As a result, few people in America were aware of the challenges that faced the Mexican American community.

Mexican educational and life experiences in the United States changed considerably as their immigration and migration patterns changed. During the 1800s, a relatively small number of Mexicans lived in the United States, and immigration rates were low (Clark, 1908; Vargas, 1999). During this period, Mexican immigration represented only about 1% of the American total immigration (Vargas, 1999). As Vargas notes, during this period, many Mexicans wanted to work in the United States, but few wanted to settle there. Over time, however, an increasing number of Mexicans desired to settle in the United States permanently, and larger numbers procured higher-paying jobs, especially in the auto industry, steel mills, and meatpacking plants (Jones, 1928; Getz, 1997; Vargas, 1999). For example, Vicki Ruiz (1993) notes, "In 1900 only 3,000 to 5,000 Mexicans lived in Los Angeles, but by 1930 approximately 100,000 persons of Mexican birth or heritage lived there" (p. 265).

The increasing propensity for Mexican people to settle in America rather than just work there meant that the United States needed to address the schooling of Mexicans in a more comprehensive way than ever before.

By the early 1900s, the generation that had lived through the Mexican-American War were no longer living, and this reduced a considerable amount of the friction that existed in the 1800s. However, three realities created segregation between White people and

Mexicans/Mexican Americans. First, these individuals tended to live in what were then called "colonies," concentrations of Mexican and Mexican American people in small areas (Cooke, 1949; Schermerhorn, 1949). Second, many Americans construed these clusters as Mexican Americans desiring to remain to themselves (Cooke, 1949; Schermerhorn, 1949). Third, many parents were concerned about their children attending schools with large concentrations of Spanish-speaking students, whom they believed would impede the instruction process (Cooke, 1949; Schermerhorn, 1949).

The third concern, in particular, led to *Mendez et al. v. Westminster School District,* California Federal District Court (1946). This case arose because California school districts in three counties, Westminster, Garden Grove, and El Modeno, had taken action to have non-English-speaking children "be required to attend schools designated by the boards separate and apart from English-speaking pupils; that such group should attend such schools until they had required some proficiency in the English language" (*Mendez et al. v. Westminster,* 1946). Although the school district decrees specified that there was to be no segregation on the basis of race, the petitioners claimed that the vast majority of the non–English speakers were Mexican and that this action by the three school districts constituted "arbitrary discrimination" (*Mendez et al. v. Westminster,* 1946).

The court sided with the plaintiff, asserting that Spanish-speaking children could not be expected to learn English well if they went to schools with little chance to be exposed to the language and that the segregation of Mexican Americans violated the California constitution (*Mendez et al. v. Westminster,* 1946; San Miguel, 1987; Tashakkori & Ochoa, 1999). Education for Mexican Americans advanced in other spheres as well. In 1948, Mexican Americans in three Texas counties filed a class action suit to abolish separate schools for their children (San Miguel, 1987; Tashakkori & Ochoa, 1999). Mexican Americans also enjoyed the benefits of individuals such as Hector Garcia to advocate advances in education and in veterans' rights for Mexican Americans (Garcia, 2002). Garcia also served on the Civil Rights Commission.

Some might wonder why *Mendez et al. v. Westminster* did not have the influence of the *Brown v. Board of Education* Supreme Court case (1954). The main reason is that the *Mendez* case involved primarily local issues (Sanchez, 1951). It was a battle over what three school districts did, an arbitrary act that was rarely practiced in American schools, regarding speaking English. Moreover, in 1946, unlike the African American population, which was spread throughout the country, the Mexican American population was concentrated in a much smaller geographic area (U.S. Census Bureau, 2001). Most of the country could not relate to the specific issues of the *Mendez* case. The practices addressed in *Brown* were much more pervasive nationally. Nevertheless, *Mendez et al. v. Westminster* set the stage for *Brown v. Board of Education* not only in terms of precedent but also because Earl Warren was Governor of California at the time of the *Mendez* case and therefore was familiar with the case.

Puerto Ricans and Education

Puerto Ricans were the other major Latino group to arrive in the United States in fairly substantial numbers in the early 1900s. The number of Puerto Ricans in the United States rose from 1,500 in 1910 to 70,000 in 1940 (Morrison, 1972). Nearly all the Puerto Ricans who moved to the United States settled in New York City. The concentration of Puerto Ricans in New York City was greater than for nearly all of the Latino and Asian minority groups in other specific locales (Morrison, 1972). This enabled school leaders to come to understand the educational needs of Puerto Ricans. As a result, the research and teaching techniques for second-language students was more advanced in New York than in other parts of the country (Morrison, 1972). The textbooks that instructors used to teach Puerto Rican students in the mid-1900s included *Fries American English Series,* which was sponsored by the Department of Education of Puerto Rico (Morrison, 1972).

As Latinos became more numerous in the United States, other issues would emerge, such as the quest for bilingual education. This issue and others relevant to Latino people will be addressed in Chapter 10 and in other sections of this book.

CONCLUSION

The educational advancements made by women and various racial minorities over the years have been remarkable. Each group has had unique challenges to overcome. The realities of industrialization, the economy, distrust, war, and residential demographics have also had a considerable impact on the education of these various groups. So much of the American educational journey does not have to do with schooling for the general population, but the way the United States has provided for the individual groups that make up the general population. As the nation continues to seek the best educational options for its various populations of people, it is important to know where the educational journey has taken the nation thus far in order to best assess where the nation's school system should go now.

DISCUSSION QUESTIONS

1. The contemporary education of Native Americans presents a very unique situation. To respect the Native American desire to preserve their culture and educate their people, most Americans find the segregation of Native American children acceptable. However, there are a growing number of people, both Native American and otherwise, who believe that many Native American children suffer because of this segregation. What do you feel is the appropriate educational policy the U.S. government should maintain with Native American students?

2. There were many turning points in the history of women's education. Which do you view as the most important of these, and why?

3. Many immigrant groups settle and concentrate themselves in certain geographical areas. What are some of the advantages and challenges faced by the immigrants themselves, educators, and society at large to these demographic realities?

4. Many of the pioneers of expanded opportunities for females were themselves women. Do you think it is preferable for women to teach girls and for men to teach boys, because of a greater ability to understand same-sex students, or do you believe that a teacher's gender does not have that much impact on teacher outcomes? Is it best for students to be exposed to teachers of both genders?

REFERENCES

Adams, J. Q. (1969). *Memoirs of John Quincy Adams, comprising portions of his diary from 1795 to 1848* (C. F Adams, Ed.). Freeport, NY: Books for Libraries Press.

Albisetti, J. C. (2000). Un-learned lessons from the New World? English views of American coeducation and women's colleges, c. 1865–1910. *History of Education, 29,* 473–489.

Barker, E. C. (1928). *Mexico and Texas, 1821–1835.* Austin: University of Texas.

Barker, E. C. (1970). *The life of Stephen F. Austin, founder of Texas 1793–1836.* New York: AMS Press.

Beard, C. A., & Beard, M. A. (1944). *A basic history of the United States.* New York: Doubleday, Doran.

Beasley, W. G. (1972). *The Meiji restoration.* Stanford, CA: Stanford University Press.

Beecher, C. E. (1874). *Educational reminiscences and suggestions.* New York: J. B. Ford.

Blinderman, A. (1976). *Three early champions of education: Benjamin Franklin, Benjamin Rush, and Noah Webster.* Bloomington, IN: Phi Delta Kappa Educational Foundation.

Boas, L. S. (1971). *Women's education begins: The rise of women's colleges.* New York: Arno.

Brauer, J. C. (1991). Editor's preface. In S. H Snyder (Ed.), *Lyman Beecher and his children* (pp. xiii–xvi). Brooklyn, NY: Carlson.

Brown v. Board of Education 347 U.S. 483 (1954).

Bryan, S. (1912). Mexican immigrants in the United States. *Survey, 20,* 726, 730.

Burroughs, C. (1827). *An address on female education.* Portsmouth, NH: Childs & March.

Burt, L. W. (1982). *Tribalism in crisis: Federal Indian policy, 1953–1961.* Albuquerque: University of New Mexico Press.

California State Senate. (1876). *Chinese immigration, the social, moral, and political effect of Chinese immigration: Testimony taken before a committee of the Senate of the State of California.* Sacramento, CA: Author.

Chen, J. (1980). *The Chinese of America.* San Francisco: Harper & Row.

Chiswick, B. R. (1992). Jewish immigrant wages in America in 1909: An Analysis of the Dillingham Commission Data. *Explorations in Economic History, 29,* 274–289.

Chronicle of Higher Education. (2003). *Notebook, 49*(42), 1–4.

Clark, V. S. (1908). *Mexican labor in the United States* (Bulletin #78). Washington, DC: U.S. Government Printing Office.

Cooke, W. H. (1949). The segregation of Mexican American children in Southern California. *School and Society, 67,* 417–422.

Crosscup, R. (Ed.). (1968). *Classic speeches.* New York: Citadel Press.

DeLeon, A. (1982). *The Tejano community, 1836–1900.* Albuquerque: University of New Mexico Press.

d'Errico, P. (2001). Native Americans in America: A theoretical and historical overview. In F. E. Hoxie, P. C. Mancall, & J. H. Merrell (Eds.), *American nations: Encounters in Indian country, 1850 to the present* (pp. 480–499). New York: Routledge.

Dickey, J. S. (1954). *Eleazar Wheelock, 1711–1779, Daniel Webster, 1782–1852, and their pioneer Dartmouth College.* New York: Newcomen Society in North America.

DuBois, W. E. B. (1912). *Disenfranchisement.* New York: National American Woman Suffrage Association.

Edwards, J. (2002). *Women in American education, 1820–1955.* Westport, CT: Greenwood Press.

Eggleston, E. (1998). *A history of the United States and its people.* Lake Wales, FL: Lost Classics.

Fairbanks, M. J., & Sage, R. (1898). *Emma Willard and her pupils; or, Fifty years of Troy female seminary, 1822–1872.* New York: Sage.

Fliegel, S., & MacGuire, J. (1993). *Miracle in East Harlem: The fight for choice in public education.* New York: Times Books.

Gamio, M. (1930). *Mexican immigration to the United States: A study of human migration and adjustment.* Chicago: University of Chicago Press.

Garcia, E. E. (1997). Effective instruction for language minority students: The teacher. In A. Darder, R. D. Torres, & H. Gutierrez (Eds.), *Latinos and education: A critical reader* (pp. 362–372). New York: Routledge.

Garcia, I. M. (2002). *Hector P. Garcia: In relentless pursuit of justice.* Houston, TX: Arte Publico.

Geiger, R. L. (2000). *The American college in the nineteenth century.* Nashville, TN: Vanderbilt University Press.

Getz, L. M. (1997). *Schools of their own.* Albuquerque: University of New Mexico Press.

Gomersall, M. (1994). Education for domesticity? A nineteenth-century perspective on girls' schooling and education. *Gender and Education, 6,* 235–247.

Gonzales, J. L. (1990). *Racial and ethnic groups in America.* Dubuque, IA: Kendall/Hunt.

Good, H, G. (1918). *Benjamin Rush and his services to American education.* Berne, IN: Witness Press.

Gordon, L. D. (2002). Education and the profession. In N. A. Hewitt (Ed.), *A companion to American women's history* (pp. 227–249). Oxford, UK: Blackwell.

Gorton, G. (1998). *What would they say? The founding fathers on current issues.* Lafayette, LA: Huntington House.

Gottheimer, J. (2003). *Ripples of hope: Great American civil rights speeches.* New York: Basic Civitas.

Henderson, J. (1998). The federal government should pursue peace with the Indians. In W. Dudley (Ed.), *Native Americans: Opposing viewpoints.* San Diego, CA: Greenhaven Press.

Hiner, N. R. (1988). The cry of Sodom enquired into: Educational analysis in seventeenth-century New England. In E. McClellan & W. J. Reese (Eds.), *The social history of American education* (pp. 3–21). Urbana: University of Illinois.

Houston, A. J. (1938). *Texas independence.* Houston, TX: Anson Jones.

Howlett, P. (2000). Evidence of the existence of an internal labour market in the Great Eastern Railway Company, 1875–1905. *Business History, 42,* 21–40.

Hoxie, F. E., Mancall, P. C., & Merrell, J. H. (2001). *American nations: Encounters in Indian country, 1850 to the present.* New York: Routledge.

Jackson, A. (1829). First annual message. In J. D. Richardson (Ed., 1897), *A compilation of the messages and papers of the presidents, 1789–1897* (pp. 1020–1022). New York: Bureau of National Literature. Retrieved August 24, 2006, from http://www.lincoln.lib.niu.edu/teachers/lesson5-groupa.html.

Jackson, A. (1830). Second annual message. In J. D. Richardson (Ed., 1897), *A compilation of the messages and papers of the presidents, 1789–1897* (pp. 1083–1086). New York: Bureau of National Literature. Retrieved August 24, 2006, from http://www.lincoln.lib.niu.edu/teachers/lesson5-groupa.html.

Jefferson, T. (1818). Letter to Nathaniel Burwell, March 14. In A. A. Lipscomb & A. E. Bergh (Eds.), *The writings of Thomas Jefferson* (pp. 104–106). Washington, DC: U.S. Government Printing Office.

Jencks, J. W., Lauck, W. J., & Smith, R. D. (1922). *The immigration problem: A study of American immigrant conditions and needs.* New York: Funk & Wagnall.

Jeynes, W. (2005). Effects of parental involvement on African American children's academic achievement. *Journal of Negro Education, 74,* 260–274.

Johnson, H. S., & Hernandez, W. J. (1970). *Educating the Mexican American.* Valley Forge, PA: Judson Press.

Jones, A. E. (1928). Mexican life in Chicago. *Social Science Review, 2*(12), 39–54.

Kalman, B. (1982). *Early schools.* Toronto, Canada: Crabtree.

Kaufman. P. W. (1984). *Women teachers on the frontier.* Englewood Cliffs, NJ: Prentice Hall.

Lee, S. J. (2004). Up against Whiteness: Students of color in our schools. *Anthropology and Education Quarterly, 35,* 121–125.

Lee, V. E., & Bryk, A. S. (1986). Effects of single-sex secondary schools on student achievement and attitudes. *Journal of Educational Psychology, 78,* 381–395.

Lee, V. E., & Marks, H. M. (1990). Sustained effects of the single-sex secondary school experience on attitudes, behaviors and values in college. *Journal of Educational Psychology, 82,* 578–592.

Lewis, J. E. (2002). A revolution for whom? Women in the era of the American Revolution. In N. A. Hewut (Ed.), *A companion to American women's history* (pp. 86–104). Oxford, UK: Blackwell.

Lord, W. (1961). *A time to stand.* New York: Harper & Brothers.

Lundy, B. (1970). *The war in Texas.* Upper Saddle River, NJ: Gregg Press.

Lyon, M. (1835). Mount Holyoke Female Seminary. *Old South Leaflets, No. 145,* 425–428. Retrieved August 26, 2006, from http://www.clio.fivecolleges.edu/mhc/lyon/b/1published/ff05/leaflet_145/01.htm.

Marshall, P., & Manuel, D. (1977). *The light and the glory.* Grand Rapids, MI: Fleming Revell.

Matthaei, J. A. (1982). *An economic history of women in America: Women's work, the sexual division of labor, and the development of capitalism.* New York: Harvester Press.

McCallum, J. D. (1939). *Eleazar Wheelock: Founder of Dartmouth College.* Hanover, NH: Dartmouth College Publications.

McKenney, T. L. (1846). *Memoirs, official and personal.* Lincoln: University of Nebraska Press.

McKenney, T. L. (1933). *The Indian tribes of North America, with biographical sketches and anecdotes of the principal chiefs* (J. Hall, Ed.). St. Clair Shores, MI: Scholarly Press.

Mendez v. Westminster, 64 F. Supp. 544, 545 (SD Cal. 1946).

Miller, L. B. (1972). *"If elected": Unsuccessful candidates for the presidency, 1796–1968.* Washington, DC: Smithsonian Institute.

Miller, W. L. (1996). *Arguing about slavery: The great battle in the United States Congress.* New York: Knopf.

Miller-Bernal, L. (2000). *Separate by degree.* New York: Peter Lang.

Miller-Bernal, L., & Poulson, S. L. (2004). *Going coed: Women's experiences in formerly men's colleges and universities, 1950–2000.* Nashville, TN: Vanderbilt University Press.

Miranda, G. E. (1990). Mexican-Americans in the history of the United States. In A. J. Wrobel & M. J. Eula (Eds.), *American ethnics and minorities: Readings in ethnic history* (pp. 71–89). Dubuque, IL: Kendall Hunt.

Morgan, T. J. (1889). *Supplemental report on Indian "education"* (House Executive Document No. 1, Pt. 5, Vol. 2, 51st Congress, 1 Sess., Ser. 2725). Washington, DC: U.S. Government Printing Office.

Morrison, J. C. (1972). *The Puerto Rican study, 1953–1957.* New York: Oriole.

Myers, J. (1948). *The Alamo.* New York: Dutton.

Newcomer, M. (1959). *A century of higher education for American women.* New York: Harper & Brothers.

Ng, F. (1998). *Adaptation, acculturation, and transnational ties among Asian Americans.* New York: Garland.

Ogbu, J. U. (1992). Adaptation to minority status and impact on school success. *Theory Into Practice, 31,* 287–295.

Ogbu, J. U. (1993). Differences in cultural frame of reference. *International Journal of Behavioral Development, 16,* 483–506.

Polakow, V. (2004). *Shut out: Low income mothers and higher education in post-welfare America.* Albany: SUNY Press.

Reynolds, A. (1933). *The education of Spanish speaking children in five southwestern states* (U.S. Office of Education, No. 11–15). Washington, DC: U.S. Government Printing Office.

Richardson, A. W. (1847). Letter to Henry Barnard, March 23, New York. *Papers of Henry Barnard.* Manuscript Collection of Trinity College Watkinson Library, Hartford, CT.

Riordan, C. H. (1990). *Girls and boys in school: Together or separate?* New York: Teachers College Press.

Rudolph, F. (Ed.). (1965). *Essays on education in the early republic.* Cambridge, MA: Belknap Press of Harvard University Press.

Ruiz, V. L. (1993). Star struck: Acculturation. Adolescence, and the Mexican American Woman, 1920–1950. In A. de la Torre & B. M. Pesquera (Eds.), *Building with our hands: New directions in Chicana studies* (pp. 109–129). Berkeley: University of California Press.

Rush, B. (1785). *Plan of education.* Carlisle, PA: Dickinson College.

Rush, B. (1786a). *A plan for the establishment of public schools and the diffusion of knowledge in Pennsylvania; to which are added thoughts upon the mode of education, proper in a republic.* Addressed to the legislature and citizens of the state. Philadelphia: Thomas Dobson.

Rush, B. (1786b). Thoughts upon female education, accommodated to the present state of society, manners, and government. In F. Rudolph (Ed., 1965), *Essays on education in the early republic.* Cambridge, MA: Belknap Press of Harvard University.

Rush, B. (1820). *A defense of the use of the Bible in schools.* New York: American Tract Society 1820.

Rush, B. (1947). *The selected writings of Benjamin Rush* (D. D. Runes, Ed.). New York: Philosophical Library.

Sanchez, G. I. (1951). *Concerning segregation of Spanish-speaking children.* Austin: University of Texas.

Sanchez, G. I. (1997). History, culture, & education. In A. Darder, R. D. Torres, & H. Gutierrez (Eds.), *Latinos and education: A critical reader* (pp. 118–134). New York: Routledge.

San Miguel, G. Jr. (1987). *Let all of them take heed.* Austin: University of Texas.

Schermerhorn, R. A. (1949). *These our people: Minorities in American culture.* Boston D. C. Heath.

Schlesinger, A. M., & Israel, F. L. (2003). *The elections of 1789 and 1792 and the administration of George Washington.* Philadelphia: Mason Crest.

Schreiner, S. A. Jr. (2003). *The passionate Beechers.* Hoboken, NJ: Wiley.

Sedillo, A. (1995). *Historical themes and identity: Mestizaje and labels.* New York: Garland.

Senese, G. B. (1991). *Self-determination and the social education of Native Americans.* New York: Praeger.

Shoemaker, E. C. (1966). *Noah Webster: Pioneer of learning.* New York: AMS Press.

Sicherman, B. (1988). College and careers: Historical perspectives on the lives and work patterns of women college graduates. In J. M. Faragher & F. Howe (Eds.), *Women & higher education in American history* (p. 136). New York: Norton.

Slotkin, R., & Folsom, J. K. (Eds.). (1978). *So dreadful a judgment: Puritan responses to King Philip's War, 1676–1677.* Middletown, CT: Wesleyan University Press.

Snyder, S. H. (1991). *Lyman Beecher and his children.* Brooklyn, NY: Carlson.

Spencer, S. (2004). Reflections on the "site of struggle": Girls' experience of secondary education in the late 1950s. *History of Education, 33,* 437–449.

Spring, J. (1997). *The American school 1642–1996.* White Plains, NY: Longman.

Sylvester, H. M. (1910). *Indian wars of New England.* Boston: W. B. Clark.

Szasz, M. (1974). *Education and the American Indian: The road to self-determination, 1928–1973.* Albuquerque: University of New Mexico Press.

Szasz, M. (1977). *Education and the American Indian: The road to self-determination, since 1928.* Albuquerque: University of New Mexico Press.

Szasz, M. (1985). *Indian education in the American colonies, 1607–1783.* Albuquerque University of New Mexico Press.

Szasz, M. (1988). *Indian education in the American colonies, 1607–1783.* Albuquerque: University of New Mexico Press.

Tashakkori, A., & Ochoa, S. H. (1999). *Education of Hispanics in the United States.* New York: AMS Press.

Tewksbury, S. (1932). *Founding of American colleges and universities before the Civil War.* New York: Teachers College Press.

Tidball, M. E., Smith, D. G., Tidball, C. S., & Wolf-Wendel, L. (1999). *Taking women seriously: Lessons and legacies for educating the majority.* Phoenix, AZ: Oryx Press.

Torres, R. (1997). Nomads and migrants. In A. Darder, R. D. Torres, & H. Gutierrez (Eds.), *Latinos and education: A critical reader* (pp. 239–258). New York: Routledge.

Troen, S. K. (1988). Popular education in nineteenth century St. Louis. In E. McClellan & W. J. Reese (Eds.), *The social history of American education* (pp. 119–136). Urbana: University of Illinois.

Urban, W., & Wagoner, J. (2000). *American education: A history.* Boston: McGraw-Hill.

U.S. Census Bureau. (2001). *The statistical abstract of the United States.* Washington, DC: Author.

U.S. Congress. (1960). *Operation Bootstrap for the American Indians.* Washington, DC: Author.

U.S. Department of Education. (2002). *Digest of education statistics.* Washington, DC: Author.

U.S. Department of Health, Education, and Welfare. (1951). *Education directory, 1949–1950.* Washington, DC: U.S. Government Printing Office.

U.S. Department of Health, Education, and Welfare. (1970). *Education directory, 1969–1970.* Washington, DC: U.S. Government Printing Office.

Vargas, Z. (Ed.). (1999). *Major problems in Mexican American history.* Boston: Houghton Mifflin.

Vigness, D. M. (1965). *The revolutionary decades: The saga of Texas, 1810–1836.* Austin, TX: Steck-Vaughan.

Viola, H. J. (1974). *Thomas L. McKenney: Architect of America's early Indian policy, 1816–1830.* Chicago: Sage.

Waldron, A., Hannan, P., & Twitchett, D. (1990). *The Great Wall of China: From history to myth.* Cambridge, UK: Cambridge University Press.

Wallace A., & Foner, E. (1993). *Andrew Jackson and the Indians: The long, bitter trail.* New York: Hill & Wang.

Ware, S. (1998). *Forgotten heroes: Inspiring portraits from our leading historians.* New York: Free Press.

Warrington, M., Younger, M., & Williams, J. (2000). Student attitudes, image, and gender gap. *British Educational Research Journal, 26,* 393–407.

Webster, N. (1807). *Education of youth in the United States.* New Haven, CT.

Webster, N. (1843). *A collection of papers on political, literary, and moral subjects.* New York: B. Franklin.

Weddle, M. B. (2001). *Walking in the way of peace: Quaker pacifism in the seventeenth century.* Oxford, UK: Oxford University Press.

Weinberg, M. (1997). *Asian-American education.* Mahwah, NJ: Lawrence Erlbaum.

Wheelock, E. (1763). *A plain and faithful narrative of the original design, rise, progress, and present state of the Indian charity-school at Lebanon, in Connecticut.* Boston: Draper.

Wilson, G. (2005, June 10). No quick fix for boys. *Times Educational Supplement,* p. 23.

Wollenberg, C. (1976). *All deliberate speed.* Berkeley: University of California.

Wollenberg, C. M. (1995). Yellow peril in the schools. In D. T. Nakanishi & T. Y. N. Nishida (Eds.), *The Asian American educational experience* (pp. 3–29). New York: Routledge.

Wollstonecraft, M. (1891). *A vindication of the rights of women.* London: Walter Scott Paternoster.

Yoo, D. K. (2000). *Growing up Nisei: Race, gender, and culture among Japanese Americans of California, 1924–1949.* Urbana: University of Illinois.

CHAPTER 6

The Widespread Growth of the Common School and Higher Education

T he rise of the common or public school and the proliferation of colleges is one of the most intriguing times in the history of American education. Although most Americans almost take for granted the presence of public schools, from their inception as a part of a national movement, these schools sparked controversy and political division (Glenn, 1988; Mondale & Patton, 2001). Nevertheless, several educational leaders led by Horace Mann, Henry Barnard, and others rose to the occasion and implemented a vision for the common schools that eventually, after the Civil War, captured the imagination and support of the American people (Mondale & Patton, 2001). The growth of higher education during the period was fundamental to building on the earlier achievements in higher education that would eventually yield the quintessential system of colleges and universities in the world.

HORACE MANN AND THE RISE OF THE COMMON SCHOOLS

Horace Mann (1796–1859) is generally regarded as the "father of the common school." Educated at Brown University, Mann was born in Franklin, Massachusetts, in the year 1796 (Messerli, 1972). Mann always wanted to make an impact on society. For this reason, in his earlier days, he studied law. However, once he had practiced law for a while, he became disillusioned. Mann claimed that education was a better means than law to change society. His reasoning was that the law dealt with adults, who were already set in their ways. Education dealt with children. Mann asserted, "Men are cast-iron, but children are wax" (as cited in M. Mann, 1907, p. 13). Mann believed that the means for extricating man from evil rested not in the law, but in education. In this sense, he transformed from an Old Testament to a New Testament type of individual. Parallel to the emphasis on fulfilling the laws in the Old Testament, Mann had previously believed that the law was the key to making people upright. However, he soon realized that the New Testament emphasis on training and teaching was the best means of truly changing society (M. Mann, 1907).

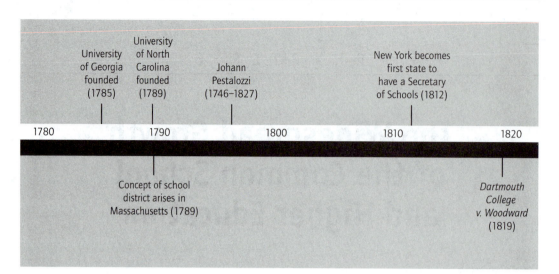

By the time Mann became the first secretary of the Massachusetts Board of Education, in 1837, New York and Massachusetts had become the prominent states in blazing the trail for the education of children in the United States (Bobbe, 1933; Bourne, 1870). Massachusetts had already established a system of public schools via taxation and the erecting of laws regarding the education of children. New York had sought to initially train their student population using private schools. Nevertheless, because of the financial strains of educating children, the charity schools of New York could not educate all the immigrants coming into America (Bourne, 1870; Clinton, 1829).

New York political and educational leaders played a major role in paving the way for the coming of Horace Mann, for in 1812, New York became the first state to create the position of state superintendent of schools (Spring, 1997). In the 1820s, some other states followed New York's lead and also developed this position for their individual states. By the 1830s, state supervisors became more common (Bobbe, 1933; Bourne, 1870). This set the stage for the proliferation of the public school movement. Normally, because of the inchoate level of communication of the era, the ascendancy of Mann and others like him would have been circumscribed to a certain geographical area. But between 1825 and 1850, educators developed dozens of journals and other periodicals. Two of the most prominent of these were based in Massachusetts and Connecticut (Barnard, 1842, 1843; Barnard & Lannie, 1974; Wertheim, 1970). The first journal was called the *Massachusetts Common School* and was edited by Mann, and the other was called the *Connecticut Common School* and was edited by Barnard (Spring, 1997).

Mann's Arguments That Common Schools Would Promote the Common Good

Mann contended that common schools would promote the common good in American education. There were a number of reasons he maintained this perspective.

Common Schools Would Level the Playing Field Between Rich and Poor Students

Mann was persuaded that the presence of common schools would level the playing field between the rich and the poor (M. Mann, 1907). He believed that affluent people had a natural advantage over the indigent in that they were able to send their children to the best schools. As a result, the children of the wealthy possessed an inherent advantage in terms of obtaining the best jobs and enjoying a high standard of living. He believed that the availability of education would make it possible for the poor to compete more adequately with the rich for the best jobs that were available. Mann thought that the wage gap that existed between the prosperous and the poor should not be solved by revolution, but by the education of the lower classes of people (M. Mann, 1907).

Mann realized that the dream of a common school needed financing. He needed to convince the American public that the common school was worthy of taxpayer-supported financing. After all, those people without young children might otherwise see little reason to pay taxes in order to send someone else's children to school. Mann (1840, 1844; M. Mann, 1907) therefore argued that the common school would not only profit the individual children who attended but would also benefit American society as a whole. First, the United States would reap advantages from having a more highly educated population (Mann, 1840, 1844; M. Mann, 1907). A more educated population would bring more wealth to each community. A higher level of education would capacitate each worker to labor more effectively and would enable him or her to do tasks that hitherto he or she could not do. Second, education would produce more tranquility in various communities across the nation, as people came to understand one another more (M. Mann, 1907). Third, education would equip more people to share in the American dream. Mann argued that the greater the number of Americans that were content, the stronger the nation would be (Mann, 1840, 1844; M. Mann, 1907).

Mann was unapologetic about the need for taxation to support schools (Mann, 1840, 1844; M. Mann, 1907). Americans valued a free education, and the charity school movement had exemplified this quest. However, it was clear that the relatively new nation simply did not possess enough wealthy individuals to support the educational needs of the populace. Taxation, in Mann's view, was both necessary and central in order to continue to provide free education for the poor (Mann, 1840, 1844; M. Mann, 1907).

Common Schools Would Promote Moral Education

Mann was a strong advocate of the primacy of moral education. Although his writings of the 1830s did impact the education world, his "Twelfth Annual Report," in 1849, had the greatest impact. In this report, Mann argued for the merits of moral education. He averred that moral education, even more than the education of the mind, was the key for changing society. Mann (1957) asserted that the most important focus that educators should have is "best expressed in these few and simple words: 'Train up a child in the way he should go, and when he is old he will not depart from it'" (p. 100, citing Proverbs 22:6). This biblical truth epitomizes the educational philosophy of Horace Mann. As Urban and Wagoner (2000) note, "For Horace Mann and the other common school reformers, moral education was the heart of the curriculum" (p. 107). In Mann's (1849) "Twelfth Annual

Report," which educators assert summarizes the essence of his educational philosophy, he declared,

> But, it will be said that this great result, in Practical Morals, is a consummation of blessedness that can never be attained without religion; and that no community will ever be religious without a Religious Education. Both of these propositions, I regard as eternal and immutable truths. Devoid of religious principles and religious affections the race can never fall so low that it may sink still lower. (as cited in Kliebard, 1969, p. 73)

Horace Mann was at heart a Christian moralist. He believed that society had a responsibility to train children not only intellectually, but also morally. Thomas Hunt and Marilyn Maxson (1981) state, "For Mann, then, moral education was the key; it was a major reason for the existence of the common school and for significantly expanding its function" (p. 14). Charles and Mary Beard (1944) state, "To the grand end of a happy and virtuous life for the individual and the progress of civilization in American society Horace Mann subordinated all other aims of education" (p. 238). Mann's strong belief in the importance of religion and morality set the stage for the strong presence of each in America's public schools. Mann (1838) stated,

> As piety is the discharge of our duty to God, and as that duty cannot be discharged, without a knowledge of his character and attributes, it follows that to teach the principles of piety, we must teach that character and those attributes. (n.p.)

Religion and morality were very important aspects of American society at this time. During his travels to America in 1831 and 1832, Tocqueville (1966), said, "There is no other country in the world where the Christian religion retains a greater influence over the souls of men than in America" (p. 268).

The 20th-century historian Ellwood Cubberley (1909) remarked, "The work of public education is with us . . . to a large degree, a piece of religious work" (p. 68). Moral education was an important component of education in Mann's day. Stephen Yulish (1980) sums up this truth well:

> The concept of moral education has always been a crucial underpinning of the American notion of a virtuous republic. Throughout its development, American leaders in education have strenuously sought to condemn mere intellectual training. Whether it was the phrenological justifications of Horace Mann for training pupils in proper laws of health and morals or the widespread perception of a need for moral training to inculcate respect for authority and law and order, the notion of moral education has historically been a crucial factor in the American experience. The deep-felt need to control behavior and conduct by moral training was undertaken by the schools alongside the instruction of the church and the home. (p. 80)

As Lawrence Cremin notes (Mann, 1957), Mann viewed "public education as a moral enterprise." Mann asserted,

> The more I see of our present civilization and of the only remedies for its evils, the more I dread intellectual eminence when separated from virtue. We are in a sick world, for whose maladies, the knowledge of truth, and obedience to it, are the only healing. (Mann, as cited in Filler, 1965, p. iii)

Filler (1965) adds, "The essence of Mann's program was moral. He believed not only that education carried moral responsibilities, but prosecuted without them, it could only produce more evil than it had ever inherited" (p. ix). Mann (1969) believed that just as mental and physical abilities increased via exercise, one's morality increased in the same way. Therefore, he argued that schools should give children the opportunity to exercise their moral facilities (Mann, 1845, 1849, 1969).

Mann (1969) believed that one of the primary jobs of the common schools was to teach children a love for the truth and that love for the truth should have as its objects both intellectual and moral truth. He was so persuaded of the salience of these facts that he was convinced that without them, those in American society not only could not weather a storm, but that "we cannot weather a calm" (Mann, 1969, p. 125). As a result of Mann's emphasis on moral education, nearly all the public schools in Massachusetts taught the Bible in the classroom (Mann, 1845).

Common Schools Would Help Ensure Quality Teaching

Mann accentuated the fact that teachers needed to be very competent at their profession. He believed that teachers could be trained to be efficacious and to maintain a good mastery over their subject matter and teach effectively (M. Mann, 1907; Messerli, 1972; Tharp, 1953). He also believed that teachers needed to be trained to be people of character in order to teach their students to possess good moral character (Mann, 1849; M. Mann, 1907; Messerli, 1972; Tharp, 1953). Mann was concerned about the American perception that city schools were of far greater quality than rural schools, and he claimed that if schools had a common curriculum, educational leaders could found teacher institutes that could train teachers to be effective no matter which common school they taught in (Mann, 1957; M. Mann, 1907; Tharp, 1953).

Once again in this case, Mann focused on educational gaps. He not only affirmed that there was a gap between rich and poor but also contended that there was an instructional gap between schools (Mann, 1849; M. Mann, 1907; Messerli, 1972; Tharp, 1953). Mann asserted that common schools were the answer to this problem, because they would cause teacher institutes to share certain common equalizing factors as well.

Mann's list of organizational features to enhance equality did not terminate at the common schools and teacher institutes. He developed a very sophisticated vision for the common schools and was an adroit organizer. He believed that in order to develop a strong common school movement, every facet of the educational enterprise had to be strong, and he insisted that every common school maintain a high level of quality (Mann, 1839, 1845). To ensure that this would take place, Mann favored a number of key actions. First, he favored the dissemination of school inspectors across the state to help guarantee that schools were meeting certain standards (Mann, 1845). Second, he favored a high degree of collaboration among schools so that they could help each other succeed (Mann, 1839). Third, he believed that school boards could function as overseers to help ensure that teachers would set a good moral example (Mann, 1846, 1849, M. Mann, 1907; Messerli, 1972; Tharp, 1953). Fourth, he favored the widespread establishment of school libraries (Mann, 1839, 1844, 1845, 1969). New York introduced the first common school library in 1835 (Mann, 1969). Fifth, Mann (1840) also believed in the fiscal accountability of his position, and he invested the education system's money wisely, doubling its worth over his years of service. Mann (1957, 1969) also had a broad vision of the common school that included addressing student hygiene in the curriculum and stating that he thought corporal punishment in the school was inappropriate.

Common Schools Would Unite the Country by Teaching Common Values

Mann believed that in order to build a common school system, teachers needed to focus on ideals that were common to all Americans. This goal pertained not only to religious values, but to political values as well. Mann (1844) exhorted teachers to veer away from the controversial political debates of the day. Nevertheless, he believed that Americans shared certain political values on which the nation was based (Kaestle & Vinovskis, 1980). Mann (1957) believed it would strengthen the nation if these shared political values were taught. He affirmed that a core set of values would strengthen the nation as a whole and reduce any violence that might result from disseverance. Mann's emphasis on common values was particularly popular once the Civil War ended, when Americans realized the urgent need of sharing common values that could help heal the country (Kaestle & Vinovskis, 1980).

Horace Mann (1849) believed, as did most Americans at the time, that the Bible should be a primary basis for those common values, as well as the moral instruction that was presented in the schools. He was nevertheless careful to include the Bible in such a way that would not produce friction between religious denominations. Mann (1849) claimed that "the laws of Massachusetts required the teaching of the basic moral doctrines of Christianity" (p. 6). He believed that the common schools needed a nonsectarian use of the Bible in which the aspects of the Bible that all denominations taught could be emphasized (Mann, 1844). This view of the place of the Bible in the public school curriculum was well received and practiced in American schools until the early 1960s (Blanshard, 1963; Kliebard, 1969).

RESISTANCE TO PUBLIC SCHOOLS

Political Opposition

We must not suppose that a grand majority of Americans supported the common school movement. In reality, whether people upheld or opposed the common school movement was divided largely along political lines (Barnard, 1842; Mann, 1840; M. Mann, 1907). By this time, the American political system was divided into two major parts. The Democratic-Republicans had previously become the dominant party, eventually forcing the Federalists into extinction. Then, John Quincy Adams became the sixth president. Adams was a Federalist at heart. With the decline of the Federalist Party, however, he joined the Democratic-Republican Party. Adams's Federalist policies aggravated many leaders in the Democratic-Republican Party, and as a result, the Democratic-Republican Party split. Andrew Jackson led the more traditional Democratic-Republicans and founded the Democratic Party (Adams, 1825, 1874b; Howe, 1973). The rest of the Democratic-Republican Party, along with other political groups, reorganized to form the Whig Party (Howe, 1973; Marshall & Manuel, 1986).

The Whig Party was more supportive of the common school movement than the Democrats were (Barnard, 1842; Mann, 1840). The Whigs believed that the United States needed a consensus on certain moral and social issues (Barnard, 1842; Howe, 1973; Mann, 1840). They believed that a system of common schools was the best medium to achieve this goal. Temperance was one of the moral issues that most concerned the Whigs (Mann, 1848; Spring, 1997). Certain members of the Whigs were also concerned about slavery (Spring, 1997).

The Democrats, in the tradition of the Democratic-Republican Party, strongly supported states' rights. They believed that Horace Mann and the Whigs were trying to thrust a singular concept of morality down the throats of the American people (Spring, 1997). The degree to which some Americans resisted Whig beliefs regarding temperance and other issues manifested itself in the burning of Lyman Beecher's church (Howe, 1979; Spring, 1997). Beecher was a well-known minister and a Whig, and he was also a moralist, advocating temperance and refraining from other moral transgressions (Beecher, 1864; Howe, 1979). When Beecher's church burned down, the volunteer fire department, which resented the moralism of the Whigs, refused to fight the flames and even sang songs while the fire raged (Beecher, 1864; Howe, 1979). In 1840, the Democrats even attempted to eliminate the Massachusetts State Board of Education. Joel Spring (1997) notes, "This action was considered a direct attack on the common school movement" (p. 122). The Democrats resented the common school movement because it was such an overt attempt to centralize the school system (Barnard, 1843; Mann, 1840). The attempt to destroy the Massachusetts State Board of Education failed in the state legislature by a vote of 245 to 182 (Kaestle & Vinovskis, 1980; Mann, 1840; Spring, 1997). Eighty percent of the Whigs voted to preserve the state board of education, helping secure its fate and Horace Mann's position as its overseer (Kaestle & Vinovskis, 1980; Mann, 1840; Spring, 1997).

One reason that Mann faced resistance is that he took strong stands on the two great moral issues of the day, temperance and slavery. Mann was an active member of the Massachusetts Temperance Society and was antislavery, as were nearly all Whigs (M. Mann, 1907). He believed that if alcohol consumption could be eliminated, it would not only benefit children directly but would also reduce poverty and criminal behavior (Mann, 1840; M. Mann, 1907).

Temperance and slavery were the primary moral issues of the day. Among the social issues of the era, ministers preached more about these topics than any others (Beecher, 1864; M. Mann, 1907).

Added Insight: The Importance of the Temperance Debate in America

Very few people would advocate alcohol temperance for contemporary society, but it was a controversial issue in the 1800s and up to the first third of the 20th century. During Horace Mann's era and throughout the 19th century, most teachers were in favor of temperance. Although this may seem like an extremist position today, teachers viewed alcohol in much the same way that most Americans view illegal drugs today. Teachers viewed themselves as defenders of children's welfare. They saw that alcoholic parents were often associated with child abuse and other forms of child mistreatment. To them, temperance was an issue of children's quality of life.

As time went on, the circumstances surrounding Abraham Lincoln's life and death only added to the conviction of many teachers that alcohol either had to be declared illegal or be subject to more substantial restrictions (Kerr, 1985; Thorton, 1992). Lincoln believed that once the victory against slavery had been won, he needed to take up a moral crusade against alcohol consumption. Although Lincoln did not appear to support declaring the drink illegal, he favored massive restrictions (Kerr, 1985; Thorton, 1992). This fact makes the circumstances surrounding the assassination of Lincoln all the more ironic. For on the day he was shot, Lincoln's bodyguard slipped away to get himself some liquor. It was at this moment that John Wilkes Booth saw his opportunity. Therefore, Booth quickly moved in to assassinate Lincoln (Clark, 1987; Reck, 1903; Roscoe, 1959). Lincoln (1842, 1863), originally a Whig, maintained a strong, typically Whig view on temperance. He said, "Intoxicating liquors . . . [came forth] . . . like the Egyptian angel of death, commissioned to slay, if not the first-born, then the fairest of every family" (Lincoln, 1842, p. 5). The intricate relationship between Lincoln's death and alcohol added to the convictions that many educators and Americans already had regarding temperance.

Parental Opposition

A lot of the resistance to the common school movement resulted from the desire not only for states rights but also for parental rights (Messerli, 1972; Tharp, 1953). Remember that traditionally, Americans viewed education as a three-way joint enterprise, involving the family, the church, and the school. Prior to this time, the school had been viewed as the least important part of this triad. In the eyes of those who opposed the common school movement, the school was now usurping the authority of the family and the church in order to proclaim itself as the foremost member of that triad (Gatto, 2001; Messerli, 1972; Tharp, 1953).

Many Americans resented people like Horace Mann, of Massachusetts, and Henry Barnard, of Connecticut, appointing the school system to be the most important member of the education triad (Gatto, 2001; Messerli, 1972; Spring, 1997; Tharp, 1953). Many people thought that if the school were to be the most important part, only the American people had the right to determine that. According to this logic, the proponents of the common school were both presumptuous and power hungry.

One might wonder why parents were raising considerably stronger objections to the public schools than they ever had to the proliferation of private schools. There are two reasons parental views were especially at variance with public schools. First, because the government sponsored public, or common, schools, parents thought the government was taking

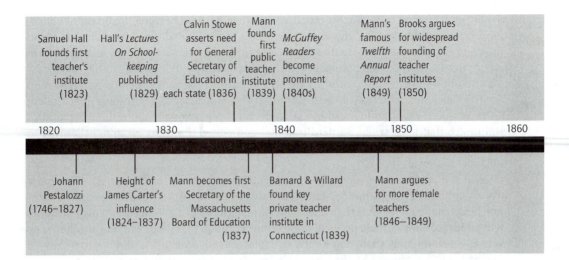

education out of the hands of the community (Downs, 1975; Gutek, 1968). Second, public schools were different from the private schools in that in many cases, parents were not familiar with the teachers (Downs, 1975; Gutek, 1968). Usually, when children attended private schools, the local church operated the school, and therefore parents and teachers were either neighbors or fellow parishioners. To many parents, schools were becoming increasingly impersonal, and the job of instruction was being given to professionals rather than parents (Downs, 1975; Gutek, 1968). To a large extent, this debate still remains with us today. Therefore, this issue will be revisited in Chapter 11.

CONTEMPORARIES OF HORACE MANN IN THE COMMON SCHOOL MOVEMENT

Henry Barnard

In terms of his influence on the common school movement, Henry Barnard (1811–1900) was second only to Horace Mann. Barnard was born in Hartford, Connecticut, in a "deeply religious family," and was inspired by "the Puritan work ethic" (Barnard & Lannie, 1974, p. 1). He went to Yale University and graduated in 1830. In 1832, Barnard became involved in Whig politics. He also later studied law, as Mann had done. He was very interested in the peace movement, and this interest inspired him to travel abroad, specifically to Europe (Barnard & Lannie, 1974). In 1835, Barnard went on a tour of Europe and witnessed the functioning of European education. After Barnard's tour of Europe, he initiated a career in education (Rippa, 1997). One of the dramatic results of his trip to Europe was that he became very interested in the education of the deaf and convinced himself that the mentally handicapped needed to be more humanely treated (Barnard & Lannie, 1974).

In 1837, Barnard was elected as a Whig to the Connecticut State Legislature. In the following year, he sponsored a bill establishing a state board of education very similar to the board of education created in Massachusetts, a year earlier. Barnard became the board of education's first secretary and left the world of politics to totally dedicate his life to education (Rippa, 1997). As a result of Barnard's experiences in Europe, he viewed humanitarian reform as perhaps the most essential aspect of his legislative agenda (Barnard & Lannie, 1974).

In addition to being influenced by his trip to Europe, Barnard's mentor was Reverend Thomas Gallaudet, who was at the forefront of the education of deaf-mutes (MacMullen, 1991). Barnard was so influenced by Gallaudet and so passionate about the education of deaf-mutes that later, when Barnard founded and edited the most prominent journal in education at the time, the *American Journal of Education,* he dedicated the first issues to Gallaudet (Barnard, 1855).

Once Barnard became secretary of the Connecticut Board of Education, he rapidly acquainted himself with Horace Mann (Barnard, 1842; Mann, 1840). They shared a common belief in the integrity of their cause and similar political challenges as Whig educators in the midst of considerable political opposition. Through their letters to one another, they were able to intimately share about their struggles and encourage one another to persevere (Barnard, 1842; Mann, 1840). In a letter on March 21, 1840, Mann wrote to Barnard after the Massachusetts legislature, for political reasons, tried to abolish the Massachusetts Board of Education: "Of course you know the result of the question about abolishing the Board. My own feelings about this from the day when the Report of the majority was made are a psychological wonder to me" (p. 1).

In the same letter, Mann (1840) wrote about the deep conviction that he had about the necessity and importance of common school education:

> I have long been accustomed to look at the great movement of education as part of the providence of God, by which the human race is to be redeemed. It is my conviction, it constitutes part of the Divine ordinances. I throw myself forward into the coming contest and see that the work has prospered. I regard it as more than a prophecy, as a fact. . . . Good-bye, my dear friend and fellow laborer in the holiest of causes. (p. 1)

The collection of correspondence between Barnard and Mann indicates that Barnard generally had a tougher time dealing with the political pressure against education than Mann did (Barnard, 1842, 1843; Mann, 1840). In Barnard's letter to Mann of March 1842, Barnard remarked, "I am sick and sad. This movement is now in the whirl of the political vortex, and I am the target of all sorts of mean and false representations" (p. 1). In another letter to Mann, on February 13, 1843, Barnard referred to the Democrats opposing common schools as "miserable demagogues" (p. 1). Barnard's battles would periodically affect his health, although he ultimately lived to the age of 89 (Barnard & Lannie, 1974; MacMullen, 1991).

Despite the challenges that Barnard faced, he, like Mann, was tenacious in maintaining the view that the common school cause was for the good of the country. He believed that democracy and education went together "in the cause of truth—the cause of justice—the cause of liberty—the cause of patriotism—the cause of religion" (Barnard, 1842, n.p.). Barnard believed the common school allowed more Americans to benefit from a comprehensive education than had ever been possible before. By "comprehensive," Barnard (1842) meant an education that addresses the "physical, intellectual, and moral powers" (p. 165).

Barnard's impact on education was broad. Not only was he the architect of the Connecticut public school system, but he also founded the *Connecticut Common School Journal* and the *American Journal of Education*. The latter became the premiere educational journal in the country (Barnard & Lannie, 1974; Thursfield, 1945). In the *American Journal of Education,* Barnard established high standards for research and for the use of educational statistics (Barnard & Lannie, 1974). He also served as the chancellor for the University of Wisconsin. Barnard, along with Emma Willard, also established the first systematic plan for the founding of many teacher-training institutes (Spring, 1997).

James Carter

Another contemporary of Horace Mann was James Carter (1795–1845). In many respects, he set the stage for Mann's success in Massachusetts. Carter is frequently called the "father" of the Massachusetts school system and of normal schools (Pulliam & Van Patten, 1991). After graduating from Harvard, in 1820, Carter launched an aggressive campaign to improve American schooling. From 1824 to 1826, Carter authored a number of widely read articles on educational issues. One of his main proposals was for the formation of normal schools to train future teachers (Carter, 1826). Carter's dedication to education was largely responsible for passing the Massachusetts school law of 1827, which provided for public secondary schools in Massachusetts. Carter also helped establish the state board of education and normal schools for training teachers in 1837 (Pulliam & Van Patten, 1991).

Calvin Stowe

Calvin Stowe (1882–1806) played a major role in the development of common schools in the Midwest. His influence over education in Ohio was similar to Mann's influence in Massachusetts (Rippa, 1997). Stowe was a professor of New Testament at Lane Theological Seminary, in Cincinnati, Ohio. He was the husband of Harriet Beecher Stowe, the author of *Uncle Tom's Cabin*. Stowe was perhaps the foremost national spokesman for the notion that the position of general secretary of education should be in place in each state (Stowe, 1836).

Stowe traveled to Europe in 1836 and reported back to American education leaders about the practices of the European schools. He pointed out that in Europe, the presence of common schools was enabling more people to be educated than ever before (Stowe, 1837). Stowe argued that public schools had a responsibility to educate the public mind. He believed that public education in Europe was having a civilizing effect on that continent because it was bringing Christianity and the teachings of democracy to the most remote parts, where despotism often ruled (Stowe, 1837).

Stowe also reported that the status of women was higher in the United States than in Europe and that it was therefore fitting for women to take a more active role in the teaching profession (Spring, 1997). Stowe (1837), like Mann, believed that moral education was the most important aspect of education. He reported that the European teachers strongly relied on the teachings of the Bible for the moral instruction that took place in their schools. In his report, he asserted that religious education was at the forefront of common school education in Europe and was responsible for much of its success (Stowe, 1836).

In his report on elementary school teaching in Europe, Stowe (1837) states,

> To leave the moral faculty uninstructed was to leave the most important part of the human mind undeveloped, and to strip education of almost every thing that can make it valuable; and that the Bible, independently of the interest attending it, as containing the most ancient and influential writings ever recorded by human hands, and comprising the religious system of almost the whole of the civilized world, is in itself the best book that can be put into the hands of children to interest, to exercise, and to unfold their intellectual and moral powers. (pp. 18–19)

Samuel Seelye

Samuel Seelye was another father of the common school movement, who often worked in conjunction with Stowe to promote the work of public education. He asserted that "Christianity is essential to education" (Seelye, 1864, p. 3). He believed that religion provided the moral and loving fiber that established a positive atmosphere in the classroom. Seelye averred that common schools needed to emphasize science instruction more than they commonly did. He believed that learning science enabled children to learn about the nature of God and about how to help society progress (Seelye, 1864).

TEACHER INSTITUTES AND NORMAL SCHOOLS

Samuel Hall (1795–1877) founded the first teacher institute, a private institute established in Concord, Vermont, in 1823 (Altenbaugh & Underwood, 1990). He wrote the first teacher-training book in the country, *Lectures on School-Keeping* (1829). The book quickly became a classic and for many years became the textbook of choice in nearly all of the teacher-training institutes in the country (Altenbaugh & Underwood, 1990). Largely because he was in New England, where many of the nation's leading educators were located, Hall quickly became well-known in the area and was asked to make speeches throughout the Northeast (Altenbaugh & Underwood, 1990). He was hired at Phillips Academy, in Andover, Massachusetts, to be the headmaster of the teachers there.

The idea for the widespread use of American teacher institutes and normal schools was actually birthed by Charles Brooks, of Massachusetts (MacMullen, 1991). Brooks, a minister, was a strong advocate of school reform. During a serendipitous meeting in Europe, a Prussian reformer, Dr. Julius, convinced Rev. Brooks of the need for a system of normal schools. Brooks (1850) stated in one of his letters, "I fell in love with the Prussian system. . . . I gave my life to it" (p. 1). For the next 2 years, Brooks worked at a feverish pace to open the minds of prominent educators to the idea of teacher institutes. Among the educators that Brooks influenced were Calvin Stowe and Henry Barnard. Stowe confirmed Brooks's perspective, arguing that teacher training was the crux of the Prussian system (MacMullen, 1991).

In 1839, Henry Barnard and Emma Willard cofounded one of the first teacher-training institutes, in Hartford, Connecticut. It was a private institute focusing on developing teachers into good moral leaders and solid instructors. Barnard and Willard were the first to establish a broad system of teacher institutes (MacMullen, 1991; Spring, 1997). They had a vision of the teacher institute or normal school that consisted of three classes of studies. The first, Acts and Arts consisted of classes on appropriate teacher behavior, reading, spelling, penmanship, and so forth. Second, Arts and Sciences focused on science and the arts. Third, Duties and Blessings consisted of the moral virtues teachers needed in order to be effective at their profession (MacMullen, 1991).

Initially, most teacher institutes were private institutes, but later they were taxpayer supported. Horace Mann opened up the first public teacher institute later in 1839, in Lexington, Massachusetts (Harper, 1939). Once again, a lot of the change in the source of support for these schools was a direct consequence of the Civil War. Before the Civil War, most Americans did not understand that public support was important to educate teachers. By the end of the Civil War, the place of the common school was in the psyche of the American mind. The one quality Willard and Barnard emphasized the most in these institutes was the moral character of the teacher (MacMullen, 1991). This does not mean that teachers functioned as preachers addressing certain moral issues. Rather, teachers, by their example, were to instill morality into the hearts of their children (Barnard, 1842, 1843; MacMullen, 1991).

From these institutes evolved the ideas of normal schools, in which America's elementary school teachers were trained. Teaching institutes were the primary means of educating teachers before the Civil War (MacMullen, 1991). After the Civil War, normal schools and universities became the primary means of preparing teachers (Jencks & Riesman, 1968). Generally, elementary school teachers were trained at normal schools. Secondary school teachers were generally trained at colleges and universities. In the minds of most educators and of Americans as a whole, it required considerably more training to teach secondary school than to teach primary school. Normal schools usually prepared teachers to give instruction in primary schools within just 1 or 2 years (Jencks & Riesman, 1968). As a result, teachers who taught primary school received a salary that was considerably less than that of their counterparts in secondary schools. Even though virtually all teachers now receive college or university training, secondary school teachers still enjoy a higher average wage than primary school teachers (U.S. Department of Education, 2000).

The nation's teacher-training infrastructure grew extensively following the Civil War (Hacker, 1970). It is quite reasonable to believe that the growth in the sophistication of the teacher-training system would not have taken place without the changes in the national consciousness that resulted from the Civil War. The training of teachers at this new higher level accomplished a number of goals educators had yearned for over the years. First, it helped ensure a certain level of quality that was not there previously among teachers in most communities. Second, the training of teachers contributed greatly not only to the secondary system of education but also the postsecondary system of education. The education of teachers gave universities a new clientele and considerably increased the total enrollment of Americans in college. Third, the presence of people training to be teachers in college helped to increase the percentage of women who attended college (Jencks & Riesman, 1968). A considerable portion of the people training to be teachers were women. Fourth, the existence of schools for teacher training helped ensure that the quality of teachers that rural schools received was similar to the quality of teachers in city schools (Spring, 1997).

THE CIVIL WAR AND THE COMMON SCHOOL MOVEMENT

Common Schools Become More Accepted

The nation's experience of the Civil War helped convince people of the need for the common school (Gutek, 1991; Jencks & Riesman, 1968). With the help of the Civil War, Americans became much more convinced that state control over the public school system was an act of progress. Nevertheless, the debate over the extent to which state input or parental input should prevail remains an issue that stirs a great deal of debate. Today, however, the movement is toward greater parental involvement in education. Many of the reform movements, including the Chicago public school reform movement, were founded largely on the basis of increased parental involvement (Hudolin, 1994). These days, it is considered progress if there is increased parental involvement rather than increased state involvement in the running of the public schools (Shaver & Walls, 1998).

Although there was an appreciable amount of disagreement about whether there should be common schools before the Civil War, the war produced a tremendous degree of consensus among most Americans about the need for common schools (Gutek, 1991; Jencks & Riesman, 1968). The Civil War was very nearly the ruination of the United States (Jencks & Riesman, 1968; Johnson, 1997). The American people were made keenly aware that division on a major issue such as slavery could destroy the country. Therefore, there was an overwhelming desire among the American people for ways to bring the country together. In this context, common schools seemed like an ideal way to unite the country with certain core beliefs that could ultimately strengthen the country (Spring, 1997).

Americans now wanted to focus on a common bond and an intermutual set of beliefs. Mann's emphasis on teaching a core set of beliefs and morals suddenly gained the widespread concurrence of many Americans, and his common schools seemed like a beautiful way to unite the North and the South. Mann's emphasis on morality was particularly attractive to many people, because the American people had become convinced that slavery was essentially a moral problem (Orr, 1989). Therefore, the American people became very agreeable to the development of a common American morality that could help prevent something like the slavery debacle. Individuals like Horace Mann and Rev. Lyman Beecher acknowledged, well before the majority of Americans did, the importance of education in terms of bringing the country together. Beecher viewed the schools not only as a means of uniting the North and the South but also of uniting the West with the rest of the country (Beecher, 1835). To Beecher, taming the West was absolutely essential to the future of America's prosperity:

> The thing required for the civil and religious prosperity of the West, is universal education and moral culture, by institutions commensurate to that result—the all-pervading influences of schools and colleges, and seminaries and pastors, and churches. When the West is well-supplied in this respect, though there may be great relative defects, there will be, as we believe, the stamina and vitality of a perpetual civil and religious prosperity. (n.p.)

Male Versus Female Teachers

Mann (1846, 1849) favored female teachers over male teachers because he believed that women were better than men at managing children and were more virtuous than their male counterparts (Elsbree, 1939; Spring, 1997). The Civil War impacted the American education system in another way as well. Prior to the war, male teachers outnumbered female instructors in the teaching force (Elsbree, 1939). But because so many men went to battle, during the Civil War, the number of female teachers outnumbered the number of male teachers. In New Jersey, in 1852, male teachers outnumbered female teachers by about 2 to 1 (Elsbree, 1939). In the midst of the Civil War, female teachers outnumbered male teachers. In Indiana, the percentage of male teachers dropped from 80% to 58% in just the short period from 1859 to 1864 (Elsbree, 1939). In both Ohio and Iowa, the percentage of male teachers was higher than that of female teachers before the Civil War, but lower than that of female teachers after the war (Elsbree, 1939).

Two other developments also helped consummate the rise of the common school to some extent before the advent of the Civil War and to some extent after the war. The first development was the rise of the educational theories of Johann Pestalozzi. The second development was the use of the *McGuffey Reader*.

Educational Debate: Females and Males in the Teaching Profession

Whether teachers should be male or female remains a touchy issue in education. Today, males make up about one quarter of the American teaching force. In addition, male teachers are largely concentrated in the secondary school level. There are doubtlessly a vast number of reasons to explain the present ratio by gender and why it differs at the elementary and secondary school level. For example, many people, including teachers themselves, perceive females as being more nurturing. Horace Mann certainly maintained this perspective. Low teacher salaries may also keep some men away, especially if they are the sole wage earners of their families.

However, the low teacher salaries do not explain why the gender differential is so much greater at the elementary school level. It is likely that some women of small physical stature may be more likely than males to shy away from teaching high school, simply because it is preferable to discipline someone who is 4 feet tall rather than someone who is 6 feet tall. There is also a sensitive issue that some may not like to address, but must be discussed. Many Americans feel uncomfortable with male elementary school teachers. This may be a result of gender discrimination but could also be out of the fear that males are more likely than females to molest children of either gender (Kincaid, 1998).

There is also a belief by some that all the issues raised to explain why there are more female elementary school teachers are a product of gender stereotyping. Still others claim that these issues are not based on stereotypes, but are founded on underlying realities.

- What do you think? What explains why there are so many more female teachers, especially at the elementary school level?

Johann Pestalozzi

Johann Pestalozzi (1746–1827) was born in Zurich, Switzerland. He authored a book entitled *Leonard and Gertrude*, in which he described the practice of education during his time. The gist of the book is that extending the maternal influence of the home to the school can lead to positive moral change. Ulich (1968) describes the book this way:

It pictures the rottenness of the life in a poor Swiss village, where Gertrude, the pious wife of a mason . . . is the only source of educational wisdom and inspiration . . . Observing how Gertrude brings up her children he and his friends realize the interdependence between family spirit and the spirit of the community, of religion and education and also of physical welfare and human dignity. (p. 230)

Pestalozzi (1898, 1916) claimed that it is the maternal nature of the mother that makes the home a wonderful place of refuge for most children. He argued that to the extent that teachers could also exert this kind of maternal influence in the schoolroom, the school could become a place of refuge for children as well. Pestalozzi believed that in such a place of acceptance and safety, a child could learn at an accelerated pace. He wanted to make the school room a comfortable place, just like their homes were, in which children could function. Therefore, he believed that the school should not be a place where students merely file into a room, sit behind desks, and listen to a lecture. Rather, Pestalozzi conceived of the classroom as a place where each child could learn by doing. The classroom, in Pestalozzi's view, should be a place of incessant activity, as the children's homes are. He believed in learning by doing and conjoining what children learned intellectually in the classroom to the real world.

A Closer Look: Johann Pestalozzi and the Maternal Role of the Schools

Johann Pestalozzi urged schools to recognize the primacy of the maternal role of the educator. As Gerald Gutek (1968) states, "Pestalozzi was deeply impressed by the mother's crucial role in the kindling of love" (pp. 61–62). Gutek also notes, "In developing educational theory Pestalozzi affirmed the crucial importance of the home circle as the origin of all education" (pp. 24–25). Pestalozzi believed that the better the teachers incorporated maternal qualities, the more effective they would be.

In Pestalozzi's view, children learned best in the home because the home was a place of love. Gutek (1968) adds, "If a child is given love and care by the mother, the child's idea of benevolence will be activated. If he continues to experience tender loving care, the child will grow into a person who is capable of giving and receiving love" (p. 62). Pestalozzi especially maintained a passion to apply his approach to benefit the poor (Heafford, 1967). Heafford affirms that "helping the poor was his life's ambition" (p. 6). Pestalozzi was able to fulfill a dream when he opened a school for the poor in 1818 (Downs, 1975). In Pestalozzi's view, education was the means by which humanity could eradicate poverty (Gutek, 1968). To him, moral education was at the heart of his educational rubric (Downs, 1975).

During Pestalozzi's lifetime, the poor did not always trust him, because they were not accustomed to the educated class reaching out to them (Gutek, 1968). Nevertheless, in the longer term, Pestalozzi served as both a theorist and practitioner who through his emphasis on the teacher functioning as a mother away from home enabled the citizenry to have a new level of trust in the public schools.

Pestalozzian practices were really the first to systematize a more liberal form of instruction method. His approach was a precursor of the philosophical perspectives of John Dewey, who later also emphasized learning by doing.

In a sense, Pestalozzian theory thrived because of the very nature of this time in American history. Urbanization was increasing, and the commencement of industrialization was taking place; and, as a result of this process, the family was retreating somewhat from its earlier role of participating in the education of children. Americans were increasingly aware of this trend and had some mixed emotions about the school taking on a larger role in education. Some people thought that the school was usurping some of the roles of education that were best left in the home. The Pestalozzian method, however, calmed a lot of the fears of people by humanizing certain aspects of school life. The teacher was designed to be a type of "mother away from home." The teacher was to provide the children with some of the moral training that children from previous generations had experienced mostly at home (Pestalozzi, 1898, 1916). As a result, myriad Americans developed an affinity for the Pestalozzian schools that enabled the school to prosper. Americans were now becoming much more aware of the changes taking place across the country, such as urbanization and industrialization. Many Americans thought that a "maternal" public school would provide a wonderful bridge between the home and the school (Spring, 1997).

The Pestalozzian schools were conservative schools in the sense that they put a great deal of emphasis on moral education (Pestalozzi, 1898, 1916). However, Pestalozzi also opened the way for the introduction of many liberal ideas that would later be espoused by John Dewey. He believed that children should learn by doing via experiencing and interacting with nature. Both conservatives and liberals influenced the Pestalozzian educational tradition (Pestalozzi, 1898, 1916).

Plato, Cicero, Augustine, and Comenius's insistence on the importance of morality of the lives of the students also shaped Pestalozzi's views (Pestalozzi, 1898, 1916). Comenius (1592–1670) was a Czech educator and religious leader who helped with school reform in Sweden, Poland, and England (Kinloch, 1969; Sadler, 1966). Pestalozzi, like Comenius, believed in the importance of a religious foundation but also appreciated the role that child-centered activity could play in education (Spinka, 1967). As Robert Ulich (1968) notes,

> Both Pestalozzi and Comenius were so intrinsically religious that their piety shines through every one of their works. They could not speak of nature without thinking of God as its creator; they could not speak of the human being without sensing the divine in even the poorest soul. For both parental love and the good family were the reflection of the fatherly love of God on the level of human relations. . . . Finally, for both, education was not merely a way of teaching and learning, but the human attempt to participate in the divine plan to unfold the best in individual man and in humanity as a whole. (p. 30)

Pestalozzi (1898, 1916) believed that moral education was important particularly in the early years of schooling. He believed that as an infant and toddler, a child developed a natural faith in his or her mother. Nevertheless, over time, a child also quite naturally grew to depend less on the mother. According to Pestalozzi, during this period of transference, it was of utmost importance that a child be taught to transfer that faith in the mother to a faith in God. Pestalozzi (1801) stated,

> It asks that we develop humanely and understandably the loving and faithful state of mind the truth and blessing of which the innocent child has so far enjoyed

unconsciously in his relation to the mother. For sooner or later this state of innocence, the faith in the mother, will weaken and vacillate. Nature then demands new means of faith. And unless we plant faith in God deeply into the child's soul, we create the danger of cutting the natural links of human development. However, in the state of early childhood, this desirable continuity can be achieved only by appeal to the child's natural sensitive faculty. The motivations of faith in God must be already provided before the child's sensuous and natural attachment to the mother is fading. Faith in God, as it were, must be melted into the maturing relation to the mother. Here is the only chance for a pure, continuous, and natural development from the innocence of childhood toward human morality, for the latter grows from the first. Only this process of growth leads to real faith and love, the lifting of sensuous affection toward the level of moral and spiritual maturity. (pp. 313–315)

Pestalozzi believed that education had strayed from its biblical roots and needed to return to the central tenet of Christianity, that is, the love of God and neighbor, which Christ asserted were the two most important commandments. On this issue, Pestalozzi (1801) states,

Thus it is evident that the truth of fundamental and organic education and the totality of its means issues from the divine spark which is planted into human nature and harmonizes with the spirit of Christianity. On the other hand, it is equally evident that our present education with all its artificiality, corruption and routine does not spring from the divine spark in the depth of man, but from his brutal and sensuous desires. Consequently, it contradicts the spirit and evidence of Christianity and can have no other effect but to undermine it. (p. 423)

On the other hand, Pestalozzi was also impacted by Rousseau's (1911) book, *Emile*. In that book, Rosseau claimed that children were incapable of reasoning until they were adolescents. The Pestalozzian method therefore consisted of little or no verbal instruction until adolescence. Pestalozzi believed that educators should emphasize the needs of the child as much as the teaching of the subject matter (Urban & Wagoner, 2000). He believed that there were important means of gaining the attention of children. His favorite method was object teaching. This was a teaching strategy that involved using a concrete object to gain the attention of the child. The object was then used to draw the child into the lesson and the educator's world (Urban & Wagoner, 2000). In other words, Pestalozzi (1898, 1916) contended it was important for young children in particular to be taught using concrete rather than abstract examples (Spring, 1997).

The Pestalozzian method became known in America as a result of American educators going to Europe and becoming apprised of the system. One educational reformer, John Griscom, was expressly responsible for conveying Pestalozzian ideas to American educators (Spring, 1997). Griscom returned from a trip to Europe with an intense approbation for Pestalozzian schools. He said, "But the greatest recommendation of the Pestalozzian . . . plan of education, is the moral charm which is diffused throughout all its operations" (Spring, 1997, p. 135). Although many educators became familiar with the Pestalozzian method by the 1840s, it was the Oswego Normal School that was most active in actually spreading his ideas in the United States. The Oswego State Normal and Training School was founded in Oswego, New York, in 1861. It played such a pivotal role in spreading Pestalozzian thinking in America that this thrust soon became known as the "Oswego Movement" (Spring, 1997).

William McGuffey

The *McGuffey Reader* also contributed to solidifying the common school. William McGuffey was born near Washington, Pennsylvania, in 1800. A publisher asked McGuffey to write a series of readers that were designed especially for public school students (Ruggles, 1950; Westerhoff, 1978). The series consisted of five readers, a primer, and a speller (McGuffey & Lindberg, 1976). From the days of Horace Mann until the end of the 19th century, the *McGuffey Reader* would sell over 100 million copies (Ruggles, 1950; Westerhoff, 1978).

The primary goals of the *McGuffey Reader* were not only to increase the overall knowledge of each student but also to teach moral lessons that could impact the individual lives of the students (Ruggles, 1950; Westerhoff, 1978). Many accounts included in the readers came from the Bible. The *McGuffey Reader* also emphasized love, nature, and the importance of diligence (McGuffey & Lindberg, 1976). The contents of the *McGuffey Reader* reflected the common core of values that Americans believed were necessary to keep the country together as one nation (Ruggles, 1950; Westerhoff, 1978).

As a result of the Civil War, Americans apprehended the need for a common school in every sense of the word. First and foremost, Americans comprehended the need for a common morality to arise in the nation. They also saw the need for a common school structure and a common type of school organization. As a result, different means of facilitating the organization of schools emerged. The concept of a school district first emerged in Massachusetts, in 1789. Although other New England states incorporated this concept into their school systems, the idea really did not disseminate to the rest of country until well into the 19th century (Jencks & Riesman, 1968).

THE GROWTH OF HIGHER EDUCATION DURING THE FIRST HALF OF THE 1800s

Dartmouth College v. Woodward, U.S. Supreme Court Case

One cannot examine the growth of higher education during the 1800s, and even the 1900s, without considering the tremendous influence of the *Dartmouth College v. Woodward Case* (1819). The *Dartmouth College* case represents the most important decision regarding education handed down by the Supreme Court during the 19th century (Current, 1964; Fribourg, 1965; Lieberman, 1976). Prior to the 1819 *Dartmouth College v. Woodward* decision, religious colleges dominated higher education in the United States (Current, 1964; Horowitz, 1987; Tewksbury, 1932). By the end of the Revolutionary War, however, some educators began to see the need for state universities to be developed. The University of Georgia was the first state university to be founded, followed by the University of North Carolina, in 1785 and 1789, respectively (Current, 1964; Horowitz, 1987; Tewksbury, 1932).

As Chapter 3 indicates, the Revolutionary War caused an increasing number of Americans to value education. They began to esteem some of the new nation's academics, with the result that in some cases, these educators rose to a level that had previously been reserved only for religious leaders. This implies that they viewed the task of educating the American populace as a necessity. The problem with this late revelation to certain secular educational leaders was that the college landscape was already dominated by religious schools. The quality of schools like Dartmouth, Harvard, and Princeton was so high that inaugurating state schools at this point to compete with these schools seemed futile (Current, 1964; Spring, 1997; Tewksbury, 1932). Yet the need of each state to educate leaders for that state was self-evident.

The solution proposed by many government leaders was for state control of all institutions of higher learning (Current, 1964; Fribourg, 1965; Lieberman, 1976; Tewksbury, 1932). In this way, it could be ensured that each college in each state would serve the public good for that state and would be responsible to more than the people of the denomination that founded the school (Current, 1964; Marshall, 1967; Spring, 1997; Tewksbury, 1932). At first, the states pushed for state representation at each of the denominational schools except for Brown, Princeton, and Rutgers (Current, 1964; Spring, 1997; Tewksbury, 1932). The state governments actually temporarily took over Columbia, the University of Pennsylvania, and Dartmouth with public approval and temporarily converted them into state institutions (Current, 1964; Marshall, 1967; Spring, 1997; Tewksbury, 1932). Other Ivy League colleges, such as Harvard and Yale, were able to avoid being taken over by the state by acknowledging some years earlier the possibility of this happening. These prestigious religious colleges, among others, had allowed state representatives to sit on their boards and to help in the decision making (Tewksbury, 1932). This flexibility helped give Massachusetts and Connecticut a sense that Harvard and Yale, respectively, were their universities. As a result, Massachusetts and Connecticut did not take over these Ivy League colleges (Tewksbury, 1932). This flexibility paid off rich dividends in the long run. Even today, there is a sense among people in those two states that Harvard and Yale are "their universities."

As government control and influence grew in the early religious schools, concern grew regarding the extent to which the state's interference with religious colleges constituted a violation of separation of church and state. A political battle ensued regarding the future form that American institutions of higher learning would take (Current, 1964; Fribourg, 1965; Lieberman, 1976; Marshall, 1967; Spring, 1997; Tewksbury, 1932). The Democratic-Republicans, led by Thomas Jefferson and James Madison, believed that education would serve the needs of the greatest number of people if private institutions such as Harvard, Yale, and Dartmouth were taken over by the state they resided in (Current, 1964; Marshall, 1967; Spring, 1997; Tewksbury, 1932). The Federalists, on the other hand, believed that if the state took over colleges that were founded as religious institutions, this amounted to a violation of church and state and an encroachment on a group's freedom of religion (Current, 1964; Marshall, 1967; Spring, 1997). The U.S. Supreme Court upheld the rights of private colleges to be free of government interference in the landmark case of *Dartmouth College v. Woodward* in 1819 (Current, 1964; Marshall, 1967). Until this Supreme Court decision, the future of denominational colleges and private colleges was in question. But in this landmark decision, the Supreme Court declared that private colleges had the right to be free from government interference (Current, 1964; Fribourg, 1965; Lieberman, 1976; Marshall, 1967).

The *Dartmouth* decision was a very salient one in the history of education in the United States. Not only did the decision encourage the further spread of denominational colleges, but it set the stage for the full fruition of state colleges across the United States. The decision encouraged the existence of both kinds of colleges (Current, 1964; Fribourg, 1965; Lieberman, 1976; Marshall, 1967; Spring, 1997).

To understand the significance of the *Dartmouth* decision, it is important to note some of the events leading up to it. Dartmouth was the last of the three Puritan colleges formed during the colonial period (Current, 1964; Marshall, 1967; Spring, 1997). The two other Puritan colleges were Harvard and Yale (Tewksbury, 1932). Of these three, Dartmouth was granted a charter with the idea that it would rely even less on government money to function than either Harvard or Yale (Spring, 1997; Tewksbury, 1932). Early on in Dartmouth's history, the government did not seem to mind that the school was so independent of government control (Current, 1964; Marshall, 1967; Spring, 1997; Tewksbury, 1932). After all, Dartmouth was a Congregational college and Congregationalists also dominated the government leadership positions. But then, John Wheelock assumed the college presidency in 1799 and proved to be something of a maverick (Current, 1964; Fribourg, 1965; Lieberman, 1976; Marshall, 1967; Spring, 1997; Tewksbury, 1932). In addition, there was a short-lived desire among many Americans at that time to have more state control of institutions of higher education (Current, 1964; Marshall, 1967; Spring, 1997; Tewksbury, 1932). After John Wheelock was removed from office in 1815, the state legislature took it upon itself to reorganize the college, in 1816. The Act of 1816 transformed Dartmouth into a state university under the name Dartmouth University. The original board of trustees strongly objected to the act and filed suit in Superior Court (Current, 1964; Marshall, 1967; Spring, 1997; Tewksbury, 1932). The Superior Court's decision favored the state, but the matter went on to the Supreme Court, which decided in favor of the college. It was a major loss for Thomas Jefferson and the Democratic-Republicans' push for states' rights (Current, 1964; Marshall, 1967; Spring, 1997; Tewksbury, 1932). The question is how the decision impacted the U.S. system of higher education in the long run.

First, the decision certainly affirmed the legality of denominational schools and other private colleges to exist. Nearly every historian views this as a constructive development, for the following reasons (Current, 1964; Fribourg, 1965; Lieberman, 1976; Marshall, 1967; Tewksbury, 1932): First, it ensured freedom of religion. Most historians believe that if the decision had gone any other way, it would have infringed upon freedom of religion. Second, religious people were among the few people who had education consistently high on their priority list. Without the freedom for religious schools to develop, it is doubtful whether the U.S. system of higher education would have developed very well at all. Third, the decision ensured the existence of both private universities and public universities. This would lead to the presence of a larger number of universities overall and hence a higher level of competition. Increased competition generally leads to higher academic quality. Fourth, the larger number of colleges, in the long run, would have another effect as well. More Americans would be able to go to college.

Amidst these advantages, however, emerges one disadvantage to this decision that most historians are also quick to point out. The *Dartmouth* case had put state colleges at a competitive disadvantage. The denominational schools had a huge head start on the state colleges. As a result, the lower-quality state colleges were slow to develop (Tewksbury, 1932).

Even to this day, America's best universities are private universities that started off as denominational colleges (Ramsey & Wilson, 1970). Even denominational colleges, like the University of Chicago and Stanford, which were founded later than many of the state institutions, were able to quickly surpass the state colleges in prestige and quality.

Even today, state universities that have obtained a high level of prestige, like UC-Berkeley, the University of Michigan, and the University of Wisconsin, generally are more competitive with private institutions at the graduate level, which developed later, than at the undergraduate level. The private institutions are still very dominant at the undergraduate level ("America's Best Colleges," 2003). In addition, most of the most prestigious state institutions are located outside the New England and mid-Atlantic states ("The Best Graduate Schools," 2003). The Ivy League schools were simply too dominant to be successfully rivaled by state schools.

Nevertheless, most historians believe the *Dartmouth* case positively impacted the U.S. system of education in the long run, for two reasons. First, the encouragement of the existence of both denominational and state colleges made it likely that there would be a large number of colleges in the United States. Second, the augmentation in the number of colleges and their diverse nature encouraged competition, which raised the overall quality of American schools. And indeed, the large number of American schools plus the quality of these schools gives the United States probably the best system of higher education in the world (Institute of Higher Education, Shanghai Jiao Tong University, 2004). Nearly 60% of Americans attend some college, and 25% have completed a 4-year college degree (U.S. Department of Education, 2000). The former number is the highest of any nation in the world, and the latter is tied with Japan for first in the world (Moore & Simon, 2000; U.S. Department of Education, 2000).

In terms of numerical growth, most of the growth from 1819 to 1860 occurred among the denominational colleges (Tewksbury, 1932). The period from 1820 to 1860 witnessed a tremendous growth in church attendance across the United States, and revivals were frequent and long lasting (Dieter, 1996; Long, 1998). By 1860, there were 180 denominational colleges in the United States (Tewksbury, 1932). Although Presbyterians made up only about 13% of the population of American Christians, they had pioneered about 27% of the denominational schools present in 1860, the most of any denomination (Tewksbury, 1932). The Methodists and Baptists, the two largest denominations in the United States at that time, ranked second and third behind the Presbyterians in the number of colleges they had founded (Tewksbury, 1932).

Although the state colleges lagged behind the denominational colleges in terms of growth, the founding of many of the state colleges during the 40-year period after the *Dartmouth* decision may have had a greater long-range impact on the U.S. system of higher education than the growth of the denominational schools (Current, 1964; Marshall, 1967; Spring, 1997; Tewksbury, 1932). Even though many state universities were founded during the 19th century, they did not grow very much, due to neglect (Jencks & Riesman, 1968; Tewksbury, 1932). State universities had not yet convinced the American people of the need for state-sponsored centers of education. State universities really did not grow dramatically until the post–Civil War period, when new needs arose that could not be completely met by the denominational schools (Jencks & Riesman, 1968; Tewksbury, 1932).

From the time the Dartmouth squabble began in 1815/1816 until 1860, a phenomenal number of the most influential state schools were founded: the University of Virginia (1816), the University of Alabama (1821), Indiana University (1828), the University of Michigan (1837), the University of Missouri (1839), the University of Mississippi (1851), Tulane University (1847), the University of Iowa (1847), the University of Wisconsin (1848), the University of Minnesota (1851), and Pennsylvania State University (1855) (Tewksbury, 1932). Other colleges were founded during this period that started off as religious colleges but later became state colleges, for example, the University of Delaware and the University of Kentucky (Tewksbury, 1932).

The fact that both denominational schools and state schools eventually flourished is a testimony to the balance that is often present in the U.S. political system. The Federalists, led by George Washington and John Adams, had faithfully worked to champion the right of private institutions of higher education to exist. Had the Democratic-Republicans had their way, nearly all American colleges would be run by the state (Current, 1964; Marshall, 1967; Spring, 1997; Tewksbury, 1932). To be sure, state schools were needed, too. The Democratic Republicans did much more to advance the cause of state-run colleges than would have been the case had the Federalists prevailed, and the state universities would be of a much lower quality than they are today. So, the positions of the Federalists and of the Democratic-Republicans tended to balance one another out.

The Revolutionary War (a) helped the number of colleges in the United States to increase exponentially and (b) helped usher in the movement for beginning state colleges. Without the war, these two events never would have happened. Both events helped ensure that an extraordinary number of Americans would be able to receive a college education. The sheer number and quality of America's institutions of higher education makes a college educa-tion available to the vast majority of Americans who desire to attend college. Most nations have a relatively small number of colleges, and many people in these nations who desire to go to college can never go (Horowitz, 1987; Jencks & Riesman, 1968; Moore & Simon, 2000). The Revolutionary War and the events that followed set into motion the greatest sys-tem of higher education in the world (Institute of Higher Education, Shanghai Jiao Tong University, 2004).

Contemporary Focus

The Advantages of Having Both Private and Public Universities

The *Dartmouth College v. Woodward* (1819) Supreme Court case is considered the most important one related to education of the 19th century. In essence, in the case, the Supreme Court declared that private colleges and universities have the right to exist. The decision had a number of profound effects. Not only did the decision declare the right for private colleges and universities to operate, but it also forced states to develop their own institutions of higher education, without the option of taking over private ones. Virtually all educators are agreed that the *Dartmouth v. Woodward* case was a positive one for education. One of the benefits is that it forced private and state universities to compete against one another, causing each to become better. As a general rule, both private and state uni-versities are better than they otherwise would be because of the presence of the other kind of insti-tution. USC (a private university) and UCLA compete not only in football but also academically, and both schools are better as a result. Stanford and UC-Berkeley compete, as do Notre Dame and Michigan.

One of the reasons educators give for the preeminence of American universities is that we are one of the few nations in the world with both strong private and public sectors among universities. Nearly all nations have one or the other sector significantly stronger than the other, and, consequently, in these nations, competition is minimized. In contrast, in the United States, there are fine private universities, such as Harvard, Yale, and Princeton, but there are significant state institutions as well, such as the University of North Carolina, the University of Michigan, and UC-Berkeley.

- What are the advantages of living in a nation with both a strong system of private and public universities?
- What are the advantages of the existence of private universities?
- What are the advantages of the existence of public universities?

WHERE STATE UNIVERSITIES GREW AND WHERE THEY DID NOT

It is very significant to note which states started state universities and which did not. As Table 6.1 indicates, 14 states founded before the Civil War did not have a state university founded before then. What is surprising, however, is that 7 of these 14 were from the original 13 states. Although the original 13 states make up 50% of the states that did not have state colleges before the Civil War, Table 6.2 indicates that they make up only 30% of the states that did possess state colleges before the Civil War.

Table 6.1   Fourteen States With No State Colleges Founded Before the Civil War

Seven Original States	Seven New States (year granted statehood)
New Hampshire	Illinois (1818)
Massachusetts	Maine (1820)
Rhode Island	Arkansas (1836)
Connecticut	Florida (1845)
New York	Texas (1845)
New Jersey	Oregon (1859)
Pennsylvania	Kansas (1861)

Table 6.2   Twenty States With State Universities Founded Before the Civil War

Six Original States	Fourteen New States (year granted statehood)
Georgia	Vermont (1791)
North Carolina	Kentucky (1792)
South Carolina	Tennessee (1796)
Maryland	Ohio (1803)
Virginia	Louisiana (1812)
Delaware	Indiana (1816)
	Mississippi (1817)
	Alabama (1819)
	Missouri (1821)
	Michigan (1837)
	Iowa (1846)
	Wisconsin (1848)
	California (1850)
	Minnesota (1858)

The Presence of Ivy League Colleges

There were a number of reasons 14 states did not establish a state university before the Civil War. To gain insight into the primary reason, all one has to do is note the surprising fact that about half the states (7) that did not start a state university before the Civil War were from the original 13 states (Tewksbury, 1932). No doubt this comes as quite a surprise to many readers. It is only natural to assume that educationally minded states, like Massachusetts, New York, Pennsylvania, Connecticut, and others, would have founded a state university before 1861. To understand why such a logical advancement did not take place, all one has to do is recall that the Ivy League universities were located in these 7 states (Brubacher & Rudy, 1958; Tewksbury, 1932). State officials did not start state universities in these states because they did not think they could adequately compete with these prestigious institutions (Tewksbury, 1932). Even so, other factors also played a prominent role in determining whether state universities opened in particular states (Brubacher & Rudy, 1958; Dyer, 1985; Fordham, 1985, Tewksbury, 1932).

Whether a state university was established in a given state was usually dependent on a number of factors, including (a) whether a state had a sufficient population to support a state university, (b) whether an existing religious university was of high enough quality that competing with that university would be difficult, (c) whether people were interested in having a state university, (d) whether there was resistance to the establishment of state colleges by the existing colleges, and (e) which political party was in power at the time (Tewksbury, 1932).

Population Factors

Population was an important factor in establishing state colleges, especially since these schools often depended on tax dollars to survive (Jencks & Riesman, 1968). Florida, Oregon, and Arkansas, for example, had very sparse populations (Tewksbury, 1932). In addition, the period before the Civil War was a very religious one. The Revival of 1857 solidified the preeminence of Christian schools in many states across the country (Dieter, 1996; Long, 1998; Orr, 1989). Despite the founding of many state colleges nationwide, most Americans viewed education as a function of the church and not the state (Brubacher & Rudy, 1958; Orr, 1989; Tewksbury, 1932).

Although Mississippi was admitted as a state in 1817, it had a hard time developing a state university. The two times the state government initiated a state college, it floundered on its own and eventually had to be turned over to religious interests. Part of the reason for these failures was the fact that when Mississippi was brought into the union, it was neither very populated nor wealthy (Tewksbury, 1932). By the 1840s, that changed as cotton became a major cash crop. As a result of the increased population and wealth that accompanied the growth of the cotton crop, the University of Mississippi began to emerge as a major academic force in the South.

Missouri also experienced something of a struggle in establishing a state university. Missouri, like Mississippi, suffered from a lack of population and resources (Stephens, 1962). The opposition of religious leaders and the divisions in the state over the slavery issue also contributed to the state university's slow start (Stephens, 1962; Tewksbury, 1932).

Proximity of Quality Religious Colleges

Whether an Ivy League institution was present in the same state was important. An additional factor was whether there were other quality religious colleges in close proximity. Both issues influenced whether a state university emerged in a given area (Brubacher & Rudy, 1958; Tewksbury, 1932).

The University of South Carolina, founded in 1801, functioned much more along the lines of what we would normally expect from a state college. The absence of any real alternative quality college aided in the founding of the school (Hollis, 1951). It is true the Episcopal school named the College of Charleston was inaugurated in 1785 (Tewksbury, 1932). But this school did not even approach the status of the Ivy League schools. Therefore, the University of South Carolina did not encounter the disadvantage of having to compete with a prestigious school. In addition, the political leaders of South Carolina were of the Jefferson wing of the Democratic-Republican Party (Hollis, 1951). Therefore, these men saw great value in advancing the cause of state colleges.

The University of South Carolina, flourished as a relatively secular institution. Jonathan Maxey, the first president, succeeded because even though the university was nonreligious in nature, he sought to be sensitive to the educational needs of the population of South Carolina. But the second president, Thomas Cooper, took the school in a secular direction to such a degree that Cooper lost a lot of support among the South Carolinian people. By 1834, Cooper was forced to resign. After that point, the University of South Carolina became more influenced by religious interests, but remained a secular university.

Interest in Founding a State University

For most of the 1700s, 1800s, and even the early 1900s, most Americans did not view college education as a primary function of the state (Ramsey & Wilson, 1970). Rather, they primarily looked to churches as possessing this responsibility (Tewksbury, 1932). As a result, in many areas of the country, people had little interest in the emergence of state colleges. This trend was true even in the South, where state universities earned their greatest foothold in the American educational scene (Tewksbury, 1932).

For example, the University of Georgia, in 1785, was the first state college founded in the United States (Dyer, 1985). Demographically, Georgia was considerably different from the New England and mid-Atlantic states. In addition, certain prominent Democratic-Republicans in Georgia were Jeffersonian in their thinking and therefore leaned toward the founding of a state institution. But the populace of Georgia, just like Virginia, was more religious than their leaders (Dyer, 1985). Hence, over time, the people of Georgia favored sending their children to church-sponsored colleges rather than to the University of Georgia (Tewksbury, 1932). Therefore, the university really did not flourish until after the Civil War (Dyer, 1985).

The University of North Carolina, founded in 1789, was the second state college founded in the United States (Conner, 1953; Fordham, 1985; Tewksbury, 1932). Although the university was founded by religious leaders like William Davie, these leaders believed in the more secular concept of a university that Jefferson advocated (Conner, 1953; Fordham, 1985; Tewksbury, 1932). Once again, however, most people who were the most concerned about education in the state were religious, and soon they were able to obtain a large degree of control over the university (Tewksbury, 1932). As a result, although the University of North Carolina was technically a state college, religious people enjoyed a considerable degree of influence in its operation (Conner, 1953; Fordham, 1985; Tewksbury, 1932).

Resistance to Establishing a State College

Among the New States that did not found a state university before the Civil War, Kansas was the last to be admitted to the Union, in 1861 (Griffin, 1974). Religious interests delayed the founding of a state university somewhat, but the University of Kansas was started just 3 years later, in 1864 (Griffin, 1974; Tewksbury, 1932). Illinois was the first of the new states admitted in 1818. The religious educational interests in Illinois were quite potent. In the years between 1835 and 1860, 12 different religious colleges were started in Illinois; only New York and Pennsylvania had more religious colleges founded before a state college was founded (Tewksbury, 1932). These two states also did not have state universities before the Civil War. Resistance by religious schools to the idea of a state college in Illinois was the primary reason a state college was not founded there prior to the war. Religious interests also opposed the founding of a state college in Texas (Tewksbury, 1932). Although Texas became a state in 1845, they would not have a state university until 1881 (Berry, 1980).

In Delaware, there were attempts to found a state college in 1821, but religious interests in the state balked at the idea (Munroe, 1986). Religious people argued that Delaware did not even have a religious college at the time (Tewksbury, 1932), and there was considerably greater demand for a religious college than there was for a state university. In 1833, the Presbyterians took the initiative to begin a college, which at the time was called Newark College (Munroe, 1986). The Presbyterian institution attempted to serve its Delaware state constituency as much as possible. Although the name of the college was changed to Delaware College in 1843, the state political leaders still were not placated. They wanted a bona fide quality state institution. However, the state did not gain control of the institution until 1913 (Munroe, 1986).

Politics

In addition to those already mentioned, one of the reasons that state universities were more likely to be started in the South than they were in the North is that Democratic-Republican, and later Democratic, governors were more likely to reside in the South (Howe, 1973). Both political parties were amenable to the idea of states' rights and state colleges (Dabney, 1981; Honeywell, 1964). Largely for this reason, Virginia did establish a state college even though there was a top-notch institution of higher education, the College of William and Mary, in the same state. The influence of Thomas Jefferson was a main reason for the establishment of the University of Virginia. Jefferson believed that it was important for Virginia to have a college that would, by definition, be sensitive to the needs of the general populace living in the state (Dabney, 1981; Honeywell, 1964; Malone, 1981; Wills, 2002). Jefferson also strongly advocated the separation of church and state. With Jefferson's support, the Virginia state government rallied behind the idea of a state university. The results of this were twofold: First, the University of Virginia emerged as one of the most respected state universities before the time of the Civil War (Dabney, 1981; Honeywell, 1964; Malone, 1981; Wills, 2002). Second, in contrast, the College of William and Mary lost much of its former status as the best college in the state of Virginia. Nevertheless, over the long run, the college generally did not lower its standards, but chose to accept only the best students (Tewksbury, 1932). As a result, William and Mary remained one of the smallest colleges founded during the colonial period. With the encouragement of Jefferson, the University of Virginia flourished (Dabney, 1981; Honeywell, 1964; Malone, 1981; Wills, 2002). But when Jefferson passed away, the strength and vitality of that state college dissipated. Ironically, religious leaders eventually stepped in to revive the university (Tewksbury, 1932).

The Growth of State Colleges in Other States

In other states, there was a large degree of variation in terms of when a state university was founded and how it fared. Other states with a top-notch school did not have the benefit of having a national leader like Thomas Jefferson advocate for state colleges (Dabney, 1981; Honeywell, 1964; Malone, 1981; Tewksbury, 1932; Wills, 2002). Among the colonial states in particular in which a state university was founded, the situations were quite different from those with Ivy League institutions (Tewksbury, 1932).

Maryland

Early in its history, Maryland had tried to fuse two private colleges, Washington and St. John's, to form a type of state college. In 1812, the College of Medicine in Baltimore became the basis of all attempts to form a state university (Callcott, 1966). This was naturally before the Supreme Court had handed down the *Dartmouth* decision. Once this decision was handed down, the government forces were forced to back off from their attempts to totally run the university. Because of this, the university remained a private institution geared toward the needs of the state. Finally, in 1920, the University of Maryland was united with Maryland State College and brought under state control (Callcott, 1966).

Federal Support of Colleges in States Not Among the Original 13

The federal government was much more supportive of founding state universities in the new states that were not among the original 13. The land grants that the government gave ensured the survival of state institutions in these new states, even when there was little public support for them (Brubacher & Rudy, 1958; Tewksbury, 1932). The federal government was especially amenable to supporting the establishment of the institutions in the new states for two reasons: First, the government wanted to encourage people to move "out West." To the extent that institutions of higher education were inaugurated, people became convinced that the federal government had every intention of developing these certain sections of the country (Brubacher & Rudy, 1958; Cross, 1999; Tewksbury, 1932). Second, the government anticipated that it had a much greater chance for success by investing in colleges in the new states, where they did not have to compete with existing eminent schools (Brubacher & Rudy, 1958; Eddy, 1956; Tewksbury, 1932).

The state of Vermont was the first state admitted to the union after the original 13. The University of Vermont was founded in 1791 (Daniels, 1991). The Puritans and Federalists were open to the idea of a state university. Nevertheless, when the Congregationalists started Middlebury College, in 1800, many people in Vermont chose to attend Middlebury. As a result, the University of Vermont was enervated and did not become a particularly strong state college until 1865, when it was reorganized (Daniels, 1991).

Ohio was the first new state to benefit by the land grant policy of the federal government. It was founded in 1802 but really did not flourish. Miami University was founded in 1809. Although it was technically a state college, in its early years, the presidents of the school were always Presbyterian.

Louisiana experimented with various semi-state-run colleges. The state government sponsored a number of institutions (Bedsole & Richard, 1959), but each of these ended in failure. Finally, Louisiana decided to concentrate its efforts on developing just one state school: Louisiana State Seminary of Learning, which eventually became Louisiana State University (LSU). LSU was founded in 1853 (Bedsole & Richard, 1959).

In Indiana, the state and the church worked closely to develop the state's system of higher education. Indiana State Seminary was chartered in 1820 and became a college in 1828. As the state felt the impact of the *Dartmouth* decision, however, it became patent that the state and the church would have to develop centers of higher education separately. So, religious groups developed private colleges, and Indiana College became more closely associated with the state and was given the name Indiana University in 1838 (Tewksbury, 1932).

Alabama was admitted as a state in 1819, 2 years after the Alabama Territory was separated from the original Territory of Mississippi. The University of Alabama was founded in 1821 and had considerably more success than did attempts to establish a state college in Mississippi (Sellers, 1953; Tewksbury, 1932). A major reason for this had to do with the school's willingness to accommodate the religious people in the state. Not only did the United

States have a large number of religious people, but, for reasons that were communicated earlier, these people generally had a much higher level of interest in education than nonreligious people. Therefore, for a school to ignore the educational needs of the religious was generally suicidal. The University of Alabama was one of the most effective universities in working with the needs of religious people. Whereas a number of state universities turned their backs on the religious community, the University of Alabama knew that because religious people were so interested in education, they formed the heart of the university's constituency (Sellers, 1953). As a symbolic acknowledgment of this fact, the University of Alabama, like Harvard, chose crimson as its official color, representing the blood of Christ (Sellers, 1953).

The University of Michigan experienced great success compared with other universities. The state legislature was fully behind the founding of the state university. In addition, the state university was sensitive to the needs of religious people, just as the University of Alabama had been (Peckham, 1967; Tewksbury, 1932). They hired professors representing some of the main religious interests of the states. From 1837, when the university was founded, until 1855, the granting of charters to denominational colleges was either strongly discouraged or strictly prohibited (Tewksbury, 1932). After a time, religious people began to resent this fact, and once they founded their own colleges, their support for the university declined somewhat (Peckham, 1967; Tewksbury, 1932). However, the University of Michigan already had a profound influence and led the way in the development of higher education in the Midwest (Peckham, 1967).

The University of Iowa was founded in 1847. During the period from 1847 until 1858, six religious colleges were founded, and this served as stiff competition for the state university (Tewksbury, 1932). As a result, the University of Iowa really did not flourish until after the Civil War (Rogers, 1979).

The University of Wisconsin, founded in 1848, also had to contend with pleasing religious and nonreligious interests. But like the University of Alabama and the University of Michigan before it, the University of Wisconsin successfully sensitized itself to these interests and therefore especially prospered after the Civil War (Curti, 1949; Tewksbury, 1932). The University of Minnesota was founded in 1851, but because of financial mismanagement, it really did not get off the ground until after the Civil War (Gray, 1951; Tewksbury, 1932).

State Universities That Started as Religious Institutions

In Kentucky, the door was left open to the founding of the University of Kentucky largely because the first private college, Transylvania College, floundered. Then in 1837, the Disciples of Christ Church founded Bacon College, the forerunner of the University of Kentucky. Bacon was forced to discontinue in 1850, but the Disciples of Christ reopened the school in 1858, on the foundation of Bacon College. Nevertheless, the university did not really become a state college until 1907 (Hopkins, 1951).

In Tennessee, as in Kentucky, a private religious college became the precursor of the eventual state university. Blount College was founded by the Presbyterians, in 1794 (Montgomery, Folmsbee, & Greene, 1984). In 1806, the U.S. Congress granted Tennessee 100,000 acres for the founding of two universities, one in the eastern part of the state and one in the western part. The congressional grant was divided between Cumberland College, a Presbyterian college in the central part of the state, and East Tennessee College, a Presbyterian college established on the foundation of Blount College in the eastern part of the state. But East Tennessee College did not really become a state college until 1879, by which time the influence of the Presbyterians had declined (Montgomery et al., 1984).

What we now know as the University of California at Berkeley, or UC-Berkeley, was originally founded by Congregational and Presbyterian interests as the College of California (Stadtman, 1970; Stone, 1970). Following the Civil War, the state received a Morrill grant, and it was evident that the state would have more money than the Presbyterians and the Congregationalists to invest in the college (Stadtman, 1970; Stone, 1970). Therefore, the trustees of the College of California thought it was in the best interests of the state to hand the college over to the state (Tewksbury, 1932).

Later in the 19th century, with the nation's higher-education system well established, many Americans viewed their nation as potentially arising as a "New Europe." To achieve this goal, educators increasingly looked to German universities as a model for a research university (Ely, 1972; Rohrs, 1995).

CONCLUSION

The 19th century, particularly the middle part of the century, was a period of tremendous educational change in the country. The state increasingly played a major role in education. Nevertheless, the government schools adhered to the same values and philosophy as the private institutions and supported the beliefs of the vast majority of Americans. As a result, most Americans eventually embraced the broader role of government in education.

DISCUSSION QUESTIONS

1. Certain individuals and groups, such as Horace Mann, Henry Barnard, the Puritans, and others, influenced education more than others. What is it about these individuals and groups that enabled them to have such a dramatic impact?

2. The United States is a much younger country than the vast majority of nations in the world. What factors enabled the nation's university system to advance to the best system of its kind in the world in such a short period of time?

3. Horace Mann and Henry Barnard had a very close relationship, in which they served as each other's confidant. What they endured politically and emotionally, they frequently endured together. To what extent do you see value for personally having a confidant in the education profession? Mann and Barnard were also concerned about producing high-quality teachers. How do their concerns connect to the contemporary concerns about producing high-quality teachers?

4. To what extent do you think a teacher should act like a mother away from home, as Pestalozzi envisioned? Is this appropriate for younger children more than older children? To what degree do teens need educators to "be parents," even if they may be resistant to this fact? If parents and children look to teachers to act as parents, to what extent is there a risk that teachers might usurp the role of parents, even if unintentionally? Does our society expect teachers to perform too many functions?

REFERENCES

Adams, J. Q. (1825, December 6.). *First annual message.* Washington, DC. Retrieved August 2, 2006, from http://www.geocities.com/presidentialspeeches/1825.htm.

Adams, J. Q. (1874a). *Memoirs of John Quincy Adams, comprising portions of his diary from 1795–1848, Vol. I.* Freeport, NY: Books for Libraries Press.

Adams, J. Q. (1874b). *Memoirs of John Quincy Adams, comprising portions of his diary from 1795–1848, Vol. VI.* Freeport, NY: Books for Libraries Press

Altenbaugh R. J., & Underwood, K. (1990). The evolution of the normal schools. In J. I. Goodlad, R. Soder, & J. I. Sirotnik (Eds.), *Places where teachers are taught* (pp. 136–186). San Francisco: Jossey-Bass.

America's best colleges. (2003). *U.S. News & World Report 135*(6), 1–60.

Barnard, H. (1842). *Papers of Henry Barnard.* Manuscript collection of Trinity College Watkinson Library, Hartford CT.

Barnard, H. (1843). *Papers of Henry Barnard.* Manuscript collection of Trinity College Watkinson Library, Hartford CT.

Barnard, H. (1855). Introduction. *American Journal of Education, 1*(1), 1.

Barnard, H., & Lannie, V. P. (1974). *Henry Barnard, American educator.* New York: Teachers College Press.

Beard, C. A., & Beard, M. A. (1944). *A basic history of the United States.* New York: Doubleday, Doran.

Bedsole, V. L., & Richard, O. (Ed.). (1959). *Louisiana State University: A pictorial record of the first hundred years.* Baton Rouge: Louisiana State University Press.

Beecher, L. (1835). *A plea for the West.* Cincinnati, OH: Truman & Smith. Retrieved August 2, 2006, from http://www.artsci.wustl.edu/ ~ acsp/courses/hist366/beecher.html.

Beecher, L. (1864). *Autobiography.* Cambridge, MA: Belknap Press of Harvard University Press.

Berry, M. C. (1980). *The University of Texas: A pictorial account of its first century.* Austin: University of Texas Press.

The best graduate schools. (2003). *U.S. News & World Report, 134*(12), 52–54.

Blanshard, P. (1963). *Religion and the schools.* Boston: Beacon Press.

Bobbe, D. (1933). *DeWitt Clinton.* New York: Minton, Balch.

Bourne, W. O. (1870). *History of the public school society.* New York: Wood.

Brooks, C. (1850). *A lecture delivered before the American Institute of Instruction at Montpelier, VT, August 16, 1849, on the duties of legislatures in relation to public schools in the United States.* Boston: Ticknor, Reed, & Fields.

Brubacher, J. S., & Rudy, W. (1958). *Higher education in transition.* New York: Harper & Row.

Callcott, G. H. (1966). *A history of the University of Maryland.* Baltimore: Maryland Historical Society.

Carter, J. G. (1826). *Essays upon popular education, containing a particular examination of the schools of Massachusetts, and an outline of an institution for the education of teachers.* Boston: Bowles and Dearborn.

Clark, C. (1987). *The assassination: Death of the president.* Alexandra, VA: Time-Life Books.

Clinton, D. (1829). In C. Z. Lincoln (Ed.), *Messages from the governors* (Vol. 5, p. 116). New York: State University of New York Press.

Connor, R. D. W. (1953). *A documentary history of the University of North Carolina, 1776–1799.* Chapel Hill: University of North Carolina Press.

Cross, C. F. (1999). *Justin Smith Morrill: Father of the land-grant colleges.* East Lansing: Michigan State University Press.

Cubberley, E. P. (1909). *Changing conceptions of education.* New York: Houghton Mifflin.

Current, R. N. (1964). The Dartmouth College case. In J. A. Garraty (Ed.), *Quarrels that have shaped the Constitution* (pp. 21–36). New York: Harper & Row.

Curti, M. E. (1949). *The University of Wisconsin: A history.* Madison: Madison: University of Wisconsin Press.

Dabney, V. (1981). *Mr. Jefferson's university: A history.* Charlottesville: University Press of Virginia.

Daniels, R. V. (1991). *The University of Vermont: The first two hundred years.* Hanover, NH: University Press of New England.

Dartmouth College v. Woodward, 17 U.S. 518 (1819).

Dieter, M. E. (1996). *The holiness revival of the nineteenth century.* London: Scarecrow Press.

Downs, R. B. (1975). *Heinrich Pestalozzi: Father of modern pedagogy.* Boston: Twayne.

Dyer, T. G. (1985). *The University of Georgia: A bicentennial history, 1785–1985.* Athens: University of Georgia Press.

Eddy, E. D. (1956). *Colleges for our land and time: The land-grant idea in American education.* New York: Harper.

Elsbree, W. (1939). *The American teacher: Evolution of a profession in a democracy.* New York: American Book Company.

Ely, R. T. (1972). American colleges and German universities. In D. N. Portman (Ed.), *Early reform in American higher education* (pp. 77–92). Chicago: Nelson-Hall.

Filler, L. (1965). *Horace Mann on the crisis in education.* Yellow Springs, OH: Antioch Press.

Fordham, C. C. (1985). *University of North Carolina at Chapel Hill: The first state university.* New York: Newcomen Society of the United States.

Fribourg, M. G. (1965). *The Supreme Court in American history.* Philadelphia: Macrae.

Gatto, J. T. (2001). *The underground history of American schooling.* New York: Oxford Village Press.

Glenn, C. L. (1988). *The myth of the common school.* Amherst: University of Massachusetts Press.

Gray, J. (1951). *The University of Minnesota, 1851–1951.* Minneapolis: University of Minnesota Press.

Griffin, C. S. (1974). *The University of Kansas: A history.* Lawrence: University Press of Kansas.

Gutek, G. L. (1968). *Pestalozzi and education.* New York: Random House.

Gutek, G. L. (1991). *Education in the United States: An historical perspective.* Boston: Allyn & Bacon.

Hacker, L. M. (1970). *The course of American economic growth and development.* New York: Wiley.

Hall, S. (1829). *Lectures on school-keeping.* New York: Arno.

Harper, C. A. (1939). *A century of public school teacher education: The story of the state teacher colleges as they evolved from normal schools.* Washington, DC: American Association of Teachers Colleges.

Heafford, M. (1967). *Pestalozzi: His thought and its relevance today.* London: Methuen.

Hollis, D. W. (1951). *University of South Carolina.* Columbia: University of South Carolina Press.

Honeywell, R. J. (1964). *The educational work of Thomas Jefferson.* New York: Russell & Russell.

Hopkins, J. F. (1951). *The University of Kentucky: Origins and early years.* Lexington: University of Kentucky Press.

Horowitz, H. L. (1987). *Campus life: Undergraduate cultures from the end of the eighteenth century to the present.* New York: Knopf.

Howe, D. W. (1973). *The American Whigs: An anthology.* New York: Wiley.

Howe, D. W. (1979). *The political culture of the American Whigs.* Chicago: University of Chicago Press.

Hudolin, G. J. (1994). Lessons from Catholic schools: Promoting quality in Chicago's public schools. *Educational Forum, 5,* 282–288.

Hunt, T. C., & Maxson, M. M. (1981). *Religion and morality in American schooling.* Washington, DC: University Press of America.

Institute of Higher Education, Shanghai Jiao Tong University (2004). *Top 500 world universities.* Shanghai: Shanghai Jiao Tong University.

Jencks, C., & Riesman, D. (1968). *The academic revolution.* Garden City, NY: Doubleday.

Johnson, P. (1997). *A history of the American people.* New York: HarperCollins.

Kaestle, C. F., & Vinovskis, M. (1980). *Education & social change in nineteenth-century Massachusetts.* New York: Cambridge University.

Kerr, K. A. (1985). *Organized for prohibition: A new history of the Anti-Saloon League.* New Haven, CT: Yale University Press:

Kincaid, J. R. (1998). *Erotic innocence: The culture of child molesting.* Durham, NC: Duke University Press.

Kinloch, T. (1969). *Pioneers of religious education.* Freeport, NY: Books for Libraries Press.

Kliebard, H. M. (1969). *Religion and education in America.* Scranton, PA: International Textbook Company.

Lieberman, J. K. (1976). *Milestones: Two hundred years of American law.* New York: Oxford University Press.

Lincoln, A. (1842). *Speech delivered before the Springfield (Illinois) Washington Temperance Society, on the 22nd February, 1842.* Springfield, IL: Springfield Washington Temperance Society.

Lincoln, A. (1863). Reply to Sons of Temperance, September 29. In R. P. Basler (Ed.), *The collected works of Abraham Lincoln, Volume VI* (p. 487). New Brunswick, NJ: Rutgers University Press.

Long, K. T. (1998). *The Revival of 1857-1958: Interpreting an American religious awakening.* New York: Oxford University Press.

MacMullen, E. N. (1991). *In the cause of true education reform: Henry Barnard & nineteenth century school reform.* New Haven, CT: Yale University Press.

Malone, D. (1981). *The sage of Monticello.* Boston: Little Brown.

Mann, H. (1838). *First annual report.* Dutton & Wentworth.

Mann, H. (1839). *Second annual report.* Dutton & Wentworth.

Mann, H. (1840). *Third annual report.* Dutton & Wentworth.

Mann, H. (1844). *Seventh annual report.* Dutton & Wentworth.

Mann, H. (1845). *Eighth annual report.* Dutton & Wentworth.

Mann, H. (1846). *Ninth annual report.* Dutton & Wentworth.

Mann, H. (1848). *Eleventh annual report.* Dutton & Wentworth.

Mann, H. (1849). *Twelfth annual report.* Dutton & Wentworth.

Mann, H. (1957). *The republic and the school: Horace Mann on the education of free men* (L. Cremin, Ed.). New York: Teachers College, Columbia University.

Mann, H. (1969). *Lectures on education.* New York: Arno.

Mann, M. P. (Ed.). (1907). *Life of Horace Mann.* Washington, DC: National Education Association.

Marshall, J. (1967). *John Marshall: Major opinions and other writings.* Indianapolis, IN: Bobbs-Merrill.

Marshall, P., & Manuel, D. (1986). *From sea to shining sea.* Grand Rapids, MI: Fleming Revell.

McGuffey, W. H., & Lindberg, S. W. (1976). *The annotated McGuffey: Selections from the McGuffey eclectic readers, 1836-1920.* New York: Van Nostrand Reinhold.

Messerli, J. (1972). *Horace Mann: A biography.* New York, Knopf.

Mondale, S., & Patton, S. B. (2001). *School, the story of American public school education.* Boston: Beacon Press.

Montgomery, J. R., Folmsbee, S. J., & Greene, L. S. (1984). *To foster knowledge: A history of the University of Tennessee, 1794-1970.* Knoxville: University of Tennessee Press.

Moore, S., & Simon, J. L. (2000). *It's getting better all the time: 100 greatest trends of the 20th century.* Washington, DC: Cato Institute.

Munroe, J. A. (1986). *The University of Delaware: A history.* Newark, DE: University of Delaware.

Orr, J. E. (1989). *The event of the century.* Wheaton, IL: International Awakening Press.

Peckham, H. H. (1967). *The making of the University of Michigan, 1817-1967.* Ann Arbor: University of Michigan Press.

Pestalozzi, J. (1801). *Leonard and Gertrude.* Philadelphia: Groff.

Pestalozzi, J. (1898). *How Gertrude teaches her children: An attempt to help mothers to teach their own children and an account of the method* (L. Hoilland & F. Turner, Trans.). Syracuse, NY: Bardeen.

Pestalozzi, J. (1916). How a child is led to God through maternal love. In J. A. Green (Ed.), *Pestalozzi's educational writings.* London: Edward Arnold.

Pulliam, J. D., & Van Patten, J. J. (1991). *History of education in America.* Upper Saddle River, NJ: Merrill/Prentice Hall.

Ramsey P., & Wilson, J. (Eds.). (1970). *The study of religion in colleges and universities.* Princeton, NJ: Princeton University Press.

Reck, W. E. (1903). *Abraham Lincoln: His last twenty-four hours*. Jefferson, NC: McFarland.

Rippa, S. A. (1997). *Education in a free society*. White Plains, NY: Longman.

Rogers, E. M. (1979). *A bibliography of the history of the University of Iowa, 1847–1978*. Iowa City: University of Iowa Libraries.

Rohrs, H. (1995). *The classical German concept of the university and its influence on higher education in the United States*. New York: Peter Lang.

Roscoe, T. (1959). *The web of conspiracy: The complete story of the men who murdered Abraham Lincoln*. Englewood Cliffs, NJ: Prentice Hall.

Rousseau, J. J. (1911). *Emile*. New York: Dutton.

Ruggles, A. M. (1950). *The story of the McGuffeys*. New York: American Book Company.

Sadler, J. E. (1966). *J. A. Comenius and the concept of universal education*. New York: Barnes & Noble.

Seelye, S. (1864). *Discourses of Rev. Samuel T. Seelye and Calvin Stowe*. New York: Gray & Green.

Sellers, J. B. (1953). *History of the University of Alabama*. Tuscaloosa, AL: University of Alabama Press.

Shaver, A. V., & Walls, R. T. (1998). Effect of Title I parent involvement on student reading and mathematics achievement. *Journal of Research and Development in Education, 31,* 90–97.

Spinka, M. (1967). *John Amos Comensios: That incomparable Moravian*. New York: Russell & Russell.

Spring, J. (1997). *The American school 1642–1996*. White Plains, NY: Longman.

Stadtman, V. A. (1970). *The University of California, 1868–1968*. New York: McGraw-Hill.

Stephens, F. F. (1962). *A history of the University of Missouri*. Columbia: University of Missouri Press.

Stone, I. (1970). *There was light: Autobiography of a university, Berkeley, 1868–1968*. Garden City, NY: Doubleday.

Stowe, C. (1836). *The Prussian system of public instruction: And its applicability to the United States*. Cincinnati, OH: Truman & Smith.

Stowe, C. (1837). *Report on elementary school instruction in Europe, made to the Thirty-Sixth General Assembly of the State of Ohio, December 19, 1837*. Columbus, OH: S. Medary, Printer for the State.

Tewksbury, S. (1932). *Founding of American colleges and universities before the Civil War*. New York: Teachers College Press.

Tharp, L. H. (1953). *Until victory: Horace Mann and Mary Peabody*. Boston: Little, Brown.

Thorton, M. (1992). *The economics of Prohibition*. Salt Lake City: University of Utah Press.

Thursfield, R, E. (1945). *Henry Barnard's American Journal of Education*. Baltimore: Johns Hopkins University Press.

Tocqueville, A. (1966). *Democracy in America*. New York: Harper & Row.

Ulich, R. (1968). *A history of religious education*. New York: New York University Press.

Urban, W., & Wagoner, J. (2000). *American education: A history*. Boston: McGraw Hill.

U.S. Department of Education. (2000). *Digest of education statistics, 1999*. Washington, DC: Author.

Wertheim, S. (1970). *Educational periodicals: Propaganda sheets for Ohio common schools* (Doctoral dissertation, Case Western Reserve University). *Dissertation Abstracts International 31*(7), 3313.

Westerhoff, J. H. (1978). *McGuffey and his readers: Piety, morality, and education in nineteenth-century America*. Nashville, TN: Abingdon.

Wills, G. (2002). *Mr. Jefferson's university*. Washington, DC: National Geographic.

Yulish, S. M. (1980). *The search for a civic religion*. Washington, DC: University Press of America.

The Effects of Events During and Between the Civil War and World War I

During the period from 1861 to 1918, from the Civil War to World War I, the United States matured into a primary economic world power. By 1900, the United States maintained the highest standard of living of any nation in the world, a position it would hold until 1973 (U.S. Department of Labor, 2005). Educators believe that the ascending American education system of the 19th and early 20th centuries contributed measurably to the puissant economy that Americans would enjoy in the 20th century (Hungerford & Wassmer, 2004). Undoubtedly, the period from 1861 to 1918 was an important one in the history of American education. Urbanization, industrialization, and immigration would all have a prominent impact. In addition, schools assumed new social roles that produced some controversy. Educators also debated about what should be the appropriate nature of education for African Americans in the post–Civil War era. This chapter of American educational history also yielded a more well-defined American education system, which in most respects resembled that which the nation's citizenry is familiar with today.

IMPACT OF THE CIVIL WAR

Many historians claim that America did not become a full-fledged nation until the conclusion of the Civil War (Johnson, 1997). There are a number of reasons historians make this assertion.

First, slavery had divided the nation prior to the Civil War. In a very real sense, as the slave trade grew, the nation became two nations under one roof (Johnson, 1997). On the basis of this reality, Abraham Lincoln (1858) made a famous speech in which he declared, paraphrasing Jesus in the New Testament, "A house divided against itself cannot stand." Certainly with such a division tearing the country apart, the United States really could not function as one nation.

Second, because the Democratic-Republicans had won the early political debates, there was a great deal more emphasis placed on states' rights than on federal rights (Johnson, 1997; Stephens, 1872). The early victories by the Democratic-Republicans both reflected and influenced the mood of the people. Truly, the American people had been accustomed to acting as separate entities for nearly 170 years, since the founding of Jamestown, in 1607, and it was difficult to alter those practices (Johnson, 1997; Stephens, 1872). This is one main reason the American people had tended to support the Democratic-Republican cause (J. Adams, 1854; J. Q. Adams, 1850). But the fact that the Democratic-Republicans did prevail also influenced the mentality of Americans. Americans were recurrently more likely to think in terms of the rights of states rather than federal rights.

Third, America's level of sophistication industrially and especially in terms of transportation was much greater after the Civil War. This made uniting the country much easier. By the mid-1800s, the United States was diligently building new railroads, and ocean travel was also becoming more sophisticated. Ships were now becoming fast and reliable enough that they were becoming a preferred means of sending mail and engaging in trade (Abdill, 1961; Beatty, 2001; Johnson, 1997). Transportation became more sophisticated particularly during the Civil War, when the transporting of military goods and soldiers made a quality transportation system that much more important (Abdill, 1961; Beatty, 2001; Johnson, 1997). The increased sophistication of the American transportation system, which resulted to a considerable degree from the Civil War, played a large role in bringing the country together.

IMPACT OF THE POST–CIVIL WAR PERIOD

The previous section explained the reasons there was not national unity prior to the Civil War and why living in a premodern society hindered the unification of a nation that occupied such a large geographical area. Two related factors, urbanization and industrialization, went a long way to help unify the nation.

Urbanization

The growth of America's urban areas was substantial following the Civil War. The growth of states with urban populations far exceeded the states with rural populations (Barth, 1980; Bender, 1975; Cremin, 1977; Cubberley, 1920; Rury, 2002; White, 1989). By 1880, there were 50 million Americans, versus only 4 million in 1790 (Cremin, 1977). By 1890, 63 million people lived in the United States (Cremin, 1977). Over half the U.S. population was concentrated in just eight urban states (U.S. Bureau of the Census, 1975). Nearly 10% of Americans lived in New York State alone, with another 7% of Americans dwelling in Pennsylvania: 1 in 6 Americans lived in these two most populous states (U.S. Bureau of the Census, 1975). Of the 10 states with the most people in 1890, the only southern state was Texas, because the Northern states were far more urbanized (U.S. Bureau of the Census, 1975). In 1890, 30% of Americans lived in cities, and by 1920, over half the American population lived in cities (Cremin, 1977).

Urbanization is the process of change associated with a town increasing in population and altering in atmosphere to become a city. Urbanization had a profound impact upon American culture and education. It meant that Americans interacted with many more people than in the past. This created a sense of being a part of a much larger nation than in the past (Barth, 1980; Bender, 1975; Cremin, 1977; Cubberley, 1920; Rury, 2002; White, 1989).

One can argue that the American fascination with individual and states' rights was influenced largely by many Americans growing up on rural farms, where there often were not any other residents for miles. However, with the inception of urbanization, people started to interface with each other a lot more. The creation of jobs that accompanied industrialization enabled urbanization to take place (Barth, 1980; Bender, 1975; Cremin, 1977; Cubberley, 1920; Rury, 2002; White, 1989). As a result of urbanization, people who would have worked separately if they were in agriculture now worked together. Church membership also rose: from 35% in 1890 to 55% by 1950 and 69% by 1960 (Cremin, 1977). Part of this increase was due to the fact that before the Civil War, church membership was not particularly emphasized (Connell, 2004; Marshall & Manuel, 1977). In fact, until after the Civil War, the only people who generally joined the church were leaders in the church (Marshall & Manuel, 1977). Nevertheless, the increase in church membership indicates that people were interacting more than ever before.

Urbanization made organizing the common school much easier. Once many cities emerged on the American scene, teachers from the same town could be easily recruited (Carter, 1826; Harper, 1939; MacMullen, 1991; Mann, 1839, 1845). Principals and superintendents could also be recruited (Harper, 1939; Stowe, 1836). When schools were located in small- to medium-sized towns, the ability to recruit educators was very dependent on their availability (Mann, 1844, 1845, 1969). Therefore, towns with a low number of available teachers usually struggled in developing a strong education system (Carter, 1826; Mann, 1839, 1845; Pulliam & Van Patten, 1991). Urbanization made it more possible for teacher-training centers to be developed in the form of normal schools and teacher colleges (MacMullen, 1991; Pulliam & Van Patten, 1991).

Added Insight: Uniting Nations and Empires

Going back to the days of the great expansionist empires, such as the Egyptian Empire, the Roman Empire, the Byzantine Empire, and so forth, one of their great challenges was to be able to expand geographically and yet establish some sense of oneness or unity within the empire. For all intents and purposes, this was never accomplished for any length of time (Brandon, 1970; Cubberley, 1920; Eisenstadt, 1967; Green, 1991; Newby, 1980). Rather, the situation was that generally one leader ruled over one of many provinces and peoples. There was very little sense of unity, even if the backgrounds of the citizens were very similar (Cubberley, 1920; Marrou, 1956). There was incredible rivalry and disunity even among cities that were culturally similar to one another (Brandon, 1970; Cubberley, 1920; Eisenstadt, 1967; Green, 1991; Marrou, 1956). The Greek rival cities of Athens and Sparta are good examples of this (Marrou, 1956).

The Macedonian leader Alexander the Great and the French leader Charlemagne brought many peoples together under one ruler (Marrou, 1956), but did the people ever feel as if they were one nation?

(Continued)

(Continued)

No. Alexander even dreamed of a single people and a single culture under his leadership, a blending of the best aspects of the Greek and Persian cultures. He even married two Persian princesses in order to help make this a reality (Green, 1991; Hammond, 1997). Nevertheless, in both the cases of Alexander the Great and Charlemagne, the empires were broken up after these men died (Green, 1991).

A person might ask why it was so difficult for these great nations to establish a sense of unity. Certainly, one reason was that in some of them, a great deal of diversity existed among the people (Brandon, 1970; Cubberley, 1920; Eisenstadt, 1967; Green, 1991; Newby, 1980). However, one should note that this was not always the case. A second factor is also important: Prior to the era of modern transportation, the lack of mobility made it difficult for people living in large geographical areas to make contact (Abdill, 1961; Beatty, 2001; Johnson, 1997; Russel, 1972).

Industrialization

Industrialization was another factor that radically changed the nature of American education (Husband & O'Loughlin, 2004; Jacob, 1997; Rury, 2002). *Industrialization* is the process of transformation from a primarily agriculturally based economy to one based on the mass production of man-made products. Perhaps the greatest way that industrialization changed education is to make education more of a necessity (Jacob, 1997; Rury, 2002). There are a number of reasons for this.

First, previously, children learned occupations from their parents and entered the same kinds of lifestyles as their parents. If a parent was a farmer, the child became a farmer; if the parent was a blacksmith, the child became a blacksmith (Bailyn, 1960; Bartlett, 1978; Beard & Beard, 1944; Brown, 1890; Cubberley, 1909, 1920). Industrialization, however, introduced all kinds of new occupations that prescribed training and additional knowledge (Cubberley, 1909, 1920; Husband & O'Loughlin, 2004; Rury, 2002). Children often could not procure this knowledge from their parents (Cubberley, 1909, 1920; Rury, 2002). Indeed, once the Industrial Revolution began, the majority of children who moved into the cities did not enter into the same occupational positions as their parents (Cubberley, 1909, 1920; Husband & O'Loughlin, 2004; Timmons, 1988). They could not learn how to function well in their new industrial trades and jobs by simply learning from their parents. This set the stage for the growth of education (Dewey, 1915, 1998).

Second, industrialization also introduced a whole list of new concepts to be learned. In fact, overall, the reality of industrialization was simply making the world more complex than it had ever been before. The complexity of the world necessitated a higher level of education and more expansive knowledge than ever before (Dewey, 1915, 1998).

Third, industrialization, in terms of increased sophistication in communication and transportation, also gave America more access to knowledge than ever before. The burgeoning amount of knowledge available also fostered a greater exigency for education. With this tremendous explosion of knowledge, Americans realized that there needed to be centers of education that could quickly disperse this information (Rury, 2002).

Fourth, industrialization made more people realize the need for education not only at an individual level but also at the national level (Cremin, 1977; Rury, 2002; Timmons, 1988).

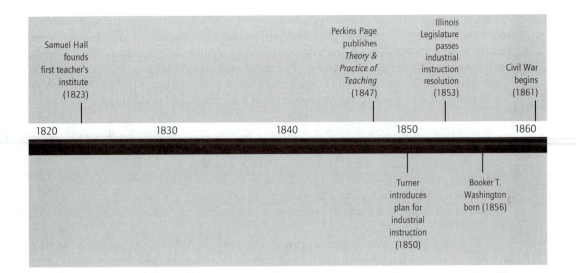

The American government and business leaders comprehended that national security, power, and standard of living would now be based on the extent to which America industrialized (Cremin, 1967; Rury, 2002; Tyack, 1967). America's religious people came to the understanding rather early that the extent to which a nation became industrialized was correlative with its knowledge level, but in the post–Civil War period, nearly all Americans understood this relationship (Marshall & Manuel, 1977; Tewksbury, 1932). Industrialization was a product of technological progress (Jacob, 1997). And technological progress was founded on knowledge. To the extent that this is true, it was the responsibility of every society to maximize the amount of knowledge available to its citizenry (Cremin, 1977; Rury, 2002; Timmons, 1988).

Before industrialization, education was thought to help people become (a) more virtuous, (b) better leaders, and (c) more open to the ideas of others (Plato, 1941, 1956). But now, industrialization had produced additional functions, such as to help (a) increase a nation's standard of living and (b) enhance the occupational survival rate of individuals (Cremin, 1977; Rury, 2002; Timmons, 1988).

DEBATE OVER AFRICAN AMERICAN EDUCATION

Following the Civil War, a growing battle emerged over the future of African American education. Two prominent African Americans were involved in the battle, Booker T. Washington (1856–1915) and W. E. B. DuBois (1868–1963). Washington was a highly respected educational leader. He wrote the book *Up From Slavery* (1901), in which he shared his experiences as a slave (Amper, 1998). One of the most memorable sections of Washington's book was his account of slaves hearing about the Emancipation Proclamation (Rippa, 1997). Washington was able to rise above any feelings of racism and was an example of love and logic in dealing with educational issues involving African Americans. He was a graduate of

the Hampton Institute and believed that African Americans should receive training in industrial education. In 1881, Washington founded the Tuskegee Institute in order to fulfill his
desires to educate the African American community (Amper, 1998). Most of the Tuskegee
curriculum was focused on teaching "industrial arts and training skills" (Rippa, 1997;
Washington, 1899). The following quote, from Booker T. Washington's (1899) *The Future of
the American Negro,* sums up some key points in his educational philosophy:

> It seems to me that there was never a time in the history of the country when those
> interested in education should the more earnestly consider to what extent the mere
> acquiring of the ability to read and write, the mere acquisition of a knowledge of
> literature and science, makes men producers, lovers of labor, independent, honest,
> unselfish, and, above all, good. Call education by what name you please, if it fails to
> bring about these results among its masses, it falls short of the highest end. (pp. 16–17)

W. E. B. DuBois was Washington's primary critic (Rippa, 1997). DuBois (1903) believed
that African Americans should aspire to higher goals than industrial education. He believed
that Washington was compromising his convictions in order to pacify the White majority
(DuBois, 1903; Rippa, 1997). DuBois said, "Mr. Washington's program practically accepts the
alleged inferiority of the Negro races" (p. 51). In his 1903 book, *The Souls of Black Folk,*
DuBois stated the following: "Mr. Washington distinctly asks that black people give up, at
least for the present, three things: First, political power. Second, insistence on civil rights.
Third, higher education of Negro youth" (p. 52).

DuBois had a more aggressive approach to obtaining equal rights for African Americans,
whereas Washington maintained a more peaceful approach. Malcolm X followed in the footsteps of DuBois, whereas Martin Luther King Jr. followed in the footsteps of Washington
(Spivey, 1978). Washington and King believed in taking the moral high ground and asserted
that this would eventually lead to equal rights for African Americans. DuBois and Malcolm
X believed in a more aggressive approach (Spivey, 1978).

As much as some people might appreciate one approach over the other, it is important
to observe that in the case of Washington and DuBois, part of their differences in approach
was due largely to their different backgrounds. Washington grew up in slavery, whereas
DuBois was raised in the free state of Massachusetts, where his family had long been free
(Rippa, 1997; Spivey, 1978). It also appears to be true that both Washington and DuBois
desired that African American people experience upward mobility, but they had different
views on how that could be best achieved (Spivey, 1978). In fact, a great deal of the tension
between Washington's view and DuBois's view revolves around an age-old question in education: In any educational aim, should one's goal be to educate the future leadership
because they have the greatest potential to change society, or to make sure the masses are
educated to perform well and function as well-informed, able citizens? DuBois believed that
schools should focus on educating what he called "the talented tenth" among African
Americans, but Washington viewed this approach as elitist and claimed that it did not serve
the interests of African Americans who were suffering the most (Washington, 1905, 1906).

The strengths of the first approach, that of DuBois, involve training the future leadership
of America, who can potentially change society and promote advances to a greater degree
than the masses might be able to do. The weakness of this approach is that it focuses on

creating a new elite rather than meeting the needs of the majority of people in a given group. The strengths of the second approach, Washington's, are that a maximum number of people are educated and literate, with numerous people being able to contribute knowledge on specific issues. The weakness of this approach is that one is not preparing people to become a new generation of leaders within a society.

Although modern educators tend to focus on the differences between Washington and DuBois, the similarities between these two men are of equal consequence. First and foremost, both men contended that education was invaluable in order to raise the status and living conditions of African Americans (DuBois, 1897, 1903; Washington, 1905, 1906). The fact that two men of distinctly different philosophies agreed on this point helped consolidate African Americans behind the notion that quality schooling was of inestimable value for the future of African American citizens. Largely because of this agreement, equal education became a major pillar of the civil rights movement that would follow. Second, both men envisioned a day in which African Americans would enjoy the privileges and joys of the American dream; they simply differed on the best way to achieve this goal.

Contemporary Focus

Affirmative Action, Japan, and the Talented Tenth

- What is the best form of affirmative action that the United States should practice to help underrepresented groups in its society?

- Should one's goal be to make sure the masses are educated to perform well and function as well-informed, able citizens, or should the focus be on educating the future leadership, because they have the greatest potential to change society?

In an ideal world, there is certainly a need to include some of both approaches. Nevertheless, some nations, like Japan, definitely emphasize the first approach more than the United States does (Stevenson & Stigler, 1992). The Japanese system of elementary and secondary schools is one of the best in the world and is regarded as far superior to the American public school system. Research indicates that Japanese students in middle and secondary schools are generally about 2 years ahead of their American counterparts in academics (Stevenson & Stigler, 1992). This should not be surprising, given the Japanese emphasis on making certain that all the people in their nation have a certain level of literacy. As a result, Japan has a 99% rate of literacy, substantially higher than that of the United States in recent years (Stevenson & Stigler, 1992). However, a higher percentage of Americans than Japanese attend at least some college (Stevenson & Stigler, 1992; U.S. Department of Education, 2003).

In terms of opening up opportunities for minorities, in recent decades, most minority leaders have preferred to focus on the DuBois-type approach of educating a new elite rather than maximizing educational opportunity for the masses (Battle & Wright, 2002; Killian, 1999). Affirmative action educational programs have focused on increasing minority representation in colleges and universities, rather than concentrating primarily on widespread literacy and core knowledge (Bergman, 1996; Hewitt, 1991). Only about 25% of Americans, as a whole, graduate from 4-year colleges (U.S. Department of Education, 2003). Therefore, to primarily focus efforts toward equality in this group is to apply the DuBois-type approach. Incorporating this approach has unquestionably given an opportunity to many minority students to go to college who otherwise would not have gone (Bergman, 1996; Zelnick, 2004). This is clearly a desirable goal.

On the other hand, some have argued that the focus of affirmative action has inappropriately favored the DuBois-type approach, leaving behind many insufficiently educated minority people to "fall through the cracks" in the system and become caught in a web of poverty that results in part from a lack of education (Battle & Wright, 2002; Killian, 1999). Therefore, there are many educators who believe that Booker T. Washington's approach is more appropriate. They argue that if America's educators emphasized the education of the masses, as Washington advocated, more minority students would eventually make their way to college not on the basis of preferential treatment, but on the basis of gains made because of an education system that offered them a quality education at a young age (Washington, 1899).

- Which vision of affirmative action do you feel is more appropriate, the DuBois approach or the Washington rubric? Why?

- Do you believe that some combination of the two approaches is ideal? Why?

INCREASED IMMIGRATION

The 50 years following the Civil War were also years of tremendous change in the number of immigrants coming to the United States. During the period of 1881 through 1925, 25 million immigrants came to America (Bayer, 1980). By 1920, 36% of the population of New York City was foreign-born, and most children in several cities in America had at least one foreign-born parent (Kessner, 1981; Spring, 1997).

After the Civil War, the United States became a much more attractive nation to which to immigrate (Johnson, 1997; Stites, 2004; Summers, 1984). Following the war, it was no longer such a divided country. The United States was not only viewed as a nation of freedom, but as a nation of prosperity (Stites, 2004; Summers, 1984). By the end of the Civil War, the United States had one of the most powerful economies on earth, and beginning in 1900, it had the largest economy in the world (Burns, 1934; Keller, 1990).

Advantages of Increased Immigration

The United States has had a long practice of encouraging immigration more than any other nation in the world. As much as this policy emanates from a historic open-mindedness to those desiring to come to this country, it traditionally has also been practiced, because Americans generally believe that there are a number of advantages to immigration both for the nation at large and for the education system (Olneck & Lazerson, 1991; Quance, 1926). Although one can consider any number of benefits, these advantages are especially worth highlighting.

Different Perspectives. The presence of immigrants in the nations from various lands brings a multitude of perspectives to the nation. Given that the United States is blessed with the presence of these perspectives, groups of people can be introduced to new ways of thinking and addressing various challenges in their work, education, and in life as a whole (Olneck & Lazerson, 1991; Quance, 1926). Americans therefore often have the benefit of attempting old tasks in a new way or having more effective results emerge from brainstorming.

Additional Workers. The large influx of immigrants makes millions of new workers available to take job positions in a growing industrial society (Olneck & Lazerson, 1991; Quance, 1926). To the extent that the economy has jobs available, this helps fuel the growth of an industrial economy by creating a larger workforce.

"Melting Pot" Effect. During the 1980s and 1990s, in many multicultural circles, the "melting pot" phenomenon became out of favor (Glazer, 1997). Instead, many multiculturalists preferred the term "salad bowl" to communicate America's diversity (D'Innocenzo & Sirefman, 1992; Glazer, 1997). A number of multiculturalists believed that this term was preferable, because they felt that a melting pot indicates a loss of identity and a salad bowl indicates that individuals' identities are maintained (D'Innocenzo & Sirefman, 1992; Glazer, 1997). In other words, in a salad, a tomato remains a tomato, and a cucumber remains a cucumber, even after the salad is mixed (D'Innocenzo & Sirefman, 1992). However, as is highlighted in "A Closer Look" in this passage, the concept of a melting pot was originally designed to communicate strength in diversity rather than a monolithic society. The melting-pot principle is based on the traditional American belief that ethnic diversity is a source of strength, rather than weakness, for the nation. Originally, the term was based on the idea that in order to strengthen a metal, for example, steel, one melts down the metal and then combines it with another kind of metal. Once the combined metals harden, a stronger metal results (Barone, 2001; Mintz, 1969). A melting pot is therefore a nation in which a diverse array of people come together, convinced that their diversity is a strength, to make a better country.

A Closer Look: The Melting Pot and Multiculturalism

The term "melting pot" is again enjoying popularity, because more people understand that the essence of the term focuses on strength in diversity (Barone, 2001). As it was originally conceived, the idea of a melting pot was based on making steel and other metals (Barone, 2001; Mintz, 1969). Steelmakers are well aware that in order to make a stronger steel, the best way to do it is to combine different metals (Barone, 2001). Therefore, the original idea of a melting pot was that the United States was made of a confluence of diverse people from all over the world forming one nation (Barone, 2001; Mintz, 1969). The gathering together of these diverse peoples made the nation stronger, as the combining of metals makes a metal stronger. The "melting pot" concept conveys the idea that America's diversity makes the nation stronger, not weaker (Barone, 2001; Mintz, 1969). The focus on steel or a related metal is also designed to communicate the strength that emerges as the final result of immigrant groups conglomerating in one nation.

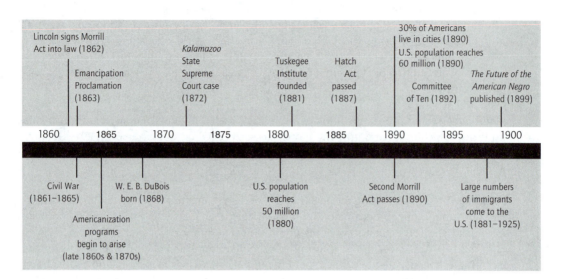

Strains of Increased Immigration

The level of immigration put certain strains on the American education system, such as (a) language considerations, (b) an elevated level of school enrollment, and (c) adaptation issues.

Language Considerations

Many immigrants who came to the United States did not speak or write English very well. Only on rare occasions did parents encourage their children to speak English (Kraut, 1986; Mutulich, 1980; Pozzetta, 1991). This created quite a challenge for American teachers. Many immigrants were fluent neither in English nor in their own native languages (Covello, 1967; Perlmann, 1988). Even among Russian Jews, some of the most academically inclined of the immigrant groups, as of 1899, illiteracy prevailed in about 30% of the children (Perlmann, 1988). For the vast majority of other immigrant groups, the rate was much higher.

Volume of Enrollment

In 1909, U.S. Immigration conducted a survey indicating that 58% of American children in America's major cities had foreign-born parents (Cremin, 1962). Some immigrant groups did particularly well in school, particularly Jewish students coming from Russia and other students from Germany (Perlmann, 1988). Nevertheless, most immigrants coming from Europe were from uneducated, lower-class stock backgrounds (Mutulich, 1980; Pozzetta, 1991). As a result, teaching this volume of students became especially difficult (Mutulich, 1980; Pozzetta, 1991).

Adaptation Issues

Any time one moves to a different country, there are going to be challenges in adapting (Pozzetta, 1991). The philosophy of the United States regarding bringing immigrants into American society was different during this period than we commonly see today. The United States today has a multicultural perspective, which asserts that the object of including immigrants in American society should not be to make them assimilate into American culture. Rather, multiculturalism asserts that it is advantageous to encourage immigrants to preserve their cultures.

The idea of assimilating into American culture was called the process of "Americanization." Americanization became a common philosophy of most American schools following the Civil War (Weiss, 1982), and many people today are critical of the practice. They ask, "Why did they not practice multiculturalism?" However, to make this assertion may be judgmental and insensitive to the historical forces that were at work at that time.

The philosophy of multiculturalism resulted from certain historical forces that were at work in the 1940s, particularly World War II and the promotion of the United States from being the world's foremost economic power to being a superpower. Later, we will examine this fact more closely. It is equally true that the Civil War played a major role in the advent of Americanization (Coben & Ratner, 1983; Weiss, 1982). The United States had just come amazingly close to being torn apart. The nation's people were terribly afraid of being destroyed by internal division (Jones, 2000). The Civil War had taught Americans that different perspectives and different worldviews could tear the country apart unless the nation did a better job of creating harmony and limiting internal divisions. The result of this concern was Americanization (Weiss, 1982).

When millions of immigrants came to the United States year after year, many Americans became concerned that the different cultures and languages that people brought with them could potentially produce a great deal of division (Cremin, 1962; Weiss, 1982). It was believed that unless the immigrants were taught the English language and the American way of life, the country could eventually be torn apart (Weiss, 1982). Contemporary Americans have never been through a Civil War. They cannot imagine the extent to which such a conflict can forever change a people's perspective on life. The Civil War remains to this day the most traumatic event that this nation has ever faced. We can only attempt to place ourselves in the shoes of the Americans who experienced it.

It should also be noted that contrary to what many modern people believe, many educators of the time did attempt to incorporate ethnic minorities into the mainstream of the school curriculum. Nicholas Montalto (1991) notes, "As early as 1920, ethnic leaders as well as mainstream educators and social workers were exerting pressure on school administrators to adapt school curriculum to the needs of white ethnic minorities" (p. 68). Montalto adds that there was a particular attempt to incorporate into the curriculum the accomplishments of individuals from various minority groups. Nevertheless, these efforts were not as determined as multicultural efforts today.

We, as contemporary Americans, might appreciate the value of multiculturalism at the expense of Americanization. But Americanization was a product of the historical forces that were at work during the post–Civil War era, even as multiculturalism is a product of the historical forces that were at work in the 1960s. It arose out of the concern that America must take action in order to ensure that the country would remain intact (Miller, 1990). It is true that even before the Civil War, nativist movements argued for the perpetuation of American culture and were concerned with excessive foreign cultural influence. However, these groups were not in the mainstream and were consistently defeated in national elections (Anbinder, 1992; Higham, 1955). In contrast, those who supported Americanization after the Civil War generally welcomed immigrants, and the movement was much more mainstream. When one considers the historical forces at work at this time, it may be seen that Americanization was probably a logical way of resolving many of the potential problems regarding division that could have arisen. Would multiculturalism have been the appropriate perspective in a period following the Civil War? Perhaps not.

SOCIAL ROLE OF THE SCHOOL

After the Civil War, as the common schools expanded, there was a great deal of emphasis on educating the poor (Cubberley, 1920). Many educators believed that just as the church worked to elevate people out of paucity, schools could perform an analogous function (Cubberley, 1920; Eavey, 1964; Stewart, 1969). Schools would not directly dispense money for families, as churches did (Eavey, 1964; Stewart, 1969). Rather, the schools would provide the educational means necessary to help the children in penurious families rise out of their poverty and live up to their fullest potential in American society (Cubberley, 1920). What educators did not initially realize, however, is that this meant that the educators would teach the children not only to read and write, but that they would also have to teach them to bathe, brush their teeth, comb their hair, and tie their shoes (Dunn, 1955). Thus, the Americanization program with immigrants involved not only the academic but also the socialization aspect of schooling (Bayer, 1980; Olneck & Lazerson, 1991; Weiss, 1982).

Naturally, a lot of teachers complained about being not only a teacher but also a nanny. To many educators, teachers were spending too much time focusing on "problem children" (Dunn, 1955). Many educators to this day believe that one of the reasons that students in American public schools trail those from other industrialized nations in academic achievement is that the American education system focuses too much on problem children (Bayer,1980; Dunn, 1955; Olneck & Lazerson, 1991; Weiss, 1982). Some educators, such as Joan Dunn (1955), in her book *Retreat From Learning,* assert that as a result, the rest of American students are suffering. The extent to which schools should serve a social function is still an area of controversy today.

Nevertheless, most educators today believe that these social roles of the school are necessary, especially in homes where children are somehow insufficiently looked after by their parents (Orr, 1987). Many social scientists believe that in an ideal world, Dunn might be right, but we do not live in an ideal world. In reality, some children come to school with lice in their hair, dirty hands, and unbrushed teeth. If part of being an effective teacher is preparing children to function as successful citizens in society, then part of that involves training children in health and hygiene.

Educational Debate: The Social Role of the Teacher

- Do you believe that teachers spend too much time tending to the sanitary and health needs of children?
- Do you think that Dunn has a point along these lines?
- In contrast, do you instead believe that tending to children's health needs is an important component of teaching, especially since many parents do not live up to their responsibilities in these areas?
- If you agree with Dunn's views, how can we better encourage parents to take responsibility for this teaching?
- If you disagree with Dunn, how can we teach those children who struggle with health and hygiene in a way that is not embarrassing to the child?

LAND GRANT COLLEGES

The Civil War also had a great impact on the emergence of *land grant colleges.* Land grant institutions are colleges that benefited from the U.S. government parceling out land to states for little or no money in order for them to strengthen or to establish state universities.

Before the Civil War, certain educators had seen a need to facilitate the development of state universities in order to encourage (a) the development of instruction in agriculture, (b) industrial education, and (c) military strategy (Anderson, 1976; Eddy, 1956). In 1847, John Turner, a Yale graduate and Illinois college professor of 14 years, announced that he would pledge himself to the "uplift of the industrial classes" (Madsen, 1976, p. 28). Although Turner certainly did not invent the idea of industrial education, he nevertheless became the movement's most outspoken advocate (Eddy, 1956). The acme of his efforts was reached in 1850, when he proposed a master plan for a state industrial institution in Illinois. Turner laid out the details of his perspective in a speech on May 13, 1850, in Griggsville, Illinois (Eddy, 1956).

Turner continued to do everything in his power to get legislation passed in sponsoring industrial education (Eddy, 1956). In 1853, the Illinois legislature passed industrial instruction resolutions to be presented before the U.S. Congress (Eddy, 1956). Horace Greeley (1811–1872), editor of the New Yorker and a well-known journalist and Whig leader, declared that the action was a major step in the right direction (Eddy, 1956).

The stage was set for some substantial contributions by Justin Smith Morrill, a Vermont politician who became a congressman in December 1855 and functioned in that capacity until serving as U.S. senator from 1867 to 1898. In 1856, Morrill attended a meeting of the Agricultural Society, in which Turner's ideas for reform were discussed (Eddy, 1956). Apparently influenced by Turner's ideas, in 1857, Morrill introduced congressional legislation to issue land grants to encourage the strengthening and initiating of agricultural, industrial, and tactical (military) instruction in colleges (Madsen, 1976; Cross, 1999). However, President James Buchanan vetoed the legislation (Madsen, 1976). Morrill bided his time, realizing that government and public support was not sufficient to result in the passage of the desired legislation.

The Civil War, however, changed the mood of the nation significantly, and by 1862, the second year of the Civil War, Morrill believed that circumstances now favored the passage of land grant legislation (Cross, 1999; Madsen 1976). The North's war effort was going miserably, and early losses at Bull Run and other battlefields were blamed primarily on the faulty military strategies of Northern generals (Cross, 1999; Madsen, 1976). Furthermore, many leaders believed that in order for the North to prevail in the Civil War, economic strength was indispensable (Madsen, 1976). Hence, when Morrill again introduced land grant legislation, in 1862, he emphasized the improvements that it would produce in military training and economic prosperity. Many leaders agreed with Morrill's assessment, and President Lincoln signed the Morrill Land Grant legislation into law in 1862 (Cross, 1999; Eddy, 1956; Madsen, 1976).

Under the Morrill Act of 1862, the federal government gave a number of states grants of public lands that could be sold so that the proceeds could be used "to promote the liberal and practical education of the industrial classes in the several pursuits and professions of life" (Morrill Act, 1862). This grant money became available only under the condition that the money be spent on education in agricultural, industrial, and tactical military education.

Contrary to popular opinion, many of the so-called land grant colleges already existed before the Morrill Act. Some may be surprised to learn that many private colleges also received land grant money (Cross, 1999; Eddy, 1956; Madsen, 1976). Nevertheless, most states specified that certain state colleges in particular would be beneficiaries of these land grants. Consequently, the colleges the states designated this way are often called *land grant institutions* (Cross, 1999; Eddy, 1956; Madsen, 1976).

Once the Morrill Act (1862) became law, three states, Michigan, Pennsylvania, and Iowa, acted the most quickly to establish a means of utilizing these land grants (Cross, 1999). As a result, Michigan State, Pennsylvania State, and Iowa State, founded in 1857, 1855, and 1862, respectively, became some of the first and finest land grant institutions (Cross, 1999). By 1870, 37 states had passed legislation for the promotion of education in agriculture, industry, and military tactics (Eddy, 1956).

If one were to examine the first 40 years following the passage of the Morrill Act (1862), one could easily conclude that the act did little to alter the educational landscape of the United States (Cross, 1999). The reason for this is that most Americans were convinced that the church was a more appropriate source for education than the state. Although the expansion of common schools in the late 1800s and early 1900s eventually did much to neutralize this attitude, this perspective regarding higher education held for many years (Tewksbury, 1932). This viewpoint manifested itself in two ways. It was apparent, first, in the attitude of leading university educators and, second, in the low enrollment figures that plagued land grant institutions for many years (Cross, 1999; Eddy, 1956; Madsen, 1976).

Regarding the first point, college presidents Charles Elliot of Harvard, Noah Porter of Yale, and James McCosh of Princeton, were critical of the land grant concept and admonished that it would cheapen and dilute the quality of education (Madsen, 1976). Nevertheless, it was probably the second point, the persistent low enrollment in land grant schools until the 20th century, that raised the greatest concerns among the leaders of these schools. For example, in 1876, both the University of Missouri and the University of Minnesota had just 117 students, Louisiana State University had only 3 students, and the Universities of Kentucky and Nebraska had 80 and 75 attendees, respectively (Eddy, 1956).

In the late 1800s, the foundation was laid to increase the influence of land grant colleges in the 20th century. From 1887 until 1914, a series of laws were passed to strengthen the breadth and influence of the first Morrill Act (Cross, 1999). These laws included the Hatch Act of 1887, the Second Morrill Act of 1890, and the Smith-Lever Act of 1914 (Cross, 1999). The Second Morrill Act was especially noteworthy because it stipulated that these subsidies be divided among White and African American colleges, in those states that practiced segregation (Cross, 1999). These bills added muscle to the land grant college momentum, causing the total number of students attending land grant colleges to increase to 133,405 by 1916 and 388,636 by 1926 (Eddy, 1956). Land grant institutions have over American history educated 20 million people (Cross, 1999).

Black Colleges Benefit

Black colleges were some of the major beneficiaries of the Morrill Act of 1862 (Cross, 1999; Eddy, 1956; Madsen, 1976). A large part of the reason for this was due to (a) the fact that the new land grant orientation gained momentum in the years following the Civil War when the education of African Americans was a central focus and (b) the need being so great (Cross, 1999; Eddy, 1956; Madsen, 1976).

About one fourth of the land grant colleges were African American colleges (Cross, 1999; Eddy, 1956). This is a very high percentage considering that African American colleges make up a tiny percentage of the total number of colleges in the United States (U.S. Department of Education, 2003). Alcorn State and Virginia's Hampton University were the first two African American land grant colleges (Cross, 1999; Eddy, 1956).

In addition to opening up educational opportunities for African Americans, the land grant institutions opened up doors of educational opportunity among women, the poor, and other minority groups, who previously had not gone to college in great numbers (Cross, 1999; Eddy, 1956; Madsen, 1976).

MAJOR EVENTS IN THE POST–CIVIL WAR PERIOD

Teacher Training Previous to This Period

The powerful role that teacher-training institutes or normal schools had on education really emerged in the post–Civil War period. However, the building blocks for the surge in teacher training between the Civil War and World War I emerged well before the Civil War.

A convergence of events set the stage for the rigorous education of teachers. The first event occurred in 1823, when a Congregationalist minister and teacher, Samuel R. Hall, opened up the first private academy, in Concord, Vermont, designed to prepare teachers (Cubberley, 1920). The fact that this teacher-training center was founded in New England is important because of its proximity to the southern New England and New York regions, which were typically the most advanced regions in educational practice (Harper, 1939). As a result, Hall's teacher-training academy gained a lot of attention among Massachusetts educators, and, in 1830, the leaders of Philips Andover Academy asked him to head up a normal department (Harper, 1939). While at Andover, Hall taught a course titled "The Art of Teaching," which caused both politicians and educators to visit him. These visits multiplied his contacts and his overall educational influence (Harper, 1939). Hall also opened up other teacher institutes (Altenbaugh & Underwood, 1990). In the minds of many, his ideas formed one of the foundations for Massachusetts educational reform. Hall wrote a book titled *Lectures on School-Keeping* (1929), which gained him even more notoriety. This textbook was the first widely used teacher-training book to be used in the United States and was the textbook of choice in most normal schools in the country during the 1840s and 1850s (Harper, 1939).

A number of other people were becoming vocal about the need for normal schools. In 1825, DeWitt Clinton, president of the Free School Society, communicated the need to train teachers (Harper, 1939). However, the efforts of two individuals, James C. Carter and Rev. Charles Brooks, really propelled teacher education forward. Carter earned the name "Father of the American Normal School" (Harper, 1939). He fought harder than perhaps anyone to gain legislation passed to establish the first state-supported normal school in Massachusetts. Carter's plea was not so much to educators, but to legislators who represented the general populace regarding the state's responsibility to make sure teachers were adequately trained (Harper, 1939).

Carter's efforts put in place the final cogs of the wheel to get the normal school movement going. However, it was the efforts of Rev. Charles Brooks that aroused the convictions of New England educators that normal schools could and should be established (Albree, 1906; Brooks, 1864). Brooks illuminated educators about the flourishing of normal schools in Prussia, Holland, and France (Harper, 1939). He argued that, certainly, if monarchs could learn to incorporate the normal school into their education systems, the American democracy surely could (Stowe, 1836, 1838). Beginning in 1835, Brooks and another educator, Calvin Stowe, husband of Harriet Beecher Stowe, launched speaking campaigns and spoke at many conventions, advocating the widespread adoption of the normal school (Stowe, 1836, 1839). These conventions were so successfully organized that both John Quincy Adams and Daniel Webster spoke at them and joined the chorus calling for the widespread application of normal schools (Harper, 1839).

The conglomeration of the combined influence of people such as Stowe, Carter, John Quincy Adams, and Webster did a great deal to cause people to really get behind the idea of the normal school.

When Horace Mann founded the first state-supported normal school, in 1839, in Lexington, Massachusetts, there was a sufficient amount of enthusiasm for state-supported normal schools that people realized that other normal schools would follow. In the same year that Mann opened the normal school in Lexington, a normal school also opened in Barre, Massachusetts (Harper, 1839). Other normal schools soon opened in Albany, New York (1844); New Britain, Connecticut (1850); Ypsilanti, Michigan (1853); Providence, Rhode Island (1854); Trenton, New Jersey (1855); Bloomington (or Normal), Illinois (1857); Millersville, Pennsylvania (1859); and Winona, Minnesota (1860).

Among the principals of these institutions, perhaps the two most influential were Rev. Cyrus Pierce, of Lexington, Massachusetts, and David Perkins Page, of Albany, New York. Pierce was well-known for his sacrificial spirit (Harper, 1939). He slept just 3 or 4 hours a night and not only carried a heavy teaching load, but did the janitorial work as well (Harper, 1839). Page, in 1847, wrote the book *Theory and Practice of Teaching,* which for many years was the most popular book written on the art of teaching. This book became a core textbook in normal schools for nearly half a century. Page also argued that teaching was not merely a set of particular practices, but a lifestyle that was an expression of the heart.

Growth of Teacher Training in the Post–Civil War Period

Although teacher-training institutes first appeared in America in the 1820s, their presence broadened and became an important part of the American scene after the Civil War. At first, educators started teacher institutes in primarily urbanized areas (Mann, 1845; Spring, 1997). Initially, teachers who received training at an institute were considered a privileged class of teachers (Harper, 1939; Monroe, 1952). Schools frequently sought out these trained individuals, believing that they were especially well equipped to teach (Mann, 1845).

As time went on, however, these institutes burgeoned all across the country (Luckey, 1903; Monroe, 1952). Concurrently, a growing number of academic leaders dedicated themselves to propounding an educational philosophy that could be communicated as a major part of the curriculum in these institutes (Rosenkranz, 1848). When these institutes emerged, the idea was that they would become the model or normal practice for other institutes to follow, and so the use of the term *normal school* arose (Harper, 1939; Monroe, 1952). Using this term for what were in reality well-developed teacher institutes was meant to convey a large degree of core content and model values, in much the same way that *common schools* communicated this message (Harper, 1939; Monroe, 1952).

As normal schools became prodigious in number, it became standard practice for preservice elementary school teachers to attend these schools for their preparation and for preservice secondary school teachers to attend college (Harper, 1939; Monroe, 1952). A high school diploma was the usual requirement for admission into normal schools (Monroe, 1952).

The early pioneers of the teacher institute movement, Henry Barnard, Emma Willard, Horace Mann, and others, believed it was essential to establish a coordinated and reasonably standardized curriculum with which to prepare teachers (Mann, 1845; Stowe, 1839). All three of these people believed that the individual character of the teachers was paramount, and therefore, the curriculum of the early teacher institutes and normal schools evinced this belief (Barnard, 1842; Goodlad & Soder, 1990; Harper, 1939; Mann, 1849).

Nineteenth-century textbooks on teaching and the philosophy of education also reflected an emphasis on teacher character. J. K. F. Rosenkranz (1848, 1872–1874) was one of the foremost European authors on the philosophy of education. Once his ideas came to America, he became one of the most preeminent writers on education of the 19th century. Rosenkranz (1848) asserted that the mind and the spirit were inextricably connected, and that in order to be effective in instruction, a teacher had to be of good character.

Following the Civil War, Americans realized that the nation was still hurting as a result of being ripped apart by such a gut-wrenching conflict. They recognized that for the nation to become strong, certain common threads of values and practices needed to become manifest in educational practice (Cubberley, 1920). This particular focus paved the way for a pervasive acceptance of common schools following the Civil War, while many Americans had demonstrated intransigence to the movement previously (Cubberley, 1920). This same desire for common educational threads caused the American Normal School Association to take action to produce more standardization in teacher preparation in 1869 (Monroe, 1952). At this time, just 4 years after the end of the Civil War, the American Normal School Association appointed a committee to determine what the science of education consisted of (Monroe, 1952).

A quarter century after the Civil War, teacher training had become a well-developed and efficacious discipline (Cubberley, 1920; Monroe, 1952). By 1889 to 1890, there were nearly 200 normal schools in the United States (Monroe, 1952). About half were public (Altenbaugh & Underwood, 1990). By this time, nearly 30% of the nation's 415 colleges and universities offered teacher education courses (Monroe, 1952). Just 6 years later, the total number of colleges and universities offering these courses would nearly double (Monroe, 1952).

Teacher education developed in two primary directions. First, teacher institutes became normal schools, and many eventually evolved into teachers colleges (Monroe, 1952). Second, many exiting universities offered teacher education courses and, ultimately, teacher education degrees (Monroe, 1952). Michigan State Normal College (now Eastern Michigan University), in Ypsilanti, became the first teachers college to give a BA (Monroe, 1952). Generally speaking, the early teachers colleges were more common in the midwestern and western states, and teacher education programs at existing universities were more common in the East (Monroe, 1952). By 1890, the United States had 18 established teacher colleges (as opposed to teacher institutes or normal schools), nearly all of which were in the Midwest and West (Monroe, 1952). However, the number of teachers colleges experienced exponential growth between 1910 and 1930, reaching 156 in number by 1931 (Monroe, 1952).

The phenomenal growth of teacher education programs was a direct outcome of the expansion of the public schools and the largest waves of immigration in American history (Monroe, 1952; Ravitch, 1974). The diffusion of teacher education courses in colleges and universities accelerated even more rapidly than the offerings at normal schools, largely because high schools were the fastest-growing component of public education. Between 1890 and 1900, the number of teachers employed in public schools grew about 16%, from 363,922 to 423,062 (Monroe, 1952). During that same period, the number of public high school teachers almost doubled (Monroe, 1952). Overall enrollment in public schools climbed nearly 70% between 1890 and 1930, reaching 23.6 million in 1930 (Monroe, 1952).

Initially, when colleges and universities offered teacher training, they combined liberal studies courses with professional training. Academic leaders believed that in order to be a proficient teacher, one needed to have both (Monroe, 1952; Willis, 1993). For example, for a person to be an effective classic literature teacher, he or she needed to be not only strong in instruction but also knowledgeable in classical literature. Most major universities that trained teachers embraced this approach (Monroe, 1952; Willis, 1993). This meant that preservice teachers often faced a demanding number of courses. Some universities, like UC-Berkeley, believed that they had no choice except to make teacher education into a 5-year program (Monroe, 1952).

Other universities, particularly on the East Coast, adapted to this dilemma by encouraging preservice teachers to get a liberal arts degree, followed by a graduate degree in education (Monroe, 1952). In 1876, Johns Hopkins emerged at the forefront of the graduate school movement (Chickering, 1981; Jencks & Reisman, 1968; Monroe, 1952). By 1890, many universities promoted strong graduate school programs in teacher education. U.S. graduate school enrollment in education went from 460 in 1880 to 1881 to 2,382 in 1890 (Monroe, 1952). By 1910, nearly 10,000 students were teacher education graduate students (Monroe, 1952). In 1907, both Columbia and New York University alone each enrolled over 250 graduate students in teacher education (Monroe, 1952). Part of the reason teacher education graduate programs grew so quickly is that teachers had the flexibility to attend graduate school during the summer.

Private universities generally emerged as the leaders in creating quality education programs. Universities such as Harvard, Columbia, and the University of Chicago were at the forefront of educational thought (Monroe, 1952). Nevertheless, state universities such as UC-Berkeley, the University of Minnesota, and Ohio State were intent on offering quality programs that provided a strong background combining liberal arts and teacher preparation (Monroe, 1952).

The incredible growth of teacher education programs had a number of remarkable effects, including substantially reducing the gender gap in America's colleges, increasing the calls for greater consistency in teacher education curriculum, and producing a large demand for teacher education textbooks (Harper, 1939; Monroe, 1952). In 1915, Charles Judd of the University of Chicago called for the standardization of normal schools (Monroe, 1952). This call to order was necessary, because normal schools varied considerably in their requirements, especially in terms of the number of units necessary for graduation (Monroe,

1952). Throughout the early 1900s, even before 1915, the use of common textbooks facilitated this move toward standardization. The call for standardization fueled the demand for these textbooks, and the existent strong demand for textbooks facilitated further standardization. Some of the most prominent textbooks included *A Cyclopedia of Education,* by William Torrey Harris, written in the early 1900s, and William Bagley's *Classroom Management,* written in 1907 (Monroe, 1952). The early 1900s also resulted in books that emphasized the psychological component of teaching and learning. William James's book *The Principles of Psychology* (1890) became a common textbook and had already become popular, but Edward Thorndike (1913, 1914) applied many of James's ideas even more directly to education. Thorndike's book *Educational Psychology: The Psychology of Learning* (1914) really helped educational psychology become a more defined discipline within education.

The continued distension of secondary schools during the early 1900s contributed greatly to the expansion of teacher education programs over the same time frame. By 1910, American secondary school students numbered over 1 million, and by 1920, this figure swelled to over 2 million, versus less than 300,000 in 1890 (Monroe, 1952). During the early 1900s, many major universities opened graduate schools for teachers, including Harvard University (Harper, 1939; Monroe, 1952). Concurrently, by 1930, most teacher colleges functioned very much like liberal arts colleges (Monroe, 1952). As a result of these developments, the 1920s and 1930s became a golden age for the introduction of new teacher education textbooks and journal articles. William Kilpatrick had a number of well-respected articles released in the *Teachers College Record* (1920s), and Edward Thorndike (1932) wrote another sentinel work, *The Fundamentals of Human Learning.* The increased systemization of teacher education programs and the use of common textbooks for preservice teachers helped give undergraduate and graduation programs for future school teachers the commonalities necessary for a mature profession. This fact was highlighted in 1926, when the American Association of Teachers Colleges called for the adoption of precise standards for accrediting teachers colleges (Monroe, 1952).

Coursework at Normal Schools

The length of coursework at the early normal schools varied to some degree, which led to the call for a greater standardization of the curriculum (Harper, 1939). Nevertheless, two trends in the length of coursework became apparent. First, over time, normal schools developed a longer list of required coursework. For example, the Lexington Normal School required 1 year of coursework when it first opened its doors and extended it to 2 years by 1860 (Harper, 1939). Second, university teacher education programs were more rigorous than those based in normal schools.

From the 1850s until 1900, the entrance and course requirements for normal schools progressively became more vigorous. To even be admitted into a normal school, candidates had to live a life of purity, have strong moral character, love children, practice good manners, be skilled in teaching, love instruction, and have a willingness to endure great sacrifices for the sake of the students (Harper, 1939). The course requirements at most normal schools evinced a belief that teachers should not only be able to teach well but should also be well-grounded in the liberal arts (Jencks & Riesman, 1968). Courses included instruction in the English language, math, writing, geography, geometry, history, and science (Harper, 1939).

The period from 1860 to 1900 was an important time for the teacher preparation movement: Normal schools spread along the Mississippi Valley and into the West. In 1860, normal schools were established in Minnesota, the first time this had taken place west of the Mississippi River (Harper, 1939). Soon, Kansas State Normal in Emporia and others followed.

The spread of teacher education institutions soon helped systematize the profession. Just before the Civil War, the first organization of normal school teachers was formed, and their first convention took place (Harper, 1939). The post–Civil War period intensified the degree of organization and systemization within the teacher education movement.

College and Universities Increasingly Found Teacher Education Departments

Another major progression during the post–Civil War period is that a growing number of colleges and universities established teacher education departments. Some of the more prestigious of the institutions included the University of Iowa (1873), the University of Michigan (1879), the University of Wisconsin (1885), Indiana University (1886), and Cornell University (1886). The establishing of teacher education departments at these institutions not only advanced the preparation of instructors in colleges but also encouraged normal schools to more directly compete with these institutions.

Increased Standardization of Teacher Education

During the 1880s, at both the university and normal school levels, there were escalated efforts to produce more standardization. During this time, Professor W. H. Payne, of the University of Michigan, called a meeting of midwestern normal school presidents in Ann Arbor to discuss standards and various other ideas that they could present to the National Education Association (NEA) (Harper, 1939).

As public school enrollment increased, normal school enrollment soared. Normal school enrollment surged from 10,000 in 1870 to 70,000 in 1900 (Altenbaugh & Underwood, 1990). By 1898, there were 331 normal schools in the country, 166 publicly run and 165 private (Altenbaugh & Underwood, 1990). Women made up the vast majority of the students in these schools (Altenbaugh & Underwood, 1990). The number of universities with teacher education courses also rose during this period, to 114 by 1892 (Altenbaugh & Underwood, 1990).

During the period from 1890 to 1920, the sophistication of teacher education continued to increase. During this time, many normal schools became colleges, and an increasing number of universities added teacher education programs (Harper, 1939; Monroe, 1952). In 1892, the New York College for the Training of Teachers became part of Columbia University (Altenbaugh & Underwood, 1990). Most other normal schools became colleges, largely because the granting of BA degrees raised the status of the college and the profession (Jencks & Reisman, 1968).

EVENTS LEADING UP TO AND INCLUDING WORLD WAR I

Added Definition to America's Education System

Over the years, the system of education in America has become more defined. In 1848, Quincy, Massachusetts, schools were the first to use grades to differentiate children by age

(Cubberley, 1920). In 1821, the first public high school opened in Boston (Cubberley, 1920). Nevertheless, the presence of high schools, especially public high schools, really was not standard in most places in America. In 1874, a key Supreme Court case in Kalamazoo, Michigan (*Stuart v. School District No. 1 of Kalamazoo*), generally referred to as the "*Kalamazoo* decision," upheld public taxation for high schools (King, 1964). This decision set the stage for the number of public high schools to eventually exceed the number of private high schools. After all, if a person wanted to send a child to a private high school, he or she would have to pay for private school tuition and pay taxes for public high schools as well. On one hand, the *Kalamazoo* decision paved the way for the expansion of public high schools, but it was also a clear disincentive for parents who wanted to send their children to private schools. As a result of the *Kalamazoo* decision, by 1890, there were 2,526 public high schools in the United States, with over 200,000 students (King, 1964). In contrast, there were about 1,600 private secondary schools and academies enrolling about 95,000 students (King, 1964). The growth of public high schools continued in the years that followed. By 1900, there were 6,005 high schools in the United States; and by 1910, that number had increased to over 10,000 (King, 1964).

In 1892, NEA established the Committee of Ten, headed by Charles Eliot, the president of Harvard (Spring, 1997). The Committee of Ten made various curricular recommendations for standardizing courses in high school (Spring, 1997). At the time, some educators wanted the high school to function as a college preparatory school, while others wanted high school courses to be more practical in nature (NEA, 1893, 1918).

The Committee of Ten meeting was particularly significant because it added substantial definition to the American education system and also triggered a clearly defined debate between instructional liberals and conservatives about the nature of the high school, a debate that still persists along the same boundaries today (Bunzel, 1985; Monroe, 1952; Nolan & Meister, 2000; Peterson & West, 2003; Ravitch & Vinovskis, 1995). The debate surrounds the central point of the purpose of the high school. Is its primary function to prepare students for college or to equip them for a broad spectrum of capacities in life (DeBoer, 1991; Monroe, 1952; Raubinger, 1969; Sizer, 1964; Willis, 1993)? The Committee of Ten's decision in 1892 definitely leaned toward the conservative perspective (Monroe, 1952; NEA, 1893). The committee determined that in order to earn a high school degree, students needed to complete 4 years of coursework in math, literature, science, civics (social studies), and foreign language (NEA, 1893). This decision clearly defined the role of high schools as educational institutions that should possess high student expectations and a college-preparatory orientation. The decisions by the Committee of Ten set the stage for all-time high levels of achievement to be reached in high school coursework and foreign-language preparation by students graduating from high school in the late 1910s, levels that have never been equaled since that time (DeBoer, 1991; Monroe, 1952; Raubinger, 1969; Sizer, 1964; Willis, 1993).

Despite the decisions reached by the Committee of Ten, the liberal-versus-conservative debate did not end with this decision, but continued in its aftermath (DeBoer, 1991; Kliebard, 2004; Monroe, 1952; Raubinger, 1969; Sizer, 1964; Willis, 1993). After World War I, the school system in America became much more clearly defined (Willis, 1993). In 1918, the Commission on the Reorganization of Secondary Education issued a report, *Cardinal Principles of Secondary Education* (NEA, 1918; Spring, 1997). The report argued that the high school should serve a comprehensive function, serving as many needs as possible of each community (NEA, 1918).

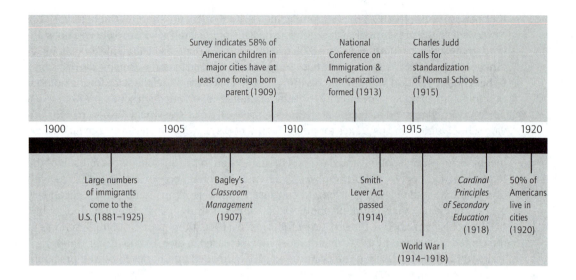

By 1918, 30 states had passed laws requiring full-time school attendance until a child reached the age of 16 (King, 1964). World War I had convinced many Americans of the importance of education in making the United States a strong and secure nation. After World War I, four aspects of the high school curriculum emerged as a result of the *Cardinal Principles of Secondary Education:* (1) the college preparatory program, (2) the business program, (3) the vocational and home economics program, and (4) a terminal program. The high school also really did not flourish until after World War I. Early on, junior high schools were simply the first 3 years of a 6-year institution. As time went on, however, especially in the 1920s and 1930s, they became separate institutions (Cremin, 1962, 1988; King, 1964; Tyack, 1967).

Other Impacts of World War I on the American Education System

Intensification of the Americanization Program

Although de facto Americanization in the schools was present by the late 19th century, it really did not have its formal beginnings until 1913 (Bayer, 1980; Covello, 1967; Olneck & Lazerson, 1991; Weiss, 1982). At that time, the National Conference on Immigration and Americanization encouraged the practice of this philosophy in American schools. The movement really gained momentum during World War I, from 1914 to 1918 (Bayer, 1980; Covello, 1967; Olneck & Lazerson, 1991; Weiss, 1982). The reason the Americanization movement gained such momentum during World War I is that the war resulted largely from ethnic divisions in Europe (Tucker & Keely, 1990) and Americans became afraid that the United States was importing some of that ethnic strife. When evidence of ethnic clashes did take place in America, some of the groups involved were related to the same groups whose ethnic tensions led to World War I in Europe (Tucker & Keely, 1990). Consequently, Americans became concerned. They generally welcomed the immigrants but increasingly felt that newcomers needed to put their ethnically based disputes behind them and view themselves as Americans (Moreo, 1996; Tucker & Keely, 1990). As a result, teachers in schools emphasized qualities that were viewed as American values, such as love, diligence, honesty, equality, loyalty, and so forth (Bayer, 1980; Covello, 1967; Olneck & Lazerson, 1991; Weiss, 1982).

Three primary emphases of the Americanization program included an emphasis on (1) literacy, (2) learning democratic values, and (3) learning habits for health and hygiene. The primary emphasis of the Americanization program was on increasing literacy, and in this respect the program reached most of its goals. The literacy rate in 1880 in the United States was 83% among those 10 years of age and older (Beard & Beard, 1944). By 1910, that literacy rate figure had risen to 92.3% (Beard & Beard, 1944). By the 1920s, the rate had reached 94% and would rise to over 99% by the 1950s, 1960s, 1970s, and the early 1980s (U.S. Bureau of the Census, 1975).

Curbs on Immigration

Americans' concerns about importing Europe's ethnic problems, which contributed so prominently to World War I, were largely responsible for the curbs on immigration that arose in 1921 (Tucker & Keely, 1990).

For the size of the U.S. population, the rate of immigration in the late 19th century was about 5 times as heavy as it was at the end of the 20th century (Ciment, 2001; Jones, 1960). One can just imagine how strong the movement to reduce immigration would be today if the rate were 5 times what it is now—which would translate into about 40 million immigrants coming into the United States every 10 years (Ciment, 2001; Jones, 1960). Although many people assume that racism was the primary motive of the 1921 law (and that may have been the motive of some), one should recall that (a) the rates of immigration before this time were astronomical compared with today or any other time; (b) the quotas arose largely as a result of World War I; and (c) the United States was far more open to immigrants coming to America from 1870 to 1920, as measured by per capita immigration rates, than is currently the case (Ciment, 2001; Jones, 1960). The curbs the United States now has in place are not only more restrictive numerically, but are far more restrictive in terms of percentage (Yans-McLaughlin, 1970). Therefore, if one argues that racism is the primary motive of immigration curbs, one can argue that the United States is more racist now than it was in 1921; then, the ones the legislation was aimed at and who suffered the most from these immigration curbs were European Whites, not people of non-White races (Ciment, 2001; Jones, 1960). They were the ones who wanted to come to America in the greatest number. Europeans fleeing Hitler also suffered greatly under these curbs during World War II (Dinnerstein, 1982; Morse, 1968). Ultimately, the immigration curbs did significantly impact Latino immigration, but this emerged as a problem primarily after World War II (Yans-McLaughlin, 1970). Some Americans wanted to continue the curbs to restrict non-White immigration into the United States (Tucker & Keely, 1990). Consequently, the United States initiated immigration reform in the early- to mid-1960s in order to lift the curbs and facilitate immigration (Bender, 1975; Yans-McLaughlin, 1970). This issue will be addressed further in Chapter 13.

CONCLUSION

The period following the Civil War up to and including World War I was one of the most dramatic periods of change in American educational history. The nation's strong education system, going back to the days of the Pilgrims and Puritans, had helped make possible a degree of progress on all fronts at a level never before seen in world history (Johnson, 1997). In less than 300 years, the most powerful and modern nation in the world had emerged, largely as a result of its educational emphasis. Now, the United States faced new responsibilities and challenges as a result of its new industrial might. However, the nation had also produced a modern education system that was designed to help the country meet these responsibilities and challenges. Over the coming decades, Americans would discover the extent to which their schools, colleges, and universities were up to the task.

DISCUSSION QUESTIONS

1. Industrialization forever changed American education. In the days following the Civil War, the invention of the telephone (1876) and the vast expansion of the railroad network changed the nation and schooling. One can argue that the computer and Internet are having a similar transforming impact on American society and schooling. In what ways do you think the computer and Internet have influenced education? In what ways do you anticipate that continued developments in these areas will produce further changes in education?

2. Booker T. Washington and W. E. B. DuBois present two different visions for affirmative action in America. To what extent do you support one vision of affirmative action over the other? Do you rather prefer some combination of the two visions for affirmative action? Why?

3. Why do you think it is harder for school leaders to adapt to an increase in enrollment due to immigration rather than a "baby boom"?

4. In American educational history, there has been a distinct tendency for education to become more standardized. In this chapter, the author examined increased standardization in teacher education. In what ways does standardization benefit education? Are there ways in which standardization in various areas in education can have negative influences?

REFERENCES

Abdill, G. B. (1961). *Civil War railroads*. Seattle, WA: Superior Publishing.

Adams, J. (1854). In C. Adams (Ed.), *The works of John Adams, second president of the United States* (Vol. IX, pp. 229). Boston: Little, Brown.

Adams, J. Q. (1850). *Letters of John Quincy Adams to his son on the Bible and its teachings*. Auburn, TX: James M. Alden.

Albree, J. (1906). *Charles Brooks and his work for normal schools*. Medford, MA: J. C. Miller.

Altenbaugh, R. J., & Underwood, K. (1990). The evolution of normal schools. In J. I. Goodlad & R. Soder (Eds.), *Places where teachers are taught* (pp. 136–186). San Francisco: Jossey-Bass.

Amper, T. (1998). *Booker T. Washington*. Minneapolis, MN: Carolrhoda Books.

Anbinder, T. (1992). *Nativism and slavery: The Northern know nothings and the politics of the 1850s*. New York: Oxford University Press.

Anderson, G. L. (1976). *Land-grant universities and their continuing challenge*. East Lansing: Michigan State University Press.

Bailyn, B. (1960). *Education in the forming of American society*. Chapel Hill: University of North Carolina.

Barnard, H. (1842). *Papers of Henry Barnard*. Manuscript collection of Trinity College Watkinson Library, Hartford, CT.

Barone, M. (2001). *The new Americans: How the melting pot can work again*. Washington, DC: Regnery.

Barth, G. P. (1980). *City people: The rise of modern city culture in nineteenth-century America*. New York: Oxford University Press.

Bartlett, R. (1978). *The faith of the Pilgrims*. New York: United Church Press.

Battle, J., & Wright, E. Jr. (2002). W. E. B. DuBois's talented tenth: A quantitative assessment. *Journal of Black Studies, 32,* 654–672.

Bayer, A. E. (1980). *The assimilation of American family patterns by European immigrants and their children*. New York: Arno Press.

Beard, C. A., & Mary R. Beard, M. A. (1944). *A basic history of the United States*. New York: Doubleday, Doran.

Beatty, J. (2001). *Colossus: How the corporation changed America*. New York: Broadway Books.

Bender, T. (1975). *Toward an urban vision: Ideas and institutions in nineteenth-century America*. Lexington: University Press of Kentucky.

Bergman, B. (1996). *In defense of affirmative action*. New York: Basic Books.

Brandon, S. G. F. (1970). *Ancient empires*. New York: Newsweek.

Brooks, C. (1864). *Two lectures: History of the introduction of state normal schools in America and a prospective system of national education in the United States*. Boston: J. Wilson.

Brown, A. (1890). *The genesis of the United States*. Boston: Houghton, Mifflin.

Bunzel, J. H. (1985). *Challenge to American schools: The case for standards and values*. New York: Oxford University Press.

Burns, A. F. (1934). *Production trends in the United States since 1870*. New York: National Bureau of Economic Research.

Carter, J. G. (1826). *Essays upon popular education, containing a particular examination of the schools of Massachusetts, and an outline of an institution for the education of teachers*. Boston: Bowles & Dearborn.

Chickering, A. W. (1981). *The modern American college*. San Francisco: Jossey-Bass.

Ciment, J. (2001). *Encyclopedia of American immigration*. Armonk, NY: M. E. Sharpe.

Coben, S., & Ratner, L. (1983). *The development of an American culture*. New York: St. Martin's Press.

Connell, J. T. (2004). *Faith of our founding father: The spiritual journey of George Washington*. New York: Hatherleigh Press.

Covello, L. (1967). *The social background of the Italo-American school child*. Leide, Netherlands: E. J. Bill.

Cremin, L. A. (1962). *The transformation of the school- progressivism in American Education, 1876–1957*. New York: Knopf.

Cremin, L. A. (1977). *Traditions of American education*. New York: Basic Books.

Cremin, L. A. (1988). *American education, the metropolitan experience, 1876–1980*. New York: Harper & Row.

Cross, C. (1999). *Justin Smith Morrill: Father of the land grant colleges*. East Lansing: Michigan State University.

Cubberley, E. P. (1909). *Changing conceptions of education*. New York: Houghton Mifflin.

Cubberley, E. (1920). *The history of education*. Boston: Houghton Mifflin.

DeBoer, G. E. (1991). *A history of ideas in science education: Implications for practice.* New York: Teachers College Press.

Dewey, J. (1915). *The school and society.* Chicago: Chicago Press.

Dewey, J. (1998). *Experience and education.* West Lafayette, IN: Kappa Delta.

Dinnerstein, L. (1982). *America and the survivors of the Holocaust.* New York: Columbia University Press.

D'Innocenzo, M., & Sirefman, J. P. (1992). *Immigration and ethnicity: American society, "melting pot" or "salad bowl?"* Westport, CT: Greenwood.

DuBois, W. E. B. (1897). Strivings of the Negro people. *Atlantic Monthly, 80,* 194–198.

DuBois, W. E. B. (1903). *The souls of Black folk.* Chicago: A. C. McClurg.

Dunn, J. (1955). *Retreat from learning.* New York: David McKay.

Eavey, C. B. (1964). *History of Christian education.* Chicago: Moody Press.

Eddy, E. D. Jr. (1956). *Colleges for our land and time.* New York: Harper & Brothers.

Eisenstadt, S. N. (1967). *The decline of empires.* Englewood Cliffs, NJ: Prentice Hall.

Glazer, N. (1997). *We are all multiculturalists now.* Cambridge, MA: Harvard University Press.

Goodlad, J., & Soder, R. (1990). *The moral dimensions of teaching.* San Francisco: Jossey-Bass.

Green, P. (1991). *Alexander of Macedon, 356–323 BC: A historical biography.* Berkeley: University of California Press.

Hall, S. (1829). *Lectures on school-keeping.* New York: Arno.

Hammond, N. G. L. (1997). *The genius of Alexander the Great.* Chapel Hill: University of North Carolina Press.

Harper, C. A. (1939). *A century of public teacher education: The story of the state teachers colleges as they evolved from the normal schools.* Washington, DC: Hugh Birch-Horace Mann Fund for the American Association of Teachers Colleges.

Hewitt, G. A. (1991). Victimized by justice. In D. Altschiller (Ed.), *Affirmative action* (pp. 144–147). New York: H. W. Wilson.

Higham, J. (1955). *Strangers in the land: Patterns of American nativism.* New Brunswick, NJ: Rutgers University Press.

Hungerford, T. L., & Wassmer, R. W. (2004). *K–12 education in the U.S. economy.* Washington, DC: National Education Association.

Husband, J., & O'Loughlin, J. (2004). *Daily life in the industrial United States, 1870–1900.* Westport, CT: Greenwood Press.

Jacob, M. C. (1997). *Scientific culture and the making of the industrial West.* New York: Oxford University Press.

James, W. (1890). *The principles of psychology.* New York: Dover.

Jencks, C., & Reisman, D. (1968). *The academic revolution.* Garden City, NY: Doubleday.

Johnson, P. (1997). *A history of the American people.* New York: HarperCollins.

Jones, M. A. (1960). *American immigration.* Chicago: University of Chicago Press.

Jones, W. L. (2000). *After the thunder: Fourteen men who shaped post–Civil War America.* Dallas, TX: Taylor.

Keller, M. (1990). *Regulating a new economy: Public policy and economic change in America, 1900–1933.* Cambridge, MA: Harvard University Press.

Kessner, T. (1981). New Yorkers in prosperity and depression: A preliminary reconnaissance. In D. Ravitch & R. K Goodenow (Eds.) *Educating urban people* (pp. 84–100). New York: Teachers College Press.

Killian, L. M. (1999). Generals, the talented tenth, and affirmative action. *Society, 36*(6), 33–40.

King, E. A. (1964). *Shaping of the American high school.* New York: Harper & Row.

Kliebard, H. M. (2004). *The struggle for the American curriculum.* New York: Routledge.

Kraut, A. (1986). *The huddled masses: The immigrant in American society, 1880–1921.* Arlington Heights, IL: Harlan Davidson.

Lincoln, A. (1858). *House-divided speech*. Address to Republicans before the Republican State Convention, June 16, 1858. Retrieved August 4, 2006, at http://showcase.netins.net/web/creative/lincoln/speeches/house.htm.

Luckey, G. W. (1903). *The professional training of secondary teachers in the United States*. New York: Macmillan.

MacMullen, E. N. (1991). *In the cause of true education reform: Henry Barnard and nineteenth century school reform*. New Haven, CT: Yale University Press.

Madsen, D. (1976). Colleges of agriculture revisited. In G. L. Anderson (Ed.), *Land-grant universities and their continuing challenge* (pp. 23–48). East Lansing: Michigan State University Press.

Mann, H. (1839). *Second annual report*. Dutton & Wentworth.

Mann, H. (1844). *Seventh annual report*. Dutton & Wentworth.

Mann, H. (1845). *Eighth annual report*. Dutton & Wentworth.

Mann, H. (1849). *Twelfth annual report*. Dutton & Wentworth.

Mann, H. (1969). *Lectures on education*. New York: Arno.

Marrou, H. I. (1956). *A history of education in antiquity*. New York: Sheed & Ward.

Marshall, P., & Manuel, D. (1977). *The light and the glory*. Grand Rapids, MI: Fleming Revell.

Miller, H. A. (1990). *School and the immigrant*. Manchester, NH: Ayer.

Mintz, P. P. (1969). *America, the melting pot*. New York: Scribner.

Monroe, W. S. (1952). *Teaching learning theory and teacher education, 1890 to 1950*. Urbana: University of Illinois Press.

Montalto, N. (1991). Multicultural education in the New York Public Schools, 1919–1941. In D. Ravitch & R. K. Goodenow (Eds.), *Educating urban people* (pp. 67–83). New York: Teachers College Press.

Moreo, D. W. (1996). *Schools in the Great Depression*. New York: Garland.

Morrill Act, 12 Stat. 503, 7 USC301 (1862).

Morse, A. D. (1968). *While six million died: A chronicle of American apathy*. New York: Random House.

Mutulich, L. (1980). *A cross-disciplinary study of the European immigrants of 1870 to 1925*. New York: Arno Press.

National Education Association of the United States, Committee of Ten on Secondary School Studies. (1893). *Report of the Committee [of ten] on secondary school studies appointed at the meeting of the National educational association July 9, 1892, with the reports of the conferences arranged by this committee and held December 28–30, 1892*. Washington, DC: U.S. Government Printing Office.

National Education Association of the United States, Commission on the Reorganization of Secondary Education. (1918). *Cardinal principles of secondary education: A report of the commission on the reorganization of secondary education*. Washington, DC: U.S. Government Printing Office.

Newby, P. H. (1980). *Warrior pharaohs: The rise and fall of the Egyptian empire*. London: Faber & Faber.

Nolan, J. F., & Meister, D. G. (2000). *Teachers and educational change: The lived experience of secondary school restructuring*. Albany: State University of New York Press.

Olneck, M. R., & Lazerson, M. (1991). The school achievement of immigrant children: 1900–1930. In G. E. Pozzetta (Ed.), *American immigration and ethnicity: Education and the immigrant* (pp. 259–288). New York: Garland.

Orr, M. T. (1987). *Keeping students in school: A guide to effective dropout prevention programs and services*. San Francisco: Jossey-Bass.

Page, D. P. (1847). *Theory and practice of teaching*. New York: Arno Press.

Perlmann, J. (1988). *Ethnic differences: Schooling and social structure among the Irish, Italians, Jews, and Blacks in an American city, 1880–1935*. Cambridge, UK: Cambridge University Press.

Peterson, P. E., & West, M. R. (2003). *No child left behind? The politics and practice of school accountability*. Washington, DC: Brookings Institution Press.

Plato. (1941). *The Republic*. New York: Modern Library.

Plato. (1956). *Protagoras and Meno*. New York: Penguin.

Pozzetta, G. E. (1991). *Education and the immigrant.* New York: Garland.

Pulliam, J. D., & Van Patten, J. J. (1991). *History of education in America.* Upper Saddle River, NJ: Merrill/Prentice Hall:

Quance, F. M. (1926). *Part-time types of elementary schools in New York City: A comparative study of pupil achievement.* New York: Teachers College Publications.

Raubinger, F. M. (1969). *The development of secondary education.* New York: Macmillan.

Ravitch, D. (1974). *The great school wars: New York City, 1805–1973: A history of the public schools as battlefield of social change.* New York: Basic Books.

Ravitch, D., & Vinovskis, M. (1995). *Learning from the past: What history teaches us about school reform.* Baltimore: Johns Hopkins University Press.

Rippa, S. A. (1997). *Education in a free society.* White Plains, NY: Longman.

Rosenkranz, J. K. F. (1848). *The philosophy of education.* New York: Appleton.

Rosenkranz, J. K. F. (1872–1874). *Journal of speculative philosophy* (Vols. 6-8, all issues). New York: Kraus.

Rury, John L. (2002). *Education and social change: themes in the history of American schooling.* Mahwah, NJ: Lawrence Erlbaum.

Russel, R. R. (1972). *Critical studies in antebellum sectionalism: Essays in American political and economic history.* Westport, CT: Greenwood Press.

Sizer, T. R. (1964). *Secondary schools at the turn of the century.* New Haven, CT: Yale University Press.

Spivey, D. (1978). *Schooling for the new slavery.* Westport: Greenwood Press.

Spring, J. (1997). *The American school 1642–1996.* White Plains, NY: Longman.

Stephens, A. H. (1872). *History of the United States.* New York: Hale & Son.

Stevenson, H. W., & Stigler, J. W. (1992). *The learning gap.* New York: Summit Books.

Stewart, G. Jr. (1969). *A history of religious education in Connecticut.* New York: Arno Press & New York Times.

Stites, B. (2004). *The Republican Party in the late 1800s: A changing role for American government.* New York: Rosen Group.

Stowe, C. E. (1836). *The Prussian system of public instruction and its applicability to the United States.* Cincinnati, OH: Truman & Smith.

Stowe, C. E. (1838). *Report on elementary public instruction in Europe made to the Thirty-Sixth General Assembly of the State of Ohio, December 19, 1837.* Harrisburg, PA: Packer, Barrett, & Parker.

Stowe, C. E. (1839). *Common schools and teachers' seminaries.* Boston: Marsh, Capen, Lyon, & Webb.

Stuart v. School District No. 1 of Kalamazoo, 30 Mich. 69 (1874).

Summers, M. W. (1984). *Railroads, reconstruction, and the gospel of prosperity: Aid under the radical Republicans, 1865–1877.* Princeton, NJ: Princeton University Press.

Tewksbury, S. (1932). *Founding of American colleges and universities before the Civil War.* New York: Teachers College.

Thorndike, E. L. (1913). *An introduction to the theory of mental and social measurements.* New York: Columbia University.

Thorndike, E. L. (1914). *Educational psychology: The psychology of learning.* New York: Teachers College Press.

Thorndike, E. L. (1932). *The fundamentals of human learning.* New York: Columbia University.

Timmons, G. (1988). *Education, industrialization, and selection.* London: Routledge.

Tucker, R. W., & Keely, C. B. (1990). *Immigration and U.S. foreign policy.* Boulder, CO: Westview Press.

Tyack, D. B. (1967). *Turning points in American educational history.* Waltham, MA: Blaisdell.

U.S. Bureau of the Census. (1975). *Historical statistics of the United States.* Washington, DC: U.S. Government Printing Office.

U.S. Department of Education. (2003). *Digest of education statistics.* Washington, DC: Author.

U.S. Department of Labor. (2005). *Bureau of Labor Statistics: National compensation survey.* Washington, DC: Author.

Washington, B. T. (1899). *The future of the American Negro*. Boston: Small, Maynard.

Washington, B. T. (1901). *Up from slavery*. New York: Doubleday, Page.

Washington, B. T. (Ed.). (1905). Introduction. *Tuskegee and its people: Their ideals and achievements* (pp. 1–15). New York: Negro Universities Press.

Washington, B. T. (1906). Tuskegee: A retrospect and prospect. *North American Review, 182,* 514–519.

Weiss, B. J. (1982). *American education and the European immigrant, 1840–1940*. Urbana, IL: University of Illinois Press.

White, D. F. (1989). *The urbanists, 1865–1915*. New York: Greenwood Press.

Willis, G. (1993). *The American curriculum: A documentary history.* Westport, CT: Greenwood Press.

Yans-McLaughlin, V. (1990). *Immigration reconsidered: History, sociology, and politics*. New York: Oxford.

Zelnick, R. (2004). *Swing dance: Justice O'Conner and the Michigan muddle*. Stanford, CA: Hoover Institute Press.

The Liberal Philosophy of Education as Distinguished From Conservatism

Changes in educational philosophy ultimately affect school practice. This cause-and-effect relationship may not emerge immediately, but may take years and decades before transformations in educational tenets imbue the classroom. The 1890s and particularly the early 1900s laid the foundation for considerable educational change in the nation's schools. During this time, the liberal school of education flowered in the United States, particularly under the tutelage of John Dewey and his colleagues (Dupuis, 1966; Walker, 1963). Dewey and his associates did not found the liberal school of philosophical thought. Rather, liberalism first emerged under the leadership of individuals such as Rousseau, Locke, and Bacon (Dupuis, 1966). Nevertheless, Dewey, especially, was responsible for putting liberalism on the map of American educational thought (Dupuis, 1966; Walker, 1963). In this chapter, we will first place the flowering of liberalism in historical context and then examine the growth of modern-day educational liberal philosophy.

SCHOOLS OF EDUCATIONAL PHILOSOPHY

History of the Philosophy of Education

The rise of the liberal school of thought in education is best understood if one first examines the historical context of its development and defines certain important terms used by educational philosophers.

Most commonly, the history of the philosophy of education is divided into six schools of thought:

1. Greeks
2. Romans
3. Early Christians
4. Renaissance humanists

211

5. Early liberals

6. Later liberals

Educational philosophers generally classify the first four schools as conservative and the latter two as liberal.

Each of the six schools of thought contributed to education progress. In the Greek school, Plato developed the idea of widespread schools (Dupuis, 1966; Marrou, 1956). As a student of Socrates, he believed that society would benefit if students were exposed to wise and brilliant instructors (Dupuis, 1966; Marrou, 1956). Plato believed that education served three purposes: (1) to train leaders, (2) to provide moral education, and (3) to enable people from different backgrounds to gather together in one place and come to understand one another. Plato developed a classical curriculum that included math, the reading of the classics, civics, science, music, art, and physical education (what Plato termed *gymnastic*). The fact that Aristotle supported Plato's rubric enhanced its support among the Greek population. Moreover, Isocrates's efforts to spread Plato's schools across Greece increased the popularity of Plato's model (Dupuis, 1966; Marrou, 1956).

The Roman school was led by Cicero and Quintilian. Cicero, one of the greatest orators in history, was a resolute supporter of Plato's model of education (Dupuis, 1966). Cicero differed from Plato's approach in only two ways. First, he asserted that students should be taught to speak well. Second, he emphasized the primacy of virtue even more than Plato did (Dupuis, 1966; Marrou, 1956). Quintilian, although lesser known than Cicero, contributed a great deal to defining many of the specific practices used in the schools today. Quintilian developed the practices of assigning term papers, recitation, and dividing up into small groups to discuss the lectures (Dupuis, 1966; Marrou, 1956).

The early Christian school was founded on the biblical principles expounded by Jesus Christ, the Apostle Paul, and Augustine. The early Christians supported the classical curriculum espoused by Plato. To the early Christians, however, the Bible was to be the central focus of the curriculum, because they maintained that the Bible had the most spiritual and moral value of any aspect of the curriculum (Dupuis, 1966; Marrou, 1956). The main contribution of the early Christians was that they asserted that all people were equal and therefore all should be educated (Dupuis, 1966; Marrou, 1956). These beliefs were based on Bible verses, such as, "There is neither Jew nor Greek, there is neither slave nor free, there is neither male nor female" (Galatians 3:28, *Holy Bible,* 1973). The declaration that all people are created equal is a concept Americans now take for granted, but it was revolutionary at the time. Before the time of Christ, there was a universal belief that leaders of certain types were superior to the general populace (Dupuis, 1966; Marrou, 1956). Political leaders were threatened by this assertion and viewed Christianity as inspiring revolt. Consequently, persecution of Christians followed. It was this Christian tenet that helps explain why 80% of the early Christians were either slaves or women (Dupuis, 1966). Early Christians were also the first to use rewards in the classroom.

The Renaissance humanists were led by individuals such as Martin Luther (1483–1546), John Calvin (1509–1564), and Desiderius Erasmus (1466–1536) (Dupuis, 1966; Harbison, 1964). The Renaissance humanists maintained the same general curriculum model as the early Christians. The primary contribution of the Renaissance humanists is that they broadened the curriculum (Dupuis, 1966; Harbison, 1964). That is, before the Renaissance humanists emerged, educators almost unanimously believed that issues such as rape, incest, and so forth were taboo and not appropriate for classroom instruction. The Renaissance humanists, on the other hand, argued that even the Bible addresses these issues, instructing readers to avoid these behaviors. Therefore, as long as the instructors emphasized that these behaviors were wrong, they should engage in discussing these realities (Dupuis, 1966; Harbison, 1964).

Contemporary Focus

What Topics Are Appropriate for Discussion in the Classroom?

The issue that Renaissance humanists addressed regarding broadening the curriculum remains a controversy to this day.

- What do you think about this issue?
- To what extent should controversial topics such as rape and incest be discussed in the classroom?
- To what extent do the answers to these questions differ depending on the age of the child?
- To what extent should teachers reach out to parents to get their feedback regarding the extent to which their own children are ready to be exposed to these topics?
- Is instruction on certain issues acceptable only if we communicate to children that certain actions are wrong?

Beyond some of the most obvious controversial issues, there is also controversy behind how one should handle a crisis such as the September 11, 2001, terrorist attacks on America or the assassination of John F. Kennedy. Some parents criticized teachers for leaving the class television on while first graders witnessed the attacks on the World Trade Center played repeatedly. This caused many of the children to conclude that there were dozens of such attacks, and they became frightened.

- To what extent should teachers address such issues as they happen, and to what extent should teachers allow parents to be the first to deal thoroughly with such topics with their children?

The early liberals were led by individuals such as Jean-Jacques Rousseau (1712–1778), John Locke (1632–1704), and Francis Bacon (1561–1626). To fathom the significance of the early liberals, one should understand that the conservatives of the first four schools of thought maintained two salient beliefs. First, they believed in dualism. *Dualism* is the belief that human beings have a virtuous part of their being and a selfish aspect (Dupuis, 1966; Strauss, 1968). The primary function of education, according to the four conservative schools of thought, is to teach the good part to prevail over the selfish aspect. For the Greeks and Romans, this meant that reason must be taught to triumph over the drives of the body. For the Christians and Renaissance humanists, this meant that one needed to be "born again" into a personal relationship with Christ (Dupuis, 1966; Marrou, 1956). The Christians asserted that only God can help one overcome one's selfish tendencies. Second, the conservatives believed that people learned either by reason alone (Greeks and Romans) or by reason and by faith/revelation (either through the Bible or a "Eureka!" experience, which people of faith believed was God-given insight given at a particular moment). The early liberals questioned these two affirmations, asserting that dualism was false and that people learned by experience.

Jean-Jacques Rousseau declared in his book *Emile* (1762/1979) that people were born inherently good, and John Locke opined that a child is born into this world as a *tabula rasa*, or "blank slate" (Dupuis, 1966; Strauss, 1968). Although a great deal of modern psychological research appears to support the belief of many parents that children are born with definite predispositions, Locke's view was significant in that it presented an alternative worldview (Dupuis, 1966; Strauss, 1968). Rousseau moved a step further than Locke, claiming that people were born good, but society corrupted them. Rousseau's conviction regained popularity particularly during the "hippie" movement of the 1960s (Dupuis, 1966; Strauss, 1968). Rousseau's belief is still in favor among many in the Western world. However, opponents of his perspective insist that his view begs this question: If people are born good, how did society become corrupt?

Rousseau, Locke, and Bacon also propounded the notion that children should learn by experience, not by reason (Dupuis, 1966; Strauss, 1968). Bacon advocated the use of the scientific method in the classroom. He envisioned teachers as facilitators who guided children through the experiencing process. To Bacon, children should not enter into the classroom with any presuppositions about how the world worked, but should discover for themselves by using the scientific method (Dupuis, 1966; Strauss, 1968). Rousseau and Locke concurred with Bacon's perspective. This was quite different from the conservative approach, which viewed the teacher as knowing more than the children and functioning as a conveyor of truth (Dupuis, 1966; Strauss, 1968).

The later liberals were led by John Dewey (1859–1952). Dewey believed that education took place by experience and that people were born inherently good. He drew from the foundation for liberalism that Rousseau, Locke, and Bacon established and made a convincing argument that the application of this rubric was appropriate for modern society. Although Rousseau, Locke, and Bacon maintained many of the same perspectives as Dewey, schooling in their era was largely a conservative enterprise. A good deal of this chapter is dedicated to examining Dewey's perspectives; therefore, his views will be examined in greater detail later in this section. One might ask why Dewey was able to usher in an era of liberal practices whereas Rousseau, Locke, and Bacon could not. There are several reasons for this. One of the most crucial is that Dewey, unlike his predecessors, was able to connect his philosophical paradigm to the transformations (due to the Industrial Revolution) that America was experiencing. Second, one should also remember that communication was limited in earlier centuries, and therefore the acceptance and implementation of new ideas took time. In addition, in earlier generations, most people believed that a person's life should be guided by certain principles (Dupuis, 1966; Strauss, 1968). The fact that Rousseau (1763/1945) admitted in *Confessions* that he fathered five illegitimate children and did not care for them impaired his reputation (Dupuis, 1966). Dewey benefited from living in an era with better modes of communication and did not engage in demonstratively controversial behavior.

Four Primary Schools of Educational Thought

There are four primary schools of thought within educational philosophy, two of them conservative and two of them liberal.

Perennialism. This is the most conservative of the four philosophies of education, as well as the oldest. This perspective "can be traced to Plato and Aristotle" (Walker, 1963, p. 8). Perennialists believe that there are certain permanent values and goals that exist throughout time and place. Perennialists assert that the teaching and application of these truths is indispensable to the success of education. Examples of this approach have been Thomas Aquinas (1225–1274) and Mortimer Adler (1902–2001).

Essentialism. Advocates of this approach believe that a more limited number of educational values and goals exist throughout time. Beyond these essential values, educational practices can change throughout time. Essentialists believe "progressive education has failed to follow established patterns but should try to get back on the right track by teaching those things that are necessary" (Walker, 1963, p. 10). They believe that progressives focus too much on the individual. Friedrich Froebel, the founder of the kindergarten, who will be discussed later in this chapter, is generally classified as an essentialist.

Progressivism. This is a moderately liberal approach that grew in popularity during the late 19th and 20th centuries. Progressives contend that schools should change as society changes, in order to meet the needs of modern-day society (Dupuis, 1966). Progressives assert that the world is in a state of constant flux and therefore teachers ought to be open to change on a periodic basis. William Kilpatrick, who will be discussed later in this chapter, was a progressive. Some of Dewey's views would also fit in this category (Walker, 1963).

Reconstructionism. This is the most liberal approach of the four schools of thought. Supporters of this perspective believe that education should be used to "reconstruct the social order" (Walker, 1963, p. 7). Moreover, many theorists of this persuasion claim that the school system is the ideal way to change society, because teachers instruct children who will one day be the leaders of society. George Counts was from this school of thought, and some of Dewey's beliefs would also represent this approach.

Additional Educational Approaches

Pragmatism. This educational approach does not rest exclusively in any of the four schools of thought. Pragmatists may be liberal or conservative in their approach. Dewey developed this philosophical rubric. The essence of this viewpoint is that the act becomes the primary focus and the idea becomes secondary in emphasis. Truth, according to pragmatists, is the successful working of ideas (Walker, 1963). Thus, the emphasis is on the method used in teaching. It is because of this emphasis that pragmatism is neither inherently liberal nor conservative, although essentialists and progressives would probably feel more comfortable with this than with those who maintain a perennialist approach.

Scientism. This perspective declares that there are no absolute values and that truth can be determined only by "laboratory analysis" (Walker, 1963, p. 15).

COMPLEXITY OF THE PHILOSOPHY OF EDUCATION

Although the four schools of thought and the liberal-conservative distinction are helpful in interpreting one's educational philosophy, in reality, the distinctions are not that simple. Most people are a combination of different liberal and conservative beliefs. In other words, most people are moderates to some degree. Beyond this, what is considered liberal or conservative can differ by time, place, and subject matter. Nevertheless, it is most important that one appreciate the fact that most people are unique mosaics of conservative and liberal beliefs. Having stated this, however, to whatever extent liberal, conservative, and these other philosophical terms are useful to distinguish views, they have a good deal of utility.

A Closer Look: Discussing the Basics of Educational Philosophy

The Limitations of Classifying Educational Philosophy: A Self-Check

Although many educators classify educational philosophies according to four different schools of thought or in the more contemporary conservative-versus-liberal mode, it is important to understand that there are limitations to this approach. Probably the most significant of these limitations is that most Americans are moderates; that is, they draw from both liberal and conservative perspectives. On your own, take this quiz with your friends and see what the results are. Score one point for either liberal or conservative, depending on the instructions for each question.

Question	Conservative	Liberal
1. Do you support affirmative action programs?	No	Yes
2. Do you support school choice programs?	Yes	No
3. Do you believe a larger role and size for government is important to solve many of society's problems?	No	Yes
4. Do you believe taxes are too high?	Yes	No
5. Do you believe there should be stricter gun control laws?	No	Yes
6. Do you believe that students ought to be able to pray or gather their thoughts during a moment of silence in the classroom?	Yes	No
7. Would you consider yourself an environmentalist?	No	Yes
8. Are you pro-life or pro-choice on abortion?	Pro-life	Pro-choice
9. Do you believe that whole language or phonics is the best method of teaching reading in the classroom?	Phonics	Whole language
10. Do you believe that judges are often too lenient on those who have committed major crimes?	Yes	No

Few people will score a perfect 0 or 10 for liberal or conservative. Most will score in the 3 to 7 range. Just as most people are liberals on some issues and conservative on others, educators also tend to combine liberal and conservative approaches when they teach in the classroom. Therefore, although liberal and conservative are useful concepts, one needs to be cautious in their application.

It is doubtlessly edifying to be familiar with the four primary schools of educational philosophy. It is also true that educators agree much more on whether a certain philosopher is conservative or liberal than they do on which of the four schools best expresses the educational philosopher's perspective. In addition, in modern society, the terms *liberal* and *conservative* are used far more than *perennialist, essentialist,* and so forth. For these reasons, liberal and conservative will be the terms most frequently used in this chapter.

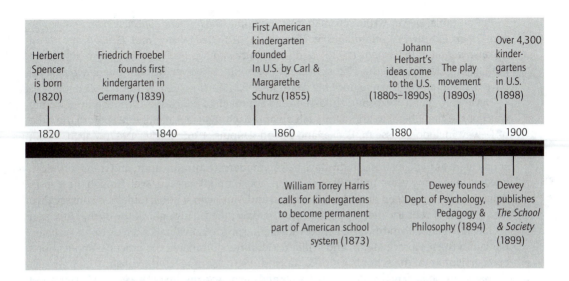

EDUCATIONAL PHILOSOPHY OF JOHN DEWEY

John Dewey (1859–1952) was a notable figure in education. The present American public school system likely bears his "fingerprint" more than that of any other individual (Dunn, 1955; Martin, 2002). Dewey was not this influential because he developed so many new ideas. Rather, he had an impact because he (a) systematized many preexisting and contemporary ideas into a coherent educational philosophy and (b) spoke convincingly of the need for education to adjust to the realities of the Industrial Revolution. Dewey's sense of timing was a crucial element of the acceptance of his ideas (Bagley, 1915).

John Dewey was born in Vermont in 1859 and therefore from an early age became well acquainted with the educational orientation of the New England area. His academic career started with professorates at the University of Minnesota and the University of Michigan. His career, however, really did not gain prominence until he founded the Department of Psychology, Pedagogy, and Philosophy of the University of Chicago, in 1894 (Martin, 2002; Schilpp, 1939). At the University of Chicago, Dewey began to develop his theories in concert with the developing school of thought called pragmatism. There, he founded and directed a laboratory school, where he was at liberty to test his experimental methods (Martin, 2002; Schilpp, 1939). His experience in Chicago led him to write his first major work in education in 1899, *The School and Society.*

Dewey eventually had disagreements with the leadership of the University of Chicago over the issue of the Laboratory School. This caused him to resign his position at the University of Chicago in 1904, after 10 years with the institution. Dewey then joined the Department of Philosophy at Columbia University, where he remained for the rest of his academic career (Martin, 2002; Schilpp, 1939). Dewey's influence at the University of Chicago remains in many respects; for example, the university still maintains his Laboratory School (Martin, 2002).

At Columbia, Dewey wrote several books, including *The Influence of Darwin on Philosophy and Other Essays in Contemporary Thought* (1910), *Democracy and Education* (1916), *Reconstruction in Philosophy* (1920), and *Experience and Nature* (1925). Dewey reached the pinnacle of his career in the 1920s, while at Columbia. However, he continued to write and have considerable influence until his death in 1952 (Martin, 2002; Schilpp, 1939).

Dewey brought a liberal and child-centered approach to education, although he certainly was not the first liberal to argue for such an approach. Educational liberals before the time of Dewey include Rousseau, Locke, and Bacon (Dupuis, 1966; Locke, 1947; Martin, 2002; Rousseau, 1762/1979; Schilpp, 1939). However, it customarily takes time for new philosophical ideas to take effect. In the days before modern communication and transportation, it would take many years. In the days of Bacon, Locke, and Rousseau, even though these individuals professed certain new ideas, European and American schools remained conservative for well over a century after their ideas were propounded. Throughout the 17th, 18th, and 19th centuries, education was a conservative enterprise. Individuals such as Noah Webster, Benjamin Rush, Horace Mann, and William McGuffey dominated the practical applications and curriculum of the schools (Hunt & Maxson, 1981; Monroe, 1940; Yulish, 1980).

Many individuals such as Rousseau, Locke, and Bacon had preceded Dewey (1915, 1990) and asserted that children knew best what they ought to learn and that teachers needed to respond to these desires (Dupuis, 1966; Locke, 1947; Martin, 2002; Rousseau, 1762/1979; Schilpp, 1939). Nevertheless, it was Dewey who put the liberal approach to education on the map (Bagley, 1915; Dupuis, 1966; Martin, 2002). Although these other educators had espoused these views, few schools actually practiced their ideas (Hunt & Maxson, 1981; Monroe, 1940; Yulish, 1980). People viewed Bacon's idea of applying the scientific method to the classroom as appropriate for scientists but not the classroom (Chamberlin, 1961; Martin, 2002). Although Rousseau (1763/1945, 1762/1979) went the farthest in developing an educational philosophy, as mentioned, his history of siring but not caring for his illegitimate children kept many from viewing Rousseau as an admirable figure on teaching children. Finally, Locke's views carried more weight in the philosophical and political sphere than they did in the schools (Cranston, 1957). Beyond these factors, the extent of external societal forces was not sufficient to produce change. All of this changed with the emergence of John Dewey on the subject of educational science.

Dewey (1915, 1990) argued that the Industrial Revolution was changing society and that the way education was practiced had to be radically changed as a result (Lawson & Lean, 1964). He claimed that two realities were especially becoming clear as a result of the Industrial Revolution. First, people in society were becoming more specialized. That is, the Industrial Revolution necessitated that in order for an industry to work effectively, each person on an assembly line had to become a specialist in a facet of producing a particular product (Dewey, 1990; Lawson & Lean, 1964). Dewey (1990) claimed that in order for education to work effectively, schools had to do likewise. Before the Industrial Revolution, people generally viewed parents as primarily responsible for educating their children (Blinderman, 1976; Gangel & Benson, 1983; Chamberlin, 1961; Morgan, 1986; Lawson & Lean, 1964). Schools were to support and supplement the efforts of parents. Now, however, with the onset the industrial age, schools were the educational specialists, according to Dewey (Dewey, 1990; Lawson & Lean, 1964). Second, the Industrial Revolution was eroding the cohesiveness and the primacy of the family. In Dewey's view, this trend was happening all around the world, and therefore it was the school's responsibility to increase the puissance of its role and execute some of the same functions previously reserved for the family (Dewey, 1964).

To many Americans, Dewey's declarations about the new pivotal role of schools appeared to make sense (Martin, 2002). In addition, because the Industrial Revolution was placing new demands upon American families, Dewey's notion of schools taking on some of the functions previously reserved for the family seemed to offer some relief for overwhelmed families (Dewey, 1964). The time-sensitive nature of Dewey's affirmations gave educational liberalism a greater audience than ever before (Bagley, 1915; Martin, 2002).

Dewey was influenced by many educators and philosophers who preceded him as well as a number of his contemporaries. He seemed to be able to coordinate many of the thoughts he had read or heard previously into an organized whole and educational philosophy (Egan, 2002). This enabled Dewey himself to influence a plethora of educators (Bagley, 1915; Martin, 2002), because he was able to skillfully articulate into a unified philosophy what many liberal educators already believed. Dewey combined the thoughts of people such as Rousseau, Spencer, Locke, Darwin, and Bacon into a cohesive theory relevant to education (Dewey, 1915, 1920, 1922, 1977a, 1977b, 1978a, 1978b, 1978c; Egan, 2002). Later, he incorporated some of the views of his contemporaries, such as William H. Kilpatrick and George Counts (Wallace, 1995). He then not only connected many of the ideas of these thinkers but also elaborated on and further developed them (Giarelli, 1995; Wallace, 1995). Consequently, Dewey's philosophy emerged to constitute the most complete declaration of the liberal philosophy of education of the 20th century (Bagley, 1915; Dunn, 1955).

What Dewey Believed

Considering Dewey's influence on the educational community, it is of great importance to define some of the highlights of what he believed.

First, Dewey advocated a child-centered education in which the children themselves determined what was learned in the classroom. That is, what the child enjoys learning should constitute that which is taught by the teacher (Dewey, 1990). He believed that in the long term, teaching children what they enjoyed learning maximized the amount that they would learn. Dewey's approach is in contrast to the conservative approach, which is preparation centered (Dupuis, 1966; Horne, 1932). Conservatives believe that teachers and adults generally know best what children need to know in order to function well in society and become successful adults. Although conservatives believe that learning should be enjoyable for children, they believe that it is possible to make material children need to know enjoyable to learn (Dupuis, 1966).

The central aspect of Dewey's philosophy of education is that it is child centered and the educational desires of the child should direct the school curriculum. In his book *The Child and the Curriculum,* Dewey (1990) states, "The child is the starting point, the center, and the end. His development, his growth, is the ideal. It alone furnishes the standard" (p. 187). What the child enjoys learning about and what produces excitement in the heart of the child should determine what is taught, for the goal of education is to make children into lifelong learners (Dewey, 1990). The teacher should attempt to do everything in his or her power to make that happen.

To be effective at this, Dewey contended educators need to bridge the gap that supposedly exists between the child and the curriculum (Dewey, 1902). According to Dewey (1990), there really need not be a gap "between the child's experience and the various forms of subject-matter that make up the course of study" (p. 189). In Dewey's view (1902, 1915),

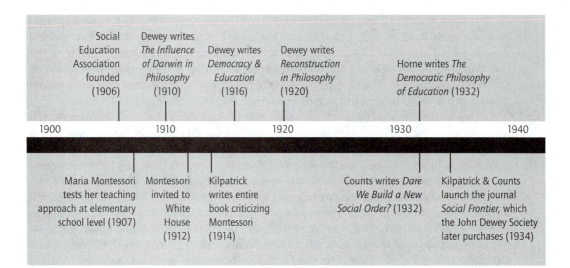

Social Education Association founded (1906)

Dewey writes *The Influence of Darwin in Philosophy* (1910)

Dewey writes *Democracy & Education* (1916)

Dewey writes *Reconstruction in Philosophy* (1920)

Horne writes *The Democratic Philosophy of Education* (1932)

1900   1910   1920   1930   1940

Maria Montessori tests her teaching approach at elementary school level (1907)

Montessori invited to White House (1912)

Kilpatrick writes entire book criticizing Montessori (1914)

Counts writes *Dare We Build a New Social Order?* (1932)

Kilpatrick & Counts launch the journal *Social Frontier,* which the John Dewey Society later purchases (1934)

teachers often make the mistake of insisting that children leave the childhood world and enter into the world of the adult and that a child rise above his or her experience to learn what there is to know about the world. From Dewey's perspective, this is truly a mistake. For via the child's own experience, he or she is able to obtain knowledge about any given subject matter.

Dewey (1915, 1978b, 1978c) believed that the child-centered approach to education was especially appropriate in a democracy and that in a democracy, a teacher should emphasize the freedom of the child. He asserted that the conservative approach to education, one focused on preparedness, is insensitive to children. Regarding the purpose of conservative education, Dewey (1998) states, "The main purpose or objective is to prepare the young for future responsibilities and for success in life, by means of information of prepared forms of skill which comprehend the material of instruction" (p. 3). Before Dewey, most educators had assumed that the primary role of the teacher was to impart truth to the student (Dupuis, 1966; Horne, 1931a). Many teachers believed truth ultimately led to freedom and enabled citizens to be enlightened participants in American democracy. Dewey's assertion that education should be child centered challenged these beliefs. The impartation of truth is not the ultimate goal of the Deweyian model (Dewey, 1922).

Dewey (1978c) was at odds with the conservative perspective on the purpose of education. He believed that this orientation, in the long run, asserted that children needed to become more like adults. In contrast, Dewey believed that the teacher needed to adapt to the learning level of the child (Dewey, 1902, 1980a). In this regard, he espoused Spencer's theory of recapitulation, which is based on the theory of evolution (Dewey, 1910, 1977a, 1980a; Egan, 2002). It asserts that as a child develops, he or she retraces the stages of evolution from lower to higher intellectual forms of life (Dewey, 1910, 1980a; Egan, 2002).

Dewey (1980a) asserted, "Education as recapitulation and retrospective . . . The individual develops, but his proper development consists in repeating in orderly stages the past evolution of animal life and human history" (p. 78). According to Spencer and Dewey, in the womb, the child physically and mentally recapitulates the earliest stages of development, and after birth, the child shows development that in many respects resembles the transitional species of apelike humans and then lower forms of human beings (Dewey, 1977a; Spencer, 1966). As a consequence of this, there are many intellectual activities that a child simply is not ready for in the early days of elementary school (Dewey, 1977a, 1977b). In other words, according to Dewey, teachers need to teach children what they want to learn because (a) children will enjoy education more and (b) teachers need to be sensitive to children's levels of development.

Dewey was greatly influenced by Darwin's theory of evolution and by Spencer's attempt to apply this theory in education. In fact, evolutionary thought so affected Dewey's philosophy that he wrote an entire book on its influence (Dewey, 1910).

A second important aspect of Dewey's philosophy was that he asserted that experience is the key to understanding the world (Dewey, 1938, 1998). In the conservative frame of mind, reason and, some also assert, revelation are the keys to knowledge (Dupuis, 1966). However, Dewey, as a true liberal along the lines of Rousseau and Bacon, argued that experience was the key to knowledge (Dewey, 1938, 1998). Dewey (1998) notes, "Everything depends upon the quality of the experience which is had" (p. 15). He believed that progressive education was rooted in experience. Education should train children to fully utilize their senses to discover the world around them (Dewey, 1938, 1998). Truth, according to the liberal school of thought, is obtained through experience. Liberals reject the notion that one can obtain truth through reason and revelation, as the conservatives contend (Dewey, 1938, 1977a, 1977c, 1978b, 1998). To Dewey (1902, 1915, 1938, 1990, 1998), the emphasis on experience was ideal for children because children are naturally curious. He believed teachers should build upon the curiosity of children to set them along the learning path (1902, 1915, 1938, 1998).

A third important aspect was that Dewey (1938, 1978a) believed that the principal role of the teacher was to guide the child through the experiencing process. He averred, in essence, that Bacon's scientific method needed to be applied in the classroom. That is, the student was like an experimenter, testing his or her theories about how the world worked (Dewey, 1902, 1938, 1998), and the function of the instructor was not to be an imparter of truth, but a facilitator for the children's learning experiences (Dewey, 1938, 1915, 1978a, 1978c).

To Dewey, in a democratic society, there are choices, and it is the function of the teacher to make those choices available to children. One of the primary roles of the teacher is therefore to inform the student about the choices available to him or her and then challenge the student to seek the choice that is best (Dewey, 1966, 1978a).

The teacher should guide children into the experiencing process in the following way (Dewey, 1938):

1. A child has an experience.

2. A child reflects over that experience.

3. A child revises his or her perspective based on the experience.

4. A child seeks to experience more and then go through further experience.

According to Dewey, education based on experience is naturally enjoyable to children, because they require activity. Children are naturally active, and the schools should capitalize on this fact (Dewey, 1902, 1915, 1938, 1990). Dewey criticized the usual method of lecturing to the students, which requires too much passivity on the part of the students. Under this method, he claimed that about the only activity the child engages in is recitation (Dewey, 1902, 1915, 1938). And recitation, according to Dewey, simply involves children showing off to the teacher what they know. To Dewey, this reflects the degree to which education focuses on the teacher rather than on the student.

Dewey stated that children could learn not only from their own experiences but also from the experiences that other children shared in class. Consequently, he believed that communication was one of the most constructive activities that could take place in class, because it maximized the usefulness of experience. In Dewey's view, communication therefore maximized knowledge (Dewey, 1915, 1938). When children shared their experiences with other students and with the teacher, they were to reconstruct their experiences and then analyze them together with the other people in the classroom (Dewey, 1915, 1938). In this process of reconstruction, the scientific method was once again to be applied to understanding the experience. Working together, the class could come to a fuller understanding of the meaning and significance of each individual's experience.

A fourth important aspect of Dewey's philosophy was that he saw a new role for the school in industrial society. He believed that the Industrial Revolution was eroding the role of the family and that the school should therefore become the primary educator of the child (Dewey, 1915, 1922). Before this time, although Americans regarded the school as very important, most Americans maintained that parents held the primary position of responsibility in educating children (Chamberlin, 1961; Hiner, 1988; Monroe, 1940). Dewey (1915, 1978a, 1978b, 1978c) argued that circumstances had now sufficiently changed so that the school should bear the primary responsibility for education. Dewey (1915) averred the two realities had changed as a result of the Industrial Revolution. First, the Industrial Revolution, by definition, had caused people's functions to become much more specialized. For example, when major products like automobiles were made, one person did not produce the entire product. Rather, each individual was now responsible for making one part of it. Dewey (1995) asserted that society needed to adapt to this transition by assigning to schools the job of educating children. Second, he claimed that given that industrialization was taking its toll on the American family, it was only natural that the schools take on some of the roles previously reserved for the family (Dewey, 1915, 1964, 1978a).

As an educator, the thought of a greater role for the school was certainly inviting for Dewey (1915, 1964). With this new influence, he and his followers saw an opportunity for the schools to influence society in a greater way than ever before (Bagley, 1915; Dunn, 1955; Egan, 2002). Naturally, in the views of Dewey and other like-minded associates, the school's newfound influence would ultimately have a positive impact on society (Egan, 2002; Giarelli, 1995; Wallace, 1995). In Dewey's view, educators now had the opportunity to produce substantial social change (Dewey, 1910, 1915, 1920, 1964; Egan, 2002; Giarelli, 1995; Wallace, 1995). As a result, although some people lamented the decline of the family, Dewey was not one of them. Dewey (1964) believed it was necessary to discourage children from developing their own value systems based on the views of their parents. Children needed to turn away from this notion to develop their own value systems based on their own experiences and the experiences of other children in the class.

Dewey (1920) believed that there was now taking place a "reconstruction of ideas" (p. iii) and a "reconstruction in moral conceptions" (p. 161), which the school needed to propel. Dewey, Kilpatrick, and others believed that children should be taught to rely on personal experience, rather than on their parents, to develop their values (Dewey, 1910, 1920, 1938, 1977b, 1980b; Kilpatrick, 1935, 1951). Children's learning about values, as with everything else, should take place through not only their own experiences, but also by listening to the communications of other children based on their experiences (Dewey, 1915, 1977b).

Dewey both had an impact and was influenced by the writings of George Counts (Egan, 2002; Wallace, 1995), who wrote a seminal book, *Dare We Build a New Social Order?* (1932). Counts (1932) boldly declared the potential of the schools to send future society in a new direction:

> Our major concern consequently should be, not to keep the school from influencing the child in a positive direction, but rather to make certain that every progressive school will use whatever power it may possess in opposing and checking the forces of social conservatism and reaction. (p. 24)

Counts's book became an influential complement to Dewey's book *Reconstruction in Philosophy* (1920).

Calls by Counts and Kilpatrick (second to Dewey as the most influential educator of the time) for education to influence society emboldened Dewey and Columbia University, where he worked (Giarelli, 1995). In 1934, Columbia University educators, led by Kilpatrick and Counts, launched the influential journal *The Social Frontier* (Giarelli, 1995). The journal attracted very prominent authors from the United States and Western Europe who argued that schools needed to have a great impact on society (Giarelli, 1995; Moreo, 1996). However, Dewey and Counts were both disappointed that the journal did not have more of an influence than it did (Moreo, 1996). Counts therefore left the journal in frustration, but the John Dewey Society bought the journal in order to promote the idea that schools could change society for the good (Moreo, 1996).

Dewey, like Counts, believed that schools had an unprecedented opportunity to influence the future of American society (Dewey, 1910, 1915, 1922, 1964; Counts, 1932). Dewey (1964) notes,

> Our special concern here is with the role of the schools in building up forces and factors whose natural effect is to undermine the importance and uniqueness of family life. It is obvious to any observer that in every western country the increase of importance of public schools has been at least coincident with a relaxation of older family ties. (pp. 84–85)

Dewey believed that the decline of the family was unavoidable in industrial society and that teachers could therefore play a new role to help children and shape society. Counts (1932) agreed with Dewey and claimed "that teachers should deliberately reach for power . . . and positively influence the social attitudes and behavior of the coming generation" (p. 28). Dewey knew that many parents would not be receptive to his ideas regarding the new role of the school, but for him, this new role was an essential part of his vision for the school.

A fifth important aspect is Dewey's assertion that the school needed to foster good habits in the lives of children. This perspective could play a prominent role in building a better society (Dewey, 1915, 1977a).

Sixth, Dewey did not believe in a transcendent reality or absolute truth (Dewey, 1915, 1920). Dewey (1920) declared, "Growth itself is the only moral 'end'" (p. 177). He also did not believe in a transcendent reality that could guide people in determining a sense of right and wrong. He believed that if we look at the world around us, we should be able to see how things should be (Dewey, 1922) and that there are no absolutes. He believed in a relativistic philosophy in which nothing is black and white. In Dewey's view, there is no transcendent reality. There is only humanity and nature. Human beings are to reconstruct nature (Dewey, 1922).

Dewey believed in Bacon's principle of applying the scientific method to all disciplines. Once again, this means putting aside all assumptions and presuppositions about what is true (Dewey, 1977a, 1977b, 1977c). Instead, each individual should test everything via experience. For Dewey (1938), the scientific approach was the only way in which one could hope to divulge truth. Dewey (1977a, 1977b) believed that this principle applied to attempting to find answers not only to general problems faced by humankind, but in our own individual lives as well. In his view, we are all to be types of scientific experimenters (Dewey, 1915, 1938).

Seventh, Dewey believed that the public school was the ideal place for education to take place (Dewey, 1910, 1915). This was a weightier declaration than it might seem today. Before Dewey's era, public education was regarded as largely a conservative enterprise (Hunt & Maxson, 1981; Monroe, 1940; Yulish, 1980). Conservatives were generally quite enthusiastic about public schools, while liberals were generally split (Barnard, 1842; Filler, 1965). Dewey's support for public schools helped usher in what many regard as a golden age for public schools, lasting from about 1920 to 1960, during which time both liberals and conservatives were generally very supportive of public schools. Ironically, beginning in the early 1960s, it would be conservatives who would often be split on their support of public schools (Ravitch & Finn, 1987).

In Dewey's (1938, 1966) mind, the existence of public schools was very important, so that this kind of dialogue regarding experience could take place. The process of experience had limited value only when it was confined to the life of the individual who was undergoing the experience (Dewey, 1938, 1966). To the extent that certain people had certain experiences, other people should be able to benefit by those experiences. Therefore, the communication of experiences was about as important as the experiences themselves. To Dewey, the public school served as the forum by which experiences can be shared.

All in all, Dewey stands out as the most influential educator of his era and of the 20th century (Bagley, 1915; Dunn, 1955; Dupuis, 1966). His ideas represent an interesting mosaic of the perspectives of those who influenced him and evolved over time. His ability to relate those ideas to the changing dynamics of his time elevated his assertions to a heightened status that few educators have enjoyed.

OTHER LIBERAL REFORMERS

Herbert Spencer

Herbert Spencer (1820–1903), an English theorist, was one of the most important figures in the progressive movement. Spencer (1908) called for what he termed "a political creed for true liberalism" (p. 227). In many respects, he established the foundation for modern-day liberalism (Duncan, 1908; Egan, 2002; Spencer, 1963). His ideas particularly influenced the educational philosophy of John Dewey (Egan, 2002; Rippa, 1997) and Jean Piaget (Egan, 1983, 2002). Rippa (1997), observes, "Spencer ranks as one of the great pioneers of American progressivism. He underscored the tenets of progressive education so forcefully that he anticipated much of the work of John Dewey" (p. 148). Egan (2002, p. 48) adds that many of Dewey's ideas were "simply echoes" of Spencer's perspective and that he drew from many of his ideas.

Spencer desired to apply Darwin's evolutionary theory to the classroom (Low-Beer, 1969; Spencer, 1963, 1966). It was actually Spencer who first coined the phrase "survival of the fittest," before it was a common phrase (Egan, 2002). He sought to apply evolution to many subjects even before Darwin's theory arose (Low-Beer, 1969; Spencer, 1932).

Spencer attempted to develop Darwin's theory of evolution into a theory that could be applied both sociologically and educationally (Low-Beer, 1969; Spencer, 1963, 1966). According to Spencer (1851, 1963, 1966), an education system should help sort out the "fittest" individuals of each generation. These "fittest" individuals would survive because of their intellect, natural abilities, and adaptability (Spencer, 1851, 1963, 1966). He argued that society needed to more fully adapt to the Industrial Revolution that was taking place (Spencer, 1902, 1966). It needed a specialized education system that would adapt to the necessity of educating the populace.

Spencer believed in a utilitarian education based on useful scientific and practical objectives. He believed that the aspects of education that should be especially emphasized are those that would help ensure the survival of the species. He supported an education that did not include (a) memorization and recitation and (b) vocational education (Low-Beer, 1969; Spencer, 1963, 1966).

Spencer (1963) believed that the purpose of education was to prepare people for life. He believed that knowledge was important because it contributed to the evolution of the human species and was helpful in self-preservation (Spencer, 1932, 1963). To maximize the school's efficacy, Spencer (1963) argued that knowledge needed to be delivered in the concrete realm and that teachers needed to direct children to make their own discoveries.

In Spencer's (1932, 1963) view, children needed to begin to learn using concrete objects before they could understand abstract concepts. To support this assertion, he drew from the evolutionary belief of "recapitulation" (Egan, 2002; Spencer, 1963). Recapitulation asserts that during a child's fetal and early childhood development, he or she progresses through the stages of the human species' development until adulthood (Egan, 2002; Krips & McGuire, 1995). Therefore, for some time, a child's intellectual abilities are similar to prehistoric humans. As a result, only as children grow older can they enter into the realm of abstract thinking. Piaget (1950) would later declare this same perspective about abstract thinking.

As a result of maintaining this perspective, Spencer (1963) thought it was imperative to create a natural learning situation for children, much as they learned from play. He declared that one of the best ways to achieve this goal was to apply Bacon's idea of using the scientific method in the classroom. In this approach, the child would not enter the classroom with any preconceived notion of truth, but would instead experience it for herself or himself (Dupuis, 1966).

Spencer (1908, 1963) believed that education should focus on furthering the advancement of the human species. Therefore, he believed the pedagogy should be reconstructed on the basis of evolutionary theory (Spencer, 1908). He believed that the key to this development is a child-centered approach to education, because children instinctively have an appetite for what they need to learn (Spencer, 1932). Given that Spencer claimed that the overall well-being of the human species should be of paramount importance, the teacher should also be concerned with the physical and moral strength of the child (Spencer, 1932, 1963).

Spencer was fascinated with progress. When he came to the United States, he was intrigued with the nation's large buildings and their focus on regulating internal and external temperature, and he predicted that the United States would soon become the world's most dominant power (Spencer, 1966). However, this same fascination with human progress caused Spencer (1902, 1908, 1963) to oppose public, that is, government-sponsored, schools.

Added Insight: Dewey's Interest in European Education

John Dewey was a strong believer in the need to learn from foreign systems of education, particularly in Europe. This is not surprising, because he was a philosopher and many of the world's leading philosophers of the time lived in Europe. In his writings, Dewey (1910, 1920, 1929) made frequent references to these philosophers and foreign systems of education.

Dewey sometimes visited Europe to interact with other educators there. The European school system that impressed him the most was in Russia. He was so impressed by the school system there that he wrote a book on it, *Impressions of Soviet Russia, and the Revolutionary World, Mexico, China, Turkey* (1929). In it, Dewey asserted that the Russian school system should be a model for the U.S. system. One should understand that many Americans at the time, and probably Dewey himself, were unaware of the Russian government's oppression of its own people. Nevertheless, Dewey's critics were quick to point out that his emphasis on the community more than the individual, together with his assertion that Russia was a model, meant that Dewey was a communist. The accusation seems to be unfair, particularly because he was later quite critical of the Russian oppression of its own people. Dewey would probably admit that he was a socialist, in much the same way that most of the Scandinavian nations are. Nevertheless, to classify him as a communist is unfair.

Dewey's claim that American educators could learn a great deal from their European counterparts was also a product of the fact that European educators, such as Johann Pestalozzi, Friedrich Froebel, Herbert Spencer, and Johann Herbart, had had such a dramatic impact on the maturation of American education. Today, many educators still believe that Americans can learn from foreign systems of education. This will be discussed further in Chapter 15.

Until the coming of John Dewey, a strong advocate of public schools, many liberal educators opposed common or public schools (Barnard, 1842; Egan, 2002). After all, the early common school movement was a conservative enterprise sponsored by traditional Whigs, such as Horace Mann (1849) and Henry Barnard (1842). Many early liberals saw the common school movement as insisting that teachers instruct in a certain way and maintain certain cultural values (Spring, 1997).

What made Spencer's view (1902, 1908, 1963) about public schooling interesting, therefore, is not his viewpoint itself, but the reason behind his opinion. Spencer (1908) did not like the public schools because he opined that such "state meddling slowed down evolutionary advancements" (Spencer, 1908, p. 472). He believed that educating the masses caused public schools to be a medium for mediocrity (Spencer, 1851). Instead, Spencer asserted that schools should focus on selecting and training the fittest individuals to lead society, and for this same reason, he also opposed special education (Cavenagh, 1932; Egan, 2002; Rafter, 2004; Sarason & Doris, 1969; Spencer, 1851, 1908).

Nevertheless, Spencer's influence in the development of educational theory is undeniable. The fact that Spencer had influence in both the scientific and educational communities caused many people to regard education as more of a science than had previously been the case (Cavenagh, 1932; Duncan, 1908; Rafter, 2004; Spencer, 1902, 1908, 1932). His application of evolution's recapitulation theory to education initially had a tremendous impact on G. Stanley Hall, perhaps the foremost early childhood educator of the day, and to a lesser extent on John Dewey (Egan, 2002).

Spencer's attempt to bridge the gap between science and education also made him accessible to critics in both of these disciplines (Rafter, 2004; Spencer, 1908). In the scientific sphere, Spencer, the evolutionist, found himself at odds with Lord Kelvin (of the Kelvin temperature scale), the creationist (Spencer, 1908). On the educational front, many educators rejected the recapitulation instructional approach because they believe it caused racism (Egan, 2002; Sarason & Doris, 1969). Nevertheless, Spencer's beliefs did much to provide a foundation for future educational thought and the fusion of science and education into a broader pedagogical paradigm.

Joseph Lee and Henry Curtis

Joseph Lee (1862–1937) and Henry Curtis (1870–1854) were major forces in education during the late 1800s and early 1900s and were the founders of the *play movement*. Both individuals redefined the meaning of play among educators, advocating the building of playgrounds in schoolyards all across the country. Lee (1915) argued,

> The thing that most needs to be understood about play is that it is not a luxury but a necessity. It is not simply something that a child likes to have; it is something that he must have if he is ever to grow up. (p. 2)

The play movement actually started during the period of 1885 to 1895, in big cities like New York, Chicago, Boston, and Philadelphia. Playgrounds were constructed to give children a place to play away from many of the negative influences of the city (Lee, 1925).

Lee (1925) asserted that play helps make children healthy and aids them in staying out of trouble and that "when conducted under wholesome conditions, it has great educational and social values" (p. 17). Lee and Curtis asserted that because social scientists universally regarded play as beneficial, playgrounds should be built not only with the school year in mind but also the entire calendar year. In other words, given that play had the year-round impact of relieving the weight of poverty and stress in the lives of children, providing relaxation, and allowing children to satisfy certain instinctual drives to play, society should encourage the use of playgrounds 12 months per year.

William Kilpatrick

William Kilpatrick (1871–1965), was the second most influential educator of his era. His influence among those in teaching programs was second only to John Dewey's (Campbell, 1970; Cousins, 1958; Douglas, 1958; Kilpatrick, 1914/1971; Kramer, 1976; Lillard, 1972; Peltzman, 1998). His reputation was great largely because he was known as a very effective instructor (Peltzman, 1998). He was called the "million-dollar professor" because some estimated that he was so popular and caused so many students to come to Columbia University, he caused a surge of tuition payments to Columbia of over $1 million (Beineke, 1998).

Kilpatrick was a loyal student of Dewey and one of the chief spokesmen of his philosophy of education (Peltzman, 1998). Kilpatrick (1951) articulated a number of themes that encompassed the essence of his educational philosophy.

First, Kilpatrick believed that a democratic society should have democratic schools. He believed that educators should also instruct using democratic methods (Kilpatrick, 1925a, 1925b, 1935). In Kilpatrick's perspective, the primary goal of the school was to prepare children to live in a democratic society. Consequently, he averred that the United States should have a democratic schooling system (Kilpatrick, 1935).

Second, Kilpatrick (1935, 1936) declared that children's desires should dictate what is taught in the classroom. He asserted that allowing children to determine the curriculum would not spoil the children. He also predicted that this child orientation would not cause children to desire to learn to use only easy material (Kilpatrick, 1925a, 1925b, 1935). In his view, teachers should allow children to actively explore their interests (Kilpatrick, 1925a, 1926). To Kilpatrick, teacher-sponsored coercion, whether expressed by forcing them to learn particular facts or in discipline, should be avoided, if at all possible (Kilpatrick, 1925a, 1926, 1935).

Third, the essence of learning is experience. Kilpatrick (1935) stated that "experience is the best educator" (p. 221). Like Dewey, Kilpatrick (1925a, 1925b, 1926, 1935) therefore contended that the teacher should be one who guides children through the experiential process rather than one who imparts truth. According to Kilpatrick (1951), we must learn what we live.

Fourth, Kilpatrick (1936, 1937) declared that society was changing and that schools needed to adapt to that change. Like Dewey, Kilpatrick believed that the Industrial Revolution had changed society in a number of ways and that schools had to adapt. Some of the ways industrialization was changing society were that it was making America's institutions more specialized and it was contributing to the decline of the family (Kilpatrick, 1925, 1926, 1951). In Kilpatrick's view, the schools needed to expand their role to incorporate some of the functions previously maintained by parents. To support the expanded role of the school, he argued for more money to go toward the support of public education (Kilpatrick, 1935).

Fifth, Kilpatrick believed that children should be taught to be socially active (Beineke, 1998). He believed that in society as a whole, people worked together to solve problems. Therefore, children should be engaged in what he called "socially purposeful acts" (Beineke, 1998). According to Kilpatrick, everyone should have moral and societal values.

Morality, especially for the public good, was a social necessity (Kilpatrick, 1951). To accomplish his vision for education, Kilpatrick (1935, 1951) believed that lower class sizes and greater financing of education was an important prerequisite for the success of schools.

Ella Flagg Young

Ella Flagg Young (1845–1918) was a student of John Dewey, while Dewey taught at the University of Chicago. Young was 50 years old when she was Dewey's pupil and unquestionably became his classroom star (Lageman, 2002). Young became so impassioned in class that she and Dewey often engaged in a discussion in class to the exclusion of the remainder of the class (Lageman, 2002; McManis, 1916). After graduation, Young was eventually the supervisor of instruction at Dewey's Laboratory School at the university, the site of the implementation of his ideas about schooling (Lageman, 2002; McManis, 1916). Young was an indefatigable proponent of teacher freedom, believing that an individual teacher was cognizant of what was best for the students in his or her care. Dewey derived many of his ideas about teacher freedom from Young (Lageman, 2002; McManis, 1916).

Many of Young's greatest contributions to schooling were administrative in nature. In 1909, the Chicago school board chose her to be superintendent. This appointment made Flagg the first woman to obtain such a position in a major city. She served on the Illinois state board of education for 20 years and was selected as its president in 1910 (Blount, 2002). Whether Young functioned as an advisor, administrator, or academic, her focus remained on teacher freedom (Blount, 2002; Lageman, 2002; McManis, 1916).

MODERATE LIBERALS

Colin Scott

Colin Scott (1861–1925) had a perspective similar to that of William H. Kilpatrick in one very important respect: He asserted that schools must "fit into the rest of society" (Scott, 1908, p. 1). He believed that for education to realize its full potential, it had to teach students to make an impact on society (Scott, 1908). Scott so completely adhered to this perspective that he founded the Social Education Association (1906). He helped popularize group activity among students and believed that since groups in society worked together to solve problems, children ought to be taught to do the same thing. Scott argued that organizing children to work together not only benefited society but also strengthened the students, because working in a group enabled them to act out of greater conviction.

Scott (1908) respected Dewey but believed that Dewey focused too much on child-centered education rather than addressing what children could do for the good of society. In Scott's view, children could not be said to be fully educated unless they learned to function in life to achieve this purpose.

Johann Herbart

Johann Herbart (1776–1841) was a German psychologist and a major force in education, although much of his influence occurred after he died (Dunkel, 1970). A number of European educators, such as Johann Pestalozzi, Friedrich Froebel, and Johann Herbart, had a considerable degree of impact on American education (Doherty, 1977; Dunkel, 1970; Slight, 1961). However, it often took time for their ideas to be practiced in the United States, for two primary reasons. First, it took time for American educators to personally witness these European theories being practiced. Second, even after American educators introduced these ideas to Americans, it took time for these concepts to be disseminated in the United States.

Charles DeGarmo first introduced Herbart's perspective to the American scene in the 1880s and 1890s (Dunkel, 1970). Herbart's greatest contribution was the lesson plan, which he believed would be suitable to every classroom. Herbart's main concern was that whatever was taught be of interest to the students. He believed he developed a lesson plan that guaranteed just that (Dunkel, 1970). Herbart believed that the best method of instruction is to present material related to the interests of the students. Therefore, ordering subject matter in a particular fashion was especially important. His lesson plan involved following five steps: (1) preparation, (2) presentation, (3) comparison and abstraction, (4) generalization or definition, and (5) application (Dunkel, 1970).

Through his book *Essentials of Method* (1889), Charles DeGarmo first brought Herbart's ideas to the United States. European educators had practiced Herbartian principles since 1865 (Dunkel, 1970).

Although Herbart's writings were not well received during his lifetime, his work had considerable influence after he died (Dunkel, 1970). He asserted that it was important not only to develop a lesson plan per se but also to determine what lessons the students most liked. He believed that whether the students enjoyed a lesson ultimately determined whether the lesson was successful (Graves, 1912). This definition of a successful lesson reflected Herbart's child-centered orientation.

Although Herbart had a typically liberal child orientation toward his educational approach, he also believed that moral education was the chief task of the school (Dunkel, 1970; Graves, 1912). Graves (1912) notes, "The making of the morally religious man is, therefore, Herbart's idea of the end of education" (p. 177). Herbart (1852) even titled one of the chapters in his book "Morality: The Sole and Total Task of Education." In this book, he stated, "Education is not merely to make man 'better' in some sense, but is to make him 'morally good.' The aim of education is virtue, morality" (p. 7).

MODERATES

Friedrich Froebel

Friedrich Froebel (1782–1852) opened the first kindergarten in Germany in 1839 (Slight, 1961). Froebel believed that the essence of the kindergarten was to help children grow up, like a garden, and experience unity with God and the people around them (Doherty, 1977; Downs, 1978; Slight, 1961). His vision for the kindergarten was what he considered a mixture of the best combinations of the conservative and liberal schools of educational thought. From the conservative perspective, he thought that the focus of the kindergarten should be on moral education. From the liberal vantage point, he averred that education should be child centered (Doherty, 1977; Downs, 1978; Slight, 1961).

Kindergartens spread during the 1840s. Although Froebel died in 1852, his ideas soon spread to the United States. Carl and Margarethe Schurz founded the first kindergarten in the United States in Watertown, Wisconsin, in 1855, although kindergartens were not very common in America in the 1850s (Baylor, 1965; Beatty, 1995). In 1861, a kindergarten was added to a New Jersey private academy. Elizabeth Peabody, a Massachusetts educator, traveled to observe European kindergartens in 1867 (Baylor, 1965; Beatty, 1995; Peabody, 1886). About a dozen kindergartens were in operation in the United States by 1873, with a total of 1,252 students (Spring, 1997).

As a minister and the son of a minister, Froebel believed in the Christian philosophy of striving for unity between people and God (Ulich, 1968), in the purity of the child's spirit, and in combining these beliefs in the kindergarten. Froebel wrote, "Education consists in leading man as a thinking intelligent being growing into a self-conscious and free representation of the inner law of Divine Unity, and in teaching him ways and means thereto" (as cited in Doherty, 1977, p. 5). The earliest American kindergartens were in private schools (Gangel & Benson, 1963; Morgan, 1986). Saint Louis, Missouri, became the home of the first public school kindergarten, in 1873 (Beatty, 1995; Shapiro, 1983). William Torrey Harris, a well-known school superintendent in Saint Louis, was the first to suggest that kindergartens become a permanent part of the nation's school system. As a result of Harris's support and work on behalf of the kindergarten, these schools spread throughout the country (Beatty, 1995; Shapiro, 1983). Initially, kindergartens functioned much like the Head Start program of today, in the sense that they were geared toward poor urban children.

Froebel's influence on American education was even greater in the 20th century than it was in the 19th century. H. A. Hamilton wrote,

> There has, indeed, been a response to Froebel in . . . America . . . primarily because of his clear religious emphasis. Some have found that they could accept an educational theory which saw the goal in terms of unity with God. (as cited in Slight, 1961, p. 178)

Froebel believed that it was very important that the school day always begin and end by praying and giving praise to God, especially by singing hymns. He generally allotted over an hour to Bible reading and praise (Slight, 1961).

Froebel claimed children at the pre-first-grade level were best equipped for life and school not by practicing long academic drills, but by maturing and developing the personality qualities most conducive to successful scholarship and citizenship (Ulich, 1957). He maintained that teachers should develop a kindergarten curriculum dedicated to developing the mind, the spirit, and the body all at the same time (Beatty, 1995; Graves, 1912). To educators such as Froebel, Pestalozzi, and Mann, the ultimate goal of early childhood education was growth and maturity.

By 1898, there were 4,363 kindergartens in the United States, reaching nearly 200,000 students (Parkway, 1998). Given that the first kindergartens were geared toward poor urban children, they helped equalize educational opportunity across the country.

Maria Montessori

Maria Montessori (1870–1952) was a remarkable individual, the first woman in Italy to graduate from medical school as well as that nation's first female doctor (Lillard, 1972; Standing, 1957). Early in her career, Montessori had no desire to be an educator. After beginning her career as a doctor, she took a position as professor of anthropology at the University of Rome (Kramer, 1976). As time went on, her work increasingly involved special education students who were mentally handicapped. Montessori developed certain "hands-on" techniques that she believed helped these children develop to their highest capacity (Applebaum, 1971; Kramer, 1976). The more Montessori experienced success with special education students, the more she realized that her techniques would work well with normal children as well (Kramer, 1976; Montessori, 1956, 1965; Standing, 1957). By 1907, Montessori was applying her approach to the broader elementary school population (Kramer, 1976; Lillard, 1972; Standing, 1957).

Many European educators noted that children were making remarkable progress using the Montessori approach, and some American educators came to Italy to witness its implementation firsthand (Standing, 1957). Soon, Montessori received invitations to introduce her program in the United States. In fact, the Montessori approach gained such favor that in 1912, she was invited to the White House (Lillard, 1972). Prominent Americans received her with such favor that President Woodrow Wilson's daughter and Alexander Graham Bell became the secretary and president, respectively, of the American Montessori school organization (Lillard, 1972). Bell was so enthusiastic about Montessori schools that one of her first schools in America was started in his home (Lillard, 1972).

Montessori had a number of deep convictions that ultimately influenced the way that her schools were run. First, she believed that schools should encourage children's spontaneous exploratory tendencies through real, hands-on activities (Montessori, 1965, Standing, 1957). In this sense, Montessori employed a liberal, child-centered approach to education. She believed that it was important for children to actually experience what they were learning (Standing, 1957). For example, one unique aspect of her approach was that children should touch the letters of the alphabet while they were learning them (Montessori, 1965).

Second, Montessori believed that it was essential for adults to guide children in the learning process. She claimed that adults knew what was best for children and therefore they should prepare the curriculum (Montessori, 1965). Montessori notes, "The child left without guidance, is disorderly in his movements. . . . We should rather give 'order' to his movements, leading them to those actions towards which his efforts are actually tending" (p. 52). According to Montessori, each child went through "sensitive periods," which were important for children to learn particular truths; only adults could know and anticipate when these periods would occur, and therefore their guidance was especially important (Montessori, 1956, 1965; Standing 1957). In this sense, Montessori was more traditional in her approach than the liberal philosophy of those such as Dewey and Kilpatrick (Kilpatrick, 1914/1971; Standing, 1957).

Montessori believed that rather than a purely child-centered approach to the curriculum, the teacher should offer the child predetermined sets of choices of what to study (Kilpatrick, 1914/1971; Montessori, 1965). Although these choices allow the child to give input into what he or she desires to learn, the structure ensures that the child will progress from easy to harder material. In Montessori's view, children will not prefer to choose more difficult material unless they are first exposed to it (Montessori, 1965; Standing, 1957). Otherwise, there is a danger that children will desire to study easy material all the time and they will be less challenged.

Third, Montessori believed in the value of moral education. As a devout Roman Catholic, she averred that the spiritual side of education was extremely important (Montessori, 1965,

p. 88). She believed that religion should play a major part in how a class should be run, especially in things such as the teaching of right and wrong and good manners (Montessori, 1965; Standing, 1957). She claimed that moral education was especially important if children were to learn self-discipline and if the world were ever to experience future peace (Montessori, 1965; Standing 1957). As a result, Montessori believed that it was important for teachers to appeal to the spirit of the child.

Fourth, Montessori (1965) argued that it was essential for adults to respect children. As one element of respect, Montessori believed that parents should be involved in their children's education (Lillard, 1972).

Although Montessori schools were initially popular after 1910, her approach did run into some problems. The first of these was that, beginning in 1914, some of the nation's most prominent liberals began to criticize her approach. The most notable attack came from William Kilpatrick, of Columbia University, the second-leading educator in the country (Kramer, 1976; Lillard, 1972). He wrote an entire book dedicated to criticizing Montessori's approach, *The Montessori System Examined* (Kilpatrick 1914/1971). In this book, Kilpatrick used strong words to denounce the approach, objecting because he found it too structured to the extent that there was a "repression" of child development (p. 30). He noted that in the mind of many Americans, children's advancements in reading emerge "in an almost occult manner" (p. 53). Kilpatrick influenced some of the most noted educators in the country, those "who had the influence and power to really accept or reject Montessori" (Applebaum, 1971, p. 232). John Dewey was also critical of the Montessori approach (Kramer, 1976).

The primary reason the nation's two leading liberals criticized Montessori is that she believed that the curriculum should be much more structured than they envisioned (Montessori, 1965). In essence, in Montessori's method, a child was given a choice of what to study, within the framework of structured choices determined by the teacher (Kramer; 1976, Montessori, 1965). For example, a Montessori teacher might give a child four books to read. The child would then choose which book he or she desired to read. After this was accomplished, the teacher would then offer a second set of four books, slightly more difficult than the first set. This process would continue with the child's choices made within a predetermined structure that ensured that he or she was reading progressively more difficult material. In addition, Montessori (1965) believed that children should repeat actions until they have mastered a certain activity.

In Montessori's (1956, 1965) view, young children in particular are not old enough to know what material they need to learn, and unless the teacher makes sure children are exposed to more difficult material, they will not learn to love harder assignments. Montessori was critical of liberal schools because in her view, they often required students to study less when they needed to study more (Standing, 1957). She challenged Darwin's notion that intelligence was fixed at birth and believed that urging children to work hard to reach their potential was key. Lillard (1972) notes, "Darwin's theory of evolution based on natural selection had left the American culture of the early 1900s with a belief in fixed intelligence. Montessori's emphasis on early cognitive development was clearly out of step with this concept" (p. 19). In contrast, Kilpatrick and Dewey were inspired by the views of Darwin and Spencer and believed that children had an innate sense of what they needed to learn (Dewey, 1966; Egan, 2002).

Montessori schools suffered because of Kilpatrick's attacks (Campbell, 1970). In addition, Montessori was very particular about how schools applied her methods, and this limited the growth of the movement (Kramer, 1976). Furthermore, some parents believed that Montessori's approach usurped the role of the parent (Appelbaum, 1971). Nevertheless, there is no question that Kilpatrick's criticism hurt the most.

Despite the decline and near extinction of American Montessori schools during the 1920s, 1930s, and 1940s, Montessori clearly had changed the nature of early childhood education. First, she added to the new emphasis the nation now placed on nursery school and kindergarten education. American nursery schools started around 1900, but really did not become popular until World War I (Forest, 1935; Davis, 1947; Meyer, 1967). Montessori's focus on early childhood development unquestionably contributed to this emphasis (Appelbaum, 1971). Although the explosive growth of the kindergarten was well in place before Montessori emerged, her philosophy confirmed this existing emphasis (Appelbaum, 1971).

Eventually, in the late 1950s, Montessori schools reemerged as an educational force. Around this time, the "*Sputnik* shock" had hit the nation. Lillard (1972) notes that by this time,

> Dewey's theories and practices supposedly held sway in the classroom. . . .
> Americans—particularly parents—were alarmed by the results of our education
> system. A significant number of children couldn't read above the most rudimentary
> level after twelve years of schooling. (pp. 16–17)

As a result, Americans became more open to alternative approaches (Lillard, 1972).

All in all, Montessori (1956, 1965) did a creative job of combining the liberal and conservative perspectives on education. She developed a classroom approach that reflected both the child-centered approach of the liberal school of thought and the preparation- and character-centered emphasis of the conservative approach.

NEOCONSERVATIVES

The neoconservative movement of the 1890s and early 1900s was an attempt to redefine conservativism in a way that was palatable to moderates, conservatives, and moderate liberals who had reservations about some dimensions of modern liberalism (Dupuis, 1966).

H. H. Horne

H. H. Horne (1874–1946) was a professor of education at New York University (NYU). He was Dewey's chief critic and even dedicated a book to the assessment of Dewey's philosophy, titled *The Democratic Philosophy of Education: A Companion to Dewey's Democracy and Education* (1932). In it, Horne voiced four main objections to Dewey's philosophy of education. First, he believed that Dewey's approach was too mechanical. Second, he asserted that Dewey was too relativistic. Third, he averred that Dewey's theories were merely opinion and had not been scientifically verified. Fourth, he warned that Dewey's approach would create friction between parents and teachers. These four aspects are described as follows.

"Too Mechanical." Horne (1932) pointed out that although Dewey spent a considerable amount of time focusing on teaching methods and the curriculum, he spent almost no time focusing on the personality traits needed to be an effective teacher. Horne (1932) notes, "The failure to appreciate the significance of personality is one of the striking features of this philosophy" (p. 531). Horne (1923, 1937) believed that the teacher should be loving, kind, supportive, and an example to the children, and he claimed that the best pedagogical techniques in the world will not compensate for these and other teacher personality qualities: "Educating is the purposeful providing of an environment. . . . It is personality in and behind the environment that counts most" (p. vii). Horne (1923, 1932) pointed out that Dewey put considerably less emphasis on teacher personality characteristics than any previous leading educator, including Noah Webster, Horace Mann, and so forth. Horne (1931a), maintained that Dewey and Spencer's theories "separate the process of education from the process of complete living" (p. 48).

To Horne (1931a, 1931b), teaching was more than just perfecting pedagogical skills and the curriculum; it was a "ministry" (p. 57). Instruction should involve not only the strengthening of children's intellectual capacities but also helping them develop "a spiritual sense" (Horne, 1923, p. 176).

In Horne's view, Dewey's approach was simply too mechanical. He believed that Dewey's assumption was that if a teacher simply used certain child-centered education techniques, children would flourish (Horne, 1931a, 1931b, 1937). He asserted that Dewey almost entirely overlooked loving responsibilities the teacher must extend toward the children and the community, which were essential for education to succeed (Horne, 1931b). For example, he believed that teachers needed to be kind enough to take interest in children between class meetings. He also advocated teachers' active involvement in helping others outside the school, asserting that "such activities include extending invitations, visiting the sick, working to improve the social conditions of the community in any way" (Horne, 1931b, p. 240). Such actions were not only important acts of love and service but would also serve as fine examples for children.

"Creates Friction Between Parents and Teachers." Horne (1923, 1931b, 1932, 1937) asserted that Dewey's emphasis that children needed to turn away from parental values and develop their own values via experience undermined parents. He believed that placing so much emphasis on one's own experiences and those of other children was capricious and was bound to create friction with parents. He averred that teachers needed to support parental values unless they were clearly destructive.

"Too Relativistic." Horne (1932, p. 137) stated that a major problem with Dewey's theory was that it contained no "ought." He further argued that Dewey's theories were "only relative and mechanical, not absolute and teleological" (Horne, 1923, p. 67). He believed that Dewey, because of his distaste for absolute values, failed to place enough emphasis on moral education and consequently did not seek to go beyond the "human point of view" (Horne, 1931a, p. 44). As a devout Christian, Horne (1931a) was unsatisfied with Dewey's and Spencer's educational theories, which he believed were "suited to an intelligent human animal, not to man made in the image of God" (p. 55).

Horne agreed with Plato's belief that no one is totally relativistic; that is, everyone has some notion that, in an absolute sense, certain things are right and certain things are wrong, (Dupuis, 1966). Plato would argue, using a contemporary example, that the Holocaust and racism are just plain wrong. In addition, he believed that everyone holds absolute beliefs regarding certain things (Plato, 2004). Along these lines, many would argue that Dewey's claim that there are no absolutes is extreme (Horne, 1932) and, furthermore, that Dewey's assertion that all we have to do is look at the world around us to discover what "should be" does not factor in the extent to which people have been deceived throughout the ages, for example, in World War II Germany.

"Not Scientifically Verified." Horne believed that Dewey introduced a plethora of interesting instruction ideas but had little evidence to demonstrate their effectiveness. He asserted that Dewey should take time out to test the validity of his theories before presenting them as truth (Horne, 1931b). Horne was just as concerned about presumptuousness of the educational world, in that they were so willing to accept Dewey's theories as being true without testing them.

Although most educators of the era ultimately chose to espouse Deweyism despite Horne's concerns, Horne's objections established a foundation on which future critics of Dewey would build.

Educational Debate: Dewey's Educational Pillars

- What do you think of Dewey's main tenets of his educational philosophy?
- What do you like?
- What do you dislike?
- What do you think of his emphasis on experience and communication among students?
- What do you believe are his strongest arguments?
- Do you, as did Horne, have concerns about some of Dewey's beliefs? If so, what are those concerns?

William James

William James (1842–1910) believed that perhaps the chief function of education was to develop good habits in students. He declared that the mind was a "mental machine" (James, 1958, p. 20) that needed to be enhanced in its effectiveness via the development of strong habits. James (1958) stated, "Education, in short, cannot be better described than by calling it the organization of acquired habits of conduct and tendencies to behavior" (pp. 36–37).

According to James (1958), for habits to become ingrained in the human mind, the student needs to (a) be completely focused on the lesson and (b) be willing to practice and repeat certain disciplines and exercises until they are nearly perfected. Furthermore,

In teaching, you must simply work your pupil into such a state of interest in what you are going to teach him that every other object of attention is banished from his mind; then reveal it to him so impressively that he will remember the occasion to his dying day. (p. 25)

James emphasized such disciplines as verbal recitation of passages of classical literature and doing written exercises repeatedly until he or she mastered certain academic abilities. James (1958) stated, "The extreme value of verbal recitation as an element of complete training may nowadays be too much forgotten" (p. 46). To hear material is important but not sufficient to be thoroughly engrained into the individual: "Habit simplifies the movements required to achieve a given result" (p. 108).

From James's (1890) perspective, habits pervade almost every aspect of life and are prerequisites if one is to fully enjoy life: "There is no more miserable human being than one in whom nothing is habitual but indecision" (p. 122). James averred that both mental and moral habits must be developed in the schoolroom. However, "the peculiarity of moral habits, contradistinguishing them from intellectual acquisitions, is the presence of two hostile powers" (James, 1958, p. 59). Therefore, in James's view, because the development of moral habits is complicated by the battle between good and evil, it is more difficult for the teacher to develop good moral habits than good intellectual habits in the lives of the students.

James's emphasis on habits and his belief that the brain acts much like a mental muscle has influenced America's education system even to this day. Many American workbooks use the terms *exercises* and *drills,* which were largely James's terms. His efforts to integrate psychological concepts into the classroom helped establish the discipline of educational psychology.

Edward Thorndike

Edward Thorndike (1874–1949) is considered the father of modern-day statistics and did much to advance the discipline of educational psychology. The fact that Thorndike played such a major role in both the development of statistics and educational psychology helped make educational psychology into a very statistics-based discipline. His publications on educational psychology read more like statistics books than theory-based works on educational psychology (Thorndike, 1910, 1931). Thorndike helped found the *Journal of Educational Psychology* and establish it as a definitively research-based academic journal (Thorndike, 1962).

Thorndike (1910, 1931, 1949) was interested in maximizing the effectiveness of teaching and learning. He believed that the use of statistical and research analysis could help determine what pedagogical approaches were best. Toward this end, Thorndike (1949) developed an approach he called "connectionism." He believed that much as in classical conditioning or the behaviorist approach to learning, children learned best when they made associations or connections between each stimulus and response. He asserted that these connections were biologically based and therefore it was imperative that teachers educate children with the goal of helping them make various connections among the truths they learn in school. As a neoconservative, Thorndike also believed that it was important for teachers to note which of their lessons enabled children to maximize their learning. In Thorndike's view, these were the lessons that teachers needed to use again. Thorndike's emphasis was in contrast to the more liberal Herbartian approach. Herbart believed that the determining factor that made a lesson successful was whether children enjoyed it (Dunkel, 1970).

Thorndike (1949) realized that mental connections could be complex. One of the chief goals of his research was to understand the nature of individual differences that might give insight into why certain connections form in certain children but not in others.

Thorndike investigated the issue of individual differences for another reason as well. He was very interested in the extent to which individual differences were due to environmental factors and how much they were due to genetic factors (Thorndike, 1910). He was interested in the influence of race, socioeconomic status, and the family (Thorndike, 1910, 1931, 1949, 1962). In the final analysis, Thorndike (1962) concluded that there are biological differences that exist at birth, but environmental influences cause differences between individuals to either increase or decrease over time.

Thorndike believed that statistical analysis could be applied to investigate a wide array of educational issues. Among these issues were the effects of class size, the age of students within a class, and the types of tests teachers administered (Thorndike, 1910, 1962). He also developed interest inventories that he believed, rightly or wrongly, could help individuals determine a career direction. He helped develop many of the principles of determining variance and comparing distributions that statisticians still use today.

Thorndike contributed a great deal to the world of schooling. Although some regard the mixing of education and statistics as producing rigidity, Thorndike focused on the ideas of testing the new educational theories of the day rather than just accepting untested theories.

CONCLUSION

The persuasiveness of Dewey helped establish liberalism as more than just a series of largely unused theoretical ideals and as practical beliefs that penetrated every level of the educational establishment. Other individuals, such as Kilpatrick, Scott, Spencer, and Counts, contributed a great deal to quickly developing a worldview that helped define what it meant to function as a liberal educator. Some of Dewey's ideas were controversial, as H. H. Horne was quick to assert. Consequently, the debate about Dewey's ideas endures to this day. Nevertheless, however one might perceive Dewey, he conspicuously changed the direction of late-20th-century educational debate.

DISCUSSION QUESTIONS

1. William H. Kilpatrick asserted that Montessori schools were too rigidly structured. Do you agree or disagree with his perspective?

2. H. H. Horne would criticize the contemporary emphasis on how to become a good teacher and claim that too little attention is paid to whether a teacher is loving, patient, and encouraging. Do you agree or disagree with Horne's assertion?

3. What do you think Friedrich Froebel would say if he were alive to see American kindergartens today?

4. Some people would respond to the idea of a "play movement" as something antithetical to education. However, there are others who believe that play is indispensable to the learning process. What role do you think play has in the educational process and in facilitating learning?

REFERENCES

Appelbaum, P. (1971). The growth of the Montessori movement in the United States, 1909–1970 (Doctoral dissertation, New York University, 1971). *Dissertation Abstracts International, 7211442.*

Bagley, W. C. (1915). Editorial. *School and Home Education, 35,* 4–5.

Barnard, H. (1842). *Papers of Henry Barnard.* Manuscript collection of Trinity College Watkinson Library, Hartford, CT.

Baylor, R. M. (1965). *Elizabeth Palmer Peabody: Kindergarten pioneer.* Philadelphia: University of Pennsylvania Press.

Beatty, B. (1995). *Preschool education in America.* New Haven, CT: Yale University.

Beineke, J. A. (1998). *And there were giants in the land.* New York: Peter Lang.

Blinderman, A. (1976). *Three early champions of education: Benjamin Franklin, Benjamin Rush, and Noah Webster.* Bloomington, IN: Phi Delta Kappa Educational Foundation.

Blount, J. M. (2002). Ella Flagg Young and the Chicago schools. In A. R. Sadovnik & S. F. Semel (Eds.), *Founding mothers and others: Women educational leaders during the progressive era* (pp. 163–176). New York: Palgrave.

Campbell, D. N. (1970). *A critical analysis of William Heard Kilpatrick's "The Montessori System Examined."* Unpublished doctoral dissertation, University of Illinois.

Cavenagh, F. A. (Ed.). (1932). *Herbert Spencer on education.* Cambridge, UK: Cambridge University Press.

Chamberlin, G. J. (1961). *Parents and religion: A preface to Christian education.* Philadelphia: Westminster Press.

Counts, G. S. (1932). *Dare the school build a new social order?* New York: John Day.

Cousins, N. (1958). T. C. in the thirties. In W. First (Ed.), *University on the heights* (pp. 73–79). New York: Doubleday.

Cranston, M. W. (1957). *John Locke: A biography.* London: Longmans.

Davis, M. D. (1947). *Schools for children under six: A report on the status and need for nursery schools and kindergartens.* Washington DC: U.S. Department of Education.

DeGarmo, C. (1889). *Essentials of method.* Boston: Heath.

Dewey, J. (1902). *The child and the curriculum.* Chicago: University of Chicago Press.

Dewey, J. (1910). *The influence of Darwin on philosophy.* New York: Holt.

Dewey, J. (1915). *The school and society.* Chicago: University of Chicago Press.

Dewey, J. (1920). *Reconstruction in philosophy.* New York: Holt.

Dewey, J. (1922). *Human nature and conduct.* New York: Holt.

Dewey, J. (1925). *Experience and nature.* Chicago: Open Court.

Dewey, J. (1929). *John Dewey's impressions of Soviet Russia and the revolutionary world: Mexico-China-Turkey, 1929.* New York: Teachers College Press.

Dewey, J. (1938). *Experience and education.* New York: Macmillan.

Dewey, J. (1964). *John Dewey's impressions of Soviet Russia and the revolutionary world: Mexico-China-Turkey, 1929.* New York: Teachers College Press.

Dewey, J. (1966). *Democracy and education.* New York: Free Press. (Original work published 1916)

Dewey, J. (1977a). *John Dewey: The middle works, 1899–1924, Volume 2: 1902–1903* (J. Boydston, Ed.). Carbondale: Southern Illinois University Press.

Dewey, J. (1977b). *John Dewey: The middle works, 1899–1924, Volume 3: 1903–1906* (J. Boydston Ed.). Carbondale: Southern Illinois University Press.

Dewey, J. (1977c). *John Dewey: The middle works, 1899–1924, Volume 4: 1907–1909* (J. Boydston, Ed.). Carbondale: Southern Illinois University Press.

Dewey, J. (1978a). *John Dewey: The middle works, 1899–1924, Volume 5: 1908* (J. Boydston, Ed.). Carbondale: Southern Illinois University Press.

Dewey, J. (1978b). *John Dewey: The middle works, 1899–1924, Volume 6: 1910–1911* (J. Boydston, Ed.). Carbondale: Southern Illinois University Press.

Dewey, J. (1978c). *John Dewey: The middle works, 1899–1924, Volume 7: 1912–1914* (J. Boydston, Ed.). Carbondale: Southern Illinois University Press.

Dewey, J. (1980a). *John Dewey: The middle works, 1899–1924, Volume 9: 1916* (J. Boydston, Ed.). Carbondale: Southern Illinois University Press.

Dewey, J. (1980b). *John Dewey: The middle works, 1899–1924, Volume 10: 1916–1917* (Boydston, J., Ed.). Carbondale: Southern Illinois University Press.

Dewey, J. (1990). *The school and society/The child and the curriculum.* Chicago: University of Chicago Press.

Dewey, J. (1998). *Experience and education.* West Lafayette, IN: Kappa Delta.

Doherty, C. H. (1977). *Kindergarten and early schooling.* New York: Prentice Hall.

Douglas, P. H. (1958). The unloosened mind. In W. First (Ed.), *University on the heights* (pp. 69–72). New York: Doubleday.

Downs R. B. (1978). *Friedrich Froebel.* Boston: Twayne.

Duncan, D. (1908). *The life and letters of Herbert Spencer.* London: Methuen.

Dunkel, H. B. (1970). *Herbart and Herbartanism: An educational ghost story.* Chicago: University of Chicago Press.

Dunn, J. (1955). *Retreat from learning.* New York: David McKay.

Dupuis, A. M. (1966). *Philosophy of education in historical perspective.* Chicago: Rand McNally.

Egan, K. (1983). *Education and psychology.* New York: Teachers College Press.

Egan, K. (2002). *Getting it wrong from the beginning.* New Haven, CT: Yale University Press.

Filler, L. (1965). *Horace Mann on the crisis in education.* Yellow Springs, OH: Antioch Press.

Forest, I. (1935). *The school for the child from two to eight.* Boston: Ginn.

Gangel, K. O., & Benson, W. S. (1983). *Christian education: Its history and philosophy.* Chicago: Moody.

Giarelli, J. R. (1995). The social frontier, 1934–1943: Retrospect and prospect. In M. E. James (Ed.), *School reconstruction through education: The philosophy, history, and curricula of a radical idea* (pp. 27–42). Norwood, NJ: Ablex.

Graves, F. P. (1912). *Great educators of three centuries.* New York: Freeport.

Harbison, E. E. (1964). *Christianity and history, essays.* Princeton, NJ: Princeton University Press.

Herbart, J. (1852). *Samtliche werke* [Complete works]. Leipzig, Germany.

Hiner, R. (1988). The city of Sodom enquired into: Educational analysis in seventeenth century New England. In E. McClellan & W. J. Reese, *The social history of American education* (pp. 3–22). Urbana: University of Illinois Press.

Holy Bible. (1973). Grand Rapids, MI: Zondervan.

Horne, H. H. (1923). *Idealism in education or first principles of making men and women.* New York: Macmillan.

Horne, H. H. (1931a). *The essentials of leadership.* New York: Macmillan.

Horne, H. H. (1931b).*This new education.* New York: Abingdon.

Horne, H. H. (1932).*The democratic philosophy of education: Companion to Dewey's democracy and education.* New York: Macmillan.

Horne, H. H. (1937).*The philosophy of Christian education.* New York: Fleming H. Revell.

Hunt, T. C., & Maxson, M. M. (1981). *Religion and morality in American schooling.* Washington, DC: University Press of America.

James, W. (1890). *Principles of psychology.* London: Macmillan.

James, W. (1958). *Talks to teachers on psychology and to students on some of life's ideals.* New York: Norton.

Kilpatrick, W. H. (1925a). *Foundations of method.* New York: Macmillan.

Kilpatrick, W. H. (1925b). How shall early education conceive its objectives? *Childhood Education, 2*(3), 1–12.

Kilpatrick, W. H. (1926). *Education for a changing civilization.* New York: Macmillan.

Kilpatrick, W. H. (1935). *Foundations of method.* New York: Macmillan.

Kilpatrick, W. H. (1936). *Remaking the curriculum.* New York: Newson.

Kilpatrick, W. H. (1937). *Education for a changing civilization.* New York: Macmillan.

Kilpatrick, W. H. (1951). *Philosophy of education.* New York: Macmillan.

Kilpatrick, W. H. (1971). *The Montessori system examined.* New York: Arno. (Original work published 1914)

Kramer, R. (1976). *Maria Montessori: A biography.* New York: Putnam.

Krips H., & McGuire, J. E. (1995). *Science, reason, and rhetoric.* Pittsburgh: University of Pittsburgh.

Lageman, E. C. (2002). Experimenting with education: John Dewey and Ella Flagg Young at the University of Chicago. In C. H. Siegfried (Ed.), *Feminist interpretations of John Dewey* (pp. 31–46). University Park: Pennsylvania State University.

Lawson, D. E., & Lean, A. E. (Eds.). (1964). *John Dewey and the world view.* Carbondale: Southern Illinois University Press.

Lee, J. (1915). *Play and playgrounds.* New York: Playground and Recreation Center of America.

Lee, J. (1925). *The normal course in play.* Washington, DC: McGrath.

Lillard, P. P. (1972). *Maria Montessori: A modern approach.* New York: Schoken.

Locke, J. (1947). *On politics and education.* New York: Classics Club.

Low-Beer, A. (1969). *Herbert Spencer.* London: Macmillan.

Mann, H. (1849). *Twelfth annual report.* Washington, DC: Massachusetts Board of Education.

Mann, M. P. (Ed.). (1907). *Life of Horace Mann.* Washington, DC: National Education Association.

Marrou, H. I. (1956). *A history of education in antiquity.* New York: Sheed & Ward.

Martin, J. (2002). *The education of John Dewey: A biography.* New York: Columbia University Press.

McManis, J. T. (1916). *Ella Flagg and a half-century of Chicago public school.* Chicago: A. C. McClurg.

Meyer, A. E. (1967). *An educational history of the American people.* New York: McGraw-Hill.

Monroe, P. (1940). *Founding of the American public school system.* New York: Macmillan.

Montessori, M. (1956). *The child in the family* (N. R. Cirillo, Trans.). Chicago: Henry Regnery.

Montessori, M. (1965). *Dr. Montessori's own handbook.* New York: Schocken Press.

Moreo, D. (1996). *Schools in the Great Depression.* New York: Garland.

Morgan, J. (1986). *Godly learning: Puritan attitudes towards religion, learning, and education.* New York: Cambridge University Press.

Parkway, F. W. (1998). *Becoming a teacher.* Boston: Allyn & Bacon.

Peabody, E. P. (1886). *Lectures in the training schools for kindergartens.* Boston: Heath.

Peltzman, B. R. (1998). *Pioneers of early childhood education.* Westport, CT: Greenwood.

Piaget, J. (1950). *The nature of intelligence.* New York: Harcourt, Brace.

Plato (2004). *Protagoras and Meno.* Ithaca, NY: Cornell University Press.

Rafter, N. (2004). The criminalization of mental retardation. In S. Noll & J. W. Trent Jr. (Eds.), *Mental retardation in America* (pp. 232–257). New York: New York University.

Ravitch, D., & Finn, C. (1987). *What do our seventeen year olds know?* New York: Harper & Row.

Rippa, S. A. (1997). *Education in a free society.* White Plains, NY: Longman.

Rousseau, J. (1945). *The confessions of Jean-Jacques Rousseau.* New York: Modern Library. Original work published 1763.

Rousseau, J. (1979). *Emile, or, on education.* New York: Basic Books. (Original work published 1762)

Sarason, S. B., & Doris, J. (1969). *Psychological problems in mental deficiency.* New York: Harper & Row.

Schilpp, P. A. (1939). *The philosophy of John Dewey.* Evanston, IL: Northwestern University Press.

Scott, C. (1908). *Social education.* Boston: Ginn.

Shapiro, M. S. (1983). *Child's garden: The kindergarten movement from Froebel to Dewey.* University Park: Pennsylvania State University Press.

Slight, J. P. (1961). Froebel and the English primary school of today. In E. Lawrence (Ed.), *Friedrich Froebel and English education* (pp. 95–124). London: Routledge.

Smith, J. K. (1994). Ella Flagg Young. In M. S. Seller (Ed.), *Women educators in the United States, 1820–1993* (pp. 553–563). Westport, CT: Greenwood Press.

Spencer, H. (1851). *Social statics, or, the conditions essential to happiness specified, and the first of them developed.* London: John Chapman.

Spencer, H. (1902). *Facts and comments.* Osnabruick, West Germany: Proff.

Spencer, H. (1908). *First principles.* London: William & Norgate.

Spencer, H. (1932). *Herbert Spencer on education.* Cambridge, UK: Cambridge University Press.

Spencer, H. (1963). *Education: Intellectual, moral, and physical.* Patterson, NJ: Littlefield, Adams.

Spencer, H. (1966). *The works of Herbert Spencer.* New York: Appleton (Original work published 1904).

Spring, J. (1997). *The American school 1642–1996.* White Plains, NY: Longman.

Standing, E. M. (1957). *Maria Montessori: Her life and work.* New York: New American.

Strauss, L. (1968). *Liberalism, ancient and modern.* New York: Basic Books.

Thorndike, E. L. (1910). *Educational psychology.* New York: Teachers College Press.

Thorndike, E. L. (1931). *Human learning.* New York: Century.

Thorndike, E. L. (1949). *Selected writings from a connectionist's psychology.* New York: Appleton-Century-Crofts.

Thorndike, E. L. (1962). *Psychology and the science of education.* New York: Teachers College Press.

Ulich, R. (1957). *Three thousand years of educational wisdom.* Cambridge, MA: Harvard University Press.

Ulich, R. (1968). *A history of religious education.* New York: New York University Press.

Walker, W. (1963). *A philosophy of education.* New York: Philosophical Library.

Wallace, J. (1995). Red teachers can't save us: Radical educators and liberal journalists in the 1930s. In M. E. James (Ed.), *School reconstruction through education: The philosophy, history, and curricula of a radical idea* (pp. 43–56). Norwood, NJ: Ablex.

Yulish, S. M. (1980). *The search for a civic religion.* Washington, DC: University Press of America.

CHAPTER 9

The Great Depression and the Long-Term Effects of World War II and the Cold War on American Education

National crises naturally exert dramatic influences on education. The Great Depression, World War II, and the Cold War presented some of the greatest challenges the United States had ever faced. Despite these formidable challenges, overall, the nation's students and schools responded well. During the Great Depression, the overwhelming majority of schools encountered significant financial cutbacks. However, both schools and students responded well. Schools learned to operate with tremendous efficiency, and student achievement ascended to great heights. World War II caused the nation and its school system to confront racial problems that still existed in the United States. Battling two largely racist countries, Germany and Japan, during World War II was a grim reminder of what racism and exclusionary politics could do if allowed to continue indefinitely. Finally, the Cold War and especially the launching of the *Sputnik* caused the United States to reevaluate its instructional priorities.

EDUCATIONAL CHALLENGES OF THE GREAT DEPRESSION (1929–1941)

Cutbacks

The financial cutbacks of the Great Depression put a great deal of strain on the education system. The extent of the Great Depression is difficult for people who didn't experience it to imagine. By its height, in 1933, unemployment was 25%, and the U.S. gross national product (GNP) had been cut almost in half (U.S. Bureau of the Census, 1975). Ultimately, the tumbling economy had a dramatic impact on the American education system (Tyack, Lowe, & Hansot, 1984). Nevertheless, amazingly, overall student academic achievement actually rose during the Depression (Jeynes, 2004; Ravitch, 1974). The question is, how could academic achievement have risen so much in the midst of such turbulent economic times? Educators frequently complained about the lack of reading materials during the Great Depression. Teachers, therefore, called on the government to invest 5-to-10 times the norm on library expenditures (Tyack et al., 1984). Educators maintained a considerable amount of anxiety over the rates of government support during the Depression. Teachers in places such as Chicago and Detroit even demonstrated, accusing the government of "undermining the whole enterprise of education" (Tyack et al., 1984, p. 45). There was a great deal of friction between teachers and the Roosevelt administration; teachers and principals felt left out of the New Deal even though they shared its goals. Although school people feared federal domination, they wanted federal money.

A lot of finger pointing persisted during the Great Depression (Graves, 2002; Moreo, 1996; Tyack et al., 1984). The schools and the country, as a whole, toiled in the midst of a crisis. Finger pointing gains popularity in times of crisis. Parents blamed the educators for canceling certain education programs, and so forth. Educators blamed Roosevelt and the federal government. David Tyack and his colleagues (1984) maintain that President Roosevelt possessed "a low opinion of educators" (p. 108), which helped explain his budget cuts. Roosevelt eventually did an excellent job of helping the nation out of the Depression, but teachers initially did not give him the appreciation that was later warranted.

With all these grim facts, we might be tempted to conclude that the Great Depression could not possibly have contributed to the academic upswing that occurred during this period. Such a conclusion, however, would be premature. In fact, some positive developments did occur in part because of the Depression. The most amazing is that student academic achievement increased considerably during the period (Berrol, 1982; Ravitch, 1974). At first, such a trend seems difficult to imagine. However, certain facts contributed to this reality.

How Students Increased Achievement During the Great Depression

1. When life is tough economically, people tend to appreciate education and try hard in school. Research indicates that students in America, and overseas as well, often work harder when the nation's economy is going through a rough time. During the Great Depression, the number of books that students read soared (New York City Association of Teachers of English, 1937). They were hungry for learning and appreciated the availability of education. During the Depression, a number of major cities kept records of the number of books read by students. Overall, the amount of time students spent reading was much higher than one sees today. Some students read more than a book a day, and reading two to three books a week was not unusual at all (New York City Association of Teachers of English, 1937). There is a strong relationship between how much students read and their test scores. Therefore, it should come as no surprise that achievement rose during the Great Depression.

2. People thought that education was a way out of economic hard times. The Great Depression actually helped the quality of education. Many people, particularly immigrants, came to the realization "that the road to alleviation was neither charity nor revolution, but in the last analysis, education" (Cremin, 1962, p. 59). There was a sense in which people viewed the school system as a potential economic salvation.

Today, people still often look to education as a means of achieving a higher level of income. College applicant numbers tend to soar during times of recession. The Ivy League

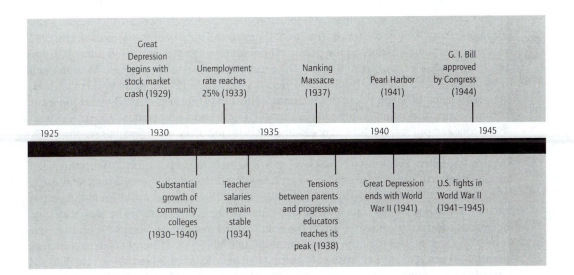

schools generally do not admit more students during recessions. Rather, because they receive more applicants, they tend to turn more away. However, the enrollment at community colleges often skyrockets during recessions, perhaps rising 20% to 40% (Brint & Karabel, 1989).

During the Great Depression, education would have been seen as a means of economic salvation even more than it is today (Tyack et al., 1984). This is because today, it is quite possible and indeed common for a person who has never attended college to make more than someone who has attended college. You can make very good money in the United States today as a truck driver or garbage collector, even if you never attended college (U.S. Department of Labor, 2005). However, 50 to 100 years ago, it was very rare for people with these kinds of jobs to make more than those with college degrees.

3. The Great Depression attracted many people to the teaching field because of reevaluated priorities. The events in New York and Washington, D.C., on September 11, 2001, caused many Americans to reevaluate their priorities and purposes in life (Friedman, 2002). Similarly, the events of the Great Depression caused Americans to assess what life was all about, and as a consequence of this, their estimation of education rose (Tyack et al., 1984). Many people concluded that they wanted to make a difference in the world by becoming teachers. The increased interest in teaching caused more qualified people to enter the field.

4. Teacher salaries remained fairly stable during the Great Depression, attracting more qualified people to the field. Selma Berrol (1982) notes,

> The onset of the depression also provided a pool of extremely well qualified teachers. . . .The twenties and thirties were a golden age in the New York schools and made it easier for everyone to forget the fact that this was an exceptional period in a previously turbulent history. (p. 40)

To say that federal spending for education decreased does not tell the whole story (Ravitch, 1974; Tyack et al., 1984). Traditionally, state and local governments have emerged as the primary contributors to the public school system. People expressed interest in the teaching profession during the Great Depression because teachers' salaries remained rather stable (Ravitch, 1974; Tyack et al., 1984). Statistics indicate that schools did make budget cuts during the Depression, but reducing capital expenditures offered by far the most common way of slashing expenditures (National Education Association [NEA], 1933). In 1932, for example, salaries for many eastern states for teachers and principals stood at 98% of the 1929 level (Tyack et al., 1984). In contrast, in the nation as a whole, by 1933, personal income had fallen 45% from its 1929 level (U.S. Bureau of the Census, 1975). With this steep drop in personal income, the relative salary level of teachers looked very attractive (Berrol, 1982; Jeynes, 2004; Ravitch, 1974). Schools did everything in their power to maintain the salaries of teachers. In the state of New York, cities, primarily represented by New York City, decreased capital outlays by 54.4% at the height of the Depression versus pre-Depression levels (Tyack et al., 1984). At the same time, expenditures for staff members decreased less than 1% (Tyack et al., 1984). Instead of cutting teachers' salaries, schools not only reduced capital expenditures but also cut certain programs that seemed less essential, for example, reducing night and adult classes as well as summer schools. Textbook orders were one of the first things to be cut (Ravitch, 1974; Tyack et al., 1984).

The decision by schools to cut back textbook purchases and capital outlays in order to keep teacher salaries stable was supported by many of the leading educators of the time. For example, John Dewey (1933) supported cutting back substantially on the ordering of textbooks, since they were "instruments of torture of a departed age" (p. 14). As Moreo (1996) notes, Dewey's statement is consistent with his emphasis on experience.

The decision to forgo the purchase of textbooks and reduce capital outlays was fairly universal across the country (Moreo, 1996). Moreo notes that schools as far west as Seattle made major cutbacks in textbook purchases in order to ensure a quality education for children in other respects via reasonable teacher salaries. The priority that many Americans placed on education was largely a result of the severe economic nature of the times: Education was seen as a way out (Moreo, 1996; Tyack et al., 1984).

A Closer Look: Tough Economic Conditions Often Produce an Appreciation for Education

Many Americans today think of education as a right. However, teachers in poor nations overseas or of certain immigrants coming to the United States point out that many of these students view education as a wonderful privilege. Economic hardship often influences the perspective of children. Teachers regularly report on some of the joys of teaching children in impoverished countries who have a real hunger to learn, because they treasure the joy of receiving an elementary school education (Baker & LeTendre, 2005). Traditionally, some of the hardest-working school children in the United States have been the sons and daughters of recent immigrants (Banks & Banks, 1995; Glazer, 1985). The parents of these immigrants often do not speak English well and are not well educated and therefore find it difficult to procure a white-collar job. However, they make sacrifices as their children study diligently, so that their children can experience the American dream.

With teachers' salaries relatively stable and the salaries of other occupations in steep decline, teaching as a profession looked especially attractive. The extent of the financial allurement of teaching becomes apparent in the following statement by Thomas Brooks (1981): "In 1934, New York City teacher salaries averaged $3,931, which compared favorably with that of doctors, $3,382, while skilled construction workers averaged $942 per year" (p. 209).

At first, these statistics stir some amazement. Yet when one recalls that a doctor's salary depends upon a steady flow of patients to see him, the above statistics are quite logical. In the midst of such severe times, many people probably abstained from seeing doctors unless it proved absolutely necessary. In all likelihood, few civilians went for their annual checkups. They simply could not afford to go. In addition, doctors probably felt pressured to significantly reduce their charges to accommodate the unemployed and the underemployed. The fact that a doctor's patients in the 1930s primarily came from the close-knit community around him probably led many doctors to see certain destitute individuals for free. We should remember that in the midst of such glaring poverty, a doctor who continued to draw wealth at the expense of the unemployed could quickly become labeled as a crooked or debauched physician.

The relatively stable teacher salaries caused many people to enter the field who perhaps would not have considered teaching as a profession.

While, on the surface, the economy seemed like it could not have helped the education system, in reality, in the form of the Great Depression, it probably did.

General Conditions in Education During the Great Depression

The economic climate for schools was more difficult away from the East Coast (Gerdes, 2002; Graves, 2002; Moreo, 1996; Tyack et al., 1984). According to a 1933 NEA report, schools in the rural areas were particularly hard-hit. For example, in Alabama, overall expenditures were down 47% in rural areas and 32% in city areas during the early 1930s. In Mississippi, rural and city school expenditures declined 42% and 24%, respectively, during the same period. In Michigan, the declines were 37% and 38%, respectively, Illinois experienced declines of 28% for rural schools and 32% for city schools. In contrast, representative declines for Eastern rural and city schools, respectively, were 18% and 13% for New York, 11% and 5% for Massachusetts, and 13% and 15% for Pennsylvania.

A number of educators became increasingly aware of the challenges faced by rural schools. In 1939, Dr. John Sexson, the Pasadena, California, superintendent of schools, declared at the annual convention of the American Association of School Administrators, "Perhaps the most tragic result of the depression is the havoc it has wrought in the educational institutions of the smaller communities" (Moreo, 1996, p. 107). The "Dust Bowl," a severe drought that struck several middle-southern states, accentuated the degree to which rural areas were hit by the Great Depression (Gerdes, 2002; Graves, 2002; Moreo, 1996; Tyack et al., 1984). The disparity between teachers' salaries in the cities versus those in rural areas widened during the Depression, so that rural teachers during this period often made between one third to one half of the pay made by city teachers (Moreo, 1996).

However, all across the country, school leaders did everything they could to maintain teacher salaries (Tyack et al., 1984). Almost without exception, this meant reducing the purchase of library books and cutting back on building maintenance and expenditures (Ravitch, 1974; Tyack et al., 1984). As has been mentioned previously, eastern city schools were quite determined to maintain teacher salaries and were very persistent in this regard. For example, between 1931 and 1934, New York cut capital outlays by 97 % but cut teacher and staff salaries by only 2 % (NEA, 1933). In Pennsylvania, city schools cut these expenditures by 71 % and 2 %, respectively (NEA, 1933). This trend, however, held for the remainder of the nation's cities as well. In Michigan, capital expenditures were down 91 %, and teacher salaries were down only 13 %, Missouri and Virginia each cut capital outlays by over 90 % and actually managed to increase teacher salaries (NEA, 1933). Utah and Colorado city schools almost totally eliminated capital expenditures, so steadfast were they in their attempts to maintain teacher salaries (NEA, 1933).

In the first years of the Great Depression, rural schools suffered economically considerably more than city schools (Tyack et al., 1984). Most people anticipated that the Depression would not last long. However, by the end of 1932, it was clear that the urban schools would soon be facing the very same challenges that rural ones faced (Tyack et al., 1984).

The most horrific years of the Great Depression for the nation as a whole were 1932 to 1934 (Graves, 2002; Moreo, 1996; Tyack et al., 1984). The same can also be said for the school system (Graves, 2002; Moreo, 1996, Tyack et al., 1984). The height of the school sacrifices occurred during this period. From 1929 to 1932, the Dow Jones average of 65 stocks lost nearly 80 % of its value (U.S. Bureau of the Census, 1975). The tax profits of American corporations dropped from $8.6 billion to negative $2.7 billion, and the nation's GNP was sliced in half (U.S. Bureau of the Census, 1975). Certain sectors of the economy were especially devastated by the Great Depression, including construction, which declined by 80 %, and manufacturing, which was cut back by two thirds (Tyack et al., 1984; U.S. Bureau of the Census, 1975). By 1932, about 55,000 businesses had closed, and by 1933, between 9,000 and 10,000 banks had failed (Graves, 2002; Tyack et al., 1984). Although schools did their best to maintain teacher salaries, over 7,000 teachers lost their jobs during the Depression (Graves, 2002; Tyack et al.,1984). By 1933, the nation's unemployment rate had surged to 25 % (U.S. Bureau of the Census, 1975). Truly, the Great Depression was the most deleterious economic situation that the United States had ever faced (Gerdes, 2002; Graves, 2002; Moreo, 1996; Tyack et al., 1984; U.S. Bureau of the Census, 1975).

The severity of the financial squeeze for schools naturally reflected the dire economic situation that the nation faced. The worst of the Great Depression struck the nation in 1932 to 1934, and these were the toughest years for the schools as well (Gerdes, 2002; Graves, 2002; Moreo, 1996; Tyack et al., 1984). In 1933, national income bottomed out at $40.2 billion, after being at $87.8 billion in 1929 (U.S. Bureau of the Census, 1975). During about the same period, overall school expenditures dropped from $2.3 billion to $1.7 billion (U.S. Bureau of the Census, 1975). Nevertheless, one should note that school expenditures did not rival the drop in personal income, which reflected the degree to which Americans viewed education as a high priority. The statistics on school capital outlays reveals the extent to which schools cut back on capital expenditures to support teacher salaries. According to the U.S. Bureau of the Census (1960), school capital outlays dropped from $371 million in 1929 to 1930, to merely $59 million in 1933 to 1934. Fortunately, this number began to recover in subsequent years, reaching $171 million in 1935 to 1936, and $239 million in 1937 to 1938 (U.S. Bureau of the Census, 1960). The figure from 1937 to 1938 is especially noteworthy because 1937 was the second dip of the Great Depression (U.S. Bureau of the Census, 1960). The extent to which the nation demonstrated a commitment to education during the Depression is also manifested in the "share of the pie" that educational expenditures accounted for in personal income during this period. In 1929, education expenditures were

3.0% of personal income (U.S. Bureau of the Census, 1960). By 1932, this percentage had soared 63%, to 4.9% of personal income, the largest increase in this percentage over such a short period in American history (U.S. Bureau of the Census, 1960).

Tensions Between Practical Parents and Idealistic Academics

The Great Depression caused a rift to develop between parents and many of the academic elite educators of the time (Moreo, 1996), who looked at the economic crisis of the time and concluded that perhaps capitalism had been revealed for its shortcomings and that a new social order was needed (e.g., Counts, 1932). Many of them thought it was the ideal time to promote their progressive agendas (Counts, 1932; Kilpatrick, 1937; Wallace, 1995). In contrast, most families at the time were in desperate financial situations and thought of education as a means of ensuring the future survival of their children (Moreo, 1996). Consequently, an odd disparity emerged for progressivism during the 1930s. During this period, the progressive movement made great progress in the halls of academia (Moreo, 1996; Wallace, 1995). In contrast, because parents were concerned with practical matters rather than ideological ones, the progressive movement faced some real resistance among parents sending their children to public schools (Moreo, 1996). Progressive attempts to influence schools in Gary, Indiana; Roslyn, Long Island; and other places eventually faced resistance from school leaders and especially from parents (Moreo, 1996).

In the case of the Roslyn, Long Island, school district parents complained that the progressive approach emphasized "activities and projects," when in order to ensure future employment, the parents wanted to return to an emphasis on reading, writing, and arithmetic (Moreo, 1996, p. 138). Many parents circulated a petition to force the schools to focus on preparation. A state report released in 1938 further convinced the parents that their children were not being properly taught and prepared (Moreo, 1996).

While the Great Depression delayed the application of progressive education in many public schools, it hastened the acceptance of progressive education among many academic educators (Spring, 1997; Wallace, 1995). This set the stage for an even more determined attempt to apply new child-centered ideas to education in future decades (Palmer, 2001).

Final Thoughts on the Great Depression and Education

The Great Depression was a challenging era in education. Nevertheless, despite the obstacles, schools served their purpose by giving people hope and a means by which the next generation could arise above the limitations of the times (Gerdes, 2002; Graves, 2002; Moreo, 1996; Tyack et al., 1984). All these factors worked together so that during a time of great economic strain, in many respects, the American education system actually flourished.

THE IMPACT OF WORLD WAR II ON EDUCATION

Foundation Stone for the Civil Rights Movement

The most poignant impact of World War II on American education had everything to do with its impact on America's willingness to deal with racism in the country. Via fighting the Nazis and the Imperial Japanese Army, Americans were confronted with the horrors of racism (Gardner, 2002; Greenberg, 1994). Seemingly, every major war in which the United States participated had a major influence on the country. The Revolutionary War facilitated a large number of Americans becoming concerned about education (Tewksbury, 1932; Urban & Wagoner, 2000). The Civil War opened the minds of the nation to the need of a common set of values to ensure that something like slavery would never happen again (Cubberley, 1909, 1920). Hence, the common school movement strengthened considerably following the Civil War. World War I helped give modern-day definition to the American public school system and also caused people to see the need for common values (Monroe, 1952). Similarly, World War II centered on fighting the racism of the Germans and the Japanese, who were both convinced that they were the superior race (Ballou, 1945; Bix, 2000; Goldhagen, 1996; Packard, 1987). In the midst of fighting such extreme forms of racism, the United States had to confront its own racism (Berman, 1970; Bernstein, 1970; Bremner & Reichard, 1982). Although America's racism was nothing like the extreme forms found in Germany and Japan, if the United States was to be the leader of the free world, racism had to be confronted.

Just as the Revolutionary War, the Civil War, and World War I impacted American education to a great degree, World War II was no exception. But the effects of World War II were quite different from those produced by the Civil War. The Civil War had caused a fear that America could easily be divided and fall apart. That concern set the stage for an emphasis on national unity, assimilation, and, ultimately, Americanization. The ethnic strife in Europe that led to World War I intensified these concerns. A greater emphasis on assimilation and Americanization prevailed.

What Americans witnessed in World War II, however, was far different from what they had seen either in the Civil War or in World War I. They fought two nations whose peoples were convinced that they were the superior race. As a result of this sense of superiority, the German Nazis and the Imperial Japanese Army exterminated millions upon millions of people simply because of their race (Dawidowicz, 1975; Edgerton, 1997; Russell, 1958; Tanaka, 1993). The idea that the Nazis would have concentration camps, put Jewish people in ovens, and even use Jewish corpses to make lampshades and soap was absolutely horrifying to Americans (Dawidowicz, 1975; Johnson, 1997). The idea that the Imperial Japanese army would also slaughter millions, leaving tens and perhaps hundreds of thousands of bodies in the Bay of Nanking in the Nanking Massacre, behead people buried up to their necks, and customarily torture and kill prisoners of war (POWs) was equally horrifying (Brook, 1999; Chang, 1997; Kerr, 1985; Levene & Roberts, 1999; Maga, 2001; Michno, 2001; Rees, 2002; Sajor, 1998). Although Americans tend to be much more aware of the German atrocities, Asians are well aware that the Japanese atrocities were also frightening in their scope (Chang, 1997; Hicks, 1995; Maga, 2001; Sajor, 1998; Tanaka, 1993).

The estimates are that Nazis slaughtered roughly about 10 million people, including 6 million Jewish people (Dawidowicz, 1975; Johnson, 1997). The other 4 million included Slavs and other ethnic minorities (Dawidowicz, 1975; Johnson, 1997). According to the beliefs of several Asian neighbors of Japan, the Japanese Imperial army slaughtered millions as well (Brook, 1999; Chang, 1997; Levene & Roberts, 1999; Li, 2003; Michno, 2001; Philippines, Resident Commissioner to the United States, 1945; Rees, 2002; Sajor, 1998). Americans are more aware of the atrocities of the Nazis than those of the Japanese Imperial Army for reasons that will be addressed shortly.

The acts of racial hatred by the Germans and Japanese during World War II speak of what can happen to a nation if it does not keep racism in check. The German war atrocities are well documented and well publicized. Among the casualties, the 6 million Jews have received the most attention (Johnson, 1997). This emphasis is justified, especially since Jewish people made up such a small percentage of the world's population. The Nazi Germans' purposeful murder of millions of Jews constitutes one of the most blatant acts of genocide in modern history, vanquishing a considerable portion of the European Jewish community (Johnson, 1997). However, even these numbers do not fully communicate the unspeakable horrors committed against the Jews. The Nazis committed millions of Jewish people to merciless concentration camps (Dawidowicz, 1975; Goldhagen, 1996). They killed their Jewish captives in ovens or in gas chambers and used the remains of Jewish people to sell for profit. They made lampshades out of the skin of Jewish people and soap out of the oil of their skin. As gruesome as the acts against the Jewish people were, German racism extended to other groups as well. They killed 4 million civilians from other ethnic groups, including Slavs and Gypsies (Dawidowicz, 1975; Goldhagen, 1996).

For various reasons, German World War II atrocities are more fully publicized by the American media than Japanese World War II atrocities even though they are more comparable than most Americans are aware (Philippines, Resident Commissioner to the United States, 1945; Tanaka, 1993). There are three reasons for this. First, Americans tend to be much more aware of European history than they are of Asian history, and Asian people are generally much more aware of the Japanese atrocities than Americans are (Tanaka, 1993). In fact, for decades, Asian politicians from China, South Korea, the Philippines, Taiwan, Hong Kong, Singapore, Malaysia, and elsewhere have bitterly complained that Japanese school children should be taught about these atrocities to make certain that they do not happen again (Li, 2003; Sajor, 1998). Second, the United States committed 85% of its war machinery to Europe (Koistinen, 2004; Mills & Rockhoff, 1993; Moore, 1944). Therefore, Americans concentrated more of their attention on Europe. The United States needed an ally in Asia to serve as a major defense against the spread of communism. To ensure that Japan would be a reliable ally against the communists, the U.S. government and military agreed not to publicly reveal many of the atrocities that took place (Tanaka, 1993). Nevertheless, as time went on, many of the atrocities became public knowledge (MacKay, 1995).

The Japanese committed many racially motivated atrocities (Brook, 1999; Chang, 1997; Levene & Roberts, 1999; Li, 2003; Michno, 2001; Rees, 2002; Sajor, 1998; Tanaka, 1993). As many Asians know, the list is a long one. The Nanking Massacre and the Rape of Manila resulted in hundreds of thousands of deaths and are the most publicized atrocities. However, many Asian nations are well aware that the list of atrocities and victims is much longer (Brook, 1999; Chang, 1997; Levene & Roberts, 1999; Li, 2003; Michno, 2001; Rees, 2002; Sajor, 1998; Tanaka, 1993). The totals may well rival the totals from Germany. Racism likely played a large role in the fact that while only 4% of Allied POWs died in German and Italian prison camps, over 27% died in Japanese prison camps (Tanaka, 1993). There are many accounts of Japanese torturing POWs, killing them, and even cannibalism. The maltreatment of POWs was commonplace and well documented (Tanaka, 1993).

As in the case of the German Nazis, the numbers tell only part of the story. Eyewitness accounts indicate that there were so many slain bodies in Nanking Harbor that it was nearly impossible to see the water, and the water that one could see was tinted red (Brook, 1999;

Chang, 1997). In other areas of Asia, civilians were frequently buried alive with only their heads showing, and then they were decapitated using machetes (Tanaka, 1993). POWs were subjected to a variety of inhumane, painful tortures, including being victimized by biological weapons while in captivity.

Both the Germans and the Japanese had one very important quality in common: They both believed that they were the superior race (Johnson, 1997). Their racist acts were a direct consequence of this belief.

Through the availability of the knowledge of the atrocities, American leaders, especially, and the American public, became more aware of the dangers of racism and what exclusionary politics can eventually lead to. As a result, World War II led to a desire to take action to reduce racism and to reduce exclusion on the basis of race (Berman, 1970; Bernstein, 1970; Gardner, 2002). Previously, as a result of the Civil War and World War I, the United States had witnessed the divisions that can result from placing too much emphasis on individual differences. As a result, the American policy in government, education, and everyday life focused on emphasizing people's similarities. As a result of World War II, Americans saw the excesses that can result if a government and culture insists that every person be the same (Berman, 1970; Bernstein, 1970; Gardner, 2002). This and another occurrence helped usher in a period that allowed for a greater tolerance of individual differences and the full flowering of the civil rights movement (Berman, 1970; Bernstein, 1970; Gardner, 2002; Harding, Kelly, & Lewis, 1997).

The other event was the fact that the United States had established itself as a superpower. Since 1900, the United States had functioned as the world's largest economy (Johnson, 1997; U.S. Bureau of the Census, 1975). But that meant less than it might seem, in terms of the international stage. The United States had been reluctant to exercise its power in world affairs (Johnson, 1997). It did not have an empire, like the colonial powers of Europe. In addition, the United States put very little money into military production and hence had a very weak military (Prange, Goldstein, & Dillon, 1981). Considering the size of its economy, the United States had an embarrassingly small military presence (Johnson, 1997). The fact that on December 7, 1941, by simply attacking one site, Japan wiped out much of the U.S. Navy demonstrates just how small the American Navy was (Prange et al., 1981). For over 40 years prior to World War II, the United States enjoyed the highest standard of living in the world, even during the Great Depression, which also indicates how poor the world economy was (Johnson, 1997; U.S. Bureau of the Census, 1975). However, if America's per capita income was high, her per capita military strength was quite low. As a result, the British pound still remained the world's dominant currency (Johnson, 1997).

All of this changed with the advent of Pearl Harbor and the Axis victories in Europe and Asia in World War II (Johnson, 1997). Before Pearl Harbor, the United States was often referred to by Europeans as the "sleeping giant" (Daniels, 1966; Johnson, 1997; Kaufmann & Kaufmann, 1996). There was seemingly an endless stream of economic power in the United States, but it appeared that Americans refused to use that power. For some time before the United States entered World War II, in December 1941, Churchill pleaded with Roosevelt to enter the war on the side of the Allies (Johnson, 1997). Although the United States provided some military supplies to Britain through the lend-lease program, Churchill was frustrated that the United States would not enter the war (Johnson, 1997). He knew how much power the United States could wield if, indeed, the government made a decision to do so (Churchill, 1941). Churchill was so convinced that the United States could tilt the scales decisively in World War II, that when he heard of Japan's attack on Pearl Harbor, his reaction was quite different than most people might expect: "To have the United States at our side was to me the greatest joy. . . . So we had won after all! Hitler's fate was sealed. Mussolini's fate was sealed. As for the Japanese, they would be ground to powder" (Churchill, 1941, p. 1). Churchill knew America's economic prowess would help ensure victory. The U.S. response to Pearl Harbor was the most massive military buildup over such a short period of time in history (Johnson, 1997). The United States built up its military to such a degree that even though only 15% of the military production was committed to the Asian front, this was more military hardware than all of the Japanese Empire, that is, Eastern Asia, produced. By the end of World War II, the United States was not only the world's foremost economic power but also the world's foremost military power (Johnson, 1997). The United States now produced most of the world's military goods and had over half of the world's GNP (Johnson, 1997; U.S. Bureau of the Census, 1975).

Added Insight: The U.S. Economy and Its Effect on Education

The primary reason Churchill believed that the U.S. entrance into the World War II would translate into victory was that the United States was the world's leading economic power. Beginning in 1900, the nation possessed the world's largest economy and the highest standard of living (Business International, 1980; O'Hara & O'Hara, 2000). Even throughout the Great Depression, the United States maintained the highest standard of living in the world. The peak of the nation's dominance was reached in the 1950s, when the United States enjoyed what was by far the world's highest economic quality of life, and even though the United States had only 6% of the world's population, the nation produced over 50% of the world's GNP (Business International, 1980; O'Hara & O'Hara, 2000). American prosperity enabled Americans to spend an unprecedented amount to support schools and colleges for a large part of the 20th century (Bernstein & Adler, 1994).

Beginning in 1973, however, the United States lost its position as the nation with the highest standard of living in the world, and now there are several nations who enjoy a higher standard living than America (Business International, 1980; O'Hara & O'Hara, 2000). Many of the country's most prodigious industrial companies of 1900 to 1973 are shadows of what they once were (Bernstein & Adler, 1994; Melman, 1985). Moreover, most economists believe that it is inevitable that China and possibly one or two other nations will, in the foreseeable future, surpass the United States in economic might (Asia Pulse News, 2003; Gittens, 2005). Few world leaders question the notion that the United States is in economic decline (Asia Pulse News, 2003; Gittens, 2005). Some are concerned about how the nation's decline could influence the country's ability to fund education at a high enough level.

- How do you feel the country's economic decline could influence the future funding of education in this country?
- Can better schools revitalize the nation's economy so that future funding issues do not become a problem?

With such great power, however, came great responsibility. The United States, torchbearer of democracy, was now in a fish bowl (Berman, 1970; Bernstein, 1970; Gardner, 2002). The world closely observed the United States to see whether it lived up to the high standards of democracy of which it spoke. In the case of the civil rights of African Americans, the United States clearly did not live up to those standards (Harding et al., 1997).

World War II, therefore, made the United States more aware than ever of its own hypocrisy. Wendell Wilkie (1945), the unsuccessful Republican presidential candidate in 1940, wrote in 1945 that the war "has made us conscious of the contradiction between our treatment of Negro minority and the ideals for which we are fighting" (p. 321). The editors of *Fortune* magazine (1945) stated, "In the consciousness of all peoples in the world this war is being fought for and against the idea of racial superiority" (p. 335).

Although the United States had fought 4 long years against the attitude of racial superiority evident among the Nazi Germans and the Imperial Japanese, too many Americans still possessed feelings of racial superiority over African Americans (Ashmore, 1994; Bartley, 1995; Harding et al., 1997). Many people thought that racism would decrease after the Civil War and the Emancipation Proclamation. But in reality, in many ways, racism increased in America following the Civil War (Hill & Jones, 1993; Johnson, 1997). There were two reasons for this: First, free African Americans both in the North and the South now competed with Whites for the same jobs (Hill & Jones, 1993). This caused many Whites, particularly in the North, to increase their resentment toward African Americans. Second, Darwinism was growing in America, and Darwin strongly believed that Whites were the superior race and that Black African tribes like the Hottentot would eventually become extinct because they were inferior (Darwin, 1859; Gould, 1981). Darwin's book, often referred to incorrectly as *The Origin of the Species,* actually has a much longer title. However, because many people find the longer title offensive, it generally is not used. The full title is *On the Origin of Species by Means of Natural Selection, or The Preservation of the Favoured Races in the Struggle for Life* (1859).

Stephen Jay Gould, a Harvard biologist, was very critical of what he perceived as the racism of Darwinists. Darwinists constantly used science as a means of proving that Whites were superior to African Americans (Gould, 1981). These scientific studies place many people in academia at the cutting edge of racism. It is clear from the content of Darwin's writings that he means exactly what "favoured races" indicates. Darwin (1859, 1871) believed that the process of natural selection truly favored certain superior races over the inferior races and that this is what enabled various species to survive. Life presented species with a continuous array of new challenges that required adaptation. To the extent that certain organisms adapted properly and improved their species, that part of the species would survive and flourish (Darwin, 1859, 1871). Evolutionists (Spencer, 1851, p. 323) called this principle "the survival of the fittest." According to Darwin's theory, these adaptations could occur along any number of dimensions. In his view, the crucial adaptation that enabled the human race to survive and distinguished it from all other forms of life was its intelligence. Darwin (1859, 1871) asserted that the "more intelligent" races would enable the human race to adapt and survive.

According to Darwin (1859, 1871), there were therefore clearly more intelligent and less intelligent races. In Darwin's view, the "intelligent races," especially the White race, would make the appropriate adaptations, carry on the gene pool, and enable the human race to survive and flourish (Darwin, 1859, 1871). Darwin stated that the smallest gap between humans and apes was between the Black African and the gorilla (Darwin, 1871). He predicted that as evolution through natural selection continued, this gap would widen because the "superior races" would carry on the gene pool. Darwin (1871) stated,

> The break will then be rendered wider, for it will intervene between man in a more civilized state, as we may hope, than the Caucasian, and some ape as low as a baboon, instead of at the present between the Negro or Australian and the gorilla. (p. 201)

Darwin's racism had a dramatic impact on American educators and, in fact, educators from all around the world. In his classic book *The Mismeasure of Man,* Stephen Jay Gould (1981), of Harvard, examined the spread of racism in education and research as a result of the spread of Darwinism. In referring to the above passage and others like it, Gould notes, "Charles Darwin . . . wrote about a future time when the gap between human and ape will increase by the anticipated extinction of intermediaries like chimpanzees and Hottentots" (p. 36). Gould presents evidence of the ramifications of these beliefs, which included researchers constantly trying to understand why Whites were superior intellectually to African Americans. The fact that Darwin's theory became so popular after the Civil War probably contributed to the slow pace of African American progress after the initial reforms of the late 1860s, 1870s, and 1880s. Many researchers and educators believed that slavery was wrong, but as a result of Darwin's thinking, they also thought it was understandable that the superior races would succeed while the inferior ones would not. In the minds of many professors and teachers, slavery was an unfortunate consequence of the superior dominating the inferior (Gould, 1981).

Had these racist beliefs, based on the Darwinian rubric, been principally held by uneducated and ignorant people, the consequences would have been minimized. However, Gould (1981) notes that the educated were the ones who most intensely held Darwin's beliefs: "The Civil War lay just around the corner, but so did 1859 and Darwin's *Origin of Species.* Subsequent arguments for slavery, colonialism, racial differences, class structure, and sex roles would go forth primarily under the banner of science" (p. 72). Because many researchers in the physical sciences, social sciences, and education embraced the tenets of Darwinism, institutions of education probably did as much to contribute to racism as any other mainstream group. The relationship between Darwinism and racism was so poignant that it caused Alfred Russel Wallace, the cofounder of the theory of natural selection with Darwin, to retract his assertion that natural selection was responsible for differing mental abilities. Gould (1981) observes,

> Alfred Russel Wallace, a co-discoverer of natural selection with Darwin, is justly hailed as an antiracist. Indeed, he did affirm near equality in the innate capacity of all peoples. Yet, curiously, this very belief led him to abandon natural selection and return to divine creation as an explanation for the human mind—much to Darwin's disgust. (p. 38)

Darwin's theory had a particular impact on education because one of his followers, Herbert Spencer (1851, 1904/1966), dedicated his life to making the theory of evolution applicable to education (Egan, 2002; Rafter, 2004). As was stated in Chapter 8, Spencer believed that for an education system to be effective, it has to be customized with the survival of the species in mind. He asserted that to maximize the efficacy of teaching, classes should be designed only with the "fittest" individuals in mind (Spencer, 1851, 1904/1966). To the extent that Darwin and his colleagues defined Whites as the "fittest" and African Americans as the "least fit," this clearly translated into the education of Whites taking precedence over the education of African Americans. Many southern educators in the 1900s used Darwin's theories as an excuse to practice segregation (Egan, 2002; Rafter, 2004).

It was well-known to Americans at this time that Hitler adhered strongly to the ideas of Darwin and Nietzsche on the issue of racial superiority (Gould, 1992). The Japanese

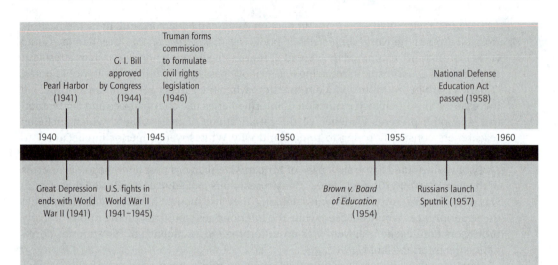

Emperor Hirohito adamantly insisted that his followers adhere to an ancient Japanese myth that asserts that Japanese are distinguished, were planted in Japan in ancient times, and are therefore unique, superior, and unrelated to the other races of the earth (Edgerton, 1997). As a result of World War II, the eyes of Americans were open to the ramifications of espousing any doctrine of racial superiority, whether it was based on evolutionary theory or the type of "ancient astronaut" theory to which the Japanese adhered. Whatever horrors the German and Japanese governments were instigating were done in the name of racial superiority, in their quest to bring what they considered "civilization" to their corners of the world. Was not the segregation of the South also done in the name of racial superiority?

Although the racial wrongs committed by Americans, especially in the South, may seem mild in comparison with those of the Axis powers, two facts stood out in the minds of Americans (Berman, 1970; Bernstein, 1970; Gardner, 2002). First, whatever the nature of racial problems in the United States, they were nevertheless based on the notion that one race can be more "fit" than another (Gould, 1981). Second, the United States, unlike Germany and Japan, was built on the notion that "all men are created equal." World War II was a reminder to the nation that although the United States was founded on this principle, Americans were not honoring that declaration in a number of respects (Finding & Thackery, 1996; Ianniello, 1965; Irons & Cuitton, 1993; Jackson, 1992). In World War II, the United States was fighting for that principle against nations set in opposition to it. After the war, Americans realized that we needed to be certain that we more completely abided by that creed ourselves.

Admittedly, it was more than World War II alone that opened the door for major civil rights reforms. The rapid spread of television during the postwar period was a dramatic blessing for the civil rights movement (Bartley, 1995; Hill & Jones, 1993). This was especially true because millions of Americans were almost totally unaware of how African Americans were treated in the Deep South (Bartley, 1995). Even though some Americans may have read of acts of mistreatment or heard about them on the radio, they found it inconceivable that African Americans could be treated with such prejudice (Bartley, 1995). Naturally, there was prejudice in the North as well. However, the difference in the way African Americans were treated in places like Alabama, Mississippi, and Arkansas was so foreign to many Americans, it was difficult to for them comprehend (Bartley, 1995). Televisions were able to bring the reality of the African American struggle in the Deep South into the homes of millions of Americans. One can argue that if the television had existed 100 years before, the original intentions of the Emancipation Proclamation and the constitutional amendments that followed would have been realized at a much earlier time.

Given that, as Wilkie declared, World War II focused on race, it is no accident that President Harry S. Truman launched a new emphasis on civil rights within months of the war's end. In 1946, the first year after the war, Truman established the Committee on Civil Rights (Berman, 1970; Bernstein, 1970; Gardner, 2002; Shull, 1999). This committee was designed to examine civil rights issues and recommend legislation. In 1947, Truman became the first president to speak before the National Association for the Advancement of Colored People (NAACP) (Berman, 1970; Bernstein, 1970; Gardner, 2002; Shull, 1999). Although many people associate the civil rights movement with events like the 1954 *Brown v. Board of Education* Supreme Court decision and the 1963 "I Have a Dream" speech, by Martin Luther King Jr., these were the climaxes of a movement that received a major "gust of wind" in its sails from the events of World War II (Berman, 1970; Bernstein, 1970; Fireside & Fuller, 1994; Gardner, 2002).

The fact that it took the most expansive war in history to cause Americans to readdress issues regarding race raises a provocative question: Why is it that it takes crises such as World War II for such pertinent issues to be addressed? Is it because without crises, humans tend to get too comfortable and even complacent to deal with some of the most pressing issues of the time? Is it because without national crises to pull a country together, the tendency is for most people to be selfish and self-absorbed? Is it because it takes a crisis to give people the wisdom to see things as they really are?

Whatever the reasons, humankind does have a tendency to prefer the path of inaction and the status quo rather than address salient issues of the day. There is probably some truth in all the statements of the previous paragraph. And if one is tempted to think that the current generation is any wiser, all one has to do is observe the changes that occurred after September 11th, 2001, to realize that similar truths hold today. The events of September 11th reminded Americans of what was important, even as World War II did, and as a product of these catastrophes, many people's values have been changed forever.

Educational Debate: Why Does It Take a Crisis to Produce Change?

American leaders partially dealt with the issue of racism in the events surrounding and following the Civil War (Johnson, 1997). The passage of the 13th, 14th, and 15th Amendments greatly ameliorated the situation faced by African Americans and other minority groups. However, as this book has repeatedly delineated, racism did not decrease to the extent that it should have. The nation finally revisited the racism issue following World War II, due to waging war against two racist countries.

- The question emerges, why does it take a crisis, such as World War II, for example, to cause a nation to deal with an issue (in this case racism) that should have been more thoroughly dealt with years before?

THE RISE OF COMMUNITY COLLEGES

The development of the public community college was an American phenomenon that started in Joliet, Illinois, in 1901 (Brint & Karabel, 1989). Private community colleges existed many decades before then, often, but not always, as women's junior colleges. These private junior colleges really did not birth a movement, but events in 1892 at the University of Chicago did. In 1892, the president of the University of Chicago, William Rainey Harper, separated instruction at the university into two sets of 2 years. By 1896, the University of Chicago called the lower set of courses "junior college" and the upper range of courses "senior college" (Brint & Karabel, 1989). In 1900, Harper convinced the leaders of the University of Chicago to award an associate's degree to those who had finished the junior college coursework. As Jencks and Riesman (1968) note, "Its aim was to provide high school graduates in a given district with two more years of free education before they either took a job or went away to college" (p. 481). In the first years of its existence, the community college often "grew up with little sense of distinctive institutional purpose. They were hodge-podges of courses and curricula, established in response to real or imagined local demands" (Jencks & Riesman, 1968, p. 481).

During the first quarter century of the public community college's existence, it did not experience a dramatic growth in enrollment. By the 1927/1928 academic year, only 44,855 people were enrolled in community colleges across the nation (Brint & Karabel, 1989). By the time the Great Depression was about to begin, only a few states pursued the establishment of the community college with any vigor. Four states together, California, Illinois, Missouri, and Texas, possessed about 60% of the nation's community college enrollment (Brint & Karabel, 1989).

However, ironically, during the Great Depression, the junior college underwent a real boost in enrollment. The Depression caused people to look to education as a means out of tough times. Beginning with the Depression, California took a clear lead in the development of junior colleges. In 1930, California had 35 junior colleges, with 13,392 students, which represented nearly one third of the total number of Americans in junior college at the time (Eells, 1931).

The junior college movement, in many respects, was a more controversial issue than most educational movements. This was because a growing number of educators, especially in California, viewed it as a means to increase educational opportunity and yet at the same time divert people away from 4-year institutions (Brint & Karabel, 1989). Interestingly enough, this approach did not have as much of an impact as one would think. Students attending junior colleges did not come from socioeconomic backgrounds much different from those of students attending state colleges, although, as one would expect, junior college students did come from different socioeconomic backgrounds than those attending private schools (Brink & Karabel, 1989).

During the Great Depression, both state and private community colleges showed strong growth. During this period, the number of community colleges in the United States grew from 277 in 1929/1930 to 456 by 1939/1940 (Brint & Karabel, 1989). Of those 456 junior colleges, 217 were public, and 239 were private (Brint & Karabel, 1989). The state junior colleges grew especially in California and in the Northeast, and private religious colleges grew in the Midwest.

By the end of World War II, due to the tremendous growth of junior colleges, the federal government was taking this institution more seriously. Shortly after the war, President Truman appointed a commission to study the junior college movement (Brint & Karabel, 1989). The commission stated that junior colleges were an important movement not only as means of improving education but also for strengthening community. For this reason, the commission recommended that the term *junior college* be changed to *community college* (Brint & Karabel, 1989). The commission stated in its 1947 report,

> The failure to provide any core of unity in the essential diversity of higher education is a cause for grave concern. A society whose members lack a body of common experience and common language is a society without a fundamental culture, it tends to disintegrate into a mere aggregation of individuals since community of values, ideas, and attitudes is essential as a cohesive force. (President's Commission on Higher Education, 1947, pp. 48–49)

In the post–World War II years, several states initiated major efforts to build community colleges. These states included New York, Florida, North Carolina, Maryland, and Washington (Brint & Karabel, 1989).

As community colleges surged in number and enrollment, it was clear that they served a number of purposes. First, they served those who did not wish to go to a 4-year college. Second, they were attended by many who were unable to be accepted by a 4-year college. Third, they aided those who could not afford to go to college (Brint & Karabel, 1989).

Since the 1950s, the main debate about community colleges is what their role should be in modern society. In the 1950s, James Conant, former president of Harvard, argued that community colleges should educate the masses. Similarly, he believed that it is necessary for only 5% of Americans to study to be professionals and that 4-year institutions could train these people (Brint & Karabel, 1989). Beginning in 1960, community college enrollment soared from 451,000, to 1.63 million in 1970, to 10 Million in 2003 (CNN, 2003).

THE COLD WAR

In many respects, the Cold War, which lasted from 1946 until about 1990 or 1991, penetrated the American psyche even more than World War II had. This was largely because although the Axis powers had designs on the United States, they never came very close to implementing them. During much of the Cold War, however, the Soviet Union possessed the ability to launch nuclear bombs at major American cities. In an instant, millions and even tens of millions of Americans could have died. The proximity and the magnitude of this threat far exceeded anything that the United States had faced during World War II.

Technically, Germany and Japan did develop a map of how they would divide up a conquered United States between them. They agreed that Germany would control the part of the United States east of the Mississippi and Japan would control the western half (Stephan,

1984). However, except for Germany's attempts to develop a more sophisticated V-2 rocket, the United States never really feared an imminent Axis invasion. Japan did make some direct attempts to inflict damage on the American mainland, but they were unsuccessful. The Japanese launched some helium balloons filled with explosives, which they directed toward the U.S. mainland (Mikesh, 1973). However, Japan quickly discontinued these attempts when nearly all the balloons failed to reach the coastline. The one or two balloons that did reach the coastline failed to arrive in populated areas (Mikesh, 1973).

The threat of the Cold War was a different matter, however. Soviet nuclear bombs could be dropped on New York; Boston; Washington, D.C.; and other major cities. In addition, the leaders of the communist world, Stalin of the Soviet Union and Mao Tse-Tung of China, were committing many of the same acts of murder and genocide that Hitler had previously committed (Fried, 1998). Seemingly, the communists had both the ability and perhaps even the will to inflict great harm upon the United States (Divine, 1993; Dow, 1991).

In American schools across the country, teachers regularly led children in atomic bomb drills designed to protect children in the advent of a nuclear attack. They directed children to hide under their desks to shield themselves from the danger of collapsing structures (Divine, 1993; Dow, 1991). American schoolchildren were well aware of what they were doing and of the potential for nuclear devastation, and many found the nuclear drills frightening. In retrospect, now that we understand the magnitude of the effects of nuclear fall-out, we realize that hiding under a desk would not significantly enhance a child's chances of surviving a nuclear holocaust. Nevertheless, at the time, American leaders believed the drills might save some who were farther from the blast. Given that the nuclear drill produced tremendous anxiety in children, many teachers sought to allay their fears by having them pray following the drill. In some kindergartens and early elementary school classes, the time of prayer was followed by a snack time of something comforting, like cookies and milk. The teachers did their best to diffuse the tension inherent in the drill (Divine, 1993; Dow, 1991).

The communist armies of the Soviet Union and China were considerably larger than the American army. Nevertheless, in the midst of a nuclear threat and with the idea of facing vast armies, Americans believed that their technology was the best in the world. In the eyes of many Americans, this technological edge would give the United States a major advantage.

Sputnik Shock

In 1957, In the midst of this rather contorted combination of American fear and complacency, America was stunned by the Soviet launch of the *Sputnik* (Logsdon & Launius, 2000), the first of a series of unmanned orbital satellites into space. This event sparked the fear not only that Soviet nuclear bombs could be transported across the ocean and dropped on the United States but also that America's technological edge was now in doubt (Logsdon & Launius, 2000). It seemed that the struggle between freedom-loving nations and the communists had expanded into the dark environs of outer space. The space race had begun (Montgomery, 1994).

Historians will argue as to whether American perceptions of the events of 1957 were accurate or infested with some degree of paranoia (Divine, 1993; Dow, 1991; Logsdon & Launius, 2000). Nevertheless, an abundant number of Americans claimed that the launching of the *Sputnik* meant that the Cold War had reached a new pinnacle of severity and historical importance (Clowse, 1981). Many military experts and scientists averred that this development meant that the Soviets had a decided advantage over the United States in their attempts to build intercontinental ballistic missiles (ICBMs), which could travel several thousands of miles over the world's largest oceans to reach their targets (Divine, 1993; Dow, 1991; Logsdon & Launius, 2000). Whether justified or not, Western leaders also feared that the Soviet Union might want to make a military base out of the moon (Logsdon & Launius, 2000). Western leaders argued that if the Soviets succeeded in doing this, it might enable them to some day intimidate other nations from outer space (Clowse, 1981). Historically, nations that were first to land on a given territory claimed it as their own. There was no reason to think that the Soviet Union would do otherwise. Should the Soviets land on the moon first, many Westerners feared that they would claim the moon as their land.

To a person who is unfamiliar with the communist call for expansionism, such a fear might appear full of hyperbole (Fried, 1998). However, to those who had witnessed the Soviet domination of Eastern Europe, the possibility of annexing the moon might not have seemed so far-fetched (Clowse, 1981). Clearly, we will never know what actions the Soviet Union would have taken had they landed on the moon first. They never had that opportunity.

Having highlighted the extent of people's alarm over the *Sputnik* launch, it comes as no surprise that Americans quickly sought to discern how this startling event could have occurred. The Soviets' success in sending up the *Sputnik* appeared to rest especially in two facts. First, a large number of aeronautic engineers had been working on the project (Clowse, 1981; Rudolph, 2002). Second, they were able to gain access to a plethora of rocketry documents written in German and French (Divine, 1993; Dow, 1991; Logsdon & Launius, 2000).

When these reasons for the Soviet success were made public, social scientists and political leaders blamed the U.S. education system for the country's failure to beat the Russians into space (Clowse, 1981; Finding & Thackery, 1996; Rudolph, 2002). Thorough investigation of scholastic trends showed that the percentages of American high school students taking advanced math, science, and foreign language courses had been in steady decline for years (Divine, 1993; Dow, 1991; Fried, 1998; Logsdon & Launius, 2000; Rudolph, 2002). Americans were shocked to hear that the percentage of high school students taking foreign-language courses had peaked in the 1910s and had steadily declined to only about half of that percentage in the 1950s (Divine, 1993; Dow, 1991; Fried, 1998; Logsdon & Launius, 2000; Rudolph, 2002). Moreover, further data analysis indicated that the reason for the declines was that high schools had consistently lowered their course requirements for nearly every major field of study, including foreign language, math, and science (Divine, 1993; Dow, 1991; Fried, 1998; Logsdon & Launius, 2000; Rudolph, 2002).

Conservatives were quick to blame liberals for the decline, citing the decisions arrived at in the *Principles of Secondary Education* (NEA, 1918) (Divine, 1993; Dow, 1991; Fried, 1998; Logsdon & Launius, 2000; Rudolph, 2002). As noted in Chapter 7, while the educational structure advocated by the NEA'S Committee of Ten in 1892 favored the conservative perspective, the *Principles of Secondary Education* document of 1918 envisioned a world in which a broad range of educational needs were addressed and the curriculum was not overly demanding.

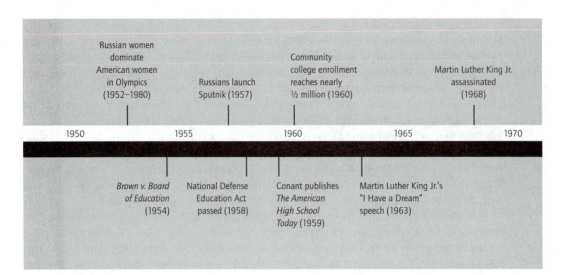

Russian women dominate American women in Olympics (1952–1980)

Russians launch Sputnik (1957)

Community college enrollment reaches nearly ½ million (1960)

Martin Luther King Jr. assassinated (1968)

1950   1955   1960   1965   1970

Brown v. Board of Education (1954)

National Defense Education Act passed (1958)

Conant publishes *The American High School Today* (1959)

Martin Luther King Jr.'s "I Have a Dream" speech (1963)

Conservatives observed that it was precisely when the *Principles of Secondary Education* were approved that the decline in the percentage of students taking foreign language declined (Clowse, 1981; Divine, 1993; Dow, 1991; Fried, 1998; Logsdon & Launius, 2000). Admittedly, many liberals around that time thought high school requirements for foreign language, science, and math were excessive and geared only toward those students preparing to enter college. Conservatives of that era, on the other hand, argued that these courses contained vital information that was necessary for all students to know (Rudolph, 2002).

Liberals similarly accused conservatives of being too reluctant to spend enough money on education to improve the quality of school facilities and to raise teacher salaries (Divine, 1993; Dow, 1991; Fried, 1998; Logsdon & Launius, 2000). As a result, liberals argued, many schools did not possess advanced scientific equipment, and too many intelligent people were not attracted into the teaching field. Although foreign scholars were quick to point out that Soviet schools were more poorly equipped than American schools and their teachers insufficiently paid, nevertheless, the earnings of teachers in the United States compared to those of other professions had been in decline for two decades.

As far as the general public was concerned, the statistics that both conservatives and liberals presented were indisputable. There had been a clear decline in academic requirements since around 1918 that had now come back to haunt the country. In addition, the United States had focused its efforts on recovering from the wars and had neglected to fully fund education.

Usually when there is an educational debate and both sides have valid points, only one side wins, because a single group is in power. However, that was not to happen in this case. There was so much mutual fear on both sides of the political aisle that liberals and conservatives actually decided to agree (Fried, 1998; Logsdon & Launius, 2000). Dwight D. Eisenhower, who, as Commander of the European Allied Forces in World War II, had unified the country under his leadership, as president now recognized the need for the nation to come together during this time of educational crisis. Conservatives and liberals decided to come together to support legislation that would increase both educational standards and funding (Rudolph, 2002). In the end, both groups of theorists won out. The liberals were able to convince the government to give generously to education. Conservatives, meanwhile, convinced the government to raise standards in mathematics, science, and language education (Fried, 1998; Logsdon & Launius, 2000; Rudolph, 2002).

The funding was used largely to facilitate strengthening standards. Both sides had won. America had won. And Americans had proved that disagreeing factions could come together in a time of crisis. The legislation that emerged was packaged primarily in what was called the National Defense Education Act (NDEA) (1958). The NDEA called for about $1 billion in expenditures over a 4-year period (Divine, 1993; Dow, 1991; Fried, 1998; Logsdon & Launius, 2000). The act contained three main provisions. First, $280 million would be supplied in federal matching funds to help both public and private schools purchase equipment to aid in the teaching of math, science, and foreign languages. Second, the government would sponsor 550 graduate fellowships in disciplines related to national defense. Third, a $295 million loan fund was formed to encourage students training to teach foreign languages, math, and science (Divine, 1993; Dow, 1991; Fried, 1998; Logsdon & Launius, 2000).

Numerous Americans called for even more substantial reforms. *Life* magazine called for schools to get away from the "John Dewey frills" (Divine, 1993, p. 160). A Gallup poll showed that 90% of the country's principals believed that school curricula were not demanding enough (*Time,* 1958). The *Sputnik* shock caused many issues about educational quality to come to the forefront, even as World War II had propelled concerns about equality to take first priority (Passow, 1979). The editors of the *Nation* also called for more reform expressed in more federal money for education. However, the editors conceded that "the bill does at last crack the ice of resistance to federal aid to education" (Divine, 1993, p. 165).

The *Sputnik* launch's short-term and probably most trenchant impact on education was to encourage higher standards for elementary and secondary school students and to devote more money to that goal (Divine, 1993; Dow, 1991; Fried, 1998; Logsdon & Launius, 2000).

The launch also had another long-term impact on the American education system. The federal government's response to the event would forever change Americans' attitudes toward federal intervention in education (Divine, 1993; Dow, 1991; Fried, 1998; Logsdon & Launius, 2000).

The issue of whether the federal government should give aid to education had been debated for some time. However, it reached the level of serious consideration only during times of national crisis (Bremner & Reichard, 1982). After the Civil War, for example, the issue of federal aid for schools was debated. After World War I, the issue again emerged as a key topic of educational debate. In the final analysis, however, any proposal for federal aid to the schools was always defeated.

Given that World War II constituted a national crisis, many educators hoped that the issue of federal funding for the schools would again be addressed. The NEA was at the forefront of the push for federal funding of the schools (Divine, 1993; Dow, 1991; Fried, 1998; Logsdon & Launius, 2000).

Two facts appeared to favor the establishment of federal support for the schools. First, Americans were aware that the military men returning home from World War II were helping to create a "baby boom." As a result of this demographic change, it was believed that the current school facilities would be inadequate to meet the demands of the next generation. Second, more people than ever before viewed obtaining a good education as necessary for experiencing success in life. As a result, there was an increase in the demand for education among the general populace. It seemed a propitious time to appeal to the Congress regarding federal aid.

The push for federal support of education started shortly after the war. Benjamin Fine, the education editor of the *New York Times,* claimed that many individuals were leaving the teaching position due to the poor level of pay they were receiving, and therefore it was time to pour more money into education to make it a more remunerative occupation (Fine, 1947).

The federal government did show some willingness to get involved in furthering education. In 1944, the G.I. Bill was passed, which offered 16 million men and women who had served in the military a federal subsidy to continue their schooling. Over the next 7 years, 7.8 million military people took advantage of the G.I. Bill and attended institutions of higher education (Spring, 1997). Truman attempted to push through a proposal for federal government funding of education. But conservatives from both the traditional mode of thinking and the business mode of thinking opposed federal intervention. They were afraid that federal funding of the schools would lead to federal control of the schools. President Eisenhower did not favor direct federal aid to the schools, but he did believe in proposing federally funded school construction programs (Divine, 1993; Dow, 1991; Fried, 1998; Logsdon & Launius, 2000). Congress defeated this proposal as well.

The launch of *Sputnik* finally propelled the country into recognizing that the federal government could play an important role in funding education (Divine, 1993; Dow, 1991; Fried, 1998; Logsdon & Launius, 2000). As mentioned, Americans viewed the *Sputnik* launch as a enormous threat because the rocketry technology could be used to destroy U.S. cities. They also knew that superior technology often determined who was the premier world power and realized that in the dangerous nuclear era, the United States could not afford to fall behind the Soviet Union technologically.

Accordingly, federal funding for education rose via the passing, as mentioned, of the NDEA (1958); the National Science Foundation flourished; and school standards did rise substantially in a very short period of time (Divine, 1993; Dow, 1991; Fried, 1998; Logsdon & Launius, 2000). SAT scores also rose during this period. However, more than this, once Eisenhower acted to provide federal funding for education, future presidents and Americans were more likely to look to the government to provide funding for other crucial causes.

A prominent written response to the *Sputnik* launching was a report by the Rockefeller Brothers' Fund (1959), "The Pursuit of Excellence," which asserted that in the pursuit of equity, the United States did not have to sacrifice academic quality. The *Sputnik* challenge gained the attention of many foundations that had previously focused their attention on higher education.

James Conant (1959), former president of Harvard, authored the book *The American High School Today.* Conant's book was a major success. He believed that a high school should offer as wide an array of courses as possible and that a high school should address the needs of all the students in a given community. Asserting that only large high schools could serve this function, he recommended the elimination of high schools that were in his opinion too small. Thus, Conant helped contribute to the belief that larger schools were preferable. In contrast, research today indicates that smaller schools may be more conducive to enhanced educational achievement. Evidence suggests that smaller schools impact student outcomes to as great a degree as small class sizes (Wenk & Harlow, 1978). Conant's (1959) recommendations played a large role in a plethora of large school buildings being built in the 1950s, 1960s, 1970s, and even 1980s.

Conant also denounced tracking, but he nevertheless believed in ability grouping. Indeed, ability grouping became popular during the 1950s as people saw the need to ensure that America's gifted children were properly trained. The gifted children of today would be able to build the rockets of tomorrow.

Lessons From *Sputnik* Shock

The fact that liberals and conservatives were able to come together during a time of crisis raises a question that is very pertinent when it comes to education and life as a whole. It is in many respects similar to the question asked in the previous section, on World War II. Why does it take times of crisis for people to unify?

Frequently, people of different political backgrounds tend to demonize the opposition. And, indeed, clearly there often is "a right" and "a wrong" to many facets of existence and behavior. However, too frequently people minimize their common goals and values. The September 11th, 2001, terrorist attacks constituted the greatest crisis to affect the United States since World War II. When the Twin Towers collapsed, spreading gray debris all over lower Manhattan, one person put it well when he noted that before that day, people defined other people as black, white, yellow, and brown. But on that day, to those who were covered with debris, skin color did not matter; everyone was gray.

In times of crisis, the superficial differences evaporate, and common humanity is valued. Crises make us realize that we had a great deal in common all along but just did not have the wisdom or humility to acknowledge this fact.

The effects of the Cold War generally declined over time because of two historical trends. First, by the mid-1960s, it was clear that the United States had caught and surpassed the Soviet Union in the "space race." The United States initiated three manned space programs during the 1960s. The first, the *Mercury* program, involved sending single astronauts into space. This took place during the early 1960s, which was largely a period of trying to play "catch-up" with the Russian space program. By the time of the second program, *Gemini,* it was clear that the United States had gained an advantage. The *Gemini* program involved sending up two spaceships in orbit and having them dock in space. This procedure was preparation for the kind of docking that would eventually be necessary to put people on the moon. The third program was the *Apollo* program, which eventually involved landings on the moon.

The second reason the effects of the Cold War on scholarly pursuits declined after a time is that by the early- to mid-1960s, educators became more concerned with equality issues than with educational quality.

Nevertheless, in the long run, the greatest effect of the *Sputnik* crisis was to create an overall belief that the federal government had an important role to play in funding education.

Contemporary Focus

What Kind of Teacher Are You?

One of the most common debates among teachers is what type of orientation they should maintain in the classroom. Should they have an approach that helps ensure that no child will "fall through the cracks," or should they focus on every child living up to his or her fullest potential, even if many are stretched? It would be very constructive for future teachers to address this question.

It is not the purpose of this book to suggest that teachers be one way or the other. In fact, both of these orientations have laudable goals. However, it is important to address the weaknesses of each so that one can prepare to take the appropriate steps to address these weaknesses. First, the weak point of the approach of teaching at a pace slow enough for everyone to keep up is that advanced children will become bored. This is still a laudable approach. After all, no one wants children falling through the cracks. However, to successfully apply this approach, a teacher should give extra work to the advanced students so that they will not become lethargic. The weak point of emphasizing that children live up to their highest potential is that by stretching them in this way, children are more likely to struggle. To prevent this from happening, if the teacher is to maintain this approach, he or she needs to be willing to meet with those struggling students to give them extra help.

These adjustments will help minimize the dropout rate and yet help ensure that children are sufficiently challenged to become all they can be.

Impact of the Cold War on Physical Education Opportunities for Women

Although the impact of the Cold War on academics waned by the mid-1960s, its impact on women's physical education increased (Bloom & Willard, 2002; Senn, 1999; Wiggins, 1995; Wu, 1997). Part of the reason for this is that by 1963, Americans did tend to become more concerned with equality than quality in education. Women's physical education was an issue that included dimensions of both equality and quality. As the reader will soon see, the Cold War raised issues of the quality of women's athletics. The civil rights movement facilitated the call for equality in access for female athletes. Both forces worked together so that in 1972, Title IX was implemented, giving women athletes the same access in funding and facilities as their male counterparts. Although Title IX is often portrayed as purely a civil rights issue, the role the Cold War played in encouraging cultural changes should not be overlooked (Horowitz, 1998; Senn, 1999; Wiggins, 1995; Wu, 1997). There is a need to examine this issue with a broader approach that encompasses international politics and culture.

Generally speaking, throughout the period of the Cold War, from 1946 to 1990 or 1991, there were four areas of heated competition between the United States and the Soviet Union. Each area was seen as a contest between the efficacy of democracy versus communism. First, there was military competition. This involved the arms race and any military conflict that involved the superpowers. Second, there was the space race or, more broadly, the technological race (Clowse, 1981). Third, economic strength was an intense arena of comparison (Clowse, 1981). Fourth, there was competition in international athletics, especially evidenced in the Olympics (Guttmann, 2002; Wiggins, 1995).

The athletic competition between the Soviet Union and the United States was certainly the most harmless of the four types of competition (Guttmann, 2002). Although, in the view of some, competition of this nature spoiled the Olympics, the politicization of the Olympics was nothing new. Most notably, Adolf Hitler had used the 1936 Berlin Olympics to showcase supposed German superiority. Although most Americans are taught how the skills of Jesse Owens and other American athletes spoiled Hitler's purpose, many Americans may not know that the Germans actually did win the most medals in that Olympics (Guttmann, 2002). The United States had to settle for second.

The Soviet Union viewed the Olympics as a superb way to showcase the superiority of the communist system. During the 1950s, 1960s, 1970s, and 1980s, the Soviets were very successful in winning the most Olympic medals of any nation (Guttmann, 2002). The Soviet claim to communist athletic superiority was aided by the fact that most of the other countries of Eastern Europe, such as East Germany, Romania, Poland, and Hungary, also performed exceedingly well in the Olympics (Guttmann, 2002). East Germany, with a population of about one tenth that of the United States, often competed with the United States for second place in the Olympic medal count.

As historian Susan Cahn (1994) notes, "Sport became part of a Cold War international contest in which the United States and USSR vied not only for athletic laurels but to prove the superiority of capitalism or communism" (p. 130). From 1896 to 1948, the United States gained more Olympic medals than any other nation (Cahn, 1994). However, Wu (1997) observes, "The U.S. performances in the Olympics during the Cold War era apparently had a negative impact on the international image of the United States" (p. 85).

The primary reason for the communist success in the Olympics rested with their women (Guttmann, 2002; Wu, 1997). American Olympic officials and members of the sports media lamented the fact that American men usually medaled more than either their Russian or German counterparts but Russian and other East European women dominated American females in competition (Guttmann, 2002; Wu, 1997). Wu (1997) notes that Soviet women sometimes won more than twice as many Olympic medals as American women. To even the casual observer, one reason was not difficult to see. The Eastern European women were often more physically fit and stronger than American women (Guttmann, 2002; Wu, 1997). The American women, perhaps in part because they were better fed, often appeared to have an extra layer of fat compared with their communist counterparts in Eastern Europe and China.

There is no question that at least part of the Eastern European advantage was due to the use of performance-enhancing drugs. After the end of the Cold War, Eastern European doctors, in particular, admitted giving hormone injections to female swimmers and runners (Haley, 2003). American female athletes often complained that East German female swimmers had deep masculine voices, and the American athletes suspected them of "doping" (Haley, 2003). Their suspicions were correct. There are even isolated cases of autopsies of Eastern European athletes who competed as women but were actually men. The most famous of these involved a Polish athlete named Stanislawa Walaziewicz. Walaziewicz was from Poland and competed from the 1930s until the early part of the Cold War. For some time, she earned the title of the "world's fastest female." However, Walaziewicz died in a shoot-out, and an autopsy revealed that the athlete was a man. Birth records also confirmed his gender (Haley, 2003).

Television commentators and Olympic leaders pointed out that much of the Eastern European athletic advantage was due to the fact that female athleticism was more acceptable in Eastern Europe than it was in the United States (Chase, 1973; Horowitz, 1998). They averred that unless the United States improved its program of women's physical education and sports, the communist nations would continue to dominate in the Olympics. Behind such declarations were concerns about far more than the results of foot races and gymnastic contests. Part of the world's impression of the effectiveness of democracy was at stake (Wu, 1997).

Thomas Hamilton (National Collegiate Athletic Association, 1961), chair of the Development Committee of the United States Olympic Association, declared,

> It is very evident that the United States must take a new and hard look at the Olympic movement and efforts. The cold war and present international climate demand that we make the strongest showing possible to uphold the prestige of the United States. . . . Now the United States is being challenged and defeated in our strong sports. . . . This condition is tragic since many people of the world have placed the fondest hopes on the image of America's strengths and ideals. We have a responsibility to these people as well as to the people of the United States to produce our best. Any effort short of the best is unworthy and unpatriotic. (p. 252)

Donald Boydston (National Collegiate Athletic Association, 1963), president of the U.S. Gymnastics Federation, said, "By building solid foundations of competition at home, we will reach our goal in track, basketball, and gymnastics, by killing the hell out of the Communists" (p. 181).

Wu (1997) summarized the situation well:

> It was, however, difficult to win the highest number of medals in the Olympics if American women did poorly—which they did. As NCAA institutions provided most of the male medal winners in the Olympics, it was only natural that a greater emphasis on women's sports might come from colleges as well. Thus, the NCAA came to see women's athletics as part of the puzzle to produce Olympic medal winners. (p. 83)

The humiliating defeats that American women faced at the hands of Soviet women provided a major impetus to improve the athletic programs that American schools and colleges offered to females (Guttmann, 2002; Wiggins, 1995; Wu, 1997).

The Olympic defeats and the desire for equal access to sports facilities were by themselves not enough to make women's athletics a mainstream American activity. Many Americans who desired change realized that there needed to be changes in cultural perceptions. Some males believed that women's participation in athletics was not particularly feminine. To a large degree, the main barrier against mainstreaming women's athletics was the attitude of women themselves (Guttmann, 2002; Wu, 1997). Many American women regarded the Eastern European athletes as offensively masculine and were often reluctant to participate in intensive sports because they did not want to build muscles or look "like a man" (Guttmann, 2002; Wu, 1997).

Some feminists saw a solution to this female-based resistance, in questioning and even belittling the concept of femininity, and those who responded to this approach came to idolize certain female athletes like Billie Jean King. However, the feminist approach was unable to bring female athleticism to the mainstream because most American women valued femininity and defined this concept more broadly than feminists did. If one defined femininity in this broad manner as "enjoying being a woman" and masculinity as "enjoying being a man," then these traits were desirable and likely to be valued (Horowitz, 1998).

In the Billie Jean King era of the late 1960s, schools and colleges grudgingly began to open the doors for additional sports activities for girls and women (Guttmann, 2002; Wu, 1997). However, many educators viewed these changes as largely addressing the desires of so-called tomboys. Women's athletics was seen not as a mainstream activity, but as opening up opportunities for a small group of athletically minded women (Guttmann, 2002; Wu, 1997). Although many women rooted for Billie Jean King, not many could relate to her.

Many Olympic officials, other athletic leaders, and members of the media desired to see educators view female and male athletes on equal footing. However, they knew that this attitude would take time to develop (Bloom & Willard, 2002; Horowitz, 1998). Beyond the mere passing of laws, fundamental changes needed to be made in the minds of men and women. Over time, three key changes took place to help mainstream the role of women's athletics in American schools.

First, there was a change in the way people perceived the balance between biology and culture in determining women's physical capabilities. Previously, many people had underestimated the role of culture in determining women's physical aptitudes. However, research comparing male and female progress in weightlifting programs indicated that female percentage strength gains (i.e., the percentage increase in the amount of weight one can lift) were greater than males'. These results indicated that females had considerably more potential for strength than was previously assumed (Ebben & Jensen, 1998; Hettinger, 1961; Holloway, 1994).

Also, certain athletic sagas unfolded that defied American biological stereotypes. One involved the track career of Chi Cheng in 1969 and 1970. Chi Cheng was originally from Taiwan. No East Asian woman had really become dominant in world-class track-and-field competition (Brown, 1979; Smith, 1998). Many assumed that this was because Asians were small and frail. Chi Cheng moved to the United States and attended California Polytechnic University. Under American tutelage, she soon smashed the biological stereotype by becoming the dominant female runner in the United States. She broke the record for consecutive track meet victories in the 100-yard dash and proceeded to break the world record in the 100-meter dash and in two other sprint categories (Brown, 1979; Smith, 1998). Her success earned her a place in the *Guinness Book* (McWhirter & McWhirter, 1972) as the world's fastest woman. Taken out of an East Asian culture that discouraged athletic prowess, Chang became the best. People saw the role of culture in influencing female athletic success.

The second event was an Eastern European phenomenon. The successes of gymnasts Russian Olga Korbut and Romanian Nadia Comaneci in the 1972 and 1976 Olympics revealed a new side of Eastern European athleticism. Here were young Eastern European women who were athletic, but also "cute" and "feminine," smashing the stereotype that women from this part of the world were all "tough" and "masculine." Each became the darling of their respective Olympics. In the aftermath of the Olympics, thousands of American girls flooded school gyms across the country for gymnastics training. In 1972, women's gymnastics had the largest television audience of all the Olympic events (Brown, 1979; Smith, 1998). Women's athletics had entered the mainstream. Schools did what they could to accommodate the sudden surge in the interest in women's sports. Also, Title IX was passed in 1972, and educators sensed that schools had entered a new era in encouraging women's athletics (Wu, 1997).

Third, largely through the actions of female athletes and celebrities, American women increasingly understood that a woman could have muscles and be athletic and still be feminine. This was a crucial realization if women's athletics were to be fully mainstreamed into

American physical education and athletic programs. The message was spread largely through celebrities famous for their femininity and female athletes who loved to dress up.

Among the first celebrities who demonstrated that the athletic look was consistent with femininity was Angie Dickinson. Angie Dickinson had established a reputation for both solid acting and femininity. In her 1970s roles in film and the television drama *Police Woman,* Dickinson played women who were both feminine and physically and psychologically strong (Strodder, 2000). Also, at about this time, her physique changed, revealing much more muscular development and definition. Given that her role as a feminine icon was already established, the changes in her appearance were well received.

Several female athletes demonstrated that femininity and athleticism were consistent. Florence Griffith Joyner, who broke the world record for the 100-meter dash in 1988, enjoyed wearing the latest fashions when she wasn't racing (Smith, 1998). Rachel McLish became a famous body sculptor. Her physical abilities appeared to confirm her femininity rather than detract from it (Smith, 1998). Kiana Tom, the so-called queen of fitness on ESPN, also appeared to view her physical conditioning as an extension of her womanhood (Tom & Rosenthal, 1995).

By the 1990s, the views of women like McLish and Tom had become mainstream in American life, with celebrities Brooke Shields, Giselle Fernandez, and many others promoting physical fitness as an expression of their womanhood rather than a detraction.

The Cold War played a major role in changing cultural beliefs about female athleticism. The effects of the Cold War in conjunction with the civil rights movement helped usher in Title IX. In addition, the Cold War worked in conjunction with other cultural transformations to make American men and women more accepting of women athletes.

CONCLUSION

As a result of two major conflicts that took place over a relatively short period of time, World War II and the Cold War, the future foundation of American education was forever altered. The civil rights movement in particular was ready to catapult into the center stage of American educational policy, and Americans saw women's education in a new light. However, it is noteworthy that the American citizenry comprehended the relationship between education and national security for only a brief time. That relationship would have to be revisited following the terrorist attacks September 11, 2001. Nevertheless, there may be no other period in American history in which international conflicts influenced the nation's educational future in such a dramatic way, in so short a period of time.

DISCUSSION QUESTIONS

1. For many decades, American educators have argued that schools should emphasize quality more or equality more. In their book, *The Pursuit of Excellence,* the Rockefeller brothers argued that educators can emphasize both at the same time. Do you agree or disagree with their conclusion?

2. In Chapter 6 of this book, evidence was presented suggesting that strong competition between the private sector and the public sector resulted in a stronger university

education system. Based on this chapter, one can argue that increased international competition from the Soviet Union contributed to passage of Title IX and the improvement in athletic opportunities for women. One can also argue that increased economic competition from East Asia is having a major impact on American education. Do you think that as everyday life becomes more influenced by global realities that global competition will increasingly influence education? If so, how? If not, why not?

3. "*Sputnik* shock" caused many liberals and conservatives, out of fear, to come together and agree on important educational legislation. Some Americans assert that the nation is currently too polarized on most educational issues and that this is not in the best interests of the country. Do you agree or disagree with this statement? If you do agree, do you think it will take another crisis or "shock" to unify the country? If you do not agree, do you think that when liberals and conservatives agree, it may not be a good thing, because principle is compromised? Do you think conservatives and liberals can agree more on key issues if they try harder?

4. The views of Darwin and Spencer and the effects that these men had on schoolteaching is a good example of how racism can be institutionalized. In other words, it is possible that racist teaching can become such a part of a school's teaching that it becomes a part of the curriculum, even without teachers and professors being aware of this. What can Americans do to reduce the presence of institutional racism? Do you believe it is possible that Americans may have a more difficult time eradicating institutional racism than individual racism? Why or why not?

REFERENCES

Ashmore, H. S. (1994). *Civil rights and wrongs: A memoir of race and politics.* New York: Pantheon.

Asia Pulse News. (2003). *China set to become world's largest economy.* Sydney, Australia: Australian Export Finance Corporation.

Baker, D., & LeTendre, G. K. (2005). *National differences, global similarities: World culture and the future of schooling.* Stanford, CA: Stanford Social Sciences.

Ballou, R. O. (1945). *Shinto, the unconquered enemy: Japan's doctrine of racial superiority and world conquest.* New York: Viking Press.

Banks, J. A., & Banks, C. A. (1995). *Handbook of research on multicultural education.* New York: Macmillan.

Bartley, N. V. (1995). *The new South, 1945–1980.* Baton Rouge: Louisiana State University Press.

Berman, W. C. (1970). *The politics of civil rights in the Truman administration.* Columbus: Ohio State University.

Bernstein, B. (1970). *Politics and policies of the Truman administration.* Chicago: Quadrangle Books.

Bernstein, M. A., & Adler, M. A. (1994). *Understanding American economic decline.* New York: Cambridge University Press.

Berrol, S. (1982). Public schools and immigrants: The New York City experience. In B. J. Weiss (Ed.), *American education and the European immigrant, 1840–1940* (pp. 31–44). Urbana: University of Illinois Press.

Bix, H. P. (2000). *Hirohito and the making of modern Japan.* New York: HarperCollins.

Bloom, J., & Willard, M. N. (2002). *Sports matters: Race, recreation, and culture.* New York: New York University.

Brandt, C. G., & Shafter, E. M. (Eds.). (1960). *Selected American speeches on basic issues, 1850–1950.* Boston: Houghton Mifflin.

Bremner, R. H., & Reichard, G. W. (1982). *Reshaping America: Society and institutions, 1945–1960*. Columbus: Ohio State Press.

Brint, S. G., & Karabel, J. (1989). *The diverted dream: Community colleges and the promise of educational opportunity in America, 1900–1985*. Oxford: New York.

Brook, T. (1999). *Documents of the Rape of Nanking*. Ann Arbor: University of Michigan.

Brooks, T. (1981). Teachers divided: Teacher unionism in New York City 1935–1950. In D. Ravitch & R. K Goodenow (Eds.), *Educating urban people* (pp. 206–218). New York: Teachers College Press.

Brown, G. (1979). *New York Times encyclopedia of sports*. New York: Arno Press.

Brown v. Board of Education 347 U.S. 483 (1954).

Business International. (1980). *BI-data printout summary*. New York: The Corporation.

Cahn, S. (1994). *Coming on strong: Gender and sexuality in twentieth-century women's sport*. New York: Free Press.

Chang, I. (1997). *The Rape of Nanking: The forgotten holocaust of World War II*. New York: Basic Books.

Chase, J. S. (1973). *Politics and nationalism in sports: Soviet and American government involvement in amateur sports as an aspect of the Cold War*. Unpublished master's thesis, San Jose State University.

Churchill, W. (1941). *Pearl Harbor*. Retrieved May 4, 2004, from http://www.spartacus.schoolnet.co .uk/2WWpearl.htm.

Clowse, B. B. (1981). *Brainpower for the Cold War: The Sputnik crisis and National Defense Education Act of 1958*. Westport, CT: Greenwood.

CNN. (2003, May 14). *Community college enrollment surges*. Atlanta: CNN.com.

Conant, J. B. (1959). *The American high school today*. New York: McGraw-Hill.

Counts, G. S. (1932). *Dare the school build a new social order?* New York: John Day.

Cremin, L. A. (1962). *The transformation of the school progressivism in American Education, 1876–1957*. New York: Knopf.

Cubberley, E. P. (1909). *Changing conceptions of education*. New York: Houghton Mifflin.

Cubberley, E. (1920). *The history of education*. Boston: Houghton Mifflin.

Daniels, J. (1966). *The time between the wars: Armistice to Pearl Harbor*. Garden City, NY: Doubleday.

Darwin. (1859). *On the origin of species by means of natural selection, or The preservation of the favoured races in the struggle for life*. London: Murray.

Darwin, C. (1871). *Descent of man*. London: Murray.

Dawidowicz, L. S. (1975). *The war against the Jews*. New York: Holt, Rinehart & Winston.

Dewey, J. (1933, 22 April). *New York Times*, p. 14.

Divine, R. A. (1993). *The Sputnik challenge*. New York: Oxford University Press.

Dow, P. B. (1991). *Schoolhouse politics: Lessons from the Sputnik era*. Cambridge, MA: Harvard.

Ebben, W. P., & Jensen, R. L. (1998). Strength training for women: Debunking myths that block opportunity. *Physician and Sports Medicine, 26*(5), 86–91.

Edgerton, R. (1997). *Warriors of the rising sun: A history of the Japanese military*. New York: Norton.

Fortune Editors. (1945). The Negro's war. In B. Moon (Ed.), *Primer for White folks* (pp. 320–335). Garden City, NY: Doubleday.

Eells, W. C. (1931). *The junior college*. Boston: Houghton Mifflin.

Egan, K. (2002). *Getting it wrong from the beginning*. New Haven, CT: Yale University Press.

Finding, J. E., & Thackery, F. W. (1996). *Events that changed America in the twentieth century*. Westport, CT: Greenwood Press.

Fine, B. (1947). *Our children are created: The crisis in American education*. New York: Holt.

Fireside, H., & Fuller, S. B. (1994). *Brown v. Board of Education: Equal schooling for all*. Hillside, NJ: Enslow.

Fried, R. M. (1998). *The Russians are coming, the Russians are coming: Pageantry and patriotism in Cold War America*. New York: Oxford.

Friedman, T. L. (2002). *Longitudes and attitudes: Exploring the world after September 11*. New York: Farrar, Strauss & Giroux.

Gardner, M. R. (2002). *Harry Truman and civil rights: Moral courage and political risks*. Carbondale: Southern Illinois University Press.

Gerdes, L. I. (2002). *The Great Depression*. San Diego, CA: Greenhaven Press.

Gittens, R. (2005, September 25). Costello counts China as world's no. 2 economy. *The Age*. n.p.

Glazer, N. (1985). *Clamour at the gates: The new American immigration*. San Francisco: ICS Press.

Goldhagen, D. J. (1996). *Hitler's willing executioners: Ordinary Germans and the holocaust*. New York: Knopf.

Gould, S. J. (1981). *The mismeasure of man*. New York: Norton.

Gould, S. J. (1992). The most unkindest cut of all. *Natural History, 101*(5), 2–7.

Graves, K. A. (2002). *Going to school during the Great Depression*. Monkato, MN: Blue Earth Books.

Greenberg, J. (1994). *Crusaders in the courts: How a dedicated band of lawyers fought for the civil rights revolution*. New York: Basic Books.

Guttmann, A. (2002). *The Olympics, a history of the modern games*. Urbana: University of Illinois Press.

Haley, J. (2003). *Performance-enhancing drugs*. San Diego, CA: Greenhaven Press.

Harding, V., Kelly, R. D. Q, & Lewis E. (1997). *We changed the world: African Americans, 1945–1970*. New York: Oxford.

Hettinger J. (1961). *Physiology of strength*. Springfield, IL: Charles C Thomas.

Hicks, G. L. (1995). *The comfort women: Japan's brutal regime of enforced prostitution in the Second World War*. New York: Norton.

Hill, H., & Jones, J. E. (1993). *Race in America: The struggle for equality*. Madison: University of Wisconsin Press.

Holloway, J. B. (1994). Individual differences and their implications for resistance training. In T. R. Baechle (Ed.), *Essentials of strength training and conditioning* (pp. 151–162). Champaign, IL, Human Kinetics.

Horowitz, D. (1998). *Betty Friedan and the making of the feminine mystique: The American left, the Cold War, and modern feminism*. Amherst, MA: University of Massachusetts Press.

Ianniello, L. (1965). *Milestones along the march: Twelve historic civil rights documents, from World War II to Selma*. New York: Praeger.

Irons, P. H., & Guitton, S. (1993). *May it please the court: The most significant oral arguments made before the Supreme Court since 1955*. New York: New Press.

Jackson, D. W. (1992). *Even the children of strangers: Equality under the United States Constitution*. Lawrence: University of Kansas.

Jencks, C., & Riesman, D. (1968). *The academic revolution*. Garden City, NJ: Doubleday.

Jeynes, W. (2004). Immigration in the United States and the golden years of education: Was Ravitch Right? *Educational Studies, 35,* 248–270.

Johnson, P. (1997). *A history of the American People*. New York: HarperCollins.

Kaufmann, J. E., & Kaufmann, H. W. (1996). *The sleeping giant: American armed forces between the wars*. Westport, CT: Praeger.

Kerr, E. B. (1985). *Surrender and survival: The experience of the American POWs in the Pacific, 1941–1945*. New York: W. Morrow Press.

Kilpatrick, W. H. (1937). *The teacher and society*. New York: Appleton-Century.

Koistinen, P. A. C. (2004). *Arsenal of World War II: The political economy of American warfare, 1940–1945*. Lawrence: University Press of Kansas.

Levene, M., & Roberts, P. (1999). *The massacre in history*. New York: Berghahn Books.

Li, P. (2003). *Japanese war crimes: The search for justice*. New Brunswick, MJ: Transaction Publishers.

Logsdon, J. M., & Launius, R. D. (2000). *Reconsidering Sputnik: Forty years since the Soviet satellite*. Sydney, Australia: Harward Academic.

MacKay, J. (1995). *The Allied-Japanese conspiracy*. Edinburgh, Scotland: Pentland Press.

Maga, T. P. (2001). *Judgment at Tokyo: The Japanese war crime trials*. Lexington: University of Kentucky Press.

McWhirter, N., & McWhirter, R. (1972). *Guinness sports record book*. New York: Sterling.

Melman, S. (1985). *The permanent war economy: American capitalism in decline*. New York: Simon & Schuster.

Michno, G. (2001). *Death of hellships: Prisoners at sea in the Pacific war*. Annapolis, MD: Naval Institute Press.

Mikesh, R. C. (1973). *Japan's World War II balloon bomb attacks on North America*. Washington, DC: Smithsonian Institute Press.

Mills, G. T., & Rockhoff, H. (1993). *Sinews of war: Essays on the economic history of World War II*. Ames: Iowa State University.

Monroe, W. S. (1952). *Teaching learning theory and teacher education, 1890 to 1950*. Urbana: University of Illinois Press.

Montgomery, S. L. (1994). *Minds for the making: The role of science in American education, 1750–1990*. New York: Guilford Press.

Moore, G. H. (1944). *Production of industrial materials in World Wars I and II*. New York: National Bureau of Economic Research.

Moreo, D. W. (1996). *Schools in the Great Depression*. New York: Garland Press.

National Collegiate Athletic Association. (1961). *1960-1961 Yearbook of the National Collegiate Athletic Association* (Vol. 19). Mission, KS: Author.

National Collegiate Athletic Association. (1963). *1962-1963 Yearbook of the National Collegiate Athletic Association* (Vol. 21). Mission, KS: Author.

National Education Association, Commission on the Reorganization of Secondary Education. (1918). *Cardinal principles of secondary education: A report of the Commission on the Reorganization of Secondary Education*. Washington, DC: U.S. Government Printing Office.

National Education Association. (1933). Current conditions in the nation's schools. *Research Bulletin, II, III*.

New York City Association of Teachers of English. (1937). *Further studies in reading*. New York: Noble & Noble.

O'Hara, F., & O'Hara, F. M. (2000). *Handbook of United States economic and financial indicators*. Westport: Greenwood Press.

Packard, J. M. (1987). *Sons of heaven: A portrait of the Japanese monarchy*. New York: Scribner.

Palmer, J. A. (2001). *Fifty modern thinkers on education*. London: Routledge.

Passow, H. A. (1979). *The gifted and the talented, their education and development*. Chicago: University of Chicago.

Philippines, Resident Commissioner to the United States. (1945). *Report on the destruction of Manila and Japanese atrocities*. Washington, D.C.

Prange, G. W., Goldstein, D. M., & Dillon, K. V. (1981). *At dawn we slept: The untold story of Pearl Harbor*. New York: McGraw-Hill.

President's Commission on Higher Education. (1947). *Higher education for American democracy* (Vol. 1). U.S. Government Printing Office.

Rafter, N. (2004). The criminalization of mental retardation. In S. Noll & J. W. Trent Jr. (Eds.), *Mental retardation in America*. New York: New York University.

Ravitch, D. (1974). *The great school wars*. New York: Basic Books.

Rees, L. (2002). *Horror in the east: Japan and the atrocities of World War II*. Cambridge, MA: Da Capo Press.

Rockefeller Brothers' Fund. (1959). *The pursuit of excellence*. Garden City, NY: Doubleday.

Rudolph, J. L. (2002). *Scientists in the classroom: The Cold War reconstruction of American of American science education*. New York: Palgaue.

Russell, E. F. L. (1958). *The knights of Bushido: The shocking history of Japanese war atrocities*. New York: Dutton.

Sajor, I. L. (1998). *Common grounds: Violence against women in war and armed conflict situations.* Quezon City, Philippines: Asian Center for Women's Human's Rights.

Senn, A. E. (1999). *Power, politics, and the Olympic games.* Champaign, IL: Human Kinetics.

Shull, S. A. (1999). *American civil rights policy from Truman to Clinton: The role of presidential leadership.* Armonk, NY: Sharpe.

Smith, L. (1998). *Nike is a goddess: The history of women in sports.* New York: Atlantic Monthly Press.

Spencer, H. (1851). *Social statics: or, The conditions essential to happiness specified, and the first of them developed.* London: John Chapman.

Spencer, H. (1966). *The works of Herbert Spencer.* New York: Appleton. (Original work published 1904)

Spring, J. (1997). *The American school 1642–1996.* White Plains, New York: Longman.

Stephan, J. (1984). *Hawaii under the rising sun: Japan's plan for conquest after Pearl Harbor.* Honolulu: University of Hawaii Press.

Strodder, C. (2000). *Swingin' chicks of the 60s.* San Rafael, CA: Cedco.

Tanaka, Y. (1993). *Hidden horrors: Japanese war crimes in World War II.* Boulder, CO: Westview Press.

Tewksbury, S. (1932). *Founding of American colleges and universities before the Civil War.* New York: Teachers College Press.

Time. (1958, April 7). p. 77.

Tom, K., & Rosenthal, K. (1995). *Kiana's body sculpting.* New York: St. Martin's Press.

Tyack, D., Lowe, R., & Hansot, E. (1984). *Public schools in hard times.* Cambridge, MA: Harvard University Press.

Urban, W., & Wagoner, J. (2000). *American education: A history.* Boston: McGraw-Hill.

U.S. Bureau of the Census. (1960). *Historical statistics of the United States.* Washington, DC: U.S. Government Printing Office.

U.S. Bureau of the Census. (1975). *Historical statistics of the United States.* Washington, DC: U.S. Government Printing Office.

U.S. Department of Labor. (2005). *Bureau of Labor Statistics: National Compensation Survey.* Washington, DC: Author.

Wallace, J. (1995). Red teachers can't save us: Radical educators and liberal journalists in the 1930s. In M. E. James (Ed.), *School reconstruction through education: The philosophy, history, and curricula of a radical idea* (pp. 43–56). Norwood, NJ: Ablex.

Wenk, E. A., & Harlow, N. (1978). *School crime and disruption.* Davis, CA: Responsible Action.

Wiggins, D. K. (1995). *Sport in America: From wicked amusement to national obsession.* Champaign, IL: Human Kinetics.

Wilkie, W. (1945). Today and tomorrow: Citizens of Negro blood. In B. Moon (Ed.), *Primer for White folks* (pp. 311–319). Garden City, NY: Doubleday.

Wu, Y. (1997). *The demise of the AIAW and women's control of intercollegiate athletics for women: The sex-separate policy in the reality of the NCAA, Cold War, Title IX* (Doctoral dissertation, Pennsylvania State University, 1997). Dissertation Abstracts International, AAT 9817607.

The Civil Rights Movement and Federal Involvement in Educational Policy

Just as the *Sputnik* launching opened the door for federal funding of education, the civil rights movement opened the door for federal involvement in education (Fried, 1998; Montgomery, 1994). This did not come directly, however. Although World War II established the foundation for the civil rights movement, many key leaders needed to act on this opportunity. This chapter traces the progress of the civil rights movement and how it affected education. The civil rights victories of the 1950s and 1960s culminated in one of the most important historical themes in education, the education of minority groups in the United States. However, the seminal case involving civil rights in education, *Brown v. Board of Education* (1954), did not occur in isolation. Events that preceded this U.S. Supreme Court decision were clearly pivotal in comprehending its importance. In addition, myriad events that happened subsequent to *Brown,* such as affirmative action and bilingual education, are essential if one is to understand the civil rights movement after this time. Granted, affirmative action and bilingual education represent some of the most controversial subjects in educational circles today. Nevertheless, the willingness to discuss these pertinent issues will strengthen the country and ultimately lead to reasonable solutions.

TRUMAN'S CONTRIBUTION

Although his name is not often associated with the civil rights movement, Harry S. Truman was really the first president to completely rally behind the goals of the civil rights movement. Truman's actions set the stage for *Brown v. Board of Education* (1954) and future civil rights legislation, which, in turn, forever transformed American education (Berman, 1970; Bernstein, 1970; Gardner, 2002). Truman had been greatly affected by the events ensuing from World War II, which opened people's eyes to the changes in racial attitudes that needed to take place in America. In 1946, just one year after World War II ended, he appointed a

President's Committee on Civil Rights to assess the situation and to recommend pertinent legislation. In the end, the committee prescribed the ending of segregation and discrimination. In 1947, Truman became the first president to accept an invitation to speak at the National Association for the Advancement of Colored People (NAACP) (Berman, 1970; Bernstein, 1970; Gardner, 2002).

Walter White, onetime president of the NAACP, said of Truman, "No occupant of the White House since the nation was born has taken so frontal or constant a stand against racial discrimination as Harry S. Truman" (cited in Bernstein, 1970, p. 11). Truman's stature as a defender of civil rights was not instantaneous. At the end of World War II, he was occupied with resolving the details of the German surrender, even more so when he was informed in July 1945 that the United States had successfully detonated a nuclear device and that it could be used in the war (Johnson, 1997). Truman now had to make the decision of his life. Would he use the nuclear bomb in the war against Japan? This quandary, coupled with later postwar decisions, would divert Truman's attention from the civil rights issues at hand. As a result, he initially faced some criticism from the African American community. For example, New York Congressman Adam Clayton Powell called Truman's wife "the last lady" rather than the first lady (Bernstein, 1970, p. 274).

Three factors made the time auspicious for Truman to pursue the civil rights agenda. First, as a result of World War II, many Americans were amenable to the idea of addressing civil rights issues (Berman, 1970; Bernstein, 1970; Gardner, 2002; Wilkie, 1945). Second, many African Americans had grown impatient with the lack of progress on various issues that concerned them during Franklin Roosevelt's terms in office, which had just recently come to an end with Roosevelt's death (Finding & Thackery, 1996; Klinker & Smith, 1999). As Bernstein notes (1970), referring to Roosevelt's African American voter support, "Roosevelt, generally assured of their support, was not prepared to risk his popularity or power aiding the struggle for equality" (pp. 270–271). The third factor needed for civil rights legislation was sufficient political support, which was there to some extent but was mostly lacking.

Despite Truman's desire to fight for civil rights, the political climate was not propitious for true change resulting from the efforts of politicians (Berman, 1970; Bernstein, 1970; Gardner, 2002). The Republicans were surely not in a position to execute reform. Many Republicans thought of themselves as the party that had secured the freedom of the slaves. In the view of the Republicans, the amendments to the Constitution that followed the Civil War had already given African Americans their civil rights (Berman, 1970; Bernstein, 1970; Gardner, 2002; Ianniello, 1965). In sense, they were right. But what they failed to acknowledge is that new laws were needed to address racist attitudes that made life difficult for African Americans (Ashmore, 1994; Hill & Jones, 1993; Klinker & Smith, 1999). The Republicans were also not in a position to help African Americans, because over the years they had grown to take the votes of African Americans for granted. From the time of Lincoln until the early 1930s, African Americans had voted strongly Republican (Berman, 1970; Bernstein, 1970; Gardner, 2002).

However, the Great Depression was a time of great suffering, and the Republicans did little to alleviate the economic distress of African Americans. In 1932, Democrat Franklin D. Roosevelt was elected president, largely as a result of people's discontent over how the Republicans had handled the economy. Roosevelt not only promised Americans that better times were ahead, but also promised them a "New Deal" in which more Americans would share in the prosperity of America. African Americans found the concept of a New Deal alluring; it was precisely what they were looking for (Berman, 1970; Bernstein, 1970; Gardner, 2002). From this time on, African Americans began to vote strongly in favor of the Democrats.

After World War II, however, the Democrats also were not in a position to initiate civil rights programs. Just as the Civil War had brought African Americans to the Republican side, it had brought southern Whites to the Democratic side. Southern Whites had never forgiven the Republicans for planning the conquering of the South during the Civil War. In fact, southern Whites voted Democratic so strongly that the South was referred to as the "Solid South," the one area of the country that could be counted on to vote Democratic (Berman, 1970; Bernstein, 1970; Gardner, 2002). Without the "Solid South," the Democrats would have had virtually no chance of procuring a majority in either the House or the Senate (Berman, 1970; Bernstein, 1970; Gardner, 2002).

When the African Americans decided to start voting mostly Democratic, the Democrats found themselves in a very awkward position. Within their party were people who favored civil rights legislation the most, African Americans; but there were also people in the party who favored civil rights legislation the least, southern Whites. While many Democrats desired to push civil rights legislation through Congress immediately following the war, others feared that doing so would risk losing the "Solid South" (Berman, 1970; Bernstein, 1970; Gardner, 2002). Also, whenever attempts were made to pass civil rights legislation, congressmen in the South stopped the initiatives (Berman, 1970; Bernstein, 1970; Gardner, 2002).

The fact that Truman formed the first Committee on Civil Rights encouraged many African Americans. This action set the stage for Truman's attempt to pass civil rights legislation and for the 1954 *Brown v. Board of Education* Supreme Court case (Berman, 1970; Bernstein, 1970; Gardner, 2002). Truman generally used his State of the Union address to advance his civil rights agenda (Brandt & Shafter, 1960). After his 1947 State of the Union address at the beginning of the year, civil rights leaders garnished Truman with a good deal of praise (Brandt & Shafter, 1960). Shortly after this time, Truman spoke before the NAACP.

Although the Civil Rights Committee eventually recommended civil rights legislation, Truman soon recognized that the issue would likely split the Democratic Party. Southern Democrats were very immutable, and Truman did not want to risk antagonizing them (Berman, 1970; Bernstein, 1970; Gardner, 2002). Truman was tempted to succumb to the southern-Democratic pressure, but political competition from the Republicans kept him from doing so (Bernstein, 1970). Thomas Dewey, the Republican candidate for president, proposed significant civil rights legislation, which would be a major part of the Republican political platform. The Republican party would support (a) equal opportunity in employment, (b) the abolition of the poll tax, (c) an anti-lynching bill, and (d) an end to segregation in the army (Bernstein, 1970).

The Republican advantage on the civil rights issue caused a keynote speaker at the Democratic Convention to say, "The Republican Party has gone much further in its advocacy of Federal interference in racial adjustments than has the Democratic Party" (Bernstein, 1970, p. 287).

Truman was faced with an important choice. Ultimately, he had to make a decision regarding whether he would side with African Americans or southern Whites. Truman elected to take up the cause of African Americans. He was determined to go in this direction for two reasons. First, he personally believed that this was morally the right thing to do.

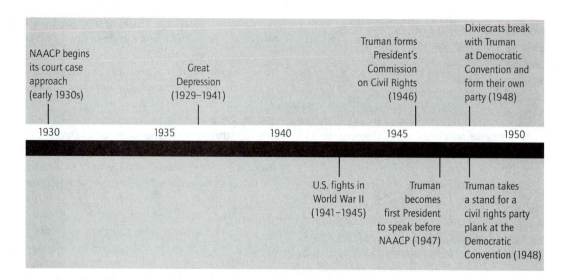

Second, it was the wisest action to take politically (Berman, 1970; Bernstein, 1970; Gardner, 2002). In the former case, Truman wanted to be on the side of right rather than wrong. It was clear that a number of state governments, particularly in the Deep South, were treating African Americans unfairly. Truman needed to address this injustice no matter what political price he paid. Second, Truman's advisors warned him that Thomas Dewey was a worthy opponent on the civil rights issue (Bernstein, 1970). They warned him that if African Americans voted on the current civil rights policy rather than on the basis of their decade-and-a-half habit of voting Democratic, the Republicans would win the majority of the African American vote (Bernstein, 1970). Governor Dewey's civil rights record was strong. He had appointed a number of African Americans to prominent posts, and his administration had taken a pro–civil rights stand on virtually every major issue verbalized by African American leaders (Bernstein, 1970). Unless Truman took the appropriate action, the party of Lincoln could again be the party of preference for most African Americans.

The civil rights issue in the 1948 presidential election was another example of how the nation benefited from the two-party system. In Chapter 3, we examined how the early political debates between the Democratic-Republicans and the Federalists fortified the strength of America's college system. Now, the competition inherent in the nation's two-party system catapulted the civil rights issue to a prominent place on the political landscape (Bernstein, 1970). Fortunately for Truman, the Democratic Convention took place after the Republican one. This gave the Democrats time to readjust their civil rights platform. Initially, they had anticipated proposing a platform that would placate the African Americans without raising the ire of the southern Democrats (especially those who opposed Truman's desire for civil rights legislation), who referred to themselves as "Dixiecrats" (Berman, 1970; Bernstein, 1970; Gardner, 2002). However, the Republican platform was sufficiently puissant and specific on civil rights that the Democrats could not seek to please both sides of the issue without appearing to be on the wrong side of the debate. Truman was pleased with this turn of events. The forces of history had now placed him in a position in which he would be compelled to take a stand for what he really believed (Berman, 1970; Bernstein, 1970; Gardner, 2002).

Surely, some credit should go to Governor Thomas Dewey for proposing a cogent and specific civil rights platform. However, one should remember that it was easier for Dewey than for Truman to take this stand politically. The South was traditionally the weakest part of the country for the Republicans and the strongest part for the Democrats (Berman, 1970; Bernstein, 1970; Gardner, 2002). Therefore, Thomas Dewey and the Republicans did not have to contend with much resistance among their political leaders.

In the 1948 Democratic Convention, Truman took a firm stand on civil rights. Many southern Democrats had made it clear that they would not support any presidential candidate that wholeheartedly endorsed major civil rights legislation (Berman, 1970; Bernstein, 1970; Gardner, 2002). However, they knew that Truman would proceed with a civil rights agenda of some kind, and they hoped to reach a compromise with him. They could live with some declaration of civil rights as long as the Democratic Party platform acknowledged that civil rights were a state issue rather than a federal concern. Southern Democrats were hopeful that if the Democratic Party made this acknowledgment, they would have the freedom to carry on segregation and other discriminatory practices (Berman, 1970; Bernstein, 1970; Gardner, 2002).

The compromise that the Dixiecrats offered was called the "Moody plank." They introduced this proposal to the floor of the Democratic Convention. Truman made it plain that he opposed the Moody plank, and he lobbied to see it defeated (Berman, 1970; Bernstein, 1970; Gardner, 2002). The closeness of the final vote on the Moody platform divulged the degree of risk that Truman was taking in promoting his pro–civil rights position. Not only was the South the major stronghold of the Democratic Party, but there also were other delegates who voted for the Moody platform because they feared that the Dixiecrats would bolt from the convention if they did otherwise. The final vote was 651 1/2 to 582 1/2 against the Moody platform (Gardner, 2002). A far more civil-rights-friendly platform was adopted instead, called the "Biemiller plank" (Gardner, 2002).

Truman knew that the defeat of the Moody plank might cause some Dixiecrats to withdraw from the convention. He also knew that depending on how many Dixiecrats departed, it might ultimately cost him the presidency (Berman, 1970; Bernstein, 1970; Gardner, 2002). However, he determined in his heart that he would do what was right, even if it cost him the election. Mayor Hubert Humphrey, of Minneapolis, one of the most respected Democrats in the country, lauded Truman for his courage. He declared, "In unmistakable terms . . . we proudly hail and we courageously support our President and leader, Harry Truman, in his great fight for civil rights in America" (as cited in Gardner, 2002, p. 98).

Within hours, the Democratic Party had been transformed. Previously, since the time of Lincoln, the Republican Party had stood at the relative forefront of civil rights issues. Suddenly, there was a change. Truman's decision would change the face of the country and postwar politics forever. Gardner (2002), explicitly states the significance of the hour,

> For the first time in the history of the country, and more than eight decades after the issuance of the Emancipation Proclamation by a Republican president, the Democratic Party's presidential candidate would be a man who publicly and unequivocally promised that he would take comprehensive federal actions to eliminate . . . racial discrimination. (p. 99)

In a sense, it is a misfortune of history that those who pay the highest price for a stand frequently do not get the credit. Instead, people tend to credit those who build on the sacrifices of those who preceded them. This is surely the case with Truman. When most Americans think of presidents who advanced the cause of civil rights, they usually think of Lyndon Johnson and to a lesser extent John F. Kennedy. However, by the time Johnson became president, the groundwork had already been laid for progress in civil rights (Berman, 1970; Bernstein, 1970; Gardner, 2002). Johnson won the presidency in 1964 by a margin almost unprecedented in modern American history. There was little political risk involved. However, Johnson enjoyed this privilege largely because President Truman, before him, had been willing to pay a high political price. (Berman, 1970; Bernstein, 1970; Gardner, 2002). Without Truman's earlier sacrifice, Johnson probably could not have so easily passed civil rights legislation years later.

As a result of the Democratic Party passing the Biemiller plank, a number of Dixiecrats did leave the Democratic convention and establish their own political ticket, the States' Rights Party. Governor Strom Thurmond, of South Carolina, was the presidential candidate for this ticket, and Fielding Wright, of Mississippi, was the vice-presidential candidate (Berman, 1970; Bernstein, 1970; Gardner, 2002). The Dixiecrats were well aware of the fact that their chance of winning the presidency was negligible. However, they were very concerned about the political landscape with Thomas Dewey and Harry Truman supporting civil rights. They realized that no matter what transpired in the election, as long as the voters decided the election, a pro–civil rights president would be elected. The Dixiecrats of the States' Rights Party therefore hoped they would win enough electoral votes to throw the election to the House of Representatives and that in this case, Truman would become more willing to recant his position on civil rights. Even if Dewey won, these Dixiecrats would have gained a type of victory in reminding the Democrats that without the support of the South, the party had little hope of winning the presidency (Berman, 1970; Bernstein, 1970; Gardner, 2002).

Truman and his advisors knew his civil rights stand could cost him the election, but he trusted that in the end, he would prevail because he had acted out of moral conviction as to what was right. His advisors were less optimistic. Gardner (2002) observes, "Most of Truman's closest friends and advisors also thought he would lose in November—a loss that was predictable in view of his stubborn refusal to equivocate on his pledge to bring about major, federally enforced civil rights reform" (p. 122).

In the final analysis, the Dixiecrats attracted support in only a few states in the Deep South. Truman edged out Dewey to win the 1948 presidential election despite the prediction of most pollsters to the contrary. Truman's victory was sweeter because he had acted out of conviction and was willing to sacrifice his position in order to do what was right.

Many southern Democrats, however, were not forgiving of Truman's failure to give in to their demands on civil rights. Although his position set the stage for future progress in civil rights, it also destined Truman to legislative defeat (Berman, 1970; Bernstein, 1970; Gardner, 2002). Embittered southern Democrats were even more adamantly opposed to Truman than they had been before. Gardner (2002) states, "Truman's attorney general in early 1949, Tom Clark, confirmed in 1972 just how hostile southern Democrats in the Congress were to any civil rights legislation—including even routine appropriations that might help advance Truman's radical civil rights program" (p. 149). Southern Democrats launched various filibusters to obstruct any kind of civil rights legislation (Berman, 1970; Bernstein, 1970; Gardner, 2002). The filibusters were so successful that on March 18, 1949, the *New York Times* declared Truman's civil rights initiatives effectively dead (Gardner, 2002, p. 151).

Republicans disagreed with the assessment of the *New York Times,* but they underestimated the determination of the southern Democrats. Truman also was not helped by the fact that strong enough Republican support for his legislative initiatives would not be forthcoming (Berman, 1970; Bernstein, 1970; Gardner, 2002). He did get a fair degree of Republican support, but, as mentioned, some believed that the Republican initiatives of the 1860s, both in freeing the slaves and the amendments to the Constitution, were sufficient for African Americans to have attained legal equality at that time (Brandt & Shafter, 1960). Others believed that since discrimination against African Americans was a matter of the heart, the solution was to enforce the laws already in place rather than passing new legislation.

Beyond the racism of certain congressional leaders in the South, the civil rights question was largely one of whether the government could legislate morality (Berman, 1970; Bernstein, 1970; Gardner, 2002). As in any debate of this nature, both sides had provocative points. In reality, changing human hearts is the ultimate goal if racism is to be eradicated. It is also true that the Emancipation Proclamation and the 13th, 14th, and 15th Amendments to the Constitution granted equal rights to African Americans as American citizens, with the right to vote and with all the rights of full citizenship (Brandt & Shafter, 1960). Of course, some acts by the Supreme Court and certain communities had weakened that sense of equality. Nevertheless, from the standpoint of federal law at the legislative level, equality had been established (Beard & Beard, 1944; Bremner & Reichard, 1982; Harding, Kelly, & Lewis, 1997; Rippa, 1997; Spring, 1990, 1997). Some Republicans felt that voting for extensive civil rights legislation would amount to asserting that Lincoln had not done enough.

Added Insight: Harry S. Truman, a Man of Conviction

Often, the greatest presidents have been men of conviction. The men whose faces appear on Mount Rushmore were all men of conviction, as well as the finest presidents of the 20th century. Harry S. Truman held on dearly to his principles. One quote of his, referring to poll numbers, gives us insight into his thinking:

> I wonder how far Moses would have gone if he had taken a poll in Egypt. What would Jesus have preached if he'd taken a poll in Israel? Where would the Reformation had gone if Martin Luther had taken a poll? It isn't the polls or public opinion of the moment that counts. It is right and wrong and leadership—men with fortitude, honesty, and a belief in the right—that makes epochs in the history of the world. (Green, 1989, p. 215)

It was this kind of conviction that enabled Truman to stand his ground on civil rights.

Truman believed that legislating morality was necessary in the case of civil rights. He knew it would not solve the problem of discrimination, but he also knew that many major actions, such as the Emancipation Proclamation, were precisely focused on this (Berman, 1970; Bernstein, 1970; Gardner, 2002). Unfortunately, Truman did not succeed. The *New*

York Times, March 1949, prediction about the end of Truman's civil rights legislation proved to be prophetic. He also became more cautious about raising the ire of southern Democrats during his second administration, for fear of ceding the long Democratic dominance of elections to the Republicans. Nevertheless, Truman established a foundation for civil rights legislation in the future (Berman, 1970; Bernstein, 1970; Gardner, 2002).

PURSUIT OF CIVIL RIGHTS LEGISLATION IN THE COURTS

Because of the political landscape in the 1940s and 1950s, it became more and more evident that the hope of the civil rights movement did not abide in the politicians, but in the court judges. The NAACP had recognized this and had begun a strategy to obtain victory in the courts back in the 1930s (Greenberg, 1994; Mauro, 2000). However, the organization now realized how crucial their court victories were for the furtherance of the civil rights movement. In the 1930s, the NAACP had initiated a plan to fight segregation by bringing various cases to court. Many of these cases focused on attempting to end segregation at certain public universities that did not admit African Americans. The NAACP was wise in that it took on only the most explicit cases. In the first case of this nature, in the mid-1930s, the NAACP represented Lloyd Lionel Gaines against the State of Missouri (*State of Missouri ex rel Gaines Canada et al.,* 1938). Gaines was a resident of St. Louis who sought admission to the University of Missouri Law School (Greenberg, 1994; Mauro, 2000). He was rejected by the all-White state law school and was advised to either apply to Lincoln, an all-Black school, in which case the state would start a law school for him there, or go to an out-of-state school, in which case the state government of Missouri would provide assistance.

On the surface, the fact that the state of Missouri offered to pay Gaines's way to go to an out-of-state school or start a law school at Lincoln just for his benefit sounds like a fairly nice offer. However, the state of Missouri was, in essence, insisting that Gaines had to go to an out-of-state university if he did not attend Lincoln: To open a law school at Lincoln for the benefit of one student would certainly not come anywhere close to matching the quality of other law schools. Experienced professors were not likely to answer an advertisement for such a position, probably resulting in the hiring of only part-time faculty, or full-time faculty who were not fully qualified to teach law.

The argument by the NAACP was that Missouri did not offer equal treatment under the Supreme Court decision of *Plessy v. Ferguson* (1896) (Greenberg, 1994). The *Plessy v. Ferguson* case was a patent example of how Supreme Court decisions sometimes have little to do with truth and taking the right action. On the surface, *Plessy v. Ferguson* had nothing to do with education; however, the Supreme Court decision had ramifications that extended to almost every facet of society, including education (Greenberg, 1994). *Plessy v. Ferguson* upheld the constitutionality of segregating Louisiana railroad cars by race. The case concluded that as long as the railroad cars were equivalent, segregation was allowed. However, the results of the case were extended to apply to the legality of segregation in other facets of life, including education. Based on *Plessy v. Ferguson,* schools in the South were segregated by race (Greenberg, 1994).

As bad a decision as *Plessy v. Ferguson* was, because it was the law, the NAACP had to argue its cases on the basis of that earlier decision (Fireside & Fuller, 1994; Horwitz, 1998;

Wilkinson, 1979). Eventually, the organization hoped to overturn the *Plessy v. Ferguson* decision, but until sufficient progress had been made, the NAACP sought to prove that the decision was not being abided by. In the early years of their court cases, the NAACP had focused their efforts on segregation in terms of African Americans gaining admittance into institutions of higher education. In these cases, the denial of equal opportunities to African Americans had been unequivocal (Greenberg, 1994).

The NAACP won the Gaines case (1938) and a similar case in Texas (Greenberg, 1994). The NAACP felt emboldened enough to address the issue of state-enforced segregation in elementary and secondary level schools. In 1950, in the case of *Sweatt v. Painter,* the Supreme Court unanimously forced Texas to admit Heman Sweatt into the formerly all-White University of Texas law school. Initially, Texas' had set up a poorly funded all-Black law school. The Supreme Court declared Texas' actions unconstitutional and forced it to accept Sweatt (Greenberg, 1994).

The Gaines and Sweatt court victories coupled with Truman's inability to pass substantial civil rights legislation in the Congress emboldened the NAACP to become more aggressive in their court strategy (Fireside & Fuller, 1994; Horwitz, 1998; Wilkinson, 1979). Victory appeared out of their reach in Congress, but attainable in the courts.

Brown v. Board of Education

In December 1952, the Supreme Court heard challenges to the segregation laws in five states, which were collectively called *Brown v. Board of Education* (Fireside & Fuller, 1994; Horwitz, 1998; Wilkinson, 1979). The appellation for the case came from what was perhaps the principal case, in Topeka, Kansas. In this case, Linda Brown was forced to attend an all-Black elementary school in Topeka, even though there was another school a good deal closer.

The *Brown v. Board of Education* decision of 1954 represents one of the most important U.S. Supreme Court decisions relating to education (Fireside & Fuller, 1994; Horwitz, 1998; Wilkinson, 1979). It ranks alongside the *Dartmouth v. Woodward* case of 1819 and the decisions regarding prayer and Bible reading in schools in 1962 and 1963. Moreover, each of these decisions influenced the larger American society, not merely the schools.

Unlike the *Dartmouth* and the prayer-in-schools Supreme Court decisions, *Brown v. Board of Education* was preceded by many other changes in favor of desegregation, so that many insightful legal analysts anticipated this type of decision coming, probably a decade or so before it was handed down. As Urban and Wagoner (2000) observe,

> Since the late 1930s, progress had been made in desegregating gradually and professional studies in southern public colleges and universities. There had also been substantial progress during the 1940s in getting white authorities on various southern locales to move toward more equal facilities in the lower schools. (p. 299)

Part of this progress was a result of political frustration that many African Americans felt with the political system. Although many considered Franklin Roosevelt an ally, he accomplished little in the name of civil rights. Harry Truman, largely as a result of the impact of World War II, made bold statements that could potentially advance the progress of African Americans (Shull, 1999). However, Truman's failure to obtain congressional support for his civil rights proposals further frustrated African Americans.

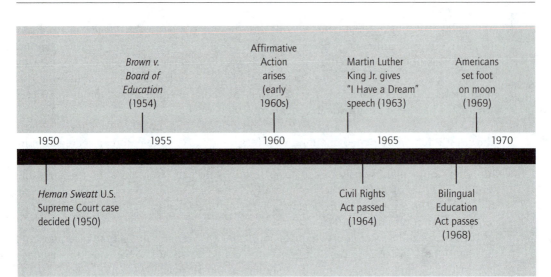

As a result of political disappointments during the Roosevelt years and unequivocal setbacks during the Truman years, increasingly, African Americans looked to the courts to advance the civil rights agenda.

Generally speaking, when similar cases come up before the Supreme Court, the justices consider these cases as a cluster in the name of efficiency (Fireside & Fuller, 1994; Horwitz, 1998; Wilkinson, 1979). Usually, the Court chooses one of the cases to be the representative case for the cluster, either by considering the strength and clarity of the case or, if the cases are similar in this regard, choosing the case based on the alphabetical order of the plaintiff's last name. In the Brown case, that honor would have fallen to the Harry Briggs case, of South Carolina. However, the Supreme Court did not wish to create more conflict in the South. Therefore, they selected the Brown case, in Topeka, Kansas, to be the representative case (Fireside & Fuller, 1994; Horwitz, 1998; Wilkinson, 1979).

In 1952 and 1953, Thurgood Marshall pled *Brown v. Board of Education* for the NAACP. Marshall was considered the NAACP's premier lawyer and would one day become the first African American Supreme Court justice (Fireside & Fuller, 1994; Horwitz, 1998; Wilkinson, 1979). Marshall made two chief arguments in *Brown v. Board of Education*. First, he claimed that under the 14th Amendment, it was unconstitutional to classify people by race. Second, as the case went on, Marshall argued that the "separate but equal" clause of the 1896 *Plessy v. Ferguson* decision was discriminatory and needed to be reversed (Fireside & Fuller, 1994; Horwitz, 1998; Wilkinson, 1979). The NAACP enlisted the help of researchers who asserted that segregation was harmful to African Americans. Among the most impressive arguments by the NAACP was the research of African American sociologist Kenneth Clark. Clark argued that being segregated accentuated feelings of inferiority (Fireside & Fuller, 1994; Horwitz, 1998; Wilkinson, 1979). Research by James Coleman, Gary Orfield, and others suggested that African Americans did better academically when they attended school with White students.

Leading the defense team was John W. Davis, a pro-segregationist from South Carolina. Davis had a long list of credits that made him a formidable opponent. He had participated in more Supreme Court cases than any other lawyer in the 20th century (Fireside & Fuller,

1994; Greenberg, 1994; Horwitz, 1998; Wilkinson, 1979). He had been the Democratic presidential nominee in 1924, solicitor general under President Woodrow Wilson, and ambassador to Great Britain. Davis was so pro-segregationalist, he decided to offer his services for Brown for free (Fireside & Fuller, 1994; Greenberg, 1994; Horwitz, 1998; Wilkinson, 1979).

Usually, when the Supreme Court hears a case, as in *Brown v. Board of Education,* in 1952, it decides and writes the case within the next several months. However, although it was clear that the Supreme Court would rule in favor of Brown and overturn *Plessy v. Ferguson,* it was obvious that the decision would not be unanimous (Fireside & Fuller, 1994; Horwitz, 1998; Wilkinson, 1979). Most of the nation hoped that the Supreme Court would deliver a strong message in *Brown* and overturn *Plessy,* but in 1953, the Supreme Court did not come through, largely because it was intimidated by the potential for upheaval in the South.

It appeared that the best supporters of *Brown v. Board of Education* could hope for was a 7-to-2 decision to overturn *Plessy.* That would get the job done, but it would not produce the trenchant message that a unanimous decision would have accomplished. Two southern justices, Reed and Clark, were not likely to vote in favor of Brown. In a controversial decision, the Supreme Court decided to rehear the case in 1953. In doing so, the Supreme Court hoped to have more time to work through differences that, if possible, would result in a more unified decision. Although the direction of the court vote was certain, the final vote was still not unanimous (Fireside & Fuller, 1994; Horwitz, 1998; Wilkinson, 1979).

In 1953, Chief Justice Vinson died, and President Eisenhower replaced him with Earl Warren, from California.

Vinson was a southerner, and many believe that the fact that Warren replaced him made it easier for the Supreme Court to produce a unanimous court decision (Fireside & Fuller, 1994; Horwitz, 1998; Wilkinson, 1979). Warren was the moderate Republican governor of California and had been the vice-presidential nominee in the 1948 election. African Americans were pleased with Eisenhower's choice because Warren had called for civil rights legislation in the past.

When Warren became chief justice, he, like Vinson, also delayed the *Brown* decision at various points. Warren knew the crucial nature of the situation. He believed it was important to get a unanimous decision because *Brown* was such an important case (Fireside & Fuller, 1994; Horwitz, 1998; Wilkinson, 1979).

Warren met with some of the justices who had some reservations about the vote. Most notably, he met with Reed, who had been firmly against ending desegregation. Warren asked Reed what it would take to get him to decide in favor of Brown. Reed said he wanted the decision to give the South time to dismantle its segregationist policy, and Warren agreed to this request (Fireside & Fuller, 1994; Horwitz, 1998; Wilkinson, 1979).

In the end, Warren was able to obtain the 9-to-0 vote that he had sought. In May 1954, the Supreme Court declared that state-imposed public school racial segregation was unconstitutional (Cremin, 1976; Fireside & Fuller, 1994; Fraser, 2001; Horwitz, 1998; Ianniello, 1965; Mauro, 2000; Wilkinson, 1979). Some say that the Supreme Court's delays and the compromise reached to ensure a unanimous vote were too high a price to pay and that handing down an uncompromising, less-than-unanimous decision a year earlier would have been more effective. Others maintain that the Supreme Court took the right action to delay handing down the decision until it was unanimous. They argue that the South would have resisted desegregation even more if some southern justices had dissented (Fireside & Fuller, 1994; Horwitz, 1998; Wilkinson, 1979).

A Closer Look: Did the Supreme Court Make the Right Move in Delaying the *Brown v. Board of Education* Decision?

Had the Supreme Court handed down its decision on *Brown v. Board of Education* in 1953, the high court would have decided 7 to 2 in favor of the Linda Brown family. Instead, the Supreme Court waited 1 year before making its decision. The reason for the delay was to enable the court to procure a unanimous decision. The belief was that the South would point to a split decision among northern and southern justices as proof that the North was coercing the South to act against its own free will. Warren asked the key dissenting justice, Reed, what was needed in order to ensure a 9-to-0 vote. Reed replied that the *Brown* decision would have to give the South more time to implement desegregation. Consequently, the final language of the *Brown* decision was weakened somewhat from what it might have been. Most notably, Warren decided to insert the phrase "with all deliberate speed" rather than specify a certain deadline. However, Warren maintained that it was essential for the United States to see that this was a unanimous decision so that it would produce the minimum amount of resistance. Indeed, the final vote on Brown was 9 to 0.

Did the Supreme Court take the right action by delaying the vote until 1954 in order to obtain a unanimous decision? Most people believe that it was the right decision. They maintain that a unanimous decision was extremely important. However, others assert that a 7-to-2 decision in favor of Brown would still have accomplished the task at hand. They argue that many in the South resisted even after the 9-to-0 decision.

- Do you think the Supreme Court employed the right strategy in delaying the *Brown v. Board of Education* decision?

Most of the states bordering the South complied quite willingly with the Supreme Court decision, but the states of the Deep South strongly resisted, and sometimes the federal government had to send in the National Guard and other military forces. In 1957, President Eisenhower showed that the federal government had every intention of enforcing the *Brown* decision by sending the National Guard and the 101st Airborne Division of the U.S. Army to Little Rock, Arkansas. The nine brave African American adolescents who were chosen to integrate Little Rock Central High are often referred to as the "Little Rock Nine." They willingly stepped into heated resistance against integration, though they were just teenagers. This turned out to be the turning point in the enforcement of the *Brown* decision (Fireside & Fuller, 1994; Horwitz, 1998; Wilkinson, 1979). After this point, the resistance became considerably lighter.

BROWN V. BOARD OF EDUCATION HELPS BUILD MOMENTUM FOR THE CIVIL RIGHTS MOVEMENT

The triumph of *Brown v. Board of Education* in 1954 accorded the civil rights movement with powerful momentum, which complemented other victories in the movement. Increasingly, African American leaders gained the respect and admiration of large numbers of both African Americans and White Americans. Martin Luther King Jr. and his trusted friend, Ralph

Abernathy, were two of these outstanding individuals. Both were Baptist preachers who believed the key to African Americans obtaining civil rights was the practice of the passive resistance that Christ had practiced (Abernathy, 1989; King, 1998; King & Washington, 1986). There is little question that the *Brown* decision gave African Americans a sense of opportunity, which, Ralph Abernathy (1989) states in his autobiography, did not exist decades before. In December 1955, in the heart of the segregated South, Montgomery, Alabama, Rosa Parks refused to give up her seat at the front of a city bus when asked to do so by a White person (Abernathy, 1989; King, 1998). Parks's action helped catapult the civil rights movement to center stage and propelled the ministries of King and Abernathy into national prominence (Abernathy, 1989; King, 1998; King & Washington, 1986).

Although King dealt with segregation in the South as a broad social issue, rather than focusing specifically on education, King's civil rights agenda ultimately had a major impact on education. In King's view, the nation needed to extricate African Americans from every manifestation of segregation, whether in society at large or in schools (King, 1998; King & Washington, 1986). There is no question that school integration would not have proceeded in as timely a fashion without the success accomplished by King. He and Abernathy worked closely as intimate friends with a common goal (Abernathy, 1989; King, 1998; King & Washington, 1986). King was the first president of the Southern Christian Leadership Conference (SCLC), and because of his trust in his friend, he personally named Abernathy as his successor. Abernathy assumed that post in 1968, following King's assassination (Abernathy, 1989). By assuming the post of SCLC president in 1968, Abernathy, along with King's widow, Coretta Scott King, became two of the primary leaders carrying on King's legacy by means of passive resistance (Abernathy, 1989). In Chapter 11, we will more thoroughly examine the influence of education on Martin Luther King Jr. and the effect he had on American education. Suffice it to say, however, that due to the leadership of King, the United States and its education system were forever changed.

One should not imagine that every attempt at integration ended in success. One initiative that initially was filled with promise was busing children to different schools in order to increase integration. However, various factors caused most Americans, White and non-White, to oppose busing (Levinsohn & Wright, 1976; Mills, 1979). First, busing went against the idea of a neighborhood school. Most parents want their children going to nearby schools. Second, because of the distance involved in busing, children often had to start the trek to school before sunrise, a fact that was not only inefficient and inconvenient but also unsafe in many cities. Third, some parents still preferred segregated schools. In addition, the soaring price of gas beginning in 1973 made the policy economically untenable (Levinsohn & Wright, 1976; Mills, 1979). Although the civil rights movement had setbacks, it was bound to expand considerably.

EXPANDING THE REACH OF THE CIVIL RIGHTS MOVEMENT: AFFIRMATIVE ACTION

By the early 1960s, there was a general consensus among most of the American political leadership that something needed to be done to ensure that members of minority groups, particularly African Americans, had greater access to 4-year institutions and various means of employment. In the early 1960s, President John F. Kennedy initiated executive orders 10925 and 1114, with the goal of "equality of prospective opportunity" in all walks of life, with a particular emphasis on job and college study opportunities (Glazer, 1975; Niel, 1991; Wilkinson, 1979). On this point, there was a genuine consensus among liberals and conservatives (Glazer, 1975).

It is important to reiterate the initial reasons for affirmative action as well as the rationale given for its continuance, because with each generation that passes, young people have less of an understanding of its presence. The original reasons for affirmative action were threefold, according to Barbara Bergman (1996). Affirmative action was designed to fight discrimination, produce integration, and "reduce the poverty of certain groups" (Bergman, 1996, pp. 9–10). The political leaders who instituted affirmative action believed that without this program, many qualified individuals of minority status and the female gender would not have a chance to excel (Bergman, 1996).

In the 1950s and 1960s, the vast majority of Americans understood that there were racial inequalities in America that needed to be resolved (Glazer, 1975; McCoy & Ruetten, 1997). The question was how to address these issues. Even before this period, Americans, even members of minority groups, were divided on the best way to approach issues of inequity in education and job opportunities. W. E. B. DuBois, for example, did not view desegregation as key to raising opportunities for African Americans, but rather to ensuring higher-quality education (Pendleton, 1991).

Initially, it appeared that affirmative action, as it was originally conceptualized in the early 1960s, would not become a controversial issue (Glazer, 1975). Even if there were differences of opinion on which was most important, desegregation, education, or job opportunities, most people comprehended that it was reasonable to initiate change in all three of these areas to ensure expeditious change (Glazer, 1975; McCoy & Ruetten, 1997). The goal would be equality of opportunity from this time forward.

However, two things happened that together caused a great deal of disharmony between liberals and conservatives on the issue of affirmative action. First, after examining affirmative action options more closely, liberals within the Democratic Party soon deduced that equality of opportunity would not be sufficient to produce equality of results. They surmised that White people had an inherent advantage over African Americans because of their edge, on average, in socioeconomic status, family structure, and other advantages, due to historical acts of discrimination (Abram, 1991; Glazer, 1975; Greene, 1989; Niel, 1991; Skrentny, 1996). In the view of these liberal Democrats, White children had an edge in much the same way that Wal-Mart has an edge in retail store competition. Yes, technically, a business could attempt to compete to be equal with Wal-Mart. However, in reality, the company has a half-century advantage that has built up in terms of distribution networks, the economies of scale, and efficiency that makes it virtually impossible to have a chance.

Even if the same rules applied to both businesses, Wal-Mart would have a competitive advantage because the company has been in a paramount position for so long. The parallel argument of liberal Democrats for this perspective was that even if African Americans were given an equal opportunity, they had been at a disadvantage educationally and occupationally for too long to actually become equal. With this argument in mind, the conclusion of the Democrats was that the only hope for African Americans was to give them an advantage that would compensate for the inherent edge that White people enjoyed (Abram,

1991; Glazer, 1975; Greene, 1989; Niel, 1991; Skrentny, 1996). Given that African Americans were at a disadvantage in competing for student admissions at universities, liberal Democrats concluded that preferential treatment in this regard might even be the superior type of affirmative action program.

This conclusion by the liberal leadership did not, in and of itself, produce friction with conservatives. But the second event together with this change in philosophy did forge discord. In 1964, Democrats behind the presidential campaign of Lyndon Johnson won a landslide election victory. As a result, Democrats enjoyed more than a two-thirds majority in both the Senate and the House of Representatives (Johnson, 1997). Never since this time has either party enjoyed such an overwhelming majority in the Congress. The extent of the majority that Democrats enjoyed meant one thing: They could push through any bill they wanted without fear of a Republican filibuster. There was virtually no need to consult Republicans at length about any important matters.

The majority the Democrats enjoyed did not so much affect the nature of the civil rights legislation that passed under Johnson in 1964. Rather, the Democratic majority influenced the way the laws were implemented and the political "spin" that was put on their passage (Abram, 1991; Glazer, 1975; Greene, 1989; Niel, 1991; Skrentny, 1996). For their part, the conservatives felt deceived (Glazer, 1975). The initial agreement over equal rights between conservatives and liberals concerned equal *opportunity*. Soon, conservatives complained that the affirmative action programs now being proposed amounted to ensuring equal *result*. The liberal/conservative camaraderie that had emerged on educational issues during the days of the *Sputnik* was dealt a serious setback (Abram, 1991; Glazer, 1975; Greene, 1989; Niel, 1991; Skrentny, 1996).

A Heated Debate Arises

Although there was agreement from both sides of the political aisle on the need for equality, it was the idea of preferential treatment that stirred heated debate. By the latter half of the 1960s, the consensus that produced the Civil Rights Act of 1964 had yielded to debates about whether preferential treatment was the best way to attempt to generate fairness and equality (Cose, 1997; Fish, 1996; Glazer, 1975; Jacoby, 1996; Steele, 1996).

As the 1960s continued into the 1970s, the debate about affirmative action became increasingly poignant, because so many individuals had different definitions of what affirmative action was (Cose, 1997). As time went on, a growing disjunction arose between those who insisted that preferential treatment was an effective remedy for past discrimination against minorities, and others who declared that it discriminated against Whites (Glazer, 1975). The dialogue became fiery at times, with Stanley Fish (1996) stating that opposition to affirmative action was "new respectable bigotry" (p. 41). Nathan Glazer (1975), on the other hand, insisted that preferential treatment had created the "Orwellian nightmare in which all animals are equal, but some animals are more equal than others" (p. 75).

The controversy over affirmative action is unlikely to subside, largely because it is so multifaceted. Most fair-minded people can visualize why preferential treatment might be a way to resolve inequality. Similarly, most fair-minded people can also see how preferential treatment might discriminate against Whites. Truly, the inequality that existed previous to and including the 1960s demanded an immediate resolution, especially rectifying the wrongs that existed as a result of the enslavement of African Americans (Jackson, 1992; Klinker & Smith, 1999; Staughton, 1966). Nevertheless, as time went on, a confounding dilemma emerged. To what degree was it ethical to ask the present generation of White people to pay for the wrongs of past generations? With each passing generation, this question becomes more difficult to resolve. In an ideal world, giving African Americans preferential treatment at the expense of those people who actually enslaved them or later discriminated against them would seem justified. The situation is further complicated by the fact that the ancestors of most Caucasian Americans came to the United States well after the time African Americans had been enslaved and thus are not descendents of those responsible for discriminating against them (Jackson, 1992; Klinker & Smith, 1999; Schwartz, 1988; Staughton, 1966).

Nonetheless, African Americans not only suffered personal discrimination but also institutional racism. *Institutional racism* results from a group of people suffering discrimination by the very way a system works, even in the absence of malicious intent (Ogbu, 1992, 1993). For example, if the way a system works is that those from wealthy families, with educated parents, living in better sections of town are at an advantage, African Americans will disproportionately be discriminated against (Bremner & Reichard, 1982; Hill & Jones, 1993; Ogbu, 1992, 1993). For years, not only have people discriminated against African Americans, but so has the "system" (Ogbu, 1992, 1993). The challenge of affirmative action is to right the wrongs of the past and yet minimize what many perceive as a new wave of discrimination, against Whites.

Some of the greatest conservative critics of the liberal approach to education include Nathan Glazer and Thomas Sowell. Glazer, a conservative education professor from Harvard, wrote the book *Affirmative Discrimination* (1975). In this book, Glazer criticizes liberals for ruining the consensus built with conservatives by changing the definition of affirmative action in midstream. He asserts that affirmative action, which had originally been concerned with equal opportunity, is now preoccupied with equal result. In Glazer's view, this approach is racist and discriminates against Whites. Thomas Sowell (1992), an African American researcher/professor from Stanford, accuses the government of attempting to achieve statistical parity.

Despite the divisions over affirmative action, such programs played a large role in increasing African American representation at American universities. From 1968 to 1974, the percentage of African Americans in undergraduate enrollment at universities increased from 6.4% to 9.2% (Glazer, 1975). Although these gains were impressive, conservatives noted similar gains for African Americans during the late 1950s and early 1960s, before affirmative action policies were set in place (Glazer, 1975).

The Allan Bakke Case

Given that affirmative action became a program of preferential treatment, it is not surprising that at least some aspects of the practice were challenged, for example, regarding the use of quotas in university admissions (Schwartz, 1988). One important case was based on the experiences of Allan Bakke *(University of California Regents v. Allen Bakke)*. His experiences of apparent discrimination occurred in 1973 and 1974, although the Supreme Court did not hand down a decision until 1978 (Ball, 2000; Schwartz, 1988; Wilkinson, 1979).

The University of California-Davis (UC-Davis) had initiated an affirmative action program designed to increase the representation of minority students. The school set aside 16 places for minorities in a special admissions program that involved considerably lower standards than the general admissions program (Ball, 2000; Schwartz, 1988; Wilkinson, 1979). Bakke, a White applicant, filed suit, claiming that the Davis quota system kept him from being admitted. When an applicant was White, he or she had no opportunity to gain entrance into those 16 slots set aside for minority students. Instead, that person could gain admittance only via the general program. However, when an applicant was a minority, he or she could be accepted into either the general program or the special program. If this individual was unable to be accepted into the general program, there was a second opportunity to be admitted via the special program (Ball, 2000; Schwartz, 1988; Wilkinson, 1979).

Bakke applied to the UC-Davis medical school in both 1973 and 1974 and was rejected both times, even though both his grade point average (GPA) and his Medical College Admission Test (MCAT) scores exceeded the majority of students admitted (see Table 10.1). Bakke asserted that he had had no chance of competing for those 16 special positions because of his race (Ball, 2000; Schwartz, 1988; Wilkinson, 1979). In other words, as stated by the U.S. Commission on Civil Rights (1979), "Davis had two admissions programs for the entering class of 100 students, the regular admissions program and the special admissions program" (p. 5). Bakke filed suit, claiming that the UC-Davis quota system had kept him from being admitted. He asserted that he had had no chance of competing for the 16 special positions because of his race, alleging that the medical schools' "setting aside of sixteen seats for minority applicants was an illegal, unconstitutional racial quota prohibited by both the Fourteenth Amendment's Equal Protection Clause and Title VI of the 1964 Civil Rights Act" (Ball, 2000, p. 53). Both a lower court and the California Supreme Court ruled in favor of Bakke and concluded that UC-Davis must admit him. In a 5-to-4 decision, the Supreme Court agreed and declared that the use of quotas was unconstitutional (Ball, 2000; Schwartz, 1988; Wilkinson, 1979). The Court did add, however, that race could be one of many factors considered in admitting (Schwartz, 1988).

One reason the Bakke case gained the attention of so many people is that such experiences were becoming very common. Many Whites with outstanding GPAs and SAT scores

Table 10.1   Allan Bakke's Grades and Test Scores Compared With Other UC-Davis Medical School Applicants From the General and Special Programs

	Science GPA	Overall GPA	Verbal (Percentile)	Quant. (Percentile)	Science	General
Bakke	3.45	3.51	96	94	97	72
Regular Program (73)	3.51	3.49	81	76	83	69
Average	3.36	3.29	69	67	82	72
Special Program (73)	2.62	2.88	46	24	35	33
Average (74)	2.42	2.62	34	30	37	18

SOURCE: Simmons (1982).

were being turned down in favor of racial minority students (Ball, 2000; Schwartz, 1988; Wilkinson, 1979).

Affirmative Action as an Ideal and in the Actual World

What a great deal of the debate about affirmative actual comes down to is that many people believe in some type of affirmative action as an ideal, but they do not like the way it is practiced in the real world. People have a number of objections to the program, to the extent that they believe that the program needs a major overhaul. First, as Skrentny (1996) and others have pointed out, affirmative action aims at the "guarantee of equal results instead of equal opportunity" (p. 1). Second, some say the program has caused us to become overly focused on race; according to Tamar Jacoby (1996), this orientation is "poisoning our lives" (p. 200). Third, some claim affirmative action does not help those who need it the most. They argue that wealthy and middle-class people of color benefit, but not those entrenched in poverty, asserting that top universities and employers look at children raised in the best families and the best schools in order to meet their goals (Kuran, 1996).

The University of Michigan Case

In 2002, the U.S. Supreme Court was confronted with the most important legal decision on affirmative action since *Bakke,* about a quarter century before (Zelnick, 2004). The University of Michigan case was actually two decisions in one. They involved affirmative action programs at the undergraduate level *(Gratz v. Bollinger)* and also for law school *(Grutter v. Bollinger).* In a sense, the ultimate decisions handed down in 2003 were predictable because they were congruent with the *Bakke* decision, in that race was allowed as one consideration in admissions decisions, but quotas and decisions based solely on race were unacceptable (Ball, 2000; Schwartz, 1988; Wilkinson, 1979; Zelnick, 2004).

The University of Michigan's undergraduate admissions program had a very specific procedure to increase its minority representation on campus (Zelnick, 2004). The university assigned students point values of up to 150 points for admission *(Gratz v. Bollinger,* 2003; Zelnick, 2004). If a student had at least 100 points, he or she was guaranteed acceptance (Zelnick, 2004). The admissions committee assigned different point values for different accomplishments. For example, if a student scored a perfect SAT or ACT score, the student received 12 points (Zelnick, 2004). The existence of a scoring system was not the focus of controversy. Rather, it was the fact that minority students were given 20 points for their racial status (Zelnick, 2004). In other words, minority students needed only 80 points to be guaranteed admittance to the university, whereas Whites needed 100 points to be guaranteed admittance (Zelnick, 2004). The result of this policy for those students with combined SAT scores of 1,000 to 1,090 was that 93.4% of underrepresented minorities with a B average were admitted versus only 19.5% of Whites and Asians "with the same qualifications" (Zelnick, 2004, p. 94).

Although the statistics might be controversial in and of themselves, it was not really the admissions statistics that led to the undoing of this program. In fact, the University of Michigan law school program possessed similar admissions statistics. From 1994 to 1995, among Americans with GPAs of 3.25 to 4.0 and Law School Admission Test (LSAT) scores of 154 to 169, 92% of African Americans and 27% of Whites were admitted (Zelnick, 2004). Ultimately, it was the University of Michigan's granting of 20 points to most racial minority groups at the undergraduate level that the U.S. Supreme Court believed constituted reverse discrimination (Zelnick, 2004). Given that the law school did not include this point system, the U.S. Supreme Court did not object to the law school admissions program. Therefore, the two decisions were split, giving very little added sense of direction to the legality of affirmative action (Zelnick, 2004).

The Future of Affirmative Action

Affirmative action continues to be an area of great controversy. The debate really focuses on the issue of what is fair. What makes the resolution of the controversy so difficult is that both sides of the debate have valid points. Can African Americans raised in the inner city compete academically with other American children raised in the suburbs? Probably not. Is it fair to deny college admittance to a White student because of the color of his or her skin in favor of a minority student? Generally not. Adding to the controversy are extremists on both the left and the right who claim that a person is racist if that individual does not see the affirmative action debate in the same way they do.

However, most fair-minded people want college admissions programs that (a) reward those who work hard and achieve at high levels without reference to the color of their skin and (b) also give opportunities to those who have grown up facing certain obstacles. Few people would disagree with either of these two objectives. To the extent that this is the case, affirmative action programs are likely to mature to be more sensitive to a wider array of people. Some people, however, want to totally eliminate affirmative action programs. In the end, it is one thing to oppose affirmative action programs that target only race and another thing to oppose affirmative action as a general concept that addresses many kinds of disadvantages.

Recent trends in Supreme Court decisions and in public attitudes indicate that the nation is probably going to keep affirmative action in some form for many years to come; however, it appears that affirmative action programs as defined by preferential treatment for minorities are probably going to decrease (Ball, 2000; Jackson, 1992; Klinker & Smith, 1999; Schwartz, 1988; Staughton, 1966; Wilkinson, 1979; Zelnick, 2004). Recent decisions by California and Texas, the nation's two most populated states, to eliminate affirmative action in college admissions appear to constitute a trend (Jones & Smith, 1998). Various Gallup Polls taken during the 1980s and 1990s suggest that many people believe that preferential treatment, although well-meaning, is no longer appropriate and may well be racist in nature. However, most Americans are also aware that children frequently face disadvantages of many types, of which race can be one, and that these disadvantages should be addressed.

The general results of the current trend appears to be, first, to define affirmative action more broadly so that it encompasses a large number of disadvantages that children can face, including socioeconomic status, personal struggles overcome by a student, parental family structure, personal responsibilities necessitated by a hard life, and so forth. Second, the trend would seem to promote initiating programs of affirmative action at a younger age, including improving schools for underprivileged children and racial minority children. Simply making it easy for these children to gain acceptance into college is a Band-Aid solution to a much deeper problem. Although educators cannot address many of the disadvantages faced by children that originate in their families and neighborhoods, there is a great deal that educators can do to make schools as equal as possible.

Educational Debate: Affirmative Action

Affirmative action is probably one of the most emotionally charged educational debates. Of all the "educational debates" that appear in this book, it may be the one people are most tempted to be silent about. However, one needs to understand that open dialogue is healthy. When the O. J. Simpson court decision was first handed down, many reporters described a stone silence that fell upon businesses in which people of varied racial backgrounds worked (Jackson, 1997). That silence or lack of communication was an indication that the United States still has some real racial tensions. Lack of communication is not the key to increased understanding and empathy; open dialogue is.

- With this in mind, what are your views on affirmative action?
- Do the present programs work?
- Should affirmative action be kept or discarded?
- Are there ways in which affirmative action programs should change?

EXPANDING THE REACH OF THE CIVIL RIGHTS MOVEMENT: BILINGUAL EDUCATION

The Roots of Widespread Bilingual Education

Bilingual education is an inherent extension of the civil rights movement (Skrentny, 2002). It is based on the theory that language minority children stand the best chance of flourishing scholastically and maintaining both their languages and cultures by being taught in school in their native languages (Casanova & Arias, 1993; Diaz, 1990; Kjolseth, 1983). The Civil Rights Act of 1964 reads that there should be no discrimination on the basis of language and no discrimination on the basis of race.

A number of laws set the stage for what we now know as bilingual education.

1. *Title VI of the Civil Rights Act of 1964.* This act prohibits denial of equal education opportunity on the basis of race, language, or natural origin. The vagueness of the legislation was intentional. It was hoped that each locality would adapt to its situation.

2. *Title VII, the Bilingual Education Act of 1968 Elementary and Secondary Education Act.* This act provides funding for bilingual education and sets guidelines. It focuses not just on Hispanic children, but on "children of limited English-speaking ability." Once again, the wording is pretty nebulous. Bilingual education is never defined.

3. *U.S. Supreme Court Decision of 1974: Lau v. Nichols.* This decision places an obligation on school districts to remove language barriers that have the effects of excluding children from full participation in public education. The *Lau v. Nichols* case was responsible for the U.S. bilingual education system as we know it. In the decision, the Supreme Court declared that it was the responsibility of the school, and not the parents, to teach children in their native languages. Prior to this time, most Americans believed that it was primarily the responsibility of the parents to maintain their children's native tongue. *Lau v. Nichols* changed the entire orientation of the schools toward language minority students.

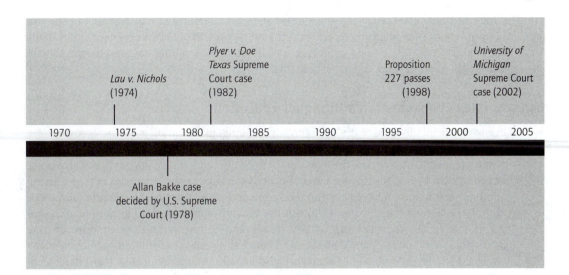

The vast majority of states in America possess bilingual education programs (U.S. Department of Education, 1995). The development of bilingual education largely arose as a result of the growing number of language minority children in the United States (Krashen, 1996). These children make up about 12% of America's schoolchildren (Cummins, 1989). However, this fact is rather deceptive in the sense that schools in some districts have a 30%-to-70% language minority enrollment. Many Americans associate bilingual education with Latino students. However, although Spanish-speaking students make up the largest group of students in bilingual education, it is actually taught in 145 different languages (Bergman, 1996; U.S. Department of Education, 1995).

Different Types of Bilingual Education Programs

One should note that bilingual education is not a singular phenomenon. There are a variety of different bilingual instruction and English immersion programs. First, there are *transitional bilingual programs.* This is the most popular approach currently used. In these programs, the subject matter is initially taught in the child's native tongue until the student's English is at a sufficient level of fluency that he or she can join in regular classroom instruction (Stewart, 1993). Second, *maintenance bilingual education* instruction is designed to preserve a child's home language and culture. Instruction can take place in both English and the child's native language. Third, two-way immersion programs teach both the student's native language and English in the same classroom.

Different Types of English Immersion Programs

English immersion programs also have a variety of orientations. First, there are *sheltered English programs.* This approach is generally used at the secondary school level. In this case, the teacher instructs using only English vocabulary that the child understands. Second, in *structured immersion programs,* the student receives all instruction in English but can use his or her native language in class (Stewart, 1993). Third, in *pulled-out immersion,* students are pulled out of their classes to receive special instruction in English geared especially to ESL (English as a second language) students.

Controversies Connected With Bilingual Education

Even aside from the issue of the extent to which bilingual education is efficacious, there are certain controversial aspects of bilingual education. First, bilingual education, as it is currently practiced, involves the preservation of not only one's native language but also one's native culture. This is controversial in the eyes of some, because they claim that preserving another person's culture goes beyond the scope of the functions of the school (Milk, 1993; Moll, 1992; Secada & Lightfoot, 1993). Some educators assert that bilingual education programs that focus on preserving both language and culture reduce the amount of time instructors spend on teaching language and hence slow down the students' ability to speak English (Milk, 1993; Moll, 1992; Secada & Lightfoot, 1993). Other educators insist that teaching students' cultures makes these children more comfortable in American schools and therefore will facilitate the learning process. Still other educators wonder whether it is appropriate for teachers to seek to preserve other people's cultures when they are not even encouraged to preserve American culture.

Another controversial aspect of bilingual education is that teachers are required to teach illegal immigrants. Former California Governor Pete Wilson claimed that his state was on the verge of bankruptcy because it was unable to care for all the educational and physical needs of illegal immigrants (Kertesz, 1996). In a case against the state of Texas, *Plyer v. Doe* (1982), the U.S. Supreme Court decision ruled that illegal immigrants must receive a public education; the state's desire to stop illegal aliens was not important enough to deny them an education. The justices stated that no one could be denied full protection under the law who is within the nation's borders. Although the concerns of California and other states that have a large number of illegal aliens are understandable, there are also many consequences if one does not educate these individuals. Unless these individuals have access to education, they are more likely to get involved with the wrong crowd, such as drug pushers, gang members, and those in organized crime, because the numbers of ways they can earn an income are reduced (*Plyer v. Doe,* 1982).

Pros and Cons of Bilingual Education

Bilingual education has been the subject of considerable debate in educational circles. Should the United States continue to use bilingual education as its main means of teaching English language learners? This question has become even more controversial with the passage of California Proposition 227, in 1998, which changed California practice by significantly limiting the extent to which bilingual education could be used in California schools. With the advent of Proposition 227, California showed preference for English immersion techniques (Alvarez, 1999).

In the bilingual education debate, there exist some convincing arguments on either side.

The Pro–Bilingual Instruction Perspective

The primary arguments of the pro–bilingual education school of thought are that (a) English-only instruction is insensitive to newly arrived immigrants who do not speak English as their first language and (b) the ability to converse in English to some degree is not sufficient to do well in school in an English-only instructional environment (Krashen, 1996; Stewart, 1993). Therefore, bilingual instruction proponents argue that schools should not initially place ESL students in English-only instructional environments (Diaz, 1990; Milk, 1993; Tabors & Snow, 2001). Let us examine these arguments more closely.

An English-only instruction environment is insensitive to ESL students. Bilingual education advocates assert that placing ESL students in all-English-speaking environments is a shock to them (Krashen, 1996). A number of researchers argue that ESL students will generally feel uncomfortable in this type of learning situation, where instruction is not given in their native languages, and cannot possibly be expected to achieve at the highest levels of which they are capable (Casanova & Arias, 1993; Diaz, 1990; Tabors & Snow, 2001). Tabors and Snow (2001) claim that ESL children in this environment will not only find adaptation difficult but that in these circumstances, "there is no possibility of the children becoming literate in their first language" (p. 173). Neuman and Dickinson (2001) go on to conclude, "Bilingual education has traditionally been justified on the grounds that children should be taught to read in the language that they know best" (p. 174).

Supporters of bilingual instruction assert that since many ESL students can already read and/or write in their native languages, it is an act of sensitivity to teach them using the language they already know (Diaz, 1990; Tabors & Snow, 2001). To do otherwise would be insensitive to these students and might impede their progress in other academic subjects (Casanova & Arias, 1993; Tabors & Snow, 2001).

Those who espouse bilingual instruction claim that anything other than bilingual instruction is insensitive not only to the student's academic adjustment but also to cultural and family dynamics (Crawford, 1989; Tabors & Snow, 2001). In their view, ESL students need to be encouraged to value and treasure their cultures especially, so they can develop high self-esteem. This can be done only if they are taught in a way that at least initially focuses on their native languages and cultures (Crawford, 1989; Neuman & Dickinson, 2001). The belief is that raising the self-esteem of these children will in the long run contribute to higher achievement. Furthermore, they believe that initially teaching ESL students in English is also insensitive in the sense that it undermines family ties (Krashen, 1996). Parents of ESL children are usually not skillful in English themselves, and if English becomes the child's dominant language, it will diminish the close ties that exist between parents and their children. Therefore, they insist that schools ought to reinforce the language that is spoken in the home. Bilingual instruction advocates claim that the only sensitive action is to initially teach ESL students in their own languages and then gradually introduce them to English, until they are also fluent in English (Casanova & Arias, 1993; Krashen, 1996; Neuman & Dickinson, 2001). Once this takes place, these children can be mainstreamed with the remainder of the school's students.

The strongest argument in favor of bilingual education is the sensitivity issue. Particularly if an immigrant is new to the United States and has little or no knowledge of English, it seems insensitive to insist that the child learn in an English immersion environment. It is true that many such classes provide interpreters to help new immigrants adjust. Nevertheless, proponents of bilingual education argue that sending a new immigrant to a class in which only English is spoken is insensitive to that student.

Some ability to converse in English is not sufficient for ESL students to succeed in an English-only instructional environment. David Stewart (1993) notes,

> The case for bilingual education rests heavily on the idea that the ability to use English develops in two stages. Basic interpersonal communication skills (BICS) come first, but although these enable the child to play and interact with other children, they do not translate into success in the classroom. (p. 148)

Therefore, as Tabors and Snow (2001) argue, "Children should be taught to read in the language that they know best" (p.174).

Stephen Krashen (1999) dismisses the argument that "many people have succeeded without" bilingual education (p. viii). Krashen asserts that this does not prove that English immersion is better than bilingual education. Instead, he claims that the level of English one uses in everyday conversation is nowhere near the level required to function well in school (Krashen, 1999).

The Pro–English Immersion Instruction Perspective

Those who prefer that children be taught using English immersion rather than bilingual approach have two primary objections to bilingual education. First, they assert that bilingual education segregates students within schools (Stewart, 1993). Second, they argue that bilingual instruction does not work and contributes to the high school dropout rate increasing among Latinos, while it has been steadily decreasing for all other major racial groups (U.S. Bureau of the Census, 2000). Let us now look at these two arguments more closely.

Bilingual education segregates students within schools. English immersion advocates believe that bilingual education does not reflect the spirit of *Brown v. Board of Education* (Baker, 1987, 1998; Rossell & Baker, 1996). Rather, it segregates students within schools, greatly discouraging their interaction. Advocates of English immersion argue that this segregation tends to "reinforce stereotypes, ghettoize immigrant children, and set them apart in programs perceived by students and teachers alike to be of inferior status" (Stewart, 1993, p. 149). Stewart adds, "Bilingual education classrooms are, by definition and of necessity 'segregated' unless they are of the type that include native English speakers who are engaged in learning another language" (p. 172).

Pro–English immersion educators are rather puzzled by most bilingual education programs because in their minds, this approach segregates students and therefore leads American education backward rather than forward (Stewart, 1993). They assert that in the Deep South in particular, before 1954, African Americans benefited the least from the nation's education system largely because they were segregated (Horwitz, 1998). Therefore, they claim, it is no surprise that the high school dropout rates of African Americans were often the highest among the various ethnic groups. Furthermore, it comes as no surprise that Latinos, who have been often segregated into specific classrooms because of bilingual education, generally have the highest high school dropout rates today (U.S. Department of Education, 2002).

European research on the effects of bilingual education indicates that this approach increases segregation between students within schools. This conclusion appears to be supported in a California study on the effects of attending mostly English immersion programs. They found that students of different racial backgrounds played with each other much more frequently than in environments in which bilingual education was practiced.

Bilingual education does not work and contributes to the elevated high school dropout rate among Latinos. Pro–English immersion educators believe that bilingual education simply does not work. They claim that bilingual instruction has had over three decades to prove that it is effective, and it has failed (Baker, 1987, 1998; Rossell & Baker, 1996). The primary evidence these advocates present is the fact that the high school dropout rate for every major race other than Latinos has gone down substantially since the mid-1970s, when bilingual education programs were first inaugurated nationwide (U.S. Department of Education, 2002). In contrast, during that same period, the high school dropout rate among Latinos has remained about the same or, by some measures, even increased (U.S. Department of Education, 2002). The English immersion proponents aver that if bilingual education worked, the high school dropout rates for Latinos, the primary target population for bilingual education, should also have declined (Baker, 1987, 1998; Rossell & Baker, 1996). Although these proponents do not put all of the blame for this lack of progress on bilingual education, they state that this instructional orientation bears substantial responsibility.

Assessing the Arguments of the Pro–Bilingual and Pro–Immersion Instructional Orientations: Can a Compromise Be Reached?

Given the extent to which both sides of the debate have convincing points, some argue that a compromise can be reached. One possibility is to place new immigrants in bilingual education classes and place those students who have been in the United States 2 to 3 years or more in English immersion classes.

Research by social scientists suggests that high-quality bilingual education programs work. However, most bilingual education classes probably do not qualify as high quality, and some educators argue that because of this, the overall program should be scrapped. However, others argue that given that some bilingual programs do work, educators should emphasize how to make most or nearly all of them work in this way. The bilingual education debate probably will not be resolved until there is further research in this area.

One reason bilingual instruction has evolved into such a contentious issue is that pro-bilingual and anti-bilingual educators are frequently far apart on the issue of how teachers should instruct ESL students. Stephen Krashen (1996, 1999) notes that social scientists from either perspective tend to cite a totally different body of research literature than those from the opposing group when attempting to substantiate their points. It may well be that spokespeople from both sides need to acknowledge the validity of a broad body of research before this debate is resolved.

One of the challenges of assessing the arguments in the bilingual debates is that both sides have valid and important points. Regarding the pro-bilingual statements, it does, in fact, seem insensitive to place new immigrants without any knowledge of English in an all-English-speaking classroom. Those who oppose bilingual education need to acknowledge this. And, indeed, it should be noted that even before bilingual education emerged on the school scene, bilingual tutors were generally present in classrooms to help ESL students adapt to an all-English-speaking classroom (Applebee, 1974). Therefore, if American schools should decline to return to an English immersion model, bilingual tutors should be provided as an act of sensitivity.

The pro-bilingual argument that ESL students who have the ability to converse in the playground may not be proficient enough to excel in school also has some truth. However, the extent to which this declaration is valid depends largely on how it is applied. After all, whether a child can converse in daily English conversation often is indicative of how the child will do in the classroom (Baker, 1987, 1998; Rossell & Baker, 1996). Therefore, while the general statement is true, one must be careful not to inadvertently communicate to children that we have low expectations of them.

The two assertions against bilingual education are also valid. There is no denying that bilingual education does segregate. Furthermore, research suggests that within-school segregation limits long-term interaction of children from different racial backgrounds (Baker, 1987, 1998; Rossell & Baker, 1996). There is a sense in which bilingual education as it is usually practiced is out of harmony with the spirit of the 1954 *Brown v. Board of Education* case. It would seem that whether one calls language instruction "bilingual" or not, it should consist of a more integrationist approach than is common today.

The second point that pro–English immersion proponents note about the substantial reduction in high school dropout rates for all major racial groups except Latinos is also noteworthy. Historically, high Latino dropout rates have resulted from a variety of factors (Krashen, 1999). Therefore, it would be unrealistic and unfair to entirely blame bilingual instruction. However, the fact that over the last three decades, Latino dropout rates have remained the same or even risen somewhat is troubling (U.S. Department of Education, 2002). Realistically, bilingual education has to take its fair share of the blame. If after 30 years of implementation, Latino graduation rates are farther behind those of Whites and other minority groups, one cannot help but conclude that bilingual education has some problems.

Proponents of bilingual education are divided as to whether the program has been a success or not. Some advocates believe that bilingual education bears no responsibility for Latino graduation rates falling farther behind those of other groups (Krashen, 1999). Other proponents believe that bilingual education has not worked especially well because either teachers have not used the best methods or the funding has been insufficient (Penedes, 1997; Valdes, 1997). In any case, the United States stands at a crossroads. The nation must decide whether to invest more time and money into bilingual education, with the hope that "practice makes perfect," or whether to return to the English immersion model, concluding that bilingual education has not lived up to people's expectations.

The Upcoming Decision

Making a decision regarding what to do about English language instruction will not be an easy task for the country. This is largely because there are valid points on both sides of the debate. Ideally, most Americans want an English instructional system that reflects the sensitivity and cognizance of children's stages of English acquisition that bilingual instruction advocates require. The majority of Americans also want an English instructional program that is integrationalist and lowers the high school dropout rate of ESL students.

The problem is that both bilingual instruction and English immersion instruction only partially fulfill these aspects. It is for this reason that the debate about bilingual education has continued almost indefinitely.

It is difficult to know just how this debate will be resolved. Perhaps because the gulf between both sets of advocates is so wide, it may be that some sort of compromise will eventually emerge. There are a number of possibilities. One option is to distinguish between students who are newly arriving immigrants and second-language students who have lived in the United States for some time. The former would be placed in bilingual instruction programs, and the latter would attend English immersion classes. The rigidity of both bilingual and English immersion programs is manifested in the degree to which these two sets of students are rarely distinguished in research and even at various times in the implementation of these programs. It may be a mistake to implement an all-or-none program of either bilingual education or English immersion.

A second option is to offer a dual-immersion approach to all students, which would create an integrated classroom. This approach is likely a more viable option in areas of the country where there is a clear dominant second language, as in a few of the southwestern states. Dual immersion in English and Spanish could well be appropriate in many classrooms in these areas. However, in about 40 states, the Latino population is only 2% to 3.5%, and such an approach would likely prove problematic. The fact that parents and children may prefer to study languages other than Spanish either because of the relevance to the business world or their overall popularity (e.g., Japanese, German, Chinese, Hindi, or French) may also make implementation more difficult.

A third option is to give parents and children more of a choice in whether the bilingual or immersion programs are offered. Different schools or districts would have the option of offering one or the other, based in part on community demand.

Although a compromise on English instruction appears to be one possible outcome, the nature of this appears uncertain.

Contemporary Focus

Those who choose to look at the bilingual education debate with a fair degree of objectivity will acknowledge that both sides of the debate possess some valid points and concerns.

- Considering these perspectives, what is your opinion of bilingual education programs?
- Do you feel that they work or not?
- Do you believe that the United States takes too much of an "all or none" approach to this issue? In other words, do you believe that there are situations in which bilingual education should be used and other times it should not?

CONCLUSION

The advance of civil rights in America was one of the most momentous periods in educational history in terms of questions of equality. It was an important enough issue that those who took a brave stand for civil rights, like Thomas Dewey and especially Harry Truman, will stand as national and educational heroes. Opponents of civil rights will be viewed in another way, even if they accomplished other things. The gains in civil rights made in the post–World War II era took the nation a step closer to realizing the age-old goal of equal education for all.

DISCUSSION QUESTIONS

1. There is little question that increasingly, America's leaders are influenced by poll numbers in directing policy. How do you think this affects school practices?

2. Countless countries have not experienced a civil rights movement. How would the world be influenced if every nation that needed a civil rights movement would have one? How would their schools be influenced?

3. According to *Lau v. Nichols,* it is now the responsibility of schools to preserve both the languages and the cultures of immigrant children coming to the United States who speak a language other than English. Do you agree with that decision? How much is it the parents' responsibility, and how much is it the schools' responsibility to maintain immigrants' languages and cultures?

4. Other types of preferential treatment exist apart from affirmative action. For example, if a parent is a graduate of a university and a generous donor to the school, a child of that parent has a better chance of being admitted than would otherwise be the case. It is highly unlikely that such preferential treatment will cease, even if some people object. The reason is that few would want to be in the position of telling a donor who just gave $100,000 to the university that his or her A- student was not admitted to the University of Chicago, Cornell, or Duke. What do you think of this form of preferential treatment?

REFERENCES

Abernathy, R. (1989). *And the walls came tumbling down: An autobiography.* New York: Harper & Row.

Abram, M. (1991). Fair shakers and social engineers. In R. Niel (Ed.), *Racial preferences and social justice* (pp. 29–44). Washington, DC: Ethics and Public Policy Center.

Alvarez, R. M. (1999). *Why did Prop. 227 pass?* (Working paper No. 1062). Pasadena, CA: California Institute of Technology.

Applebee, A. N. (1974). *Tradition and reform in the teaching of English.* Urbana, IL: National Council of Teachers of English.

Ashmore, H. S. (1994). *Civil rights and wrongs: A memoir of race and politics.* New York: Pantheon.

Baker, K. (1987). Comment on Willig's "A Meta-Analysis of Selected Studies in the Effectiveness of Bilingual Education." *Review of Educational Research, 57,* 351–362.

Baker, K. (1998). Structured English immersion. *Phi Delta Kappan, 80,* 199–204.

Ball, H. (2000). *The Bakke case: Race, education, and affirmative action*. Lawrence: University of Kansas Press.

Beard, C. A., & M. R. Beard, M. A. (1944). *A basic history of the United States*. New York: Doubleday, Doran.

Bergman, B. (1996). *In defense of affirmative action*. New York: Basic Books.

Berman, W. C. (1970). *The politics of civil rights in the Truman administration*. Columbus: Ohio State University.

Bernstein, B. (1970). *Politics and policies of the Truman administration*. Chicago: Quadrangle Books.

Brandt, C. G., & Shafter, E. M. (Eds.). (1960). *Selected American speeches on basic issues, 1850–1950*. Boston: Houghton Mifflin.

Bremner, R. H., & Reichard, G. W. (1982). *Reshaping America: Society and institutions, 1945–1960*. Columbus: Ohio State Press.

Brown v. Board of Education, 349 U.S. 294 (1954).

Casanova, U., & Arias, M. B. (1993). Contextualizing bilingual education. In M. B. Arias & U. Casanova (Eds.), *Bilingual education: Politics, practice, and research* (pp. 1–35). Chicago: National Society for the Study of Education.

Cose, E. (1997). *Color-blind: Seeing beyond race in a race-possessed world*. New York: HarperCollins.

Crawford, J. (1989). *Bilingual education: History, politics, theory, and practice*. Trenton, NJ: Crane.

Cremin, L. A. (1976). *Traditions of American education*. New York: Basic Books.

Cummins, J. (1989). *Empowering minority students*. Ontario, CA: California Association for Bilingual Education.

Dartmouth v. Woodward, 17 U.S. 518 (1819).

Diaz, R. M. (1990). Bilingualism and cognitive ability: Theory, research, and controversy. In A. Barona & E. E. Garcia (Eds.), *Children at risk: Poverty, minority status, and other issues of educational equity* (pp. 225–238). Washington, DC: National Association of School Psychologists.

Finding, J. E., & Thackery, F. W. (1996). *Events that changed America in the twentieth century*. Westport, CT: Greenwood Press.

Fireside, H., & Fuller, S. B. (1994). *Brown v. Board of Education: Equal schooling for all*. Hillside, NJ: Enslow.

Fish, S. (1996). Opposition to affirmative action among Whites is racist. In P. A. Winters (Ed.), *Race relations* (pp. 36–42). San Diego, CA: Greenhaven Press.

Fraser, J. W. (2001). *The school in the United States*. Boston: McGraw-Hill.

Fried, R. M. (1998). *The Russians are coming, the Russians are coming: Pageantry and patriotism in Cold War America*. New York: Oxford University Press.

Gardner, M. R. (2002). *Harry Truman and civil rights: Moral courage and political risks*. Carbondale: Southern Illinois University Press.

Glazer, N. (1975). *Affirmative discrimination*. New York: Basic Books.

Gratz v. Bollinger, 539 U.S. 244 (2003).

Green, M. P. (Ed.). (1989). *1500 illustrations for biblical preaching*. Grand Rapids, MI: Baker.

Greenberg, J. (1994). *Crusaders in the courts: How a dedicated band of lawyers fought for the civil rights revolution*. New York: Basic Books.

Greene, K. (1989). *Affirmative action and principle of justice*. New York: Greenwood Press.

Grutter v. Bollinger, 539 U.S. 306 (2003).

Harding, V., Kelly, R. D. Q., & Lewis, E. (1997). *We changed the world: African Americans 1945–1970*. New York: Oxford University Press.

Hill, H., & Jones, J. E. (1993). *Race in America: The struggle for equality*. Madison: University of Wisconsin Press.

Horwitz, M. (1998). *The Warren Court and the pursuit of justice: A critical issue*. New York: Hill & Wang.

Ianniello, L. (1965). *Milestones along the arch: Twelve historic civil rights documents, from World War II to Selma*. New York: Praeger.

Jackson, D. W. (1992). *Even the children of strangers: Equality under the U.S. Constitution.* Lawrence: University of Kansas.

Jackson, J. L. Jr. (1997). Why race dialog stutters. *Nation, 264*(12), 22–24.

Jacoby, T. (1996). Integration in a color-blind society should be the goal. In P. A. Winters (Ed.), *Race relations* (pp. 200–204). San Diego, CA: Greenhaven Press.

Johnson, P. (1997). *A history of the American people.* New York: HarperCollins.

Jones, J., & Smith, E. L. (1998). Affirmative action onslaught persists. *Black Enterprise, 29*(1), 22.

Kertesz, L. (1996). Wilson slashes immigrant-care funds. *Modern Healthcare, 26*(36), 28–29.

King, M. L. Jr. (1998). *The autobiography of Martin Luther King Jr.* (C. Carson, Ed.). New York: Warner.

King, M. L. Jr., & Washington, J. M. (Ed.). (1986). *A testament of hope: The essential writings of Martin Luther King Jr.* San Francisco: Harper & Row.

Kjolseth, R. (1983). Cultural politics and bilingualism. *Society, 20*(4), 40–48.

Klinker, P. A., & Smith, R. M. (1999). *The unsteady march: The rise and decline of racial equality in America.* Chicago: University of Chicago Press.

Krashen, S. (1996). *Under attack: The case against bilingual education.* Culver City, CA: Language Education Associates.

Krashen, S. (1999). *Condemned without a trial: Bogus arguments against bilingual education.* Portsmouth, NH: Heinemann.

Kuran, T. (1996). A backlash against affirmative action is growing among Whites. In P. A. Winters (Ed.), *Race relations* (pp. 29–35). San Diego, CA: Greenhaven Press.

Lau v. Nichols, 414 U.S. 563 (1974).

Levinsohn, F. H., & Wright, B. D. (1976). *School segregation: Shadow and substance.* Chicago: University of Chicago.

Mauro, T. (2000). *Illustrated great decisions of the Supreme Court.* Washington, DC: CQ Press.

McCoy, D. R., & Ruetten, R. T. (1973). *Quest and response: Minority administration.* Lawrence: University Press of Kansas.

Milk, R. D. (1993). Bilingual education and English as second language: The elementary school. Contextualizing bilingual education. In M. B. Arias & U. Casanova (Eds.), *Bilingual education: Politics, practice, and research* (pp. 88–112). Chicago: National Society for the Study of Education.

Mills, N. (1979). *Busing in the U.S.A.* New York: Teachers College Press.

Moll, L. C. (1992). Bilingual classrooms and community analysis: Some recent trends. *Educational Researcher, 21*(2), 20.

Montgomery, S. L. (1994). *Minds for the making: The role of science in American education, 1750–1990.* New York: Guilford Press.

Neuman, S. B., & Dickinson, D. K. (Eds.). (2001). *Handbook of early literary research.* New York: Guilford Press.

Niel, R. (1991). *Racial preference and racial justice: The new affirmative action controversy.* Washington, DC: National Book Network.

Ogbu, J. U. (1992). Adaptation to minority status and impact on school success. *Theory Into Practice, 31,* 287–295.

Ogbu, J. U. (1993). Differences in cultural frame of reference. *International Journal of Behavioral Development, 16,* 483–506.

Passow, H. A. (1979). *The gifted and the talented, their education and development.* Chicago: University of Chicago.

Pendleton, C. M. (1991). Equality of opportunity or equality of results. In D. Altschiller (Ed.), *Affirmative action* (pp. 7–16). New York: H. W. Wilson.

Penedes, C. (1997). Bilingual education: Boom or bust? *American Language Review, 1*(4), 6–8

Plessy v. Ferguson, 163 U.S. 537 (1896).

Plyer v. Doe, 457 U.S. 202 (1982).

Rippa, S. A. (1997). *Education in a free society*. White Plains, NY: Longman.

Rossell, C. H., & Baker, K. (1996). Educational effectiveness of bilingual education. *Research in the Teaching of English, 30*(1), 7–74.

Schwartz, B. (1988). *Behind Bakke: Affirmative action and the Supreme Court*. New York: New York University Press.

Secada, W. G., & Lightfoot, T. (1993). Symbols and political context of bilingual education in the United States. In M. B. Arias & U. Casanova (Eds.), *Bilingual education: Politics, practice, and research* (pp. 36–64). Chicago: National Society for the Study of Education.

Shull, S. A. (1999). *American civil rights policy from Truman to Clinton: The role of presidential leadership*. Armonk, NY: M. E. Sharpe.

Skrentny, J. D. (1996). *The ironies of affirmative action: Politics, culture, and justice in America*. Chicago: University of Chicago Press.

Skrentny, J. D. (2002). *The minority rights revolution*. Cambridge, MA: Harvard University Press.

Simmons, R. (1982). *Affirmative action: Conflict and change in higher education after Bakke*. Cambridge, MA: Schenkman.

Sowell, T. (1992). *Inside American education*. New York: Free Press.

Spring, J. (1990). *The American school 1642–1990*. New York: Longman.

Spring, J. (1997). *The American school 1642–1996*. New York: Longman.

State of Missouri ex rel Gaines Canada et al. 305 U.S. 337 (1938).

Staughton, L. (1966). *Nonviolence in America: a Documentary history*. Indianapolis, IN: Bobbs-Merrill.

Steele, S. (1996). Self-segregation should be condemned. In P. A. Winters (Ed.), *Race relations* (pp. 209–215). San Diego, CA: Greenhaven Press.

Stewart, D. W. (1993). *Immigration and education*. New York: Lexington Books.

Sweatt v. Painter, 339 U.S. 629 (1950).

Tabors, P. O., & Snow, C. (2001). Young bilingual children and early literacy development. In S. B. Neuman & D. K. Dickinson (Eds.), *Handbook of literary research* (pp. 159–178). New York: Guilford Press.

University of California Regents v. Allen Bakke, 438 U.S. 265 (1978).

U.S. Bureau of the Census (2000). *Historical statistics of the United States*. Washington, DC: U.S. Government Printing Office.

U.S. Commission on Civil Rights. (1979). *Toward an understanding of Bakke*. Washington, DC: Author.

U.S. Department of Education. (1995). *Digest of statistics for limited English proficient students*. Washington, DC: Author.

U.S. Department of Education. (2002). *Digest of education statistics*. Washington, DC: Author.

Urban, W., & Wagoner, J. (2000). *American education: A history*. Boston: McGraw-Hill.

Valdes, G. (1997). Dual-language immersion programs: A cautionary note concerning the education of language minority students. *Harvard Educational Review, 67,* 391–429.

Wilkie, W. (1945). Today and tomorrow: Citizens of Negro blood. In B. Moon (Ed.), *Primer for White folks* (pp. 311–319). Garden City, NY: Doubleday.

Wilkinson, J. H. (1979). *From Brown to Bakke: The Supreme Court and school integration*. New York: Oxford University Press.

Zelnick, R. (2004). *Swing dance: Justice O'Connor and the Michigan muddle*. Stanford, CA: Stanford University, Hoover Institution Press.

CHAPTER 11

The Turbulence of the 1960s

The 1960s was a time of phenomenal change in American education. When people think of the turmoil of the 1960s, they often think of the student demonstrations that stretched across many college campuses and the discontent they expressed, particularly toward the Vietnam War (Miles, 2004; Ravitch, 1983). And, indeed, the student demonstrations had a pervasive impact on American education and society not only in the short term, but in the long term as well. However, there were also other major movements that influenced education, most notably the New York City teachers' strike of 1968 (Podair, 2002), the civil rights movement lead by Martin Luther King Jr., the mainstreaming of educational practices espoused by many academic theorists (Palmer, 2001), and taking voluntary prayer out of the schools (Michaelsen, 1970).

These events constituted some of the most important changes to come to education in the 20th century. Amazingly, they all transpired during just one decade. In this chapter, we will address each of these issues and discover why American education was considerably different at the end of this decade than it was at the beginning. We will examine each of these trends, as well as others, and how they influenced education and American society as a whole.

THE VIETNAM WAR AND STUDENT ACTIVISM

Just as the other major wars in American history impacted schooling to a great degree, the Vietnam War was no exception (Ravitch, 1983). The student activism of the 1960s cannot be separated from the existence of the Vietnam War. Without the Vietnam War, demonstrations that students initiated would likely have been isolated and would not have possessed the intensity of those during the Vietnam War (Goines, 2001).

Some Context Regarding Student Demonstrations

Those who do not remember the 1960s might wonder why the student demonstrations concerning the war became so poignant. There are a number of reasons for this, but a prominent one is that many Americans were simply becoming satiated with war (Johnson, 1997). From 1941 to 1945, Americans were engaged in World War II; during the early 1950s,

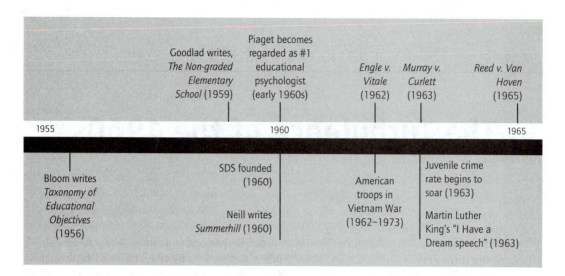

tens of thousands of GIs lost their lives in the Korean War; then there was the Bay of Pigs invasion, the Cuban Missile Crisis, and interventions in Greece and Central America. Finally, in the 1960s, there was yet another conflict, the Vietnam War. Americans were becoming satiated with war and the fact that many nations somehow expected the United States to be the world's police force (Miles, 2004).

The Vietnam War constituted one of the major events of the Cold War. The French tried and failed to fend off the communist takeover of South Vietnam led by Ho Chi Minh. Once the French realized that victory in the war was not achievable for them, they desired to "hand the baton" to the United States (Smith, 1983). However, having just completed the Korean War, President Eisenhower showed no particular predilection for committing American troops to Vietnam (Johnson 1997; Smith, 1983). He did send a small group of military advisors, but he did not anticipate that any greater commitment would be needed (Morin, 1969; Smith, 1983).

Once he assumed the role of president, John F. Kennedy was much more concerned about the situation in Vietnam. The Cuban Missile Crisis convinced Kennedy that to lose key battles in the Cold War could bring the threat of communism in close proximity to America's shores (Kaiser, 2000; Paterson, 1989). Kennedy had run against Richard Nixon, claiming that Eisenhower had been too soft on communism (Johnson, 1997; Kaiser, 2000; Paterson, 1989). This claim, we now know, has a certain irony to it, given that it was Eisenhower's threat of using nuclear weapons that helped end the Korean War (Morin, 1969). Neither Kennedy nor the American public was cognizant of this fact at the time (Kaiser, 2000; Paterson, 1989). Consistent with Kennedy's position in reference to Nixon, he had developed a reputation of being a staunch anticommunist, and he displayed this trait in his dealings with Cuba and Vietnam (Kaiser, 2000; Paterson, 1989). Kennedy sent numerous military advisors to Vietnam and anticipated that sending American troops might be necessary. Nevertheless, Kennedy sent far fewer U.S. troops than did Lyndon Johnson, who would eventually replace Kennedy as president, and there was still very little concern about Vietnam among college students (Kaiser, 2000; Paterson, 1989).

In retrospect, the American people were initially quite patient with the Vietnam troop buildup. As early as 1962, during the Kennedy administration, the United States already had 12,000 troops in Vietnam and spent half a billion dollars a year to support South Vietnam forces (Kallen, 2001). Despite this, the first large student demonstration did not occur until 1964 at the University of California, Berkeley, and this was primarily about issues other than Vietnam (Goines, 2001). The first antiwar marches were in 1965 in Washington, D.C., and attracted about 15,000 people (Miller, 2001).

The Rise of Student Demonstrations

The student demonstrations would not have been as extensive and potent had it not been for several factors. First, a large student organization was established in 1960 that played a preeminent role in the eventual mobilization of student protests in the mid-1960s (Ravitch, 1983). In 1960, in Ann Arbor, Michigan, the Students for a Democratic Society (SDS) formed out of another student group and set about their goal of building a "new left" among American college students (Kallen, 2001). SDS leader Tom Hayden fabricated the organization around issues such as the risks of nuclear war, the presence of racism, and the belief that anticommunist sentiment was overblown (Ravitch, 1983). Although many people did not share the left-wing views of the SDS, many people from a gamut of political persuasions appreciated the idealism behind the group's views (Ravitch, 1983). No one interpreted the formation of the SDS as an event that would set in place the organization necessary to mobilize hundreds of student demonstrations in the 1960s.

Many of the leaders of the SDS were inspired by the successes of the civil rights movement and were emboldened because they thought what they were fighting for was also morally right. Although they were inspired by the victories wrought by Martin Luther King Jr., they used entirely different tactics (Ravitch, 1983). King was a Baptist minister who was inspired by Christ's teachings on pacifism and the pacifism practiced by others, such as the Puritans, the Quakers, and Gandhi. He believed there was moral power in passive resistance (King & Washington, 1986). In contrast, the roots of the student movement were not religious and were not pacifistic. They believed that the only way to instill change in American society was through promoting their alternative lifestyle and using whatever means necessary to get the attention of "the establishment" (Ravitch, 1983). Sometimes they were able to gain attention through peaceful means, but as time went on, they increasingly resorted to force (Miller, 2001). Although the SDS was vocal and willing to exercise controversial actions to achieve their goals, other factors worked in conjunction with the organization to bring about the protest movement of the 1960s (Miller, 2001).

A second factor that contributed to the demonstrations was that the students perceived that the way individuals over the age of 30 treated younger people was unjust (Miller, 2001; Podair, 2002; Ravitch, 1983). To say that nearly all the student demonstrations of the 1960s were directly about the Vietnam War would be inaccurate (Ravitch, 1983). It would, however, be accurate to say that most of the student demonstrations were "anti-establishment" and the Vietnam War was the primary reason students had such resentment (Astin, Astin, Bayer, & Bisconti, 1975; Kallen, 2001). Therefore, it is fair to say that even if a given student demonstration was not focused on Vietnam, the war was always in the backs of people's minds (Miller, 2001). To the student demonstrators, it seemed that adults were always telling them what to do but had little sensitivity to the needs of the younger generation (Goines, 2001). Two primary student complaints were that (1) university leaders dictated university policy but generally allowed little or no student input and (2) the U.S. government sent 18-year-olds to war, but these young people did not have the right to vote (Miller, 2001; Ravitch, 1983).

As for the first complaint, in the early 1960s, liberals had seized strong control over American public schools. Public schools now emphasized the liberal persuasion of a child-centered education rather than the conservative approach of a preparation-centered education (Miller, 2001; Ravitch, 1983). Deweyism pervaded most of the public schools. The universities, however, were much more preparation centered, that is, conservative, than were America's public schools (Ravitch, 1983). When students attended school at America's universities, this preparation-centered philosophy came as an unwelcome surprise. According to national polls, most of the voting public had little or no objection to the way the universities were run (Ravitch, 1983). However, the student demonstrators were vocal, and they were determined. According to these students, American society as a whole was focused too greatly on preparation and delayed gratification (Ravitch, 1983). And what good was preparation if you could be drafted and die in Vietnam a month later? These students saw value in "gratification now" and doing "what felt good" (Miles, 2004). Therefore, many sought immediate pleasure through sex, drugs, and alcohol (Miles, 2004; Ravitch, 1983).

The SDS and other student groups fought for greater student input in the decision making of universities (Ravitch, 1983). UC-Berkeley, for example, experienced mass demonstrations in 1964, because the school limited the degree to which political recruitment and fund-raising could take place on campus (Goines, 2001; Ravitch, 1983). As a state-funded campus, UC-Berkeley needed to avoid political controversy. But the students on the left resented this and demanded not only that this rule be changed but also that grades for undergraduates and dormitory rules be abolished. These students also insisted on student involvement in university decisions (Goines, 2001; Ravitch, 1983). Student demonstrations on the Berkeley campus continued sporadically throughout the 1960s until about 1970. The 1964 Berkeley demonstration set the stage for student demonstrations at key universities across the country (Goines, 2001).

A third factor that contributed to the demonstrations was the exponential increase in the nation's military involvement in Vietnam under President Lyndon Johnson. Johnson especially intensified the American arms buildup beginning in 1965. Repeatedly, Johnson committed more troops to Vietnam, until the number of U.S. troops was over a half million, nearly as large as the population of Boston today (Berman, 1989; VanDeMark, 1991). Although the students were often violent and destructive, it is important to understand their perspective during that time. From the 1940s to the 1960s, the United States had been involved in more military conflicts and lost more soldiers in the battlefield than during any period in its history (Berman, 1989; VanDeMark, 1991). One should note, however, that if one includes civilian deaths and the proportion of the American population that perished, the Civil War was the nation's deadliest war (Richardson, 1960). Nevertheless, students, particularly male students, were the individuals being drafted to fight for the United States. The bottom line is that this generation was fed up with all wars (Archer, 1986).

A fourth factor contributing to the demonstrations was that radical leftists obtained leadership positions in the student movement. The major turning point in the student protest movement occurred in 1965, when the Soviet-influenced Progressive Labor Party (PL) joined the SDS (Ravitch, 1983). Within the SDS, the PL demanded that the SDS always abide by its stand. In addition, the PL leaders were more vocal and persuasive than the "new left" SDS leaders, and therefore those from the PL assumed many key leadership positions within the SDS. Consequently, the PL members drove the SDS too far to the left of the political spectrum (Ravitch, 1983). By 1967, members of the SDS were meeting with revolutionaries from "North Vietnam, Cuba, and other Communist countries" (Ravitch, 1983, p. 199). By 1967, the SDS had been driven far enough to the left that they became one of the centerpieces of the "hippie" countercultural movement (Miles, 2004; Ravitch, 1983).

Student Demonstrations Intensify

As the severity of the war increased from 1965 to 1968, student demonstrations increased in intensity and drew greater numbers of students (Astin et al., 1975). The student movement gained a lot of media attention and aroused the concerns of many university leaders. Student takeovers of university buildings occurred at many universities, including Columbia, the University of Wisconsin, and Harvard (Ravitch, 1983). Student bombings killed people at various schools, including the University of Chicago and the University of Wisconsin. As Astin and his colleagues (1975) note, student violence "became almost commonplace" (p. 26). Furthermore, "Terrorist acts—including bomb threats, planting of bombs, and attempts to intimidate administrators and unsympathetic faculty members—also grew more frequent" (p. 26).

A major psychological turning point took place in 1968 when the North Vietnamese launched the TET offensive. In this strategy, the North Vietnamese initiated about 100 "mini-offensives" in a wide range of places in order to communicate that they could attack anywhere and at any time (Kallen, 2001). Although American troops repelled the offensive, the expansive nature of the attacks convinced many Americans that President Johnson's claims that victory was near were hollow (Kallen, 2001). With over a half million American troops in Vietnam and many thousands of them dying, the students lost patience with President Lyndon Banes Johnson (LBJ), frequently chanting, "Hey, hey, LBJ, how many kids did you kill today?" (Kallen, 2001, p. 23). As antiwar sentiment spread to many Americans, Johnson realized that he could not win reelection and stepped down from the effort early in the primary season.

In 1969, Richard Nixon became president, largely because he promised that he would get American troops out of Vietnam with honor (Kimball, 1998). He nevertheless communicated with the American people that this process would take time, and this antagonized many students who wanted the troops removed immediately (Kimball, 1998; Ravitch, 1983). The demonstrations therefore continued (Miles, 2004). The combination of students' distrust of the "over-30 establishment" and Nixon's secretive nature led to the infamous Kent State demonstrations of 1970 (Kimball, 1998).

The geographical realities of war led the North Vietnamese to develop a certain strategy to conquer South Vietnam. Rather than invade head-on from North Vietnam into the northern part of South Vietnam, the North Vietnamese concluded that they should focus on conquering Saigon, the capital of South Vietnam, located in the southern portion of the country (Smith, 1983). To do this, they moved military supplies along the Ho Chi Minh Trail, which stretched across North Vietnam, Laos, and Cambodia. Cognizant of this fact, in 1970, Nixon ordered American planes to bomb Cambodia. However, Nixon did not openly communicate this fact to the American people, but, rather, newspapers released this information. Students interpreted Nixon's actions as expanding the Vietnam War, contradicting his promise to gradually end it (Kimball, 1998; Smith, 1983). Furthermore, when Nixon also ordered ground assaults in Cambodia, this further enraged many students (Ravitch, 1983). Had Nixon previously openly explained that he was not expanding the war, but was trying to remove a threat, most Americans, even if they disagreed with Nixon, would have likely accepted his explanation. However, Nixon's attempt to keep the matter secret hurt him in this case.

As a result of the situation, students demonstrated at Kent State University, in Ohio. There, they rioted, "burned the campus ROTC building, and prevented firemen from saving the building" (Ravitch, 1983, p. 219). As a result, the political leaders of Ohio sent in the National Guard to restore order. The students threw stones and other objects at the men. Unfortunately, the National Guardsmen were not given shields to protect themselves. The turning point happened when 600 Kent State students surrounded about 100 National Guardsmen and pelted them with rocks (Grant & Hill, 1974). Student demonstrators typically engaged in this activity because they believed the response would always be minimal. However, in this case, the National Guard fired on the students, killing four of them (Aron, 1997). The troops claimed that the students fired first, and the students asserted the reverse. Some claimed that a student sniper initiated the gunfire, but one was never found. What is clear is that the National Guardsmen thought they were in danger (Grant & Hill, 1974). An initial government investigation indicated that the troops had shot first (Aron, 1997). The chronology of events remains controversial. Although there was a temporary student backlash over the killings, the SDS had moved so far to the left that it no longer enjoyed enough popularity to mobilize students much further. As a result, the pinnacle of the student demonstration movement also spelled a turning point, and major student protests subsided in the aftermath of the Kent State incident (Ravitch, 1983)

Long-Term Effects of Student Demonstrations

Astin et al. (1975) assert that although the student protests abated during the period from 1970 to 1971, they had the considerable long-term impact of causing people to question authority. Garry Willis (1999) asserts, "Some believe that this massive challenge to authority loosened the whole fabric of society" (p. 185). A second central long-term effect has been seen in the trend toward historical revisionism.

Questioning Authority

At the heart of the student demonstrations of the 1960s was a sense that the Vietnam War was wrong (Miles, 2004; Ravitch, 1983). According to the student demonstrators, it was the United States and not the communists who were the "bad guys" in the war (Goines, 2001). Of course, many Americans disagreed. This group of Americans argued that our primary mistake in the Vietnam War was that we had a defensive strategy and did not make a full attempt to win the war. Instead, the United States vowed only to protect South Vietnam, rather than launch a land invasion of North Vietnam (Head & Grinter, 1993). Nevertheless, there remained a considerable percentage of Americans who believed that the war in Vietnam was a civil war in which it was not America's business to intervene (Head & Grinter, 1993) and therefore America was errant to fight in Vietnam.

Whether or not the United States was right to fight in Vietnam is not the issue that we want to dwell on in this book. Rather, we want to focus on the results that emerged due to that conclusion by many student demonstrators. That is, there arose a new distrust of almost every U.S. major institution: the presidency, Congress, the media, the schools, and so forth. The interesting fact is that this wariness did not abate after the Vietnam War. In fact, when the Watergate scandal broke in the early 1970s, surveys indicated that the confidence that Americans possessed in most of our institutions fell even further (Head & Grinter, 1993). There was a pretty strong surge in Americans' confidence in their institutions during the 1980s, especially when it was clear that the Cold War was terminating (Gallup Poll, 2005). However, with the recent scandals of the 1990s and the attacks of September 11th, 2001, the public's faith in America's institutions dipped to new lows during the 1990s and into the early 2000s (Gallup Poll, 2005). During that time, however, one institution has managed to maintain fairly high confidence levels among the American people in the last 25 years, consistently ranking highest, and that is the military (Head & Grinter, 1993). After Vietnam, the military was held in disdain by many student demonstrators and other Americans (Ravitch, 1983). However, during the 1980s, Americans again started to hold the military in high esteem (Gallup Poll, 2005). Of course, the military has been beset by some scandals in recent years, but not as many significant scandals as other institutions, and its performance in Granada, Haiti, former Yugoslavia, and the Persian Gulf War bolstered the confidence of many.

Historical Revisionism

The second long-term effect of the student demonstrations is the emergence of historical revisionism. That is, before the Vietnam War, it was believed that in most armed conflicts the Americans had engaged in, they were on the side of right. Now, however, as a result of the Vietnam War, many young people believed that if the United States had been on the side of wrong in the Vietnam War, it seemed probable that the United States had been wrong in most, if not all, of its wars. Many in the younger generation became just as convinced of this as past generations were convinced that the United States was right in nearly all of its conflicts (Head & Grinter, 1993). One by one, the history of various conflicts was rewritten by historians such as Harry Magdoff, Adam Jones, Philip Foner, and Amy Kaplan to portray the United States as being on the "wrong side" (Flynn, 2002; Loewen, 1996; Nash, 1997). To some extent, the revisionism was not all deleterious, because it caused Americans to reexamine some exaggerated portrayals of history (Head & Grinter, 1993). Nevertheless, revisionism reached such a level in the 1980s that there was an attempt by some to portray Hitler as being unaware of the concentration camps and as really not such a bad person. This assumption was apparently based on a diary by Adolf Hitler, in which he was portrayed as a reasonable fellow, deceived by his subordinates (Hamilton, 1991; Harris, 2001). The debate became so prominent that it reached the covers of many of the most prestigious American and European news magazines. However, the diary and other documents, which the revisionist historians were convinced proved Hitler's innocence, were proven to be forgeries (Hamilton, 1991; Harris, 2001). Similar attempts were made to censure the United States for the World War II battle with Japan. Revisionist historians argued that the United States was the primary guilty party because it had dropped the atomic bomb (Mee, 1975). And not only that, the United States was racist because it had dropped the atomic bomb on Japan instead of Germany (Mee, 1975). Of course, revisionists who assert this forget two important truths: (1) The atomic bomb was designed principally with Germany in mind (Irving, 1968), and (2) in fact, we could not have dropped the bomb on Germany, anyway, for the very simple reason that the Germans surrendered in May 1945 and the atomic bomb was invented in July 1945 (Mee, 1975). The United States could not have dropped an atomic bomb on Germany, because it had not yet been invented while they were still engaged.

A serious aspect of historical revisionism involves a change in which historical sources are considered to be the most accurate descriptions of history. For centuries, it was believed (and many maintain the same position today) that the most accurate historical sources were those closest in time to the actual event that occurred. Documents and diaries that were "straight from the horse's mouth" were considered most accurate (Head & Grinter, 1993). Under the historical revisionism approach, just the opposite situation is the case. It is now the opinion of many that recent writings are the most reliable. In defense of the young generation of individuals who started the movement of historical revisionism, they thought they had been lied to about Vietnam by the older generation. Their argument was that if they had been lied to about Vietnam, perhaps they had been lied to about everything. Hence came historical revisionism.

Changes in Students Over Time

Although most social scientists acknowledge that the student activism of the 1960s forever changed the cultural and political landscape of America, it should also be noted that the extent of that change could have been even greater (Mitchell & Block, 1983). Mitchell and Block administered a longitudinal study examining the degree to which UC-Berkeley students in 1967 maintained or changed their "values and attitudes" (p. 229) from 1967 to 1979. Their study distinguished between students who were activists during the 1960s and those who had not participated in the demonstrations. The results indicate that the student activists whose views were far to the left of the rest of the student body tended to moderate after they became 21 years of age (Mitchell & Block, 1983). By 1979, the student demonstrators were considerably less supportive of the views they once held and tended to have views similar to UC-Berkeley students who had not participated in the 1960s demonstrations (Mitchell & Block, 1983).

Similarly, when one considers the lifestyle changes that many hippies espoused, such as communal living and cohabitation rather than a family unit based on marriage, one should note that Americans generally do not regard communal living as a viable alternative to marriage (Davidson, 1971; Leary, 2001). It is true that the rates of cohabitation are significantly higher than they used to be (Jeynes, 2000). Nevertheless, many cohabitating couples view their family structure as a premarital arrangement. Consequently, although there have been some lifestyle changes since the 1960s, the vast majority of Americans still prefer marriage rather than cohabitation.

| **Contemporary Focus** |

Student Demonstrations for Today

Among students who demonstrated in the 1960s, many bemoan the fact that students are not as polit-ically active today as they were (Loeb, 1994; Raffini, 1988). In the opinion of an abundance of past demon-strators, college students today are too passive and do not take an active role in attempting to better American society (Loeb, 1994; Raffini, 1988). These people also argue that participation in what Kilpatrick (see Chapter 9) called a "socially purposeful act" was meritorious and educational. However, others assert that we are fortunate to live in a much more tranquil age than the 1960s (Kaldor & Holden, 1989). In addition, they claim that students may not be as politically inspired as they once were but that those that are air their views in a much more constructive manner than in the 1960s. What do you think?

- Are contemporary students as politically involved as those in the 1960s?
- Should they be as involved?
- Which do you value more, political activity or societal tranquility?
- Do you ever think similar demonstrations will occur again, especially in a society that has eradicated the draft and now allows 18-year-olds to vote?

CIVIL RIGHTS AND EDUCATION

There is no question that the civil rights movement forever influenced American education. This is especially evident in the *Brown v. Board of Education* (1954) decision, affirmative action, and other events. However, it is also patent that education had a considerable impact on the civil rights movement. When one thinks of that movement, Martin Luther King Jr. is the indi-vidual who generally first comes to mind. Without question, King's efforts dramatically impacted American education. Nevertheless, it is also true that education has had a dramatic impact on King as well. This is particularly salient because, as Stephen Oates declares (1982), "In truth . . . King did more than any other leader in his generation to help make emancipation a political and social reality in the racially troubled South" (p. ix). Oates adds, "King was all things to the American Negro movement—advocate, orator, field general, historian, fundraiser and symbol" (p. xi). Given King's prominence in his generation, his century, and for all history, it is particularly noteworthy to point out the effect that education had on him.

Naturally, King's first educating experiences were in the home. He was the son of a Baptist minister, Martin Luther King Sr., who was the pastor of Ebenezer Baptist Church in Montgomery, Alabama (Branch, 1988; King, 1998). Martin Luther King Jr. was born in 1929 into a loving family. As King (1998) asserts in his autobiography, "It is quite easy for me to think of a God of love mainly because I grew up in a family where love was central" (p. 2). King had a considerable amount of respect for his father both at a personal and a ministerial level. King states that his father had a great deal of influence in the African American community and commanded a certain degree of respect among the White population. On a personal level,

King (1998) also notes, "The thing that I admire most about my dad is his genuine Christian character" (p. 5). He also received much of his education, both as a child and an adolescent, at his father's church, which Oates (1982) declares was King's "second home" (p. 3).

Aside from his experiences at home and the church, King's college schooling helped shape the future leader's mind and heart (Branch, 1988; King, 1998; Oates, 1982). On September 20, 1944, King became a freshman at Morehouse College. In high school, King had been exceptionally bright, which enabled him to enter the 10th grade at the age of 13. Also, due to many college-age students being drafted, many colleges were in dire straits financially during World War II (Branch, 1988). Morehouse College was no exception, and therefore in order to stay solvent, it lowered its minimum standards for admittance. Consequently, King applied and was admitted to Morehouse and never went to the 12th grade (Branch, 1988; King, 1998). At Morehouse, King was influenced especially by two professors, Dr. George Keley, director of the Department of Religion, and Dr. Benjamin Mays. Both men encouraged King to read and integrate his knowledge of the Bible with the classic writings of literature (Branch, 1988; Oates, 1982). Oates (1982) observes that Mays "was out to renew the mission of the black church" (p. 19). According to Oates, Mays's goal "was not turning out doctors or lawyers or preachers, Mays said he was turning out men" (p. 19). Mays helped King understand what Oates calls "liberation through knowledge" (p. 19). Education, he told his students, allowed the Negro to be intellectually free. Mays enabled King to see that he wanted to be a minister and that this was the greatest way he could make a difference for humanity. As a result, King became an ordained minister in 1947 and assumed the position of assistant pastor of Ebenezer Baptist Church (Oates, 1982).

While at Morehouse, King read many of the classics on social thought. He perused works by W. E. B. DuBois, Booker T. Washington, and Karl Marx. Although he thought each of these writers had provocative insights, he came away dissatisfied with their approaches to the social ills of the day (King, 1998; Oates, 1982). King did not feel comfortable either with DuBois's solution of self-segregation or Washington's tendency toward accommodation (Oates, 1982). King especially felt uneasy with Marx's notion of communism because it was atheistic and totalitarian, and he felt corruption and dictatorial excess would result from this system (King, 1998; Oates, 1982). On June 8th, 1948, King graduated from Morehouse with a BA in sociology. As a result of going to Morehouse, King believed even more resolutely than before that Christ's teachings of love and passive resistance were the key to addressing the social ills and racism so persistent in the South. However, Christ was a religious and moral teacher and not a politician. Therefore, King did not yet perceive how these teachings could be applied not only at the individual level, but in the political sphere as well (Branch, 1988; King, 1998; Oates, 1982).

On September 14th, King entered Crozer Theological Seminary (King, 1998). Crozer was attractive to a number of African Americans and others desiring to enter the ministry because it was a high-quality, primarily White institution that was quite racially diverse (Branch, 1988). Walter Rauschenbusch now influenced King the most of all the authors he had read during his higher-education journey (Branch, 1988; Oates, 1982). According to Oates (1982), "Rauschenbusch summoned Christians to build a new social order, a new Christian commonwealth—in which morality would replace Darwin's law of the jungle" (p. 25). Rauschenbusch argued that most of the world was being engulfed by the survival of the fittest and "a whole era of competition, greed, and plunder" (Oates, 1982, p. 25). King realized through Rauschenbusch that new hearts and attitudes geared toward love and cooperation were needed instead of individual competition and materialism, which caused people to overlook the injustices of the day.

At Crozer, King was influenced by other thinkers and leaders who practiced and encouraged pacifism. Most notably, the theologian Reinhold Niebuhr affected King's thinking. Niebuhr declared that Christian pacifism could and should be applied to yield political and social change (Branch, 1988; King, 1998). The Quakers were among those who had demonstrated the utility of this principle, by their practice of pacifism and also their boycott of products made by slaves prior to the Civil War (Ammerman, 1995; Vahey, 1998). King was also impressed by a lecture on Gandhi delivered by Howard University President Mordecai Johnson (King, 1998). He was intrigued by the pacifism of Niebuhr, the Quakers, Gandhi, and Henry David Thoreau (Oates, 1982). Branch (1988) asserts that Niebuhr particularly affected King, because King cited him in his books much more than the others. The more he studied pacifism and civil disobedience, the more King came to apprehend that the principles of Christ could be applied to the political and social sphere in order to combat racism (King, 1998; Oates, 1982).

Despite King's joy over coming to this understanding, he was also saddened by his studies. He stated, "The more I observed the tragedies of history and man's shameful inclination to choose the low road, the more I came to see the depths and strengths of sin" (King, 1998, p. 25). Niebuhr was especially instrumental in honing this truth in King's mind. One facet of Niebuhr's writings that especially impressed King (1998) is that he was not deluded by what he called the "false optimism" (p. 27) that humans were inherently good, which plagued many idealists of the 1960s. However, King remained a realistic optimist, believing that God was capable of drawing out "man's potential for good" (p. 27) when people "allowed themselves to be coworkers with God" (p. 30). King became even more grounded in this perspective when he began his doctoral studies at Boston University, in September of 1951, because there, according to King, both Dean Muelder and Dr. Chambers held precisely this view. King more than ever realized the formidable nature of his task to fight segregation in the South. Nevertheless, he knew there was hope.

In Boston, in 1952, King met Coretta Scott, whom he quickly realized would become his wife. On June 18, 1953, Martin Luther King Sr. officiated at the marriage of his son and Coretta Scott, in Marion, Alabama (King, 1998). King was now ready to assume a role in American life that would forever change American education and the nation as a whole. Until 1954, American education had affected King. Now King would influence education and the nation.

In 1954, Dexter Avenue Baptist Church, in Montgomery, Alabama, requested that King become their pastor (King, 1998). King's decision to go to Montgomery would forever change his life and the direction of the entire nation. Consequently, 1954 emerged as a landmark year in American education and everyday life, not only because of the *Brown v. Board of Education* decision, but because of King's decision to pastor in Montgomery. Less than a year after King became pastor at Dexter, Rosa Parks, secretary of the Montgomery National Association for the Advancement of Colored People (NAACP) chapter, informed King that he had been elected to the executive committee of the chapter (King, 1998). On December 1, 1955, Rosa Parks was arrested in Montgomery for resisting the city's bus segregation laws. Four days later, supporters elected King head of the nascent protest group the Montgomery Improvement Association (MIA). Following this event, King delivered what he considered to be the most important speech of his life in Montgomery, Alabama, asserting that Rosa Parks's civil rights had been violated and that segregation needed to come to an end. King (1998) noted, "That night we were starting a movement that would gain national recognition" (p. 58).

King decided to launch an African American protest against the buses. African Americans provided, by many accounts, a majority of the passenger income for the Montgomery city bus system (Branch, 1988; Fredrickson, 2002; King, 1998; Oates, 1982). Consequently, King and his colleagues believed the bus boycott, because of its economic impact, had the potential for being a formidable tool for fighting segregation in Alabama. To ensure that African Americans could still fulfill their daily responsibilities and routines, African American churches and the NAACP organized to provide carpool transportation for those who normally rode the bus (Branch, 1988). On February 21, 1956, the Montgomery grand jury indicted King and other MIA leaders for violating the antiboycott law. The grand jury sentenced King to 386 days in jail and a $500 fine. The case was appealed (Branch, 1988; King, 1998).

The Montgomery bus episode was extremely challenging for King (King, 1998; Oates, 1982). He was suffering a great injustice in his battle for what was right. During the Montgomery bus boycott episode, King prayed,

> Oh Lord, I'm down here trying to do what is right. But, Lord, I must confess that I am weak now. I'm afraid. The people are looking to me for leadership and if I stand before them without strength and courage, they too will falter. I am at the end of my powers. I have nothing left. I can't face it alone. (as cited in Oates, 1982, p. 88)

But then, King sensed "an inner voice speaking to him" (Oates, 1982, pp. 88–89). The voice said "'Martin Luther, stand up for justice. Stand up for truth. And lo, I will be with you even to the end'" (King, as cited in Oates, 1982, pp. 88–89). "It was the voice of Jesus telling him *still* to fight on" (p. 89). King regarded the Montgomery experience as the key turning point of his public life (Branch, 1988; King, 1998; Oates, 1982). Ultimately, he led the way to victory, because on November 13, 1955, the U.S. Supreme Court asserted that segregation laws were unconstitutional. The decision broadened *Brown v. Board of Education* to apply to more than just education, but all walks of life. The integration of the South had now gained a prodigious amount of momentum.

King's influence increased further when on February 14, 1957, he became the head of the Southern Leaders Conference, which would later become the Southern Christian Leadership Conference. In May of 1957, King delivered a well-publicized address at Prayer Pilgrimage for Freedom, in Washington, D.C. (Branch, 1988; King, 1998; Oates, 1982). In September 1957, King (1998) praised President Eisenhower's decision to call in the military to enforce *Brown v. Board of Education* in Little Rock, Arkansas. In 1958, King and other civil rights leaders met with President Eisenhower. The White House gathering symbolized the amazing progress that the civil rights movement had made over such a brief period.

In 1960, King moved his family back to Atlanta to copastor with his father at the Ebenezer Baptist Church, in Atlanta, and to increase his presence at the headquarters of the Southern Christian Leadership Conference, also based in Atlanta. King (1998) declared that the desegregation of schools in the Deep South was taking place at such a gradual rate that it was intolerable (Branch, 1988; Oates, 1982). Consequently, he decided to implement a broad offensive against segregation in the South. He launched this initiative in Greensboro, North Carolina, by beginning a series of "lunch counter sit-in" demonstrations (King, 1998, p. 135).

In 1963, King (1998) focused his energy on Birmingham, Alabama, which he called "probably the most thoroughly segregated city in the United States" (p. 189). As King and others brought their civil rights activities to Birmingham to fight segregation, King paid a high price by being jailed there (Branch, 1988, 1998; Oates, 1982). Despite this, King realized the tremendous progress that the movement was making and firmly adhered to the strategy of passive resistance as the key to victory. In "A Letter From Birmingham Jail," King (1998) averred, "I have consistently preached that nonviolence demands that the means we use must be as pure as the ends we seek. I have tried to make clear that it is wrong to use immoral means to attain moral ends" (p. 202).

Although King generally focused on noneducational forms of segregation, his efforts spawned victories in schools and colleges in the South. Two months after King's letter from the Birmingham jail, President Kennedy had to federalize the Alabama National guard in order to enable two African Americans to enroll at the University of Alabama, despite the stern resistance of Alabama Democratic Governor George Wallace. In the 18 months that followed, King's life reached a climax with his "I Have a Dream" speech, in Washington, D.C., in August 1963, and his receiving of the Nobel Peace Prize, in 1964. King then directed his attention to Selma, Alabama, in 1965, like Birmingham, the site of a key civil rights thrust (Branch, 1998; Fredrickson, 2002; King, 1998; Oates, 1982).

Not everyone appreciated King's emphasis on passive resistance. Malcolm X called for African Americans to arm themselves and ready themselves for violence, which greatly concerned King. He believed that Malcolm X's approach had the potential of undermining many of the gains procured using passive resistance:

> I feel that Malcolm has done himself and our people a great disservice. Fiery, demagogic oratory in the Black ghettos, urging Negroes to arm themselves and prepare to engage in violence, as he has done, can reap nothing but grief. (King, as cited in Oates, 1982, p. 291)

King (1998) did have compassion for Malcolm X and attributed Malcolm X's attitude to the fact that "in his youth there was no hope, no preaching, teaching, or movements of nonviolence" (p. 267).

Martin Luther King Jr. was a beaming light rarely seen in a generation. Education helped shape him into the great spiritual and intellectual force that he was. King, in turn, fought against segregation and discrimination, especially in the Deep South, and helped cement the gains made in *Brown v. Board of Education*. In 1968, an assassin's bullet killed Martin Luther King Jr. African Americans mourned; Americans mourned; and the world mourned.

Added Insight: Martin Luther King Jr. and Education

Martin Luther King Jr. was not only an outstanding moral leader but also had an amazing intellect. From his early schooling, he was regarded as both a virtuous and extremely bright child. He was able to play well with children of different races, and this exposure made him aware of the value of each individual (Oates, 1982). His advanced intellect enabled King to swiftly go through his years of schooling and enter college and finish graduate school with his youth and vigor still intact. King's inspiring moral leadership, his acute mind, and his persuasive oratory all helped make him into the memorable leader that he was.

- Why was the combination of these three traits so important?
- Could King have lacked in any of these three areas and still had the impact that he did?
- In what ways were each of these three qualities helpful to accomplishing the progress that Martin Luther King Jr. sought?

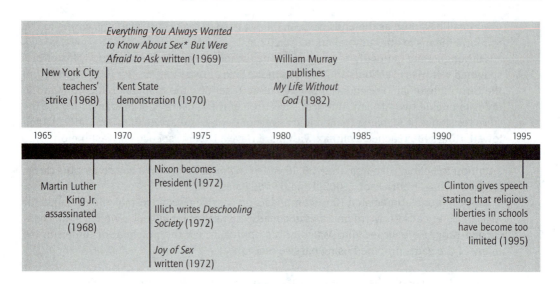

The timeline contains the following entries:

New York City teachers' strike (1968)

Everything You Always Wanted to Know About Sex* But Were Afraid to Ask written (1969)

Kent State demonstration (1970)

William Murray publishes My Life Without God (1982)

Martin Luther King Jr. assassinated (1968)

Nixon becomes President (1972)

Illich writes Deschooling Society (1972)

Joy of Sex written (1972)

Clinton gives speech stating that religious liberties in schools have become too limited (1995)

Timeline years: 1965, 1970, 1975, 1980, 1985, 1990, 1995

THE NEW YORK CITY TEACHERS' STRIKE

The Tumultuous National Background

The turbulence of the 1960s not only inundated college campuses with demonstrations and uncertainty but also spilled over into conflicts that resulted in teachers' strikes (Goldbloom, 1973; Podair, 2002). Naturally, teachers' strikes were not new, but the late 1960s emerged as a unique period in this regard because of the frequency, the length, and the severity of these strikes (Goldbloom, 1973). The late 1960s was a politically and emotionally charged period of transformation, which helps explain the intensity of the strikes of the period.

The most notable strike of the 1960s was the New York City school strike of 1968 (Goldbloom, 1973; Mayer, 1969). The crisis that emerged in New York was significant certainly because New York was the nation's largest city but also because the issues of race, autonomy, and unionism that arose in New York City were representative of the forces that were unleashed in many urban areas across the country (Cohen, 1973; Podair, 2002). Beyond this, because New York City schools were in the largest city and the place that had historically served as a beacon of educational light, the city was, in many respects, the battlefield of choice for educational clashes.

Barbara Carter (1971) eloquently summarized the challenge facing New York City urban schools:

> Here was the nub, the heart of the thing—the profound frustration over the failure of the system to improve education in the ghetto. . . . For all that the system had tried, and it had made many attempts—special serve schools, after-school reading clinics, Head Start centers, tutorial programs—little impact had been made. (p. 9)

Only 10 years before, the New York City public school system published and distributed annual reports that were disseminated all over the world, because during the 1930s, 1940s, and 1950s, the city's school system was not only the envy of the nation, but of the world (Jeynes, 2004; U.S. Department of Health, Education, and Welfare, 1957). By the late 1960s, however, New York City school students had slipped behind the national norm in achievement test scores (Carter, 1971).

The New York City school strike of 1968 was significant not only because of its status and locale but also because of its timing. One can argue that the summer and fall months of 1968 represented the most tense period during the tumultuous 1960s (Mayer, 1969; Podair, 2002). During this period of time, the Vietnam War was at its height. President Johnson had committed over half a million troops to Vietnam, and there appeared little chance that he would reduce the nation's troop commitments (Berman, 1989; VanDeMark, 1991). Concurrently, the United States was holding one of the most contentious presidential elections in its history (Johnson, 1997). Vice President Hubert Humphrey, a Democrat, promised the American people that victory would eventually come in Vietnam, while former Vice President Richard Nixon promised that he would secure peace with honor in the war (Berman, 1989; VanDeMark, 1991). That is, he promised that he would gradually reduce the number of American military personnel fighting in Vietnam, and he declared that he could accomplish this while departing with a sense of having successfully accomplished a task. The subsequent election was one of the closest in American history, revealing the deeply divided nature of the country (Kimball, 1998). Perhaps most significant of all, on April 4, 1968, Martin Luther King Jr. was assassinated. His death would leave a void not only in African American leadership, but in the nation's leadership. That is not to say that there were not other leaders of significance in both the African American and national community, but when a leader of the caliber of King passes on, decades often pass before someone of the same quality rises again. Moreover, with the death of King, many African Americans reexamined the issue of whether passive resistance was really the most efficacious form of protest (Oates, 1982).

The timing of the New York teachers' strike added to the intensity of the divide between the minority parents and the teachers' unions (Mayer, 1969; Podair, 2002). Given that the strike took place at the height of the Vietnam War, in the midst of a potential executive-branch-based change in military strategy and months after the assassination of King, in this atmosphere, the strike became even more politically charged than would have otherwise been the case (Mayer, 1969; Podair, 2002).

Perspectives of African American and Other Minority Parents

African American parents, in particular, in certain sections of New York City voiced their desire for more autonomy in hiring decisions and in school policy and curriculum issues (Podair, 2002; Urofsky, 1970). The reason African American families placed such an emphasis on greater community control as the key can be attributed to two issues. First, over the years, educators and politicians had tried virtually every other means of raising the level of inner-city student achievement, for example, raising school expenditures, providing extra tutoring, reducing class sizes, and so forth (Carter, 1971). Second, since the early 1930s, the New York City school system had become increasingly centralized to the degree that by 1967, people recognized that it had devolved into an inefficacious bureaucracy:

> During the course of political reform in the 1930s, control of the New York City school system was narrowly concentrated in a central office. In the 1950s and

early 1960s the machinery grew too complicated and too rigid for its purposes, and the system became increasingly unresponsive to both the teachers in the classrooms and the parents whose children were in the schools. . . . From 1961, when the state legislature mandated "revitalization" of the local school boards, which had been allowed to atrophy since the 1930s, there had been a political drive toward "decentralization" of the school system. (Mayer, 1969, p. 16)

The student body at Ocean Hill-Brownsville was about 75% African American and 20% Puerto Rican (Pritchett, 2002). Rhody McCoy (1969) states,

In Ocean Hill-Brownsville, there are people groping in the dark; they are people who for a long time have felt themselves outside the mainstream of public concern. . . . These residents have been frustrated at every turn in their attempt to reverse the process. (p. 52)

McCoy asserts that "the alarming turnover in staff, coupled with high pupil mobility" (p. 52) were two major factors contributing to school problems. The significant rate of turnover was especially important with regard to teachers, because over the 12 months leading up to the strike, many parents in the Ocean Hill-Brownsville area became convinced that the teachers were not committed to their children (Berube, 1969; Mayer, 1969).

Parents in the Ocean Hill-Brownsville district were frustrated with a stubborn tradition of low scores and high dropout rates among the students in the heavily African American area (Berube, 1969; McCoy, 1969; Podair, 2002; Pritchett, 2002). Although a host of factors contributed to this phenomenon, the residents of the area became convinced that lack of local control and the presence of the tenure system were two major reasons for the high student failure rate (Cohen, 1973). They believed that the tenure system allowed some incompetent and racist teachers to remain in the schools, when it was best for the students for the teachers to be fired (Cohen, 1973; Ravitch, 1974). The Ocean Hill-Brownsville residents wanted to possess the authority to fire these teachers and hire new ones (Cohen, 1973; Podair, 2002). They came to the conclusion that the teachers' union, the United Federation of Teachers (UFT), was the greatest obstacle to bringing this to pass (Mayer, 1970; Podair, 2002).

Two growing realities caused African Americans in the Ocean Hill-Brownsville District to believe that they were justified in insisting on greater community control of the schools. First, many people had become disillusioned with the educational policies of the 1960s, to the point that many African Americans believed that these policies had failed (Cohen, 1973; Silver, 1981). Specifically, they believed that the sharp increase in funding for African American students and desegregation had not raised African American scores (Cohen, 1973). Previously, African Americans had held high hopes for these policies, and they were greatly disappointed. In addition, Goldbloom (1973) notes that class size in inner-city schools had also decreased substantially, but test scores among African American and Latino students remained unaffected.

A second reason African Americans in the Ocean Hills-Brownsville District believed their complaints were justified is that during the 1960s, many Americans, not just Blacks, felt a loss of a sense of community control and connection with the schools. For example, many

Whites complained that busing was causing them to lose a sense of community (Podair, 2002). There was also a general consensus among all groups that New York City had what Podair (2002) called a "culture of centralization" (p. 23) that discouraged community control. African American leaders had become aware of the Coleman Report (U.S. Center for Education Statistics, 1966), which concluded that the family, rather than the school, was the main factor that influenced achievement (Cohen, 1973). African Americans were very desirous of finding a solution to the problems of underachievement and concluded that parental involvement and community control might be a more effective solution than government-sponsored policies (Cohen, 1973).

Even though there was great frustration among the residents of Ocean Hill-Brownsville, most people did not suspect that disagreements between these residents and the UFT would yield a teachers' strike, technically a series of three successive strikes, that the participants would not resolve until almost Thanksgiving of 1968 (Podair, 2002; Urofsky, 1970). Newly elected New York City Major John Lindsay was sympathetic to the parents' frustrations and believed that it was important for the city to increase its sensitivity to the needs of racial minority parents and students (Ravitch, 1974). Lindsay was open to the legislature's directive to "prepare a decentralization plan for the city's schools" (Ravitch, 1974, p. 329). The legislature passed this bill in April 1968.

On these bases, Lindsay established a committee to produce a paper eventually called the "Bundy Plan" in order to take action to increase the amount of autonomy parents and communities had in school affairs (Mayer, 1969; Podair, 2002). Soon, the commission drafted a proposal that would be introduced in the New York Legislature, significantly expanding the role that parents and local communities could play in the affairs of their local schools. Initially, many politicians and educators believed that the initiative represented a sufficient move in the direction of local autonomy that would preclude any immediate demands for greater control of school affairs (Mayer, 1969; Podair, 2002). However, the majority of these leaders underestimated the degree of frustration and tenacity of parents in the Ocean Hill-Brownsville school district (Mayer, 1970). Eugenia Kemble (1969) articulated the extent of this frustration well:

> The painfully obvious results of a failing school system—low reading
> schools . . . hostility and animosity both against those responsible for the
> educational inadequacy of the schools as well as against the teachers who
> work in them. (p. 33)

To the residents of Ocean Hill-Brownsville, a major turning point in their perceptions of the UFT emerged when their leader, Albert Shanker, called for a 2-week teachers' strike in the fall of 1967 (Carter, 1971). The union had just won huge salary increases, but now it wanted smaller class sizes (Carter, 1971; Podair, 2002). Many inner-city parents viewed the union members as selfish and unconcerned about the children who suffered as a result of the strike. In addition, the residents regarded the teachers as greedy and insensitive to children (Carter, 1971, Pritchett, 2002). Indeed, teachers' strikes, which previously were almost unthinkable and were very rare, were now becoming alarmingly frequent. In 1965, there were only 2 teachers' strikes nationwide, but in 1967, that number swelled to 80 (Carter, 1971). Even before the prodigious teachers' strike of 1968, many New Yorkers viewed the ease with which the UFT called a strike as calculating and power driven (Carter, 1971; Pritchett, 2002).

United Federation of Teachers' Perspective

The UFT viewed schools and students in an entirely different way than did the people of Ocean Hill-Brownsville (Mayer, 1969, 1970). First, the UFT believed that many of the students had attitude problems and that teachers were not allowed to deal with these students appropriately, either for the good of the students or the teachers (Carter, 1971). Second, the UFT believed that more money needed to be spent per pupil (Mayer, 1969; Podair, 2002). The UFT "requested that teachers have the right to suspend disruptive students from class" (Ravitch, 1974, p. 319) and that funding be increased. The view of the Ocean Hill-Brownsville parents was that funding per pupil had already been increased to a vast degree but students had shown no improvement in achievement (Carter, 1971; Podair, 2002). In their view, the union approach simply did not work.

African American parents interpreted the union's demand for teachers to be able to suspend students as being racist (Carter, 1971; Ravitch, 1974). The UFT interpreted the African American parents' demands also as racist and antiunion, because they directed all their complaints against White teachers, and nearly all these teachers were Jewish (Podair, 2002). In addition to these perspectives, both the Ocean Hill-Brownsville parents and the UFT opposed the Bundy Plan, but for entirely different reasons (Podair, 2002). The teachers' union claimed that the plan would give parents too much control over the activities in the local school districts, while the Ocean Hill-Brownsville district believed the initiative did not grant enough autonomy (Carter, 1971; Podair, 2002).

The turning point in the developing dispute came in the fall and winter of 1967, when the Ocean Hill-Brownsville district governing board concluded that not only was the autonomy promised by the Bundy decentralization plan insufficient, but to approve such a plan was worse than having no plan at all (Carter, 1971; Mayer, 1970). To achieve their goal of local autonomy, the people of Ocean Hill-Brownsville took actions that bypassed contract agreements and school authority. In the eyes of the teachers' union, this action virtually guaranteed that there would be a long strike. The union believed that to give in to these actions would set a terrible precedent for education nationwide (Mayer, 1970; Podair, 2002). As a result, the UFT significantly toughened its stance against any degree of decentralization and specifically showed stiff opposition to the Bundy Plan (Mayer, 1969; Podair, 2002). Mayor Lindsay tried to broker a compromise, but neither side was willing to find a middle ground (Mayer, 1970).

Laudable Goals But Misguided Strategy

Although the desire of African American parents, in particular, for greater local control over the schools was understandable, their strategy in Ocean Hill-Brownsville area did not reflect the King rubric of passive resistance that had earned so many victories previously (Branch, 1988, 1998; King, 1998; Oates, 1982). Perhaps this was understandable, given that King had just been assassinated. With King's assassination, new doubts arose over the effectiveness of his techniques (Oates, 1982). There was a leadership void not only within the African American community but also within the United States as a whole. Naturally, there were other leaders of various hues, but the stature of King's leadership was one that people witness only rarely in a lifetime. King had a way of leading the way to victory, even against tremendous odds (Branch, 1988, 1998; King. 1998; Oates, 1982). In the absence of the King rubric of passive resistance, what should have been a victory, based on principle, produced disappointing results (Mayer, 1970; Podair, 2002). As perhaps the first major civil rights engagement since King's assassination, his absence was evident. The goals of the Ocean Hill-Brownsville parents were consistent with other civil rights struggles, but the ensuing strategy lacked the acumen and sensitivity of King. Even the most successful historical tides have setbacks, and the civil rights movement is no exception. Nevertheless, a movement for justice generally eventually prevails, despite occasional setbacks.

If there was any doubt whether the Ocean Hill-Brownsville governing board would abide by its all-or-nothing approach to local autonomy, that doubt was lifted in April 1968 (Podair, 2002; Ravitch, 1974). At this point, it was clear that the legislature would pass the Bundy Plan (Mayer, 1969; Podair, 2002). Claiming that the plan was insufficient, the Ocean Hill-Brownsville governing board took matters into its own hands and terminated the employment of 19 educators (Podair, 2002; Ravitch, 1974). The teachers were even more taken aback when the governing board specified the powers that would constitute the level of local control that it considered acceptable (Ravitch, 1974). Among the demands were that the governing board would have control over all the school money, the hiring and firing of all school personnel, the purchasing of all textbooks, and decisions to build (Podair, 2002; Ravitch, 1974).

The Ocean Hill-Brownsville governing board claimed the teachers' unions were insensitive to the needs of individual students (Mayer, 1970; Podair, 2002). Although there was probably a good deal of truth in this assertion, it was the board's inexorable actions that stood out in people's minds (Mayer, 1970; Podair, 2002). The board claimed that the 19 teachers had been trying to "sabotage" local control and that the community had "lost confidence" in them (Carter, 1971, p. 5). The teachers in the district were dumbfounded. As Carter observes, "What Ocean Hill had done had never been done before" (p. 82). In retrospect, most historians believe this action was a strategic mistake. They assert that the residents of Ocean Hill-Brownsville had a valid desire to have more local control but by their actions, they had provided the teachers' union with a valid complaint as well (Mayer, 1969). As Carter (1971) notes, "No matter how much sympathy one might have for the local board, there is no question that their method of handling the 19 has been grossly irregular and even brutal" (p. 62).

Unless the governing board quickly relented, its actions guaranteed that its members would end up the losers in this battle. With their action, the primary issue was no longer a difference in educational philosophy, in which the African American parents had some valid points, but a matter of illegal actions and insubordination to government and educational leaders (Mayer, 1970; Podair, 2002; Ravitch, 1974).

The logic of the African American parents was in many respects understandable. However, the degree to which they took matters into their own hands overruled the rights of teachers and infuriated the union and other people as well (Ravitch, 1974). In fact, Ocean Hill-Brownsville demonstrators would not allow teachers to enter the schools (Podair,

2002). The teachers' union quickly appealed to Mayor Lindsay to act on their behalf to establish order. However, Lindsay asserted that he thought the teachers' union was being insensitive to the desire for more community control (Podair, 2002).

First, a Localized Teachers' Strike

As a result of the governing board's decision in April 1968, the UFT called a teachers' strike against the Ocean Hill-Brownsville district (Mayer, 1969, 1970). The strike further embittered residents, because the localized 5-week teachers' strikes coupled with the 2-week strikes at the beginning of the school year meant that their children had gone without instruction for 7 weeks (Mayer, 1969, 1970). In the minds of the residents, if the teachers' union really cared about children, they would not strike so frequently and for such extended periods of time (Mayer, 1969, 1970). However, many New York residents were also bothered by the governing board, because the timing of their actions coincided with the otherwise likely passage of a decentralization plan and their sudden actions virtually guaranteed that the legislation would not pass. In addition, many New Yorkers thought that the governing board was also insensitive to their district's children, because they surely knew that their actions would likely cause the union to strike (Mayer, 1969; Podair, 2002).

The Citywide Teachers' Strike of 1968

Unfortunately, the teachers' union and the governing board were unable to resolve their differences during the summer, and at the beginning of the school year, the UFT called a citywide teachers' strike (Mayer, 1969, 1970; Podair, 2002). The UFT action would raise the ire of many New Yorkers. After all, the dismissal of the 19 educators was a local dispute with the Ocean Hill-Brownsville district. Why should 1,500,000 New York City schoolchildren pay for a localized dispute? The UFT actions over the next 2½ months confirmed the impression by a growing number of people that the UFT was impervious to the needs of children (Mayer, 1969, 1970; Podair, 2002).

Over time, 9 of the 19 educators either dropped their charges against the governing board or reluctantly accepted the transfers out of the district. This development along with the fact that an agreement between the Ocean Hill-Brownsville governing board and the teacher's union appeared imminent led many New Yorkers to the conclusion that the strike would not last that long (Mayer, 1970). In fact, shortly after the UFT called a strike, what turned out to be a very tentative agreement was reached. On September 11, 1968, the teachers temporarily returned to work. However, at Junior High School 271 in Ocean Hill-Brownsville, Sonny Carson led a group that blocked the teachers from entering the school (Carter, 1971; Mayer, 1969, 1970). Meanwhile, Principal William Harris told the teachers to gather at the auditorium of I.S. 55, a middle school, for an orientation with Rhody McCoy. When the 83 teachers arrived, they were greeted by 50 African American men carrying sticks (Carter, 1971; Mayer, 1969, 1970). Some of the men threw 30-caliber cartridges at the teachers, and at least one warned the teachers that if they returned, they would "go out in a pine box" (Carter, 1971, p. 93; Mayer, 1970, p. 201). The teachers discovered they had not been given teaching assignments, and the students were encouraged to leave the school (Mayer, 1969, 1970; Podair, 2002). Harris locked the teachers in a room for their own protection "and arranged a police escort for them out of the building at 2:15" (Mayer, 1969, p. 201). As a result of this incident, the UFT called for a resumption of the strike (technically, a second strike).

One of the complicating factors involved in the New York City teachers' strike is that the tensions developed pronounced racial overtones. There was, of course, the fact that Oceans Hill-Brownsville was then 95% minority, although in past decades, the area had been predominantly Jewish (Pritchett, 2002). This helped contribute to a teaching force in Ocean Hill-Brownsville that was not only 70% White but was also over 50% Jewish (Ferretti, 1969). Further exacerbating the imbalance was the fact that New York City's adult population was only 27% minority but its population of children was over 50% minority (Mayer, 1969, 1970). Tensions between the African American and Jewish population became especially intense (Ferretti, 1969). The 10 remaining dismissed teachers who were the centerpiece of the dispute were all Jewish, while the governing board was nearly all African American (Mayer, 1969, 1970).

In his autobiography, Martin Luther King Jr. (1998) addressed the reason that certain African Americans in the North, but not so much in the South, were anti-Semitic. He noted that in the North, although many Jewish people were supportive of the civil rights movement, an average northern African American "meets them daily as some of his most direct exploiters in the ghetto as slum landlords and gouging shopkeepers" (King, 1998, p. 310). This tension was intensified because Jewish educators held many of the highest positions in the city's educational leadership and were the most plentiful group teaching the young in Ocean Hill-Brownsville (Pritchett, 2002).

John Hatchett, an African American teacher wrote,

> We are witnessing today in New York a phenomenon that spells death for the minds and souls of our Black children. It is the systematic coming of age of Jews who dominate and control the educational bureaucracy of the New York public school system. . . . Our Black children are being educationally castrated. . . . The reader may ask why have I singled out the Jews? . . . It is not a matter of singling out; it is a statistical fact that Jewish teachers comprise 80–85 percent of the teaching staff. (as cited in Carter, 1971, p. 95)

Tension continued to grow when a prominent African American teacher read one of his student's poems on WBAI radio, called, "Anti-Semitism, Dedicated to Albert Shanker" (Pritchett, 2002). New Yorkers interpreted the reading as anti-Jewish. Rather than appealing to humankind's more principled intentions, the UFT sought to strengthen its position in the public relations battle by magnifying every expression of anti-Semitism by Ocean Hill-Brownsville leaders (Carter, 1971; Mayer, 1969, 1970; Podair, 2002). Some assert that the UFT even fabricated or exaggerated some of the evidence it used to foster public opinion (Mayer, 1969).

Given that a great moral leader, Martin Luther King Jr., had just been assassinated and that a number of the African American concerns were understandable, the parents in the Ocean Hill-Brownsville district had a real opportunity to gain the moral high ground. However, Podair (2002) notes that anti-Jewish scapegoating by African Americans totally undermined this potential advantage, and other historians concur with Podair's assessment (Carter, 1971; Mayer, 1969). Podair (2002) notes, "The existence of anti-Jewish sentiment in the Black community during the Ocean Hill-Brownsville dispute . . . robbed Black leaders of the moral authority they needed to give their message weight in the political dialogue of the city" (p. 208).

As a result of the uncompromising actions taken by both sides, a citywide teachers' strike ensued, technically consisting of three successive strikes, resulting in nearly all New York City schools being closed from about Labor Day almost until Thanksgiving of 1968 (Podair, 2002; Ravitch, 1974). For a time, the tensions between the UFT and the Ocean Hill-Brownsville school district ran so deep, there was even talk of canceling the entire school year. Given that the strike lasted almost until the holiday season, most schools emphasized reviewing the past grade-level material until well after the first of the year. To make up for the loss of school days, usually both the school day and the school year were lengthened, so that many New York City students attended school until the middle of the summer (Podair, 2002).

The breadth and length of the strike were almost unfathomable. Mayer (1969) notes a provocative irony regarding Albert Shanker, the UFT president:

> In person and in print, he had long advocated a partnership between union
> teachers and Negro parents as the only hope for success in the struggle to improve
> urban education, now he led a series of strikes which destroyed any chance of
> such a partnership. (p. 13)

Mayer also notes a harsh reality about the teachers' strikes, which helps enlighten the reader as to why a strike of this nature could possibly be so protracted:

> By the end of the third strike parents were frantic and furious. Perhaps it may
> be noted here without comment that none of the principal figures—not
> Shanker, not McCoy . . . not Mayor Lindsay . . . had children in New York City
> public schools. And perhaps it should also be noted that all the children of
> these worthies, and of the teachers, are well fed at home while for tens of
> thousands of colored children in New York the free lunch they now missed was
> the one good meal they ate. (p. 89)

In retrospect, the teachers' union also should have taken more of a conciliatory stance regarding parental frustration about their lack of input and the inefficiency of the tenure system. In addition, the teacher's union was remarkably callous to call for such a protracted strike that involved all 1.5 million of the city's public school children (Carter, 1971; Mayer, 1969). Also, the Ocean Hill-Brownsville parents probably would have gained more if they had argued for a broader Bundy Plan than had they not taken such an uncompromising attitude (Mayer, 1969; Podair, 2002). Carter (1971) summarizes the situation well: "But what happened in New York was of a far different order than any strike, anywhere, ever. It was a strike that went completely berserk, beyond reason, or logic, or hope" (p. 107). In the end, the teachers' strike was so disruptive that it is difficult to discern whether there were any winners. However, one conclusion is clear: The big losers were New York City public schoolchildren.

Educational Debate

The 1968 teachers' strikes in New York and many other educational ideological clashes over the years have resulted from different perspectives regarding whether the parents or teachers have the primary responsibility for teaching children. From the days of Horace Mann to the days of John Dewey to the period of the New York City teachers' strike, parents have sometimes felt that schools were taking too much authority from them. Recently, there have been isolated incidents of parents suing the school systems because their children graduated illiterate from high school (Ridgeway, 2002; Sykes, 1995). In other words, the parents blamed the schools for their children's illiteracy. However, school officials doubtlessly responded by saying something like this to the mother, "Where were you all these years? You must have known your child was struggling in reading? Why did you not talk to the teachers or use the school's free tutors?"

- Whose responsibility is it to make sure children are properly educated?
- Is it primarily the parents' responsibility or the teacher's responsibility?
- Furthermore, as the child becomes an adolescent, how much is success in education the responsibility of the youth?

THE PRIMACY OF NEW EDUCATIONAL THOUGHT

One of the major reasons for the 1960s tumult is that such clashes between major disagreeing parties occurred along so many dimensions (Kallen, 2001), including the following: the "hawks" and the "doves," adults and teenagers, women and men, communists and free-market supporters, traditionalists and nontraditionalists, and minority parents and teacher unions. The tensions of the 1960s were also substantial because the turbulence occurred not only at the overt behavioral level but also at the more covert philosophical level. The coexistence of both these kinds of clashes was a strong reminder to people of how philosophical battles generally eventually produce behavioral- and practical-level battles (Kallen, 2001).

With the preceding thoughts in mind, when addressing the turbulence of the 1960s, one should not only address the behavioral dimensions as they relate to education, but the philosophical dimensions as well. Without question, the American school and universities systems were impacted by the behavioral confrontations that took place during the 1960s. Nevertheless, it is also true that the changes of the 1960s presented an opportunity for Deweyism to come to the forefront of educational thought (Sowell, 1992). Beyond this, it is patent that one cannot totally separate the philosophical and behavioral realms. That is, ultimately, behavioral confrontations are a direct result of previous and ongoing philosophical differences (Dupuis, 1966). With this in mind, we now turn to examining some of the major educational philosophers of the time and their proposals for change. The progressive or reconstructionist advocates that were prevalent during this time included educators such as A. S. Neill, John Goodlad, Jean Piaget, Jerome Bruner, Lawrence Kohlberg, and Ivan Illich.

Rethinking Educational Philosophy

A. S. Neill

A. S. Neill (1883–1973) was Scottish, but he had a tremendous influence on American educational thought. In the 1920s, he opened an English school called Summerhill. As Palmer (2001) writes, "There Neill began to implement systematically his revolutionary ideas of pupil freedom and the lack of teacher authority" (p. 1). In 1960, Neill wrote a book called *Summerhill,* in which he advocated the child-centered approaches that he practiced at this school. As a result of his book, Neill became one of the most influential educators on the American landscape in the 1960s (Palmer, 2001).

Neill (1968) advocated an educational atmosphere in which the teacher was not considered above the students, but a part of the group, largely as Dewey had initially imagined. "I believe that to impose anything by authority is wrong. The child should not do anything until he comes to the opinion—his own opinion—that it should be done" Neill (1960, p. 111). Neill (1968) emphasized freedom, because he believed in the innate goodness of the child. He rejected "both moral and religious education" (Neill, 1960; Palmer, 2001, p. 2). According to Neill, "The child should never be forced to learn," and "attendance at lessons is voluntary whatever the age of the child" (as cited in Palmer, 2001, pp. 1–2).

The influence of Neill on American educational thought during the 1960s is difficult to overstate, especially because *Summerhill* sold over 2 million copies, though he did have his critics during the 1960s and beyond. This primary objection of Neill's critics is that he was too inexperienced in mainstream education to generalize the practices of Summerhill school to what conventional educational practices should be. The entire Summerhill school had only 40 students (Palmer, 2001). Therefore, many educators pointed out that Summerhill constituted more of a miniature experimental design rather than anything that approximated a real school (Neill, 1960). Indeed, one might find it hard to imagine how a man who ran a school with only 40 students could have such a prodigious degree of influence on liberal educational thought (Palmer, 2001). However, the 1960s was a period typified as one in which people became the center of attention who years before never would have enjoyed such a large audience (Kallen, 2001).

John Goodlad

John Goodlad (1920–present) was an educator whose writing often reflected the mood of the times. During the 1960s, Goodlad represented cutting-edge liberal education thought. In 1959, he published a book titled *The Non-Graded Elementary School,* which became a centerpiece of the push for change in the 1960s. There is no question that Goodlad's approach caused many teachers to change their grading practices (Palmer, 2001). Although most schools maintained some sense of the practice, many schools reduced the number of distinctions in their grading systems (Ravitch, 1983). For example, some schools and universities deleted the use of " + " and "–" in their grading. Other schools dropped letter grading all together, in favor of phrases such as "outstanding," "satisfactory" and "unsatisfactory" (Palmer, 2001).

As time passed, in the 1970s and 1980s, and the nation entered a more stable era, Goodlad's works tended to become more mainstream in nature, and he focused on the general need for school reform (Goodlad, 1984). Nevertheless, Goodlad's call for nongraded schools earned him a special place in the liberal educational establishment of the 1960s (Palmer, 2001).

Jerome Bruner

Jerome Bruner (1915–present) was born in New York City and was educated at Harvard and Duke. After World War II, he became a leading educational psychologist and one of the primary leaders of the "cognitive revolution." He placed an emphasis on human perception and cognition and focused on children's expectations and interpretations of how they perceived the world around them (Palmer, 2001). In 1959, under the auspices of the National Academy of Sciences and the National Science Foundation, Bruner was asked to chair a pivotal meeting of educational scholars at Woods Hole, on Cape Cod, Massachusetts, in 1959 (Orlofsky, 2001). As a result of the gathering, Bruner wrote his book *The Process of Education* (1960). This book elaborated on some key themes of that meeting and was a key factor in the development of a wide range of educational programs and experiments in the 1960s (Orlofsky, 2001). At the end of the decade, Bruner turned his attention to children learning language (Palmer, 2001). Later in his career, he would focus on cultural psychology (Bruner, 1996).

All in all, Bruner demonstrated that learning should not be viewed as mechanical set of routines (Bruner, 1966). Rather, children process information on the basis of who they are as people. In Bruner's view, this truth should be considered whenever children are taught.

Jean Piaget

Jean Piaget's (1896–1980) ideas had actually been present well before the 1960s. Educational psychologists in Europe had been applying his theories for decades. American educational psychologists also became aware of his views decades before, but the introduction of his ideas across American schools came gradually. By the early 1960s, Piagetian views enjoyed overwhelming support among American educational psychologists and public school educators (Flavell, 1963). Piaget presented a cognitive theory of child development that was helpful, practical, and could easily be applied by American teachers (Case, 1992). Piaget (1950) argued that children passed through cognitive stages that emerged at specific ages and lasted particular lengths of time. Furthermore, he developed tests that teachers could use to help determine when a child had passed through one stage into the next. He demonstrated that these tests were not only helpful, but could be easily administered by teachers (Jeynes, 2006).

By the early 1960s, Piaget became probably the most highly regarded educational psychologist of his era (Flavell, 1963). He ushered in a greater emphasis on cognitional processes and testing that progress than had been present ever before (Case, 1992; Perrone, 1990). As a result of Piaget's work, there was a new emphasis on giving instruction that was "developmentally appropriate" for the child, that is, sensitive to his or her stage of development (Piaget, 1950). Teachers also became more convinced of the need for assessment (Flavell, 1963). Therefore, testing of both Piagetian and standardized varieties started to surge in the early 1960s, at a rate of 20% per year (Perrone, 1990). Piaget's theories helped spawn an era of cognitive focus in America's schools (Case, 1992).

Educators today are not quite as enamored with Piaget's beliefs as they were in the 1960s (Case, 1992). American educators were introduced belatedly (due greatly to the Cold War) to the works on Lev Vygotsky (1978), who tested Piaget's stage theory and found his stages of development to be far too rigid. Piaget also based his theories on observing his own children, which doubtlessly limited the validity and generalization of his findings (Flavell, 1963). Nevertheless, his views spawned an era in which the cognitions of children were examined more closely than ever before.

Lawrence Kohlberg

Lawrence Kohlberg (1927–1987) tried to bring balance to Piaget's cognitive emphasis by proposing a theory of moral development. He was influenced by Piaget's stage theory but argued that children's moral development was also extremely important (Kohlberg, 1981; Kohlberg & Mayer, 1972). It should be noted that Piaget did write on moral education but his overwhelming focus was on cognitive development (Piaget, 1950).

Although Kohlberg enjoyed a good deal of influence in educational psychology, he did not rival Piaget (Kohlberg, 1981; Kohlberg & Mayer, 1972). Part of this is because by the 1960s, the first and second priorities of schools were generally the experiences and cognitive development of the child. Before the 1920s, moral and intellectual development were the primary emphases, with a slow shift taking place between the 1920s and the 1960s. Therefore, by the time Kohlberg's theory of moral development emerged, moral education no longer enjoyed the primacy it once had (Anderson, 1992; Flanagan, 1984). Nevertheless, Kohlberg's theory provided a balance to what some perceived to be an overemphasis on cognitive development (Kohlberg, 1981; Kohlberg & Mayer, 1972).

To be sure, Kohlberg's stage theory is subject to some of the same kinds of criticisms as Piaget's theory. To assert that moral development must take place in a set of ordered stages is quite rigid. Some educational psychologists also assert that Kohlberg's tests are not very statistically reliable and can be biased (Gregory, 2004). However, nearly everyone praises Kohlberg for his assertions that moral education is an important part of a child's development.

Ivan Illich

Ivan Illich (1926–present) is an important contributor within the liberal education movement (Barrow, 1978). Nevertheless, one should point out that he is extreme enough in his views that even the vast majority of liberals do not agree with him. Illich's most well-known work is titled *Deschooling Society* (1972). The title of this book reflects the true nature of his viewpoint that American society should do away with schools as we know them. His book has become a classic that many professors, all across the country use as a required textbook in their classes (Barrow, 1978). One might ask that given that Illich's overall assertion is so extreme, why would professors use his book as a main text? The answer is. simply. because Illich's assertions make one think about why society has schools in the first place.

Illich (1972) believes that educators support the concept of schooling because they have four misconceptions about education:

1. Teacher-dominated behavior is valuable to schools and society.

2. Children and adolescents require socialization in the schools.

3. Children should delay efforts to change society until they have finished school.

4. School requires structure.

Illich (1972) is very strong in his criticism of the schools. He believes that there are many problems present in society but is totally convinced that the present education system is not the way to solve them. He asserts, "The failures of school are taken by most people as proof that education is a very costly, very complex, always arcane and frequently almost impossible task" (p. 11). Illich believes that people of all classes rely too much on the schools to help relieve poverty and disadvantage that many people face. He notes, "It should be obvious that even with schools of equal quality a poor child can seldom catch up with a rich one" (p. 9). Illich questions the efficiency of many of the pillars of schooling today, including the effectiveness of teacher certification, and states that teacher curriculum is so expensive that it benefits businesspeople more than students.

Illich (1972, p. 43) further contends that because schools are so thoroughly institutionalized into the American system, this causes people to rely on schools for their "salvation" rather than on their own individual efforts. He opines that people tend to rely on schools as the means of education, "instead of becoming themselves the means of education" (p. 11). He avers that the dependence of schools as an institution of education has become so complex that it "renders individual accomplishment suspect" (p. 3).

Illich (1972) further contends that the problems associated with schooling run so deep that "school has become a social problem" (p. 71). His declarations to this effect could not be stronger. He claims, "The paradox of school is evidence: increased expenditure escalates their destructiveness at home and abroad. . . . The escalation of the schools is as destructive as the escalation of weapons but less visibly so" (pp. 13–14).

Illich presents (1972) evidence suggesting that most learning takes place outside of school and that this should be encouraged. According to Illich, school is the wrong place for learning to take place. He believes in the ultimate child-centered approach to education; that is, instead of having teachers instruct students, resources ought to be placed in front of the children to use as the children see fit. Along these lines, he states, "We can depend on self-motivated learning instead of employing teachers to bribe or compel the student" (p. 104).

Illich's perspective gained attention because it made people reexamine why the world has schools and because his book was released at the tail end of the hippie movement, when most of society's institutions were under attack (Leary, 2001). Although few would agree with Illich's specific conclusions, there is a grain of truth to many of his assertions, and his views are thought-provoking.

Rethinking Research and Pedagogy

Although there emerged new patterns of philosophical orientation in education, other individuals focused on the importance of productive research or pedagogy, including Lee Cronbach, David Campbell, and Benjamin Bloom. Cronbach and Campbell were cognizant of the evolving role that research was playing in education. Bloom addressed issues of effective pedagogy in the context of the maturation of the learning process.

Lee Cronbach and David Campbell

Lee Cronbach (1916–2001) may be considered the most influential statistician of the modern era. Although his initial great contributions were made in the immediate post–World War II period, as technology and the sophistication of social scientific research advanced in the 1960s, the significance of Cronbach's work became even more evident (Cronbach, 1949, 1951; Palmer, 2001).

Donald Campbell (1916–present) helped provide some of the missing ingredients to help further the discipline of statistics as applied to the social sciences. His book *Experimental and Quasi-Experimental Design for Research,* coauthored by J. C Stanley, was published in 1966. This book has sold over 300,000 copies, which is remarkable for a book of this type. Campbell, in addition to Cronbach, help set in motion the explosive growth in social science experimentation in the 1960s, 1970s, and beyond (Palmer, 2001).

Benjamin Bloom

Benjamin Bloom (1913–1999) was less interested in progressive education and focused more on the science of education (Palmer, 2001). Bloom coauthored the book *Taxonomy on Educational Objectives* in 1956. In the 1960s, he further developed his emphasis on the science of education by developing a theory of "mastery learning." In this theory, Bloom (1976) argued that nearly all children, perhaps 90% to 95%, are able to learn basic skills if they are given enough time. He argued that the bell-shaped curve that often emerges from the results of a standardized test are more a product of the different amounts of time it takes children to learn rather than primarily a result of differences in levels of understanding (Bloom & Krathwohl, 1956).

A Closer Look: Ivan Illich and Why We Have Schools

There is no question that Ivan Illich's views of education are quite extreme, even for those whose views are well to the left of center. Despite this, Illich's book *Deschooling Society* (1972) is used as a main textbook by many professors across the country. How could this be the case? The answer is that whatever one might think of Illich's conclusions, his assertions challenge one's mind and daily assumptions. It causes one to think about why it is that society develops school systems and in many cases makes attendance mandatory. It challenges a person to reconsider the purposes, functions, and goals of an education system that demands that nearly all children depart from the security of the home to be taught by relative strangers. Such questions ideally cause people to either rediscover why they believe what they believe or to be awakened into improving the current educational system.

There is no doubt that the timing of the release of *Deschooling Society,* in 1972, during the hippie movement, contributed to the book's success. Hippies questioned almost every institution and practice that was conventional, and there are few institutions more conventional than schools. Although sometimes a meticulous examination of traditions may overturn the conventional, often it serves to eventually reinforce the conventional and perhaps make long-held traditions stronger and better. Many people believe that *Deschooling Society* fulfills that function.

THE REMOVAL OF PRAYER FROM SCHOOLS

In three 1962 to 1963 Supreme Court decisions, prayer and Bible readings were removed from the public schools. The first of these Supreme Court decisions was *Engel v. Vitale* (1962), which forbade school prayer (Blanshard, 1963; Kliebard, 1969; Louisell, 1964; Michaelsen, 1970; Sikorski, 1993). *Murray v. Curlett* (1963) disallowed not only school prayer but also Bible reading (Murray, 1982). As a result of this case, Madeline Murray O'Hare became the most well-known atheist leader in the United States. Her son Bill, who was the child directly involved in the case, later came to feel remorse over his role in the case and wrote a letter of apology to the American people in a Baltimore newspaper, where the family had lived (Murray, 1982). He later converted to Christianity.

The *Engel v. Vitale* case was a very unusual Supreme Court decision. As Michaelsen (1970) notes, "In a most unusual fashion, Justice Black, in writing the opinion of the Court in Engel, did not appeal to a single court case as precedent setting" (p. 199). In the *Engel* decision and in the 1963 case of *School District of Abington v. Schempp,* Black and the other Supreme Court justices who sided with him based their rulings on the "separation principle," which, although the concept of "separation of church and state" never appears in the Constitution, was relied on to argue the case (*Engel v. Vitale,* 1962).

Many legal experts objected to the Supreme Court's decisions on the basis of not only the decisions themselves but also the unusual lack of judicial experience of the justices (Michaelsen, 1970). In almost every case, the justices were appointed to the Supreme Court following a long history of political rather than judicial experience (Michaelsen, 1970). Chief Justice Earl Warren had served as Governor of California for 10 years before his appointment; Justice William Douglas was chairman of the Security and Exchange Commission; Justice Hugo Black had been a U.S. Senator for 10 years; Justice Arthur Goldberg served as secretary of labor; and Justice Felix Frankfurter was an assistant to the secretary of labor and served as a founding member of the American Civil Liberties Union (ACLU). Ironically, the only justice with extended federal constitutional experience before he began his service on the Supreme Court, Justice Potter Stewart, was also the only justice to object to the removal of prayer and Bible reading (*McCollum v. Board of Education,* 1948).

The *Engel v. Vitale* case involved a prayer that the Board of Regents of New York State encouraged schools to use as part of the state's program of moral education. It was titled "Statement on Moral and Spiritual Training in the Schools": "Almighty God, we acknowledge our dependence upon Thee, and we beg Thy blessings upon us, our parents, our teachers, and our country" (Kliebard, 1969, p. 198).

This prayer was used in the Supreme Court proceeding itself, and the justices acknowledged that no student was compelled to say the prayer. Any child who so desired did not have to take part (*Engel v. Vitale,* 1962). In fact, as Paul Blanshard (1963) observes, the prayer was doubly voluntary. Not only could parents opt out of the prayer, but so could local school boards. The justices also acknowledged that this practice in New York schools was essentially the same as the practice of the U.S Supreme Court beginning each day by asking for God's blessing, and Justice Douglas also specifically noted that this prayer certainly did not establish a religion (*Engel v. Vitale,* 1962). Despite this, the Supreme Court disallowed the prayer. In his dissent, Judge Stewart stated that the decision in the resulted in "the establishment of a religion of secularism" (*Engel v. Vitale,* 1962).

The reaction by the American public and its leadership was not positive. Dwight Eisenhower responded by saying,

I always thought that this nation was essentially a religious one. I realize, of course, that the Declaration of Independence antedates the Constitution, but the fact remains that the Declaration was our certificate of national birth. It specifically asserts that we as individuals possess certain rights as an endowment from our Creator—a religious concept. ("President Urges Court Be Backed," 1962, p. 1)

Former President Hoover said the Supreme Court decision constituted "a disintegration of a sacred American heritage" and added, "The Congress should at once submit an amendment to the Constitution that establishes the right to religious devotion in all government agencies—national, state, or local" (*National Catholic Almanac,* 1963, p. 69).

The members of Congress strongly disapproved of the Court's decision. According to the *Congressional Record* for the following day, not one member of Congress defended the Court's decision (Blanshard, 1963). An unsuccessful movement urged impeachment of Supreme Court Chief Justice Earl Warren (Blanshard, 1963). Senator Eugene Talmadge claimed that "the Supreme Court has set up atheism as a new religion" (House Committee on the Judiciary, 1962, p. 140). Many strong opinions were voiced by both religious and political leaders in the days immediately following the Supreme Court's *Engel* decision, in June 1962. Congressman Frank Becker, a Catholic, called the decision "the most tragic in the history of the United States" (*Congressional Record,* 1962).

A Gallup Poll in 1963 indicated that Americans were opposed to the *Engel, Murray,* and *Schempp* decisions by a 3-to-1 margin (Sikorski, 1993). Even the newspaper media, often criticized for being left of center politically, was about twice as likely to express opposition to the decisions (Sikorski, 1993).

In *School District of Abington v. Schempp* (1963), the Supreme Court heard a case about the reading of the Bible in the classroom. Pennsylvania possessed a law that stated,

At least ten verses from the Holy Bible shall be read, without comment, at the opening of each public school on each school day. Any child shall be excused from such Bible reading or attending such Bible reading, upon the written request of a parent or guardian. (24 Pa. Stat. 15-1516, as amended, Pub. Law 1928)

Murray v. Curlett (1963) involved a similar situation. In this case, the Board of School Commissioners of Baltimore allowed for the opening exercises of a school to include primarily the "reading, without comment, of a chapter in the Holy Bible and/or the use of the Lord's Prayer" (Kliebard, 1969, p. 213). The three decisions had a considerable impact on school practices. A study indicated that in four eastern states (New Jersey, Pennsylvania, Maine, and Massachusetts), 96% of the schools did have Bible readings before 1962. and 97% did not have Bible reading after 1962 (Sikorski, 1993).

Other court cases were handed down as well. including *Reed v. Van Hoven* (1965), a Michigan Supreme Court Case. In this case, the courts declared that saying grace over one's lunch at school was allowed only if one did not move his or her lips. And, indeed, many children have been suspended from school for saying grace aloud (Barton, 1990).

The *Engel, Schempp,* and *Murray* court decisions eliminated public school prayer, religious-released time off taking place on school premises, and school-sponsored group prayer (Michaelsen, 1970). Although these three court decisions curtailed the expressions of people of faith in the classroom, certain activities involving religion were still allowed. First, religious-released time off was allowed on school premises. In *Zorach v. Clauson* (1952), this type of religious expression was allowed as long as it was not done on public school property (Michaelsen, 1970). Second, ceremonies that were patriotic or civic in purpose with religious references were also acceptable. Third, the objective study of teaching about religion was also permitted (Michaelsen, 1970).

Arguments in Favor of the Supreme Court Decision

Some people supported the Supreme Court decisions. Some believed that the presence of any form of religious expression in the schools is equivalent to the establishment of religion, as dictated by the government. This perspective was later articulated in Ronald Flowers's (1994) book, *That Godless Court?* Flowers argues that to the extent that the government establishment of religion means an "official, formal, symbiotic relationship between religion and civil authority, the prayer decisions were correct" (p. 9). In the opinion of Flowers and others, the presence of prayer overlooked atheists, despite the fact that children could opt out of any expressions of school prayer. Although supporters of prayer believe that the Supreme Court decision violates the First Amendment right to the freedom of religious expression, opponents of voluntary prayer in the schools believe that voluntary prayer is inappropriate in what they perceive to be a secular institution, that is, the public schools. They believe that prayer should be allowed to be expressed either in religious institutions or within one's home.

Misapplication of the Supreme Court Decisions

A debate has since ensued about what these court cases mean. Many educational leaders, either out of ignorance or other motives, have suspended many children for bringing their Bibles to school (House Committee on the Judiciary, 1995). The problem has become sufficiently pervasive that in late June 1995, the Committee on the Judiciary of the House of Representatives convened to hold hearings on the issue of school authorities suspending students who brought Bibles to school, who prayed individually, and engaged in other religious activities, such as wearing religious clothing (House Committee on the Judiciary, 1995). One of the cases that emerged during these hearings was that of April Fiore. Ms. Fiore's daughter Rebecca and two of her friends sometimes carried Bibles in the school. The school warned them to stop bringing their Bibles to school or they would be suspended from school for 10 days (the same punishment as for possession of illegal drugs). The girls asserted that they were being denied their right of freedom of religion. When they were caught holding their Bibles on another occasion, they were suspended from school for 10 days, and the school officials strongly urged the parents to send their children to another school (House Committee on the Judiciary, 1995).

The Hearings before the House Committee on the Judiciary created such a stir that shortly after the completion of the hearings, on July 12, 1995, President Bill Clinton felt compelled to speak to the issue of religious freedom in the public schools (Religious Tolerance, 2002). In a speech at James Madison High School, in Vienna, Virginia, Clinton stated, "Nothing in the first Amendment converts our public schools to religion-free zones or requires all religious expression to be left at the schoolhouse door" (Religious Tolerance, 2002).

Despite Clinton's remarks, a considerable number of reports continue to emerge of students who felt their rights to religious freedom of speech had been violated. On May 19, 2000, a teacher at Lynn Lucas Middle School, in Texas, threw the Bibles of Angela and Amber Harrison in the trash, asserting, "This is garbage!" (Religious Tolerance, 2002). Praying in school and Bible reading are probably the most common types of religious expressions that are punished by suspension (Dominion School, 2002). A first grader at Haines Elementary School was sent to the principal's office for reading a Bible passage, even though the teacher had asked the students to read aloud any literature passage of their choice (Libertocracy, 2002). Another student was suspended for saying, "Jesus Christ is Lord" in the classroom (Spin-Tech, 1999).

In February 2000, a principal forbade a Bible club from using the cross as a club symbol (Religious Tolerance, 2002). Religious clothing has also been an area of concern. In 1997, school officials told two Texas students that they could not wear rosaries (Jeremiah Project, 2002). An Alabama school blocked students from wearing crosses (*Maranatha Christian Journal,* 1999). A girl whom the Anti-Defamation League (2002) referred to only as "Ann" was suspended for wearing a Star of David necklace. Another student was forbidden from wearing a shirt that promoted family values (World Net Daily, 2002). Incidents such as these are numerous, and many social scientists and political leaders believe that these actions restrict the freedom of religion (Religious Tolerance, 2002).

Although most Americans do not want teacher-led prayer, Gallup and Harris polls indicate that about 75% of Americans do want voluntary prayer in the schools (Barton, 1990). Most Americans believe that there should be a period of silence given to children, whatever their religious or personal beliefs, during which they can pray or just simply collect their thoughts.

Possible Price of Taking Prayer and Moral Education out of Schools

The removal of vocal prayer and Bible reading from the public schools had a dramatic impact on the teaching of moral education in the public schools. Previous to 1962, moral education was founded on the Bible. Once Bible reading was forbidden, schools no longer emphasized moral teachings such as "turning the other cheek," "one should not covet," and "honoring one's mother and father" for fear that many would interpret these as religious and moral teachings.

The removal of moral teaching from the public schools quickly became associated with a religious and moral decline in the nation as a whole. It is difficult to determine how much of this decline resulted from the removal of vocal prayer and Bible readings from the school and how much the moral decline influenced the Supreme Court decisions on this matter. The direction of causality is likely in both directions. Nevertheless, the removal of Bible reading and verbal prayer had a dramatic impact on the extent to which teachers dared address moral education (Sikorski, 1993). Vitz (as cited in Kennedy, 1994) also notes that following

1962, public school textbook manufacturers substantially reduced the number of moral lessons that had previously been a recurring thread in many American textbooks.

Based on statistical information, it is clear that beginning in 1963, American juveniles experienced a sudden increase in immoral behavior. How much of this sudden and unexpected increase was due to America's overall moral decline and how much was due to the absence of many moral teachings in the public schools is debatable. Surely, there were several factors involved. Theoretically, the surge in immoral behavior could have been entirely coincidental. However, very few people believe this.

Here are some interesting statistics, many of which compare the late 1990s with 1962:

1. Murder arrests among 13- to 18-year-olds are nearly 5 times their 1962 level.

2. Murders by girls are also 5 times their 1962 level.

3. Aggravated assaults by girls 13 to 15 are 5 times their 1962 level.

4. Rape arrests among 13- to 14-year-old boys are 3 times their 1962 level.

5. Teenage pregnancies among unwed girls are 7 times their 1962 level.

6. Half of sexually active adolescent males have had their first sexual experiences between the ages of 11 and 13.

7. In the case of teenage pregnancies, about 80% of the girls end up on welfare. Nearly 50% of all people on consistent welfare started there as unwed teens (U.S. Department of Health and Human Services, 1998; U.S. Department of Justice, 1999).

Again, most of these surges started in 1963. Could it all be coincidence? Most people think that it is not. Surely, other factors were involved. Indeed, removing prayer out of the schools was not only a cause but also an effect, for it resulted partially from a decreased emphasis on morality and discipline in the country as a whole.

Although it is difficult to determine the forces of cause and effect of this behavioral change, there seems little doubt that these trends are part of a larger moral and religious puzzle. The removal of vocal prayer and Bible-based moral teaching is likely an important component of this puzzle. As previously mentioned, there were other pieces of evidence suggesting an overall national moral decline. Illegal drug use skyrocketed beginning in the early- to mid-1960s (U.S. Department of Health and Human Services, 1992; U.S. Department of Justice, 1993). Most notably, the divorce rate, which had been in slight decline since 1948, suddenly began to soar in precisely 1963. The divorce rate then peaked in 1980, and since then has remained slightly under the 1980 level (Glenn, 1999). To the extent that parents and schools are the two institutions that impact children the most, it is hard to imagine that the moral decline present in each of these institutions, especially evident following 1962, did not impact juvenile behavior.

The influence of moral education on juvenile behavior is recognized by many of the most advanced public education systems in the world. Asian nations have noted that when moral education programs are reduced or eliminated, rates of juvenile crime and violence rise quickly. As a result, moral education programs have been reinstituted or reinvigorated in these countries.

Prayer, Bible reading, and moral education will continue to be hot topics in educational circles as long as Americans are concerned about the nation's moral decay and the removal or reduction of these school practices is regarded as a major contributing factor to that decay. In addition, opponents of voluntary school prayer are in the awkward position of having to explain why schools should be inclusive when it comes to culture but not religion, which is often the first or second most important component of one's culture. Given that people are encouraged to participate in events that celebrate their ethnic cultural heritage, why is it not permissible to participate in events that celebrate their religious cultural heritage? For these reasons, the debate over voluntary prayer in the schools is likely to continue for many years to come.

SEX EDUCATION

Clearly, many real family and educational changes resulted from the cultural changes of the 1960s. Before this period, most Americans believed that sex education was not an appropriate topic of discussion (Irvine, 2002). However, the college students called for freer discussion and attitudes toward sex, and many Americans, including academics such as Masters and Johnson tended to agree (Irvine, 2002).

The Sex Information and Education Council of the United States (SIECUS) was formed to promote health and sex education in the public school classroom. Although SIECUS stirred some controversy in the mid-1960s by espousing sex education, it did originally support sex only within stable relationships (Irvine, 2002). Conservative groups ideally wanted stable relationships defined as marital bonds, and the SIECUS perspective of the time at least suggested that sex only within a married relationship was the ideal (Irvine, 2002).

The late 1960s and early 1970s, however, produced a great deal of change. Freer sex practiced by many college students ultimately influenced mainstream attitudes (Melody & Peterson, 1999). In 1969, the book *Everything You Always Wanted to Know About Sex, but Were Afraid to Ask* was released (Reuben, 1969). In 1972, *The Joy of Sex* was published (Comfort, 1972). By the late 1960s and early 1970s, SIECUS supported sex in a wider range of relationships (Irvine, 2002). The fact that teen pregnancy rate rose during the late 1960s and throughout the 1970s caused many conservatives to conclude that the freer SIECUS stand on sexual relationships bore considerable responsibility for this trend (Irvine, 2002; Melody & Peterson, 1999). Consequently, the abstinence movement was born (Irvine, 2002).

Because of the proliferation of the AIDS virus in the late 1980s and 1990s, sex education reached a new place of centrality within the school curriculum, (Feldman & Miller, 1998). School leaders initiated renewed efforts to teach students to engage in "safe" rather than "unprotected" sex. School officials and teachers had a particularly strenuous time adjusting to the reality of the situation, because in the early years of the AIDS epidemic, researchers and physicians possessed limited knowledge of how the infection spread and often disseminated advice that seemed nebulous. Health officers also did not know how rapidly the AIDS virus would spread and how prevalent mutations of the disease would become (Feldman & Miller, 1998). The fact that contracting the AIDS virus could be deadly also provided new impetus to the abstinence program, the proponents of which argued that abstinence was the best way to stem the growth of the disease and save lives (Irvine, 2002). The best way to teach sex education remains a controversy to this day.

CONCLUSION

Perhaps more than any other decade in the 20th century, the 1960s was all about change. The country would never be the same after the 1960s. The student demonstrations, the teachers' strikes, the removal of prayer from the public schools, and sex education all hurled great currents of change at America's institutions of education. Just as *Brown v. Board of Education* and the Cold War defined the 1950s for America's educational system, so these events defined the 1960s. Whatever one might think of the overall ramifications of these changes in the 1960s, education in the United States had changed.

DISCUSSION QUESTIONS

1. Of all the educators mentioned under the heading "New Educational Thought," which one do you think had the greatest impact, and why?

2. In 1995, President Bill Clinton made a speech attempting to stem the tide that restricted religious liberty in the schools. Do you think his speech has changed the trends addressed in this chapter, or is more action needed to ensure that schools do not communicate that students must leave their religious inclinations at the front door of the school?

3. Martin Luther King Jr. had many admirable qualities. What actions and traits do you most admire in him?

4. It is indisputable that just about every war, including the one in Vietnam, has had a considerable impact on education. Why? Is there an intensity that accompanies war? Is it that wars often represent a transition into a new era? Is it because people are fighting for what they believe?

REFERENCES

Ammerman M. (1995). *Roger Williams*. Uhrichsville, OH: Barbour.

Anderson, D. C. (1992). *The loss of virtue: Moral confusion and social disorder in Britain and America.* London: Social Affairs Unit.

Anti-Defamation League. (2002). *Ann.* Retrieved June 11, 2002, from http://www.adl.org/religion_ps/dress_codes.asp.

Archer, J. (1986). *The incredible Sixties: The stormy years that changed America.* San Diego, CA: Harcourt, Brace & Jovanovich.

Aron, P. (1997). *Unsolved mysteries of American education.* Thorndike, ME: G. K. Hall.

Astin, A. W., Astin, H. S., Bayer, A. E., &. Bisconti, A. N (1975). *The power of protest.* San Francisco: Jossey-Bass.

Barrow, R. (1978). *Radical education: A critique of deschooling and freeschooling.* New York: Wiley.

Barton, D. (1990). *Our Godly heritage* [Video]. Aledo, TX: Wallbuilders.

Berman, L. (1989). *Lyndon Johnson's war: The road to stalemate in Vietnam.* New York: Norton.

Berube, M. R. (1969). The unschooling of New York's children. In M. R. Berube & M. G. Gittell (Eds.), *Confrontation at Ocean Hill-Brownsville* (pp. 136–139). New York: Praeger.

Blanshard, P. (1963). *Religion and the schools*. Boston: Beacon Press.

Bloom, B. (1976). *Human characteristics and school learning*. New York: McGraw-Hill.

Bloom, B., & Krathwohl, D. (1956). *Taxonomy of educational objectives*. New York: McKay.

Branch, T. (1988). *Parting the waters: America in the King years 1954–1963*. New York: Simon & Schuster.

Branch, T. (1998). *Pillar of fire: America in the King years 1963–1965*. New York: Simon & Schuster.

Brown v. Board of Education 347 U.S. 483 (1954).

Bruner, J. (1960). *The process of education*. Cambridge, MA: Harvard University Press.

Bruner, J. (1966). *Toward a theory of instruction*. Cambridge, MA: Harvard University Press.

Bruner, J. (1996). *The culture of education*. Cambridge, MA: Harvard University Press.

Campbell, D. T., & Stanley, J. C. (1966). *Experimental and quasi-experimental designs for research*. Chicago: Rand McNally.

Carter, B. (1971). *Pickets, parents, and power*: The story behind the New York City teachers' strikes. New York: Citation Press.

Case, R. (1992). Advantages and limitations of the Neo-Piagetian position. In R. Case (Ed.), *The mind's staircase* (pp. 37–51). Hillsdale, NJ: Lawrence Erlbaum.

Cohen, D. K. (1973). The price of community control. In C. Greer (Ed.), *The solution as part of the problem* (pp. 42–65). New York: Harper & Row.

Comfort, A. (Ed.). (1972). *The joy of sex*. New York: Crown.

Congressional Record. (1962, June 26). Vol. 108.

Cronbach, L. (1949). *Essentials of psychological testing*. New York: Harper & Row.

Cronbach, L. (1951). Coefficient alpha and the internal structure of tests. *Psychometrika, 16*, 297–334.

Davidson, S. (1971). The hippie alternative: Getting back to the communal garden. In A. S. Skolnick & J. H. Skolnick (Ed.), *Family in transition* (pp. 527–541). Boston: Little, Brown.

Dominion School. (2002). Retrieved June 11, 2002, from http://www.dominionschool.com/

Dupuis, A. M. (1966). *Philosophy of education in historical perspective*. Chicago: Rand McNally.

Engel v. Vitale 370 U.S. 421 (1962).

Feldman, D. A., & Miller, J. W. (1998). *The AIDS crisis: A documentary history*. Westport, CT: Greenwood Press.

Ferretti, F. (1969). Who's to blame in the school strike? In M. R. Berube & M. G. Gittell (Eds.), *Confrontation at Ocean Hill-Brownsville* (pp. 283–313). New York: Praeger.

Flanagan, O. J. (1984). *The science of the mind*. Cambridge: MIT Press.

Flavell, J. H. (1963). *The developmental psychology of Piaget*. Princeton, NJ: Van Nostrom.

Flowers, R. (1994).*The godless court?* Louisville, KY: Westminster John Knox Press.

Flynn, D. (2002). *Why the left hates America: Exposing the lies that have obscured our nation's greatness*. Roseville, CA: Forum.

Fredrickson, G. M. (2002). *Racism: A short history*. Princeton, NJ: Princeton University Press

Gallup Poll. (2005). *Surveys from 1960–2005*. Washington, DC: Gallup. Retrieved from http://www.Gallup.com.

Glenn, N. D. (1999). Further discussion on the effects of no-fault divorce on divorce rates. *Journal of Marriage and the Family, 61,* 800–802.

Goines, D. L. (2001). The free speech movement in Berkeley. In S. A. Kallen (Ed.), *Sixties counterculture* (pp. 33–43). San Diego, CA: Greenhaven Press.

Goldbloom, M. J. (1973). The New York school crisis. In C. Greer (Ed.), *The solution as part of the problem* (pp. 66–92). New York: Harper & Row.

Goodlad, J. (1984). *A place called school: Prospects for the future*. New York: McGraw-Hill.

Goodlad, J. I., & Anderson, R. H. (1959). *The non-graded elementary school*. New York: Harcourt & Brace.

Grant, E., & Hill, M. H. (1974). *I was there: What really went on at Kent State*. Lima, OH: CSS.

Gregory, R. J. (2004). *Psychological testing*. Boston: Allyn & Bacon.

Hamilton, C. (1991). *The Hitler diaries: Fakes that fooled the world*. Lexington: University of Kentucky.

Harris, R. (2001). *Selling Hitler*. London: Arrow.

Head, W. P., & Grinter, L. E. (1993). *Looking back on the Vietnam War*. Westport, CT: Greenwood.

House Committee on the Judiciary. (1962). *Hearings before the Committee on the Judiciary*. Washington, DC: U.S. House of Representatives.

House Committee on the Judiciary. (1995). *Hearings on religious freedom in the schools*. Washington, DC: U.S. House of Representatives.

Illich, I. (1972). *Deschooling society*. New York: Harper & Row.

Irvine, J. M. (2002). *Talk about sex*. Berkeley: University of California.

Irving, D. C. (1968). *The German atomic bomb*. New York: Simon & Schuster.

Jeremiah Project. (2002). Available at http:// www.jeremiahproject.com.

Jeynes, W. (2004). Immigration in the United States and the golden years of education: Was Ravitch right? *Educational Studies, 35,* 248–270.

Jeynes, W. (2006). Standardized tests and Froebel's original kindergarten model. *Teachers College Record, 108*(10), 1937–1959.

Jeynes, W. H. (2000). Effects of several of the most common family structures on the academic achievement of children. *Marriage and Family Review, 30*(1/2), 73–97.

Johnson, P. (1997). *A history of the American people*. New York: HarperCollins.

Kaiser, D. E. (2000). *Kennedy, Johnson, and the origins of the Vietnam War*. Cambridge, MA: Harvard University Press.

Kaldor, M., & Holden, G. (1989). *The new détente: Rethinking East-West relations*. London: United Nations University.

Kallen, S. A. (2001). Introduction. In S. A Kallen (Ed.), *Sixties counterculture* (pp. 3–32). San Diego, CA: Greenhaven Press.

Kemble, E. (1969). Ocean Hill-Brownsville. In M. R. Berube & M. G. Gittell (Eds.), *Confrontation at Ocean Hill-Brownsville* (pp. 33–51). New York: Praeger.

Kennedy, J. (Ed.). (1994). *The hidden agenda* [Video]. Ft. Lauderdale, FL: Coral Ridge Presbyterian Church.

Kimball, J. P. (1998). *Nixon's Vietnam War*. Lawrence: University of Kansas.

King, M. L. Jr. (1998). *The autobiography of Martin Luther King Jr*. (C. Carson, Ed.). New York: Warner.

King, M. L. Jr., & Washington, J. M. (Ed.). (1986). *A testament of hope: The essential writings of Martin Luther King Jr*. San Francisco: Harper & Row.

Kliebard, H. M. (1969). *Religion and education in America*. Scranton, PA: International Textbook Company.

Kohlberg, L. (1981). *The philosophy of moral development*. San Francisco: Harper & Row.

Kohlberg, L., & Mayer, R. (1972). *Development as the aim of education*. Cambridge, MA: Harvard University Press.

Leary, T. (2001). Spreading the psychedelic message. In S. A. Kallen (Ed.), *Sixties counterculture* (pp. 115–131). San Diego, CA: Greenhaven Press.

Libertocracy. (2002). *Web essays*. Retrieved June 11, 2002, from http://www.libertocracy.com/ webessays/religion/persecution.

Loeb, P. R. (1994). *Generation at the crossroads: Apathy and action on the American campus*. New Brunswick, NJ: Rutgers University Press.

Loewen, J. W. (1996). *Lies my teacher told me*. New York: Simon & Schuster.

Louisell, D. W. (1964). The man and the mountain: Douglas on religious freedom. *Yale Law Journal, 73,* 975–988.

Maranatha Christian Journal. (1999). *Alabama school stops student from wearing cross*. Retrieved June 11, 2002, from http://www.mcjonline.com.

Mayer, M. (1969). *The teachers strike, 1968*. New York: Harper & Row.

Mayer, M. (1970). The full and sometimes very surprising story of Ocean Hill, the teacher's union, and the teachers' strikes of 1968. In A. Meier & E. Rudwick (Eds.), *Black protest in the sixties* (pp. 169–229). Chicago: Quadrangle.

McCollum v. Board of Education, Dist. 71. 333 U.S. 203 (1948).

McCoy, R. (1969). The year of the dragon. In M. R. Berube & M. G. Gittell (Eds.), *Confrontation at Ocean Hill-Brownsville* (pp. 52–63). New York: Praeger.

Mee, C. L. (1975). *Meeting at Potsdam.* New York: M. Evans.

Melody, M. E., & Peterson, L. M. (1999). *Teaching America about sex.* New York: New York University Press.

Michaelsen, R. (1970). *Piety in the public school.* London: Macmillan.

Miles, B. (2004). *Hippie.* New York: Sterling Press.

Miller, J. (2001). The anti-war movement is born. In S. A. Kallen (Ed.), *Sixties counterculture* (pp. 57–66). San Diego, CA: Greenhaven Press.

Mitchell, V., & Block, J. H. (1983). Assessing personal and social change in two generations. In M. Horner, C. C. Nadelson, & M. T. Notman (Eds.), *The challenge of change: Perspectives on family, work, and education* (pp. 223–262). New York: Plenum.

Morin, R. (1969). *Dwight D. Eisenhower: A gauge of greatness.* New York: Simon & Schuster.

Murray v. Curlett 374 U.S. 203 (1963).

Murray, W. (1982). *My life without God.* Nashville, TN: Thomas Nelson.

Nash, G. (1997). *History on trial: Culture wars and the teaching of the past.* New York: Knopf.

National Catholic Almanac. (1963). Vol. 24. Patterson, NJ: St. Anthony's Guild.

Neill, A. S. (1960). *Summerhill.* New York: Hart.

Neill, A. S. (1968). *Summerhill.* Harmondsworth, UK: Penguin.

President urges court be backed on prayer issue (1962, June 28). *New York Times*, p. 1.

Oates, S. B. (1982). *Let the trumpet sound: The life of Martin Luther King Jr.* New York: Harper & Row.

Orlofsky, D. D. (2001). *Redefining teacher education: The theories of Jerome Bruner and the practice of training teachers.* New York: Peter Lang.

Palmer, J. A. (2001). *Fifty modern thinkers of education: From Piaget to present.* London: Routledge.

Paterson, T. G. (1989). *Kennedy's quest for victory.* New York: Oxford.

Perrone, V. (1990). How did we get here? Testing in the early grades: The games grown-ups play. In C. Kamii (Ed.), *Testing in the early grades* (pp. 1–13). Washington, DC: National Association for the Education of Young Children.

Piaget, J. (1950). *The nature of intelligence.* New York: Harcourt, Brace.

Podair, J. E. (2002). *The strike that changed New York.* New Haven: Yale University Press.

Pritchett, W. (2002). *Brownsville, Brooklyn, Blacks, Jews, and the changing face of the ghetto.* Chicago: University of Chicago Press.

Raffini, J. P. (1988). *Student apathy: The protection of self-worth.* Washington, DC: National Education Association.

Ravitch, D. (1974). *The great school wars.* New York: Basic.

Ravitch, D. (1983). *The troubled crusade: American education 1945–1980.* New York: Basic Books.

Reed v. Van Hoven 237 F. Supp. 48 (W.D. Mich. 1965).

Religious Tolerance. (2002). *News.* Retrieved June 11, 2002, from http://www.religioustolerance.org/lawmenu.htm.

Reuben, D. R. (1969). *Everything you wanted to know about sex but were afraid to ask.* New York: McKay.

Richardson, L. F. (1960). *Statistics of deadly quarrels.* Pittsburgh, PA: Boxwood.

Ridgeway, I. (2002). *A survey into the physical and psychological differences of the American, German, and Japanese educational methods in teaching the subject of mathematics.* Master's thesis, University of Wisconsin at Stout.

School District of Abington v. Schempp 374 U.S. 203 (1963).

Sikorski, R. (1993). *Controversies in constitutional law.* New York: Garland.

Silver, H. (1981). Education against poverty: Interpreting British and American policies in the 1960s and 1970s. In E. B. Gumbert, H. Silver, M. F. Young, & E. Z. Friedenberg, (Eds.), *Poverty, power, and authority in education* (pp. 13–33). Atlanta: Georgia State University.

Smith, R. B. (1983). *An international history of the Vietnam War*. New York: St. Martin's Press.

Sowell, T. (1992). *Inside American education*. New York: Free Press.

Spin-Tech. (1999). *Spin-Tech letters to the editor*. Retrieved June 11, 2002, from http://www.spintech .mag.com.

Sykes, C. J. (1995). *Dumbing down our kids*. New York: St. Martin's Press.

Urofsky, M. (Ed.). (1970). *Why teachers strike*. Garden City, NY: Doubleday.

U.S. Center for Education Statistics. (1966). *Equality of educational opportunity*. Washington, DC: U.S. Center for Education Statistics.

U.S. Department of Health and Human Services. (1992). *Statistical abstracts of the United States*. Washington, DC: Author.

U.S. Department of Health and Human Services. (1998). *Statistical abstracts of the United States*. Washington, DC: Author.

U.S. Department of Health, Education, and Welfare. (1957). *Progress of public education, 1956–1957*. Washington, DC: Author.

U.S. Department of Justice. (1993). *Report to the nation on crime and justice*. Washington, DC: Author.

U.S. Department of Justice. (1999). *Age-specific arrest rate and race-specific arrest rates for selected offenses, 1965–1992*. Washington, DC: Author.

Vahey, M. F. (1998). *A hidden history: Slavery, abolition, and the underground railroad in Cow Neck on Long Island*. Port Washington, NY: Cow Neck Peninsula Historical Society.

VanDeMark, B. (1991). *Into the quagmire: Lyndon Johnson and the escalation of the Vietnam War*. New York: Oxford.

Vygotsky, L. (1978). *Mind in society: The development of higher psychological processes*. Cambridge, MA: Harvard University Press.

Willis, G. (1999). A necessary evil: A history of American distrust of government. New York: Simon & Schuster.

World Net Daily. (2002). *News*. Retrieved June 11, 2002, from http://www.worldnetdaily.com/nes/ article.asp/ARTICLE_ID=22891.

Zorach v. Clauson 343 U.S. 306 (1952).

CHAPTER 12

The Rise of Public Criticism of Education

Historically speaking, Americans have varied in terms of their support for public education. From the 1830s to about 1920, conservatives tended to be more supportive of public education than liberals were, largely because the national public school movement was birthed by conservatives, led by Horace Mann (Hunt & Maxson, 1981; Yulish, 1980). However, when John Dewey expressed uncompromising support for public schools, an unprecedented number of liberals also advocated the expansion of the public school system. The surge in liberal support ushered in a golden age of popularity for public schools, which lasted from the early 1920s until the early 1960s. During this period, both conservatives and liberals demonstrated enthusiasm regarding public education (Jeynes, 2004). However, in about 1963, this pervasive support came to an end as evidence mounted that the nation's schools suffered from academic decline. Many individuals reached this conclusion because of the steep decline in achievement test scores that took place from 1963 to 1980, most notably in SAT scores (formerly known as "Scholastic Aptitude Test" or "Scholastic Achievement Test") (Ravitch & Finn, 1987; Wirtz, 1977). During the 1960s and 1970s, public criticism of the public school system reached new levels (Breland, 1977).

Few topics create as much dissension and contention as the debate over whether the U.S. system of public education suffered from a protracted decline in academic achievement or had a productive learning environment from 1963 to 1980 (Bloom, 1987; Breland, 1977). The dialogue invariably gravitates to a discussion about achievement test scores and, more recently, about violence and racism in the schools (Ravitch & Finn, 1987; Sowell, 1993; Wirtz, 1977). Achievement test scores arise in the conversation because they represent the most objective and standardized way of assessing academic progress in the schools. But educators address a variety of other measures as well.

As with so many educational issues, the debate about a purported decline in the quality of America's public schools tends to exhibit a high degree of polarization (Bloom, 1987; Ravitch & Finn, 1987; Sowell, 1993; Wirtz, 1977). On one hand, some educators deny that U.S. public schools suffer from any decline at all and claim they even manifest some signs of improvement (Bracey, 1992a, 1992b, 1993a, 1993b). On the other hand, others declare that the academic decline is not only real and sharp, but that the drop in achievement test scores results completely from academic factors (Ravitch & Finn, 1987; Sowell, 1993).

Much of the argument surrounding the question of educational decline not only addresses the drop in achievement test scores in general but also specifically the drop in SAT scores. From 1963 to 1980, SAT scores declined for 17 consecutive years (Wirtz, 1977). The SAT stands as the oldest and most prestigious standardized test of its kind. This extended decline in SAT scores caused considerable consternation among many educators. Nevertheless, using the SAT as a national measure of educational achievement presents some limitations. First and foremost, those who take the SAT consist of students who maintain at least some interest in pursuing a college education (Wirtz, 1977). Thus, the sum of the SAT-test-taking population does not truly represent the aggregation of American public and private school students (Wirtz, 1977).

There do exist other standardized tests, which record data from a more representative sample of American students (Stedman & Kaestle, 1985a, 1985b). Most of these other tests possess some utility in helping to assess whether U.S. schools suffered from academic decline from 1963 to 1980. Perhaps the most notable of these is the National Assessment of Educational Progress (NAEP). According to Stedman and Kaestle (1985a), "The NAEP tests are probably the best indicators of national trends" (p. 204). Numerous educators hold the NAEP in high regard largely because results are "statistically weighted to produce a sample that is representative of the whole population" (Ravitch & Finn, 1987, p. 44). Unfortunately, however, administration of the NAEP did not begin until 1969, and educators did not administer the NAEP math to a nationally representative sample until 1973 (U.S. Department of Education, 1990). Fully nonestimated math scores became available beginning in the 1978 admission (U.S. Department of Education, 1990). Therefore, the NAEP, unlike the SAT, can help us dissect only the latter half or so of the achievement test score decline.

Fortunately, other modes of educational assessment, such as the Iowa Tests of Educational Development (ITED) and the Iowa Tests of Basic Skills (ITBS), can also serve as supplements in examining the achievement test score decline (Forsyth, 1994; U.S. Department of Education, 2000).

Each of the achievement tests commonly used for student assessment possesses some elements of weakness. These shortcomings act as limiting factors in arriving at the widespread conclusions educators would like to make from them regarding a so-called academic decline in America. Any approach, therefore, that would examine achievement test scores and other indicators collectively seems wise. While this chapter will give special attention to the SAT because of its prominence both in terms of reputation and in scholarly analysis, we should give careful consideration to whether other achievement scores confirm the SAT trends.

BASIC ARGUMENTS

Educators in the Excellence Movement

Those who assert that America suffers from educational decline claim that the U.S. education system tolerates a new standard of "mediocrity" among its students (Boyer, 1985, p. 16). The National Commission of Excellence in Education (1983) report, *A Nation at Risk,* epitomized many of the concerns of this school of thought (Boyer, 1985). The report pointed to the now infamous 90-point drop in SAT scores, a concomitant decline in some SAT achievement test results, and a steady increase in remedial math courses needed in the nation's 4-year public colleges (National Commission on Excellence in Education, 1983). In addition, several writers in the book *Nation Reformed? American Education, 20 Years After "A Nation at Risk"* (Gordon, 2003) assert that little progress has been made since that report was released.

A Closer Look: To Test or Not to Test? That Is the Question

The question of how tests should be used and whether they should be used at all stands as a debate that has persisted for centuries. The main reason this debate continues is that on one hand, teachers need to be able to assess just how well they are teaching and how well the students are prepared to use the knowledge they have gained, and, on the other hand, tests can be stressful, and it would seem plausible that teachers should find ways to alleviate stress.

How one resolves this debate usually comes down to whether the essence of one's philosophy is conservative, that is, perennialist or essentialist, or whether one is a liberal, that is, a progressive or reconstructionist (see Chapter 8) (Dupuis, 1966; Strauss, 1968; Walker, 1963). There are two distinctions that are especially pertinent in this discussion. First, what is the best type of assessment? Liberals believe that examinations are stressful and should be avoided, if at all possible. Instead, they prefer teachers to engage in more student-friendly, subjective means of assessment, such as teacher ratings, grading homework, and examining portfolios (Dupuis, 1966; Strauss, 1968). They aver that students will perform best in a stress-free environment. Conservatives believe that the liberal approach permits too much room for teacher bias (Dupuis, 1966; Walker, 1963). They claim that nearly all students have endured the experience of having a teacher grade him or her down (or up) because of teacher bias. It is too risky to have one's future determined on the subjective views of a teacher (Dupuis, 1966; Walker, 1963). Instead, more objective modes of assessment are needed.

A second distinction is based on what is perhaps the most salient difference between the liberal and conservative approaches to education. That is, liberals think that education should be child centered, and conservatives believe that it should be preparation centered. Liberals believe that one should teach children what they want to learn, because when children enjoy the material, they will learn more (Dupuis, 1966; Strauss, 1968). Using this approach, liberals claim, will be more likely produce lifelong learners. This, they contend, is the ultimate goal of education. With this in mind, if children do not like taking examinations, test administration should be avoided. To test children when they do not wish to be tested will dampen the zeal that many children possess for learning (Dupuis, 1966; Strauss, 1968). On the other hand, conservatives argue that a main function of schools is to train children to learn how to become fulfilled in life. They assert that to achieve this goal, children have to be prepared in order to fulfill their desires (Dupuis, 1966; Walker, 1963). For example, like it or not, modern American society virtually requires one to know Microsoft Word, Excel, and Power Point in order to obtain a good job. Schools, from the conservative view, need to prepare children for these realities (Dupuis, 1966; Walker, 1963).

Both liberals and conservatives have some valid points along these lines. Perhaps one might even suggest that schools can concurrently be child centered and preparation centered.

- Do you think schools should be child centered or preparation centered?
- How do you think children should be evaluated?
- Should standardized tests be used?
- If standardized tests are used, how often should they be given?

Reports inundated the newspapers regarding the widespread nature of the problem of illiteracy. David Harman (1987), author of *Illiteracy: A National Dilemma,* notes,

> The problem isn't confined to school dropouts and the disadvantaged members of minority groups, although they account for the greatest number of illiterates; more and more working members of mainstream America are found to be either totally illiterate or unable to read at the level presumably required by their job or their position in society. (p. 1)

Wherever the problem persists, there arises growing alarm over reports of high school graduates who cannot read. Jonathan Kozol (1985), author of the book *Illiterate America,* calls the situation an abomination.

Estimates vary considerably regarding the extent to which illiteracy plagues the American landscape. The variations result largely from differences in definition of just what constitutes illiteracy. Officially, the United States still boasts a 97% literacy rate, a relatively high percentage when compared with other countries (U.S. Census Bureau, 2001). Yet increasingly, Americans in business and education view this basic definition of *literacy* as antiquated. *Functional literacy* stands as the phrase currently in vogue (U.S. Census Bureau, 2001). Yet researchers rarely agree on what exactly constitutes functional literacy. Therefore, while the U.S. Census Bureau (2001) contends that 3% of Americans above the age of 20 are illiterate, Jonathan Kozol puts the number much higher, 60 million, and still others estimate that 72 million Americans are "functionally illiterate" (Kozol, 1985). This would amount to about 20% to 25% of the American population.

Those who perceive a school system in decline frequently cite lower educational standards as an indicator (National Commission on Excellence in Education, 1983). They point to statistics that indicate that American students do less homework now than in earlier years (Cintora, 1999). Concurrent with this trend emerges a continuing trend of grade inflation. Thomas Sowell (1993) believes that there exists a direct connection between falling test scores and grade inflation:

> These two trends—grade inflation and declining test scores—are by no means unconnected. Without the systematic deception of parents and the public by rising grades, it is highly unlikely that the decline in performance could have continued so long. (p. 2)

The American College Testing Program (ACT) reports that the average grade point average (GPA) rose from 2.59 in 1966 (using a 4.0 scale) to 2.85 in 1976 (Singal, 1991). Other sources confirm that the proportion of A's and B's given in grading rose during that period (Sowell, 1993). Carl Singleton (1985) displays a degree of contempt for a system of education that he contends almost refuses to give F grades and that makes grade-level promotion virtually automatic. Singleton avers, "School systems have contributed to massive ignorance by issuing unearned passing grades over a period of some 20 years" (p. 264).

Some excellence-oriented educators, such as Diane Ravitch and Chester Finn (1987), assert that diminished requirements at America's universities have contributed to the academic deterioration in the public schools. Many institutions of higher learning maintain

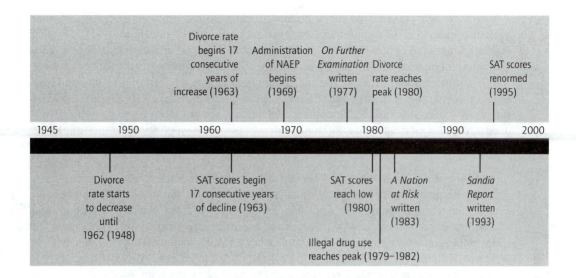

more lax math, history, and literature requirements for their high school applicants than they did 30 years ago (Ravitch & Finn, 1987). Thomas Sowell (1993) notes that despite this, ironically, a lower percentage of the top applicants (as measured in grades and test scores) are gaining acceptance in the nation's top universities than in past years:

> [At] Amherst College, for example, among those applicants from the class of 1991 who scored between 750 and 800 on the verbal SAT, less than half were admitted—while 26 other students who scored 400 on the same test were admitted. A very similar pattern is found at Stanford University, which rejected a majority of applicants who scored between 700 and 800 on the verbal SAT, while admitting more than a hundred other students who scored below 500 on the same test. (pp. 122–123)

Sowell (1993) adds that while MIT offered admission to two thirds of the applicants who scored between 750 and 800 on the quantitative math portion of the SAT in 1968, that percentage dropped to 40% by 1987. Of course, one could argue that a great deal of what Sowell observes simply indicates that 4-year institutions place a higher value on grades than they do on SAT scores. That is, a student with a C average will not gain admittance to a top school no matter what SAT scores he or she gets. Dinesh D'Souza's (1991) research, however, indicates that similar trends to those found by Sowell regarding SAT scores also apply to grades. America's top colleges turn down numerous students with 4.0 GPAs and/or high SAT scores (Sowell, 1993). Sowell adds, "Among the non-academic criteria which help explain such anomalies are personal qualities (real or imagined by the admissions committee), geographical distribution, alumni preferences, and ethnic 'diversity' or racial quotas" (pp. 122–123). As a consequence of these changes, advocates of excellence argue that less incentive exists for students to do well, because grades and scores mean less than they did 30 years ago (Sowell, 1993).

Educators who assert that the academic decline is real point to a variety of other indicators to support their contention. For example, Professor David Singal (1991) states that in 1989, a national poll indicated 75% of professors thought "undergraduates were 'seriously under prepared in basic skills,' while only 15% of the professors thought otherwise" (p. 59). Some scholars claim that the vocabulary of the contemporary elementary and high school student is declining at a rate of about 1% per year (Kennedy, 1994). There is evidence that even students acknowledge that the U.S. school system lacks vigor. Joseph Adelson asserts that 48% of students do not think their schoolwork is tough enough (Adelson, 1985).

Thomas Sowell (1993) summarizes the excellence ideology well:

> The general decline in education performance that began in the 1960s encompassed elementary and secondary education, as well as education at the college level. The evidence of this decline include not only results on a variety of objective tests, but also first-hand observations by teachers and professors, and dismaying experiences by employers who have found the end-product seriously lacking. The most widely known decline was in the scores of the Scholastic Aptitude Test (SAT). However, scores also declined on the rival American College Testing Program (ACT) examination, as well as on the Iowa Test of Educational Development and on a variety of local tests. As of 1991, only 11 percent of eighth-grade students in California's public schools could solve seventh-grade math problems. (p. 1)

Initially, conservatives were the ones who argued that the American education system suffered from a malaise of mediocrity (Sowell, 1993). However, soon many progressives like Albert Shanker and various minority leaders issued rallying cries that America's schools needed substantial reform (Stedman, 1994). Jonathan Kozol (1985), another liberal educator, claims that if the achievement and literacy problems are not rectified, poor and minority students will suffer the most. Many of the ideas for reform held by these conservatives and progressives fueled the excellence movement of the 1980s and 1990s (Finn, 1991; Sowell, 1993). Many of those calling for reform agreed on several of the reasons the American education system had, in their view, declined. These reasons included the attenuation of the work ethic, the reduction in the percentage of students taking challenging courses, the deterioration of moral values in America, the increased role of television in America, and a reduction in the percentage of children coming from two-parent homes (Finn, 1991). Paul Cooperman (1985) summarized well the views of those in the excellence movement when he stated,

> Each generation of Americans has outstripped its parents in education, in literacy, and in economic attainment. For the first time in the history of our country, the educational skills of one generation will not surpass, will not equal, will not even approach, those of their parents. (p. 23)

Educators Who Disagree With the Excellence Movement

A considerable number of educators disagree with the conclusions propounded by those in the excellence movement. These individuals feel that the case for academic deterioration is hyperbolic (Berliner & Biddle, 1995; Bracey, 1993a, 1993b; Stedman, 1994). They do not deny that our schools face problems, but they affirm that academic trends over the last 30 years indicate stability rather than decline (Berliner & Biddle, 1995; Stedman, 1994). Many educators, for example, assert that the decline in SAT scores from 1963 to 1980 resulted almost entirely from the changing composition of the population applying for college (Gough, 1993). After all, the push for equality during the 1960s resulted in an unprecedented number of African Americans and other minorities applying for college and taking the SAT (Wirtz, 1977). The SAT decline therefore might actually reflect a success in educational policy rather than a failure worthy of national angst (Wirtz, 1977).

Those who defend the public school system in this way also tend to view the goals of education from a different angle than those who emphasize excellence. Defenders of public education feel that equality of educational opportunity represents as laudable a goal as excellence in education. Cynthia Brown, for example, worries that the excellence movement may hurt equality (Brown, 1985). Milton Schwebel (1985) believes that inequity constitutes the greatest problem facing schools:

> Like it or not, the United States has two school systems. The system that serves the more favored students compares favorably with those of other nations. . . . This other system is characterized by lower student achievement, lower per capita educational expenditures, and lower social-class status of parents. (pp. 237–238)

Some liberals deride the tendency for school critics to sound alarmist about declining test scores without seriously considering other factors that may contribute to dropping achievement test scores (Levin, 1985):

> I would like to argue that, to a major extent, the much lamented deterioration of basic skills, declines in test scores, shifts in curriculum, inflation of grades, and ease of getting into college with substandard skills are much more a result of the economic situation than the cause of it, and that Back to Basics measures will improve neither the economy nor the schools. (p. 232)

As a result of taking this perspective, many defenders of public education believe we should target inner-city schools as the principal part of any reform efforts (Stedman, 1994). Many of these educators also believe that the school's attempt to establish and reinforce a child's self-esteem enjoys as central a role in any school's success as raising grades and scores (Finn, 1991).

As time went on, two schools of thought arose among those who pleaded for public education, and they gained a good deal of attention. First, a "revisionist" school arose that claimed that American public schools had actually fared quite well from 1963 to 1980 compared with past accomplishments (Carson, Huelskamp, & Woodall, 1993). Second, some researchers questioned the usefulness of standardized tests (Finn, 1991).

The Revisionist View of Achievement During the 1960s and 1970s

Revisionists gained increased prominence among those who maintained a buoyant view on the progress of our public school system (Berliner & Biddle, 1995; Stedman, 1994). These "revisionists," led by Gerald Bracey and C. C. Carson, delineated a much brighter picture of the education trends from 1963 to 1980 than did most conservatives and progressives (Stedman, 1994). Revisionists asserted that the entire decline in SAT scores found its roots in demographic factors (Berliner & Biddle, 1995; Stedman, 1994). They noted that the percentage of elementary school students who eventually received high school and college diplomas rose during this period (Berliner & Biddle, 1995; Carson et al., 1993). The dropout rate, particularly among African Americans, continued to fall, and the revisionists also noted that SAT scores for minority students rose steadily during the 1980s (Carson et al., 1993). Educators in the revisionist school claimed that many achievement test scores showed either steady or rising patterns after 1980, including Graduate Record Examinations (GRE) scores (Carson et al., 1993). In addition, revisionists claimed that there did not exist sufficient data to conclude how American students stacked up in achievement versus their foreign counterparts (Carson et al., 1993). Furthermore, revisionists questioned the validity and utility of international comparisons (Berliner & Biddle, 1995; Carson et el., 1993).

Carson et al. (1993), in the "Sandia Report," concluded that the SAT score decline of 1963 to 1980 was due entirely to demographic factors. Gerald Bracey (1993a, 1993b), probably the most prolific revisionist, concluded, "No decline exists or ever existed. . . . Even if we are cautious in our interpretations, we can conclude that there has not been a decline in SAT scores" (pp. 106, 107). Those who defended the U.S. system of public schools are divided as to whether they endorse all the revisionist views. Nevertheless, revisionists gained a growing audience among many of public education's greatest advocates. The revisionist argument caused many researchers to take a second look at the available data to see whether the United States really did experience an academic decline.

Those Who Question the Utility of Standardized Tests

Some researchers point out that some children do not test well and that as a general rule, the United States should avoid an excessive reliance on standardized tests (Crouse & Trusheim, 1988). Carson et al. (1993) also point out that standardized tests, of which the SAT is only one, indicate a child's cumulative knowledge rather than what they learned from a particular course. Some argue that children become overly anxious when they know they are being evaluated. In addition, others claim that some children know more than performance on short-answer and essay tests might indicate. Some children even cheat to obtain higher scores.

Naturally, one can also apply a large portion of these objections to grading in schools (Goodlad & Anderson, 1959). Teachers grade largely on the basis of tests; some children cheat; and there exists a tendency for educators to heavily rely on grades and even label unique individuals by their GPAs (Levy & Dweck, 1999). Given this propensity, several educators have propounded the notion of ungraded schools (Brown, 1963; Goodlad & Anderson, 1959). After all, many of America's finest leaders, including Noah Webster, Horace Mann, and Martin Luther King Jr., asserted that the state of the heart is more important than the condition of the mind (King, 1998; Mann, 1849; Webster, 1834).

There is little question that those have a point who aver that the grading system, whether measured by one's GPA or SAT score, has only a certain degree of value (Brown, 1963; Goodlad & Anderson, 1959). Most people would also agree American children today are overtested (Carson et al., 1993; Crouse & Trusheim, 1988). These assertions patently place the test score decline in a helpful context. Educators who emphasize the overreliance on tests are nevertheless also concerned about the test score decline. Whether a certain individual thinks Americans are overtested or not, no one wants test scores to decline so steeply over such a prolonged period of time.

Some educators also claim that the SAT is biased against certain groups (Crouse & Trusheim, 1988). Although the SAT has fared well in most assessments of bias, this term will sometimes emerge with reference to even the best tests and other grading systems because of the considerable disagreement over what constitutes bias (Donlon, 1984; Gregory, 2004; Nash, 1979). In addition, research indicates that even the Culture Fair IQ test shows essentially the same patterns as other standardized intelligence or achievement tests, like the SAT (Gregory, 2004). Nevertheless, those who question the utility of the SAT emphasize other issues more than bias, because all classifications of groups experienced a substantial decline in scores from 1963 to 1980 (Wirtz, 1977).

ADDRESSING THE DATA

In assessing the arguments of those in the excellence movement who insist there was a real academic decline from 1963 to 1980 and those that disagree with them, ultimately, one needs to look at the evidence.

The Trends in Achievement Test Scores

Whether there was real academic decline from 1963 to 1980 will be addressed in the next section. However, in order to understand the trend, one should take note of the achievement test score trend before this time. Virtually all major achievement test scores showed stability from 1920 to 1963 (Cooperman, 1978). In fact, most major achievement test scores showed a steady increase during that period, particularly during the post-*Sputnik* era, from 1957 to 1963 (Armbruster, 1977). The College Board first released specific statistics on verbal and math SAT scores beginning in 1951. From 1951 to 1963, SAT scores rose from 970 to 980. The verbal score rose from 476 to 478, and the math score rose from 494 to 502. During that period, there appeared very little fluctuation in SAT scores, except for a small drift upward (Armbruster, 1977).

In 1963, the trend suddenly shifted downward. In every year following 1963 until 1980, SAT scores dropped (Lipsitz, 1977; Wirtz, 1977). The decline was unparalleled in the history of the SAT. Scores had never before declined for more than 2 consecutive years (Armbruster, 1977; Wirtz, 1977). Between 1963 and 1970, SAT scores plummeted 32 points, and by 1980, the drop totaled 90 points. Since then, SAT scores have stabilized and have even shown a slight increase in math scores (U.S. Department of Education, 2005). Yet even in the 1990s, SAT scores stubbornly remained 80 points below their 1963 levels (U.S. Department of Education, 2000).

Since 1995, this fact was masked by an Educational Testing Service decision to renorm SAT scores (Feinberg, 1995; Young, 1995). Consequently, the results of the verbal and math scores, though totaling in the low 900s, were now renormed to equal 1,000 (Feinberg, 1995; Young, 1995).

To comprehend where American students stand academically, we must come to an understanding of just what happened to cause the steep decline in SAT scores.

Attempting to Explain the Academic Decline

Given the controversy surrounding the achievement test score decline generally and the SAT score decline specifically, the Educational Testing Service initiated the largest organized effort ever amassed to assess standardized test score trends (Wirtz, 1977). In 1977, because of the extensive debate surrounding the SAT decline, the College Board organized a panel of approximately 20 to 25 renowned educational researchers to address the question of what caused the protracted decline in SAT scores. To date, this analysis provides us with the most elaborate analysis of the SAT score decline, and therefore researchers quote this work, titled *On Further Examination* (Wirtz, 1977), with great frequency. This panel specifically addressed the question of what proportion of the SAT score decline resulted from compositional and other factors affecting academics, respectively. The Educational Testing Service statistically considered all the possible reasons for the SAT score decline and asserted that a case could be made for both compositional changes and real academic deterioration contributing to the SAT score decline (Wirtz, 1977).

The Case for Compositional Change

Whether the composition of the student body to which the SAT was administered changed significantly from 1963 to 1980 carries a great deal of importance. Those who defend the U.S. system of public education assert that nearly all the SAT decline finds its roots in the presence of such compositional change (Bracey, 1993a, 1993b).

The panel concluded that there existed considerable evidence for a compositional change contributing to the decline in SAT scores. The College Board dissected their argument into two parts: (1) that an increasingly large percentage of high school students took the SAT, particularly between 1963 and 1970, and (2) that an increasing percentage of students who took the SAT came from groups that traditionally attained lower-than-average SAT scores (Wirtz, 1977). The panel concluded that the latter effect proved especially puissant from 1963 to 1970.

Increased Percentage of Students Taking the SAT

Indeed, the percentage of 18-year-olds taking the SAT increased from 33.5% in 1962/1963 to 43.6% in 1967/1968 (Wirtz, 1977). The assumption researchers make regarding these statistics is that the additional 10.1% of students, on average, probably earned lower SAT scores and lower grades than the 33.5% (Wirtz, 1977). This is true because the additional numbers taking the SAT resulted directly from the conscious decision by schools and lawmakers to increase the availability of a college education to the American public. Clearly, this development is a positive one. Virtually all Americans want more people and a more diverse group of people to go to college (Lawrence-Lightfoot, 1983). In this sense, part of the SAT score decline actually reflects an ameliorative trend (Lawrence-Lightfoot 1983). In 1977, the panel observed the following:

Twenty-five years ago, only half of all young Americans were staying in school through the 12th grade; this fraction grew by 1964 to two thirds and by 1970 to three fourths. The proportion going on to college was about one fourth in 1952, about a third in 1964, and almost half by 1970. (Wirtz, 1977, p. 13)

In addition, a growing percentage of those who took the SAT chose to attend "colleges and universities with less selective or even open admission policies" as well as 2-year colleges and technical schools (Wirtz, 1977, p. 15). This fact patently impacted the overall average SAT score. The panel concluded,

There are average score differentials of from 60 to 85 points (1) between test takers going on to four-year colleges (who average higher scores) and those who subsequently enter two-year colleges, and (2) between test takers who go directly from high school to college (averaging higher scores) and those who do not. (p. 17)

The percentage of students taking the SAT from the lower-scoring groups rose from 8% in 1960 to 15% in 1972 (Lipsitz, 1977; Wirtz, 1977). Lower-scoring groups generally means those of lower socioeconomic status (SES). No matter what a child's background, students of lower SES do not do as well as their more privileged counterparts (Lipsitz, 1977; Stedman, 1994; Stedman & Kaestle, 1985b). Once again, the fact that a larger number of poor children took the SAT is an ameliorative development. These students are often the first in their families to go to college. Consequently, any trend that expands the percentage of poor students going to college broadens the scope of educational opportunity in America. This trend reflects not only a change in the number of students desiring to go to college but also the growth of community colleges and flexible admission policies. The SAT "came to be taken increasingly by a much wider variety of students with more diverse prospects in mind" (Wirtz, 1977, p. 18). The change in admission policies may have reduced the number of people taking the SAT twice, which also mildly reduced the average SAT scores. Repeaters generally lift their SAT scores 15 to 30 points (Wirtz, 1977). Nevertheless, other factors, such as a decline in the work ethic, may have contributed to fewer students taking the SAT twice (Wirtz, 1977).

Of course, we should exhibit some degree of caution when we relate the growth in the number of people going to college to the decline in SAT scores. First, we should note that during the 1960s and 1970s, an increasing number of schools did not require students to take the SAT (or even the ACT) to obtain admission; in particular, most community colleges did not require students to take the SAT (G. Marco, personal communication, November 2, 1994). Second, the increase in the percentage of high school students taking the SAT may not be as telling as it might seem. For while the percentage of 18-year-olds taking the SAT rose from 33.5% in 1962/1963 to 43.6% in 1967/1968, this percentage began to fall the following year. In fact, by 1975/1976, the percentage stood at 33.2% and would fall still farther in coming years (Cooperman, 1978). The percentage of 18-year-olds taking the ACT shows the same general trend. Although this percentage for SAT scores was actually lower than the 33.5% recorded in 1962/1963, just before the SAT decline, the scores in 1975/1976 were 81 points lower than in 1962/1963 (Wirtz, 1977). Critics of the panel's conclusion regarding student composition also note that the percentage of high school students taking the test rose from 3.9% in 1951/1952 to 33.5% in 1962/1963 but SAT scores rose during that time (Wirtz, 1977).

While these objections caution us against overestimating the role of compositional change, it does not deny the effect of compositional change. First, the fact that SAT scores fell significantly, despite a return to 1962/1963 levels of the percentage of 18-year-olds taking the test, simply indicates the presence of other factors influencing SAT scores as well. Second, the stability of SAT scores from the 1951/1962 period, despite the increase in the percentage of students taking the SAT, may indicate that nationwide achievement rose during the period. As a result, the effect of compositional change was neutralized. The results of other achievement tests document an achievement test score rise during the 1950s and early 1960s. The Iowa Test of Basic Skills (ITBS), for example, rose somewhat during this period (Armbruster, 1977). The ITBS does not cover high school students, but nevertheless does possess some comparative usefulness. A renorming study by test maker Harcourt Brace Jovanovich also confirms a rise in achievement test scores from Grades 1 through 9 between 1958 and 1964 (Cooperman, 1978). Particularly impressive improvements came at the 8th- and 9th-grade levels. The primary achievement test used then to assess high school achievement, the Iowa Test of Education Development (ITED), did not confirm these upward trends, but did remain relatively stable during this time. The results of these achievement tests carry a great deal of significance because compositional change occurs much more slowly in the general student population than it does in those taking college entrance examinations.

Third, the College Board admits that a compositional change previously affected the results of the SAT. Between 1941, when the College Board originally normed the SAT at 1,000 for the combined verbal and math scores, and 1951, the composition of the test takers changed so dramatically that the Educational Testing Service will not even publish the results of those tests. The number of students taking the SAT soared over sevenfold during that period (Cooperman, 1978).

Fourth, although the increase in the percentage of 18-year-olds taking the SAT was sharper from 1951 to 1963 than it was immediately following 1963, the nature of the compositional change after 1963 may be greater than in the former period. In other words, even though the percentage of students taking the SAT increased substantially from 1951 to 1963, the additional students were more frequently of the same race and class than was the case with the additional students who took the exam from 1963 to 1970.

Regarding the place of compositional change from 1963 to 1970, the College Board panel made the following the conclusions:

> We find, therefore, that the largest part of the SAT score decline between 1963 and about 1970 was identifiable with compositional changes in the mix of the SAT-taking group, considered both in terms of the test takers coming from higher- and lower-scoring groups and in terms of their plans for going to college. Although precise identification of the degree to which these changes explain that part of the decline is impossible, fairly careful calculation indicates that they account for between two-thirds and three-fourths of it. (Wirtz, 1977, p. 18)

Of the 32 points the SAT declined from 1963 to 1970 (using the mean of two thirds and three fourths; i.e., 71%), about 22.7 points of the decline resulted from compositional factors, and 9.3 points of the decline resulted from factors creating an academic decline (Wirtz, 1977). This conclusion naturally assumes that the SATs in 1963 and 1970 possessed the same level of difficulty, which is actually not the case. But we will scrutinize that matter at a later point.

Some members of the excellence movement claim the College Board underestimated the contribution of the academic decline. On the other hand, Lawrence Stedman and Carl Kaestle (1985b, p. 88) clearly misquote the College Board panel by saying that their conclusion referred to the period of 1963 to 1973, rather than 1963 to 1970. Clearly, individuals on "both sides of the aisle" would like the College Board panel's conclusion to read differently, but the panel's figures represent the most complete data available.

The panel adds an important statement, however, to keep the debate from becoming too imbalanced: "Already, appearing during the period, however, were indications of a broader set of influences on these scores—which were subsequently to emerge more plainly and strongly" (Wirtz, 1977, p. 18).

Compositional factors played a lesser role in the decline from 1970 to 1980, as we will soon see.

The Case for Academic Decline

The case for an academic decline from 1963 to 1980 originates from the study of a number of achievement tests and international comparisons, as well as from the reports on literacy and various other statistics mentioned at the beginning of this paper.

Achievement Tests Administered From 1963 to 1970

One of the most penetrating arguments in favor of an academic decline beginning around 1963 revolves around the fact that so many other achievement tests showed commensurate declines during the same period (Clearly & McCandless, 1976). The SAT's sister test, the ACT, also showed declining scores beginning in the mid-1960s (Clearly & McCandless, 1976). In the case of the ACT, however, the math score declined more than the English score, whereas on the SAT, the verbal score declined more than the math score. Between 1967 and 1983, the ACT composite score declined from 19.9 to 18.3. GRE scores also showed a similar decline from 1965 to 1979. During that time, GRE scores declined 70 points (U.S. Department of Education, 2000). GRE scores constitute a less useful comparison, however, because they reflect on the quality of America's postsecondary institutions as well as the quality of U.S. primary and secondary education.

The ITED composite score also declined starting in the mid-1960s. ITED comparison tests prove especially useful when using Iowa students, because the use of the test is widespread and because Iowa maintains a "highly stable" composition of students:

> For high school seniors and juniors, but also for students in grades 10 to 9, we basically find the same trend as in the SAT. The mean scores of all seven sub-tests have been declining since the mid-sixties in all assessed grade levels, grades 9 through 12. (Harnischfeger & Wiley, 1975, p. 43)

The national trends for the ITED show remarkable similarity to the SAT pattern. Harnischfeger and Wiley (1975) note, "The national data show consistent drops between

1963 and 1970 in a majority of the sub-scales: reading, language and Mathematics skills" (p. 50). Once again, 1963 appears as the turning point in ITED scores. In virtually every major nationwide achievement test used in the period, a decline in achievement scores began during the period from 1963 to 1965. PSAT (Preliminary SAT) math scores initiated their drop in 1963, and verbal scores started to drop in 1964 (Harnischfeger & Wiley, 1975). By 1970, the PSAT composite score had dropped by almost exactly the same degree as the SAT composite score (Harnischfeger & Wiley, 1975).

State achievement tests also confirm the decline. Dr. Farr, an educational statistician, tried to obtain data from all 50 states on public school achievement scores. Only 17 sent him the statistics he requested, which he felt could bias the scores upward. Instead, the majority of the states reported declines between the mid-1960s and early 1970s (Cooperman, 1985). Frank Armbruster undertook a similar study of statewide achievement test results, consisting of results from the 21 states from which he obtained responses (Cooperman, 1985). Of the states that responded, seventy percent showed declining test scores from 1965 to 1973 (Cooperman, 1985). The remainder showed either steady or improving scores. Ohio, New York, California, Hawaii, and Iowa were some of those states reporting declines. California state test results recorded a drop in every subject every year for both high- (75th percentile) and low-scoring students from 1969 to 1973 (Armbruster, 1977). Armbruster notes that the much publicized drop in the New York state reading and math achievement test scores hit the suburban and rural areas of the state as well as the cities.

One can argue that compositional factors produced some degree of the change in the achievement test results. Certainly, such an argument would likely carry a good deal of credence when applied to the ACT, the PSAT, and the GRE. But such an argument loses much of its strength when applied to the ITED and other statewide achievement tests. States show very little demographic change year to year, and many of the states that showed considerable academic declines had virtually no demographic change from 1963 to 1980.

Other tests exist of lower grade levels that confirm the SAT trend as well, such as the ITBS. These tests of lower grade levels, however, possess only a limited degree of utility, because they measure very different grade levels. In comparing scores for 1971 versus 1964 and 1973 versus 1963, ITBS scores revealed stable or somewhat improving scores for Grades 2 through 4 and significant declines for Grades 5 through 8 in all areas of the test. The higher the grade level, the larger the drop in scores. The ITBS results highlighted another interesting fact: The scores of high-achieving students were falling as fast or faster than were the scores of average and below-average students (Harnischfeger & Wiley, 1975). California states achievement tests for Grades 6 through 12 confirm this data (Harnischfeger & Wiley, 1975).

The Stanford Achievement test comparing 1964 and 1973 achievement for Grades 1 through 8 also demonstrates a trend similar to that of the ITBS. Reading and math scores showed slight increases for Grades 1 and 2. Scores for 1973 dropped for Grades 3 through 8, with the greatest decreases coming in the highest grades (see chart below).

The general trend listed above also appears in the Comprehensive Test of Basic Skills (CTBS) for Grades 2 through 10, the SRA Achievement Test, and the Metropolitan Readiness Test Composite (Clearly & McCandless, 1976). The rise in the scores of first and second graders may result from the proliferation of preschools and educational shows for children in the late 1960s.

Table 12.1   Decline in Academic Achievement on the
Stanford Achievement Test, 1964–1973

Grade	Reading	Math
8	−8	−18
7	−5	−14
6	−7	−12
6	−4	−9
4	−5	−4
3	−4	−2
2	+1	+4
1	+3	n.a.

SOURCE: Cooperman (1985).

NOTE: "n.a." indicates "not available." Unit of measure is months of loss.

Added Insight: Preschool Television and Rising Test Scores for Young People

As one examines the result of the Stanford Achievement Test, one notices a distinct tendency for scores to decline the older the cohort of children examined. Consistent with this trend is one bright spot that emerged, that the first- and second-grade children actually had their scores rise during the period of 1964 to 1973. Some researchers give credit for this trend to the several preschool programs that were birthed during the late 1960s and early 1970s, including *Sesame Street* (Cooperman, 1985; Harnischfeger & Wiley, 1975). If these observations about the benefit of preschool educational programs are correct, it raises a number of interesting questions for people to consider.

- First, do you believe that this suggests that one's level of preschool academic stimulation contributes to early academic success?
- Second, to the extent that the score increase did not last beyond the second grade, does this suggest that television producers ought to consider airing more programs designed for students in the third grade and beyond?
- Third, how should these results affect the way teachers counsel parents regarding the influence of a high-stimulating home environment?
- Fourth, how should these results affect the way teachers counsel parents and students regarding their use of leisure and television time?

Even the degree of decline among tests, which measure a similar pool of students, punctuates the convincing nature of the ostensible academic decline. Between 1965 and 1976, both the SAT and the ACT suffered from an average decline of 3% of a standard deviation a year (Clearly & McCandless, 1976; Lipsitz, 1977). The Minnesota Scholastic Aptitude Test (MSAT) suffered from an average decline of 2% of a standard deviation per year (Clearly & McCandless, 1976).

There do exist a few exceptions to this downward trend. These exceptions emerge in a few state achievement tests, as we have mentioned, as well as in some tests that students take nationwide. TALENT tests, for example, show large declines in most, but not all subject areas. TALENT Reading Comprehension scores for Grades 9 through 11 were as high in 1975 as they were in 1960 (Clearly & McCandless, 1976). On the math phase of the test, although scores fell on two sections of the test, they held steady on another.

Achievement Tests Administered From 1970 to 1980

SAT scores plummeted from 1970 to 1980. After falling 32 points from 1963 to 1970, SAT scores dropped another 58 points by 1980 (Wirtz, 1977; U.S. Department of Education, 2000). The College Board panel believes that this second stage of the decline was of a different nature than the first stage. The panel asserts that this second stage, beginning in 1970, was dominated by factors affecting academic performance rather than compositional factors. The panel declares regarding this period, "What showed up increasingly was an across-the-board score decline, the apparent consequence of more 'pervasive' changes or influences affecting higher- and lower-scoring groups alike" (Wirtz, 1977, p. 13).

The panel continues by stating that by 1970, many compositional changes of the previous 7 years had either slowed, remained steady, or reversed. The percentage of low-SES students, for example, taking the SAT remained roughly the same throughout the 1970s and beyond (Wirtz, 1977). Concomitant to this came a large drop in the number of students scoring 600 or above on either the verbal or math section of the SAT. While the number of students taking the SAT did drop between 1970 and 1976 by 10%, the number of high-scoring students dropped 43%. The panel also conducted a special study of valedictorians, which indicated a serious drop in their scores as well, beginning in the late 1960s (Lipsitz, 1977; Wirtz, 1977).

Other achievement tests, once again, tend to confirm the SAT decline. The deterioration of scores on the ACT also intensified by 1970. The Science Research Association (SRA) test for reading, for example, showed a drop of between one half and one full grade level between 1971 and 1978 (Cooperman, 1985). English, literature, and vocabulary tests showed declines averaging 2% to 3% of a standard deviation per year. ITED social studies tests showed even greater declines (Clearly & McCandless, 1976). The ACT social studies test from 1965 to 1976 manifested "the most rapid decline observed, about 5 percent of a standard deviation per year" (Clearly & McCandless, 1976, p. 10).

Other achievement tests covering lower grades proved less revealing but nevertheless serve to add insight into the overall academic trend of the 1970s. Stephen A. Roderick performed a study using 1973 ITBS scores. He concluded that the 1973 results represented the worst of all other periods under study. Roderick notes a positive trend in scores from 1936 to the early to mid-1960s: "Student mathematics achievement in grades six and eight in 1973 is clearly inferior to the achievement of similar students in 1936" (as cited in Armbruster, 1977, p. 40).

NAEP results for 17-year-olds tend to confirm the overall trend in SAT and other achievement test scores, except in the area of reading. NAEP scores from 1969 fell substantially in science, civics, and writing. Math scores also dropped, although the decline was not as severe as in the case of the other subjects (U.S. Department of Education, 1993). The NAEP results also indicate that the average 17-year-old was reading as well as the very best 9-year-olds. The top 5% of 9-year-olds were better at mathematics than the bottom quarter of 17-year-olds (U.S. Department of Education, 1993).

Although this period lies outside our primary frame of focus (i.e., 1963–1980), we should note that most achievement test results remained steady or increased slightly during this period (Koretz, 1986).

International Comparison Tests

The performance of American students on international comparison tests often elicits a considerable degree of embarrassment on the part of U.S. educators. On most of the major international tests of recent years, U.S. students have fared badly. On the 1988 International Assessment of Educational Progress, for example, the United States finished 12th out of the 12 nations that participated (National Center for Education Statistics, 1989).

Critics, however, point to a few flaws in the international comparison format. A principal criticism involves the fact that in high school comparison tests, the United States suffers from an unfair disadvantage. The United States keeps a lot of children in high school that many nations either allow to drop out or place on vocational tracks (Stedman, 1994). This fact tends to inflate the scores of some nations. Beyond this, Iris Rothberg (1990, p. 287) contends that another weakness of international comparison relates to sampling methodology. Specifically, it is important to know how research design controls for differences in the proportion of the age group actually attending school in each of the countries and grades tested and whether the geographical and socioeconomic composition of the sample is a fair reflection of an entire country.

The first problem, retention, does not appear particularly consequential. After all, this problem does not affect the results of international tests for 9- and 13-year-olds. Yet American children generally trail children from other nations at these ages as well (Lynn, 1988). Also, Japan and some other Asian nations actually possess as high a rate of high school retention as the United States yet frequently outperform American students on international comparison tests (Lynn, 1988).

Contemporary Focus

The Efforts of Teachers Today Are Likely to Produce a Stronger National Economy in the Future

Teachers sometimes wonder whether their efforts and the achievement of their students today really produce a stronger country in the future. There is a considerable amount of evidence that the sacrifices of teachers today as manifested in the educational outcomes of their students yield impressive economic outcomes in the future.

Now that many nations have been engaged in widespread test administration for some time, one trend is becoming quite patent. That is, how a nation's children perform on domestic and international comparison tests often presages how fast a nation's economy will grow in the future (Hunt, 1984; Lin,

2003; Lynn, 1988; Stevenson & Stigler, 1992). Although these trends may seem only correlative in nature, research has suggested that there is a substantial cause-and-effect component to this relationship; and, moreover, most international leaders formulate educational policy based on this belief (National Commission on Excellence in Education, 1983; Hunt, 1984; Lin, 2003 Stevenson & Stigler, 1992).

For example, based on domestic assessments, achievement by American students rose steadily from 1930 to 1963 (Jeynes, 2004; Wirtz, 1977). Eleven years after this trend started, in 1941, the U.S. standard of living started to surge, ending in 1973, 10 years after achievement ceased to rise (U.S. Census Bureau, 2006). In Japan, student educational outcomes surged from the early 1960s until about 1980 (Duke, 1986; Lynn, 1988). Ten years after this trend started, the Japanese economy soared until its growth leveled out in about 1991 (*The Directorate,* 1999). Similarly, Chinese (including Hong Kong) student outcomes, as measured by international comparison tests, grew considerably beginning in the early 1980s (International Association for the Evaluation of Educational Achievement, 1985a, 1985b, 2000a, 2000b; Stevenson & Stigler, 1992). Since 1990, the Chinese economy has been the fastest-growing economy in the world (Academic International, 2005).

Although the relationship between students' outcomes and economic growth may vary to some degree, teachers can take heart because there is evidence to suggest that teacher efforts translating into strong academic outcomes among youth, in turn, translate into a higher standard of living in the future.

The second problem, about ensuring representative student samples, poses more of a problem. Organizations administering these tests increasingly recognize these problems and either exclude some nations from the official results or list them separately (Lynn, 1988). Nevertheless, because of this problem, we need to approach the results of international comparison tests with caution.

The results of international comparison tests may, however, confirm the trend of educational inadequacy in the U.S. education system. U.S. students badly trail Japanese students in both mathematics and science achievement, and the gap increased between international test administrations in 1967 and 1982. Some might argue that this substantiates America's educational decline. But we should note that Japanese achievement scores assessed at virtually all grade levels increased significantly during the same period. Hence, we face a formidable task of deciding how much of the widening of the Japanese lead results from Japanese advances and how much results from American declines.

The College Board panel examined the same data elaborated on in this chapter (excluding results occurring after 1977) and concluded as follows:

From about 1970 on, the composition of the SAT-taking population has become comparatively more stabilized with respect to its economic, ethnic, and social background. Yet the score decline continued and then accelerated. . . . Only about a quarter of the decline since 1970 can be attributed to continuing change in the make-up of the test-taking group. . . . With a handful of exceptions, the drop in scores in recent years has been virtually across the board, affecting high-scoring and low-scoring groups alike. (Wirtz, 1977, p. 46)

The College Board panel affirmed that three fourths of the decline from 1970 to 1977 found its root in "more pervasive" forces. SAT scores declined 49 points between 1970 and 1977. This translates into a 12.25-point decline due to compositional factors and a 36.75-point decline due to factors affecting academic ability. The College Board also believes that 100% of the academic decline from 1977 to 1980 was due to real academic change (Marco, personal communication, November 2, 1994). In addition, the College Board also examined the possibility that the SAT had become more strenuous over the period in question, even though there is an immense effort by the College Board to keep the test statistically consistent (Lipsitz, 1977; Wirtz, 1977). The College Board tested this hypothesis by giving students an SAT test from 1963 and one from the 1970s (Wirtz, 1977). To the amazement of the College Board, the results indicated that the test had actually become 20 points easier (Wirtz, 1977). Hence, the 90-point drop was actually a 110-point drop. Table 12.2 breaks down the conclusions of the College Board panel (Marco, personal communication, November 2, 1994). Given that the College Board discovered that the SAT became easier during the period in question by a total of 20 points, this is also factored into the results of Table 12.2 (Wirtz, 1977).

POSSIBLE EXPLANATIONS FOR THE REAL ACADEMIC ACHIEVEMENT DECLINE

There is a general assumption among many that a drop in student achievement automatically means that the schools were to blame. David Harman (1987) observes that "blaming the schools has become a national pastime" (p. 47). However, the conclusion of the

Table 12.2   Factors Contributing to the SAT Score Decline

Period	Compositional Factors (Points)	Factors Affecting Academics (Points)
1963–1970	22.7 (71%)	9.3 (29%)
1970–1977	12.25 (25%)	36.75 (75%)
1977–1980	0	10.00
Test change	7.6	12.4
	42.55 (37.7%)	68.45 (62.3%)

SOURCE: Computation based on Wirtz (1977).

College Board was that a vast array of factors contributed to the scholastic slide of 1963 to 1980. In fact, from the College Board's standpoint, they found the factors external to the school easier to quantify than those inherent to the school system.

Decline of the Family

For example, just as SAT scores started a sudden and precipitous decline beginning in 1963, so did the stability of the intact family. Divorce rates, which had been in a gradual decline from 1948 to 1962, suddenly started to surge precisely in 1963 (U.S. Census Bureau, 2001). Ironically, just as SAT scores declined 17 consecutive years before bottoming out in 1980, divorce rates rose 17 consecutive years, topping out in 1980 (U.S. Department of Education, 2000). Between 1963 and 1980, the divorce rate rose 117% (U.S. Census Bureau, 2001). Regarding the these two trends, the College Board concluded, "There is probably more than coincidence between the decline in SAT scores and the drop in the number of children living in two-parent homes" (Wirtz, 1977, p. 34). Given this confluence of statistics, most social scientists agree that the decline of the family impacted achievement test scores from 1963 to 1980.

The panel adds,

> Yet if the question is why those scores have been going down, few would respond without recognizing that part of the answer is almost certainly hidden in these gaps in present knowledge—about the effects of change on the whole meaning of family and youth decline. (Wirtz, 1977, p. 35)

The panel asserted that from 1963 to 1980, parents spent less time teaching their children than before. Ernest Boyer (1985) argues that teachers are discouraged by problems originating with students' families. According to the 1987 Metropolitan Life Survey of the American Teacher, teachers listed "having parents spend much more time with their children in support of school and teachers" as the number-one step that would "help a lot to improve education" (p. 1). It is noteworthy that 84% of the teachers questioned view this as very important (U.S. Department of Education, 1990). Children from nonintact homes are considerably more likely to end up in prison than are children from two-parent homes (U.S. Department of Justice, 1983). Children from one-parent homes have a greater tendency to use illegal drugs, alcohol, and cigarettes than do children from two-parent homes (Jeynes, 2001a, 2001b, 2002).

Decline of the Work Ethic

The College Board avers that there was also a decline in the work ethic during the 1960s and 1970s. It maintains that there is "observable evidence of diminished seriousness of purpose in students of the post-1963 era" (Wirtz, 1977, p. 48). The panel contends, "For whatever combination of reasons, there has been an apparent marked diminution in young people's learning motivation" (Wirtz, 1977, p. 48). It points out, as have other social scientists, that increasingly, children were choosing to watch television rather than do their schoolwork (Schramm, 1977; Winn, 2002). However, the College Board acknowledges that the declining work ethic was likely not only a cause but also a result of other broader factors at work in society. It concludes, "It can hardly be coincidence that problems of discipline and absenteeism appear at a time when changing life styles and values in adult society, earlier physical maturity, higher mobility, drugs, and the pill are all interacting" (Wirtz, 1977, p. 35).

Changes in 1960s Culture

The panel assembled a considerable list of cultural changes that took place in the 1960s, including an increase in the use of illegal drugs, increases in teenage violence and teenage pregnancy, and the removal of prayer from the schools. The College Board panel addresses these issues by stating,

> Still others attribute the decline to a "growing rejection of traditional Western religions" and . . . concern about a crisis in values is widely expressed . . . a revolution in values, including a decline in the Protestant work ethic. . . . In general we find the sum of these contributions substantially helpful in suggesting the character of a period, covered by the score decline, which has been an unusually hard one to grow up in. (Wirtz, 1977, pp. 42, 43)

Some interesting facts rest in the data that the College Board examined along these lines. After long periods of stability, rates of teenage pregnancy, sexually transmitted diseases, and so forth all started to surge in 1963 or, in one case, 1964 (Barton, 1990). Some specific issues that the College Board observed along these lines were a tendency toward increased violence and a lack of discipline during from 1963 to 1980. For example, the percentage of parents who believed schools "were too lax" jumped from 39% in 1969 to an extraordinary 84% in 1978, according to a Roper Poll (Adelson, 1985). Almost concurrently, a 1970 Gallup poll indicated people of color were more likely than Whites to regard schools as "not strict enough" (Adelson, 1985, p. 321). In terms of violence, the rise in the juvenile crime rate doubled from 1963 to 1980, flattening out only toward the end of that period (U.S. Department of Justice, 1983). In fact, the juvenile crime rate rose so much that there existed a greater chance for a 12- to 19-year-old to suffer as a victim of violence or theft than for any other age group (spanning an equal 8-year range) (U.S. Department of Justice, 1983).

The panel also notes changes in the consumption of illegal drugs and sexual behavior that probably influenced academic achievement (Lipsitz, 1977; Wirtz, 1977). The pattern of teenage drug use followed the general trend that divorce and teenage violence showed, as described earlier, surging in the 1960s and 1970s and reaching an apex somewhere between 1979 to 1982 (U.S. Department of Education, 1993).

Table 12.3 shows the peak years in the percentage of 12- to 17-year-olds reporting that they used certain illegal drugs.

In terms of sexual behavior, between 1963 and 1988, preteenage pregnancy rose 553% (U.S. Department of Health and Human Services, 1998; U.S. Department of Justice, 1999). Few would argue with the assertion that it is extremely difficult to concentrate on academics and on the opposite sex at the same time. Critics differ in terms of where they place the blame for this upsurge, but most social scientists believe every major institution probably deserves a good portion of the blame, especially because the increase is so large (Barton, 1990). Parents, schools, the media, peers, pregnancy centers for young girls that offer abortions and counseling, and so forth likely each deserve a good part of the responsibility for such an unparalleled increase.

Table 12.3   Peak Year of the Percentage of 12- to 17-Year-Olds Reporting the Use of Illegal Drugs

	Peak Year
1. Any illicit use	1979
2. Marijuana	1979
3. Cocaine	1979 and 1982[a]
4. Nonmedical stimulants	1982
5. Alcohol	1979

SOURCE: U. S. Department of Education. (1993).

a. Those reporting using cocaine in the last 30 days peaked in 1979.
   Those reporting using cocaine in the last year peaked in 1982.

The College Board panel concludes as follows:

Although the panel's attention has been directed repeatedly to the facts of increased school ground violence and crime and juvenile alcoholism and drug addiction, we can add nothing here to what common knowledge and common sense already establish. These aberrations obviously affect not only the individuals directly involved, but the broader educational process, and they have been increasing as the SAT scores have been going down. . . . What is causing the delinquent behavior? (Wirtz, 1977, p. 41)

Educational Debate: Societal Trends and the Decline in SAT Scores

Many Americans blame teachers for the decline in achievement test scores from 1963 through 1980 (Sykes, 1995). However, the College Board Report *On Further Examination* indicates that societal factors probably played a larger role than school factors in causing the decline (Wirtz, 1977). Indeed, the trends in societal changes parallel the academic downtrend almost exactly (Wirtz, 1977; U.S. Department of Justice, 1983, 1999). Divorce rates, which had been in slight decline from 1948 to 1962, suddenly began to surge in 1963 and then climbed 17 consecutive years during the precise time period that SAT scores declined 17 consecutive years (U.S. Census Bureau, 2001; U.S. Department of Education, 2000). The increase in illegal drug use demonstrated a very similar trend, climbing significantly in almost exactly the same years that SAT scores were falling (U.S. Department of Education, 1993). Other societal changes such as the removal of voluntary prayer from schools also took place in 1963, which many people believe affected students' morality, which is generally associated with achievement levels (Murray, 1982; Wirtz, 1977).

Many studies have confirmed that a relationship exists between family structure, illegal drug and alcohol consumption, and religiosity, on one hand, and academic outcomes, on the other (Albrecht & Heaton, 1984; Jeynes, 2002; Hetherington & Clingempeel, 1992; McLanahan & Sandefur, 1994; Zill & Nord, 1994).

- Do you believe that the changes in the societal factors mentioned by the College Board in their report *On Further Examination* as well as other factors contributed to the achievement test score decline, or do you believe that the confluence of these factors is merely coincidental?

What Does the College Board's Assessment Mean?

It is undeniable that the achievement test score decline from 1963 to 1980 was real. However, there are some important truths to note about the trend. First, part of the decline (about 38%) was due to compositional or demographic factors. These are actually good changes. Certainly, the nation wants more poor people, people of color, and high school students in general applying to college. But there is an irony here, because on one hand, clearly some of the decline represents a greater variety people striving to attain the American dream. That is what this country is all about. On the other hand, the academic decline was also real. There is surely a need for Americans everywhere to address some of the causes. From 1963 to 1980, American students clearly slipped and fell well behind their counterparts in most of the industrialized world. Although some progress has been made since, the United States has never regained its reputation of having the finest elementary and secondary school students in the world.

Third, it is important to note that although the College Board places some of the blame for the academic decline on the schools, the majority of the blame falls on forces outside the schools. This is not to say that the schools escape blame, but it does mean that one can argue that being a teacher in the post-1980 world is more difficult than at any other time in recent memory.

Fourth, the debate over scholastic decline from 1963 to 1980 has wide implications. A large majority of the educational reforms in the decades that followed have roots in this debate about educational decline, a debate that seems never to end.

ADVANCES IN PUBLIC EDUCATION FROM 1963 TO 1980

Undoubtedly, Americans directed much more criticism than praise toward the public schools from 1963 to 1980. Nevertheless, one should note that schooling in the United States also experienced what most people would label advances during this period (Bracey, 1997). Moreover, apologists of public education are quick to cite these contributions as evidence that public education was not ensnared in the quagmire that many parents claimed (Bracey, 1997).

First, there can be no question that the civil rights movement continued to influence the number of students of color who were able to attend better schools and eventually go to college (Bracey, 1997). Second, the percentage of American students who graduated from high school rose during this period (U.S. Department of Education, 2005). This development is more controversial than the first because, on average, course requirements for high school graduation also lightened considerably during this period. Some argue that without this loosening of graduation requirements, there would have been little or no change in graduation trends (Chavez, 1999; Stotsky, 1999; Sykes, 1995). Nevertheless, graduation rates did rise (U.S. Department of Education, 2005).

Third, Congress passed the Elementary and Secondary Education Act in 1965 (Payzant & Levin, 1995; Smith, Scoll, & Plisko, 1995). This initiative broadened government involvement in schooling, particularly by increasing funding for public schools and inaugurating efforts to ameliorate instruction of poor and other disadvantaged students (Payzant & Levin, 1995; Smith et al., 1995). A vast array of federal programs either started or began concurrently with this federal initiative, including the Title I and Head Start programs, which were focused on several specific groups of at-risk children, including poor children and certain minority youth (Carleton, 2002; Payzant & Levin, 1995; Smith et al., 1995). School lunch programs, which had started in 1946 under President Harry S. Truman, were also expanded (Carleton, 2002). The Head Start program was conceived on the premise that gaps in academic achievement developed primarily before kindergarten and that, furthermore, these gaps were the product of a lack of educational emphasis and orientation in various families and communities across the United States (Carleton, 2002; Mills, 1998). Government leaders initiated the Head Start program to bridge these achievement gaps by promoting preschool education programs for those children who would normally run the risk of falling behind.

Although Americans often debate about the merits of the government's educational initiatives of the mid-1960s, the Head Start component enjoys bipartisan support (Mills, 1998). The only significant difference among the major political parties regarding Head Start is that Republicans want to begin Head Start at an earlier age (Mills, 1998) and Democrats instead want to broaden the program to include more children (Mills, 1998).

THE INFLUENCE OF RISING CRITICISM ON SCHOOLS

One of the first effects the rising criticism of public schools was that by the early 1980s, Americans became less likely to support tax increases in order to fund public schooling (Sowell, 1993; Sykes, 1995). During the 1960s and 1970s, local, state, and federal governments had successfully executed the largest increase in public school education expenditures in American history to that date (Flora & Heidenheimer, 1981; U.S. Department of Education, 2005). Therefore, parents were dismayed that despite this increase, scores had declined so rapidly. The fact that schools were now better supplied than ever before and enjoyed a steady reduction in class size was not enough to allay parents' concerns about issues of academic decline. Parents often declared that they would support higher taxes if scholastic achievement indicated they were worthy of that support (Harnischfeger & Wiley, 1975; Sowell, 1993; Sykes, 1995). In the views of many parents, they had generously fulfilled their financial commitment to the schools, and now it was the public education system's responsibility to use that added funding to increase academic outcomes (Harnischfeger & Wiley, 1975; Sowell, 1993; Sykes, 1995).

As the statistics in this chapter indicate, however, many of the national trends that caused the academic decline were due to family and societal factors that were largely beyond the school's score (Wirtz, 1977; Jeynes, 2004). This is not to say that schools deserve none of the blame for the academic decline, but they certainly did not deserve all, or even a majority, of the blame (Wirtz, 1977). However, one can argue that the parents were as much or more to blame for the academic decline as the teachers.

CONCLUSION

Although witnessing academic scores decline for 17 years made educators feel helpless, there is no question that the educational community took many steps in order to understand the reasons behind this decline. As Americans arrived at certain conclusions regarding why the decline took place, they discovered that not all of the decline was purely academic. The period of 1963 to 1980 was a time of decline, but it was also an era of increased opportunity for many Americans who probably would not have attended college years earlier. It is also true that one positive result of this educational deterioration has been that American leaders and individuals are aggressively addressing educational challenges more than ever before. Therefore, if the decline served as a wake-up call for American education, long-term benefits could result if the right changes are made.

DISCUSSION QUESTIONS

1. Some experts say that personal factors that influence achievement are often "contagious." For example, if many in a society possess a strong work ethic, it is easier to be diligent. If numerous people in a person's environment take illegal drugs, taking them is a more potent temptation for that individual. Do you agree or disagree with this assessment? How might scholastic outcomes be influenced if this statement is right or wrong?

2. Is it beyond the realm of government and society to reduce undesirable trends such as a rising divorce rate? Why or why not? If it is not beyond the scope of government and society to affect these trends, in your view, what can be done to reverse specific trends?

3. Does the widespread presence of television and video games make it inevitable that students in the future will read less than in the past? If so, what do schools need to do more to adjust to this reality? What should schools do to adapt more successfully?

4. The 1983 report *A Nation at Risk* asserts that low achievement will ultimately lower our economic competitiveness in the world. Do you agree that there is a "risk" that this will happen, or is this argument overstated?

REFERENCES

Academic International. (2005). *China facts and figures annual.* Gulf Breeze, FL: Academic International Press.

Adelson, J. (1985). Educators are stuck in the 60s. In B. Gross & R. Gross (Eds.), *The great school debate* (pp. 317–331). New York: Simon & Schuster.

Albrecht, S. L., & Heaton, T. B. (1984). Secularization, higher education, and religiosity. *Review of Religious Research, 26*(1), 43–58.

Armbruster, F. E. (1977). *Our children's crippled future.* New York: New York Times.

Barton, D. (1990). *Our Godly heritage* [Video]. Aledo, TX: Wallbuilders.

Berliner, D. C., & Biddle, B. J. (1995). *The manufactured crisis: Myths, fraud, and the attacks on America's public schools.* Reading, MA: Addison-Wesley.

Bloom, A. (1987). *The closing of the American mind.* New York: Simon & Schuster.

Boyer, E. (1985). Introduction. In B. Gross & R. Gross (Eds.), *The great school debate* (pp. 15–20). New York: Simon & Schuster.

Bracey, G. (1992a). Curriculum reform, test reform. *Phi Delta Kappan, 73,* 809–811.

Bracey, G. W. (1992b). Discriminating among the top of the top. *Phi Delta Kappan, 74,* 181–182.

Bracey, G. (1993a). Growth on NAEP scales or not? *Phi Delta Kappan, 74,* 807–808.

Bracey, G. (1993b). The third Bracey report on the condition of public education. *Phi Delta Kappan, 75,* 104–116.

Bracey, G. W. (1997). *Setting the record straight.* Alexandria, VA: Association for Supervision and Curriculum Development.

Breland, H. (1977). *Family configuration effects and the decline in college admissions test scores: A review of the Zajonc hypothesis.* Princeton, NJ: Educational Testing Service.

Brown, C. (1985). Is excellence a threat to equality? In B. Gross & R. Gross (Eds.), *The great school debate* (pp. 298–301). New York: Simon and Schuster.

Brown, F. B. (1963). *The nongraded high school.* Englewood Cliffs, NJ: Prentice Hall.

Carleton, D. (2002). *Landmark congressional laws on education.* Westport, CT: Greenwood Press.

Carson, C. C., Huelskamp, R. M., & Woodall, R. D.(1993). Perspectives on education in America. *Journal of Educational Research, 86,* 259–310.

Chavez, L. (1999). Multiculturalism does not benefit society. In M. B. Williams (Ed.), *Culture wars* (pp. 148–156). San Diego, CA: Greenhaven Press.

Cintora, A. (1999). Civil society and attitudes: The virtues of character. *Annals of the American Academy of Political and Social Science, 565,* 142–147.

Clearly, T. A., & McCandless, S. A. (1976). *Summary of score changes (in other tests).* Princeton, NJ: Educational Testing Service.

Cooperman, P. (1978). *Literacy hoax.* New York: William Morrow.

Cooperman, P. (1985). In B. Gross & R. Gross (Eds.), *The great school debate* (pp. 23–49). New York: Simon & Schuster.

Crouse, J., & Trusheim, D. (1988). *The case against the SAT.* Chicago: University of Chicago Press.

The Directorate. (1999). *Handbook of international economic statistics.* Washington, DC: Author.

Donlon, T. F. (1984). *The College Board technical handbook for the scholastic aptitude and achievement tests.* New York: College Entrance Examination Board.

D'Souza, D. (1991). Sins of admission: Affirmative action on campus. *New Republic 204*(7), 30–31.

Duke, B. (1986). *The Japanese school.* New York: Praeger.

Dupuis, A. M. (1966). *Philosophy of education in historical perspective.* Chicago: Rand McNally.

Feinberg, L. (1995). A new center for the SAT. *College Board Review, 174,* 8–13, 31–32.

Finn, C. E. Jr. (1991). *We must take charge.* New York: Free Press.

Flora, P., & Heidenheimer, A. J. (1981). *The development of welfare states in Europe and America.* New Brunswick, NJ: Transaction Books.

Forsyth, R. (1994). *Iowa Testing Program.* Iowa City: University of Iowa.

Goodlad, J. I., & Anderson, R. H. (1959). *The non-graded elementary school.* New York: Harcourt & Brace.

Gordon, D. T. (2003). *A nation reformed? American education 20 years after "A Nation at Risk."* Cambridge, MA: Harvard University Press.

Gough, P. B. (1993). A view from the outside. *Phi Delta Kappan, 74,* 669.

Gregory, R. J. (2004). *Psychological testing: History, principles, and applications* (4th ed.). Boston: Allyn & Bacon.

Harman, D. (1987). *Illiteracy: A national dilemma*. New York: Cambridge Book.

Harnischfeger, A., & Wiley, D. (1975). *Achievement test score decline: Do we need to worry?* Chicago: Camrel.

Hetherington, E. M., & Clingempeel, W. G. (Eds.). (1992). Coping with marital transitions: A family systems perspective. *Monographs of the Society for Research in Child Development, 57*(1).

Hunt, J. B. (1984). Education for economic growth: A critical investment. *Phi Delta Kappan, 65,* 538–541.

Hunt, T. C., & Maxson, M. M. (1981). *Religion and morality in American schooling*. Washington, DC: University Press of America.

International Association for the Evaluation of Educational Achievement. (1985a). *TIMSS 1984 International Mathematics Report*. Chestnut Hill, MA: International Study Center.

International Association for the Evaluation of Educational Achievement. (1985b). *TIMSS 1984 International Science Report*. Chestnut Hill, MA: International Study Center.

International Association for the Evaluation of Educational Achievement. (2000a). *TIMSS 1999 International Mathematics Report*. Chestnut Hill, MA: International Study Center.

International Association for the Evaluation of Educational Achievement. (2000b). *TIMSS 1999 International Science Report*. Chestnut Hill, MA: International Study Center.

Jeynes, W. (2001a). The effects of recent parental divorce on their children's consumption of alcohol. *Journal of Youth and Adolescence, 3,* 305–319.

Jeynes, W. (2001b). The effects of recent parental divorce on their children's consumption of marijuana and cocaine. *Journal of Divorce and Remarriage, 35* (3/4), 43–65.

Jeynes, W. (2002). The relationship between the consumption of various drugs by adolescents and their academic achievement. *American Journal of Drug and Alcohol Abuse, 28*(1), 1–21.

Jeynes, W. (2004). Immigration in the United States and the golden age of education: Was Ravitch right? *Educational Studies, 35,* 248–270.

Kennedy, J. (1994). *Public education: The hidden agenda*. Fort Lauderdale, FL: Coral Ridge Presbyterian Church.

King, M. L. Jr. (Ed.). (1998). *The autobiography of Martin Luther King Jr.* (C. Carson, Ed.). New York: Warner.

Koretz, D. (1986). *Trends in educational achievement*. Washington, DC: U.S. Congressional Budget Office.

Kozol, J. (1985). *Illiterate America*. Garden City, NY: Anchor.

Lawrence-Lightfoot, S. (1983). *The good high school: Portraits of character and culture*. New York: Basic Books.

Levin, H. (1985). Education and jobs: The weak link. In B. Gross & R. Gross (Eds.), *The great school debate* (pp. 231–236). New York: Simon & Schuster.

Levy, S. R., & Dweck, C. S. (1999). The impact of children's static versus dynamic conception of people on stereotype formation. *Child Development, 70,* 1163–1180.

Lin, T. C. (2003). Education, technical progress, and economic growth: The case of Taiwan. *Economics of Education Review, 22,* 213–220.

Lipsitz, L. (1977). *The test score decline: Meaning and issues*. Englewood Cliffs, NJ: Educational Technology Publications.

Lynn, R. (1988). *Educational achievement in Japan*. Armonk, NY: M. E. Sharpe.

Mann, H. (1849). *Twelfth annual report*. Dutton & Wentworth.

McLanahan, S., & Sandefur, G. (1994). *Growing up with a single parent: What hurts, what helps*. Cambridge, MA: Harvard University Press.

Mills, K. (1998). *Something better for my children: The history and the people of Head Start*. New York: Dutton.

Murray, W. (1982). *My life without God*. Nashville, TN: Thomas Nelson.

Nash, S. C. (1979). Sex role as a mediator of intellectual functioning. In M. A. Wittig & A. Peterson (Eds.), *Sex-related differences in cognitive functioning* (pp. 57–72). New York: Academic Press.

National Center for Education Statistics. (1989). *Trends in international mathematics and science study, 1988*. Washington, DC: Author.

National Commission on Excellence in Education. (1983). *A nation at risk*. Washington, DC: Author.

Payzant, T. W., & Levin, J. (1995). Improving America's schools for children with the greatest need. In J. F. Jennings (Ed.), *National issues in education: Elementary and Secondary Education Act* (pp. 55–75). Bloomington, IN: Phi Delta Kappan.

Ravitch, D., & Finn, C. (1987). *What do our 17-year-olds know?* New York: Harper & Row.

Rotberg, I. (1990). I never promised you first place. *Phi Delta Kappan, 72*(4), 296–303.

Schmitt, J. S. (1991). They no longer ask the big questions. In S. M. Krason (Ed.), *The recovery of American education* (pp. 9–16). Lanham, MD: University Press of America.

Schramm, W. L. (1977). *Television and test scores.* Princeton, NJ: College Board.

Schwebel, M. (1985). The other school system. In B. Gross & R. Gross (Eds.), *The great school debate* (pp. 236–246). New York: Simon & Schuster.

Singal, D. (1991). The other crisis in American education. *Atlantic Monthly, 268*(5), 59–74.

Singleton, C. (1985). Let there be "F"s. In B. Gross & R. Gross (Eds.), *The great school debate* (pp. 264–270). New York: Simon & Schuster.

Smith, M. S., Scoll, B. W., & Plisko, V. W. (1995). Improving America's schools acts: A new partnership. In J. F. Jennings (Ed.), *National issues in education: Elementary and Secondary Education Act* (pp. 3–17). Bloomington, IN: Phi Delta Kappan.

Sowell, T. (1993). *Inside American education.* New York: Free Press.

Stedman, L. C. (1994). The Sandia Report and U.S. achievement. *Journal of Educational Research, 87*(3), 133–147.

Stedman, L. C., & Kaestle, C. F. (1985a). The test score decline is over: Now what? *Phi Beta Kappan, 67,* 204–210.

Stedman, L. C., & Kaestle, C. F. (1985b). Weak arguments, poor data, simplistic recommendations. In B. Gross & R. Gross (Eds.), *The great school debate* (pp. 83–105). New York: Simon & Schuster.

Stevenson, H. W., & Stigler, J. W. (1992). *The learning gap.* New York: Summit Books.

Stotsky, S. (1999). *Losing our language: How multicultural classroom instruction is undermining our children's ability to read, write, and reason.* New York: Free Press.

Strauss, L. (1968). *Liberalism, ancient and modern.* New York: Basic Books.

Sykes, C. (1995). *Dumbing down our kids.* New York: St. Martin's Press.

U.S. Census Bureau. (2001). *Census 2000.* Washington, DC: Author.

U.S. Census Bureau. (2006). *Statistical abstracts of the United States, 2006.* Washington, DC: Author.

U.S. Department of Education. (1990). *1989 education indicators.* Washington, DC: Author.

U.S. Department of Education. (1993). *Digest of education statistics, 1992.* Washington, DC: Author.

U.S. Department of Education. (2000). *Digest of education statistics.* Washington, DC: Author.

U.S. Department of Education. (2005). *Digest of education statistics.* Washington, DC: Author.

U.S. Department of Health and Human Services. (1998). *Statistical abstracts of the United States.* Washington, DC: Author.

U.S. Department of Justice. (1983). *Report to the nation on crime and justice.* Washington, DC: Author.

U.S. Department of Justice. (1999). *Age-specific arrest rates and race-specific arrest rates for selected offenses, 1965–1992.* Washington, DC: Author.

Walker, W. (1963). *Philosophy of education.* New York: Philosophical Library.

Webster, N. (1834). *Value of the Bible, and the excellence of the Christian religion: For use of families and schools.* New Haven, CT: Durrie & Peck.

Winn, M. (2002). *Television, computers, and family life.* New York: Penguin.

Wirtz, W. (1977). *On further examination.* New York: College Entrance Examination Board.

Young, J. W. (1995). Recentering the SAT score scale. *College and University, 70*(2), 60–62.

Yulish, S. M. (1980). *The search for a civic religion.* Washington, DC: University Press of America.

Zill, N., & Nord, C. W. (1994). *Running in place.* Washington, DC: Child Trends.

CHAPTER 13

The Rise of Multiculturalism and Other Issues

More than ever, by the 1960s, inclusiveness had become a major theme in American education (Banks, 1975, 1997). As much as any movement, multiculturalism represents this emphasis on inclusion. With the increased immigration of the 1960s and as a by-product of the civil rights movement, multiculturalism ascended as a new emphasis in American education and society. Advocates propounded several convincing reasons the United States should adhere to a multiculturalist perspective (Banks, 1997; Grant, 1999; Sleeter & McLaren, 1995). As the multiculturalist movement expanded, however, a variety of different social scientists defended multiculturalism in different ways (Murrell, 2002; Pollard & Ajirotutu, 2000). Consequently, in addition to examining the arguments given in support of multiculturalism, we will also examine the assertion by many social scientists that multiculturalism will succeed only if it includes certain qualities (Chang, 1999; Kalakowski, 1989; Kane, 1994; Gardels, 1986). In addition, some social scientists oppose multiculturalism, and their perspectives will be examined as well (Schlesinger, 1992). Finally, some theorists believe that multiculturalism has served its purpose and the United States needs to move ahead to the next educational and sociological paradigm, which some call a "post-ethnic" America (Hollinger, 1995; Lind, 1995).

Although *inclusion* as expressed in multiculturalism is a key educational concept, it encompasses other areas of schooling as well, including education for children with special needs, the disabled, and those who desire vocational education (Bratten, 1995; Brint & Karabel, 1989; McLeskey & Pacchiano, 1994). Education for children with special needs has made a considerable amount of progress over the years but has also come full circle in certain respects. In the early days of the country, care for these individuals was family- and community based. Then, in the late 1800s and the first half of the 1900s, Americans often institutionalized these individuals. In recent decades, family- and community-based education has emerged as the preferred approach (Jones, 2004; Metzel, 2004; Nehring, 2004).

Vocational education is also an attempt to make education more inclusive. Its proponents argue that schooling needs to prepare children along a variety of dimensions (Brint & Karabel, 1989). However, vocational education also has its critics who maintain that it impedes many individuals from maximizing their potential (Rippa, 1997).

THE RISE OF MULTICULTURALISM

Multiculturalism arose as a direct result of the increase of immigration that took place in the early 1960s (Banks, 1997; Banks & Banks, 1995; Grant, 1999; Sleeter & McLaren, 1995). Although heavy levels of immigration emerged in the second half of the 19th century, the vast majority of immigrants came from Western Europe. Therefore, even though there were cultural differences between these groups, there were also a lot of cultural similarities (Calderon, 1998; Cremin, 1962; Johnson, 1997; Vernez & Abrahamse, 1996; Weiss, 1982; White & Kaufman, 1997). But by the 1960s, the world had become much smaller; transportation had become much cheaper; and, increasingly, the United States was receiving immigrants from all over the world (Parrington, 1994; Reed, 1994). As a result, far more diverse groups of immigrants were coming to the United States than had come previously. There was a sense that the extent of America's new diversity needed to be addressed (Banks, 1997; Parrington, 1994; Reed, 1994). An emphasis on Americanization no longer seemed appropriate. The cultural differences between these new immigrants and those in the United States seemed too vast to encourage each group to become Americanized.

What Made a Multicultural Orientation Possible?

A number of changes taking place in America made multicultural education possible. First, in the 1960s, bilingual education rose as a powerful emphasis within education circles (Banks, 1997; Banks & Banks, 1995; Lambert & Reynolds, 1991). There was no longer an emphasis on learning English at the intense level that had been encouraged previous to this time (Calderon, 1998; Cremin, 1962; Johnson, 1997; Vernez & Abrahamse, 1996; Weiss, 1982; White & Kaufman, 1997). It is true that bilingual education started primarily as a movement that focused purely on language, but the emphasis evolved into preserving not only various people's languages but also their cultures. Therefore, many of multiculturalism's current roots are found in the bilingual education movement (Banks, 1997; Banks & Banks, 1995; Lambert & Reynolds, 1991).

Second, the United States was a far stronger and steadier country in the 1960s than was the case in the late 19th century. It had been many years since the Civil War, and the fear of the nation falling apart had virtually disappeared (Johnson, 1997). Americanization had been viewed as a means to keep the country together (Weiss, 1982), but once the United States was more unified, many people believed that Americanization no longer needed to be emphasized. The increased feeling of security in the United States made the situation more conducive to multiculturalism. As long as the generation that had fought in the Civil War had been alive, there was no chance that multiculturalism could exist in the United States, but by the 1960s, people realized the nation was steadier.

Third, as mentioned by the 1960s, the extent of diversity among the immigrants had increased since the 19th century, when newcomers were mostly from Western Europe (Johnson, 1997; Weiss, 1982). Therefore, the primary cultural adaptation that these individuals made was in terms of language (Calderon, 1998; Cremin, 1962; Johnson, 1997; Vernez & Abrahamse, 1996; Weiss, 1982; White & Kaufman, 1997). The immigrants who arrived beginning in the 1960s especially were vastly different not only from the prevailing culture in the United States but also from each other (Parrington, 1994; Reed, 1994). Thousands of people were coming from the Middle East, the Orient, Africa, and so forth

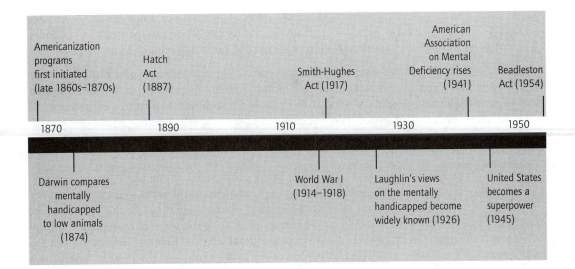

Americanization programs first initiated (late 1860s–1870s) | Hatch Act (1887) | Smith-Hughes Act (1917) | American Association on Mental Deficiency rises (1941) | Beadleston Act (1954)

1870 | 1890 | 1910 | 1930 | 1950

Darwin compares mentally handicapped to low animals (1874) | World War I (1914–1918) | Laughlin's views on the mentally handicapped become widely known (1926) | United States becomes a superpower (1945)

(Parrington, 1994; Reed, 1994). To ask that people from these cultures become Americanized seemed inexpedient.

The issues surrounding what would later be known as multiculturalism arose following the Civil Rights and the Immigration Act of 1965 and continued into the 1970s and 1980s. James Banks, Christine Sleeter, and Carl Grant were some of the leaders of this movement (Banks & Banks, 1995; Grant, Boyle-Baise, & Sleeter, 1980). Initially, they argued for the inclusion of greater amounts of minority people's history in the standard textbooks and curricula used in American schools (Banks, 1975; Banks & Banks, 1970; Banks & Grambs, 1972; Gitlin, 1994; Grant et al., 1980). Some outstanding members of minority groups, particularly African Americans, were already included; nevertheless, it was clear that greater representation was needed (Banks, 1997; Giroux, 1996; Gitlin, 1994; Parrington, 1994; Reed, 1994). It was believed that including more of the history of other cultures would raise the self-esteem of children from these minority groups (Giroux, 1996; Gitlin, 1994).

As the integration of material about other cultures was integrated into American textbooks, Banks and others asserted that a multicultural approach should pervade the American educational landscape more completely (Giroux, 1996; Gitlin, 1994; Parrington, 1994; Reed, 1994). Banks believed that all students should be required to examine other cultural perspectives and to become bilingual (Banks, 1997; Banks & Banks, 1995). He believed that every element of the school life (assemblies, the celebration of holidays, public displays) should reflect a multicultural perspective. Some African American leaders, including Molefi Kete Asante (1993), called for ethnocentric schools that could focus on learning the histories and cultures of various groups. Several of the largest public school systems have implemented ethnocentric curricula and schools (Murrell, 2002; Pollard & Ajirotutu, 2000).

Multiculturalism Replaces Americanization

Some Americans remain puzzled as to why recent immigrants coming to the United States have resisted Americanization and instead have preferred a multicultural approach. There were a number of reasons for this change.

1. *The civil rights movement made people aware of the extent to which African Americans had American culture thrust upon them involuntarily.* Other groups began to wonder whether through the Americanization program, the same had happened to them.

2. *The United States had become a superpower with greater cultural clout than ever before.* Many immigrants had already felt inundated with the pressure to Americanize even within their own homelands. Never in the history of mankind had a culture experienced so much potency that nearly every other culture in the world felt constrained to Americanize. There was a tendency among immigrants, therefore, to resist that pressure more than they had in the 19th century (Asante, 1993; Banks, 1997; Vann & Kunjufu, 1993).

3. *As the world's foremost superpower, many peoples around the world envied and even resented the United States.* Some of these people came as immigrants to the United States. Millions of immigrants came to the United States not because they like the United States, but because of financial, family, or other reasons. During the wave of immigration during the 19th century, the United States was not that great a power. However, recently, given the status of the United States as a superpower, naturally, envy and resentment have arisen among some foreigners, and this has sometimes translated into greater resistance to the process of Americanization among some immigrants (Banks, 1997).

4. *The differences between the cultures of some immigrants arriving in the United States and American culture were greater than they had been in past years.* During the time when immigrants were primarily made up of Europeans, the differences between the immigrant cultures and American culture were not that great. But once immigrants began coming to the United States from all over the world, the cultural differences became greater (Banks, 1997; Banks & Banks, 1995; Grant, 1999; Grant et al., 1980; Sleeter & McLaren, 1995).

As a result of these developments, many immigrants coming to the United States preferred a "salad bowl" concept of American cultural contributions, rather than a "melting pot." The salad bowl, at least for a time, became the favored expression because each part of a salad maintains its identity in the mixture; for example, a cucumber remains a cucumber, and a tomato remains a tomato. Many immigrants believed the idea of a melting pot symbolized the loss of one's identity (Banks, 1997; Banks & Banks, 1995; Grant, 1999; Grant et al., 1980; Sleeter & McLaren, 1995; Weyr, 1988). However, the term "melting pot" is regaining some of its lost popularity, because people are coming to understand its original meaning. Originally, the term was based on the idea of strengthening metals: The way to create a stronger metal is to combine it with other metals. Melting pot, in its original intent, was meant to convey the idea that the United States is made up of many different people, or in this analogy "metals." The idea is that by combining these metals, the nation is made stronger. In other words, America's diversity is a source of strength and not weakness (Johnson, 1997). There is a sense of oneness advocated in the analogy, but it does not mean that each metal becomes any less of a metal.

Whatever analogy one chooses to use to describe the American cultural phenomenon, one development was clear. Many immigrants wanted to maintain their cultural traditions and did not look favorably upon the idea of "When in Rome, do as the Romans do." This perspective would have a substantial impact on American school curriculum (Banks, 1997; Banks & Banks, 1995; Grant, 1999; Grant et al., 1980; Sleeter & McLaren, 1995; Weyr, 1988).

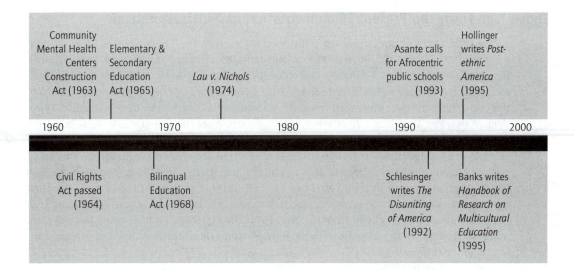

The Success of Multicultural Curricula

There is no question that the adoption in public schools of the multicultural curricula has been a great success in many ways. One of the most objective ways of addressing its success is assessing what historical events and individuals American students are most familiar with and asking them to identify the contributions of these events and individuals. By far, the most recognized speech in American history is the "I Have a Dream" speech, by Martin Luther King Jr. (Colonial Williamsburg Foundation, 2003; Ravitch & Finn, 1987). In addition, some notable ethnic minorities are in the top 10 most recognized historical figures, including Harriet Tubman and Martin Luther King Jr. (Colonial Williamsburg Foundation, 2003; Ravitch & Finn, 1987). Research by Applebee (1989) and others also indicates that the percentage of books in American classes written by racial minorities is approaching the percentage of ethnic minorities in the American population (Stotsky & Anderson, 1990).

THE DEBATE ABOUT MULTICULTURALISM

Multicultural education has been accepted in many circles but still remains a controversial topic (Parrington, 1994; Reed, 1994). People generally fall into one of three categories in their philosophies regarding multicultural education. First, there are those who favor the present nature of its implementation (Parrington, 1994; Reed, 1994). Second, there are those who favor many of the tenets of multiculturalism but want to make sure that the kind of multiculturalism that is practiced is indeed appropriate (Applebee, 1989; Chang, 1999). Third, there are those who think that multiculturalism is inappropriate and is an expression of political correctness taken to an extreme (D'Souza, 1991).

Those Who Favor the Present Implementation of Multiculturalism

Those who favor multiculturalism point to the fact that the United States is becoming increasingly diverse and must make adjustments to sensitize itself to various cultural groups (Banks, 1975, 1997; Banks & Banks, 1970; Ovando & McLaren, 2000; Sleeter & McLaren, 1995). Banks (1997) and others (Pallas, Natriello, & McDill, 1989) predict that by the year 2020, well over 40% of the nation's student population will be people of color. They declare that the American education system needs to alter the way it teaches the curriculum in order to adjust to these realities. Multicultural advocates assert that American schools need to teach subject matter that is relevant to the students who are in the classroom. Ladson-Billings (1998) calls this a "culturally relevant" pedagogy, and Geneva Gay (2002) goes one step further and advocates a "culturally responsive" pedagogy. To encourage the self-esteem of these students, teachers should emphasize the accomplishments and cultural traditions of people of color (Giroux, 1996; Gitlin, 1994). Such an emphasis will also increase student awareness of the racial, ethnic, and cultural diversities that are present in the United States (Banks, 1975, 1997; Banks & Banks, 1970; Ovando & McLaren, 2000; Sleeter & McLaren, 1995).

Reasons for a Multicultural Approach

1. The United States is traditionally a land of immigrants. The United States has long had the reputation of admitting more immigrants and being more open to foreigners than any other nation in the world. Consistent with this openness, should not the United States do what it can to facilitate the transition for foreigners so that they can adapt easily to their new home (Brown & Ling, 1991; Diamond, 1963; Kennedy, 1964)? Most nations in the world do not welcome foreigners and have restrictions that make it difficult or even impossible for a foreigner to become a citizen, obtain a college education, or run for political office, and even some industrialized countries are only just beginning to lift restrictions along these lines (Claude, 1976; Commission on the Programme to Combat Racism, 1986; Gurr, 1993; Hicks, 1997; Human Rights Watch, 1997; Upham, 1987; Walden, 2004). The vast majority of nations in the world use the word *foreigner* in a derogatory way that translated means "barbarian" or something similar. Ethnic purity and residence are emphasized in many of these nations, such that unless someone is of pure blood and was born in that country, that person is regarded as a foreigner and has circumscribed rights (Claude, 1976; Commission on the Programme to Combat Racism, 1986; Gurr, 1993; Hicks, 1997; Human Rights Watch, 1997; Upham, 1987; Walden, 2004).

In the midst of these practices, the United States stands as an exception, a nation that has long proclaimed that its diversity is a strength and not a weakness (Brown & Ling, 1991; Diamond, 1963; Kennedy, 1964) To many people, a multicultural approach is consistent with a nation that has opened its borders to foreigners to a degree previously unseen in history (Parrington, 1994; Reed, 1994).

2. The United States should be an example to the world of how diverse groups can live together. The value that the United States places on diversity is not a common belief in most nations of the world today. In most nations, there is active, condoned discrimination (Commission on the Programme to Combat Racism, 1986; Gurr, 1993; Hicks, 1997; Human Rights

Watch, 1997; Thomas, 1996; Walden, 2004). In many nations, those of minority racial heritage have to obey separate laws, are not able to run for political office, and cannot hope to go the college. Those of minority races are often blatantly denied access to housing or are charged higher train and bus fares simply because of their ancestry or place of birth. Those of mixed racial heritage are subject to beatings, harassment, and even death in various nations of the world (Claude, 1976; Commission on the Programme to Combat Racism, 1986; Gurr, 1993; Hicks, 1997; Human Rights Watch, 1997; Upham, 1987; Walden, 2004). Hicks (1997) calls these tendencies a "hidden apartheid" (p. i). Historically, in many nations around the world, various ethnic groups have been compelled to flee their homelands because of persecution. Even slavery is still practiced in certain nations in Africa (Commission on the Programme to Combat Racism, 1986; Human Rights Watch, 1997).

Nevertheless, it is clear that the world is becoming "smaller." That is, more and more people of different ethnic backgrounds are interacting with one another. One argument in favor of multiculturalism is that in light of these developments, the United States should serve as an example of how a multicultural society should exist (Frias & Anderson, 2003). Naturally, it will take time for such a philosophy to penetrate the world. In fact, America's multicultural orientation is regarded as a threat and a decadent philosophy in particular to many third-world countries (Commission on the Programme to Combat Racism, 1986; Human Rights Watch, 1997). Despite this, many people in the world view the world trend toward multiculturalism as inevitable and feel the United States needs to serve as an example of how this orientation is practiced (Brown & Ling, 1991; Diamond, 1963; Kennedy, 1964).

3. Given that the United States has undergone significant changes demographically, should not its curriculum reflect this fact? Pro-multicultural individuals argue that the teaching in schools should reflect the diversity of the American people (Walker, 1998). Given that the nation has changed demographically, particularly since the 1960s, the curriculum should reflect this fact (Walker, 1998). There is no question that American textbooks have changed over the last 40 years (Banks, 1975, 1997; Banks & Banks, 1970; Ovando & McLaren, 2000; Sleeter & McLaren, 1995). For example, many textbooks now include a higher percentage of pictures of people of color than exist in the general population (e.g., Ceaser, 1997; Daniel, 2000b; Merki, 1999). Studies by Stotsky and Anderson (1990) and Applebee (1989) show that the books that teachers use in classrooms have dramatically changed since the early 1900s. These studies indicate that only about 16% of books used in most American schools in 1907 are currently used today (Applebee, 1989; Stotsky & Anderson, 1990). Naturally, the transition has been slower in history books, because Whites tended to represent nearly 85% to 90% of the U.S. population until around 1965 (U.S. Census Bureau, 2001).

James Banks (1997) points out that there are cities in the United States where people of color are already in the majority in many schools, and it is important to be sensitive to this younger generation of Americans. Pallas et al. (1989) point out that not only is Banks's assertion true, but schools are also trending in the direction of having increasingly high percentages of racial minority students.

4. A multicultural curriculum is needed to raise the self-esteem of racial minority students. Sleeter and McLaren (1995) assert that there is still a large degree of racial inequality in the nation by income, occupation, and other factors and that it is the responsibility of the schools to combat these problems. Many multiculturalists argue that one of the ways to bridge these gaps is by raising the self-esteem of minority students by highlighting the accomplishments of people of color throughout history (Asante, 1991; Murrell, 2002; Vann & Kunjufu, 1993)

Naturally, there is still a great deal of debate about the cause-and-effect relationship between academic achievement and self-esteem (Edwards & Warin, 1999; Gregory, 2000; Richards, 1983; Schmidt & Padilla, 2003; Sykes, 1995). There is a considerable amount of evidence indicating, as one might expect, that doing well in school raises one's self-esteem (Edwards & Warin, 1999; Richards, 1983; Sykes, 1995). The possibility that a heightened self-esteem raises achievement is more controversial, but many multiculturalists make this claim (Pollard & Ajirotutu, 2000; Vann & Kunjufu, 1993). Furthermore, even if increased self-esteem does not raise achievement, there is no question that high self-esteem is a positive psychological attribute that school leaders should attempt to foster in children (Pollard & Ajirotutu, 2000; Vann & Kunjufu, 1993).

5. Multiculturalism may help alleviate poverty. A number of multiculturalism advocates believe that their programs of diversity will alleviate poverty (Banks, 1997; Tracy & Tracy, 2000). Tracy and Tracy (2000) state that there is "interdependency between public education and social welfare policies for poor, minority, and marginalized populations in the United States" (p. 331). In other words, politicians and educators frequently view education primarily as a type of welfare program, to help Americans under the poverty level rise above their circumstances. Tracy and Tracy convincingly argue that politicians, economists, and educators see "public education as a component of welfare policy to improve the employ-ability of people of welfare in the hope of getting—and keeping—them off welfare through education" (pp. 331–332). To the extent that people of color are still somewhat more likely than White people to be on welfare, many view multiculturalism as a means of helping impoverished minority students rise above their circumstances by emphasizing the value of their cultural heritage and contributions (Aaron, Mann, & Taylor, 1994; Athanases, Christiano, & Lay, 1997). Although multiculturalism does not focus on the problem of White children on welfare, it nevertheless is seen by its advocates as a way of helping people of color, who represent about 45% of the welfare recipients (U.S. Department of Health and Human Services, 1998).

6. Multiculturalism supporters view an emphasis on diversity as consistent with "the rights revolution" that gained momentum in the 1960s (Walker, 1998). In contrast to many nations, for example, many of those in East Asia where the good of society is valued over what is right for the individual, the United States, particularly since the 1960s, has emphasized the welfare of the individual. Walker (1998) and others (Aaron et al., 1994; Athanases et al., 1997; Banks & Banks, 1995) note that multiculturalism is a result of the emphasis on individual rights. In fact, the essence of multiculturalism is teaching children to respect individual differences.

7. Multiculturalists believe that children need to become more aware of other cultures. Multiculturalists declare that children are often lacking sufficient knowledge about others' cultures (Banks, 1997; Milner, 2005; Walker, 1998) and therefore schools should introduce children to other cultures (Milner, 2005).

The teaching of multiculturalism not only emphasizes the salience of children of color learning about their own cultures but also helps young people become cognizant of one another's cultures (Banks, 1997; Milner, 2005; Walker, 1998). Proponents of multiculturalism assert that White children particularly need to learn about other cultures and to also perceive themselves as cultural beings (Milner, 2005). This not only helps children to understand one another but also to overcomes a sense, perceived or real, of White hegemony. That is, it addresses a perception by minority groups that public schools are dominated by White people (Banks, 1975; Milner, 2005).

Those Who Support Many Manifestations of Multiculturalism but Are Concerned About the Kind of Multiculturalism That America Supports

A large number of social scientists support multiculturalism as an idealistic principle that encompasses respect and tolerance (Aaron et al., 1994; Athanases et al., 1997). However, these individuals have some real concerns about the kind of multiculturalism that is emerging today or is likely to arise based on current trends (Chang, 1999). Spokespersons maintaining these concerns generally fall into one of three groups: integrationalists, national unity advocates, and absolute-values supporters. We will now address the concerns of each of these groups.

Integrationalists

Integrationalists are those who support multiculturalism as a means of promoting mutual respect but have concerns about a number of segregationalist trends within the multicultural movement (Glaster & Hill, 1992; Lageman & Miller, 1996; Orfield & Eaton, 1996; Smelser & Wilson, 2001). Gary Orfield notes that the United States is becoming resegregated to levels that are approaching those evident before the 1954 *Brown v. Board of Education* decision (Orfield & Eaton, 1996). Some facets of the multicultural movement resegregate children at both the school and college levels (Glaster & Hill, 1992; Lageman & Miller, 1996; Orfield & Eaton, 1996; Smelser & Wilson, 2001). Molefi Kete Asante (1991) is a leading multiculturalist scholar who believes in ethnocentric schools and is the primary sponsor of the ethnocentric-school concept. As a result of the influence of Asante and others, a number of school districts are experimenting with Afrocentric public schools, and curricula are now in cities such as Detroit; Washington, D.C.; Atlanta; Milwaukee; Indianapolis; Pittsburgh; Philadelphia; Baltimore; and Camden (Murrell, 2002; Pollard & Ajirotutu, 2000; Schlesinger, 1992). In addition, some dorms, at the request of certain minority groups, are open only to African Americans and Latinos (D'Souza, 1991; Hill, 1996). As Juan Williams of the *Washington Post* puts it, "self-segregation is in" (as cited in Wilkinson, 1997). Cornell University even has study areas reserved for members of specific minority groups (Hill, 1996; Wilkinson, 1997).

Added Insight: The Difficult Fight Against Segregation

In 1954, *Brown v. Board of Education* supposedly ended forced segregation in the schools. *Brown* was unquestionably a landmark Supreme Court decision. Nevertheless, in the aftermath, social scientists and political leaders have found a much more obstinate problem than people originally imagined: self-segregation (Clotfelter, 2004; Jencks & Peterson, 1991; Steinberg, 1998). This assertion does not depreciate the significance of the *Brown* case, which ended forced segregation in the Deep South. This fact is a laudable and immense triumph. However, once the nation had dealt with forced segregation, people soon comprehended the extent to which de facto segregation is a much more difficult problem from which to extricate oneself. *De facto segregation* means "in-fact segregation," although it is not forced and results primarily from residential segregation. That is, ethnic groups tend to congregate in certain residential areas. School demographics generally represent those of the neighborhood. Therefore, residential segregation consistently leads to school segregation.

De facto segregation is hard to fight, because residential segregation is usually based on freedom of choice. Americans have the right to live where they choose. The reality of the matter is that most racial and cultural groups tend to choose to live in close proximity to each other (Clotfelter, 2004; Jencks & Peterson, 1991; Steinberg, 1998). Lest one be overly critical of this tendency, people who speak the same language often congregate together in order to facilitate survival (Clotfelter, 2004; Jencks & Peterson, 1991; Steinberg, 1998). If one is not accustomed to how the laws and regulations of a nation work and he or she speaks a language other than English, it is certainly understandable why that person would want to live around others who could help explicate how the system frequently works. There was a time in which cities like New York prided themselves on possessing a Chinatown, a Little Italy, a Little Tokyo, and a Little Dominican Republic. Now some immediately associate these "mini-cities" with residential segregation.

Making residential segregation even more difficult to fight is the fact that this type of segregation often results from socioeconomic factors. In many areas of the Midwest, there is a phrase used, the "wrong side of the tracks," because often the railroad tracks divide a city or town into a poor and wealthy section. If, for example, there is one elementary school on the "right side of the tracks" and one on the "wrong side of the tracks," this can result in racial segregation. In fact, if families of color generally make less money in a town of this kind, it will lead to de facto segregation, because people of color will be disproportionately represented on one side of the tracks but not the "other" (Clotfelter, 2004; Jencks & Peterson, 1991).

Residential segregation produces de facto segregation, and this is difficult to fight without imposing on people's individual liberties. Americans generally value both integration and liberty. The challenge arises when values such as these conflict with one another. This is why de facto segregation is so difficult to combat.

Desegregationalists warn that if multiculturalism leads to ethnocentric schools, the United States would be returning to the practice of segregating schools. One of the chief proponents of this view is Gary Orfield, of Harvard. He is a strong believer in the merits of desegregation (Orfield & Eaton, 1996) and claims that desegregation is the only means by which educational equality can be achieved. Nevertheless, some educators who generally support desegregation dissent from Orfield's view. They believe that since the idea for resegregating schools was sponsored by minority groups, segregation is acceptable (Asante, 1991; Murrell, 2002; Pollard & Ajirotutu, 2000). Other educators, however, expressed concern that resegregation would only increase racial divisions within the country (Glaster & Hill, 1992; Lageman & Miller, 1996; Orfield & Eaton, 1996; Smelser & Wilson, 2001).

David Hollinger, author of *Post-Ethnic America: Beyond Multiculturalism* (1995), has expressed concerns about the present system of multiculturalism. He asserts that multiculturalism tends to pigeonhole members of ethnic groups into "ethnic boxes," which can contribute to self-segregation. Consequently, Hollinger supports a more integrationalist approach in which children are taught to respect different racial backgrounds but are not so focused on ethnic differences for establishing their identity. Is the multiculturalism that is promoted in the country one in which students learn about various cultures or one in which they learn only about their own cultures?

Those Concerned With National Unity

A number of political leaders and scholars support the idea of respect promoted by multiculturalism but believe that the way multiculturalism is presently taught needs to change. They argue that teachers currently focus almost totally on cultural differences and almost never mention cultural similarities (Chang, 1999; Wilkinson, 1997). Those concerned about national unity assert that unless a greater balance is brought to multicultural teaching, it will be difficult to build bonds of unity across different ethnic groups in America (Chang, 1999; Wilkinson, 1997). Supporters of this perspective aver that teaching about ethnic differences is good and should continue. However, they hold that cultural similarities should be taught just as enthusiastically as cultural differences (Chang, 1999). Some social scientists have expressed concern that unless this balance is sought and attained, the nation runs the risk of contradicting the national motto of *e pluribus unum* ("out of many, one") with *e pluribus plenum* ("out of many, many") (Ravitch, 1993, p. 175).

One of the greatest spokesmen for those concerned about a multiculturalism that unifies rather than divides is J. Harvie Wilkinson. Wilkinson (1997) observes, "As the United States becomes a multicultural nation, we must consider what form that multiculturalism will take" (p. viii). Wilkinson posits that the kind of multiculturalism that schools promote could not be a more crucial issue. He notes, "America may be a stronger nation by 2100 or it may no longer be one nation at all" (p. viii). Wilkinson argues that multiculturalism must unify the country and not divide it and therefore cultural similarities should be taught concurrently with cultural differences.

Contemporary Focus

Differences and Similarities Among Cultures

Some social scientists believe that multiculturalism is a good ideal but that Americans often teach it the wrong way. They claim that American multiculturalism today often instructs children about cultural differences but almost never examines cultural similarities. These individuals believe that this is an unhealthy balance (Chang, 1999; Wilkinson, 1997). Although they do agree that it is essential that children learn and appreciate their cultural differences, they think that children need to also become cognizant of cultural similarities (Chang, 1999; Wilkinson, 1997). They believe that on the basis of these cultural similarities, children can understand that they share a great deal in common with others who may appear very different. To support their point, advocates of this position point to the fact that a multicultural marriage is built on commonalties between a man and a woman far more than it is constructed on differences (Hamon & Ingoldsby, 2003; McGoldrick, 1998). To the extent that a successful multicultural marriage is a microcosm of a multicultural society, it may well be true that the same is true of a successful multicultural society (Hamon & Ingoldsby, 2003; McGoldrick, 1998).

Those Concerned With Absolute Values

A number of social scientists support the notion of respect and tolerance promoted in multicultural education but also believe that multiculturalism in its present form is devoid of any sense of absolute values (Weeks, 1995). These individuals assert that multicultural education should also have a sense of right and wrong. Robert Kane (1994) describes this perspective well when he states,

> [There is] a pervasive temptation to embrace relativism, the view that there are no objective or absolute values that hold for all persons and all times. Judgments about the good and the right, it is said, can only be correct for some persons or societies or time. (p. 1)

Kane further argues that multiculturalism in its present form is causing a relativism that is producing "the loss of a sense of (1) absolute value, of (2) the uniqueness and dignity of persons and of (3) the roots, or an historically defined sense of belonging" (p. 98). Scholars with Eastern European roots have especially warned that multiculturalism must contain absolute values—or the same moral relativism that infected communist society and undermined it will distend in the United States (Kalakowski, 1989; Gardels, 1986). Specifically, Milosz (as cited in an interview with Gardels, 1986) states that multiculturalism has led to "an indifference to basic values" (p. 35). Kane (1994) argues that this trend is serious because "inalienable rights with no absolute values" is an impossibility.

The absence of absolute values could hurt the cause of multiculturalism for a number of reasons. According to those concerned about the consequences of implementing multiculturalism as it presently stands, there are 5 reasons for concern:

1. Virtually all people have some absolute values, even if it involves, for example, murder. In fact, virtually every member of American society shares certain absolute values with other Americans, and these values should not be overlooked (Dahl, 1989; Johnson & Phillips, 2003; Kalakowski, 1989; Kane, 1994; Gardels, 1986).

2. Ironically, by insisting that all cultural values are relative, we are actually making it more difficult for many immigrants to adapt to this country. Many immigrants say they have difficulty adapting to American customs because we are a country that does not believe in any black-and-white principles (Kalakowski, 1989; Kane, 1994; Gardels, 1986). Rather, we believe in "gray areas." The vast majority of other nations, however, believe in many moral absolutes.

3. Multiculturalism will lead to moral decay, because students in school are taught that all options in life are considered equal (Kalakowski, 1989; Kane, 1994; Gardels, 1986).

4. Multiculturalism will lead to inaction regarding issues in which there is a "right" and a "wrong" (Kalakowski, 1989; Kane, 1994; Gardels, 1986).

5. Multiculturalism is just as much a form of moral absolutism as the point a view of those who espouse that all values are absolute (Kalakowski, 1989; Kane, 1994; Gardels, 1986). Instead of asserting that everything is either black and white and there are no gray areas, multiculturalism could lead to cultural self-destruction among certain cultures. For if we see members of a culture engaging in a certain practice that may be culturally destructive in the long run, the tenets of multiculturalism require us to abstain totally from judging or speaking out against the practice. Some conservative African Americans assert that Whites are doing little or nothing to solve the problem of a disintegrating family structure in the African American community yet consistently applied moral relativism justifies this inaction. They claim that Whites either do not care or that they are using multiculturalism as an excuse for doing nothing.

Although the social scientists mentioned raise concerns about the kind of multiculturalism that is taught, one should not conclude that these individuals are against multiculturalism. Rather, they claim that multiculturalists would be remiss if they taught in a way that was not consistent with integration, national unity, or the presence of absolute values.

Those Who Oppose Multiculturalism

Although some social scientists believe that multiculturalism is beneficial as long as it is taught with certain issues in mind, other individuals think that multiculturalism itself is harmful.

First, a number of social scientists state that the historical claims of multiculturalists are frequently inaccurate, that is, that multiculturalists often exaggerate the contributions of their cultures in order to earn a place in history books (Glazer, 1994, 1997; Schlesinger, 1992). This became a real issue in New York when some African Americans claimed that ancient Egyptians were Black (Glazer, 1997). In addition, some social scientists complained that because minority historical figures were identified by race while White figures often were not, students sometimes assumed, for example, that White inventors were people of color (D'Souza, 1991). Arthur Schlesinger (1992) is probably the primary spokesman for this particular point of view. As a historian with "impeccable liberal credentials," Schlesinger (1992) stated,

> For better or for worse American history has been shaped more than anything else by British tradition and culture. Like it or not, as Andrew Hacker the Queens political scientist puts it, "For almost all this nation's history the major decisions have been made by white Christian men." To deny this perhaps lamentable, but hardly disputable fact, would be to falsify history. (p. 53)

A second reason some social scientists oppose multicultural education is that they believe that it takes too much time away from other academic subjects (Ravitch, 1993; Stotsky, 1999). Some educators have suggested that in an age in which the United States is falling well behind other industrialized and nonindustrialized nations in achievement, the best thing we can do to raise the hopes and job prospects of children of color is not to spend so much time teaching them about other cultures, but to hone their skills in the areas most needed to excel in a global economy (Chavez, 1999; Stotsky, 1999). These opponents of multiculturalism believe that children naturally should learn about other cultures, but they object to the multicultural view that this should be the primary goal of education (Stotsky, 1999).

Third, opponents of multiculturalism object to political correctness, which they perceive is a major component of the multicultural curriculum (D'Souza, 1991; Elder, 2000). This is one of the most divisive areas of the multicultural debate, and opinions vary widely on whether political correctness is a good or bad development (Berube, 1992; D'Souza, 1991; Elder, 2000; Fish, 1993).

Proponents of political correctness assert that people need to be taught to be sensitive to the feelings of minority groups by not stating ideas that may be offensive to people of color, gays and lesbians, women, and other groups (Berube, 1992; D'Souza, 1991; Elder, 2000). Multicultural opponents believe that political correctness is a facade that masks a broader agenda (D'Souza, 1991). They assert that political correctness is far from sensitive because it allows for offensive speech about Whites, Christians, and males (Berube, 1992; D'Souza, 1991; Elder, 2000; Wilkinson, 1997). Therefore, they assert that multiculturalism involves deprecating Western cultures and values and elevating non-Western ways (Orwin, 1997).

The issue of political correctness has become problematic for multiculturalists. Some multiculturalists themselves have become critical of political correctness and have stated that the multicultural insistence on political correctness is sabotaging the future of the multicultural movement (Chang, 1999; Hollinger, 1995). Hollinger (1995), a strong advocate of diversity, mourns the fact that the multicultural movement has hurt its own cause in its tactics along these lines. *Newsweek* even called political correctness "the new McCarthyism" (Hollinger, 1995). Opponents of multiculturalism present an endless list of examples of professors who were suspended or fired for using terms such as *Indian* in place of *Native American* and students who were flunked because they dared to question a multiculturalist claim made by a professor (D'Souza, 1991).

THE FUTURE OF MULTICULTURALISM

There are two ways in which multiculturalism thrives and will likely continue to thrive. First, the United States is increasingly a land made up of people from many different cultures, and this is simply a matter of fact. Second, the ideas of respect and tolerance are ideals that have their roots in the documents of the nation's founders and represent American aspirations. With this in mind, Nathan Glazer (1997) has declared that "we are all multiculturalists now."

The future of multiculturalism may well depend on the ability of its supporters to live up to its ideals. It is ironic that the opponents of multiculturalism believe that the Achilles heel of the movement is its lack of tolerance and respect for diverse points of view, especially manifested in political correctness (Berube, 1992; D'Souza, 1991; Elder, 2000). For now, most Americans appear to view multiculturalism favorably, despite its apparent weaknesses (Banks 1997, Banks & Banks, 1995; Glazer, 1997).

Beyond this, there is no question that multiculturalism has radically changed the material that teachers use in the schools. Studies indicate that books by European authors, which used to dominate the list of required readings, are rarely used and that the percentage of racial minority authors is beginning to approach the percentage of minorities in the American adult population (Stotsky, 1997). It is true that many scholars believe that this has caused many classics, such as *Hamlet,* the Bible, and *Pride and Prejudice,* to be removed from the reading list of many school classes, but it does demonstrate the widespread impact that the multicultural orientation is having (Reeves, 1997). Another indication that multiculturalism is impacting school curricula is that Martin Luther King Jr.'s "I Have a Dream" speech is the most recognized speech in American history and many people of color are some of the most recognized individuals in American history (Ravitch & Finn, 1987).

For the time being, the primary debates about multiculturalism focus on what kind of multiculturalism the nation should have. Should it be integrationalist or segregationalist, include absolute values or not, or encourage national unity or only distinctiveness? How these questions are resolved will go a long way in determining how multiculturalism looks in the coming years. Indeed, multiculturalism has changed over the years (Banks, 1975, 1997; Banks & Banks, 1995). The multiculturalism of the 1960s, which emphasized being "color-blind" and an integrationalist approach, is different from the multiculturalism that is practiced or at least debated today. Hence, it is inevitable that multiculturalism will continue to change.

Going Beyond Multiculturalism

In addition to the debate about the kind of multiculturalism the United States should have, since the 1990s, a new debate has emerged: Should the nation go beyond multiculturalism to another rubric? Michael Lind (1995) calls this "The next American nation . . . the fourth American revolution." Hollinger (1995) calls this rubric "post-ethnic America." Lind, Hollinger, and others argue that multiculturalism focuses on race as the primary means of determining one's identity and that this is simplistic and out-of-step with what is needed to make the United States a strong nation. They assert that in the coming generations, the United States will need to emphasize ethnicity less and not more, especially because the fastest-growing sector of the population is that of mixed racial heritage. Lind (1995) and Hollinger (1995) call for an educational approach that emphasizes one's heart, rather than the color of one's skin, as a means of establishing individual identity.

When multiculturalism is viewed in the context of history, there is little question that it will last for a time and then yield to another movement. Each generation longs to initiate its own movement and declare its own identity, hoping that their movement will be better than the last.

> ## Educational Debate: What Schools of Thought Within the Multicultural Debate Do You Most Agree With, and Why?
>
> In this chapter, we examine a number of schools of thought regarding multiculturalism. Some social scientists are strong advocates of multiculturalism (Banks, 1997; Ovando & McLaren, 2000; Sleeter & McLaren, 1995). Those supporting this view give several reasons they believe multiculturalism is a healthy development, not only because it raises the self-esteem of minority students but also because it is consistent with the increasing diversity of the country. Conditional advocates include the integrationalists, those concerned about national unity, and others (Chang, 1999; Kalakowski, 1989; Kane, 1994; Gardels, 1986; Sobol & Glazer, 1991). In addition, some individuals oppose multiculturalism largely due to reasons related to historical inaccuracy and political correctness (D'Souza, 1991; Elder, 2000; Schlesinger, 1992). Finally, there are those who believe the country needs to move beyond multiculturalism into a "fourth revolution" or "post-ethnic" society (Hollinger, 1995; Lind, 1995).
>
> - Which perspectives do you agree with the most?

VOCATIONAL EDUCATION

Vocational education gained a new degree of respect and attention in the 1960s as educators became more determined than ever to eliminate the specter of poverty that dampened the hopes of many young women and men (Brint & Karabel, 1989). There is no question that vocational education took on a broader and more integral role as a result of this focus. Nevertheless, the history of vocational education goes back much further.

In the days of the Puritans, parents were seen as the primary providers of vocational education (Bailyn, 1960). This pattern held for many years until the founding of the first farmers' institutes, in 1854, designed to train agricultural experts (Pulliam & Van Patten, 1999). This heightened interest in agriculture contributed to the passage of the Morrill Acts of 1862 and 1890, mentioned in Chapter 7, which granted college status to institutions that specialized in the teaching of agricultural and mechanical disciplines (Cross, 1999; Eddy, 1956). The Hatch Act of 1887 provided federal funds for agricultural experiments, which gave further respect to the vocational movement. In 1914, Congress passed the Smith-Lever Act, which led to the formation of agricultural courses and 4-H clubs (Pulliam & Van Patten, 1999).

The vocational movement was also enhanced by John Dewey's (1915) emphasis on children learning simple practical activities. Vocational education had been called "industrial education" in the early 1900s, largely because the need kept growing for schools to offer this type of education as the nation industrialized (Jacob, 1997; Rury, 2002). The strong connection between industrialization and vocational education especially became apparent when the National Society for the Promotion of Industrial Education was formed in 1960 (Urban & Wagoner, 2000). The passage of the Smith-Hughes Act in 1917 also added momentum to the movement because it provided funding for vocational high school teachers that provided training for them (Cross, 1999; Eddy, 1956). The *Cardinal Principles of Secondary Education* (1918) formalized the place of vocational education in the high school curriculum (Tyack, 1967).

Despite these developments, controversy often surrounded vocational education. Many argued that focusing too much on vocational education directed the poor, the principal participants in vocational education, to lower occupational tracks in life (Brint & Karabel, 1989; DuBois, 1903; Rippa, 1997). The belief by some was that many people in vocational education were capable of more in life than these labor-intensive jobs and that emphasizing vocational education was relegating them to unwanted positions (Brint & Karabel, 1989). This belief was further enhanced by the attacks made by W. E. B. DuBois against Booker T. Washington on the latter's emphasis on industrial education (DuBois, 1903; Rippa, 1997; Washington, 1899). DuBois felt that Washington's emphasis on industrial or vocation education caused African Americans to fall short of their potential and become stuck in a secondary economic role in American society (Rippa, 1997).

The opposition of critics caused many educators to view vocational education as not much more than a necessary evil. Clearly, a classical education was best. This attitude changed considerably with the passage of the Elementary and Secondary Education Act of 1965. As one prong in the war against poverty, this legislation supplied funding for school textbooks and other materials for any school practicing vocational education. This federal legislation was the most prominent step the federal government had ever taken in promoting vocational education (Brint & Karabel, 1989). Although some still felt that vocational education encouraged students to fall short of their potential, supporters argued that without prominent vocational education programs, students would fall even further short of their potential (Brint & Karabel, 1989). Consequently, a general consensus formed that vocational education was necessary, particularly in families and communities in which poverty had been passed on from generation to generation.

During his first term, President Bill Clinton advocated the passage of the School-to-Work Act of 1994. Educators are mixed on whether this helped or hindered the development of vocational education. On one hand, numerous educators have either compared this program to or equated it with a vocational education experience (Jennings, 1995; Kantor, 1994). These individuals point out that the school-to-work initiative prepares students for work through their schooling (Jennings, 1995; Sykes, 1995). On the other hand, some social scientists note that Clinton's program often bypasses high schools and focuses on school-to-work training in community colleges, arguing that all Americans should have at least a community college education (Jennings, 1995; Kantor, 1994). Consequently, after 1994, many high schools discontinued their vocational education emphases (Hettinger, 1999). In the long term, it may be that Clinton's emphasis will simply transfer the primary site of vocational education from high schools to community colleges.

EDUCATION FOR CHILDREN WITH SPECIAL NEEDS OR DISABILITIES

Education for the children with special needs or disabilities has changed considerably over the years. From the days of the European settlements until the early 1900s, people had little knowledge of the precise nature of mental handicaps (Jones, 2004; Nehring, 2004). Americans who lived during this era realized that accidents could cause brain damage. However, beyond this medical fact, people had limited knowledge of how specific parts of the brain worked and what biological phenomena could cause a person to be mentally handicapped.

Due to this dearth of awareness, before the 1850s, communities did not provide special education and services for the children with special needs. Instead, families generally cared for the mentally handicapped in much the same way that they would take care of any individuals who were struggling to take care of themselves. The understanding in each given town was that families were responsible for taking care of their own, and if the community was able to help out financially, that was done. However, people did not believe that the government itself had any responsibility to care for the mentally handicapped. The overall system of care that existed before the 1850s can be characterized as simple but personal, being family- and community based (Jones, 2004; Metzel, 2004; Nehring, 2004).

Beginning in the 1850s, the usual American approach to educating and caring for the mentally challenged transformed. Just prior to this period, Europeans had experienced some success in educating the mentally handicapped (Metzel, 2004). As a result of this progress, private and state schools opened in the United States to train such individuals. The hope was that once these children with special needs were trained at these schools, they could return to their families as "productive family members" (Metzel, 2004, p. 423). One American advocate of this approach was Gridley Howe, who began asserting in the late 1840s that one could teach the mentally challenged (Schwartz, 1956). Howe (1848) presented a report to the Massachusetts legislature in which he argued that both the state legislature and private groups should promote and fund education for the mentally handicapped. Based on his research of 77 Massachusetts towns, Howe estimated that there were between 1,200 and 1,500 mentally handicapped people in the state (Schwartz, 1956; Noll & Trent, 2004). Howe (1848) emphatically stated,

> It is recommended that measure be at once taken to rescue this most unfortunate class from the dreadful degradation in which they now grovel. . . . The moral evils resulting from the existence of a thousand and more such persons in the community are still greater than the physical ones. The spectacle of human beings being reduced to a state of brutishness . . . is not only painful, but demoralizing in the last degree. (p. 24)

The Massachusetts legislature responded to Howe's declarations and decided to invest money in a state-funded pilot program to see whether mentally handicapped people did respond to the teaching and training that Howe recommended and if so, to what extent (Schwartz, 1956).

A Closer Look: Children With Special Needs and Disabled Children

One of the greatest questions facing instructors of special education children is to what extent is mainstreaming or individual instruction the ideal teaching approach? Certainly, there are advantages to either approach. The primary advantage of mainstreaming is that it places a child into a much more normal environment, in which the child can build relationships with all types of children and not have as much of a sense of being different. On the other hand, children with special needs and disabled youth may have needs that require special attention in order to function at their highest potential.

- Do you support more of a mainstreaming approach or a strategy that focuses on individual attention to certain student needs?
- Do you think the answer depends on the type or degree of the handicap?
- Might the answer vary depending on the age of the child?

The teaching of children with special needs underwent a major transformation in the 1870s (Rafter, 2004). Herbert Spencer and Charles Darwin wrote a number of works on the place of the mentally handicapped in the evolution of the species. Nicole Rafter (2004) notes, "Herbert Spencer and other so-called social Darwinists advised that socially problematic groups should be left to die out, like inferior species" (p. 234). For example, in 1851, Spencer wrote, "Under the natural order of things society is constantly excreting its unhealthy, imbecile, slow, vacillating, faithless members" (pp. 323–324). Rafter (2004) notes Spencer's (1851) use of the term "purifying process" of extinction when she observes that in Spencer's view, "to aid the unfit would merely thwart this 'purifying process' of extinction" (pp. 234–245). Rafter (2004, p. 234) notes that Darwin and other evolutionists viewed being mentally handicapped as "reversion" to a lower form of life. Darwin (1874), in his book *The Descent of Man and Selection in Relation to Sex,* stated, "The several and moral faculties of man have been gradually evolved. . . . We may trace a perfect graduation from the mind of an utter idiot, lower than that of an animal low in the scale, to the mind of Newton" (p. 495).

The claim by Darwin that some mentally handicapped had the intelligence of a low animal alarmed many scholars and helped launch the eugenics movement (Rafter, 2004; Sarason & Doris, 1969). The movement was designed to develop a biologically, evolutionarily, and sociologically based strategy to improve the genetic makeup of the human race (Rafter, 2004; Sarason & Doris, 1969).

As a result of this more scientifically based depiction of children with special needs, three patterns began to emerge. First, because the mentally handicapped were seen as a reversion to a "lower species," Rafter notes that there began to emerge a "criminalization of mental retardation." Unfortunately, this meant that the country's policies reflected more of a desire to protect people from those facing severe mental challenges rather than to benefit the mentally challenged (Dugdale, 1877; Metzel, 2004). Second, the eugenics movement desired to develop national policies that would limit the ability of the mentally handicapped to reproduce and to receive the education they needed (Dugdale, 1877; Gelb, 2004; Laughlin, 1926; Metzel, 2004; Rafter, 2004; Sarason & Doris, 1969). Third, scholars wanted to gain a greater understanding of what caused a person to become mentally handicapped in the first place (Dugdale, 1877; Fish, 1879; Metzel, 2004).

It took time for these factors to completely change the national policy toward the mentally handicapped, but change it did. Richard Dugdale's book *The Jukes: A Study in Crime, Pauperism, Disease, and Heredity; Also Further Studies of Criminals* (1877) went a long way in developing a perceived link between retardation in mental abilities and criminality (Rafter, 2004). William Fish's (1879) work, *A Thesis on Idiocy,* was less judgmental but still tainted people's perception of children with special needs. He declared that parental alcoholism could sometimes influence a child's genetic makeup if alcohol was consumed while the baby was in the womb and that, consequently, this could sometimes cause brain or genetic damage in the child. Some contemporary biologists have noted similar relationships between illegal drug consumption and mental defects at birth (Church, 1993; Elliot & Coker, 1991). Nevertheless, in a scholastic atmosphere that had already turned decisively negative toward the mentally handicapped, Fish's comments were not helpful. Unlike a number of his contemporaries, however, Fish still maintained the conviction that with proper training, many of the mentally handicapped could be taught to partially or totally earn their own living (Fish, 1879).

During the 1870s and 1880s, the eugenics movement gained momentum under the leadership of the primary American spokesperson for the movement, Josephine Lowell (Rafter, 2004). Lowell became the main advocate of the building of asylums, where mentally handicapped people could be placed so that they would not harm those around them (Metzel, 2004; Rafter, 2004). Rafter (2004) states, "Lowell's first major accomplishment on the charity board was to define feebleminded women as a biological threat to society, what later generations would label 'born criminals'" (p. 233). Lowell's views were founded in Spencer's teachings, mentioned earlier. Although Lowell did not found the first asylum, she called for their rapid expansion (Rafter, 2004). As a result of these beliefs of the period, many educators believed the mentally retarded person was "a person who was vulnerable to criminal exploitation and vice" (Metzel, 2004, p. 423). This view was crucial in establishing the asylum movement of the 1880s and 1890s.

The asylum movement had enough momentum to carry it well into the 20th century. Another eugenicist, Harry Laughlin (1926), continued the movement where Lowell had left off. In 1926, Laughlin wrote a journal article titled "The Eugenical Sterilization of the Feeble-Minded." He argued that the way to ensure a reduction in the number of "feeble-minded" was to sterilize "feeble-minded" and "potentially feeble-minded" people. Laughlin served as the director of the Eugenics Record Office of the Department of Genetics of the Carnegie Institute from 1910 to 1940. Noll and Trent (2004) state, "His model sterilization laws were used by several of the thirty states that passed sterilization laws. Nazi Germany's 1933 sterilization laws were also modeled after Laughlin's" (p. 502).

The excesses of World War II played a large role in reversing the movement toward putting the mentally challenged in asylums, though even just prior to World War II, organizations like the American Association on Mental Deficiency placed a great deal of emphasis on the social control of these individuals (Gelb, 2004). During the 1940s and 1950s, people organized into groups to once again make the treatment of the mentally handicapped more humane (Gelb, 2004; Jones, 2004). Some politicians began to work with parents of children with special needs to help make the education system more amenable to mentally challenged children. Alfred Beadleston, a Republican assemblyman from New Jersey, sponsored the Beadleston Act in 1954. This piece of legislation was designed to identify and educate children who were being left behind by the system (Jones, 2004). In 1955, the National Association for Retarded Children (NARC) began to lobby Congress to establish child development clinics that could diagnose, evaluate, and provide counseling for children who were possibly mentally handicapped (Nehring, 2004).

Although there was progress in the treatment of the mentally challenged in the post–World War II period, psychologists and counselors still encouraged their institutionalization (Jones, 2004). Psychological experts of the 1950s stated that if families maintained the burden of caring for the mentally handicapped, it would place too much pressure on the family (Jones, 2004). Therefore, many psychologists argued that institutionalization was the best thing for the entire family. Even the esteemed psychoanalyst Erik Erikson and his wife, Joan, followed this advice in 1944, when their son was born with Down syndrome (Jones, 2004). To support family harmony, Erikson hid the existence of the child from the other children and instead said that the child had died at birth (Jones, 2004).

By the 1970s, however, there was a movement toward the deinstitutionalization of children with special needs. Social scientists concluded that there was a need to "return to the community" in terms of caring for these people (Metzel, 2004, p. 434). This orientation came on the heels of the congressional passage of the Mental Retardation Facilities and Community Mental Health Centers Construction Act of 1963. This act sponsored university- and community-based programs for the mentally handicapped (Nehring, 2004). The return to an emphasis on family- and community-based care and a renewed commitment to the mentally handicapped indicated that there were days of promise ahead.

In addition to the reemergence of an emphasis on home and community care, Congress passed legislation designed to enhance teacher and staff sensitivity to the needs of handicapped children. The Education of All Handicapped Children Act of 1975 (Pub. Law 94-142) was formulated to ensure that children with disabilities received a full and adequate education (Beyer, 1989; Crocket, 1999; Maag & Katsiyannis, 2000; Martin, 1996). The law mandates that each disabled child receive instruction in the least restrictive environment (Abeson, Bolick, & Hass, 1975; Bolick, 1975). Consequently, children who previously were taught separately in special classes were now mainstreamed (Abeson et al., 1975; Beyer, 1989). Public Law 94-142 necessitates that special education students spend as much of the day as is feasible with other classroom children. It requires that an individualized education plan be created for each child by the collaborative efforts of local educators and the child's parents or guardians (Abeson et al., 1975; Beyer, 1989).

Public Law 94-142 was designed to address a number of salient issues. First, it would facilitate socializing between disabled and nondisabled students' guardians (Abeson et al., 1975; Beyer, 1989). Second, it would enable nondisabled students to feel more comfortable knowing when to help disabled students and when the latter students prefer to act independently. Third, it would provide disabled students with additional models that would yield a more competitive learning environment (Crocket, 1999; Maag & Katsiyannis, 2000; Martin, 1996).

In 1997, Congress passed the Disabilities Education Act Amendments (IDEA), which sought to establish formulas for how money should be distributed among states, depending on state demographics. The legislation considered issues of poverty and also provided special assistance to historically Black colleges and universities with large minority populations (Crocket, 1999; Maag & Katsiyannis, 2000; Martin, 1996).

One should point out some people think although tending to children with special needs is important, educators pay far too little attention to gifted and talented students (Davidson, Davidson, & Vanderkam, 2004; Yecke, 2003). Estimates differ, but generally only 1% to 3% of the educational dollar goes toward educating gifted and talented children (Davidson et al., 2004; Yecke, 2003). Given that these children are often the inventors and creative geniuses of the future and some are likely to fuel future job growth, many Americans believe that educating the gifted and talented has become neglected to the detriment of these children and the future of the country (Davidson et al., 2004; Yecke, 2003). Although advocates of instruction for the gifted propound these arguments, there is little question that presently, at least, there is far greater emphasis placed on meeting the needs of special needs and disabled children (Davidson et al., 2004; Yecke, 2003). It may well be that at some time in the future, American education will more completely recognize the importance of honing educational opportunities for advanced students, but presently most Americans can derive satisfaction from knowing that there have been many advancements in the education of children with special needs and disabilities.

CONCLUSION

In the past several decades, inclusion has become a centerpiece of American education. By the very nature of the word *inclusion,* one might conclude that the development is a positive one (Banks, 1975, 1997). However, the practical applications of inclusion in education are multifaceted (Hollinger, 1995; Wilkinson, 1997). Schools are faced with a limited time frame, and, ultimately, including one element of a new curriculum means excluding something else (Banks & Banks, 1995; Stotsky, 1999). In addition, whether one is talking about cultural practices, children with special needs or disabilities, or vocational education, people often disagree about how much inclusion is truly appropriate. Can including certain cultural distinctions inadvertently divide people? To what extent does mainstreaming benefit the mentally handicapped, and to what degree do they need special attention? Does including a vocational track in school better prepare students for the job market, or foster a trail of unfulfilled potential?

During the past 40 or 50 years, inclusion has become a cherished value by millions of Americans. However, although many Americans agree on the importance of this value in an idealistic sense, they often differ on how it should be applied. Consequently, issues of inclusion stir a great deal of debate among educators today.

DISCUSSION QUESTIONS

1. Some multiculturalism advocates see the movement as a permanent fixture in American society, and others, such as Lind and Hollinger, view it as a movement that will serve its purpose for a time and then yield to another movement. Which of these two perspectives do you have regarding multiculturalism?

2. Do you agree that vocational education runs the risk of placing a student on an occupational track that fails to utilize that student's highest potential? Why or why not? If you do believe there is such a risk, how great is that risk? If such a risk does exist, is it worth it because of the potential benefit to society?

3. Particularly since the 1850s, society has had a tendency to classify people based on their intelligence. This is especially clear with how theorists and educators treated the mentally handicapped, even to the point of referring to an "idiot, lower than that of an animal low in the scale." Why are some people so inclined to classify people on the basis of their intelligence rather than on their character and "heart"?

4. Do you believe that academic proficiency raises one's self-esteem? Do you also think that raising one's self-esteem raises achievement? According to the International Assessment of Educational Progress (IAEP), American students have the highest self-esteem of all the nations they tested. However, the IAEP also found that American students are the most likely of those tested to overestimate their scholastic prowess. To what extent should a teacher attempt to raise the self-esteem of students? How does a teacher determine the balance between encouraging self-esteem and causing students to have unrealistic perceptions of themselves?

REFERENCES

Aaron, H. J., Mann, T. E., & Taylor, T. (1994). Introduction. In H. J. Aaron, T. E. Mann, & T. Taylor (Eds.), *Values and public policy* (pp. 1–15). Washington, DC: Brookings Institution.

Abeson, A. R., Bolick, N., & Hass, J. (1975). *A primer on due process: Education decisions for handicapped children*. Reston, VA: Council for Exceptional Children.

Applebee, A. (1989). *A study of book-length works taught in high school English, Report Series 1.2*. Albany: Center for the Learning and Teaching of English Literature, SUNY

Asante, M. K. (1991). Multiculturalism without hierarchy: An Afrocentric reply to Diane Ravitch. In F. J. Beckwith & M. Bauman (Eds.), *Are you politically correct?* (pp. 185–193). Buffalo, NY: Prometheus.

Asante, M. K. (1993). *Malcolm X as cultural hero and other Afrocentric essays*. Trenton, NJ: Africa World Press.

Athanases, S. Z., Christiano, D., & Lay, E. (1997). Fostering empathy and finding common ground in multiethnic classes. In R. E. Long (Ed.), *Multiculturalism* (pp. 57–70). New York: H. W. Wilson.

Bailyn, B. (1960). *Education in the forming of American society*. Chapel Hill: University of North Carolina.

Banks, J. (1975). *Teaching strategies for ethnic studies*. Boston: Allyn & Bacon.

Banks, J. (1997). *Educating citizens in a multicultural society*. New York: Teachers College Press.

Banks, J. A., & Banks, C. A. (1970). *Teaching the Black experience*. Belmont, CA: Fearon.

Banks, J. A., & Banks, C. A. (1995). *Handbook of research on multicultural education*. New York: Macmillan.

Banks, J., & Grambs, J. D. (1972). *Black self-concept*. New York: McGraw-Hill.

Berube, M. (1992). Public image limited: Political correctness and the media's big lie. In P. Berman (Ed.), *Debating P.C.* (pp. 124–139). New York: Dell.

Beyer, H. A. (1989). Education For All Handicapped Children Act: 1975–1987: A judicial history. *Exceptional Parent, 19*(6), 52–54, 56, 58.

Bolick, N. (1975). *Digest of state and federal laws: Education of handicapped children*. Arlington, VA: Council on Exceptional Children.

Bratten, S. (1995). Public Law 94-142. Twenty years and counting and where do we stand? *Preventing School Failure, 39*(3), 4–5.

Brint, S. G., & Karabel, J. (1989). *The diverted dream: Community colleges and the promise of educational opportunity in America, 1900–1985*. New York: Oxford University Press.

Brown v. Board of Education 347 U.S. 483 (1954).

Brown, W., & Ling, A. (1991). *Imagining America: Stories from the promised land*. New York: Persea Books.

Calderon, M. (1998). *Adolescent sons and daughters of immigrants: How schools can respond*. Chicago: National Society for the Study of Education.

Ceaser, L. (Program Advisor). (1997). *Choices in literature: Where paths meet*. Upper Saddle River, NJ: Prentice Hall.

Chang, H. N. (1999). Multiculturalism benefits society. In M. B. Williams (Ed.), *Culture wars* (pp. 140–147). San Diego, CA: Greenhaven Press.

Chavez, L. (1999). Multiculturalism does not benefit society. In M. B. Williams (Ed.), *Culture wars* (pp. 148–156). San Diego, CA: Greenhaven Press.

Church, M. W. (1993). Does cocaine cause birth defects? *Neurotoxicology and Teratology, 15,* 289.

Claude, R. P. (1976). *Comparative human rights*. Baltimore: Johns Hopkins University Press.

Clotfelter, C. T. (2004). *After Brown: The rise and retreat of school desegregation*. Princeton, NJ: Princeton University Press.

Colonial Williamsburg Foundation. (2003). *American history poll*. Williamsburg, VA: Author.

Commission on the Programme to Combat Racism. (1986). *Racism in Asia*. Geneva, Switzerland: World Council of Churches.

Cremin, L. A. (1962). *The transformation of the school- progressivism in American Education, 1876–1957*. New York: Knopf.

Crocket, J. B. (1999). The least restrictive environment and the 1997 IDEA Amendments of federal regulations. *Journal of Law & Education, 28,* 543–564.

Cross, C. (1999). *Justin Smith Morrill: Father of the land grant colleges*. East Lansing: Michigan State University.

Dahl, R. (1989). *Democracy and its critics*. New Haven, CT: Yale University Press.

Daniel, K. (2000a). *Elements of literature, first course*. Austin, TX: Holt, Rinehart, & Winston.

Daniel, K. (2000b). *Elements of literature, second course*. Austin, TX: Holt, Rinehart & Winston.

Darwin, C. (1874). *The descent of man and selection in relation to sex*. New York: A. L. Burt.

Davidson, J., Davidson, B., & Vanderkam, L. (2004). *Genius denied: How to stop wasting our brightest young minds*. New York: Simon & Schuster.

Dewey, J. (1915). *The school and society*. Chicago: Chicago Press.

Diamond, S. (1963). *The nation transformed: The creation of an industrial society*. New York: Braziller.

D'Souza, D. (1991). *Illiberal education: The politics of race and sex on campus*. New York: Free Press.

DuBois, W. E. B. (1903). *The souls of Black folk*. Chicago: A. C. McClurg.

Dugdale, R. L. (1877). *The jukes: A study in crime, pauperism, disease, and heredity; also further studies of criminals*. New York: Putnam & Sons.

Eddy, E. D. Jr. (1956). *Colleges for our land and time*. New York: Harper & Brothers.

Edwards, A., & Warin, J. (1999). Parental involvement in raising the achievement of primary school pupils: Why bother? *Oxford Review of Education, 25,* 325–341.

Elder, L. (2000). *The ten things you can't say in America*. New York: St. Martin's Press.

Elliot, K. T., & Coker, D. R. (1991). Crack babies: Here they come, ready or not. *Journal of Instructional Psychology, 18*(1), 60–64.

Fish, S. (1993). There's no such thing as free speech and it's a good thing too. In F. J. Beckwith & M. Bauman (Eds.), *Are you politically correct?* (pp. 43–55). Buffalo, NY: Prometheus.

Fish, W. B. (1879). *A thesis on idiocy*. Albany, NY: Albany Medical College.

Frias, G. A., & Anderson, G. A. (2003). *What is the role of the United States of America in the world?* Washington, DC: Center for Latin American Studies, Georgetown University. (Available at http://www.georgetown.edu/sfs/programs)

Gardels, N. (1986, February 27). An interview with Czeslaw Milosz. *New York Review of Books,* pp. 34–35.

Gay, G. (2002). Culturally responsive teaching for ethnically diverse students: Setting the stage. *International Journal of Qualitative Studies in Education, 15,* 613–619.

Gelb, S. A. (2004). Mental deficients fight fascism: The unplanned normalization of World War II. In S. Noll & J. W. Trent (Eds.), *Mental retardation in America: A historical reader* (pp. 308–321). New York: New York University.

Giroux, H. A. (1996). *Fugitive culture*. New York: Routledge.

Gitlin, T. (1994). The classics must be broadened to include multicultural literature. In F. Whitehead (Ed.), *Culture wars* (pp. 23–27). San Diego. CA: Greenhaven Press.

Glaster, G. C., & Hill, E. W. (1992). *The metropolis in black and white: Place, power, and polarization*. New Brunswick, NJ: Center for Urban Policy Research.

Glazer, N. (1994). Multiculturalism and public policy. In H. J. Aaron, T. E. Mann, & T. Taylor (Eds.), *Values and public policy* (pp. 113–115). Washington, DC: Brookings Institution.

Glazer, N. (1997). *We are all multiculturalists now*. Cambridge, MA: Harvard University Press.

Grant, C. (1999). *Multicultural research: A reflective engagement with race, class, gender, and sexual orientation*. London: Falmer.

Grant, C., Boyle-Baise, M., & Sleeter, C. (1980). *The public school and the challenge of ethnic pluralism*. New York: Pilgrim.

Gregory, S. T. (2000). *The academic achievement of minority students: Perspectives, practices, and prescriptions*. Landham, MD: University Press.

Gurr, T. R. (1993). *Minorities at risk: A global view of ethnopolitical conflicts*. Washington, DC: United Institute of Peace Press.

Hamon, R. R., & Ingoldsby, B. B. (2003). *Mate selection across cultures*. Thousand Oaks, CA: Sage.

Hettinger, J. (1999). House recommends increase for vocational education, cut for STW. *Techniques: Making Education and Career Connections 74*(1), 6.

Hicks, G. (1997). *Japan's hidden apartheid*. London: Ashgate.

Hill, M. J. (1996). Do theme dorms sanction self-segregation? *Christian Science Monitor, 88*(160), 12.

Hollinger, D. A. (1995). *Post-ethnic America: Beyond multiculturalism*. New York: Basic Books.

Howe, S. G. (1848). *A report made to the legislature of Massachusetts upon idiocy*. Boston: Collidge & Wiley.

Human Rights Watch. (1997). *Iran: Religious and ethnic minorities: Discrimination in law and practice*. New York: Author.

Jacob, M. C. (1997). *Scientific culture and the making of the industrial West*. New York: Oxford University Press.

Jencks, C., & Peterson, P. E. (1991). *The urban underclass*. Washington, DC: Brookings Institute.

Jennings, J. F. (1995). *National issues in education: Goals 2000 and school-to-work*. Bloomington, IN: Phi Delta Kappan.

Johnson, L., & Phillips, B. (2003). *Absolute honesty*. New York: American Management Association.

Johnson, P. (1997). *A history of the American people*. New York: HarperCollins.

Jones, K. W. (2004). Education for children with mental retardation: Parent activism, public policy, and family ideology in the 1950s. In S. Noll & J. W. Trent (Eds.), *Mental retardation in America: A historical reader* (pp. 322–350). New York: New York University.

Kalakowski, L. (1989). *Modernity on endless trial*. Chicago: University of Chicago.

Kane, R. (1994). *Through the moral maze: Searching for absolute values in a pluralistic world*. New York: Paragon House.

Kantor, H. (1994). Managing the transition from school to work: The false promise of youth apprenticeship. *Teachers College Record, 95*, 442–461.

Kennedy, J. F. (1964). *A nation of immigrants*. New York: Harper & Row.

Ladson-Billings, G. (1998). Teaching in dangerous times: Culturally relevant approaches to teachers assessment. *Journal of Negro Education, 67*, 255–267.

Lageman, E. C., & Miller, L. P. (1996). *Brown v. Board of Education: The challenge for today's schools*. New York: Teachers College Press.

Lambert, W. E., & Reynolds, A. G. (1991). *Bilingualism, multiculturalism, and second language learning*. Hillsdale, NJ: Lawrence Erlbaum.

Laughlin, H. (1926). The eugenical sterilization of the feeble-minded. *Journal of Psycho-Asthenics, 31*, 210–218.

Lind, M. (1995). *The next American nation: The new nationalism and the fourth American Revolution*. New York: Free Press.

Maag, J. W., & Katsiyannis, A. (2000). Recent legal and policy developments in special education. *NASSP Bulletin, 84*(613), 1–8.

Martin, E. W. (1996). The legislative and litigation history: History of special education. *Future of Children, 6*(1), 25–39.

McGoldrick, M. (1998). *Re-visioning family therapy: Race, gender, and culture in clinical practice*. New York: Guilford Press.

McLeskey, J., & Pacchiano, D. (1994). Mainstreaming students with learning disabilities: Are we making progress? *Exceptional Children, 60*, 508–517.

Merki, M. B. (1999). *Teen health course 3.* Woodland Hills, CA: Glencoe/McGraw Hill.

Metzel, D. S. (2004). Historical social geography. In S. Noll & J. W. Trent (Eds.), *Mental retardation in America: A historical reader* (pp. 420–444). New York: New York University.

Milner, R. (2005). Developing a multicultural curriculum in a predominantly White teaching context. Lessons from an African American teacher in a suburban English classroom. *Curriculum Inquiry, 35,* 391–427.

Murrell, P. C. (2002). *African-centered pedagogy: Developing schools of achievement for African American children.* Albany: SUNY.

Nehring, W. M. (2004). Formal health care at the community level: The child development clinics of the 1950s and 1960s. In S. Noll & J. W. Trent (Eds.), *Mental retardation in America: A historical reader* (pp. 371–383). New York: New York University.

Noll, S., & Trent, J. W. (2004). Introduction. In S. Noll & J. W. Trent (Eds.), *Mental retardation in America: A historical reader* (pp. 1–19). New York: New York University.

Orfield, G., & Eaton, S. E. (1996). *Dismantling desegregation.* New York: New York University Press.

Orwin, C. (1997). Fostering empathy and finding common ground in multiethnic classes. In R. E Long (Ed.), *Multiculturalism* (pp. 45–56). New York: H. W. Wilson.

Ovando, C. J., & McLaren, P. (2000). *The politics of multiculturalism and bilingual education.* Boston: McGraw-Hill.

Pallas, A. M., Natriello, G., & McDill, E. L. (1989). The changing nature of the disadvantaged population: Current dimensions and future trends. *Educational Researcher, 18*(5), 16–22.

Parrington, V. L. (1994). The principles of Puritanism would be a destructive influence. In F. Whitehead (Ed.), *Culture wars* (pp. 51–55). San Diego, CA: Greenhaven Press.

Pollard, D. S., & Ajirotutu, C. S. (2000). *African-centered schooling in theory and practice.* Westport, CT: Bergin & Garvey.

Pulliam, J. D., & Van Patten, J. J. (1999). *History of education in America.* Upper Saddle River, N J: Merrill/Prentice Hall.

Rafter, N. (2004). Criminalization of mental retardation. In S. Noll & J. W. Trent (Eds.), *Mental retardation in America: A historical reader* (pp. 232–257). New York: New York University.

Ravitch, D. (1993). Multiculturalism without hierarchy. In F. J. Beckwith & M. Bauman (Eds.), *Are you politically correct?* (pp. 175–198). Buffalo, NY: Prometheus.

Ravitch, D., & Finn, C. (1987). *What do our seventeen year olds know: A report on the first national assessment of history and literature.* New York: Harper & Row.

Reed, I. (1994). An emphasis on Western civilization is outdated. In F. Whitehead (Ed.), *Culture wars* (pp. 23–27). San Diego, CA: Greenhaven Press.

Reeves, W. (1997). Will zealots spell the doom of great literature. In R. E. Long (Ed.), *Multiculturalism* (pp. 86–95). New York: H. W. Wilson.

Richards, J. M. (1983). The validity of locus of control and self-esteem measures in a national longitudinal survey. *Educational & Psychological Measurement, 43,* 897–905.

Rippa, S. A. (1997). *Education in a free society.* White Plains, NY: Longman.

Rury, J. L. (2002). *Education and social change: Themes in the history of American schooling.* Mahwah, NJ: Lawrence Erlbaum.

Sarason, S. B., & Doris, J. (1969). *Psychological problems in mental proficiency.* New York: Harper & Row.

Schlesinger, A. (1992). *The disuniting of America.* New York: Norton.

Schmidt, J. A., & Padilla, B. (2003). Self-esteem and family challenge: An investigation of their effects on achievement. *Journal of Youth and Adolescence, 32*(1), 37–46.

Schwartz, H. (1956). *Samuel Gridley Howe: Social reformer, 1801–1876.* Cambridge, MA: Harvard University.

Sleeter, C., & McLaren, P. (1995). *Multicultural education, critical pedagogy, and the politics of difference.* Albany: SUNY.

Smelser. N. J., & Wilson, W. J. (2001). *America becoming: Racial trends and their consequences.* Washington, DC: National Academy Press.

Sobol, T., & Glazer, N. (1991). *One nation, many peoples: A declaration of cultural interdependence.* New York: Social Studies Review and Development Committee.

Spencer, H. (1851). *Social statics: or, The conditions essential to happiness specified, and the first of them developed.* London: John Chapman.

Steinberg, S. (1998). *Race and ethnicity in the United States: Issues and debates.* Malden, MA: Blackwell.

Stotsky, S. (1997). Changes in America's secondary school literature programs. In R. E. Long (Ed.), *Multiculturalism* (pp. 71–84). New York: H. W. Wilson.

Stotsky, S. (1999). *Losing our language: How multicultural classroom instruction is undermining our children's ability to read, write, and reason.* New York: Free Press.

Stotsky, S., & Anderson, P. (1990). Variety and individualism in the English class: Teacher recommended lists of reading for grades 7–12. *Leaflet, 1,* 1–11.

Sykes, C. J. (1995). *Dumbing down our kids.* New York: St. Martin's Press.

Thomas, J. E. (1996). *Modern Japan.* London: Longman.

Tracy, M. B., & Tracy, P. D. (2000). Education and social welfare policy. In T. Midgley, M. B. Tracy, & M. Livermore (Eds.), *The handbook of social policy.* Thousand Oaks, CA: Sage.

Tyack, D. B. (1967). *Turning points in American educational history.* Waltham, MA: Blaisdell.

Upham, F. K. (1987). *Law and social change in postwar Japan.* Cambridge, MA: Harvard University Press.

Urban, W., & Wagoner, J. (2000). *American education: A history.* Boston: McGraw-Hill.

U. S. Census Bureau. (2001). *Census 2000.* Washington, DC: Author.

U.S. Department of Health and Human Services. (1998). *Statistical abstracts of the United States.* Washington, DC: Author.

Vann, K. R., & Kunjufu, J. (1993). The importance of an Afrocentric multicultural curriculum. *Phi Delta Kappan, 74,* 490–491.

Vernez, G., & Abrahamse, A. (1996). *How immigrants fare in U.S. education.* Santa Monica, CA: RAND.

Walden, R. (2004). *Racism and human rights.* Leiden, Netherlands: Nijhoff.

Walker, S. (1998). *The rights revolution.* New York: Oxford University Press.

Washington, B. T. (1899). *The future of the American Negro.* Boston: Small, Maynard, & Co.

Weeks, J. (1995). *Invented moralities: Sexual values in an age of uncertainty.* New York: Columbia University.

Weiss, B. J. (1982). *American education and the European immigrant, 1840–1940.* Urbana: University of Illinois Press.

Weyr, T. (1988). *Hispanic USA: Breaking the melting pot.* New York: Harper & Row.

White, M. J., & Kaufman, G. (1997). Language usage, social capital, and school completion among immigrants and native-born ethnic groups. *Social Science Quarterly, 78,* 385–398.

Wilkinson, J. H. (1997). *One nation indivisible: How ethnic separatism threatens America.* Reading, MA: Addison-Wesley.

Yecke, C. P. (2003). The war against excellence: The rising tide of mediocrity in America's middle schools. Westport, CT: Praeger.

Educational Reform Under Republicans and Democrats

From the 1980s onward, American presidents became more consistently involved in educational policy than ever before (Spring, 1997). A large part of this involvement emerged from the rising degree of public criticism of public education during the late 1960s and the 1970s (Cooperman, 1985).

During the period beginning in 1981, both Democrats and Republicans proposed a number of reforms to improve the educational outcomes of American students (Spring, 1997). In this chapter, we focus on three reforms each by the Democratic and Republican presidents that emerged during this period. For both political parties, of these three reforms, one was clearly successful and the other two were more controversial.

The Republicans initiated three noteworthy programs: the Back to the Basics movement, under Ronald Reagan; the School Choice initiative, especially under George H. W. Bush; and the No Child Left Behind program, under George W. Bush. The Democrats, under the leadership of Bill Clinton, undertook policies to promote computer literacy, school choice limited to public schools, and the implementation of national standards for schools. The different perspectives of Republicans and Democrats on school choice in particular present an interesting contrast.

REFORMS UNDER REPUBLICAN PRESIDENTS RONALD REAGAN, GEORGE H. W. BUSH, AND GEORGE W. BUSH

The Back to the Basics Movement

The Back to the Basics movement was an educational reform movement initiated by the presidential administration of Ronald Reagan (from 1981–1989). Of the three reforms inaugurated by the Republicans since 1980, this is the one that is generally regarded as being the most successful (Bell, 1988; Garrett, 2005; Zak, 2000).

The Back to the Basics movement started largely as a result of the decline in achievement test scores that took place from 1963 to 1980 (Reagan, 1983). Although, as we discussed in

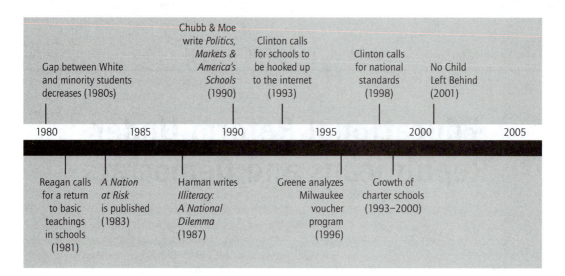

Gap between White and minority students decreases (1980s)

Chubb & Moe write *Politics, Markets & America's Schools* (1990)

Clinton calls for schools to be hooked up to the internet (1993)

Clinton calls for national standards (1998)

No Child Left Behind (2001)

1980   1985   1990   1995   2000   2005

Reagan calls for a return to basic teachings in schools (1981)

A Nation at Risk is published (1983)

Harman writes *Illiteracy: A National Dilemma* (1987)

Greene analyzes Milwaukee voucher program (1996)

Growth of charter schools (1993–2000)

Chapter 12, one cannot blame all (and perhaps even most) of the decline in test scores on school factors, the Reagan administration focused primarily on school components in the Back to the Basics movement. Reagan declared that to raise the educational accomplishments of children, schools needed to return to teaching the most essential aspects of knowledge and self-discipline. The liberal policies of John Dewey were finally in place by the early 1960s. Many people, mostly conservatives and some moderates, blamed the academic decline over the next two decades on the implementation of liberal child-centered policies. The Reagan administration asserted that part of the reason academic achievement was down was that American schools had become so child centered that they no longer maintained the preparation-centered nature that had made American schools great (Reagan, 1983).

Certain reports, research studies, and books came out during the Reagan and George H. W. Bush administrations that appeared to support the notion that America's public schools were in decline and were in serious need of reform. In the early 1980s, the National Commission of Excellence in Education (1983) released the report *A Nation at Risk.* The report pointed to the now infamous 110-point drop (using the College Board's adjusted figure) in SAT scores (formerly known as the Scholastic Aptitude Test or Scholastic Achievement Test), a concomitant decline in some SAT results, and a steady increase in the need for remedial math courses in the nation's 4-year public colleges. The report also lamented the falling scores of American students in international test scores. In 1987, another influential book was published, written by David Harman, titled *Illiteracy: A National Dilemma,* in which he asserted that many Americans could not read well enough to perform adequately at their jobs. It is not clear just what America's literacy rate is at this time. It depends on the definition of *literacy* that is used. Official estimates vary from 79% to 97% for the *basic* type of literacy (U.S. Census Bureau, 2001). The U.S. Census Bureau (2001) contends that America's *functional* literacy rate is about 87%.

Bill Bennett, secretary of education under Ronald Reagan, encouraged schools to focus on teaching basic material such as reading, math, and science. Bennett asserted that the traditional basal approach to reading should be taught, rather than the whole-language approach. The traditional basal approach emphasized phonics and accurate pronunciation in reading (Stahl, 2001). Historically, teachers have employed a basal paradigm to their instruction because English is a phonetic language (Jeynes & Littell, 2000; Stahl, 2001). The whole-language approach was a more child-centered approach that emphasized teaching whole words and teaching material that was enjoyable to children (Goodman, 1989, 1992; Jeynes & Littell, 2000). The belief was that if children enjoyed reading, they would learn to read more in the long run. In the whole-language approach, instructors focused more on whether children enjoyed reading rather than on their accuracy (Goodman, 1989, 1992). Most schools did not listen to Bennett until the early 1990s, when California and Texas declared their whole-language programs to be failures.

During the 1980s and early 1990s, the gap between the performance of African Americans and Whites on standardized tests decreased substantially for the first time. Many educators credit the Back to the Basics movement with this decrease, but other factors were probably involved as well (Conciatore, 1990; Haycock, 2001; Haycock & Jerald, 2002; Jerald & Haycock, 2002; Jones, 1984; Walberg, 1986). There is research indicating that basal instruction especially benefits minority children (Haycock, 2001; Haycock & Jerald, 2002; Jerald & Haycock, 2002; Wilson & Daviss, 1994). It is not difficult to fathom why focusing on the basics at school will tend to benefit poor and minority children the most. Children from affluent homes have parents who can afford to make certain that their children get the basics despite whatever shortcomings a school might have. They have the resources to afford ordering "Hooked on Phonics" for a few hundred dollars even if their children do not receive the basics at school. However, for many poor families, this alternative would be a great financial strain.

To give historical substantiation to his work, Reagan quoted Thomas Jefferson, who said, "If a nation expects to be ignorant and free . . . it expects what never was and never will be" (as cited in Reagan, 1983, p. v). To provide factual substantiation for his views, Reagan drew from the report *A Nation at Risk,* as mentioned, a report by the National Commission of Excellence in Education, in 1983, which lamented the decline in American student achievement and presented evidence indicating that the decline was putting American students well behind their counterparts in other industrialized countries. The report argued that if current trends continued, the United States risked having a lower standard of living and reduced power status in the world.

Reagan (1983) averred that something far more than just increased government spending on public education was needed to remedy the nation's education woes. He supported this claim with the fact that for many years, educational expenditures had risen at twice the rate of inflation and yet test scores had fallen. In his view, more money was not the primary answer. Although many educators nevertheless remained committed to more money for education, most were puzzled as to why the unprecedented increases in educational expenditures during the 1960s and 1970s had not yielded higher test scores (Garrett, 2005; Ravitch, 1974).

President Reagan (1983) recommended that six steps be taken in his Back to the Basics plan. First, he called for school standards to be raised. He pointed out that 35 states required only one high school math course in order to graduate from high school. Similarly, he pointed out that 36 states required students to take just one science class to graduate from high school. This was a contrast to the 4-course math and science requirement typical of American high schools in the late 1800s and early 1900s (National Education Association, 1893, 1918).

Second, Reagan called for greater teacher empowerment in administering classroom discipline. He asserted that too many students were assaulting teachers and that teachers often lacked the authority to quiet children down and to get them to do their homework.

Third, Reagan called for Americans to take action along a multidimensional front to reduce student drug and alcohol abuse. Reagan believed that this behavior had a baleful impact on school outcomes.

Fourth, Reagan believed that teachers needed to have higher expectations of students and assist more of them to take college preparatory classes.

Fifth, Reagan called for a higher level of parental involvement. He argued that students absorb the most when parents and teachers work together for the good of the children.

Sixth, Reagan called for basic virtues to be taught in the school, that is, moral or character education.

At first, Reagan's call to focus on the basics was controversial. However, over the long run, people realized that the movement was necessary (Kearns & Doyle, 1989; Garrett, 2005). School standards were simply intolerably low, and many companies complained about the low quality of high school graduates (Kearns & Doyle, 1989). Standardized test scores did begin to edge upward after the Back to the Basics movement was set in place (U.S. Department of Education, 2000). However, the biggest accomplishment of the Back to Basics movement was that for the next decade, the achievement gaps between White and minority students, as well as wealthy and poor students, showed some significant reduction for the first time (Conciatore, 1990; Haycock, 2001; Haycock & Jerald, 2002; Jerald & Haycock, 2002; Jones, 1984; U.S. Department of Education, 2000). To be sure, although the Back to the Basics supporters would like to take all the credit for narrowing this gap, it is likely that other factors also contributed (Hedges & Nowell, 1999). Nevertheless, the reduction is consistent with other research that suggests that poor and minority children are the ones who benefit the most when the basics are taught (Haycock, 2001; Haycock & Jerald, 2002; Jerald & Haycock, 2002; Wilson & Daviss, 1994). When all children are taught the basics in school, the playing field becomes more level.

Overall, the Back to the Basics movement was probably the most productive Republican educational reform movement of the era from 1980 to the present.

Added Insight: Why Does Teaching the Basics Help Poor Children?

Research indicates that when the basic subjects (e.g., math, phonics, science, and social studies) are emphasized, poor children of all backgrounds and minority children, who are still somewhat more likely to be poor than Whites, benefit the most (Haycock, 2001; Haycock & Jerald, 2002; Jerald & Haycock, 2002; Jeynes & Littell, 2000; Wilson & Daviss, 1994). This finding is important because mastering the basics is unequivocally essential if students are to succeed in school and in life as a whole (Boyer, 1995; Sykes, 1995). If an individual cannot do simple math or read at a certain level, job opportunities will be minimized and the realization of one's dreams might be truncated (Boyer, 1995; Sykes, 1995).

The question emerges as to why teaching the basics benefits poor children the most? The answer is simply that children from affluent homes receive basic instruction whether their schools impart these teachings to them or not (McCabe, 2003). Pecunious parents can afford to buy the best materials, send their children to the best tutors or after-school tutelage, or share from their own repositories of knowledge. Indigent families are unlikely to possess any of these advantages. Therefore, when instructors do not teach the basics, impoverished children suffer the most and the achievement gap tends to widen. In contrast, when teachers train children in the basics, the achievement gap abates.

School Choice

Both the Republicans and Democrats had school choice initiatives during the period since 1980; however, they were somewhat different. Both political parties believed school choice would benefit the nation's education system. However, the Democrats under President Bill Clinton favored a choice system that was limited to public schools, and Republicans favored extending the choice to include private schools as well (Doerr & Menendez, 1991; Kirkpatrick, 1990; Manno, 1995).

The Republican movement to initiate school choice programs that included private schools grew under Reagan, George H. W. Bush, and George W. Bush (Edwards, Hawley, Hayes, & Turner, 1989; Kirkpatrick, 1990; Minutaglio, 1999). Although their desire for private school choice has never been adopted except at an experimental level, it remains a major plank of the Republican Party's platform. It is more controversial in its impact than the Back to the Basics movement, and this is a major reason it has not been more fully applied.

Although Reagan supported school choice, the movement really did not gain much momentum until the publication of Chubb and Moe's book, *Politics Markets and America's Schools* (1990). In their book, Chubb and Moe ask an interesting question: Why is it that America's university system is generally regarded as the best in the world but our public school system is regarded as below average? Chubb and Moe hypothesize that the reason is that at the university level, schools in the private and public sectors compete against one another, while at the elementary and secondary school levels, public schools have a virtual monopoly. At the university level, institutions such as Stanford (private) and UC-Berkeley (public) as well as USC (private) and UCLA (public) compete against one another, and each institution is made better by that competition. However, at the elementary and secondary school levels, the school tax burden is substantial enough so that most people feel they cannot afford to send their children to private schools (Chubb & Moe, 1990).

Chubb and Moe (1990) assert that to restore American elementary and secondary school education to a high quality, private schools must be allowed to compete on more equal footing with the public schools. They argue that if the government allows this to transpire, two positive educational effects will occur. First, more American children will attend private school, where they will receive a better education, on average, than they would in a public school. Second, the competition from private schools would compel public schools to become better. Consequently, Chubb and Moe maintain, America's entire elementary and secondary school system would improve.

The way to end the public school monopoly, Chubb and Moe (1990) assert, is to ease the financial burden of parents by giving a voucher to each family that sends its children to private school. This voucher would partially compensate for the fact that families pay taxes to support public schools even if their children do not receive their training through public education. Other proponents of school choice have recommended that tax breaks be given to parents engaging in choice instead of vouchers (Bryk, Lee, & Holland, 1993). One potential advantage of this approach is that it might be easier to adjust the tax break to the income of the family. For example, a given school choice plan would likely give a larger tax break to the poor than to the wealthy. In contrast, one advantage of granting a voucher is that it might be easier to give school choice benefits to those individuals who do not pay any taxes.

Experimentation but Not Wide Implementation of School Choice

Although the Republican presidents have backed school choice in principle, the implementation of school choice has been limited to isolated efforts in cities such as Milwaukee and Cleveland (Greene, Peterson, Du, Boeger, & Frazier, 1996; Jeynes, 2000; Peterson, Greene, & Noyes, 1996). At first, this may seem surprising, because one of the groups whose support is important to school choice, African Americans, is generally the most enthusiastic ethnic group when it comes to school choice (Phi Beta Kappa/Gallup Poll, 2002). Not only do polls indicate a high degree of African American support for school choice, but many African Americans have protested outside the White House, declaring that the federal government was not doing enough to promote school choice (Green, 2000).

The primary reason for the strong African American support is easy to understand. Many African Americans live in dilapidated urban areas, where public schools are dens for drug pushers and gangs (Green, 2000; Irvine & Foster, 1996; Phi Beta Kappa/Gallup Poll, 2002). Concurrently, most African American parents cannot afford to send their children to religious and other types of private schools where gangs and drug pushers are rare (Green, 2000; Jeynes, 2000). Many African American parents would love the opportunity to be given a tax break or a voucher so that they could afford to do so. As has already been intimated, a primary reason African Americans want school choice is often more out of a desire to remove their children from baneful influences than it is for scholastic reasons (Green, 2000; Irvine & Foster, 1996).

It is largely because of the support among African Americans that school choice initiatives have been launched in Milwaukee and Cleveland (Greene et al., 1996; Howell & Peterson, 2002). Nevertheless, it is noteworthy that despite the support of three Republican presidents in the last quarter century, school choice has not emerged as a large-scale practice (Jeynes, 2000). One of the primary reasons for this is that while many Americans would feel comfortable with poor urban and rural Americans getting a tax break or voucher, most would not feel at ease with the affluent or upper middle class getting such a boon. It is very likely that if school choice is ever implemented on a large scale, tax breaks and vouchers would have to be distributed on a sliding scale. That is, the poor would get a large benefit, the middle class some degree of benefit, and the wealthy would receive no benefit at all. There are some states, such as Florida and Colorado, that allow parents of children doing poorly in school and attending schools that have been designated as failing to use public funds to send their children to better-performing schools, whether it be public, Evangelical, Catholic, or other private schools (Greene & Winters, 2006). In Florida, Pennsylvania, and

Arizona, individuals and corporations can make tax-deductible contributions that fund scholarship-granting programs, and scholarships can be used to cover the cost of private school tuition or tutoring (Greene & Winters, 2006).

Early assessments of the school choice programs presently in place indicate that children generally do receive a moderate academic benefit from attending a private school instead of a public one, although the first year of attending a different school is often a period of adjustment for the children (Greene et al., 1996). Research also suggests that even when adjusting for socioeconomic status, children attending religious schools outperform children from public schools (Coleman, Hoffer, & Kilgore, 1982; Jeynes, 2002). However, not all social scientists are convinced that the analyses of school choice programs in Milwaukee and Cleveland offer decisive evidence in favor of these programs (Witte, 1999, 2000; Rouse, 2004).

It is difficult to determine the degree to which Republican presidents will pursue the practice of school choice. In the ideal world, it is clearly one of the party's top priorities (Garrett, 2005). However, while many Americans support the poor having school choice, presently Republicans do not have the backing of a majority of Americans for a broad-based plan. Therefore, instead of initiating extensive school choice programs, Presidents George H. W. Bush and George W. Bush chose to sponsor initiatives that will facilitate school choice program implementation at a later time (Howell & Peterson, 2002). For example, during his administration, President Bush Sr. called for the establishment of magnet schools across the country (Bush, 1989). He also initiated a $13 million federal government investment in expanding experimental educational programs, including school choice (Bush, 1989; Edwards et al., 1989).

Analyzing the Possible Effects of School Choice

One of the greatest problems in assessing the effects of school choice abides in the lack of relevant data collected on its impact on children. In addition, almost none of this research has examined the effects of school choice on academic achievement. Gewirtz, Ball, & Bowe (1995) observe that "most of the empirical research is piecemeal and tends to be very specifically focused" (p. 3). Gewirtz et al. therefore contend that much of the research on school choice has been "inadequate" (p. 6). To be sure, some recent data indicate that school choice may positively impact academic achievement (Greene et al., 1996; Peterson et al., 1996; Witte & Thorne, 1996), but overall, the evidence is sparse. There are three reasons for coming to this conclusion. First, the number of studies that social scientists have done measuring the influence of school choice is relatively small. Second, for those studies that have attempted to assess the effects of school choice, it is not clear whether this is in fact what has ultimately been measured. Many studies have focused on how choice affects (a) the distribution of students among schools (Gewirtz et al., 1995; Woods, Bagley, & Glatter, 1998) and (b) what parents consider when making their choices (Woods et al., 1998). Third, the dynamics of school choice are complex and difficult to examine. For example, the effects of school choice are going to differ in urban areas, where there will be more choices, versus rural areas, where choices are limited (Gewirtz et al., 1995). School choice will often differ depending on how schools promote themselves and will have various effects rooted in copious education philosophies (Colopy & Tarr, 1994; Pardey, 1991). Fourth, the school choice debate has become so politicized, it has become hard to disentangle the research of many social scientists from their political views.

Beyond these problems, it is not clear how many of the effects found in favor of choice or nonchoice students are actually a product of choice and how many result from simply changing schools or from certain students dropping out of a choice program. Greene and his colleagues (1996) found, for example, that children participating in the Milwaukee voucher program obtained an academic advantage over similar Milwaukee children not participating in the program by the third year of participation. Opponents of choice may note that choice did not produce an academic edge for choice students during the first 2 years of the program. However, the fact that it took over 2 years for differences to emerge could be explained in large degree by the fact that changing schools is a difficult experience for many children (McLanahan & Sandefur, 1994). Nevertheless, supporters of choice can take some satisfaction in the fact that academic achievement rose by the third year. One can argue that this may partially be a result of children who struggle in their new schools, often dropping out of the project by the third year, leaving only those students who are doing reasonably well as the study's sample. Overall, Greene's study appears to partially support some of the merits of school choice programs that include private schools, but more research needs to be done. Although broad programs of school choice have not yet been implemented, school choice including private schools remains one of the chief educational desires of the Republican Party, though it also remains a controversial part of the Republican perspective.

No Child Left Behind

George W. Bush's No Child Left Behind initiative also represents a controversial Republican educational policy. President Bush signed the policy into law on January 8, 2002. Initially, No Child Left Behind earned bipartisan praise as an educational act that could help many disadvantaged children. David Broder, the dean of the Washington Press Corps, stated that he thought the legislation was the most essential piece of educational legislation in 35 years (Moranto & Coppetto, 2004). Even the name of the plan seemed ideal. After all, who could argue with a plan whose goal it was to ensure that no child would be left behind? The initial response to the legislation was helped by the fact that President Clinton's Secretary of Education Richard Riley (2002) indicated that Clinton had anticipated going in a similar direction.

President Bush's goals were certainly commendable, but the actual implementation of the plan ultimately stirred up controversy (Yeagley, 2003). No Child Left Behind possessed the primary goal of assisting the educational achievements of the economically disadvantaged, increasing the pool of highly qualified teachers, increasing the literacy rate of students, and holding schools accountable for the success or failure of their students (Poswick-Goodwin, 2003). Bush also authorized one of the greatest increases in federal spending for education in the post–World War II era, 41% in just the 3-year period from 2000 to 2003, and federal funding for Title I schools in particular has risen substantially (Poswick-Goodwin, 2003).

No Child Left Behind sets specific standards that schools need to abide by using standardized tests to ensure that they are meeting those goals (Office of Educational Research and Improvement, 2001). The aim of No Child Left Behind is to ensure that schools achieve 100% proficiency for all students in reading and math by the year 2014 (U.S. Department of Education, 2002). To monitor whether these goals are met, No Child Left Behind requires that children be tested in reading and math from third through eighth grade (U.S. Department of Education, 2002).

One of the most novel and controversial aspects of No Child Left Behind is that it contains specific directives for schools that fail to show improvement over various lengths of time. For example, if schools do not show progress in meeting proficiency standards after 2 years, they are placed in a "school improvement" category. At this stage, a school needs to develop a 2-year improvement plan and use 10% of its Title 1 funds for professional development (U.S. Department of Education, 2002). Over time, if schools do not improve, there are additional actions that they must take, including providing tutoring services for students and paying transportation costs for children who choose to go to different schools (U.S. Department of Education, 2002).

If a school has still failed to show academic progress after 4 years, it is placed in the "corrective action" category, which results in requirements such as implementing new curriculum, replacing staff, and possibly extending the school day or year. After 6 years, if a school is chronically failing, it then goes through a "restructuring" phase, which may take any number of different forms. Most frequently, the principal will be replaced. However, it is also possible the school could be closed and then reopened as a charter school or, under certain circumstances, might even be bought out by a private company (U.S. Department of Education, 2002).

No Child Left Behind also strongly discourages the use of emergency credential teachers and requires a certain length of time for them to complete their credentials in order to continue in the teaching profession (U.S. Department of Education, 2002). President Bush has stated that the reason for this requirement is that a disproportionate number of emergency credential teachers are giving instruction in the poorest schools (Office of Educational Research and Improvement, 2001). Virtually all educators acknowledge that although there are many fine emergency credential teachers, on average they are not as well trained and experienced and therefore on average will be less effective than those with credentials (Office of Educational Research and Improvement, 2001). Therefore, Bush argues that having a disproportionate number of emergency credential teachers in the nation's poorest schools will only exacerbate the gap that already exists between wealthy and poor students (Office of Educational Research and Improvement, 2001).

Many states in the United States are having no problem meeting the goals and directives of No Child Left Behind, because they are largely already in place (Ritter & Lucas, 2003). However, there are other states, most notably California, that have had a high percentage of emergency credential teachers and relatively low standards (Neu & Hale, 2000). These states are finding No Child Left Behind a shock to the school system (Gardner, 2003; Posnick-Goodwin, 2003). California had a phenomenal number of emergency credential teachers at the time that No Child Left Behind was first implemented (Ritter & Lucas, 2003; Neu & Hale, 2000). Even though Californians acknowledged that this was a problem and was harmful, especially toward impoverished children, politicians and educators did little to alleviate the problem (Neu & Hale, 2000). When No Child Left Behind was set in place, it forced states like California to address the problem (Office of Educational Research and Improvement, 2001). Nevertheless, most educators believe that although rectifying the situation was necessary, the Bush administration allowed too short a time period for states inundated with emergency credential teachers to adjust to the new mandates.

Criticisms of No Child Left Behind

The previous section leads us to now address the principal criticisms of No Child Left Behind. First, as mentioned, the legislation leaves little time for states with a high number of emergency credential teachers to adjust to the new mandates. This argument has a great deal of credence and may reflect the fact that many Washington policymakers do not have much experience in the classroom.

Second, some educators claim that the federal government is not providing enough money to meet the mandates. Although it is true that schools can always use more money, this argument is weakened by the fact that Bush has authorized one of the greatest increases in federal educational spending in memory and at a rate of increase about 4 times greater than the rate of inflation (Poswick-Goodwin, 2003).

Third, some educators claim that many public schools will not be able to meet the standards of No Child Left Behind and that hundreds of schools will eventually close (Yeagley, 2003). Some skeptics even claim that the legislation is part of a long-term plan to eventually force privatization of schools (Bracey, 2003). Based on Bush's past preference as governor of the state of Texas to work toward the improvement of public schools rather than privatization, this criticism lacks substantiation (Moranto & Coppetto, 2004). It is possible, although unlikely, that countless schools will close down. However, if this happens, what is very likely is that many principals and staff members will lose their jobs.

The fact that many principals and staff members will lose their jobs raises two salient controversial aspects about No Child Left Behind. First, the legislation clearly shifts the burden of failure from the children to the schools. President Bush makes it clear that he will no longer tolerate children "falling through the cracks" because of inadequate schools (Moranto & Coppetto, 2004). Instead, the schools must either train children properly or face considerable staff changes. Such a change in orientation is likely to face massive resistance on the part of teachers' unions, instructors, and principals. Beyond this, although No Child Left Behind conveys the impression that it contains a no-nonsense approach to incompetence in educational leadership, in reality, because of the tenure system, principals and staff who are fired will probably just transfer to other school districts.

The fourth criticism of No Child Left Behind is that it does not adequately acknowledge that some schools, especially those operating in rapidly declining neighborhoods, are more difficult to improve than others (Bracey, 2003). While this criticism is probably one of the most valid, it is also true that it is a formidable task to obtain an objective measure of such things. Given that No Child Left Behind is the most recent Republican initiative, the jury is still out on what its long-term effects will be. Its aims are honorable, but its implementation is currently controversial.

The Republican Party has initiated other reforms and proposals, such as merit pay for teachers and increased federal support for traditionally Black colleges (Bush, 1989; Edwards et al., 1989; Reagan, 1983). In 1991, President Bush also propounded America 2000, which included several goals that he believed must be met in order to raise the nation's educational prowess (Finn, 2002; Manno, 1995). First, it required raising standards for all students. Seconds, tests needed to be implemented to meet those standards. Third, it called for a reduction in federal government red tape that would allow for more educational innovations by schools, families, and communities. Fourth, it encouraged school choice. Fifth, Bush urged that control of the schools be shifted from professionals and teacher unions, that is, the producers, to parents, civilians, and other community leaders, that is, the consumers (Manno, 1995).

Although the Republicans proposed these other initiatives, the Back to the Basics Movement, school choice, and No Child Left Behind are the most salient.

Contemporary Focus

No Child Left Behind

No Child Left Behind has become one of the most hotly debated educational initiatives in recent memory. The aims are certainly laudable, to ensure that all children are able to reach their full educational potential. Also meritorious is the fact that George W. Bush authorized one of the most substantial increases in federal spending for education in the post–World War II era by raising this 41% in just his first 3 years in office (Poswick-Goodwin, 2003). However, two aspects of No Child Left Behind have been especially controversial. First, the initiative insists that poorly performing schools raise their academic performance or they could potentially face rigorous federal action (Moranto & Coppetto, 2004; U.S. Department of Education, 2002). Some school authorities are concerned that some public schools will be unable to meet these standards and will be compelled to make formidable staff changes and could conceivably eventually face closure (Bracey, 2003). Second, critics contend that No Child Left behind does not allow schools in states with low standards sufficient time to execute transitions (Bracey, 2003).

Overall, critics of No Child Left Behind assert that although this rubric may possess meritorious aspirations, it is replete with uncertainty. On the other hand, proponents argue that if the nation's schools are not held to certain minimum standards, the children who can least afford to suffer from ineffectual schools, poor and at-risk students, will be the ones who pay the highest cost.

- What do you like and dislike about No Child Left Behind?
- What do you think of this initiative overall?

REFORMS UNDER DEMOCRATIC PRESIDENT BILL CLINTON

Preparing Students for the Technological World

President Bill Clinton's emphasis on schools adapting to the technological revolution was clearly his most triumphant educational reform during his presidential term (1993–2001). Just as the Back to the Basics movement represents the Republicans' educational jewel of the post-1980 world, Clinton's insight into the important relationship between education and technology was the Democratic jewel. He argued that in the technological age, computer literacy was becoming almost as important as other forms of literacy, and he particularly emphasized schools being hooked up to the Internet. By the time Clinton left office, 98% of public schools were connected to the Internet (McLarty, Panetta, Bowles, & Podesta, 2001). The percentage of public school classrooms connected to the Internet rose from 3% in 1994 to 77% in 2000 (McLarty et al., 2001).

President Clinton believed that increased technological access was key for students to learn how to compete in a computer-based global economy (Shapiro, 1998). He initiated the greatest outlay in federal expenditures for educational technology that the nation had seen to that day, increasing federal expenditures from $23 million in 1993 to $872 million in 2001 (McLarty et al., 2001; Tatalovich & Frendeis, 2000). The latter amount included $65 million for community technology centers to reach over 180 disadvantaged communities (McLarty et al., 2001). Clinton's Technology Literacy Challenge program not only focused on connecting each public school to the Internet but also sought to increase the number of multimedia computers in the classroom (McLarty et al., 2001).

Although most Americans now view President Clinton's technological initiatives as an important component of educational policy, he did have his share of critics at the time. Clinton's policies focusing on technology to prepare children for the job market were too centrist for some of his educational supporters, who wanted him to focus on fostering student cooperation in the schools and child-centered education (Shapiro, 1998). There was a sense among some liberals that Clinton had "sold out" to the business community by focusing on education as a job creator rather than on more idealistic themes (Shapiro, 1998). Nevertheless, as time went on, Gallup Polls indicated that the American people steadily increased their support of Clinton's educational policies (Harvey, 2000). Furthermore, he eventually silenced his critics by advocating additional policies, including advocating hiring 100,000 new teachers to reduce class size and give children the individual attention they need (Guth, 2000; McLarty et al., 2001).

Clinton's technology-in-education policy reflected his fundamental belief that students needed to be prepared for the new economy that awaited them after graduation (Coleman, 2000). His forward-looking policy was a key accomplishment in his administration.

Public School Choice

Clinton, like the Republicans, believed that to revive American education, the nation's public schools needed to be infused with new levels of competition (McLarty et al., 2001). Unlike his Republican counterparts, however, Clinton claimed that simply creating increased public school choice would be sufficient competition to produce the desired effect. He encouraged various communities and states to develop programs of school choice to stimulate competition among the schools, believing this increased competition would lead to higher levels of quality (McLarty et al., 2001). In some respects, Clinton followed through with George H. W. Bush's (1989) call for increased public school choice. However, since Bush was more amenable toward school choice including private schools than he was of public school choice, he did not pursue public school choice with the same energy that Clinton did (McLarty et al., 2001).

President Clinton personally met with governors across the country and encouraged them to launch public school choice programs. The charter school movement especially grew under Clinton's two terms in office (McLarty et al., 2001). Technically, Albert Shanker (1996) was the first to introduce the idea of charter schools in the 1970s. However, with the exception of a schooling experiment based in Philadelphia, there was little effort to apply the charter school paradigm until Clinton was elected into office (Bradley, 1994). At that time, the fledgling charter school movement was just getting off the ground. However, by the time Clinton left office, there were more than 2,000 charter schools in the country, in 34 states and the District of Columbia (McLarty et al., 2001). For his last year in office, Clinton secured a $45 million increase in funds designed to increase public school choice (McLarty et al., 2001).

Although there is no question that Clinton made a great deal of progress in promoting school choice, the benefits of these actions are debatable. The evidence that is available to date shows that students in charter schools do no better academically than their counterparts in regular public schools (Sarason, 1999). Advocates of private school choice have pointed to these results as evidence that choice will produce the needed level of competition only if private schools are included (Chubb & Moe, 1990; Kirkpatrick, 1990). On the other hand, opponents of school choice assert that Clinton's efforts were simply a waste of time because choice does not work (Sarason, 1999).

Admittedly, there are some indications that school choice may do some good in the lives of the participants. Minnesota possesses the most developed system of public school choice in the country. Barbara Zohn (personal communication, 1994, May 14) reports that self-report surveys by the students involved in the Minnesota choice program are "very good." She notes that a much higher percentage of "choice students" desire to pursue a college education than do students who remain in their districts. Zohn adds that the survey results indicate that many students who once "did not think" of going to college now anticipate attending. The second result is especially salient because of the makeup of the students that participate in Minnesota's choice program. The largest of Minnesota's choice programs involves "students at risk." These are students in Grades K–12 that schools identify as at-risk students. They generally are from homes in which there are problems with chemical dependency or teenage parents. The schools supply child care for teenage parents and even night school for those students who find it difficult to attend during the day. Of Minnesota's 40,000 students involved in the choice programs, nearly half are at-risk students (Colopy & Tarr, 1994; B. Zohn, personal communication, 1994, May 14). Nevertheless, it is clear that more research needs to be done to determine whether public school choice is really effective, especially since some, like Lewis Finch (1989), claim that "supporters of choice base claims of success on contrived data" (p. 13). To date, there really does not appear to be strong evidence suggesting that public school choice aids academic achievement.

The Participation Rate Issue

Beyond these arguments emerges the issue of the small number of students who are likely to participate in school choice even if such programs are available on a wide scale. Generally speaking, the rate of participation in school choice programs internationally and domestically are about 12% to 15% (Jeynes, 2000). This trend holds whether one is talking about school choice programs that involve just public schools or those that include private schools. Given this fact, it appears unlikely that school choice will emerge as the grand source of reform that its advocates promise (Jeynes, 2000). As a result, few children will benefit from the program, and few schools will possess the incentive to change significantly. Having stated this, it may well be that even this level of participation in choice will force public schools to increase their quality and become more competitive. Indeed, one can argue that competition is more likely to increase especially if private schools are included. To whatever extent minority and poor school children continue to be the focus of most school choice programs, this may also make such programs remunerative. However, based on such low participation rates, it is hard to argue that school choice programs will revolutionize American education.

The early research indicates that private school choice (the Republican plan mentioned earlier in the chapter) probably does raise academic achievement, but private school choice remains problematic for two reasons. First, many Americans would favor the poor and the middle class getting tax breaks but would balk at the wealthy getting a tuition tax break. Second, the participation rate in other nations tends to be low. On the other hand, Clinton's public school plan avoids the tax break controversy. However, the academic benefits of charter schools, magnet schools, and other expressions of public school choice have not been convincing. Consequently, the school choice debate will continue to be heated and controversial.

Educational Debate: Which School Choice Program Do You Prefer—the Democrat or the Republican Model?

Both Democrats and Republicans have propounded school choice paradigms. The Democratic initiative involves school choice in the realm of public schools. This strategy eschews the controversy inherent in choice programs involving tax breaks or vouchers to enable parents to send their children to private schools. Most Democrats believe that public school choice will supply a sufficient degree of competition to improve school outcomes (McLarty et al., 2001). The Republican approach calls for school choice in both the private and public school sectors. Advocates of this approach, such as Chubb and Moe (1990), believe that a sufficient degree of competition can be reached only if the nation's best schools, which are frequently private schools, are included in a choice program.

- Which school choice program do you prefer, school choice that includes public schools or an approach that includes both public and private schools? Why?

Nationalized Standards

President Clinton also expressed concern about the achievement gap between White and Asian American students, on one hand, and other minority groups, on the other (Coleman, 2000; Shapiro, 1998). He stated, and George W. Bush later agreed, that this chronic achievement gap was one of the most pressing problems facing American education (Shapiro, 1998).

Clinton was convinced that one of the reasons for the gap was that students in poor urban schools were not receiving the same level of demanding instructional material as their counterparts in suburban schools. To reduce this inequity, he proposed that national standards be established to ensure that all students at various grade levels are taught certain key concepts (Shapiro, 1998). Furthermore, Clinton stated that nationwide standardized tests be given at the fourth-grade level for reading and at the eighth-grade level for math that would monitor whether teachers were inculcating these concepts (Shapiro, 1998).

National tests were one of the most important facets of Clinton's educational program. He believes that children need to master the basics and that tests are vital to see that they are doing so (Coleman, 2000; Shapiro, 1998). Most other developed countries have similar tests, but some people are solicitous about too prodigious a role played by the federal government in education (Shapiro, 1998). To address this concern, Clinton said he would make the tests voluntary. The tests would be based on the National Assessment of Educational Progress (NAEP), a highly esteemed test that was already used extensively in the country. Senators from both parties were quite amenable to the idea, but many Republicans insisted that Clinton transfer the oversight of the testing from the U.S. Department of Education to the more neutral NAEP.

The Clinton initiative for higher standards and an augmented role for the federal government in education was prominent in Goals 2000, or the Educate America Act (Manno, 1995). Goals 2000 wrote into law the national education goals established by President George H. W. Bush in 1991, in his America 2000 plan (Manno, 1995). In addition, Goals 2000 called for the reauthorization of the Elementary and Secondary Education Act of 1965 (Smith, Scoll, & Plisko, 1995). Clinton desired to place special attention on Title I programs that "in 1965 . . . symbolized a new era of federal involvement in education, with federal involvement in education with federal assistance focusing on students who needed it the most: poor and disadvantaged children" (Payzant & Levin, 1995, p. 55).

For the most part, educators embraced Goals 2000 as a whole, although there were some critics. The component of the legislation that called for nationalized standards and testing was a controversial one. Critics claimed that Clinton was centralizing the decentralized system of which most Americans were so fond (Powell, 1999; Shapiro, 1998). Clinton denied this claim and stated that he was simply trying to make adjustments to a generally decentralized system. Other critics claimed that under Clinton, "schools and schooling are dominated by a concern with testing" (Shapiro, 1998, p. 46). Shapiro notes that "during the 1980s and 1990s, the number of standardized tests administered to students during their pre-college years has increased by almost 400 percent" (p. 46). And furthermore, according to Shapiro, "The language of increased content, higher levels of performance, and important test scores—sadly, the language of your administration's education policies—will only contribute and exacerbate the confusion of schooling with some genuine, humanly liberating and meaningful education" (p. 50).

Some argued that Clinton was inaugurating a precipitous turn toward centralization of America's schools (Manno, 1995). For example, Howard Howe (1995), a former U.S. commissioner of education and professor at Harvard Graduate School of Education, asserted that Clinton was creating "an elaborate bureaucratic structure that brings Uncle Sam into the classrooms of 2 1/2 million American public school teachers" (pp. 374, 376). The extent to which American students may be overtested and required to satisfy a plenary set of standards is controversial and remains a subject of much debate (Howe, 1995; Perrone, 1991; Powell, 1999).

A Closer Look: The Essence of the Debate About Standards: Necessity Versus Liberty

There is no question that the educational community and the nation's leadership stand at a crossroads regarding educational policy. A decentralized education system is a long-standing tradition in the American experience that dates back to the early political debates between the Democratic-Republicans and the Federalists, addressed in Chapter 3. Liberty is one of the traditions that Americans most value. A decentralized system of schooling is largely a result of the American love for liberty in education. Through this system of schooling, many citizens believe that schools can maximize their sensitivity to

(Continued)

(Continued)

> students, parents, and innovative teachers. In recent years, however, it has become patent that decentralization exacerbates inequality. In a decentralized system, children, by definition, are not taught much of the same information that is shared at other schools. Moreover, the standards at schools across the country vary considerably.
>
> Presidents Clinton and George W. Bush believe that reducing the achievement gap must be a national priority and that part of the solution is establishing national standards.
>
> Just how far the Clinton and Bush initiatives will take the nation on the road to centralization is incalculable. Attempts to make specific conclusions will produce nebulous arguments at best. However, what is certain is that the nation is now involved in a debate that confronts the value of liberty with the reality of necessity.
>
> - In your view, in which direction should the country go in this debate?

In defense of President Clinton, like many political leaders, he was at a loss about how to reduce the achievement gap. Although the gap had finally been narrowed during the 1980s, it still remained unacceptably large after four decades of trying one reform after another to hasten the process (Green, 2001; Slavin & Madden, 2001). Per-student expenditures had soared since the 1950s; schools were integrated, with millions of dollars spent to bus students; bilingual education was introduced and backed by millions of dollars of expenditures; multicultural education became a staple of American public school education; and experiments were undertaken to give parents more localized control of schooling (Podair, 2002; Ravitch, 1974; U.S. Department of Education, 2004). After all of these attempts, the achievement gap stubbornly remained, and Clinton's actions reflected a deep frustration. Something had to be done to deal with this persistent problem. As a result, he acted forcefully in making these recommendations (Shapiro, 1998).

Although standardized testing had been on the increase since the 1960s, conjoining this method with national standards gave new importance to the move toward increased testing (Shapiro, 1998). It also paved the way for George W. Bush's No Child Left Behind policy, examined earlier, which called for even more standards and testing than Clinton had envisioned (U.S. Department of Education, 2002). Bush, in essence, gave the same rationale for his education policy as Clinton had given for his: The achievement gap had to be eradicated.

There is no question that Clinton and Bush have both concluded that a decentralized system breeds inequality. The question that emerges from both of their policies is whether in the name of equality, the United States is now headed toward having a much more centralized system of education. For the moment, both Clinton and Bush assert that this is not so. We probably will not know the full answer for decades. Nevertheless, the possibility is real. John Coleman (2000) notes that "education . . . is becoming increasingly nationalized as an issue" (p. 164); and, consequently, greater centralization seems inevitable. Many factors, including national dialogue, parental frustrations, teachers' unions, national reports, and a slow-growing economy, have all contributed to the nationalization of the educational dialogue.

The reality is that there is presently a powerful degree of momentum in the direction of increased standardization and testing. There is little reason to think this trend will change any time soon. For the moment, many political leaders feel they must either choose decentralized system or greater equality, and for the foreseeable future, they have chosen greater equality.

The Democratic Party also initiated other reforms, including Clinton's attempt to reduce the student-teacher ratio by using federal funds to hire more teachers (Guth, 2000; McLarty et al., 2001). This initiative came out of the belief that children perform better when they are in smaller class sizes because they receive more individual attention. Reducing class sizes in this way would require considerable federal expense. On one hand, many educators supported this initiative because in the United States, there is a correlation between class size and student achievement (Guth, 2000; McLarty, et al., 2001). However, many social scientists believed that although Clinton's intentions were good, the education money could be spent in better ways (Hanushek, 1995; Woessmann & West, 2002). They asserted that based on international and national data combined, the relationship between class size and achievement was not that strong (Hanushek, 1995; Woessmann & West, 2002). Clinton (1995) also propounded the Gun-Free Schools Act, designed to reduce acts of gun violence, which had become more frequent in the nation's schools (Coleman, 2004).

Finally, another educational trend resulted from both Republican and Democratic initiatives of this era, an increased engagement in education at the state level. A good deal of this development can be attributed to President Reagan's efforts at creating a "New Federalism," which encouraged more self-governance at the state level (Busch, 2001; Conlan, 1988). Reagan's belief was that encouraging states to become more active in initiating reforms was more efficient and more congruent with what the framers of the Constitution had originally intended (Busch, 2001; Conlan, 1988). In many respects, President Clinton continued this emphasis on encouraging states to undertake educational reform initiatives, such as school choice at the public school level (McLarty et al., 2001).

THE POLITICAL ATMOSPHERE TODAY

The initiatives presented in this chapter are indicative of the fact that especially since 1980, education has earned a central place in the nation's political dialogue (McLarty et al., 2001; Manno, 1995). On the whole, this is probably a positive development. Many educators are now more content because politicians juxtapose educational quality with some of the most essential contemporary policies, including economic prosperity, alleviating crime, and fighting poverty (McLarty et al., 2001; Manno, 1995). However, one should also acknowledge that the new place of centrality that education possesses also translates into a politicizing of the educational debate. Teachers' unions and parents' groups, in particular, are becoming active political entities that are often at odds philosophically (Liebermann, 1997; Loveless, 2000). Each espouses a perspective that sometimes approaches an assertion that if one is a true teacher or parent, one should advocate a particular political view. Although this is understandable, it introduces the risk of prompting politicians to act out of political expediency rather than considering what is educationally productive (Liebermann, 1997; Loveless, 2000). Nevertheless, one can only hope that the primacy that education now enjoys in the political sphere will translate into reasoned judgments and responsible decisions that will make a stronger United States of America.

CONCLUSION

Both political parties have made contributions to education that are either clearly positive or more controversial. Even though, from the contemporary American standpoint, the controversial actions may be more numerous than the clearly enlightened ones, we should also recall that many of the most long-lasting and influential educational movements also started off as controversial. The final analysis of the Republican and Democratic initiatives of the last 25 years will not be written for some time to come.

DISCUSSION QUESTIONS

1. Most Americans treasure the notion of individualism as much as any nation in the world. Not surprisingly, people from other countries believe that Americans often prize individualism to the detriment of the good of society. Most trends in American society as a whole are toward greater individualism. However, some argue that with the government's insistence on setting nationwide standards and its reluctance to allow a broad program of school choice, American education is going in the direction of being less individualistic. Why is American education going in the direction opposite that of American society on this issue? Is more individualism good or bad in education and society as a whole?

2. Some educators argue that the technological and Internet revolution will change college education to such a degree that distance education (education over the Internet) will become the standard practice and that eventually most college classes will not involve going to class. Do you agree or disagree with this perception?

3. Do you think that the best educational ideas emerge by combining the perspectives of both political parties, or from each political party working primarily among its own members? Why?

4. Some educators claim that with all the changes that take place in society, children will always need the basics or fundamentals of education. Do you agree or disagree with this statement? Why?

REFERENCES

Bell, T. H. (1988). *The thirteenth man: A Reagan cabinet memoir*. New York: Free Press.

Boyer, E. (1995). *The basic school*. Princeton, NJ: Carnegie Foundation.

Bracey, G. (2003). The 13th Bracey report on the condition of public education. *Phi Beta Kappan, 85,* 148–164.

Bradley, A. (1994). Student-achievement gains in Philadelphia charter schools. *Education Week, 13*(28), 10.

Bryk, A., Lee, V., & Holland, P. (1993). *Catholic schools and the common good*. Cambridge, MA: Harvard University Press.

Busch, A. (2001). *Ronald Reagan and the politics of freedom*. Lanham, MD: Rowman & Littlefield.

Bush, G. (1989). *Building a better America*. Washington, DC: U.S. Government Printing Office.

Chubb, J. E., & Moe, T. M. (1990). *Politics, markets, and America's schools.* Washington, DC: Brookings Institution.

Clinton, B. (1995). *Proposed legislation: The Gun-Free Zones Amendments Act of 1995.* Washington, DC: U.S. Government Printing Office.

Coleman, J., Hoffer, T., & Kilgore, S. (1982). *High school achievement: Public, Catholic, and private schools compared.* New York: Basic Books.

Coleman, J. J. (2000). Clinton and the party system in historical perspective. In S. E. Schier (Ed.), *The postmodern Presidency: Bill Clinton's legacy in U.S. politics* (pp. 145–166). Pittsburgh, PA: University of Pittsburgh Press.

Coleman, L. (2004). *The copycat effect.* New York: Paraview.

Colopy, K. W., & Tarr, H. C. (1994). *Minnesota's public school options.* Washington, DC: Policy Studies Associates.

Conciatore, J. (1990). Nation's report card shows little progress: Black students close gap. *Black Issues in Higher Education, 6*(22), 30–31.

Conlan, T. J. (1988). *New federalism.* Washington, DC: Brookings Institution.

Cooperman, P. (1985). A nation at risk. In B. Gross & R. Gross (Eds.), *The great school debate.* New York: Simon & Schuster.

Doerr, E., & Menendez, A J. (1991). *Church schools and public money.* Buffalo, NY: Prometheus.

Edwards, C., Hawley, J., Hayes, L., & Turner, C. (1989). *Federal funding priorities under the Bush administration.* Arlington, VA: Government Information Services.

Finch, L. W. (1989). Choice: Claims of success, predictions of failure. *Education Digest, 55,* 12–15.

Finn, C. E. Jr. (2002). Leaving many children behind. *The Weekly Standard, 7*(47), 26.

Gardner, W. (2003, October 4). History lesson: Schools' golden age is a myth. *Los Angeles Times,* p. B21.

Garrett, M. (2005). *The enduring revolution.* New York: Crown Forum.

Gewirtz, S., Ball, S., & Bowe, R. (1995). *Markets, choice, and equity in education.* Buckingham, UK: Open University.

Goodman, K. S. (1989). Whole language research: Foundations and development. *Elementary School Journal, 90,* 207–221.

Goodman, K. S. (1992). Why whole language is today's agenda in education. *Language Arts, 69,* 354–363.

Green, M. (2000, October). *Jesse Jackson's education amendment: Don't drink the water.* New Visions Commentary paper. Washington, DC: National Center for Public Policy Research.

Green, S. R. (2001). Closing the achievement gap: Lessons learned and challenges ahead. *Teaching and Change, 8,* 215–224.

Greene, J. P., Peterson, P. E., Du, J., Boeger, L., Frazier, C. L. (1996, August 30). *The effectiveness of school choice in Milwaukee: A secondary analysis of data from the programs of evaluation.* Paper presented at the annual meeting of the American Political Science Association, San Francisco.

Greene, J. P., & Winters, M. A. (2006). The effect of residential school choice on public high school graduation rates. *Peabody Journal of Education, 81,* 203–216.

Guth, J. L. (2000). Clinton impeachment and the culture wars. In S. E. Schier (Ed.), *The postmodern Presidency: Bill Clinton's legacy in U.S. politics* (pp. 203–222). Pittsburgh, PA: University of Pittsburgh Press.

Hanushek, E. A. (1995). Moving beyond spending fetishes. *Educational Leadership 53*(3), 60–64.

Harman, D. (1987). *Illiteracy: A national dilemma.* New York: Cambridge Books.

Harvey, D. H. (2000). The public's view of Clinton. In S. E. Schier (Ed.), *The postmodern Presidency: Bill Clinton's legacy in U.S. politics* (pp. 124–142). Pittsburgh, PA: University of Pittsburgh Press.

Haycock, K. (2001). Closing the achievement gap. *Educational Leadership, 58*(6), 6–11.

Haycock, K., & Jerald, C. (2002). Closing the achievement gap. *Principal, 82*(2), 20–23.

Hedges, L. V., & Nowell, A. (1999). Changes in the Black-White gap in achievement test scores. *Sociology of Education, 72*(2), 111–135.

Howe, H. (1995). In J. F. Jennings (Ed.), *National issues in education: Elementary and Secondary Education Act* (5th ed.). Bloomington, IN: Phi Delta Kappan.

Howell, W. G., & Peterson, P. E. (2002). *The education gap: Vouchers and urban schools.* Washington, DC: Brookings Institution.

Irvine, J. J., & Foster, M. (1996). *Growing up African American in Catholic schools.* New York: Teachers College.

Jerald, C., & Haycock, K. (2002). Closing the gap. *School Administrator, 59*(7), 16, 18, 20, 22.

Jeynes, W. (2000). Assessing school choice: A balanced perspective. *Cambridge Journal of Education, 30*, 223–241.

Jeynes, W. (2002). Educational policy and the effects of attending a religious school on the academic achievement of children. *Educational Policy, 16*, 406–424.

Jeynes, W., & Littell, S. (2000). A meta-analysis of studies examining the effect of whole language instruction on the literacy of low-SES students. *Elementary School Journal, 101*(1), 21–33.

Jones, L. V. (1984). White-Black achievement differences: The narrowing gap. *American Psychologist, 39*, 1207–1213.

Kearns, D., & Doyle, D. (1989). *Winning the brain race.* San Francisco: ICS Press.

Kirkpatrick, D. W. (1990). *Choice in schooling.* Chicago: Loyola University Press.

Liebermann, M. (1997). *The teacher unions: How the NEA and AFT sabotage reform and hold students, parents, teachers, and taxpayers hostage to bureaucracy.* New York: Free Press.

Loveless, T. (2000). *Conflicting missions? Teachers unions and school reform.* Washington, DC: Brookings Institution.

Manno, B. V. (1995). Reinventing education in the image of the Great Society. In J. F. Jennings (5th ed.). *National issues in education: Elementary and Secondary Education Act* (pp. 3–54). Bloomington, IN: Phi Delta Kappan.

McCabe, J. (2003). *The wasted years: American youth, race, and the literacy gap.* Lanham, MD: Scarecrow Press.

McLanahan, S., & Sandefur, G. (1994). *Growing up with a single parent: What hurts, what helps.* Cambridge, MA: Harvard University Press.

McLarty, T. F., Panetta, L., Bowles, E. B., & Podesta, J. D. (2001). *A record of accomplishment.* Little Rock, AR: William J. Clinton Foundation.

Minutaglio, B. (1999). *First son: George W. Bush and the Bush family dynasty.* New York: Random House.

Moranto, R., & Coppetto, L. (2004). The politics behind Bush's No Child Left Behind initiative. In B. Hilliard, T. Lansford, & R. P. Watson (Eds.), *George W. Bush: Evaluating the president at midterm* (pp. 105–119). Albany: SUNY Press.

National Commission on Excellence in Education. (1983). *A nation at risk.* Washington, DC: Author.

National Education Association of the United States, Commission on the Reorganization of Secondary Education. (1918). *Cardinal principles of secondary education: A report of the Commission on the Reorganization of Secondary Education.* Washington, DC: U.S. Government Printing Office.

National Education Association of the United States, Committee of Ten on Secondary School Studies. (1893). *Report of the Committee [of ten] on secondary school studies appointed at the meeting of the National Educational Association, July 9, 1892, with the reports of the conferences arranged by this committee and held December 28–30, 1892.* Washington, DC: U.S. Government Printing Office.

Neu, B., & Hale, W. (2000). Supervising emergency credential teachers. *Thrust for Educational Leadership, 29*(3), 38–39.

Office of Educational Research and Improvement. (2001). *Implications of the No Child Left Behind Act of 2001 for education.* Washington, DC: Author.

Pardey, D. (1991). *Marketing for schools.* London: Kogan Page.

Payzant, T. W., & Levin, J. (1995). Improving America's schools for children with the greatest need. In J. F Jennings (Ed.), *National issues in education: Elementary and Secondary Education Act* (pp. 55–75). Bloomington, IN: Phi Delta Kappan.

Perrone, V. (1991). On standardized testing. *Childhood Education, 67*(3), 131–142.

Peterson, P. E., Greene, J. P., & Noyes, C. (1996). School choice in Milwaukee. *Public Interest, 125,* 38–56.

Phi Beta Kappa/Gallup Poll. (2002). *School Choice Poll.* Princeton, NJ; Gallup.

Podair, J. E. (2002). *The strike that changed New York.* New Haven, CT: Yale University Press.

Poswick-Goodwin, S. (2003, February). Sizing up the ESEA. *California Educator,* pp. 7–19.

Powell, S. D. (1999). Teaching to the test. *High School Magazine, 6*(5), 34–37.

Ravitch, D. (1974). *The great school wars.* New York: Basic Books.

Reagan, R. (1983). Foreword. In R. Reagan, W. Bennett, & E. W. LeFever (Eds.), *Reinvigorating our schools.* Washington, DC: Ethics and Public Policy Center.

Riley, R. (2002). Education reform through standards and partnerships. *Phi Delta Kappan, 83,* 700–707.

Ritter, G. W., & Lucas, C. J. (2003). Puzzled states. *Education Next, 3*(4), 54–61.

Rouse, C. E. (2004). Private school vouchers and student achievement: An evaluation of the Milwaukee parental choice program. In *Efficiency, competition, and policy, the Elgar Reference Collection* (pp. 320–369). Cheltenham, UK: Elgar.

Sarason, S. B. (1999). Charters: The next flawed reform? *School Administrator, 56*(7), 32–34.

Shanker, A. (1996). AFT endorsement. *Teacher Magazine, 8*(1), 8.

Shapiro, S. (1998). Clinton and education: Policies without meaning. In S. Shapiro & D. E. Purpel (Eds.), *Critical social issues in American education: Transformation in a post-modern world* (pp. 44–45). Mahwah, NJ: Lawrence Erlbaum.

Slavin, R. E., & Madden, N. A. (2001, April). *Reducing the gap: Education for all and the achievement of African American and Latino students.* Paper presented at the annual meeting of the American Educational Research Association, Seattle, WA.

Smith, M. S., Scoll, B. W., & Plisko, V. W. (1995). Improving America's Schools Act: A new partnership. In J. F. Jennings (Ed.), *National issues in education: Elementary and Secondary Education Act* (pp. 3–17). Bloomington, IN: Phi Delta Kappan.

Spring, J. (1997). *The American school 1642–1996.* New York: Longman.

Stahl, S. A. (2001). Teaching phonics and phonological awareness. In S. B. Neuman & D. K. Dickinson (Eds.), *Handbook of early literacy research* (pp. 333–347). New York: Guilford Press.

Sykes, C. J. (1995). *Dumbing down our kids.* New York: St. Martin's Press.

Tatalovich, R., & Frendreis, J. (2000). Clinton, class, and economic policy. In S. E. Schier (Ed.), *The post-modern presidency: Bill Clinton's legacy in U.S. politics* (pp. 41–59). Pittsburgh, PA: University of Pittsburgh Press.

U.S. Census Bureau. (2001). *Census 2000.* Washington, DC: Author.

U.S. Department of Education. (2000). *Digest of education statistics.* Washington, DC: Author.

U.S. Department of Education. (2002). *No Child Left Behind.* Washington, DC: Author.

U.S. Department of Education. (2004). *Digest of education statistics.* Washington, DC: Author.

Walberg, H. J. (1986). What works in a nation still at risk. *Educational Leadership, 44*(1), 7–10.

Wilson, K. G., & Daviss, B. (1994). *Redesigning education.* New York: Holt.

Witte, J. (1999). The Milwaukee voucher experiment: The good, the bad, and the ugly. *Phi Delta Kappan, 81,* 59–64.

Witte, J. (2000). Selective reading is hardly evidence. *Phi Delta Kappan, 81,* 391.

Witte, J. F., & Thorn, C. (1996). Who chooses voucher and interdistrict choice programs in Milwaukee? *American Journal of Education, 104,* 186–217.

Woessmann, L., & West, M. R. (2002). *Class-size effects in school systems around the world: Evidence from between-grade variation in TIMSS.* Cambridge, MA: Harvard University.

Woods, P. A., Bagley, C., & Glatter, R. (1998). *School choice and competition: Markets in the public interest?* London: Routledge.

Yeagley, R. (2003). The demands of data under NCLB. *School Administrator, 60*(11), 22–25.

Zak, M. (2000). Back to the basics for the Republican Party. Chicago: Zak.

C H A P T E R 1 5

Other Recent Educational
Issues and Reforms

As education has moved well into the 21st century, it stands in a place of centrality that means that schooling has become the subject of many reform initiatives and controversial issues. Although these reforms and issues frequently vary considerably from each other, the gamut of topics is a reminder of the extent to which the influence of educational events is pervasive and that school issues are inextricably connected with the welfare of youth and national health.

Equalization of school funding represents one of the most intriguing of these topics, particularly since about half of the states in the union have implemented equalization requirements (Education Trust, 2002; Quade, 1996). Perhaps the most publicized set of educational events in recent years has been the series of school shootings that has afflicted dozens of suburban and rural schools beginning in 1996. Probably the most important questions related to these events involve how they can be stopped (Coleman, 2004; Matera, 2001). A growing list of schools has inaugurated policies that require students to wear uniforms in order to combat socially undesirable behavior (Starr, 2000; Brunsma, 2004). Some school officials claim the donning of uniforms accomplishes the desired goals, but skeptics are not quite so sure (Starr, 2000; Brunsma, 2004).

In recent years, educators have also become aware of the primacy of the family in affecting educational outcomes and the need to learn from foreign systems of education (Jeynes, 2002, 2003, 2005a; Stevenson & Stigler, 1992). Many social scientists aver that American educators need to learn and apply certain principles from each of these fields in order to maximize educational efficiency (Jeynes, 2002, 2003, 2005a; Stevenson & Stigler, 1992).

Issues regarding the implementation of teaching practices related to technology will also play a prominent role in future curricular instruction (Cuban, 2001; LeFevre, 2004; Shapiro, 2004; Wilson, 2004). Teachers who use technology in an efficacious way will enhance the preparedness of future graduates.

EQUALIZATION OF SCHOOL EXPENDITURES

Currently, in U.S. schools, wealthy school districts (defined as the 75th percentile) spend about $900 more per student than schools in poor school districts (defined as the 25th percentile) (Education Trust, 2002). The difference is even greater at the most extreme parts of the distribution (Education Trust, 2002). In the United States, where equality is regarded as one of the highest virtues, such a state of affairs seems intolerable (Yinger, 2004). This type of inequality appears to discriminate against the poor.

The push for equalization of funding was first made in the early 1970s (Benson, 1975). The primary argument for this was as a matter of justice and that in order to more effectively battle poverty, public school expenditures should be equalized so that each school spends the same amount per student as other schools (Benson, 1975).

The primary reason for differences in educational spending per student can be traced to the fact that local property taxes are such a major source of educational revenue (Benson, 1975; Guthrie, 1975). Under plans of equalization, some property tax income from wealthy districts would be redistributed to poorer schools and districts so that school-funding equalization can be achieved (Benson, 1975; Guthrie, 1975). As an issue of justice, one can certainly see why school funding should be equalized within each state. However, there are some issues that may make the implementation more difficult and produce less impressive results that one might want ideally.

In one sense, equalization of funding has similar qualities to school choice. Some educators believe that if the United States will simply promote school programs to include private schools, the education system will be saved. There are some who feel the same way about equalization of school expenditures. However, just as there are practical issues that would likely limit the effectiveness of school choice, there are factors that make the application of equalization of school funding either more difficult or less efficacious than it otherwise would be.

First, it is far more difficult than it might seem to determine what is fair and equal. To illustrate this fact, let us imagine for a moment a situation that is reasonably close to reality. Let us say that among public schools, an urban public school spends $6,800 per student, a suburban school spends $7,800 per student, and a rural school spends $5,800 per student. One might argue that in order to equalize funding among these schools, each should receive about $6,800 per student and all would be resolved. However, the solution is not that facile. Some schools spend more than others for such things as hiring security guards in high-crime areas, having a larger proportion of special education children than most schools, having a higher percentage of high school students than most districts, and having more acts of vandalism done against the school building, books, and so forth (Benson, 1975; Guthrie, 1975; Quade, 1996). One might also argue that different levels of teacher salary might be needed for certain situations. For example, there are certain rural areas in the desert, in mountainous areas, or in extremely remote regions in which a school would need to offer more money to teachers simply because few people would want to move there. It would also likely take a more generous monetary offer to attract teachers to a high-crime area. Many cities recognize this fact and therefore offer teachers more money to come to such areas (Yinger, 2004). Guthrie (1975) points out that to ensure true equality and fairness, different types of students and situations would have to receive different weighting. For example, special education and high school students require more money than typical elementary school students (Guthrie, 1975). Issues regarding the destruction of school buildings are especially touchy, because under an equalization plan, some people and schools might resent paying for vandalism perpetuated at a distant school that might have been done by the students of that school. There might be some disagreement about what is fair in such circumstances. Gloria Ladson-Billings (2000, p. 208) addresses the issue of whether "equality means sameness" to some degree, asserting that the two are not identical concepts. However, even if one agrees that two concepts are not the same, determining equality becomes very subjective if there is not some element of equity.

Second, even if equalization of school spending is the right thing to do, it probably will not have the effect of reducing the achievement gap between rich and poor. There are two reasons for this. The first reason is that in states that have equalized school funding (a total of 24), there has been very little reduction in the achievement gap (Downes, 2004; Flanagan & Murray, 2004). The second reason is that there is not a very strong relationship between state expenditure per student and student performance on academic tests. There is somewhat of a positive correlation, but it is quite modest (U.S. Department of Education, 2003). If one examines the educational expenditures per student and achievement in the 50 states plus the District of Columbia, one finds some interesting facts. For example, of these 51 entities, Washington, D.C., spends the most per student (U.S. Department of Education, 2003). And yet Washington, D.C., ranks 51st, or last, in academic achievement (U.S. Department of Education, 2003). Similarly, Utah ranks 51st in expenditures per student but usually ranks in the top six academically (U.S. Department of Education, 2003). Although virtually all Americans would like to see the achievement gap reduced, it is unlikely that equalization would have the impact that its advocates desire.

Third, early indications are that states that have equalized funding may have residents who are less willing to have their taxes raised in order to support schools (Yinger, 2004). That is, it may be that residents in more prosperous areas of these states are less willing to be taxed more, because nearly all the money will go to students in other areas of the state (Cullen & Loeb, 2004; Yinger, 2004).

The Movement Toward Equalized Funding

Although equalized school funding probably will not raise the educational outcomes of poor districts very much, one can argue that the country should implement equalization as a matter of fairness. The issue of fairness in school funding became especially apparent in 1971, when, in the case of *Serrano v. Priest,* the California Supreme Court ruled that the state's system of financing was unfair. The court ruled that California relied too much on property taxes to finance education, creating a degree of inequality that violated the California constitution (Yinger, 2004). The significance of the *Serrano v. Priest* decision is that it opened up the door for equalization cases being decided on the basis of provisions in state constitutions (Yinger, 2004). As a result, on the basis of the *Serrano* decision, dozens of states heard similar cases. However, at the U.S. Supreme Court level, the results were quite different. In the case of *San Antonio Independent School District v. Rodriguez* (1973), the U.S. Supreme Court concluded that "similar disparities in the Texas school system did not violate the federal equal protection clause" (Lukemeyer, 2004, p. 60). The significance of the

San Antonio decision is that it forced plaintiffs to take their cases to the state level rather than to the federal courts (Lukemeyer, 2004). In 18 cases, State Supreme Courts have upheld the existing educational finance systems; however, many states have had their finance systems declared unconstitutional (Yinger, 2004).

State-based equalization battles still continue, although they are usually initiated in conjunction with other educational goals as well. One example took place in California in what is now called the "Williams lawsuit" (California League of Middle Schools, 2004). The Williams lawsuit claimed that California schools were not only unequal in their funding, but were underfunded in even many wealthy districts. Without admitting wrongful distribution of funds, the state of California settled with the plaintiffs and developed a plan to further equalize funding and increase funding across the state districts (California League of Middle Schools, 2004).

Should the United States Equalize Funding?

Even though equalization of funding is unlikely to have much of an effect on either educational outcomes in urban areas or on the achievement gap, as an issue of fairness, the nation will probably continue to move in the direction of equalization. The Education Trust (2002) reports that low-poverty districts spend between $900 and $1,000 more per student than high-poverty districts. It would seem that as an issue of fairness, this gap should be reduced.

To be sure, there are potential pitfalls to implementing equalization policies. For an equalization policy to work, people in affluent areas need to act altruistically, and the state political leadership needs to be dedicated to school improvement (Benson, 1975; Yinger, 2004). Indeed, Hoxby (2001) asserts that pecunious and upper-middle-class parents will send their children to private schools rather than see their tax money depart from their own children's education.

Nevertheless, there are definite advantages to equalization of school funding. In addition to creating a more equitable school system, Benson (1975) claimed that it would "encourage state governments to take the matter of raising productivity in education seriously" (p. 10). Furthermore, school-funding equalization may have a mild impact of increasing the property values of rural and inner-city homes and decreasing the value of suburban homes. Naturally, we do not know what the full effect of equalization would be, but the nation is clearly moving in that direction. No one argues for equalization of funding for all the nation's schools, because the variation in the cost of living is so great across the country. However, many educators support school-funding equalization within states. Only time will tell how far the country will go in the direction of equalization.

SCHOOL SHOOTINGS

Beginning in 1996, Americans across the country were alarmed to hear of many incidents of horrifying shootings initiated by youngsters in public schools in primarily suburban and rural areas across the country (Coleman, 2004).

It should be pointed out that the problem of school shootings did not begin in 1996. In reality, school shootings have been common since the 1960s in urban areas (Kopka, 1997).

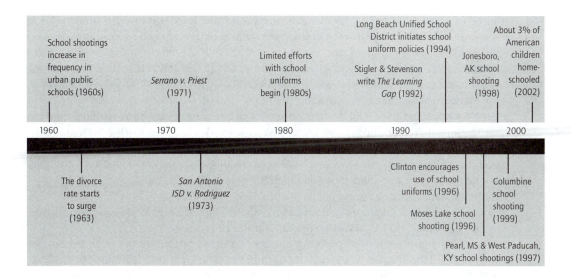

Urbanites are quick to point this out and often resent the fact that many Americans believe that the school shooting rampage began in 1996. Urbanites complain that there is a sense that when a shooting occurs in an urban area, people respond by saying, "Well, that's too bad. But that's just Philadelphia (or some other urban area) for you." However, when the same people hear that a shooting has occurred in a suburban or rural setting, they say, "Oh, my goodness, what is this world coming to! How could this happen?" As a result of this propensity, the American public did not become aware of the school shooting quandary until the late 1990s.

Although 1996 was not the first year of school shootings, it was the time these events came to suburban and rural America. On February 2, 1996, Barry Loukaitis, a 14-year-old from Moses Lake, Washington, killed two students and a math teacher. Loukaitis claimed he was greatly influenced by the Stephen King novel *Rage,* about a school killing (Coleman, 2004). He even quoted the book at the time of the killing, saying, "It sure beats algebra, doesn't it?" Loukaitis also stated that he was influenced by Pearl Jam's video *Jeremy,* as well as the movies *Natural Born Killers,* by Oliver Stone, and *Basketball Diaries* (Coleman, 2004). Coleman notes, "Today, Stephen King says he wishes that he had never written *Rage*" (p. 4).

In Beth, Alaska, Evan Ramsey said he thought it would be "cool" to gun down people and then proceeded to shoot his principal and a classmate (Matera, 2001). In October of 1997, in Pearl, Mississippi, a boy who was a Satan worshipper and was enraged at his former girl-friend stabbed his brother to death and killed the ex-girlfriend and another student. He was a member of a gang called "the Kroth."

In late 1997 and the first half of 1998, the school rampages continued. In West Paducah, Kentucky, on December 1, 1997, Michael Carneal barged in on a prayer meeting before school and shot 8 students, killing 3 (Matera, 2001). One of the most publicized shootings before the Columbine incident was in March 1998, in Jonesboro, Arkansas. At this locale, two boys, ages 11 and 14, opened fire on students, killing 4 classmates and a teacher and wounding 10 other students (Matera, 2001). The boys stated that their motive was that they wanted to scare people. This incident received a tremendous amount of publicity for a number of reasons: its occurrence in the open air where the carnage could easily be televised, the disturbing nature of the children's motives, and the extent of the injuries.

Some social scientists hypothesize that the extent to which the media covered the Jonesboro massacre resulted in the "copycat effect" (Coleman, 2004). The day after this incident, a student shot himself in Coldwater, Michigan, and 6 days after the Jonesboro incident, a female student in Chapel Hill, North Carolina, shot herself. Furthermore, within 2 months after the Jonesboro shooting, three major shootings took place. On April 24, 1998, a boy shot his teacher. On May 19th, in Fayetteville, Tennessee, a boy shot another boy who had dated his ex-girlfriend. On May 21st, a boy in Springfield, Oregon, killed one student, wounded 23 others, and then shot and killed his parents.

Other school shootings occurred in Stamps, Arkansas; Conyers, Georgia; Deming, New Mexico; Fort Gibson, Oklahoma; Mount Morris Township, Michigan; El Cajon, California; Santee, California; and Lake Worth, Florida (Matera, 2001).

The most infamous school shooting episode occurred at Columbine High School, in Littleton, Colorado (Brown & Merritt, 2002; Carlston, 2004; Scott & Nimmo, 2000; Zoba, 2000). In April 1999, Eric Harris and Dylan Kliebold exploded 30 bombs and blasted 188 shots, resulting in the death of 15 students and the wounding of 14 others (Matera, 2001). Their hideous acts actually fell well short of their goal because two massive 20-pound propane bombs in the cafeteria failed to detonate. Had they succeeded, "authorities believe that 488 people in the bustling lunchroom would have perished, as well as 56 who were quietly studying in the library one floor above" (Matera, 2001, p. 2). Harris and Kliebold had 76 hand-made pipe bombs and a vast array of semiautomatic guns and shotguns.

Perhaps the most amazing aspect of the Columbine massacre is that there were so many warning signs to which people should have responded. Harris had a Web site that declared his beliefs and intentions. On it, Harris stated, "My belief is that if I say something, it goes. I am the law, if you don't like it you die. If I don't like you or I don't like what you want me to do, you die" (as cited in Brown & Merritt, 2002, p. 84). He also stated, "I will rig up explosives all over a town and detonate each of them at will after I mow down the whole [expletive] area" (as cited in Scott & Nimmo, 2000, p. 150). Harris wrote in Dylan's handbook, "God I can't wait until they die. I can taste the blood now. . . . You know what I hate? MANKIND! Kill everything. . . . Kill everything" (as cited in Brown & Merritt, 2002, p. 94).

Like most of the students involved in school shootings, Harris and Kliebold loved the music of Marilyn Manson and played violent video games. Football players also bullied them. In addition, Harris had been hurt by a girl he had once dated, and he sought revenge against her. One student said, "Eric held grudges and never let them go" (Brown & Merritt, 2002, p.75).

Since Columbine, there has been an increase in the number of school shootings planned but a decrease in the number of those succeeding (Matera, 2001; Coleman, 2004). The failure of several planned attacks is due largely to increased vigilance by school authorities, the FBI, and the police. Some of the plans, if successful, would have made the Columbine shootings seem meager. For example, officers of the law intercepted an e-mail the day before a planned series of multiple explosions and shootings that, if successful, would have blown up an entire school in New Bedford, Massachusetts, in 2001 (Newman, 2004).

Reasons for the Shootings

Those who instigated these crimes were clearly disturbed and angry people, but the causes of their emotional instability varied (Brown & Merritt, 2002; Coleman, 2004; Matera, 2001; Newman, 2004). Many of the students were infatuated with guns and violence. Some were bullied or teased. Others recently had girlfriends break up with them. Others received failing grades at school. Some of the students simply wanted to scare people and get reactions. Generally speaking, the habits of the shooters had more commonalities than their experiences. The students tended to idolize guns and listened to and watched media that condoned violence. However, Newman (2004) notes that all the individuals tended to be low on the totem poll of the student hierarchy.

How Widespread Is Juvenile Violence and Crime?

The school shootings that have gained so much publicity since 1997 have caused Americans to take a closer look at the extent of juvenile violence and crime. As mentioned earlier, it is unfortunate that it took these rural and suburban massacres to inform parents of the problem, when, in reality, the increase in school and teenage violence really began to surge in the 1960s, though these incidents were almost exclusively in urban areas (Kopka, 1997). Consequently, many Americans shrugged off the significance of such incidents by stating that events like this happened only in "bad" areas, and then often proceeded to move to the suburbs (Kopka, 1997).

Teenagers are generally not as malicious as they are portrayed to be on the evening news, nor are most schools as hazardous as they are sometimes depicted. Nevertheless, there are some troubling statistics. First, there are generally over 400,000 incidents of crime per year on America's school campuses (Burns et al., 1998). Research studies differ on whether or not schools are safer than homes and communities (Centers for Disease Control and Prevention, 1989; Snyder & Sickmund, 1995). Nevertheless, this debate is largely irrelevant, because many conflicts that begin on campus are resolved off school grounds. Juvenile crime has considerable deleterious effects wherever it might occur. In 1998, school campuses reported 253,000 serious violent crimes, defined as aggravated assault, against students (Kaufman et al., 2000). The National Education Association estimates that each school day, 160,000 students miss school in order to avoid other students who wish to do them physical harm (Lal, Lal, & Achilles, 1993).

Evidence suggests that the greater predictors of whether it is likely that there will be violence on a school campus are the presence of gangs in the school and whether drug pushers disseminate drugs in school (Kaufman et al., 2000; Lal et al., 1993). This is especially troubling because as early as the eighth grade, 11% of American school children admit they are in gangs, and that percentage is much higher if one examines just boys in the sample (Esbensen & Deschenes, 1998). In addition, about one third of American students state that drug pushers have either sold or offered them illegal drugs on campus (Kaufman et al., 2000). Although school shootings are rare, violence in the schools and disciplinary problems are common.

President Clinton's Gun-Free Schools Act, discussed in Chapter 14, was designed to inaugurate a zero-tolerance policy toward student possession of guns and other weapons (Clinton, 1995; Coleman, 2004). Schools became much more aggressive in implementing this policy once the school shootings became more common in the suburbs starting in 1996 (Casella,

2003; Coleman, 2004). However, social scientists are mixed in their assessment of this zero-tolerance policy. Some of them claim that it reduces school violence, but others assert that it indiscriminately results in the expulsion of countless youth; for example, one whose parents accidentally drop a kitchen knife in the car that school officials later find (Casella, 2003).

Possible Solutions to School Shootings

Two of the most common solutions to school shootings that social scientists and national leaders propose are gun control and moral education. There is no question that there are a lot of guns in the United States. In fact, although estimates vary, there are about as many guns as people in the nation (Gahr, 2002). Guns are relatively easy to obtain, and, on this basis, many people argue that the nation needs stricter gun control laws. However, others argue that there are already laws on the books that should have prevented these adolescents from procuring guns (Armstrong, 2002). Despite this fact, each of these students obtained guns. In fact, Eric Harris even made a video in which he proclaimed that gun laws could not have stopped him from obtaining guns (Scott & Nimmo, 2000). Gun control might well curb adult crime, but it is less certain whether gun control would reduce adolescent crime.

Another suggestion is to reintroduce moral education in the schools. When moral education had a much more prominent role in American education, teachers taught more actively about love, the Golden Rule, forgiveness, managing anger, and not picking on anyone who is different for any reason (Coleman, 2004). Those who advocate this position believe that increasing the number of metal detectors, zero-tolerance programs, and other initiatives deals only with the symptoms of the problem, when it is the condition of the human heart that must be addressed.

A third suggestion that some educators favor is reducing school size. Virtually all the school shootings occurred at large schools. For example, Columbine High School was greatly expanded to become a school of 2,000 shortly before the shootings (Carlston, 2004). As discussed in Chapter 10, there are also some academic reasons that some educators argue in favor of reducing school size. The issue of how to reduce the school shootings has become a key educational debate as a result of the school violence.

Educational Debate: What Is the Best Solution to Prevent Future School Shootings?

Although all Americans are agreed that more needs to be done to prevent school shootings, there is some disagreement on how to best realize this goal. Some social scientists argue that the nation needs more restrictive gun control laws. However, others argue that the laws presently on the books already prohibit adolescent gun purchases and yet these youth were somehow able to obtain guns. Some educators assert that reducing class size is the solution, especially since the majority of school shootings occurred at large schools. Finally, some social scientists assert that the country needs to return to its pre-1963 practice of a moral education emphasis. In this way, teaching students to forgive, control their anger, and not to bully will become common practices once again. Consequently, these deleterious behaviors will decrease.

SCHOOL UNIFORMS

School uniforms are one of the most popular reforms currently being applied or under consideration by many school districts (Brunsma, 2002). The idea of school uniforms is hardly new. In fact, requiring students to wear uniforms for school was the general practice for many years in many private and public schools across America (Brunsma, 2004). Moreover, it still remains the preferred manner of attire in many nations around the world, many of which based their school system on the Western model (Stevenson & Stigler, 1992). The first use of the school uniform dates back to 1222, when Stephen Langton, then the Archbishop of Canterbury, called for its implementation (Brunsma, 2004). As individualism increasingly became a sacred value, especially during the hippie movement, the practice of wearing school uniforms fell out of favor. In addition, certain American court cases upheld the rights of students to wear to school what they chose. Therefore, schools could not constrain students to wear particular kinds of clothes (Brunsma, 2002, 2004).

Conservatives lamented over the stylistic and legal trends mentioned and claimed that the absence of uniforms would lead to a further deterioration of student self-discipline, already a problem in the 1960s and 1970s (Brunsma, 2002, 2004). Nevertheless, the cultural and legal trends were clear, and the conservatives had to admit defeat.

Surging rates of juvenile crime caused the issue of school uniforms to resurface again. In the late 1970s, the juvenile crime rate had risen to such levels that an adolescent was 32 times as likely as in 1950 to be arrested for committing a crime (Bennett, 1983). Marion Barry, Democratic mayor from Washington, D.C., "began discussing with his administration the possibility of proposing a standardized dress code for D.C.'s public schools" (Brunsma, 2004, p. 14). It was Barry's belief that political leaders needed to take swift action to stem the surge in juvenile crime. In the early to late 1980s, public schools discussed the matter of school uniforms, and, in some cases, there were isolated and limited attempts to initiate such programs (Brunsma, 2004). Naturally, many private schools continued to require school uniforms. However, the first American public school in the last quarter of the 20th century to highly publicize a school uniform code was Cherry Hill Elementary school, in Baltimore, Maryland, in the 1980s (Brunsma, 2004). Via initiatives in the Washington, D.C., and Baltimore area, by the fall of 1988, 23 schools in the Washington-Baltimore area had inaugurated school uniform programs (Starr, 2000; Brunsma, 2004).

The school uniform movement gained considerable momentum when New York City Mayor Ed Koch called for the city to launch a pilot school uniform program (Brunsma, 2004). The mayor of the nation's largest city was now onboard. After Mayor Koch announced his support for school uniforms, many of America's schools initiated uniform programs, including Chicago, Detroit, Los Angeles, Philadelphia, Miami, and others (Brunsma, 2004).

The Long Beach Unified School District (LBUSD) in California became the first entire school district to implement a school uniform policy (Melvin, 1994). The school board unanimously decided that a school uniform policy would be launched for all public schools in Long Beach. The unanimous decision was reached largely because they regarded a previous experimental 5-year, 11-school uniform program to have been a real success (Melvin, 1994).

The board gave the following reasons for LBUSD inaugurating a districtwide uniform policy: (a) to combat gang warfare, since certain colors were associated with certain gangs; (b) to quell competition, theft, and violence over designer clothing; (c) to help students focus on school; and (d) to de-emphasize the existence of economic inequality in the schools (Melvin, 1994).

If Mayor Koch was the source of momentum in the period from 1988 to 1994, it was Republican Governor Pete Wilson of California who provided additional momentum in the fall of 1994. Governor Wilson signed a California bill stating that public schools could require their students to wear uniforms (Brunsma, 2004). Wilson's bill stipulated that children of families who opposed the school uniform policy would still receive an appropriate education (Brunsma, 2004). The bill also stipulated the following: (a) School districts needed to consult with parents, principals, and teachers before they undertook a school uniform policy; (b) schools needed to give parents 6 months' notice; and (c) parents could opt out of any school uniform plan if they showed there was a good reason (Brunsma, 2004).

Long Beach Claims Success

In the years immediately following LBUSD's implementation of their school uniform policy, the district undertook an analysis to see if the program had worked (LBUSD, 2003). By the 1998/1999 school year, district officials reported an 86% drop in school crime, a 93% reduction in sex crimes, and a 73% drop in assault and battery (LBUSD, 2003). Robbery declined 84%, and vandalism fell 93% (LBUSD, 2003). School attendance also rose 93.8% in the 1993/1994 school year to 99% in 1998/999 (LBUSD, 2003). District officials claim that the higher attendance figures reflect that families believed that the schools were now safer (LBUSD, 2003).

School Uniform Programs Greatly Expand

Once preliminary results indicated that the LBUSD uniform plan was a success, President Bill Clinton decided to take action. On February 24, 1996, "Clinton instructed the Department of Education to distribute manuals to the nation's 16,000 school districts advising them how they could legally enforce a school uniform policy" (Brunsma, 2004, p. 20).

The fact that LBUSD had experienced such success and that three of the nation's most powerful politicians (Clinton, Wilson, and Koch) were now onboard catapulted the school uniform movement to center stage. By 1997, many educators estimated that half of the urban districts in the United States had instituted school uniform policies (Melvin, 1994). Eighty percent of Chicago public schools implemented school uniform policies, 66% of Cleveland's public schools, and 60% of Miami's public schools (Brunsma, 2004).

On March 25, 1998, New York City's board of education passed a resolution that allowed more schools to require school uniforms. Consequently, about 72% of the city's elementary schools adopted uniform guidelines (Brunsma, 2004). Philadelphia adopted school uniform guidelines in 2000. The school uniform movement was in full force.

Do School Uniforms Really Help?

On the basis of the statistics regarding reduced crime that LBUSD supplied, one might be tempted to immediately conclude that school uniforms must indeed work. Some schools have reported such results (Brunsma, 2004). However, the debate over this issue is complicated by one major factor. That is, in nearly every case in which schools and their districts adopted school uniform policies, they concurrently implemented other programs that were also designed to reduce crime (Brunsma & Rockquemore, 1998). Among these other programs were parental involvement initiatives and character education programs (Brunsma, 2002, 2004). As a result, it is not clear how much the improvements noted by these schools have been due to school uniform policies and how much they have been due to the implementation of other programs. For example, Brunsma and Rockquemore (1998) compared schools that had school uniform policies versus those schools that did not, using the National Education Longitudinal Study (NELS) of 1988. They found that after controlling for a variety of school-based and individual factors, school uniforms had minimal influence on school outcomes and measures of crime. From these findings, these researchers concluded that school uniforms have no real impact on student behavior (Brunsma & Rockquemore, 1998).

The Brunsma and Rockquemore (1998) study is intriguing because it does use a nation-wide data set and acknowledges that other factors, such as parental involvement and character education, may be acting concurrently with school uniform policies. Nevertheless, the 1988 NELS data set would have predated the implementation of these uniform programs, and this is problematic. In the NELS 1988 data set, private schools had school uniform policies, and public schools did not (U.S. Department of Education, NELS, 1992). The vast majority of private schools are religious in nature, and it is highly unlikely that school uniforms would have much of an impact in schools where the religious culture of the school is regarded as the primary force influencing educational outcomes (Coleman, Hoffer, & Kilgore, 1982; Hoffer, Greeley, & Coleman, 1987). It is therefore highly unlikely that when controlling for variables for religious culture, statistically significant effects for school uniforms would emerge.

The Brunsma and Rockquemore (1998) study therefore has one primary contribution and one outstanding weakness. Its major contribution is that unlike district- and school-based studies that have considered only the implementation of school uniform policies apart from the presence of other programs, this study considers the presence of other variables. However, the Brunsma and Rockquemore (1998) study makes a questionable generalization by assuming that the influence of school uniforms in private schools is the same as one would find in public schools. It is likely that none of the public school uniform programs that have been initiated since the public school uniform movement was launched in the mid-1980s are included in this study. Consequently, it is hard to use the results of this study as a means of contradicting the claims of school districts that assert that school uniform policies produce results.

THE INFLUENCE OF THE FAMILY

There are a number of ways that the family influences school outcomes. Two of those ways will be dealt with here: parental family structure and parental involvement. One needs to remember that when addressing the influence of each of these factors, we are dealing with average effects and that the actual impact varies from one child to another.

Family Structure

Generally speaking, the trend in the influence of family structure is that the further one goes from the biological two-parent family, the greater the extent to which family structure has a downward impact on educational outcomes (Jeynes, 2002; Wallerstein & Kelly, 1980). For example, on average, living in a single-parent divorced family structure does have a downward impact on children's achievement (Jeynes, 2002; Wallerstein & Kelly, 1980). However, residing in a never-married single-parent family structure generally influences achievement even more negatively (Jeynes, 2002). This is because in the case of divorce, marital dissolution usually occurs a considerable time after a child has been born (Jeynes, 2002; Wallerstein & Kelly, 1980). Furthermore, children often continue to have a relationship with the noncustodial parent after the divorce (Hetherington & Jodl, 1994). In the case of a never-married single-parent family structure, the access to the noncustodial second parent is often minimal (Jeynes, 2002), It follows that, on average, children from a never-married single-parent family structure have less access to their parents than in a divorced single-parent family structure (Jeynes, 2002). Consequently, one should not be surprised to find that the never-married single-parent family structure exerts more of a negative impact on achievement than the divorced single-parent family structure (Jeynes, 2002). In addition, single-parent homes account for 85% of young people in prison, 63% of youth suicides, 90% of homeless/runaway children, 85% of children with behavior problems, and 71% of high school dropouts (National Center for Health Statistics, 2003; U.S. Bureau of the Census, 2001).

A second trend in the influence of family structure is that the greater the number of family structure transitions or adjustments a child must go through, the greater the impact on the child (Amato & Ochiltree, 1987; Baydar, 1988; Downey, 1995; Hetherington & Clingempeel, 1992; Hetherington, Stanley-Hagan, & Anderson, 1989). For example, parental divorce or the death of a parent exerts downward pressure on academic achievement, but parental remarriage following each of these events, on average, exerts additional pressure on academic achievement. This is because the addition of a new adult in the house represents an additional transition for the child that requires emotional and psychological adjustment (Amato & Ochiltree, 1987; Baydar, 1988; Downey, 1995; Hetherington & Clingempeel, 1992; Hetherington et al., 1989). Similarly, when one adjusts for socioeconomic status (SES), cohabitation exerts greater pressure on academic achievement than being from a never-married single-parent family (Amato & Ochiltree, 1987; Baydar, 1988; Downey, 1995; Hetherington & Clingempeel, 1992).

Nearly all researchers now understand that children from nonintact families are at an academic and psychological disadvantage compared with children from intact families (Amato & Ochiltree, 1987; Baydar, 1988; Downey, 1995; Hetherington & Clingempeel, 1992; Hetherington et al., 1989). Some years ago, some social scientists debated whether parental remarriage following divorce has a positive or negative overall impact on the children who formerly lived in divorced or widowed single-parent families (Beer, 1992; Coleman & Ganong, 1990; Jeynes, 1998). Some therapists even encouraged parents to remarry for the sake of the children (Beer, 1992; Coleman & Ganong, 1990; Jeynes, 1998). In recent years, however, social scientists have accumulated a sizable amount of evidence indicating that remarriage is indeed a challenging transition for many children (Dawson, 1991; Hetherington & Jodl, 1994; Popenoe, 1994; Zill, 1994; Zill & Nord, 1994).

Many children view the new parental figure as a stranger in their homes (Hetherington & Clingempeel, 1992; Kelly, 1992; Visher & Visher, 1988). Children in reconstituted families often struggle with rivalries with their stepbrothers and stepsisters. Moreover, they may grapple with the suspicion that the stepparent is robbing them of necessary access to their biological parent (Hetherington & Clingempeel, 1992; Kelly, 1992; Walsh, 1992). The presence of a stepparent often reduces the intimacy of the relationship that the children have with the biological parent (Hetherington & Clingempeel, 1992; Walsh, 1992). In addition, remarriage often produces an increased tension between the biological parents, and this fact can have detrimental effects on the psychological well-being of a child (Walsh, 1992). Reconstituted marriages are also less stable and more likely to end in divorce than first-time marriages, and this may have several effects on the child (Booth & Edwards, 1992; Popenoe, 1994). Recent research also indicates that reconstituted families are much more physically mobile than intact families (McLanahan & Sandefur, 1994). Many researchers believe that as a result of these factors, many children from reconstituted homes become frustrated and show a greater tendency to be aggressive, agitated, and unhappy than children from intact families (Nunn, Parish, & Worthing, 1993; Wallerstein & Kelly, 1980). These researchers believe that while some moderating influences may exist in certain families that can lighten the impact of remarriage following divorce (the extent of communication between the stepchild and the stepparent, the length of time a child has lived in a reconstituted family, etc.), it nevertheless has many negative consequences for children (Hetherington & Clingempeel, 1992; Walsh, 1992).

Although a new consensus is developing among social scientists regarding the impact of remarriage on children of divorce, very few principals and teachers are aware of this fact. If indeed America's schools are to be sensitive to children of divorce from reconstituted families, educators must not assume that remarriage following divorce generally benefits children. Educators need to familiarize themselves with the challenges that this large group of children face, in order to make America's schools more effective in reaching out to this "minority" population.

It may be that the cohabitation family structure has the negative impact it does on academic achievement for much the same reason that divorce followed by remarriage and widowhood followed by remarriage generally exert a downward pressure on academic achievement (Jeynes, 2002). First, in many cohabitation relationships, only one of the adults is the child's biological parent (Jeynes, 2002). When this situation occurs, any children living in the household probably face many of the same disadvantages as in any household in which the child has only one biological parent. Even when both biological parents are present, cohabitation often involves a lower level of commitment by the adults to the continuation of family union and to any children that might abide in the household (Forste & Tanfer, 1996; Nock, 1995). Second, in those households in which one of the parents is not the natural parent, the same kind of friction and adjustments that often arise between stepparents and their stepchildren can develop between the child and the nonbiological parent.

Parental Involvement

Parental involvement is another area that has been subject to a great deal of research. For the purpose of this section, *parental involvement* will be defined as the participation of parents in the various dimensions of a child's educational experience, both in establishing the atmosphere of the home and in explicit activities. The modern-day interest in parental involvement grew in part out of the concern with the increasing number of dissolved marriages (Jeynes, 2003, 2005a). Clearly, parental involvement is facilitated when there are two parents rather than one involved in raising a child (Jeynes, 2003, 2005a). Nevertheless, parental involvement has evolved to be an educational topic in its own right, because it is important no matter what a child's family structure is and there are plenty of two-parent families that despite having the potential availability of two adults are nevertheless relatively uninvolved in their children's education.

Many social scientists believe parental involvement is vital to improving educational outcomes. Hara (1998), for example, claims that increased parental involvement is the key to improving the academic achievement of children. Various studies indicate that parental involvement is fundamental in inducing children to excel in school at both the elementary and secondary school levels (Christian, Morrison, & Bryant, 1998; Mau, 1997; McBride & Lin, 1996; Muller, 1998; Singh et al., 1995). Meta-analyses by Jeynes (2003, 2005a) and a study by Singh and colleagues (1995) suggest that the influence of parental involvement may be greater at the elementary school level than at the secondary school. The impact of parental involvement manifests itself in reading achievement (Jeynes, 2003; Shaver & Walls, 1998); mathematics achievement (Muller, 1998; Peressini, 1998; Shaver & Walls, 1998); and in other subjects as well (Jeynes, 2003, 2005a; Zdzinski, 1996).

The impact of parental involvement is so considerable that it holds across all level of parental education, ethnicity, and locale (Bogenschneider, 1997; Deslandes, Royer, Turcotte, & Bertrand, 1997; Griffith, 1996; Hampton, Mumford, & Bond, 1998; Jeynes, 2003, 2005a; Mau, 1997; Villas-Boas, 1998).

Research indicates that parental involvement makes it more likely children will do their homework (Balli, 1998; Balli, Demo, & Wedman, 1998; Villas-Boas, 1998); improve their language skills (Bermudez & Padron, 1990); have low school absentee rates (Nesbitt, 1993); and even have strong musical skills (Zdzinski, 1992). Parental involvement research has been on the increase during the last two decades. Social scientists are giving parental involvement a special place of importance in influencing the academic outcomes of the youth.

LEARNING FROM FOREIGN SYSTEMS OF EDUCATION

There is no question that since the early 1960s, American citizens have been increasingly critical of the American system of education (Stevenson & Stigler, 1992; Wirtz, 1977). The fact that American students generally perform poorly versus their counterparts in other nations, especially in East Asia and Europe, has led some to conclude that the United States should attempt to learn from foreign systems of education, particularly in East Asia (Stevenson & Stigler, 1992). Furthermore, this advantage has grown considerably since the mid-1960s, when American schools fared better than they do now on international comparison tests (International Association for the Evaluation of Educational Achievement, 1985a, 1985b, 2000a, 2000b; International Project for the Evaluation of Educational Achievement, 1967; Lynn, 1988).

When one examines the issue of the extent to which American educators need to learn from the Japanese school system, two questions immediately emerge: (1) To what degree are school systems in Japan, Korea, Taiwan, China, and other Asian nations worthy of emulation? and (2) to what extent can American schools learn from these systems of education?

To What Degree Are East Asian Schools Worthy of Emulation?

Harold Stevenson and James Stigler (1992) conducted extensive research comparing Japanese and American students at various grade levels. They concluded that by the fifth grade, only the top American students could match the average mathematics achievement level attained in Japan. Lynn's (1988) analysis of international comparison tests confirms the findings of Stevenson and Stigler. He found that 98% of the Japanese students did better than the average American. Lynn notes that this advantage was much larger than it had been in the 1960s. In the most recent Trends in International Mathematics and Science Study (TIMSS), the nations of Singapore, Taiwan, Korea, and Japan were always among the top five nations in achievement (International Association for the Evaluation of Educational Achievement, 2000a, 2000b).

Benjamin Duke (1991) explains the findings of the body of research on Japanese education in the following way:

> Japan has undoubtedly out paced all the other major nations of the world in what should be the fundamental task of schooling, imparting to virtually all students adequately high levels of the basic skills, such as literacy and high competence in mathematics, needed for life in the modern world. (p. xviii)

Even when adjusting for differences in the representative nature of the samples and SES, the East Asian education advantage is quite clear (Stevenson & Stigler, 1992).

To What Extent Can American Schools Learn From Other Systems of Education?

Some educators believe that we cannot learn much from the education systems of other nations, because those school practices exist in other cultural contexts. However, Stevenson and Stigler (1992) and other social scientists argue that the United States can learn from the East Asian systems of education, especially because most of them were built using the American (and to a lesser extent the British and French) model (Shimizu, 1992).

Japan was the first nation to base its educational system on the Western rubric. In 1868, Emperor Meiji became leader and declared that unless Japan incorporated certain Western modern developments, Japanese society would not flourish (Shimizu, 1992). From 1872 to 1873, Meiji inaugurated a series of reforms that called for a radical level of Western-style changes, including hiring many American educators to fabricate the Japanese education system (Shimizu, 1992). In 1872, the Meiji Restoration resulted in the establishing of the Japanese education system (Shimizu, 1992). Emperor Meiji then requested that hundreds of Western educators come to Japan and formulate a Japanese education system that would be based on the Western paradigm. David Murray, from Rutgers University, led this group of educators and was largely responsible for formulating the modern Japanese education system (Amano, 1990). Murray's impact was so remarkable that Keenleyside and Thomas (1937) observe, "Dr, Murray himself probably did more than any other one man to influence the trend of educational development in Japan" (p. 92).

In 1879, Japan initiated a new wave of educational reforms that favored American practices over European ones (Keenleyside & Thomas, 1937). In addition, in the post–World War II period, the United States enjoyed another period of significant influence on the Japanese education system (Benjamin, 1997; Stevenson & Stigler, 1992).

To the degree that the United States has influenced Japan's education system the most of any nation in the Orient, South Korea probably ranks second. In the years following these changes in Japan, American and European missionaries founded Western-style schools in Korea. Many of Korea's finest universities and elementary and secondary schools were founded by Western missionaries (Duke University, 2002). China's education system was influenced by several Western nations, and by 1920, China had 6,301 Western-style schools (Cui, 2001). Other East Asian nations, such as Singapore and Taiwan, were similarly influenced (Lee, 1991; Miller, 1943).

Therefore, when educators argue that there is much that the United States can assimilate from the East Asian systems of education, what they are really saying is that there is much that America can relearn. The concepts that a number of these social scientists believe Americans can learn from the East Asian education system include parent/teacher partnerships, efficacious whole-class teaching, moral education, and an emphasis on effort more than ability (Benjamin, 1997; Khan, 1997; Stevenson & Lee, 1995; Stevenson & Stigler, 1992; White, 1987). It is also true that in most East Asian countries, the school year is longer than in the United States, which means there is more overall study time.

Added Insight: The United States Is Very Open to Cultures Within Its Borders, But Not to Cultures Beyond Its Borders

The United States today prides itself on its multicultural emphasis, that is, that Americans are open-minded to the practices of other cultures. Based on the issues addressed in Chapter 13, this is evidently true when focusing on cultures within American borders. In this sense, the United States may well be the most open-minded nation in the world. However, according to Stevenson and Stigler (1992) and others who have written on the East Asian educational phenomenon, this attitude does not persist when it comes to learning from other nations outside of American borders (Benjamin, 1997; Duke, 1991; White, 1987). Some social scientists observe that the United States is especially disinclined to learn from nations that do not practice multiculturalism (Fallows, 1989; Pye & Pye, 1985). This attitude is particularly problematic because there are only a handful of nations in the world that value multiculturalism. If the United States remains adamant in its reluctance to learn from nations that do not practice multiculturalism, it will be refusing to learn from the overwhelming majority of nations in the world.

Researchers and educators who study East Asia insist that there is a great deal that the United States can learn from school systems there (Benjamin, 1997; Duke, 1991; Stevenson & Stigler, 1992; White, 1987). However, East Asian nations do not hold multiculturalism in especially high esteem. In fact, East Asian nations value assimilation and conformity (Benjamin, 1997; Duke, 1991; Jeynes, 2005b; Stevenson & Stigler, 1992; White, 1987). Many Americans look down on East Asians because of their emphasis, which seems totally antithetical to the tenets of multiculturalism (Fallows, 1989; Pye & Pye, 1985).

- If Americans are accepting only of multicultural countries, are we as accepting as we claim?

Many researchers believe the United States can learn a great deal from East Asian school systems, particularly since their education systems were based largely on the American model (Benjamin, 1997; Duke, 1991; Jeynes, 2005b; White, 1987). However, according to Stevenson and Stigler, few Americans are willing to do so.

TECHNOLOGY IN THE SCHOOLS

The place of technology has increased in the schools. The importance of computer literacy has soared at an astronomical rate. There is no question that the future economic growth of the country is largely dependent on the ability to inculcate American students with technological know-how. Coates (2004) avers that teaching children how to use the Internet is particularly important, because it will lead to more efficient businesses. As Honey (2004) argues, computer technology is rapidly changing American society, and schools must adapt to that change. Eaton (2004) claims, "It's impossible to overstate the impact of the Internet" (p. 39), predicting, "very soon if you aren't computer literate, you won't be literate" (p. 40).

Some social scientists have made incredible predictions about the extent to which technology will revolutionize education. Davey (2004) said that to the extent to which the Internet made distance learning possible education would be revolutionized and predicted that distance learning would become a vital part of American education.

However, Larry Cuban (2001) argues that computers currently are not used enough in the classroom. He believes that whether computers are located in individual classrooms or whether they form computer clusters, computers are frequently left unused by educators. Cuban notes that compared with 1986, teachers do use computers in the classroom somewhat more frequently. However, the increase in classroom computer time is not as great as one might think. Cuban's research indicates that only 1 out of 10 teachers uses technology in the classroom daily and only 1 in 3 use technology occasionally.

Although virtually all social scientists agree that computer literacy is important, some of them nevertheless believe that the emphasis on technology is overdone (LeFevre, 2004; Shapiro, 2004; Wilson, 2004). For example, LeFevre (2004) argues that "technology will not . . . propel a poor student to the honor role" (p. 22). Some social scientists in fact argue that because schools are emphasizing technology too much, certain important aspects of education are being lost in the process (LeFevre, 2004; Shapiro, 2004; Wilson, 2004). Some of the problems with technological education that these individuals are concerned may be overlooked include the following.

First, some argue that the calculator is being introduced too early and that, consequently, students are losing the ability to do math without the calculator (LeFevre, 2004). Second, they are concerned that teachers tend to use the computer like a babysitter for playing and listening to music rather than having its main functions be academically related. Some are concerned, in fact, with Larry Cuban's (2001) approach of having children play with the computer in the same way that children play with blocks.

Third, some are concerned that the emphasis on computer instruction is taking children away from learning how to interact with one another one-on-one (Shapiro, 2004). Regarding college education, they argue that the learning that takes place via distance learning can never replace the level of education that takes place in personal education in a classroom (Wilson, 2004).

Fourth, some believe that some educators are forcing academic technologies on children at too early an age. Cuban (2001) for example, calls for "cyberteaching in preschools and kindergarten" (p. 49). Some believe that although some degree of exposure to the computer is good at this age, this academic emphasis only contributes to the trend toward making kindergartens more like first grade (Jeynes, 2006). Increasingly, it appears that modern kindergartens are laying aside the foundational nature of Froebel's original model of the kindergarten and are becoming focused on the academic (Jeynes, 2006).

A Closer Look: How Much Does Technology Really Help?

There is no question that computer literacy is constantly growing in importance. To procure some of the nation's better jobs, knowledge of the Internet, Microsoft Word, Excel, and Power Point are becoming requisite. Increasingly, teachers must train students in computer literacy. And over time, an increasing number of corporate executives regard this training as a fundamental part of the educational process. However, a growing number of people question the wisdom of how schools frequently implement technology training in the classroom (Loveless & Couglan, 2004). Specifically, these individuals tend to raise two concerns. First, they assert that schools rely so much on the calculator that students today have considerably less developed mathematics abilities than their counterparts from 30 or more years ago (Loveless & Couglan, 2004; Thompson & Sproule, 2000). There are many cases introduced as evidence indicating that many students lack multiplication, division, and addition skills as a result (Loveless & Couglan, 2004; Thompson & Sproule, 2000). Therefore, an increasing number of elementary school teachers are forbidding their students from using calculators in class until they reach a certain age (Loveless & Couglan, 2004; Thompson & Sproule, 2000). Second, many claim that teachers frequently use technology, such as television and computers, as babysitters more than as sophisticated and effective educational tools (Celano & Neuman, 2000; Loveless & Couglan, 2004).

- Do you believe that teachers should always seek to incorporate more technology in the classroom, or do you have concerns?
- Do you think there can be some disadvantages of incorporating technology in the classroom without monitoring how it is used?
- How do you imagine you will incorporate technology in the classroom?

Educators need to increasingly incorporate technology in the classroom. However, given that the computer is a relatively new addition to the classroom, it may take some time to resolve these debates to maximize the effectiveness of the use of technology in the classroom.

HOMESCHOOLING

Approximately 1.8 to 2.0 million, or 3%, of American children are homeschooled (Barfield, 2002). Although a number of famous individuals, such as Abraham Lincoln and Thomas Edison, were homeschooled, the modern-day movement really did not begin until the early 1980s (Mayberry, Knowles, Ray, & Marlow, 1995). Homeschooling is legal in all 50 states, although states vary in the extent to which they have certain restrictions. Southeastern states tend to have the most restrictions, and the industrial Midwest tends to have the least (Mayberry et al., 1995). Parents and children choose to homeschool for a variety of reasons.

Some of the most common are concerns about the lack of moral and religious teaching in public schools and a sense that public schools do not maintain high academic standards (Mayberry et al., 1995; Ray & Wartes, 1991). Many of these families are not particularly wealthy, and therefore the cost of sending their children to private schools is prohibitive. The average household income for a homeschool family is approximately $10,000 below the national median level, largely because many times, one parent does not work (Golden, 2000). Given the considerable expense of the private school option, these parents choose to homeschool their children.

People generally have two concerns about homeschooling: academic and social. The academic concerns emerged largely because people were concerned about the type of parents who would be attracted to the idea of homeschooling their children. Would they be the type, for example, who slept in and just did not feel like taking their children to school? As a result of these academic concerns, the early state restrictions on homeschooling were greater than they are today.

Research on the academic achievement of children indicates that homeschooled children do quite well academically, averaging about 2 years ahead of public school students and about 9 months ahead of private school students (Mayberry et al., 1995; Ray & Wartes, 1991).

In recent years, the primary concern that educators have had regards the social effects of homeschooling (Barfield, 2002; Mayberry et al., 1995). This concern largely stems from a stereotype that many people have of homeschooled children, that they are alone with their mothers or fathers all day long. In reality, most homeschooled children belong to homeschooling associations that go on field trips together, have physical education classes together, and do other activities together (Barfield, 2002; Orr, 2003; Stevens, 2001). Beyond this, many private educational businesses offer classes especially designed for home-schoolers. They especially focus on teaching subjects that parents do not feel comfortable with, such as chemistry, art, music, and foreign languages (Barfield, 2002; Orr, 2003; Stevens, 2001). In addition, homeschooled children sometimes attend some public school classes, and often they play on public school sports teams (Barfield, 2002; Orr, 2003). They have the right to be involved in public school activities because they pay the same level of taxes that everyone else pays.

Homeschool parents generally make certain that their children are involved in many social activities and organizations in order to compensate for not being in school, such as the Girl or Boy Scouts, dance classes, gymnastics, lifeguarding, and church (Orr, 2003). Homeschooled children often have the time and flexibility of schedule to engage in other activities as well, including Dale Carnegie speech classes and instruction in American Sign Language (Orr, 2003). Given that homeschooled children are generally quite socially involved, they tend to score at least as well as public school children on psychological tests (Mayberry et al., 1995).

Probably the most interesting aspect of the homeschooling movement is that the academic achievement of these children appears unrelated to SES (Mayberry et al., 1995; Ray & Wartes, 1991). This is highly unusual. In America's schools, there is a strong relationship between SES and academic achievement (Barfield, 2002; Orr, 2003; Stevens, 2001). Because the homeschool relationship between academic achievement and SES is the ideal, the question naturally arises as to why this is the case. The first reason that is generally given is that homeschooling represents a high degree of parental involvement (Barfield, 2002; Orr, 2003; Stevens, 2001). This involvement is facilitated by the fact that homeschooled children are more likely than their public school counterparts to come from two-parent homes and from families in which only one parent works outside the home (Mayberry et al., 1995; Ray & Wartes, 1991). The second reason is that homeschooled children receive a great deal of individual attention. The research on homeschooling suggests that this individual attention is not merely a phenomenon that takes place during the school day, but carries over into other activities. For example, research indicates that nearly two thirds of homeschooled fourth graders watch less than 1 hour of television per day (Mayberry et al., 1995; Ray & Wartes, 1991). These facts may give public and private school educators some insight into improving educational outcomes.

Contemporary Focus

Choosing an Educational Reform to Strengthen American Schools

In this book, *American Educational History: School, Society, and the Common Good,* we have examined an abundance of educational themes and issues. Below are listed six of the most common reforms that educators, social scientists, and political leaders cite as a means to improve the U.S. education system.

If you could choose one of the following programs to help American students in school, which would it be, and why?

1. Expand the affirmative action program

2. Expand programs of school choice

3. Teach children better morals/character and allow moral expression, such as voluntary prayer, in the schools

4. Increase teacher salaries

5. Learn from foreign systems of education regarding how they run their programs

6. Have an equalization of school expenditures

CONCLUSION

One can argue that the topics addressed in this chapter constitute some of the greatest changes that American education has ever faced. Indeed, that may well be the case. School expenditure equalization, school shootings, uniforms, learning from foreign systems of education, the changes in family structure since the early 1960s, and the technological revolution represent prodigious transformations that will help guide American education in one direction or the other. Unquestionably, depending on one's perspective, some people will view some of these changes as positive developments, and others will view some of them as events that have gone awry. Nevertheless, for good or ill, change is part of the American educational landscape.

Although the transformations addressed in this chapter seem major, and they patently are, they are probably no more trenchant than some of the changes that American education has encountered in past decades and centuries. For example, within just a short span of years, the Puritans guided New England from having virtually no formal education at all to establishing compulsory education and Harvard College. The Revolutionary War helped catapult the nation into a breeding ground for higher education. Horace Mann and his colleagues forever changed the way most American children receive their education. Various minority groups, as well as women, experienced prodigious changes in educational experiences, particularly during the 1800s. John Dewey laid his imprint on American education in a way that perhaps no other man had done. America's Civil War, World Wars I and II, the Great Depression, and the Cold War all had dramatic effects on the ways American schools functioned. The civil rights movement also decidedly impacted American education. The 1960s was one of the most turbulent decades in American history and produced changes in American schools and universities that may well surpass any other decade. Educational transformations are a part of U.S. history.

The United States is constantly trying to improve its education system. If the nation is to strengthen its education system, a primary need is to learn from the history of education. There are many lessons to be learned from the great accomplishments as well as the mistakes that have been made over the years. One can only hope that as time passes, the accomplishments will breed further success, and the mistakes will be corrected. This truth makes the study of educational history an exciting experience, a journey through time, with many applications for today.

DISCUSSION QUESTIONS

1. Do you favor the use of school uniforms in schools? Why or why not?

2. Obviously, Eric Harris and Dylan Kliebold spread a great deal of hate in their world, and they clearly had some deep-rooted psychological problems. What can teachers and parents do to reduce the likelihood that children with such problems and hatred will do harm to other students?

3. Some claim that the homeschooling movement has emerged out of a sense of frustration that a fair number of parents have with the public schools. Do you agree with this statement? Do you think that there are actions that public schools could take to win back these parents?

4. Given that family factors affect the educational outcomes of students the way they do, family and educational researchers frequently contend that teachers ought to function as surrogate parents for children. Do you agree with this statement? To what extent can teachers function as surrogate parents?

REFERENCES

Amano, I. (1990). *Education and examination in modern Japan.* Tokyo: University of Tokyo.

Amato, P. R., & Ochiltree, G. (1987). Child and adolescent competence in intact, one-parent, and step-families, an Australian study. *Journal of Divorce, 10,* 75–96.

Armstrong, A. (2002). Guns have been wrongfully blamed for school shootings. In L. K. Egendorf (Ed.), *School shootings* (pp. 36–39). San Diego, CA: Greenhaven Press.

Balli, S. J. (1998). When mom and dad help: Student reflections on student involvement with homework. *Journal of Research and Development in Education, 31*(3), 142–146.

Balli, S. J., Demo, D. H., & Wedman, J. F. (1998). Family involvement with children's homework: An intervention in the middle grades. *Family Relations, 47*(2), 149–157.

Barfield, R. (2002). *Real-life homeschooling.* New York: Fireside.

Baydar, N. (1988). Effects of parental separation and reentry into union on the emotional well-being of children. *Journal of Marriage and the Family, 50,* 967–981.

Beer, W. R. (1992). *Americans stepfamilies.* New Brunswick, NJ: Transaction Publishers.

Benjamin, G. (1997). *Japanese lessons.* New York: NYU Press.

Bennett, W. J. (1983). Authority, discipline, excellence. In R. Reagan, W. Bennett, & E. W Lefever (Eds.), *Reinvigorating our schools.* Washington, DC: Ethics and Public Policy Center.

Benson, C. S. (1975). *Equity in school financing: Full state funding.* Bloomington, IN: Phi Delta Kappan.

Bermudez, A. B., & Padron, Y. N. (1990). Improving language skills for Hispanic students through home-school partnerships. *Journal of Educational Issues of Language Minority Students, 6*(1), 33–43.

Bogenschneider, K. (1997). Parental involvement in adolescent schooling: A proximal process with transcontextual validity. *Journal of Marriage and the Family, 59,* 718–733.

Booth, A., & Edwards, J. N. (1992). Starting over: Why remarriages are more unstable. *Journal of Family Issues, 13,* 179–194.

Brown, B., & Merritt, R. (2002). *No easy answers: The truth behind death at Columbine.* New York: Lantern Books.

Brunsma, D. L. (2002). *School uniforms: A critical review of the literature.* Bloomington, IN: Phi Delta Kappa.

Brunsma, D. L. (2004). *The school uniform movement and what it tells us about American education.* Bloomington, IN: Phi Delta Kappa.

Brunsma, D., & Rockquemore, A. (1998). Effects of student uniforms on attendance, behavior problems, substance use, and academic achievement. *Journal of Educational Research, 92*(1), 53–62.

Burns, S., McArthur, E., Heaviside, S., Rowand, C., Williams, C., & Farris, E. (1998). *Violence & discipline problems in U.S. public schools: 1996–1997.* Washington, DC: U.S. Department of Education.

California League of Middle Schools. (2004, July 21). *Legislative update.* Retrieved April 28, 2005, from http://www.clms.net/legislation/leg0704.htm.

Carlston, L. (2004). *Surviving Columbine.* Salt Lake City, UT: Deseret.

Casella, R. (2003). Zero tolerance policy in schools: Rationale, consequences, and alternatives. *Teachers College Record, 105,* 872–892.

Celano, D., & Neuman, S. B. (2000). Channel one: Time for a TV break. *Phi Delta Kappan, 76,* 444–446.

Centers for Disease Control and Prevention. (1989). *Cost of injury in the United States.* Atlanta, GA: Author.

Christian, K., Morrison, F. J., & Bryant, F. B. (1998). Predicting kindergarten academic skills: Interactions among child care, maternal education, and family literacy environments. *Early Childhood Research Quarterly, 13,* 501–521.

Clinton, B. (1995). *Proposed legislation: The Gun-Free Zones Amendments Act of 1995.* Washington, DC: U.S. Government Printing Office.

Coates, J. E. (2004). The information revolution will continue to benefit society. In L. K. Egendorf (Ed.), *The information revolution: Opposing viewpoints* (pp. 152–159). San Diego, CA: Greenhaven Press.

Coleman, J., Hoffer, T., & Kilgore, S. (1982). *High school achievement: Public, Catholic, and private schools compared.* New York: Basic Books.

Coleman, L. (2004). *The copycat effect.* New York: Paraview.

Coleman, M., & Ganong, L. (1990). Remarriage and stepfamily research in the 1980s: Increased interest in an old family form. *Journal of Marriage and the Family, 52,* 925–940.

Cuban, L. (2001). *Oversold and underused.* Cambridge, MA: Harvard University.

Cui, D. (2001). British Protestant educational activities and nationalism of Chinese education in the 1920s. In G. Peterson, R. Hayhoe, & L. Yongling (Eds.), *Education, culture, and identity in twentieth century China* (pp. 137–160). Ann Arbor: University of Michigan.

Cullen, J. B., & Loeb, S. (2004). School finance reform in Michigan: Evaluating Proposal A. In J. Yinger (Ed.), *Helping children left behind: State aid and the pursuit of educational equity* (pp. 215–249). Cambridge: MIT Press.

Davey, K. B. (2004). The information revolution has improved off-campus education. In L. K. Egendorf (Ed.), *The information revolution: Opposing viewpoints* (pp. 83–88). San Diego, CA: Greenhaven Press.

Dawson, D. (1991). Family structure and children's health and well-being: Data from the 1988 National Health Interview Survey on Child Health. *Journal of Marriage and the Family, 53,* 573–584.

Deslandes, R., Royer, E., Turcotte, D., & Bertrand, R. (1997). School achievement at the secondary level: Influence of parenting style and parent involvement in schooling. *McGill Journal of Education, 32*(3), 191–207.

Downes, T. (2004). School finance reform and school quality: Lessons from Vermont. In J. Yinger (Ed.), *Helping children left behind: State aid and the pursuit of educational equity* (pp. 59–85). Cambridge: MIT Press.

Downey, D. B. (1995). Understanding academic achievement among children in stephouseholds: The role of parental resources, sex of stepparent, and sex of child. *Social Forces, 73,* 875–894.

Duke, B. C. (1991). *Education and leadership for the twenty-first century.* New York: Praeger.

Duke University. (2002). *Big list of Korean universities.* Retrieved June 11, 2003, from http://www.duke.edu/~myhan/c_blku.html

Eaton, R. J. (2004). The Internet has transformed the economy. In L. K. Egendorf (Ed.), *The information revolution: Opposing viewpoints* (pp. 38–43). San Diego, CA: Greenhaven Press.

Education Trust. (2002). *The funding gap: Low-income and minority students receive fewer dollars.* Washington, DC: Author.

Esbensen, F., & Deschenes, E. P. (1998). A multisite examination of youth gang membership: Does gender matter? *Criminology, 36,* 799–828.

Fallows, J. M. (1989). *More like us.* Boston: Houghton Mifflin.

Flanagan, A. E., & Murray, S. E. (2004). A decade of reform: The impact of school reform in Kentucky. In J. Yinger (Ed.), *Helping children left behind: State aid and the pursuit of educational equity* (pp. 59–85). Cambridge: MIT Press.

Forste, R., & Tanfer, K. (1996). Sexual exclusivity among dating, cohabiting, and married women. *Journal of Marriage and the Family, 58,* 33–47.

Gahr, E. (2002). Access to guns can lead to school shootings. In L. K. Egendorf (Ed.), *School shootings* (pp. 33–35). San Diego, CA: Greenhaven Press.

Golden, D. (2000, February 11). A class of their own: Home-schooled kids defy stereotypes, ace SAT test. *Wall Street Journal,* p. 1).

Griffith, J. (1996). Relation of parental involvement, empowerment, and school traits to student academic performance. *Journal of Educational Research, 90*(1), 33–41.

Guthrie, J. W. (1975). *Equity in school financing: District power equalizing.* Bloomington, IN: Phi Delta Kappan.

Hampton, F. M., Munford, D. A., & Bond, L. (1998). Parental involvement in inner city schools: The project FAST extended family approach to success. *Urban Education, 33,* 410–427.

Hara, S. R. (1998). Parent involvement: The key to improved student achievement. *School Community Journal, 8*(2), 9–19.

Hetherington, E. M., & Clingempeel, W. G. (1992). Coping with marital transitions: A family systems perspective. *Monographs of the Society for Research in Child Development, 57*(2–3), Serial No. 227.

Hetherington, E. M., & Jodl, K. M. (1994). Stepfamilies as settings for child development. In A. Booth & J. Dunn (Eds.), *Stepfamilies: Who benefits? Who does not?* (pp. 55–79). Hillsdale, NJ: Lawrence Erlbaum.

Hetherington, E. M., Stanley-Hagan, M., & Anderson, E. R. (1989). Marital transitions: A child's perspective. *American Psychologist, 44,* 303–312.

Hoffer, T., Greeley, A. M., & Coleman, J. S. (1987). Catholic High School effects on achievement growth. In E. H. Haertel, T. James, & H. Levin (Eds.), *Comparing public and private schools* (pp. 67–88). New York: Falmer Press.

Honey, M. (2004). Technology has improved education. In L. K. Egendorf (Ed.), *The information revolution: Opposing viewpoints* (pp. 70–77). San Diego, CA: Greenhaven Press.

Hoxby, C. M. (2001). All school finance equalizers are not created equal. *Quarterly Journal of Economics, 66,* 1189–1232.

International Association for the Evaluation of Educational Achievement. (1985a). *TIMSS 1984 International Mathematics Report.* Chestnut Hill, MA: International Study Center.

International Association for the Evaluation of Educational Achievement. (1985b). *TIMSS 1984 International Science Report.* Chestnut Hill, MA: International Study Center.

International Association for the Evaluation of Educational Achievement. (2000a). *TIMSS 1999 International Mathematics Report.* Chestnut Hill, MA: International Study Center.

International Association for the Evaluation of Educational Achievement. (2000b). *TIMSS 1999 International Science Report.* Chestnut Hill, MA: International Study Center.

International Project for the Evaluation of Educational Achievement. (1967). *International Study of Achievement in Mathematics: A comparison of twelve countries, Vol. 2.* Hamburg, West Germany: Author.

Jeynes, W. (1998). Does divorce or remarriage following divorce have the greater impact on the academic achievement of children? *Journal of Divorce and Remarriage, 29*(1/2), 79–101.

Jeynes, W. H. (2002). *Divorce, family structure, and the academic success of children.* Binghamton, NY: Haworth Press.

Jeynes, W. (2003). A meta-analysis: The effects of parental involvement on minority children's academic achievement. *Education and Urban Society, 35,* 202–218.

Jeynes, W. (2005a). A meta-analysis of the relation of parental involvement to urban elementary school student achievement. *Urban Education, 49,* 237–269.

Jeynes, W. (2005b). Parental involvement in East Asian schools. In D. Hiatt-Michael (Ed.), *International perspectives on parental involvement* (pp. 151–177). Greenwich, CT: Information Age Press.

Jeynes, W. (2006). Standardized tests and Froebel's original kindergarten model. *Teachers College Record, 108*(10), 1937–1959.

Kaufman, P., Chen, X., Choy, S. P., Ruddy, S. A., Miller, A. K., & Fleury, J. K. (2000). *Indicators of school crime and safety 2000.* Washington, DC: U.S. Department of Justice.

Keenleyside, H. L., & Thomas, A. F. (1937). *History of Japanese education and present educational system.* Tokyo: Hokuseido Press.

Kelly, J. (1992). *Conflict and children's post-divorce adjustment: A closer look.* Paper presented at the National Council for Children's Rights, Arlington, VA.

Khan, Y. (1997). *Japanese moral education: Past and present.* Madison, NJ: Fairleigh Dickinson University Press.

Kopka, D. L. (1997). *School violence: A reference handbook.* Santa Barbara, CA: ABC-CLIO Press.

Ladson-Billings, G. (2000). Fighting for our lives: Preparing teachers to teach African American students. *Journal of Teacher Education, 51,* 206–214.

Lal, S. R., Lal, D., & Achilles, C. M. (1993). *Handbook on gangs in schools: Strategies to reduce gang-related activities.* Thousand Oaks, CA: Corwin Press.

Lee, W. O. (1991). *Social change and educational problems in Japan, Singapore, and Hong Kong*. New York: St. Matthew's Press.

LeFevre, A. T. (2004). Technology alone has not improved education. In L. K. Egendorf (Ed.), *The information revolution: Opposing viewpoints* (pp. 78–82). San Diego, CA: Greenhaven Press.

Long Beach Unified School District. (2003). *Crime data*. Retrieved September 3, 2006, from http://www.lbusd.com.

Loveless, T., & Couglan, J. (2004). The arithmetic gap. *Educational Leadership, 61*(5), 55.

Lukemeyer, A. (2004). Financing a constitutional education: Views from the bench. In J. Yinger (Ed.), *Helping children left behind: State aid and the pursuit of educational equity* (pp. 59–85). Cambridge: MIT Press.

Lynn, R. (1988). *Educational achievement in Japan*. Armonk, NY: M. E. Sharpe.

Matera, D. (2001). *A cry for character*. Paramus, NJ: Prentice Hall.

Mau, W. (1997). Parental influences on the high school students' academic achievement: A comparison of Asian immigrants, Asian Americans, and White Americans. *Psychology in the Schools, 34,* 267–277.

Mayberry, M. J., Knowles, G., Ray, B., & Marlow, S. (1995). *Homeschooling parents as educators*. Thousand Oaks, CA: Corwin Press.

McBride, B. A., & Lin, H. (1996). Parental involvement in prekindergarten at-risk programs: Multiple perspectives. *Journal of Education for Students Placed at Risk, 1,* 349–372.

McLanahan, S., & Sandefur, G. (1994). *Growing up with a single parent: What hurts, what helps*. Cambridge, MA: Harvard University Press.

Melvin, T. (1994, August 7). Blackboard: Uniform diversity in California. *New York Times*, p. A7.

Miller, B. W. (1943). *Generalissimo and Madame Chiang Kai-Shek: Christian liberators of China*. Grand Rapids, MI: Zondervan.

Muller, C. (1998). Gender differences in parental involvement and adolescents' mathematics achievement. *Sociology of Education, 71,* 336–356.

National Center for Health Statistics. (2003). *Marriage and divorce*. Hyattsville, MD: U.S. Department of Health & Human Services.

Nesbitt, G. K. (1993). The effects of three school-to-home parental involvement communication programs on reading achievement, conduct, homework habits, attendance, and parent-student-school interaction (Doctoral dissertation, Georgia State University). *Dissertation Abstracts International, 54/11,* 3993.

Newman, K. S. (2004). *Rampage: The social roots of school shootings*. New York: Basic Books.

Nock, S. L. (1995). A comparison of marriages and cohabiting relationships. *Journal of Family Issues, 16*(1), 53–76.

Nunn, G. D., Parish, T. S., & Worthing, R. J. (1993). Perceptions of personal and familial adjustment by children from intact, single-parent, and reconstituted families. *Psychology in the Schools, 20,* 166–174.

Orr, T. (2003). *After homeschool*. Los Angeles: Parent's Guide Press.

Peressini, D. D. (1998). The portrayal of parents in the school mathematics reform literature: Locating the context for parental involvement. *Journal for Research in Mathematics Education, 29,* 555–582.

Popenoe, D. (1994). The evolution of marriage and the problem of stepfamilies: A biosocial perspective. In A. Booth & J. Dunn (Eds.), *Stepfamilies: Who benefits? Who does not?* (pp. 55–79). Hillsdale, NJ: Lawrence Erlbaum.

Pye, L. W., & Pye, M. W. (1985). *Asian power and politics: The cultural dimensions of authority*. Cambridge, MA: Belknap Press.

Quade, Q. L. (1996). *Financing education*. New Brunswick, NJ: Transaction Publishers.

Ray, B. D., & Wartes, J. (1991). Academic achievement & affective development. In J. Van Galen & M. A. Pitman (Eds.), *Homeschooling: Political, historical and pedagogical perspectives* (pp. 43–62). Norwood, NJ: Ablex.

San Antonio Independent School District v. Rodriguez (411 U.S. 1 (1973).

Scott, D., & Nimmo, B. (2000). *Rachel's tears.* Nashville, TN: Thomas Nelson.

Serrano v. Priest 487 P.2d 1241 (1971).

Shapiro, A. L. (2004). The Internet discourages social interaction. In L. K. Egendorf (Ed.), *The information revolution: Opposing viewpoints* (pp. 57–65). San Diego, CA: Greenhaven Press.

Shaver, A. V., & Walls, R. T. (1998). Effect of Title I parent involvement on student reading and mathematics achievement. *Journal of Research and Development in Education, 31*(2), 90–97.

Shimizu, K. (1992). Shido: Education and selection in Japanese middle school. *Comparative Education, 28,* 114–125.

Singh, K., Bickley, P. G., Trivette, P., Keith, T. Z., Keith, P. B., & Anderson, E. (1995). The effects of four components of parental involvement on eighth grade student achievement. *School Psychology Review, 24,* 299–317.

Snyder, H. N., & Sickmund, M. (1995). *Juvenile offenders and victims: A focus on violence.* Pittsburgh, PA: National Center for Juvenile Justice.

Starr, J. (2000). School violence and its effect on the constitutionality of school uniform policies. *Journal of Law & Education, 29*(1), 113–118.

Stevens, M. L. (2001). *Kingdom of children.* Princeton, NJ: Princeton University Press.

Stevenson, H. W., & Lee, S. (1995). The East Asian version of whole class teaching. *Educational Policy, 9,* 152–167.

Stevenson, H. W., & Stigler, J. W. (1992). *The learning gap.* New York: Summit Books.

Thompson, A. D., & Sproule, S. L. (2000). Deciding when to use calculators. *Mathematics Teaching in the Middle School, 6,* 126–129.

U.S. Bureau of the Census. (2001). *Statistical abstract of the United States.* Washington, DC: U.S. Government Printing Office.

U.S. Department of Education. (1992). *National education longitudinal study, 1988: First follow-up, 1990. Vol. 1: Student data.* Washington, DC: Author.

U.S. Department of Education. (2003). *Digest of education statistics.* Washington, DC: Author.

Villas-Boas, A. (1998). The effects of parental involvement in homework on student achievement in Portugal and Luxembourg. *Childhood Education, 74,* 367–371.

Visher, E. B., & Visher, J. S. (1988). *Old loyalties, new ties: Therapeutic strategies with stepfamilies.* New York: Brunner/Mazel.

Wallerstein, J. S., & Kelly, J. B. (1980). *Surviving the breakup.* New York: Basic Books.

Walsh, W. M. (1992). Twenty major issues in remarriage families. *Journal of Counseling and Development, 70,* 709–715.

White, M. (1987). *The Japanese educational challenge: A commitment to children.* New York: Free Press.

Wilson, D. (2004). The information revolution has not improved off-campus education. In L. K. Egendorf (Ed.), *The information revolution: Opposing viewpoints* (pp. 89–92). San Diego, CA: Greenhaven Press.

Wirtz, W. (1977). *On further examination.* New York: College Entrance Examination.

Yinger, J. (2004). State aid and the pursuit of educational equity. In J. Yinger (Ed.), *Helping children left behind: State aid and the pursuit of educational equity* (pp. 3–57). Cambridge: MIT Press.

Zdzinski, S. F. (1996). Parental involvement, selected student attributes, and learning outcomes in instrumental music. *Journal of Research in Music Education, 44*(1), 34–48.

Zill, N. (1994). Understanding why children in stepfamilies have more learning and behavior problems than children in nuclear families. In A. Booth & J. Dunn (Eds.), *Stepfamilies: Who benefits? Who does not?* (pp. 109–137). Hillsdale, NJ: Lawrence Erlbaum.

Zill, N., & Nord, C. W. (1994). *Running in place.* Washington, DC: Child Trends.

Zoba, W. M. (2000). *Day of reckoning: Columbine and the search for the American soul.* Grand Rapids, MI: Brazos Press.

Index